ENDLESS EMPIRE

And Jupiter, king of the gods, said:
"Young Romulus
Will take the leadership, build walls of Mars,
And call by his own name his people Romans.
For these I set no limits, world or time,
But make the gift of empire without end."

—Virgil, *Aeneid* (1:371–75)

Marble statue installed inside the U.S. Capitol Rotunda in 1841 showing George Washington seated like Zeus at Mt. Olympus, with right arm raised in the manner of a Roman emperor addressing his legions. (Smithsonian Institution)

ENDLESS EMPIRE

Spain's Retreat, Europe's Eclipse,
America's Decline

Edited by

Alfred W. McCoy, Josep M. Fradera, Stephen Jacobson

THE UNIVERSITY OF WISCONSIN PRESS

Publication of this book was aided by a grant from the research project Imperial Transitions, funded by Spain's Ministry of Science and Innovation (HAR2009-14099-CO2-01).

The University of Wisconsin Press
1930 Monroe Street, 3rd Floor
Madison, Wisconsin 53711-2059
uwpress.wisc.edu

3 Henrietta Street
London WCE 8LU, England
eurospanbookstore.com

Printed in the United States of America

Library of Congress Cataloging-in-Publication Data
Endless empire : Spain's retreat, Europe's eclipse, America's decline / edited by
Alfred W. McCoy, Josep M. Fradera, and Stephen Jacobson.
p. cm.
Includes bibliographical references and index.
ISBN 978-0-299-29024-5 (pbk. : alk. paper) — ISBN 978-0-299-29023-8 (e-book)
1. Imperialism—History. 2. United States—Foreign relations—History. 3. Spain—
Foreign relations—History. 4. Europe—Foreign relations—History. I. McCoy,
Alfred W. II. Fradera, Josep Maria. III. Jacobson, Stephen, PhD.
D32.E54 2012
325´.32—dc23
2012010172

Dedicated to

DAVID K. FIELDHOUSE *and* STANLEY J. STEIN

whose work on modern empires has
influenced generations of scholars

CONTENTS

ACKNOWLEDGMENTS

Sensing the current world order at the cusp of major change, a global network of 140 historians gathered from four continents for an intense dialogue at a succession of conferences in Madison (2006), Sydney (2008), Manila (2008), and Barcelona (2010). The purpose of these meetings was to gain a comparative perspective on the subject of modern imperial transitions, which would have been impossible had we limited ourselves to specific area specialties or established academic traditions.

The first two gatherings resulted in the publication of *Colonial Crucible: Empire in the Making of the Modern American State* (2009), edited by Alfred W. McCoy and Francisco A. Scarano. The present volume, *Endless Empire*, is the fruit of a symposium held at the Universitat Pompeu Fabra, Barcelona, in June 2010, which probed the processes of imperial decline within six modern maritime empires.

In the context of this wide-ranging inquiry into imperial history, *Colonial Crucible* explored the rise of the U.S. global power while this current volume examines the dynamics of its decline. In sum, these two books represent nothing less than an assessment of history's most powerful empire, both its rise and possible demise. In that vast void between the enormity of American power and the paucity of its critical study, it is our hope these publications will serve as both contribution and corrective, placing current debates about the changing world order in a broader historical context.

Three institutions have been responsible for putting these conferences together—the Harvey Goldberg Center at the University of Wisconsin–Madison (http://history.wisc.edu/goldberg/goldberg.htm); the World University's Network in collaboration with the University of Sydney; and the Research Group on Empires, Metropolises, and Extra-European Societies (GRIMSE) organized within the Humanities Department at the Universitat Pompeu Fabra (http://www.upf.edu/grimse). In convening the Barcelona symposium, we are indebted to the administrative staff, which coordinated the sensitive business of grant applications, translation services, program scheduling, airline tickets, and hotel bookings. In particular, Ms. Cinta Campos and Ms. Yolanda Pueyo undertook the logistical and organizational work for the well-organized Barcelona conference.

To carry out this ambitious project, the question of funding was paramount. The principal backing for the Barcelona symposium came from Spain's Ministry of Science and Innovation, which provided support through the Imperial Transitions Research Group (HAR2009-14099-CO2-01) and a supplementary grant for the conference itself (HAR2009-07974-E). Other contributors included the Department d'Humanitats, the Institut Jaume Vicens Vives d'Història, the UNESCO Chair for Iberian Cultures, the UNESCO Chair for Intercultural Studies, and the Statebuilding in Latin America Research Project, sponsored by the European Research Council (Seventh Framework Program, no. 230246). We thank the respective directors, coordinators, administrative staffs, and the anonymous judges and peer referees who gave our proposal a high priority. Given the global financial climate, which grew ever more difficult in the months of planning that preceded this conference, we are particularly grateful for being entrusted with these scarce resources.

Various colleagues from multiple academic institutions lent their expertise by attending and chairing panels at the Barcelona conference, contributing the insights, comments, and criticisms reflected in these pages. To this end, we would like to express our gratitude to professors Albert Carreras, Alex Coello, Robert Fishman, Juan Carlos Garavaglia, Jordi Ibañez, Vina Lanzona, Eloy Martín, Juan Pan-Montojo, Martín Rodrigo, Florentino Rodao, Mauricio Tenorio, and Enric Ucelay-Da Cal.

The University of Wisconsin–Madison was equally generous in its support for the research and editorial work needed to transform a lively symposium into a publishable volume. The International Institute provided, through Dean Gilles Bousquet and his associate Guido Podesta, funding for the Empires in Transition Research Circle, which helped convene these scholarly symposia. At the University of Wisconsin Press, the volume benefited greatly from the rigorous editing of Dr. Gwen Walker, the careful supervision of Adam Mehring, and the support of their director Shelia Leary. The Press also solicited reviews from three external readers—Anne Foster, Franklin Knight, and John Sidel—whose close reading and thoughtful comments inspired significant revisions to almost all the essays in this volume.

More broadly, this volume owes multiple debts, personal and professional, to the earlier generations of gifted scholars who have tracked the course of modern empires. We feel a particularly strong sense of gratitude to historians David K.

Fieldhouse and Stanley J. Stein who, as scholars and mentors, nurtured this field and made our own work possible. To acknowledge their lasting contribution to the field of comparative imperial history, this volume is gratefully dedicated to them.

Though grateful for all this support, the editors and contributors to this volume remain responsible for any faults or flaws in their work.

PART I

INTRODUCTION

Destruction (detail), 1836, the fourth painting in Thomas Cole's five-part series titled *The Course of Empire*. (Collection of the New York Historical Society)

Fatal Florescence

Europe's Decolonization and America's Decline

ALFRED W. MCCOY

For NEARLY TWO CENTURIES, the United States has shown a deep ambivalence about its path from republic to empire. As the country began its conquest of a continent in the 1830s, Congress commissioned a marble colossus for the Capitol Rotunda, the nation's symbolic center. When delivered from Italy, this massive twelve-ton, toga-clad statue portrayed George Washington with a mix of classical metaphors—seated like the god Zeus at Mt. Olympus, right arm raised magisterially in the *adlocutio* (oratorical) manner of Roman emperors, and left arm thrusting forward a short Roman sword. All these imperious gestures were evocative of the poet Virgil's lines about the King of the Gods giving ancient Rome "the gift of empire without end."[1] In those same years, American artist Thomas Cole invoked this Roman analogy to make a very different argument in five monumental canvases titled *The Course of Empire*—showing the progress of a metaphorical valley from wilderness in *The Savage State* to lush arcadia in *The Pastoral State*, imperial grandeur as a city resembling Rome in *The Consummation*, the fiery sacking of that same city in *Destruction*, and ruins reclaimed by forest in *Desolation*.[2]

In less than two centuries, the United States passed through the first three of Cole's canvases to reach the imperial grandeur of his *Consummation*. At its peak of power circa 1990, America controlled the global economy, exercised unchallenged military power, and set the political agenda for much of the world. But by 2010, after a decade of war and economic crisis, U.S. dominion seemed at the brink of decline, prompting President Barack Obama to warn Congress of serious challenges to America's global power. "China is not waiting to revamp its economy. Germany is not waiting. India is not waiting," he said. "These nations aren't playing for second place." Then, in a rhetorical flourish that brought thunderous bipartisan applause, he announced, "Well, I do not accept second place for the United States of America."[3]

Reprising that theme a few days later, Vice President Joseph Biden cited historian Paul Kennedy's 1987 book attributing Europe's retreat from global power to imperial overstretch and predicting the United States would soon suffer a similar decline. Disagreeing sharply, Biden ridiculed the idea that Americans "are destined to fulfill Kennedy's prophecy that we are going to be a great nation that has failed because we lost control of our economy and overextended." With seeming confidence that America's growth would soon recover, Biden stressed, "We will continue to be the most significant and dominant influence in the world as long as our economy is strong."[4]

By referencing Paul Kennedy's work, Biden spoke directly to contemporary concerns that Europe's past is somehow a harbinger of America's future. Indeed, imperial analogies, usually with Rome or Britain, now abound in U.S. academic and public discourse, used variously to analyze America's ascent or warn of its retreat.[5] After Washington elites began calling for a new "national strategic narrative . . . with a . . . projected happy ending that will transcend our political divisions," neoconservative historian Robert Kagan argued, in an influential 2012 essay, that the United States today, with its unrivaled military, diplomatic, and economic clout, "is not remotely like Britain circa 1900 when that empire's relative decline began." Thus, America alone, he added, can decide whether its world power will "decline over the next two decades or not for another two centuries."[6] Whatever the merits of all these analogies might be, this debate raises an important question: Does Europe's decolonization over the past two centuries offer insights about the ongoing decline of U.S. global power?

Europe's Empires

Even now, a half century after the end of Europe's global empires, the character of their colonization and the consequences of their decolonization still elude us. From 1500 onward, each century brought a new layer in Europe's overseas expansion, culminating in an accelerated advance in the late nineteenth century when a half dozen powers carved up Africa and Asia.[7] Then, after four centuries of relentless imperial expansion that encompassed half of humanity by 1920, Europe's five major overseas empires were erased from the globe in just a quarter century—giving way, between 1947 and 1974, to nearly a hundred new nations, over half of today's sovereign states. In twenty years after World War II, the British Empire's population fell from seven hundred million to only five million.[8]

Though marked by seemingly small acts, the flick of a pen and the folding of a flag, the decolonization of Europe's empires after World War II plunged many societies worldwide into wrenching transitions while precipitating sweeping changes in the international order. These hundred new nations had to detach themselves from the economic tendrils of empire, starting troubled transitions to nationhood. In the former metropoles, there was often a brooding sense of cultural malaise, economic dislocation, and political recrimination sometimes escalating into civil war—*vide* Spain after 1898 and France after Algeria. Simultaneously, the great land-based empires also collapsed, four of them in the aftermath of World War I (China, Russia, Austro-Hungary, and the Ottoman Empire) and the last, the Soviet Union, by 1991.[9]

Yet the dissolution of these European empires did not mean the end of empire as a system of global governance. These fading dominions became the foundation for an expanding American imperium, allowing Washington to extend its hegemony across four continents after World War II with a surprising speed and economy of force. Whether by negotiations with the Dutch in 1949 or entente with Britain during the 1950s, Europe's retreat meant America's advance. Such change did not bring the erasure of these European powers, but instead their subordination within a new global order marked by U.S. military dominion, shared economic governance, and a myriad of sovereign nations.

At their peak circa 1900, the great European empires seemed to enjoy an illusory omnipotence. Yet even at the apex of power, empires germinate seeds of decline unnoticed until they burst forth in a fatal florescence that brings defeat

Mehmed VI, last sultan of the Ottoman Empire, departing Istanbul for exile in 1922, the symbolic end of the world's oldest empire. (Otrakji family collection on mideastimage.com)

and retreat, sometimes slow, often rapid. Empires decline and disappear. But empire in some form has persisted over the millennia, and will likely continue into the foreseeable future.

COMPARATIVE ANALYSIS OF EMPIRES

To engage the enormity of such global transitions, 140 historians from four continents met periodically, from 2006 to 2010, at Madison, Sydney, Manila, and Barcelona for wide-ranging reflections comparing Europe and America, past and present. In *Colonial Crucible*, our first volume, we explored U.S. empire during its formative years, when the challenge of ruling a string of far-flung territories created the need and opportunity for the American imperial state to undertake bold social experiments across a broad range of institutions, including policing and prisons, education, public health, law, the military, and environmental management. In these discussions we drew on a vast literature to define *colonial empire* as a form of global governance in which a dominant power exercises control over other peoples through direct territorial rule (e.g., colonies, mandates, or protectorates) involving military domination, economic exploitation, and cultural conditioning.[10]

In this present volume, the culmination of our five-year collaboration, we follow the arc of empire to its endpoint, at the same time broadening the scope of our inquiry to offer a comparative analysis that builds on the history of four major maritime empires—Spanish, British, French, and American. We have, moreover, moved beyond direct colonial rule to include "informal empire," which we describe, following Gregory Barton's essay in this volume, as "a relationship in which a national . . . imperial elite . . . exercises a dominant influence over . . . the subjected elite in another nation . . . with none of the formal structures of empire." Methodologically, this volume treats empires at two levels: first, as an extension of the state beyond its national boundaries, concentrating on political and military institutions, their coercive capacity, the imperial ideologies that legitimate this force, and the reformist or anti-imperial ideals that question such coercion; and, second, as "social units" with class, status, and racial distinctions shaped by elite interactions from the metropole to the far-off periphery.

In seeking a conceptual frame for this vast terrain, the editors, like the larger discipline of history since the ascent of theory, struggled for a balance between themes manifest across the broad sweep of imperial history and their resonances within specific empires. Like shards making a mosaic, these essays, arrayed by time and place, now form a larger design—manifest in the clear chronological progression in the studies of Spanish imperial history; the thematic complementation between the essays on U.S. dominion in Latin America; the contrast between British information versus its American counterpart; and the tight topical interface among the essays on postwar U.S. power. The sum of this scholarship allows us to construct an analytical frame, a model if you will, for comparative analysis of imperial decline over the span of three centuries.

Looking backward to examine both formal and informal empire, we now ask: What impact did the end of the European maritime empires that once ruled half the globe have on their former colonies, fading metropoles, and an evolving global system? Looking laterally to assay the present, how did Europe's retreat influence America's ascent to global power? Looking forward, what does Europe's rapid imperial recessional in the twentieth century tell us about America's slow decline in the twenty-first century, both its causes and consequences?

So complex, so vast is this global change that much of current writing fails, as Gary Wilder argues below, to "treat decolonization as an epochal process of global restructuring that unfolds on a vast political terrain which includes numerous and diverse actors and entails multiple levels of causation." Instead of the usual narrative of a single empire or the most common alternative, analysis of one or two factors at the global level, the sum of these essays finds that modern European empires were, in both their rise and retreat, a confluence of five interrelated military, economic, and political factors.

Europe's great empires did not spectacularly rise and fall. Rather, they were fluid systems, political as much as military and economic, that transmuted into successor empires. At the broadest level, the fate of these European empires was shaped by two overarching, intertwined forces—economic strength and military capacity. Without the revenues that are almost organic to a conventional, contiguous state, empires must somehow find funds to sustain the enormous expense of their overseas operations, both civil and military. While citizen militias or conscript armies can guard a nation's frontiers at a sustainable cost, the projection of force beyond those borders entails extraordinary expenses that must be somehow covered by exceptional revenues, whether from plunder, heavy metropolitan taxes, or exploitative colonial imposts. Once these revenues falter, the military power so essential to maintenance of any empire soon fails—a weakness often manifest in strategic miscalculations or waning combat capacity.

Just as economic growth produces innovative military technology decisive during an empire's expansion, so fiscal problems can bring a loss of technological prowess that contributes to retreat or defeat. But, as our study shows, state coffers alone do not determine the course of empire. Not only must an empire secure such scarce resources, but it must expend them wisely, literally picking its battles. During such a demoralizing decline, imperial armies, so lethal and rational during an empire's ascent, can err by plunging into draining, even disastrous "micromilitary" misadventures—psychologically compensatory efforts to salve the loss of power by occupying new territories whose symbolism often exceeds any real economic or strategic value. In addition to exhausting the imperial treasury, such geopolitical gambits can also expose the humiliating fact of an empire's fading power.

Among the many military aspects of empire, our study draws attention to the importance of imperial information systems and communications networks for securing accurate intelligence and shaping public opinion. No matter how lavishly funded, intelligence operations can break down or even backfire as their seeming sophistication inspires an illusion of control. Both British and U.S. intelligence exhibited, as the essays by Tony Ballantyne and myself argue, the religious and racial intolerance that Edward Gibbon once found so fateful for Rome, thus suffering an inability to interpret information about other cultures. Yet in the fluid state of empire, the value of even a flawed information system may accrue over time through the complex ways in which scientific and technical knowledge grows, with one discovery unexpectedly opening the door to another—thus making this factor an important wild card in the game of empire.

Between the bounds of these economic and military fundamentals, our investigation also shows that no empire is sustainable without astute statecraft, both diplomacy to court peers and dominance to control subordinates. Empires exercise much of their authority through alliances with peer states that encourage, condone, or at least tolerate their exercise of global influence. Always in flux, these relationships with other powers can elide into conflict through diplomatic breaches, economic competition, or war, thereby weakening the dominant state. Equally important, empires depend on relationships with the leaders in their subject spheres—whether tribal chiefs under formal colonial rule or national leaders in an "informal empire" like America's. When an empire loses its leverage over these "subordinate elites," it founders through lack of support by those best positioned to translate its global power into local control.

In the chapters that follow, we explore the effect of these factors on imperial decline within four contexts—Britain, France, Spain, and the United States—using these cases not for the usual point-by-point comparison but instead to add depth and resonance to each facet. Thus, the essays that focus on individual empires explore not only their decline but a particular factor or combination of factors germane to each case.

Just as these factors influence imperial decline, they are also central to the rise and rule of most empires, albeit with adjustment for particular circumstances. At its peak circa 1900, the British Empire dominated the world economy through the City of London's unequaled foreign investments of £3.8 billon, trade treaties with sovereign states, and global economic leadership through the gold standard and the pound sterling. Of equal import, Britain ruled colonies that covered a quarter of the globe through subordinate elites ranging from Malay sultans to African chiefs. And it controlled an informal empire encompassing another quarter of humanity in nominally independent states in China, Persia, Siam, and Latin America. Moreover, multilingual British diplomats were famously skilled in negotiating force-multiplier alliances with other major powers such as France, Japan, Russia, and, above all, the United States. As the steel behind this diplomacy, the British navy of three hundred warships ruled the seas from a global network of thirty bastions, controlling maritime chokepoints from Gibraltar through the Suez Canal to the Straits of Malacca.[11] Reflecting British industrial innovation, in 1906 its dockyards launched the HMS *Dreadnought*, the world's first battleship, armed with powerful twelve-inch guns, torpedo tubes, advanced armor, and steam-driven turbine engines. With a standing British Army of only ninety-nine thousand men, the entire U.K. defense budget consumed just 2.5 percent of the country's gross domestic product, an extraordinary economy of global force.[12]

Using these same five factors, our analysis draws on and extends the existing scholarship on imperial decline—a topic that, unlike the vast literature on empires' rise and rule, is relatively sparse and often under-theorized. Though far fewer than scholars of empires' expansion, historians of their eclipse have crafted a useful literature that usually relies on just a few causal factors to explain this sweeping global change.

To begin at the beginning of modern imperial historiography, the eighteenth-century English scholar Edward Gibbon, in his monumental *The Decline and Fall of the Roman Empire*, attributed this "inevitable" collapse to several distinct causes. First, poor intelligence made Romans "ignorant of the extent of their danger . . . beyond the Rhine." Second, their empire "depended upon the personal merit of one or two men . . . whose minds were corrupted by education, luxury and despotic power." And, finally, the abandonment of military service, which had once hardened the Romans, made them dependent, fatally, on "the rude valour of the barbarian mercenaries."[13] At the broadest level, Gibbon attributed Rome's fall to the rise of Christianity, which ended its successful imperial strategy of assimilating local gods into "the capacious Roman pantheon"—a conclusion contemporary historians have interpreted to mean that empires, like America's, intolerant of religious and racial differences are destined for decline.[14] Beyond these particulars, Gibbon's influential work inclined succeeding generations of historians to see even the greatest of empires not as fixed or static but as fluid, even ephemeral, moving inexorably across time through phases of ascent, dominion, and decline.

More recently, Paul Kennedy has attributed the retreat of European powers over the past five centuries to the interplay of just two factors. If a state diverts resources from "wealth creation" or wages wars whose "potential benefits . . . may be outweighed by the great expense," then the result is imperial decline. He warned, in 1987, that America's future as "the global superpower" was threatened by such imbalance, while China, though then "the poorest of the major Powers," seemed to be "evolving a grand strategy altogether more coherent and forward-looking than that which prevails in Moscow, Washington, or Tokyo."[15] Embracing this same fiscal-military binary, British historian Eric Hobsbawm observed that "empires were mainly built, like the British Empire, by aggression and war," and it was usually winning or losing big wars "that did them in." In between this military rise and decline, "empires depend not just on military victories or security but on lasting control" through economic power.[16]

In explaining the causes of decolonization, other prominent British imperial historians privilege different factors: first, an empire's waning coercive capacity; and, second, its loss of control over colonized elites.[17] Offering an elegant iteration of this argument, Piers Brendon posits that the British Empire contained a fatal "ideological bacillus" in its doctrine that "colonial government was a trust." With its contradictory motto "Imperium et Libertas," the British Empire necessarily became, as the London *Times* said in 1942, "a self-liquidating concern." Once the "temporary circumstances" that allowed Britain's ascent had faded—naval dominance, industrial preeminence, and "the relative weakness of rival states"—its empire's "ultimate reliance on coercion" could no longer hold.[18] Employing the same factors, but privileging the agency of local actors in this struggle, historian Ronald Robinson famously argued that imperial rule ended "when colonial rulers had run out of indigenous collaborators," with the result that the "inversion of collaboration into non-cooperation largely determined the timing of decolonization."[19]

Among recent scholarship, our approach to imperial transitions shares most with that of John Darwin who warns against sharp dividing lines between colonization and decolonization, seeing instead continuities as empires succeeded one another over the past six hundred years. Empires are "unavoidably subject to . . . an ultimate fall" whose prime causes include loss of "loyalty of subject elites," conflict with old allies, imperial "wars of mutual destruction," domestic fiscal fatigue, or mismanagement by privileged metropolitan elites.[20] Even while analyzing crisis and decline, we are, like Darwin, speaking about metamorphosis, with each empire's eclipse eliding into imperial succession in a process that is more comma than period.

To compare these processes of imperial decay, the essays below begin by closely studying Spain's protracted retreat, and then move through Europe and various thematic issues, eventually arriving, in the last section, at the subject of America's decline. Instead of the usual emphasis on postwar British and French decolonization, our volume's focus on Spain shows how empires in eclipse adapt to changing circumstances, go through epicycles of expansion and contraction, adopt new fiscal-military and socioeconomic models, persist, and even modernize. Such an approach is, we feel, relevant to the U.S. decline, which seems to resemble the slow Spanish retreat more than the sudden British or French collapse during the Cold War.

Applying the factors extracted from the eclipse of these European empires, we conclude that the American century of global dominion, proclaimed at the start of World War II, will end after just eighty years—dawning in 1945, declining by 2020, and eclipsed by 2030. Whether a more just global order will follow, or the world will look back on this American century with nostalgia, we cannot say. But we do seem poised at the brink of major geopolitical change.

Europe's Decolonization

As arguably the most complex of all political systems, empires are subtle synergies of economic, political, military, and technological forces that played, in varying combinations, a central role in Europe's imperial decline. While the history of an individual empire might weave such facets imperceptibly into a narrative, comparative imperial history, the subject of this volume, is best done by extracting key factors from Europe's eclipse before applying them, at the end of this essay, to the ongoing decline of U.S. global power—first, the erosion of economic strength needed for military power on a global scale; next, weakened control over the subordinate elites critical for any exercise of international influence; third, breakdown of alliances among major powers; fourth, misuse of military might through micromilitary misadventures; and, finally, insufficient technological innovation to sustain global force projection.

Economy

First and fundamentally, empires lack the natural revenues of a normal state and must find funds to sustain their costly foreign operations. Unlike nation-states, whose revenues rise almost naturally from their territories, global governance is both costly and lacking in any reliable income. Hence, empires are both predatory and fragile. They are famously predatory in their relentless quest for plunder or profit—witness Spain's silver mines in the Americas, the Atlantic slave trade, the Belgian Congo's rubber lust, or the India-China opium commerce. When they fail to find such revenues, empires seem fragile—witness the collapse of the Soviet sphere as its command economy imploded.

To cite the best-documented decline, six years of global warfare had exhausted Britain's revenues by 1945, and its leaders soon faced an irresolvable conflict between "domestic recovery and their imperial commitments." During the brief hiatus before the start of the Cold War in 1947, Washington was cool toward the notion of bailing out the British Empire.[21] The U.S. Congress rescued the British people from "starvation corner" by forgiving their wartime Lend-Lease debt, but it extended further credits of £3.5 billion only on the condition that London "make the pound convertible into the dollar within twelve months. The imperial economy, in effect, was dismantled," and the empire's dissolution soon followed.[22]

Subordinate Elites

Great empires may rule the waves or the skies, but when they touch ground they need local allies who can serve as intermediaries in controlling complex, often volatile social formations. No matter how extensive an empire, its power is usually synonymous with such "subordinate elites"—whether local notables under colonial rule or national leaders in an informal empire. Absent such support, how could Britain, with an army of only ninety-nine thousand men in 1900, rule a global empire of some four hundred million, nearly a quarter of all humanity? These local and national leaders—who are so essential to the rise of any empire, formal or informal—can also precipitate its decline when they move from alliance to opposition.

In his study of British dominion, Gregory Barton argues that the imperial visionary Lord Henry Palmerston fostered Britain's informal empire in the mid-nineteenth century through alliances with elites across Latin America and Asia, remarking that "to trade with civilized men is infinitely more profitable than to govern savages."[23] By 1890, London reigned over an informal empire through local allies that included emperors from Beijing to Istanbul, kings from Bangkok to Cairo, and presidents from Santiago to Caracas. Indeed, as imperial historians John Gallagher and Ronald Robinson explained so famously, "[I]t is only when and where informal political means failed to provide the framework of security for British enterprise . . . that the question of establishing formal empire arose."[24] If we apply cost-benefit analysis, remarked John Darwin, informal empire was "imperialism at its highest stage."[25]

As Britain's formal colonial empire expanded in the late nineteenth century, "traditional tribal structures and support for those rulers who headed them were . . . established as the ways to govern this new imperium."[26] But the British also stiffened these loose structures, bargaining with India's Brahmans "to harden caste status into an administrative system" and transforming African clans into "'tribes' with chiefly rulers as their ancestral leaders." Thus, British rule ramified across Asia via Malay sultans and Indian maharajas, and across Africa via Kikuyu chiefs, Sudanese sheikhs, and Nigerian emirs.[27]

Just as the choice of these "indigenous collaborators," wrote Ronald Robinson in 1972, "determined the organization and character of colonial rule," so the rupture in these relations led to rapid decolonization.[28] Thus, the end of Spanish rule in Latin America arose, as Josep Delgado Ribas and Josep Fradera argue, from erosion of Spain's economic relations with local elites in the late eighteenth century, culminating in the national revolutions of the 1820s, which soon made the continent part of Britain's growing informal empire. "Spanish America is free," remarked Britain's foreign minister paradoxically in 1824, "and if we do not mis-manage our matters sadly, she is English."[29] Indeed, by 1860 Britain held 76 per-cent of Latin American government bonds and controlled mines, railways, and public utilities across the continent.[30]

In a parallel process at century's end, Cuban and Puerto Rican elites, in a bid to control their plantation laborers, rebelled against Spain and then, as Francisco Scarano explains, formed a close collaborative relationship with the United States. As London's influence in the region faded circa 1900, an American visionary of Lord Palmerston's stature, Secretary of State Elihu Root, crafted a similar system of informal U.S. empire in Latin America. Through Root's deft diplomacy, the continent's leaders allied with Washington, as Greg Grandin and Courtney Johnson explain, to jointly advocate a world order grounded in sovereignty and international law—an extraordinary example of agency by nominally subordi-nated elites. In the Philippines, similar elites, María Dolores Elizalde argues, found the stagnation of Spanish rule increasingly intolerable, first rising in revolt against Spain and later accepting the collaborative U.S. colonialism that Root framed for their country.

In time, these educated elites rejected formal empire entirely, playing key roles in anticolonial revolutions. To overturn the racial order embedded in empire, emerging Indonesian elites delineated a democratic polity through deliberations dating back to the 1920s—challenging, as Warwick Anderson and Hans Pols argue, the idea that postcolonial democracy was an imperial creation. National narratives have often focused on legal and historical knowledge as the well-springs of anticolonial resistance, but Filipino and Indonesian leaders, many of them doctors, derived a "mode of modern self-consciousness" from their med-ical educations, which inspired them to "mobilize the masses for the nation."

Profound geopolitical change was also necessary to give these nascent national leaders access to the rural districts and a mass audience for their ideas. In the Netherlands Indies, as Remco Raben explains, the Japanese occupation during World War II allowed Sukarno and his nationalist allies the opportunity to con-vene mass rallies and draft a constitution for their new Indonesian nation. At a particularly low ebb in their wartime fortunes in 1942, Britain committed itself to postwar independence for India and Queen Wilhelmina made similar prom-ises for Indonesia before the U.S. Congress.

In Africa, Southeast Asia, the Caribbean, and the Pacific where their colo-nies survived into the 1950s, European empires suddenly found themselves confronted with mass movements unimaginable only a decade earlier. As "past masters" of divide and rule, colonial states, Darwin's essay explains, had a long history before the war of maintaining local control by "devolving political power to very local elites, discouraging lateral links between different districts, and avoiding colonial initiatives that might rally more general opposition." But after the war London and Paris, desperate for colonial revenues, imposed extractive policies that brought "more taxation, more centralization, and an activist state whose grasping, governing hand would reach down far deeper into rural society." Confronted with such an aggressive centralization, "colonial communities made common cause," rural unrest spread, and the "vacuous rhetoric of café politicians acquired novel force." Finding their local security forces inadequate to repress this ferment, Britain and France decided to collaborate with the new nationalist leaders in negotiating rapid decolonization.

While colonialism required collaboration by countless local chiefs, after World War II the Soviet and U.S. empires needed allies among the leaders of the world's hundred new nations, producing an intense worldwide competition for their loyalties. Illustrating the critical role of these new leaders, Indonesia's President Sukarno forged a third world bloc that defied the Cold War's bipolar division, while Senegal's Leopold Senghor articulated an alternative path to modernity for his continent. After the French National Assembly rejected his bid for a transformative, transnational francophone union, writes Gary Wilder, Senghor took Senegal toward "African socialism." As Cold War divisions deepened, Sukarno, as Raben recounts, launched the nonaligned movement by convening twenty-nine African and Asian leaders, who represented half of humanity, at Bandung in 1955. If Lord Palmerston and Secretary Root were world historical figures who oversaw vast informal empires, then Sukarno and Senghor were bold visionaries—"canny readers of the historical conjuncture" in Wilder's words—who challenged the postcolonial global order. Indeed, a dozen such leaders—Allende, Árbenz, Castro, Gadhafi, Ho, Kenyatta, Lumumba, Mao, Mosaddegh, Mugabe, Nasser, and Nyerere—were so profoundly disruptive of U.S. hegemony that they seem to confirm the astuteness of Palmerston and Root in subordinating such dynamic elites.

Just as empires deployed colonial police to surveil their local surrogates, so, as decolonization segued into the Cold War, the world's four major powers used their espionage agencies to manipulate the leaders of nominally sovereign nations. The Soviet Union's Committee for State Security (KGB) and its surrogates, such as the Stasi and Securitate, enforced conformity among the fourteen Soviet satellite states in Eastern Europe, while the U.S. Central Intelligence Agency (CIA) monitored the loyalties of national leaders on four continents. As their empires receded, both Britain's Secret Intelligence Service (MI-6) and the French Service de Documentation Extérieure et de Contre-Espionnage (SDECE) engaged in extraordinary postcolonial intrigues within their former spheres, the British to facilitate an orderly imperial retreat and the French to forge a postcolonial empire in francophone Africa.

After 1962 France responded to the traumatic loss of its global empire with a postcolonial dominion over the dozen nations that had emerged from its rule in West Africa—an easy elision from formal to informal empire facilitated by a constitutional tradition that Emmanuelle Saada styles "colonial exceptionalism." Over the next thirty years, as Robert Aldrich tells us, Paris would sanction twenty military coups to advance reliable allies within an imperium called "Franç-afrique." In this shadow realm between empire and independence, the Élysée Palace exercised covert controls via presidential advisers such as Jacques Foccart, manipulating African presidents through coup and co-optation.[31]

Apart from this new role for subordinate elites, the most dramatic change brought about by decolonization, the shift in a people's status from subject to citizen, began before and continued long after the end of empire. As Europe's empires expanded from 1870 to 1920, indigenous demands for rights and imperial manipulations of racial categories grew in almost equal measure, making contestation over civil liberties a common feature of colonial rule. When Portuguese colonies reduced the rights of Africans from a quasi-citizenship to the tutelary category of "indigenous person" before World War I, Cristina Nogueira da Silva finds that educated native elites preferred legal wrangling over their status within the empire to addressing larger questions of home rule—a choice that postponed struggles over independence for several generations. By contrast, the breakup of the British Empire into sovereign states after World War II brought, as Joya Chatterji argues, a complex, contested shift from subjecthood to citizenship in both South Asia and Britain itself.

Rival Powers

Like subordinate elites, peer states are pragmatic, adjusting alliances in accordance with their evolving interests. Articulating Britain's version of this cold realpolitik, Lord Palmerston told Parliament in 1848, "We have no eternal allies and we have no perpetual enemies. Our interests are eternal and perpetual."[32] Thus, a fading power is often closely allied with its would-be successor, which exploits the partnership to assist its own ascent.[33] Indeed, the major transitions studied in this volume—Spain to Britain in Latin America after the continent's liberation in 1824 or Britain to the United States since 1945—involve a rising power superseding not an enemy but an ally.

Although London was Madrid's sometime patron throughout much of the nineteenth century, the British quickly extended their informal empire into Spain's domain after the Latin American republics rebelled in the 1820s. These republics then moved from British informal empire to a U.S. sphere after 1890 though what Courtney Johnson styles "alliance imperialism" between London and Washington. Simultaneously, the United States, with Britain's support, declared war to seize Madrid's remaining island colonies in the Caribbean and Pacific, ending the Spanish empire after four hundred years.

Beyond bilateral relations, modern empires operate within multilateral diplomatic systems exemplified by the Congress of Vienna that liquidated the Napoleanic and Holy Roman empires in 1815, the 1885 Conference of Berlin when European powers partitioned Africa, the Versailles peace conference that broke up the Hapsburg and Ottoman empires after World War I, and the San Francisco conference that established the United Nations in 1945. Under the standard for international relations shaped by the Conference of Berlin, with liberal norms for independence and dependence, the great powers could not colonize or recolonize countries with constitutions and parliaments but could impose conditions that made for winners and losers. This modernization of empires during the nineteenth century was, of course, preceded by the transformation of their metropoles from old regimes into modern liberal states—a path blazed by England and Holland and then pursued by France, Spain, and Portugal. Such reinvention of the state involved new constitutions for the metropole (discussed by Saada and Fradera), legislation concerning the rights of European and non-European colonials (as Silva argues for Portugal), and new information systems for control of overseas territories (analyzed by Ballantyne and myself).

This imperial transition from Spain to the United States in 1898 thus entailed competing cultural claims to modernity and legitimacy. The transfer of Madrid's surviving colonies to Washington was justified, as Elizalde argues, by depicting Spain not as a liberal parliamentary state with modern colonial governance but as a semiabsolutist relic incapable of ruling Cuba, Puerto Rico, and the Philippines. After 1898, as Johnson explains, Latin American elites attempted to advance a global Hispanic cultural union in opposition to Anglo-Saxon dominance. But Washington soon countered successfully with an ideology of Pan-American amity between the United States and its southern neighbors. After supplanting Spain, reports Christopher Schmidt-Nowara, U.S. empire builders began identifying with Spanish imperial grandeur, appropriating Columbus as an American hero and celebrating the Hispanic origins of European settlement in Florida and California.

Even as an aspiring empire maneuvers to replace an erstwhile ally, a receding power may knowingly assist in the transition after a calculated decision to divest itself of global responsibilities. In the imperial shift from the United Kingdom to the United States after World War II, much of Washington's rising global influence, as Greg Bankoff tells us, came from provision of reconstruction aid to a war-torn world, allowing the United States to dominate a ravaged Europe. Ironically for a nation born of anticolonial revolt, the United States, Julian Go argues, regarded Europe's empires as anticommunist bulwarks and supported their cautious decolonization during the early years of the Cold War—thereby gaining the right to site many of its overseas bases in these imperial territories.

In the mid-1950s, the delicate geopolitical balance that had allowed the survival of European empires, with U.S. support, suddenly shifted. This global change, as Darwin's essay explains, arose from a confluence of causes, including wars, political leadership, economic change, and ideological trends. The Korean War drew the United States into anticommunist containment on the Asian mainland, first in Korea and then in Indochina, making Washington "reluctant to back the old order against its local opponents" elsewhere in the world. At the Bandung nonaligned conference in 1955, India, China, Indonesia, and Egypt reached an "informal agreement . . . to pull down what remained of the imperial order." While Joseph Stalin had been cautious and concentrated on the Soviet sphere in Eastern Europe, his more venturesome successor, Nikita Khrushchev, armed Gamel Abdel Nasser of Egypt in 1955 and challenged the United States in "a global competition for influence in the ex-colonial world." In the aftermath of Britain's disastrous Suez invasion of 1956, Washington decided, "Empire must die if the Cold War was to be won."

Ultimately, each European retreat after 1945 facilitated America's advance, making U.S. global hegemony an aggregation of antecedent empires. In picking its battles, the United States was often motivated by a desire for global stability and reliable anticommunist allies. When the Netherlands clung to its Indonesian colony after World War II, Washington shifted quickly from wartime ally to postwar antagonist, first pressuring The Hague to recognize Indonesia's independence in 1949 and then to yield western New Guinea in 1962.[34] Although it conceded Indochina begrudgingly to Washington's sphere after 1954, France responded to the trauma of defeat in Algeria through a neo-imperial foreign policy marked by withdrawal of its forces from the North Atlantic Treaty Organization (NATO), a nuclear "force de frappe," support for a "Québec Libre," and, above all, dominion over francophone West Africa. When Portugal liquidated its overseas empire so suddenly during the 1970s, Washington employed realpolitik diplomacy to deny power to radical liberation movements—sanctioning Indonesia's bloody conquest of East Timor, supporting South Africa's pressure on Mozambique, and authorizing a costly CIA proxy war in Angola.

Washington's relations with London followed this pattern of alliance opportunism, exploiting Britain's economic crisis to depose the pound sterling as global reserve currency, while cooperating in defense, intelligence collection, and covert operations. In March 1946, the two powers laid the foundation for their "special relationship" by signing the top secret British-U.S. Communication Intelligence Agreement (BRUSA) to share intercepts of foreign communications. Building on close ties between the U.S. National Security Agency and Britain's Government Communications Headquarters (GCHQ), the agreement expanded during the next decade into a worldwide listening apparatus by adding

Australia, Canada, and New Zealand as BRUSA partners and allies such Norway, Germany, Italy, and Turkey as adjuncts in the Echelon network.[35] Throughout the Cold War, moreover, British MI-6 collaborated with CIA covert operations to topple insubordinate leaders in Guatemala, Iran, Congo, Indonesia, and elsewhere.[36] Simultaneously, Britain's fusion of formal and informal empire in the Middle East passed into Washington's ambit during the 1950s and 1960s, usually with London's support.[37] Across Asia and Africa, London thus cooperated with Washington to facilitate its own imperial retreat by transferring local allies to U.S. influence, covert assets to the CIA, and oil operations to national and multinational corporations. By the mid-1970s, historian William Roger Louis would summarize this turn in Anglo-American relations, saying, "If foreign loans and economic assistance are considered as vehicles of economic imperialism, then, especially from the vantage point of the British, the post-war era can be seen as one of American 'informal empire.'"[38]

Micromilitarism

As their power wanes, empires often plunge into micromilitary misadventures with hemorrhaging expenditures or humiliating defeats. While the judicious application of armed force is central to the conquest and control of overseas dominions, fading empires can embarrass themselves through these ill-considered displays of power, plunging deeper into military misadventures until defeat becomes debacle.

Whether under British or American dominion, colonial rule, as Kelvin Santiago-Valles argues, sparked an eruption of peasant and worker resistance that required years of efficient pacification to establish even a rudimentary order—an analysis that illustrates the agency of indigenous actors in shaping both specific colonial conquests and the course of entire empires. As imperial power trends downward, however, such military vigilance can easily spiral into micromilitary misadventures aimed at seemingly easy conquests to salve the sting of retreat. Such micromilitarism can also exacerbate the destabilizing impact of imperial decline on the former capitals of empire.

In its long imperial retreat, Spain provides an exemplary case of such micromilitarism, which Stephen Jacobson analyzes as an unsustainable, sometimes nonrational reaction to the pressures of decline or decolonization. In response to the loss of Latin America in the 1820s, Madrid later launched a half dozen imperial adventures ranging from Cochinchina in 1858 to Peru in 1864. Amidst these demoralizing defeats, one imperial general, Juan Prim, came home the hero after a rare victory in North Africa to lead the liberal Revolution of 1868 against a moribund monarchy—a harbinger of later political "blowback" from micromilitary misadventures along Spain's colonial periphery. Then, after losing its remaining colonies in 1898, Spain began to expand out of its small coastal enclaves at Morocco in 1909, establishing a protectorate over the north after winning the bloody Rif War with the aid of France in the 1920s. Across the span of a century, however, the mass appeal of empire faded within Spain itself, notably in the imperial entrepôt Barcelona where, as Albert Garcia Balañà observes, public sentiment shifted from enthusiastic enlistment for Cuba in the 1860s to violent protests against the later mobilization for Morocco.

Even so, Spanish leaders reacted to defeat in the decades after 1898 by seeking regeneration through colonial conquest. Though facing extraordinary resistance, Madrid clung to northern Morocco during the 1920s, dispatching the Spanish Foreign Legion, largely led by Francisco Franco, for a protracted pacification of Berber guerrillas that featured both mass slaughter and military innovation, including history's first sustained aerial bombardment with poison gas and first successful amphibious landing. In a sense, Franco's later dictatorship arose from the ashes of empire, taking form in Morocco and full flight when his Army of Africa launched the Spanish Civil War in 1936. Similarly, the bloodstained French struggle to hold Algeria culminated, at the moment of its defeat in 1961–62, in a two-year military revolt by the Organisation de l'armée secrète, which started in Algiers and spread to France itself. Both in Morocco during the 1930s and Algeria in the 1960s, colonial officers were empowered commanders who proved most dangerous when repatriated.[39]

Although micromilitarism often attacks targets of dubious economic value or objectives that prove strategically unsustainable, the psychological pressures on declining empires are so strong that nations gamble their prestige in such misadventures. During its carefully managed decolonization, London generally avoided imperial backlash. Even so, the suffocating stress of imperial retreat eventually pushed British conservatives into a disastrous micromilitary intervention at the Suez Canal in 1956, causing a "deep moral crisis in London" and what one British diplomat called the "dying convulsion of British imperialism."[40] Similarly, the Dutch held on to western New Guinea for a decade after Indonesian independence until U.S. pressure forced a withdrawal that left them "internally divided, frustrated, and humiliated."[41]

Information Systems

Just as a technical advantage in warfare eases imperial expansion, so shifts in military technology can contribute to an empire's eclipse. For over four centuries, from 1500 to 1940, European empires were synonymous with naval power. Hence, small states with weak armies—Portugal, Holland, and England—could parlay maritime prowess into vast overseas dominions. In equal measure, technology often determined the fate of these far-flung empires. Britain's development of history's first four-ocean navy defeated its Bourbon rivals, France and Spain, in the global Seven Years' War (1756–63). During World War II, Britain's skillful code breaking gave it the edge of victory over Germany's formidable Luftwaffe, U-boats, and surface ships,[42] while America's deployment of radar, submarines, and air power swept Imperial Japan's navy from the Pacific. In postwar decades, the transfer of global hegemony from London to Washington was accompanied by a parallel shift in strategic dominion from the Royal Navy to the U.S. Air Force.

Beyond the firepower of the man-of-war and strategic bomber, imperial rule rests on accurate, timely information. As its dominion expanded during the nineteenth century, British imperialists, Ballantyne argues, filtered local knowledge through cultural frames for both preemptive action and lethal response to any resistance, whether by Maori warriors or Indian mutineers. Even this elaborate system, generally successful in containing indigenous resistance at the high tide of imperialism, showed consistent failings that indicate, ultimately, it could slow but not stop the surge of nationalism that would emerge with such fatal force a half century later.

AMERICA'S DECLINE

The eclipse of European empires in the mid-twentieth century offers insight into the dynamics of U.S. decline during the twenty-first century. At the start of its rise to world power after 1945, the United States had impressive assets for the exercise of global dominion. During World War II, America's role as the "arsenal of democracy" meant massive industrial expansion, no damage to domestic infrastructure, and comparatively light casualties—405,000 dead versus twenty-four million for Russia, ten million for China, and seven million for Germany. While rival industrial nations struggled to recover from the ravages of history's greatest war, America "bestrode the postwar world like a colossus." With the only intact industrial complex, the U.S. economy accounted for 35 percent of gross world output and half of its manufacturing capacity. Militarily, Washington had a monopoly on nuclear weapons and a navy of unprecedented power that ruled the seas. Reflecting its global diplomatic influence, the United States was supported by allies from Europe to Japan and an informal empire in Latin America secured by the Rio mutual-defense treaty.[43] In geopolitical terms, this "colossal imperium" became the first in five centuries with sufficient military force to entrench itself "at both ends of Eurasia," an unprecedented global position that would make Washington the world's preeminent power for half a century.[44]

At the end of World War II, the U.S. invested all this prestige and power in forming an array of permanent institutions for a new world order—the United Nations, the International Monetary Fund, the World Bank, and the General Agreement on Tariffs and Trade (predecessor to the World Trade Organization).[45] In the years that followed, U.S. hegemony built "a hierarchical order with liberal characteristics" based on "multilateral institutions, alliances, special relationships, and client states."[46]

Despite these extraordinary assets, U.S. global dominion exhibited many essential attributes of its British and European predecessors. Instead of London's ad hoc economic leadership, Washington established formal international institutions under the 1944 Bretton Woods Agreements, supplemented by trade and development aid, to dominate the global economy. Apart from some differences in administrative form, both global regimes, British and American, promoted a "liberal international order" founded on free trade, free markets, and freedom of the seas.[47] While the British Empire had covered half the world through direct colonial rule and indirect controls, U.S. envoys used bilateral diplomacy to court allies worldwide while forging multilateral alliances—from NATO to SEATO (Southeast Asian Treaty Organization)—to check rival communist powers. Just as London used the Royal Navy to confine rivals France and then Germany to the continent, so Washington deployed its air and sea power to contain the Soviet Union and China behind the iron curtain.

Yet there were also some significant differences. After completing his ten-volume history of human civilizations in 1961, Arnold Toynbee observed that "the present-day American Empire" had two features that distinguished it from Great Britain's: military bases and economic aid. Following the Roman practice of respecting "the sovereign independence" of weaker allies and asking only a "patch of ground for . . . a Roman fortress to provide for the common security," so Washington sought no territory and instead signed agreements for hundreds of military bases on foreign soil. And in a policy "unprecedented in the history of empires," America was making "her imperial position felt by giving economic aid to the peoples under her ascendancy, instead of . . . exploiting them economically." Indeed, as a defining feature of its global reach, the U.S. has eschewed territorial conquest and instead occupied, after 1898, a half-dozen naval bastions reaching from Puerto Rico to the Philippines that grew, after World War II, into a worldwide matrix of 500 air and naval bases in 1949 and nearly 800 by 1988.[48] In testimony to the success of this strategy, the Soviet empire imploded in 1990 without a single American casualty.

By the close of the Cold War, America was so dominant in every sphere that its intellectuals could triumphantly proclaim, in all seriousness, "the end of history"—meaning that the world now bore an American imprint so deep, so lasting that it would continue in this form unchanged for countless generations to come.[49] Just a decade later, however, such exuberance would seem little more than ill-considered imperial hubris.

To see the shape of our global future a bit more clearly, we can apply the five factors extracted from the eclipse of European empires, coming step-by-step to the conclusion that Washington's unchallenged military dominion has been giving way, in history's relentless imperial cycle, to a new global order in which the United States will become one power among several or, should the decline prove precipitous, a secondary state. The question is not whether America is losing its unchallenged global power but whether it will be the soft landing currently envisioned by Washington's elites or a more wrenching collapse.

In examining this process, the analysis below will compare the social, educational, and cultural changes unleashed by the eclipse of Europe's overseas empires to the current waning of U.S. global power, raising questions about the relationship between domestic decline and imperial retreat. Through application of the key facets of Europe's eclipse to America's ongoing decline, this volume thus seeks to bridge long-standing academic divisions that have generally precluded close study of a problem that lies at the intersection of domestic and imperial history, at the juncture of past and present. But, above all, by exploring five comparable factors in the process of imperial eclipse, these essays indicate some striking continuities between Europe's past and America's future.

Economy

The slow slide in U.S. economic power will someday force a retreat in Washington's global reach. As rival nations grew rapidly in the prosperous years after World War II, the U.S. share of the world's gross product slipped from an estimated 50 percent in 1950 to only 25 percent by 1999.[50] Even so, at the close of the Cold War in 1990, U.S. multinational corporations were still the engines of global growth, its inventors led the world in patents, its scientists won over half the Nobel Prizes, and its economy still accounted for a substantial share of gross world output.[51] Sustained by this economic and scientific strength, the U.S. military maintained 700 overseas bases, an air force of 1,763 jet fighters, an armada of over 1,000 ballistic missiles, and a navy of 600 ships, including 15 nuclear carrier fleets—all linked by the world's only global system of communications satellites.[52] Indicating a possible chink in all this armor, U.S. global defense consumed a heavy 5.2 percent of the country's gross domestic product (GDP) in 1990—twice the British rate at its peak in 1900.[53]

In the twenty years following the Cold War's end, U.S. preeminence in the global economy ebbed, China emerged as the United States' chief competitor, and a multipolar system eroded the preeminence of any single superpower. In 2004, Washington's Institute for International Economics reported that, with the rise of China and the European Union, "the United States is no longer the world's dominant economic entity."[54] Indeed, by 2008 the United States had fallen to number three in worldwide merchandise exports, with just 11 percent compared to 12 percent for China and 16 percent for the European Union. More specifically, China's exports to the United States grew steadily from a nugatory $2 billion in 1984 to a substantial $221 billion in 2009, representing 14 percent of all U.S. imports.[55] A year later China sped past America to become the world's top energy consumer, putting it on track to surpass U.S. economic output.[56] Foreign policy specialist Michael Klare argues that, after "becoming the world's leading energy consumer" in 2010, "China will . . . set the pace in shaping our global future."[57]

Long-term forecasts have predicted a continuing contraction in U.S. economic power. According to Goldman Sachs' 2003 projections, China would become the world's second-largest economy by 2025 and surpass the United States by 2041. By 2007, these accelerating trends forced Goldman to revise its forecast, projecting China to supplant the U.S. by 2027 and India to challenge America for the number two slot by 2050, if not earlier.[58] In fact, China jumped Japan to become the world's second-largest economy in 2010, far sooner than expected, indicating that these earlier estimates were much too conservative.[59] That same year, 2010, China became the world's leading manufacturing nation, ousting the United States from a position that it held for over a century.[60] By April 2011, the International Monetary Fund (IMF) was projecting that China would overtake the United States in real GDP to become the world's largest economy in just five years—with China's share of world gross output surging to 18 percent by 2016, and rising, while America's share would slide to an historic low of 17.7 percent, far below its peak of 50 percent in 1950.[61]

The United States was also losing its leadership in technological innovation. Between 2000 and 2008, America's worldwide patent applications grew by a modest 40 percent to 232,000 and placed second behind Japan; but China was closing fast at 195,000 after a blistering 800 percent increase.[62] Moreover, a survey of "global innovation-based competitiveness" in 2009 found that the United States still clung to sixth place overall but ranked rock bottom among the forty nations surveyed in the rate of change during the preceding decade.[63] Adding substance to these statistics, in October 2010 China's Defense Ministry launched the world's fastest supercomputer, the Tianhe-1A, with so much additional power that, said one U.S. expert, it "blows away the existing No. 1 machine" at a national laboratory in Tennessee.[64]

The American education system, the source of future scientists and engineers, was also falling far behind its competitors. After leading the world for most of the twentieth century, the U.S. performance in secondary education stagnated after 1970 while a dozen other nations shot ahead.[65] In 2009 China "stunned" American educators when Shanghai students came in first in a worldwide survey of fifteen year olds and a comparable U.S. cohort placed at a lowly number twenty-four in math and thirty-one in science.[66] If this test is accurate, by 2025 those Shanghai high school students will be China's rising generation of scientists and engineers. After decades of leading the world in twenty-five to thirty-four year olds with university degrees, America had fallen to number 12 by 2010, and foreign graduate students in the sciences had begun returning home instead of staying in the United States as they once did.[67] Moreover, the World Economic

Forum ranked the United States at number 52 among 139 nations in quality of university math and science instruction. As one U.S. space expert noted in 2009, "China's core space scientific . . . cadre is about two decades younger than its counterparts in the United States and Russia, which are now retiring," giving China an "expanding pool of young, talented, and motivated space scientists."[68]

Similarly, the National Academies warned, in September 2010, that unless the United States recovers its technological edge by investing in education and research, "the nation's ability to provide financially and personally rewarding jobs for its own citizens can be expected to decline at an accelerating pace."[69] With rising social disparities pushing the United States down to number fifty-six in income equality worldwide, American families will increasingly lack the resources to close this talent gap by investing in their children's education.[70] By 2030, America's current cohort of engineers and scientists will retire without sufficient replacements from an ill-educated younger generation, and the country could well lack the economic wherewithal to compete for substitutes internationally.

These global shifts are producing some blunt challenges to America's economic leadership and the dollar's role as world reserve currency. At the peak of its Cold War power, Washington exported the cost of its Vietnam debacle to allies by unilaterally ending the dollar's convertibility to gold in 1971. But the dollar's position recovered in 1974 when Saudi Arabia agreed that oil would be traded in U.S. currency, allowing Washington, a decade later, to close its trade deficit by pressing Germany and Japan to accept the dollar's unilateral devaluation. By 2005, analysts could argue that "the core advantage of the U.S. economy . . . is the peculiar role of the U.S. currency," which allows it "to keep hundreds of thousands of troops stationed all over the world," import goods cheaply, and enjoy "limitless spending power" funded by "its twin deficits (fiscal and trade)."[71] With the world's central banks holding an astronomical $4 trillion in U.S. Treasury notes by 2009, it was time, said Russian president Dmitri Medvedev, to end "the artificially maintained unipolar system" based on "one formerly strong reserve currency"—a view seconded by the governor of China's central bank.[72]

A year later, when the Obama administration failed to close America's trade deficit by forcing China to revalue its currency, former Federal Reserve chair Paul Volcker observed that "the time is gone when the U.S. could lay claim as the putative superpower with both unchallenged economic and military might" and expressed doubt that "the exceptional role of the dollar can be maintained."[73] After President George W. Bush (2001–8) raised U.S. debt to unsustainable levels by doubling defense expenditures and cutting taxes, Washington became gridlocked over fiscal solutions, prompting Standard & Poor's to take "the unprecedented step" in mid-2011 of cutting the country's credit rating below AAA.

In response to this clear sign of U.S. decline, China commented that the United States must cut its "gigantic military expenditure" and the world needed to replace the dollar with a "secured global reserve currency . . . to avert a catastrophe caused by any single country."[74]

Significantly, the U.S. National Intelligence Council has conceded, for the first time, that American global power is receding. In its 2008 study *Global Trends, 2025*, the council cited "the transfer of *global wealth and economic power* now under way—roughly from West to East— . . . without precedent in modern history" as the primary factor for predicting that, by 2025, the "United States' relative strength—even in the military realm—will decline." Russia, along with Iran and Qatar, will hold 57 percent of the world's natural gas reserves by 2025. Adding oil to natural gas, just "two countries—Russia and Iran—emerge as energy kingpins."[75]

Other countries around the globe are meeting this energy threat with aggressive survival strategies—a solar and wind power grid in Portugal (45 percent of all energy), passive solar houses in Germany (95 percent energy savings), surging mass production of solar panels and wind turbines in China (25 and 50 percent of world capacity, respectively), nuclear electrical generation in France (80 percent of all power), wind farms in Denmark (19 percent of electricity), and high gas prices to encourage fuel-efficient cars in the Netherlands ($6.50 a gallon).[76] And America's strategy? Although increased production of domestic natural gas and Western Hemisphere oil will mitigate its dependence, in 2025 America will cover only 12 percent of its energy needs from alternative sources and will remain dependent on imported oil for half its fuel consumption.[77]

These indices of declining U.S. competitiveness, China's economic surge, and the rise of Brazil, Russia, and India are all clear signposts on America's retreat from global dominion. By 2011, Brazil's national development bank was making $83 billion in foreign loans annually, overshadowing the World Bank's lending of $57 billion and challenging U.S. economic leadership in Latin America.[78] Instead of responding to these challenges with a political consensus for reform and renewal, Washington wasted a trillion dollars in micromilitary misadventures in Afghanistan and Iraq during a decade, 2001 to 2011, while its own infrastructure, alternative energy, scientific research, and public education withered from want of capital.[79] After the 2008 banking crisis, a costly mix of military operations and corporate bailouts forced fiscal legerdemain to sustain domestic employment and social welfare, alienating allies and weakening the dollar's credibility as an international currency.[80] Over the longer term, America's social welfare costs will rise from 4 percent of GDP in 2010 to 18 percent by 2050, confronting Washington with the same choice between domestic welfare and overseas military operations that London faced in the 1950s and, in all likelihood, forcing a similar retrenchment of the U.S. global presence.[81]

Subordinate Elites

While European colonial rule rested on local leaders from African chiefs to Indian maharajas, America's informal empire required alliances with national leaders achieved through coaxing, coercion, and manipulation. By applying Robinson's colonial model of subordinate elites in a post-colonial context, we gain a new lens to perceive larger patterns at play in U.S. foreign policy across disparate continents, to see some logic underlying its seemingly contradictory choices during the Cold War, whether CIA coups, alliances with anti-democratic dictators, or preference for military aid over development assistance. When decolonization and the Cold War coincided during the 1950s, the Eisenhower administration was forced, as Brett Reilly's essay argues, to develop a new system of global dominion, replacing Europe's fading empires of local subordinate elites with a worldwide network of national leaders—whether autocrats, aristocrats, or pliable democrats. In effect, the fulcrum for imperial controls had moved upward from countless colonial districts to the national capitals of a hundred new nations. Thus, history's most powerful empire would, like the British before it, be founded on the gossamer threads of personal ties to subordinate elites.

With his experience commanding allied forces during World War II, President Eisenhower revitalized the U.S. national security apparatus, adapting it for the challenge of a world being changed by rapid decolonization. Under the National Security Act of 1947, Washington had already forged the basic instruments for its exercise of global power—the Defense Department, the U.S. Air Force, the National Security Council (NSC), and the Central Intelligence Agency (CIA). Under Eisenhower, an expanded NSC served as his central command for fighting the Cold War, meeting weekly to survey a fast-changing world and plan foreign policy, while the CIA became his strike force for securing this new system of subordinate elites.

From its founding in 1947, the CIA had seemed incapable, even incompetent in its main mission of penetrating the Soviet Union or communist China. But the agency proved surprisingly adept at managing the global network of subordinate elites on the U.S. side of the iron curtain. After shifting the agency away from Soviet espionage toward political enforcement in the emerging nations of Asia and Africa, Eisenhower authorized, during his eight-year term, 170 major covert operations in forty-eight nations. In industrial societies, the CIA cultivated allies with electoral cash, cultural suasion, and media manipulation, thereby building long-term alliances with Christian Democrats in Italy, the Socialist Party in France, and the Liberal-Democratic Party in Japan. In the developing world, the agency brought compliant leaders to power through a string of coups from Iran in 1953 to Congo and Laos in 1960. Under the Eisenhower administration's Overseas Internal Security Program, the CIA also served as lead agency in strengthening the repressive capacity of Washington's Third World allies, creating secret police units for a dozen such states and, in 1958 alone, training 504,000 officers in twenty-five nations.[82]

Throughout the Cold War, the United States favored, with some variation, military autocrats in South America, monarchs across the Middle East, and a mix of democrats and dictators in Asia. In a top-secret analysis of Latin America in 1954, the CIA suggested that "long-standing American concepts of 'fair play' must be reconsidered" if the U.S. were to arrest the region's "irresponsible and extreme nationalism, and immunity from the exercise of U.S power."[83] That December when the NSC met to review challenges to U.S. influence in Latin America, treasury secretary George Humphrey suggested that they should "stop talking so much about democracy" and instead "support dictatorships of the right if their policies are pro-American." You mean, interjected President Eisenhower, "they're OK if they're *our* s.o.b.'s."[84] In this moment of crystalline clarity, the president had articulated the system of global dominion that Washington would implement for the next forty years—setting aside democratic principles for a realpolitik policy of backing almost any reliable leader.

To cultivate a new democratic cohort across Asia, in 1954–55 the NSC promoted "the development of indigenous leadership within Southeast Asia." Concerned about the "surging nationalism of many Asian countries" and aware that "Asian unification must be made through Asians," the Defense Department suggested that its ally President Ramon Magsaysay of the Philippines had "the logical potential" to advance a form of nationalism that complemented U.S. policy.[85]

In Asia, Latin America, and the Middle East, U.S. military aid inflated the political strength of armed forces, while training missions cultivated institutional ties and alternative leadership within the local officer corps. In the quarter century after World War II, U.S. military advisers trained more than 300,000 soldiers in seventy countries, acquiring thereby access to this influential elite within emerging nations worldwide. Under a formal agency finding, adopted in 1968, that "Latin American military juntas were good for the United States," the CIA supported the right-wing leaders of eleven nations with intelligence, covert funds, and military training. When civilian leaders became disruptive, Washington, working through CIA covert operations, could install a sympathetic military successor—replacing, among others, Patrice Lumumba with Colonel Joseph Mobutu in Congo, Sukarno with General Suharto in Indonesia, Salvador Allende with General Augusto Pinochet in Chile, and Mohammed Mosaddegh with General Fazollah Zahedi in Iran. As its Near East director put it, the agency saw every Muslim leader who was not pro-American as "a target legally authorized by statute for CIA political action." The sum of these policies was a distinct "reverse wave" in the global trend toward democracy from 1958 to 1975, as military coups seized power in more than three-dozen nations, representing a full quarter of the world's sovereign states.[86] Thirty years later, in 2009–10, Washington still lavished $1.3 billion in aid on Egypt's military, while economic development languished with just $250 million. As demonstrations toppled the staunch U.S. ally Hosni Mubarak a year later, the *New York Times* reported that "a 30-year investment paid off as American generals . . . and intelligence officers quietly called . . . friends they had trained with," successfully urging the army's support of a peaceful transition to, not surprisingly, military rule.[87]

Elsewhere in the Middle East, Washington has, since the 1950s, followed the British imperial preference for Arab monarchs by cultivating allies that included a shah (Iran), sultans (Abu Dhabi, Oman), emirs (Bahrain, Kuwait, Qatar, Dubai), and kings (Saudi Arabia, Jordan, Morocco). Across this volatile region, Washington courted royalist regimes with military alliances, CIA intelligence, a safe haven for their capital, and special favors for local aristocrats, such as education in the United States or access to Department of Defense overseas schools.[88]

From its inception, the U.S. system of subordinate elites did not create mere surrogates or puppets, but allies who worked, albeit from a weaker position, to maximize their nation's interests through a complex bargaining relationship. Even at its peak of global power in the 1950s, Washington was forced into tense political give-and-take with allies such as Magsaysay, Syngman Rhee, and Ngo Dinh Diem, though it still held ample authority to dominate. Within a decade, as Reilly's essay demonstrates, Washington had to concede President Park Chung Hee billions of dollars in exchange for deployment of fifty thousand Korean troops to Vietnam, providing capital sufficient to spark South Korea's economic miracle and confidence for Seoul to aggressively shape decision-making in Washington.[89]

In less than a generation, South Korea moved from mendicant and manipulated under Rhee in the early 1950s to assertive and manipulating under his successor Park by the late 1960s—illustrating the fluid, ever-shifting power balance between a hegemon and its satellites. As Ronald Robinson once argued so persuasively for the British Empire, the U.S. discovered that even the most pliant of its subordinate elites could soon become assertive, even independent, eroding the foundations for its global power. As secondary states like Germany and South Korea prospered under U.S. dominion, gaining industrial strength and commensurate diplomatic influence, the power balance slowly shifted and Washington's authority inexorably waned, making its informal empire, like the British before it, "a self-liquidating concern."

In the twenty years since the Cold War's end in 1990, Washington found its control over once loyal surrogates fading as globalization fostered both a multipolar system and denationalized corporations that, in tandem, reduced the dependency of developing economies on any single power. With its capacity to control subordinated elites thus receding, Washington's worldview faced, in the twenty-first century, ideological competition from Islamic fundamentalism, European regulatory regimes, Chinese state capitalism, and Latin American economic nationalism. In addition to the fundamentals of military and economic power, "every successful empire," observes Joya Chatterji in her essay below, "had to elaborate a universalist and inclusive discourse" to win support from these subordinate elites. Just as Spain espoused Catholicism and Hispanism, the Ottomans Islam, the Soviets communism, or post-colonial France a cultural *francophonie*, so the United States, at the dawn of its global dominion after 1945, appealed to allies worldwide through soft-power programs promoting democracy and development.

As its leadership was battered by the Iraq War and the Abu Ghraib torture scandal after 2001, Washington, like London in its day, found control over key subordinate elites becoming ever more tenuous. Indeed, the most visible U.S. attempts to control such leaders began to fail—including efforts to topple America's bête noire, Hugo Chávez of Venezuela, in a badly bungled 2002 coup; to detach ally Mikheil Saakashvili of Georgia from Russian orbit in 2008; and to oust nemesis Mahmoud Ahmadinejad in the 2009 Iranian elections. While a CIA coup or covert operation once sufficed to remove a nettlesome leader, in 2003 the Bush administration required a massive invasion to topple just one troublesome dictator, Saddam Hussein, and then found its plans for subsequent regime change in Syria and Iran blocked when those states sponsored a devastating insurgency against U.S. forces inside Iraq.[90]

Even client regimes installed in Afghanistan and Iraq by U.S. forces during the War on Terror were quick to spurn Washington's leadership. After eight years pacifying Iraq at a cost of 4,800 lives and a trillion dollars, the U.S. found, once its combat forces withdrew in late 2011, that its supposed ally Prime Minister Nuri Kamal al-Maliki suddenly asserted his nation's sovereignty, forcing Washington to slash staff and curtail plans for making its massive, 104-acre Baghdad embassy a bastion of American power in the Middle East.[91] Despite billions in foreign aid, Washington could not control Afghan president Hamid Karzai, who told U.S. envoys, memorably, "[I]f you're looking for a stooge and calling a stooge a partner, no. If you're looking for a partner, yes."[92]

Washington's waning influence over leaders worldwide was exposed in November 2010 when the activist news service WikiLeaks released 251,000 recent U.S. diplomatic cables, many rich in timely insights into U.S. relations with these subordinate elites. As the influential Israeli journalist Aluf Benn observed in the newspaper *Haaretz*, "[T]he cables . . . depict the fall of the American empire, the decline of a superpower that ruled the world by the dint of its military and economic supremacy." Today, he added, U.S. envoys are "tired bureaucrats [who] spend their days listening wearily to their hosts' talking points, never reminding them who is the superpower and who is the client state."[93]

To generalize from a myriad of details, these State Department cables show Washington struggling, by means fair and foul, to manage an unruly global system of subordinate elites—intrigue to collect personal data, friendship to coax compliance, threats to coerce cooperation, and billions in misspent aid to court influence. In a move reminiscent of colonial policing, the State Department instructed embassies worldwide, in 2009, to collect comprehensive data on local leaders, including "Biographic and biometric data, including health, opinions toward the U.S., training history, ethnicity (tribal and/or clan), and . . . email addresses, telephone and fax numbers, fingerprints, facial images, DNA, and iris scans."[94] Indicating the need for incriminating information, the department pressed its Bahrain embassy for details, damaging in an Islamic society, on the kingdom's crown princes, asking, "Is there any derogatory information on either prince? Does either prince drink alcohol? Does either one use drugs?"[95]

Indicative of its declining influence, in early 2011 Washington faced an eruption of protests against pro-American autocrats from North Africa to the Persian Gulf, threatening a crucial cohort of its subordinate elites. President Zine el-Abidine Ben Ali of Tunisia had long kept Islamic radicals at bay. Colonel Muammar Gadhafi of Libya was "a strong partner in the war against terrorism." Hosni Mubarak repressed the radical Muslim Brotherhood in Egypt. President Ali Abdullah Saleh of Yemen allowed the United States an "open door on terrorism." King Abdullah II of Jordan was a key defender of Israel. King Hamad of Bahrain provided port facilities for the U.S. Fifth Fleet in the oil-rich Persian Gulf and favored "his relations with the U.S. intelligence community above all others."[96]

While these leaders served Washington, they also subjected their own peoples to decades of corruption and repression, a policy whose ultimate failure prompted a frank admission from U.S. Secretary of State Condoleezza Rice in 2005. "For 60 years," she said, "the United States pursued stability at the expense of democracy . . . in the Middle East, and we achieved neither."[97] By 2011, these failures fueled protests that rocked U.S. client regimes across the Middle East. Although the U.S. ambassador to Tunisia reported in 2009 that police repression and corruption had increased "the risks to the [Ben Ali] regime's long-term stability," the envoy still recommended that Washington "dial back the public criticism" and rely only on "frequent high-level private candor"—a policy that failed to produce any reforms before demonstrations toppled that government in just eighteen months.[98]

Similarly, in late 2008 the American embassy in Cairo reported that "Egyptian democracy and human rights efforts . . . are being suffocated," but still insisted, "[W]e would not like to contemplate complications for U.S. regional interests should the U.S.-Egyptian bond be seriously weakened."[99] When Mubarak visited Washington a few months later, the embassy urged the administration "to restore the sense of warmth that has traditionally characterized the U.S.-Egyptian partnership."[100] Consequently, President Obama hailed this dictator as "a stalwart ally" and "a force for stability and good in the region."[101] When massive demonstrations demanded Mubarak's ouster just eighteen months later, Washington discouraged sudden democratic reforms and backed General Omar Suleiman, the president's "consigliere" and intelligence chief who, according to embassy cables, had a "strong and growing relationship" with the CIA.[102]

Amidst these mass protests that filled Cairo's Tahrir Square for eighteen days in early 2011, Mubarak's stunning downfall and the sudden eclipse of his chosen successor Suleiman represented, wrote a *New York Times* commentator, "an historic eclipse of U.S. power." Indeed, in the year that followed this Arab spring, Islamist leaders whom Washington had long disdained rode to power in Egypt, Tunisia, and elsewhere in the Middle East on a wave of anti-American rhetoric.[103] Taking a broader view of this failure, Egypt's respected opposition leader Mohamed ElBaradei complained bitterly that, after forty years of U.S. dominion, the Middle East was "a collection of failed states that add nothing to humanity or science" because "people were taught not to think or to act, and were consistently given an inferior education."[104]

Rival Powers

For decades the United States successfully managed its relations with rival powers, building its informal imperium on the foundations of Europe's formal empires. Since the end of World War II, the United States "operated within layers of regional and global economic, political, and security institutions" that made its overwhelming power predictable and thus reduced "the incentives for other states to undermine it by building countervailing coalitions."[105] By the dawn of the twenty-first century, Washington exercised its global sway through ententes with major powers, leadership in international organizations, and fifty formal military alliances with both major and midrange nations.[106] But after expending its economic and diplomatic capital in an Iraq War replete with false intelligence and lurid tortures, Washington's global leadership waned. As former U.S. national security adviser Zbigniew Brzezinski put it, this "unilateral war of choice against Iraq precipitated a widespread delegitimation of U.S. foreign policy even among its friends."[107] Meanwhile, new powers had gained a competitive edge. European, Russian, and Chinese leaders grew more assertive after 2001, challenging Washington's ability to set the international agenda.

During this decade of misbegotten warfare after 2001, signs of America's fading leadership have come in rapid succession: the failure, for the first time, to win majority support from the UN Security Council for its 2003 invasion of Iraq; the raucous booing of U.S. envoys by delegates at the Bali climate conference in 2007; and Obama's exclusion from key meetings at the Copenhagen climate summit in 2009. A year later, as the president flew back from visiting Asian allies, the *New York Times* summed up Washington's waning influence with a front-page headline: "Obama's Economic View Is Rejected on World Stage—China, Britain, and Germany Challenge U.S.—Trade Talks with Seoul Fail, Too."[108] A year later, the downward trend continued at the 2011 session of G-20 powers when Washington pressed Europe, unsuccessfully, to solve its fiscal crisis internally and thus avoid aid from China or the International Monetary Fund that would diminish U.S. influence.[109] Amidst its own crippling fiscal crisis, Washington no longer had the wherewithal to fund anything equivalent to the Marshall Plan that had rebuilt a ravaged Europe after World War II.

In the strategic second tier of global power, key U.S. allies Turkey and Australia have grown increasingly independent in their foreign policy. Indeed, Turkey's military, long a bulwark of NATO, staged its first joint air force exercises with China in 2010, angering Washington, which feared a leak of communication codes from Ankara's American-made F-16 fighters.[110] Simultaneously, Australia, reflecting its growing dependence on mineral exports to China, staged its first joint maneuvers with the Chinese navy in the Yellow Sea, and Beijing's warships reciprocated with an historic first visit to Sydney Harbor.[111] These rising states, for decades the most reliable of U.S. allies, were adjusting to the emergence of a new power, calibrating their loyalties carefully.

Just as Washington played on its close alliance with London to appropriate much of Britain's global influence after 1945, so China is using its integration into the U.S. economy to fund a military challenge to America's dominion over Asia and the Pacific. To meet the threat from China and Iran in "two areas of vital interest: the Western Pacific and the Persian Gulf," the U.S. Air Force and Navy signed a secret memorandum in September 2009 forging a new operational doctrine called "AirSea Battle" to explore "power-projection options" in regions that "are primarily aerospace and maritime domains."[112] For conventional force projection, the Pentagon has expanded its bases at Diego Garcia and Guam as anchors in a ring of alliances and installations intended to encircle China—or, as security analyst John Pike put it, to be able "to run the planet from Guam and Diego Garcia by 2015."[113]

With its growing economic resources, Beijing has moved aggressively to establish unchecked control over a vast maritime arc from Korea to Indonesia, waters long dominated by the U.S. Navy. On its southern frontier, Beijing reacted angrily to Secretary of State Hillary Clinton's assertion, in July 2010, that the United States has a "national interest" in mediating China's claims to the South China Sea—a role Washington then reinforced with naval maneuvers there led by the nuclear carrier USS *George Washington*. "The U.S.-China wrestling match over the South China Sea," observed Beijing's *Global Times*, "has raised the stakes in deciding who the real future ruler of the planet will be."[114]

A 2010 Pentagon study reported that China has launched "a comprehensive transformation of its military," focused on improving the ability of the People's Liberation Army (PLA) "for extended-range power projection." With the world's "most active land-based ballistic and cruise missile program," Beijing could target "its nuclear forces throughout . . . most of the world, including the continental United States," while accurate antiship missiles provide "the PLA the capability to attack ships, including aircraft carriers, in the western Pacific Ocean." China was also contesting U.S. dominion over space and cyberspace, with plans to dominate "the information spectrum in all dimensions of the modern battlespace." With the development of the Long March V booster rocket and the launch of five satellites by mid-2010, China was building "a full network" of thirty-five satellites for independent global positioning, communications, and reconnaissance to be completed by 2020.[115]

Micromilitarism

As empires sink into a demoralizing decline, their militaries are prone to ill-considered micromilitary operations, sometimes successful, often disastrous. Just as a dying imperial Spain occupied northern Morocco after 1909 and a fading British Empire attacked Suez disastrously in 1956, so the United States reacted to the trauma of defeat in Vietnam by invading tiny Grenada triumphantly with a full carrier fleet in 1983, sparking a momentary burst of patriotic pride.

Looking back on the early twenty-first century, however, future historians will likely view Washington's 2003 invasion of Iraq as micromilitarism at its most disastrous, a misguided geopolitical gambit that accelerated America's decline. For eight years, argues former U.S. national security adviser Brzezinski, the Bush administration remade America into "a crusader state," leading Washington to neglect "its long term interests," and leaving it unprepared "to face the novel challenges of the twenty-first century."[116]

After the terror attacks of September 2001, Washington became obsessed with the Islamist threat to its Middle East influence, which was, in retrospect, a distraction from the deeper Arab democratic revolution that would, starting in early 2011, sweep away the autocrats who had long been the foundation of U.S. power. By the time the terrorist leader Osama Bin Laden was killed in May 2011, these mass pro-democracy movements had, said Pentagon analysts, weakened his appeal and freed Arabs from a choice "between police-state autocracies and seventh-century theocracies"—raising questions about the wisdom of the U.S. decision to spend several trillion dollars on wars in Iraq and Afghanistan.[117] Instead of recalibrating and correcting this strategic miscalculation, Washington increased its troops in Afghanistan to one hundred thousand in 2010 and then extended its military operations to 2014, courting misadventures large and small in this graveyard of empires.

Information Systems

If the micromilitarism exemplified by Iraq was a corrosive force, then advanced military information systems remain Washington's best hope to retain global power in the face of inexorable economic decline. From 1898 to the present, the U.S. military has responded to difficult overseas operations by developing advanced information systems for both counterinsurgency and conventional combat. During the pacification of the Philippines after 1898, the U.S. Army applied data management to amass intelligence, creating a labor-intensive information infrastructure superseded, during the Vietnam War, by computerized intelligence and air operations.

Even as U.S. economic fortunes trended downward in 2010–11, Washington was determined to maintain a technological advantage for the exercise of international influence in excess of waning fiscal strength. Through a fusion of scientific research and military power, discussed in my own essay below, the Pentagon has planned new technologies for global dominion via space and cyberspace, elevating its forces into an ether beyond the tyranny of terrestrial power. By 2020, the United States will deploy a triple-canopy aerospace shield, advanced cyberwarfare, and digital surveillance to envelop the earth in a robotic grid capable of blinding entire armies on the battlefield or atomizing a single insurgent in field or favela. In a decade-long attempt to effect the technological transformation of warfare, the Pentagon was spending, starting in 2009, $55 billion annually to replace piloted aircraft with drones and to develop robotics for a data-dense interface of space, cyberspace, and terrestrial battlespace.[118]

Alternatively, if Washington is unable to sustain the high cost of technological development, America's economic decline could precipitate a chain reaction of adversity—loss of scientific superiority, forces vulnerable far from home, and pressures for retreat from overseas bases. Simultaneous with China's emergence as an economic power in 2009–10, Beijing began challenging U.S. military dominance—brashly in the western Pacific and obliquely in space and cyberspace. In 2010, China launched fifteen rockets into space, the first time any nation equaled America, carrying satellites that will, by 2020, give China a global system of orbital satellites—ending America's monopoly and allowing Beijing an independent platform for communications, surveillance, and cyberattacks.[119] "The expected next revolution in high technology involving the convergence of nano-, bio-, information, and materials technology could further bolster China and India's prospects," the U.S. National Intelligence Council predicted in 2005, forcing the United States to "compete with Asia to retain its edge," which, the council conceded, could be lost "in some sectors."[120]

Weighing alternatives, history offers some mixed messages, both positive and negative, about Washington's chances for preserving its power by means of technology alone, whether innovative weaponry or information infrastructure. In the last years of World War II, Germany defended its continental empire through a daunting array of advanced weaponry, with V-2 rockets devastating London and Me-262 jet fighters downing U.S. bombers. In the end, however, the Allied juggernaut of tanks, trucks, and troops—all mobilized by America's raw industrial might—simply rolled over Hitler's "secret weapons," ending his bid for sheer technological triumph over larger geopolitical forces.[121]

The history of imperial information offers similarly pessimistic lessons. As its empire expanded in the nineteenth century, Britain relied on systematic cultural study and colonial policing to control local elites and contain uprisings. By contrast, America's proconsuls have eschewed, from 1898 to the present, such deep cultural knowledge and instead favored voluminous yet serviceable empirical data. Although British cultural knowledge and American data processing had their successes, both forms of intelligence were inclined, through imperial hubris, toward an assumption of perfect information that led to imperfect decisions. If British cultural mastery failed spectacularly in its inability to preempt the 1857 Indian mutiny, then American computerized data processing fostered delusions of victory as Washington plunged toward defeat in Vietnam.

Elsewhere, imperial history offers analogies indicating that the tensions between irrational micromilitarism and rationalizing military technology might possibly be resolved in ways that will extend U.S. global hegemony. Reeling from the shock of military defeat and imperial retreat after 1898, Spain sought national revitalization through renewed empire in nearby northern Morocco, plunging into a protracted colonial war that brought bloody riots at home and military disaster abroad. Nonetheless, the Spanish military persisted, overwhelming guerrilla resistance with innovative aerial and amphibious technology and, ultimately, forging its Army of Africa into a hammer that built an empire in Morocco and brought fascism to power in Madrid. In a narrowly self-referential sense, these rationalizing forces rescued the Spanish army from an irrational attachment to empire by taking it on a path to domestic political power. Similarly, the U.S. military's information infrastructure, revitalized amid searing strategic miscalculations in Vietnam and Iraq, has used aerospace innovation to compensate for Washington's waning economic clout, launching a bold bid to extend its global reach deep into the twenty-first century. Whether Washington's fusion of space and cyberspace for a potent global reach will incline it toward micromilitary disaster or extend its global hegemony beyond economic strength is something for future historians to analyze.

GLOBAL TRAJECTORY

If we draw together all this diverse data enumerated above, the negative trends for U.S. global power start aggregating by 2020 and seem to reach a critical, fatal mass around 2030. Under current projections, America's economic output will fall to second place behind China's sometime between 2016 and 2025. Beyond raw economic power, Chinese technology will be on a trajectory toward world-class innovation in applied science and military systems just about the time that America's supply of leading scientists and engineers is dwindling. Moreover, Russia, together with Iran, will hold nearly 60 percent of the world's natural gas—the wherewithal for enormous leverage over an energy-starved Europe.

By 2040, if not earlier, the combined output of Brazil, Russia, India, and China (the BRIC group) will have surpassed the current G-8 of advanced nations. Indeed, the aggregate GDP of the BRIC nations quadrupled in the first decade of the twenty-first century, providing a full third of global economic growth and accounting for 20 percent of world trade. And rising fast behind these four dynamos were the "next eleven" whose economic leaders—Indonesia, Mexico, South Korea, and Turkey—became significant growth centers by 2011 and were on track to surpass several of the G-8 economies by 2050.[122] Exemplifying the new assertiveness of these dynamic second-tier states, Turkey's deputy prime minister told a public meeting with U.S. officials in late 2011 that his nation, not America or Europe, would win the twenty-first century, saying: "The fast fish, not the big fish, eats the small fish." To that prediction of U.S. decline, Vice President Biden could only reply that the United States was still the whale in this sea of young sharks.[123]

This combined shift of economic and military power will diffuse influence within a more multipolar global system and erode Washington's control over such restive subordinate elites in Asia, Africa, and Latin America. Complicating matters incalculably, these economic, military, and technological trends will not operate in tidy isolation. As happened to European empires after World War II, these negative forces might well become synergistic, combining to overcome the U.S. military's technological prowess and spin its global power into an irreversible downward spiral.

SCENARIOS FOR A NEW WORLD ORDER

Even if future events prove duller than the dramatic projections outlined above, every significant trend points toward a significant decline in U.S. power sometime around 2025. If Washington's global reach does in fact recede, a broad spectrum of possibilities exists for a future world order. At one extreme, we cannot rule out the rise of a new global superpower. Yet there does not seem to be any state with the requisite mix of appealing ideology, administrative apparatus, and military power to replace the United States as sole superpower. Searching the world for possible successors, both China and Russia evince inward-looking defense, self-referential cultures, recondite nonroman scripts, nondemocratic political structures, and underdeveloped legal systems that will deny them key instruments for global dominion. Successful imperial transitions driven by the hard power of guns and money often require the soft-power salve of cultural suasion, much as the shift from British to U.S. dominion over Latin America circa 1900 sparked sweeping cultural realignments on three continents.[124] For the first time in four centuries, there is no single state on the horizon to assume the mantle of world power from a fading global hegemon.

Looking for alternatives, a new world order of law and international institutions, first envisioned by Secretary of State Root in 1906, might form a genuine transnational community through shared governance of their strained global commons—its threatened environment, depleted seas, scarce water, and warming Arctic rich in resources.[125] As political scientist G. John Ikenberry argued circa 2011, the U.S. ability to shape world politics will decline, but "the liberal international order will survive and thrive." While the U.S. "hegemonic organization of the liberal international order" will recede as other powers rise, the global system's core elements such as multilateral governance, open markets, free global trade, human rights, and respect for sovereignty will persist.[126]

In a dystopian version of such global governance, a coalition of transnational corporations, multilateral forces such as NATO, and an international elite self-selected at Davos and Bilderberg could forge a single, supranational nexus that would make it no longer meaningful to speak of any national empire. As sketched out in Michael Hardt and Antonio Negri's books *Empire* and *Multitude*, denationalized corporations and multinational elites would rule such a world from secure urban enclaves, pushing increasingly impoverished masses to the economic and ecological margins. There, across the global south by 2025, a billion people will be crowded into "feral, failed cities" and nearly three billion more will want for water. As these authors imply, transnational corporations are quasi-governmental units untethered physically, psychologically, or fiscally to any location, and thus capable of agile global movement to maximize profit and minimize costs.[127]

About midpoint on this spectrum of future scenarios, a new global oligopoly might emerge with the rising BRIC nations plus a perfected European Union using their massive manpower, industrial dynamism, and natural resources to collaborate with receding powers such as the United States and Japan in an ad hoc global dominion, similar to the loose European alliance that ruled much of the world through colonies and informal empires circa 1900. "The arriviste powers China, India, and perhaps others such as Brazil and Indonesia," advises the U.S. National Intelligence Council's report *The 2020 Global Landscape*, "have the potential to render obsolete the old categories of East and West, North and South, aligned and nonaligned, developed and developing."[128]

At the other antipode of future possibilities, we might see the rise of regional hegemons, each ruling what we might call, with a bow to Secretary John Hay's "open door" policy, a "backdoor empire." Such a new world order would be the sum of midsize powers that combine territorial proximity with counterinsurgency, regional free trade, and an international imprimatur of legitimacy. Indeed, a number of such regional blocs have already formed, from the European Union to Latin America's Mercosur (Mercado Común del Sur).[129] In this violent neo-Westphalian world order, a multipolar system would be marked by workaday warfare waged on any insurgents that challenge a hegemon's authority. Through such a fusion of international legitimacy and raw power, each regional center would dominate its immediate hinterland—Brasilia over South America, Washington over North America, Beijing over Southeast Asia, Moscow over Eastern Europe, New Delhi over South Asia, Teheran over Central Asia, Ankara over the Middle East, and Pretoria over southern Africa.[130] Coordinating these regional blocs, a broader configuration for global governance might emerge beyond the current club of North Atlantic powers. Thus, the G-8 of older economies would give way to a G-20 of rising nations or something akin to the Shanghai Cooperation Organization, with the global economic agenda now set in Beijing and New Delhi rather than London or New York.

CONCLUSION

If we draw on Europe's experience of imperial decline, America seems headed for a painful imperial transition. By managing and often initiating its decolonization, Great Britain emerged from its empire's retreat reduced but unscarred. Understanding its limits as a small island with a vast empire, Britain conducted a generally careful recessional that enfolded former colonies into the Commonwealth, preserved the City of London's financial clout, retained international influence as Washington's partner, and maintained global cultural authority through civil institutions—the Anglican Communion, the British Broadcasting Corporation, and leading universities. By contrast, the French, Spanish, and Portuguese, with their national identities enmeshed with empire, clung determinedly to their colonies and suffered wrenching imperial transitions marked by revolution abroad and military revolt at home. Similarly, the United States, suffering from imperial hubris in the form of "American exceptionalism," seems incapable of recognizing the limits of its power and planning rationally for its declining global influence, increasing the likelihood of a troubled transition.

In the aftermath of U.S. imperial expansion circa 1898, Mark Twain wrote an imagined history of America from a far-off future. "It was impossible to save the Great Republic. It was rotten to the heart. Lust for conquest had long ago done its work," he wrote, for "trampling upon the helpless abroad had taught her, by a natural process, to endure with apathy the like at home." Adding to these tribulations, wars had bankrupted the nation, both morally and economically. "The country's conquests, so far from being profitable to the Treasury, had been an intolerable burden from the beginning," Twain continued. "The pensions, conquests, and corruption together, had brought bankruptcy in spite of the maddest taxation, the government's credit was gone, the arsenals empty, the country unprepared for war."[131] After watching the U.S. occupation of the Philippines descend into a bloodstained pacification, replete with torture and atrocities, Twain felt that America's bid for empire had betrayed the democratic principles at the core of its civilization. Whether the United States will emulate Britain in a managed global retreat with minimal domestic damage or fulfills Twain's dismal vision by clinging doggedly to its fading world power and thus diminishing its legacy is something for future historians to decide.

Clearly, an ideology that evokes some broad if not universal principles is central to the success of a world power, facilitating the tolerance of peer states and support from subordinate elites. Indeed, empires, particularly informal empires such as Britain and America's, are alliances between a dominant power and subordinate elites held together, above all, by ideals, whether religious or secular, royalist or liberal, communism or Catholicism. If the London *Times* in 1942 was correct referring to the British Empire as "a self-liquidating concern" by virtue of its dual mission of "Imperium et Libertas," then its careful recessional fulfilled that implicit social contract with the colonized peoples whose support for empire was ebbing.

On a similar note, America's trusteeship of a troubled globe, which started at the end of World War II when Europe was war ravaged and its empires birthed a hundred unstable nations, might finally be coming to an end. After presiding over a half century of sustained economic growth free of the devastation of world war, Washington is now confronted with the emergence of a prosperous multipolar world that neither needs nor wishes its global guardianship. Instead of recognizing this sweeping geopolitical change and planning accordingly, Washington has tried to extend its hegemony by expending trillions of dollars in unilateral wars since 2001, which alienated peer powers, exposed its weakness to secondary states, diverted scarce capital from domestic enterprise, and degraded its moral leadership—thereby accelerating its decline as a global power. Whether America will continue this slow slide or instead will adapt to changing geopolitics in ways that preserve some residual power, by military technology or other means, remains, at this writing, an unanswered question.

No matter what our shared global future might be, it seems likely to entail a new world order based on wide disparities in economic and military power that future historians will one day identify as another in history's endless succession of empires. Europe's empires are gone, and America's imperium is going. But we are not likely, in our lifetimes, to see the end of empire as a system of global governance.

PART 2

Spain's Long Imperial Retreat

Reflecting U.S. attitudes toward a fading Spanish empire, a New York satirical magazine comments, "She is getting too feeble to hold them." (*Puck*, November 16, 1896, Library of Congress Prints and Photographs Division)

Eclipse and Collapse of the Spanish Empire, 1650–1898

JOSEP M. DELGADO RIBAS

IT IS APPROPRIATE THAT A VOLUME entitled *Endless Empire* should begin with Spain—an empire in retreat—which seems to have lasted longer than its fiscal, military, and geopolitical strength should have warranted. Spain is an exemplary case of imperial flexibility and longevity, defying easy "fiscal-military" equations and causing historians to reexamine the durability of empires and to rethink the mechanics of imperial transition. It is clear that a pure and simple geopolitical approach would be insufficient to explain an imperial retreat in which multiple administrative and fiscal reforms reconstructed an empire, first said to be in decline in the late seventeenth century. Indeed, such a process of perceived decline followed by imperial reconstruction occurred at various points within the history of the empire in consonance with world developments. To paraphrase Mark Twain, rumors of its death were greatly exaggerated. As we shall see, the case of Spain also demonstrates that the impressions of decline or collapse, at the time that such words were bandied about, were not always the same as, and sometimes radically different from, those perceived centuries later.

It is perhaps helpful to begin with this problem of characterizations and perceptions. Social scientists have adopted two words from the field of astrophysics—*collapse* and *eclipse*—to describe the decline and fall of empires. *Collapse* is reminiscent of the sudden implosion of a star, the result of a gravitational disequilibrium between the external pressure of gravity and an internal expansive force released by the combustion of hydrogen. The outcome is a constellation of new celestial bodies such as white dwarves, neutron stars, supernovas, planets, satellites, and black holes. *Eclipse* refers to a full or partial covering of the sun or moon observed from earth, which casts a shadow over the location of the observer. The sun or moon is obscured but does not disappear. *Eclipse* refers to a transient situation, conditioned by the perspective of the observer. For their part, historians usually refer to *collapse* to mean the definitive and rapid disintegration of an imperial structure, even though the causes may have developed over a much longer period. Archetypical examples include fifth-century Rome, Romanov Russia in 1917, the Soviet Union in 1989–91, and the Spanish empire in the Americas from 1810 to 1824. *Eclipse* has more contemporary connotations. At the present time, scholars use the term to describe the uncertainty surrounding U.S. hegemony in the aftermath of September 11, 2001, leading to talk of American decline and even imminent collapse.[1] Historians started to use *eclipse* in the interwar period to refer to the decline of Great Britain. Authors such as Richard Jebb described this eclipse as a transient occurrence—a temporary dimming of an imperial splendor that would someday eventually return.[2] Following the World War II, misgivings and doubts became certainties, and the eclipse of Great Britain came to be irretrievably linked to the encroaching hegemony of the United States.[3]

With respect to the Spanish empire, historians have, until recently, preferred the word *collapse* rather than *eclipse*.[4] However, confusion still prevails, given that this expression has not always referred to the same phenomenon, nor has everyone been in agreement over when such a collapse occurred. For example, in 1898 the *Calcutta Review* published an article on the war between the United States and Spain, succinctly titled "The Collapse of Spain." It reiterated the British prime minister Lord Salisbury's famous prediction, made some months earlier in a speech to the conservative Primrose League, that old empires, such as those of Spain and the Ottomans, were "dying nations" soon to be replaced by ascendant powers.[5] The collapse was the closing stages of a lengthy illness caused by the debilitating effects of corruption and misgovernment on the body politic. For the contemporary U.S. press, Spain's collapse was consummated when its plenipotentiaries, negotiating in Paris at the end of November 1898, agreed to transfer sovereignty over the Philippines to the United States. Thus did the entire Spanish colonial edifice founder.[6]

By contrast, historians of Spain have consigned the expression "vertiginous collapse" to the early decades of the nineteenth century. The actual causes of such ruin continue to be disputed.[7] According to the historian David Ringrose, what added a truly catastrophic dimension to the collapse of empire and monarchy during the period of the Napoleonic Wars was the fact that Spain exited the ranks of the great powers. Following the Congress of Vienna (1815), it was excluded from the Concert of Europe and had hence been reduced to a mere supernumerary in the new state system.[8] To be sure, geopolitical decline was seconded by overwhelming economic and fiscal repercussions. The loss of the colonies not only seriously affected Spanish industry and trade, but seriously compromised the fiscal foundations of the absolute monarchy itself.[9]

Curiously, this general agreement among historians clashes with impressions at the time. In 1824, as defeated Spanish armies returned from the Americas, practically no one talked of decline, collapse, or empire. While in 1898 Spaniards continually sought to come to terms with and lamented the end of empire, and endlessly bandied about such expressions, memoirs from the 1820s reveal nothing of the sort.[10] Scholars attempting to explain the absence of a discourse of decadence have pointed to three reasons. First, the return of absolute monarchy following the Napoleonic Wars conditioned the debate. Under the despotic government of Ferdinand VII (1814–20, 1823–32), the monarchy treated its colonial possessions as private patrimony rather than a public good. Moreover, the regime distorted and limited the distribution of information concerning events taking place in the Americas. For example, the defeat at Ayacucho in December of 1824, signaling the capitulation of Spanish armies on the continent, was only made public in April. Even when the event could not be denied, official voices questioned whether the outcome had been so catastrophic. Second, Spanish liberals, who also suffered under the yoke of absolute monarchy, sympathized with the plight of their American counterparts. In 1820, Spanish soldiers rebelled in the southern town of Cabezas de San Juan, refusing to be sent overseas to fight in a colonial expedition to reconquer the Río de la Plata region. This mutiny sparked a revolution in Spain, inaugurating a period of liberal rule known as the Constitutional Triennium (1820–23). Following the restoration of absolutism in 1823, Ferdinand VII and his advisers continued to insist that it was possible to reconquer continental America, yet many liberals simply disagreed. Third, economic factors weighed heavily. Beginning in the 1830s, the Cuban boom led many to posit that a slimmed-down version of the empire could be just as, or even more, profitable than its bulky predecessor.[11]

With the coming of the constitutional monarchy of Isabel II (1833–68), elites sensed the dawning of a new era of imperial opportunities despite economic losses stemming from the disintegration of the continental American empire. The Cuban boom, the potential of Puerto Rico, and the vast resources of the Philippines opened a door of opportunity for Spanish imperialists to mend their old colonial ways and construct a new model of liberal colonialism. According to the Constitution of 1837, the colonies were to be governed by "special laws," an arrangement that had the effect of preventing colonial inhabitants from enjoying rights and liberties that were slowly gaining ground on the Iberian Peninsula. There was much continuity during the transition from absolutism to liberalism in the 1830s. A political oligarchy, which had thrived behind the scenes of the absolutist state, adjusted to changing times and formed an alliance with a financial and trade elite whose wealth, often of dubious origins, was based on colonial business ventures.[12] This alliance would remain intact throughout the nineteenth century. It would only come apart following the loss of the colonies in the Spanish-American War of 1898 when the high bourgeoisie of the Spanish periphery, which had grown wealthy from Cuban, Puerto Rican, and

Philippine commerce, began to break with the political elite of the Restoration Monarchy (1876–1923). The loss of the colonies in 1898 did not put an end to debates concerning Spain's imperial future. Indeed, during the first third of the twentieth century, Spanish governments intensified their presence in Morocco and the Gulf of Guinea. Nonetheless, while governing elites continued to believe in the need to rebuild an empire, the bourgeoisie on the periphery no longer believed that the Spanish state was up to the task. Rather, this elite supported Catalan (and later Basque) nationalist movements, which incidentally were pregnant with imperial pretensions.[13]

Regeneration after 1898

One of the most striking articles published in Spain during the war with the United States explicitly argued against interpreting the events of 1898 as an irreversible imperial eclipse. Written by Gonzalo de Reparaz, "The Spanish Empire: What There Was and *What Remains*," appeared in the weekly broadsheet *Blanco y Negro*. Writing on August 13, 1898, the very day Manila capitulated to General Wesley Merritt, the author expressed a desire to continue an empire project even in the face of defeat.[14] Interestingly, the article caught the eye of the British ambassador in Madrid, who included an extract in one of his reports to the Foreign Office. According to the ambassador, a profound sadness imbued Reparaz's observations. The article did not focus on 1898 but reflected on the lengthy imperial trajectory of what had once been the "most powerful of all nations." The author referred to four "dismemberments" that had weakened the empire since Philip II unified the peninsula by annexing Portugal in 1580. These dismemberments were illustrated in a simple but telling graph depicting, using circles of decreasing size, the eclipse of an empire from the first dismemberment of 1668—

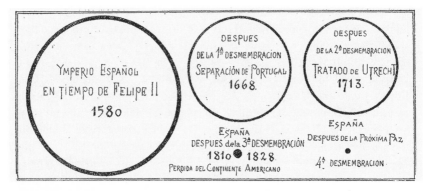

Representation of Spain's imperial decline, showing a marked contraction in the Spanish empire's size from the seventeenth to nineteenth centuries. (Gonzalo de Reparaz, *Blanco y Negro*, August 13, 1898)

the separation of Portugal—to the latest, though not definitive, dismemberment of 1898. Reparaz was an "Iberianist," arguing that the loss of Portugal was "the most painful of those suffered by Spain." Like many other publicists of the period, he was also a "regenerationalist," believing that defeat in the Spanish-American War offered an opportunity for regeneration. The "continuity of our decline," he argued, was due to the absence of a manifest destiny that should replace the "discovering and colonizing mission imposed by Providence" in the sixteenth century. According to the author, Spain's new manifest destiny should be to exert its influence in Morocco.[15]

Aside from the author's predictive capacities concerning Morocco, the article is interesting for two reasons. First, Spain continued to be perceived as an empire, one in decline, but an empire nonetheless. Two centuries of misguided policies had dragged it down. Second, the author argued that if errors were not put right, the decline would continue with new amputations: "We are in a bad way, we are worth little, and if we fail to admit to it and start to mend our ways, we will soon be worse off and entirely worthless."[16]

THE DISCOURSE OF DECLINE

Was the Spanish empire slowly declining over the previous 250 years, as Reparaz would have it? Or was this notion of an empire in permanent decline nothing more than what one historian has called a "paper tiger"?[17] What is certain is that this "discourse of decline" had been omnipresent in the writings of Spanish bureaucrats, theologians, jurists, and protoeconomists since the closing decades of the sixteenth century.[18] These writings reflect the ongoing work of an "imperial think tank" relentlessly searching for solutions to problems that had never been encountered in Europe. How could territories be governed when it took months for news to reach the peninsula? How could overseas provinces be administered in the name of a monarch but without his presence? How could Spaniards ensure submission and obedience of an Amerindian labor force without a costly occupation force? How could a regular flow of the precious metals—the lynchpin of the Hapsburg's power in Europe since the time of Charles V—be guaranteed and protected from pirates? These are only some of the questions that imperial administrators had to confront.

To address such issues, the monarchy created ad hoc boards, comprised of a wide range of experts, to examine specific problems, such as how to distribute noble patents and titles of conquest, how to regulate and enforce the just treatment of Indians, and how to organize the licensing of companies granted monopolies over parcels of the slave trade. Such intellectuals also served as magistrates, judges, inspectors, and advisers to the Council of the Indies, the chief governing and jurisdictional body for the colonies. To no one's surprise, this organizational structure was never cited as a cause of decline. After all, those responsible for diagnosing ills were usually the same Hapsburg policy makers who benefited from the system. In the last third of the seventeenth century, when Spain's precipitous decline in Europe, in the wake of the Thirty Years' (1618–48) and Franco-Spanish wars (1635–59), was the talk of all diplomatic (and non-diplomatic) circles, this situation changed. Spaniards came to increasingly criticize the imperial administration. However, such criticisms tended to focus on how administrators had indifferently ceded control of trade with the Americas to emerging European powers, such as Holland, France, and Great Britain. Proposed remedies steered clear of a wholesale reorganization of the imperial administration. Instead, reformers stressed the urgency of reorganizing Atlantic trade according to the chartered company model, which other countries had been using with great success in their overseas possessions.[19]

Yet, just as the Hapsburg monarchy was foundering in the face of emerging fiscal-military powers, Spain's colonial empire managed to survive intact. Remarkably, the monarchy adjusted to inter- and intraimperial dynamics. Its adaptive capacity was severely tested during the second half of the seventeenth century, but it managed to survive due to two major changes, the first ideological and the second economic. First, imperial administrators came to an agreement with creole, mestizo, and native elites in the Americas concerning the redefinition of the empire. The idea of "conquest" was abandoned and replaced with that of a "pact"—a "blood pact" (*pacto de sangre*)—an expression borrowed from the Philippine political tradition. Second, Hapsburg administrators implemented a series of reforms, opening up its colonial markets to European maritime powers.

THE FLEXIBILITY PRINCIPLE

This new imaginary foundational pact, consecrating the Crown's dominion over its overseas territories, proved quite durable. It remained in place until the monarchy of Charles III (1759–88) abolished it with a series of enlightened reforms. It became so engrained in the imperial *mentalité* that when Charles unilaterally broke the pact, the colonists themselves invoked its veracity. The pact involved what the historian John L. Phelan has convincingly described as the "flexibility principle."[20] In essence, the colonial bureaucracy exercised discretionary nonapplication of the laws and royal commands transmitted from the metropolis by the Council of the Indies. According to the jargon of the period, this tacit right of remonstration was expressed by the saying "We obey but do not comply" (*Se obedece, pero no se cumple*). As such, the legislative imperium of the Crown was preserved while the colonial institution enjoyed a considerable degree of autonomy. Viceroys, governors, and *audiencias* (high judicial and administrative bodies) used this arrangement in order to adapt broad-ranging colonial policies dictated from the metropolis to local interests; by so doing, they ensured the support, cooperation, and complicity of local groups. The pact also allowed creoles to take up key posts in the colonial administration by selling public offices, which were often temporary but sometimes permanent and even heritable. In 1557, the Crown initiated this process, and by 1633 some of the most important posts in the administration of justice and tax collection were venal. In addition to solidifying the pact, the sale of offices constituted a crucial source of revenue. Of course, the price of flexibility was the sacrifice of efficiency. Widespread corruption enabled creoles to populate the colonial bureaucracy in furtherance of private interests. Purchasers of public offices were not primarily concerned with developing an imperial career in order to gain prestige or personal fulfillment. What mattered was the ability to leverage their positions for illicit gains. On balance, the flexibility principle minimized the risk of internal dissent and secession while drastically reducing the cost of defending the empire—but at the price of widespread corruption in justice and administration.

The Crown also employed the flexibility principle in its dealings with emerging powers such as Holland, France, and Britain. The historians Stanley and Barbara Stein have pointed out that the Treaty of Westphalia (1648) marked Spain's "definitive transition from power to inferiority."[21] As a result, Spain entered a number of unequal trade agreements with European maritime powers. These effectively removed protective barriers that had previously ensured the Spanish monopoly over trade in the Americas. The Peace of Münster (1648) and the Treaty of The Hague (1661) gave such privileges to the United Provinces, the Treaty of the Pyrenees (1659) extended these to France, and in 1667 Stuart England came to a similar agreement with Hapsburg Spain. In the latter decades of the seventeenth century, Spain signed on to a number of other general and specific tariff concessions, further opening up the empire to trade with the great powers. According to Gonzalo de Reparaz, the loss of monopoly trade represented "a descent a few more rungs down the ladder."[22] At the time, though, negotiators were aware that this was the price that an empire in eclipse had to pay in order to maintain its territorial integrity, given that its economic and military potential had been clearly surpassed by the maritime powers of northern Europe. By means of these mechanisms, the last Hapsburg, Charles II (r. 1665–1700), managed to bequeath, almost intact, the patrimonial inheritance received from his ancestors to his House of Bourbon successors.

During the War of the Spanish Succession (1701–14), the creole elite in the Americas remained faithful to the cause of the Bourbon pretender, Philip of Anjou, who in fact was the testamentary heir of the last Spanish Hapsburg. As a result, there was no conflict between peninsulars (persons born in Spain who lived in the colonies) and Americans in the Americas. The English and Dutch, who supported the alternative Hapsburg candidate, came to understand that support for their cause would not be forthcoming from the Americas. At one point, the Dutch contemplated fomenting an uprising against Philip V. Organized from

Curaçao, the plan was to stir up support for the Hapsburg pretender by landing a force in Central America as a way to gain access to Peru, Mexico, Venezuela, and the Philippines. The project was abandoned before such a landing took place when it became apparent that it could only count on a small group of supporters in Venezuela, who would have been unable to rally the rest of the population.[23]

BOURBON REFORMS

The Bourbons prevailed in the War of Spanish Succession, and Philip V, the grandson of Luis XIV, ascended to the throne. Unlike the Hapsburgs, the Bourbons were less willing to pay such a high price for flexibility in interimperial relations. The Treaty of Utrecht (1713), ending the war, confirmed the contents of the previous bilateral peace and trade treaties, ratified further tariff reductions granted in the latter decades of the seventeenth century, and ceded new trading privileges to Britain. In a nutshell, it represented an insurmountable obstacle to the development of mercantilist policies similar to those of France or England. Spanish legislators were well aware of the steps necessary to move toward mercantilism, but they simply could not get around the impositions stemming from Utrecht and previous agreements. During the first half of the eighteenth century, reformers writing on the ills of the imperial economy were well aware of these limitations. Hamstrung by Utrecht, they could only propose minor or cosmetic improvements to the old colonial edifice.

This price, paid by the Bourbons to safeguard the empire from intervention, became increasingly burdensome as Spain gradually emerged from its eclipse. The recovery in remittances from the West Indies in the first half of the eighteenth century and new sources of revenue from the territories of the Crown of Aragon improved the state of the treasury. It must be realized that the Crown of Aragon, with its traditional capital in the city of Barcelona, was also part of the imperial structure even though it was on the peninsula. It included the regions of Catalonia, Valencia, and Aragon, which had supported the Hapsburg pretender during the War of Spanish Succession by allying itself with Britain, Holland, and Austria against France and Castile. However, the British had sold out the Crown of Aragon at the negotiating table in Utrecht, returning it to Spain without exacting any guarantees. Thereafter, the Bourbon monarchy imposed a series of "New Foundation" (Nueva Planta) decrees (1716–17) under which these regions not only lost their representative institutions but were also subject to punitive taxation. The new revenues not only funded the Italian policies of the monarchy, which were aimed at recovering some of the territories lost at Utrecht, but also enabled the treasury to bear the cost of an army of occupation in Catalonia, which, until 1770, was more numerous than that deployed in all the mainland American colonies. Still, new revenues did not solve the Crown's fiscal problems. In 1739, the treasury again went bust. Indeed, the imperial state was stretched to its financial limit, as taxes were insufficient to support the price of administering and defending the empire, including the Crown of Aragon.

To resolve these fiscal problems, royal administrators implemented two reforms. The first was the handiwork of the Marquis de Ensenada, the enlightened adviser of Ferdinand VI (r. 1746–59). It did not address the tax status of the Americas but that of Spain. In essence, it rationalized tax administration in all of Spain by implementing a system of direct taxation that replicated that which had worked well in the Crown of Aragon since the New Foundation decrees. The reform failed to produce the desired financial results, but improvements in administration did allow Ensenada to capitalize on a time of peace inaugurated by the Treaty of Aix-la-Chapelle (1748) to rebuild the Spanish navy. By the mid–eighteenth century, the Spanish fleet was the third largest in the world.

The second major reform of the fiscal system took place in the wake of Spain's first colonial "disaster," that of 1762. In 1761, Charles II had reestablished the "Family Pact" with Louis XV and entered into the Seven Years' War (1756–63) on the side of France. The results of this alliance were disastrous for Spain, as Great Britain occupied the ports of Havana and Manila. Ultimately, the efforts of the new dynasty to rebuild the Spanish navy and improve the treasury's finances had not brought about an end of the eclipse. In Spain, the Seven Years' War did not cause such serious financial problems as it did in France, Britain, and Prussia. However, it did force enlightened reformers to realize that the monarchy could only be revived by reworking its relationship with the Americas. The key document signaling the path of future reforms was the *Discourse on the Utility to Be Derived by Spain from the Misfortune of the Loss of Havana*, authored by Francisco de Craywinckel, a Spanish official of Flemish origin. "Moved by the pain of the loss of Havana," his goal was to draw conclusions from the latest war to provide the means so that Spain "could begin to flourish and, with time, become richer and more powerful" than Britain.[24]

This dry internal, administrative document was not laden with the elegant and propagandistic phrases then permeating the printed works of enlightened minds. All the same, it came to have a massive impact on imperial policy. According to Craywinckel, military and naval power depended not so much on a country's wealth as on the state's ability to tax this wealth. During the Seven Years' War, Britain had managed to raise 108 million pesos from its taxpayers, whereas Charles III had barely raised 20 million. The British were thus able to equip 372 warships in comparison with Spain's 84. Britain's main source of wealth was trade, and, in Craywinckel's opinion, trade had furnished the resources that enabled British military power to surpass that of Spain. In the same year as Craywinckel penned this piece, his enlightened friend and royal adviser Pedro Rodríguez de Campomanes wrote *Reflections on Trade in the Indies*. The two shared similar views—to follow the British example, Spain had to treat the

American territories not as provinces but as colonies. As such, the colonies should shoulder the brunt of imperial rearmament. This would involve constructing new fortifications in the nodes of imperial governance, frequently dispatching veteran troops from the peninsula, strengthening creole militias, and increasing the presence of Spanish warships in American waters. Charles III took up the suggestions of Campomanes and Craywinckel by implementing a reform plan from 1765 to 1787. Initially under the supervision of the Marquis de Esquilache and later under José de Gálvez, the reforms were couched in a enlightened language promising good government and augmenting the happiness of the people. Underneath this convincing prose, though, fiscal motivations were paramount.

Compromised Reforms

Did this effort to end the eclipse of the Spanish empire and halt the march of British hegemony lead to the imperial collapse of 1810–24? On one level, Charles III's coterie of reforms undoubtedly intended to end the tradition of *pactisme* with colonial subjects, a strategy that led the subjects to grow increasingly skeptical of Crown reforms. The monarchy no longer sold offices or tolerated noncompliance. What is more, in a stated attempt to combat corruption—and an implicit attempt to strengthen control—the Crown limited the number of creoles who could serve in key places in the colonial administration. Instead, it greatly augmented the number of peninsulars (persons born in Spain) in such positions, who were theoretically more faithful to the Crown and less susceptible to corruption. Taken together, these measures ended the foundational myth of the pact of blood, restricted local autonomy, and blocked qualified elites from ascending to important posts, angering the creole community and planting the seeds of future dissent during the era of independence. Yet this standard explanation does not sufficiently explain the effect of the reforms.

On another level, many of the intended reforms did not serve to reassert Crown control but paradoxically created mechanisms that favored colonial autonomy, hence maintaining the spirit of the flexibility principle. For example, the reforms converted the American militias into the central component on which the defense of the empire rested.[25] This reform worked well in Cuba, as well as other places, because it provided creole elites with the opportunity to receive military training and strengthen its leadership over mestizo and *pardo* (black and mulatto) militiamen.[26] The militias were essentially private, as they were raised and financed by wealthy creoles with official posts who paid for uniforms or equipment and covered delays in paying salaries. As head of both the War and Treasury ministries, Esquilache decided that the militias would be the center of colonial defenses; this would curb growing military spending without compromising the security of the empire.[27] This decision had as a precedent Philip V's reorganization of the peninsular militia in 1734. Interestingly, this reform excluded the rebellious Crown of Aragon, which had fought against Philip V in the War of Spanish Succession. Here even the nobility was not allowed to bear arms.[28] The lack of faith in Catalan, Aragonese, and Valencian loyalty to the Crown, however, did not extend to the American territories. Across the Atlantic, the army and the militias would only be necessary "in the event of a war; they were not necessary to uphold authority, because the temperament of these natives is such that he who commands is willingly obeyed."[29] As later events would prove, this calculation was wrong. During the Napoleonic invasion of 1808, the Catalan and Aragonese formed militias faithful to the Crown, while many of the American ones worked toward autonomist or secessionist ends.

Moreover, these reforms did not succeed in asserting greater central control over the city and *cabildos* (town councils). On the peninsula, the Bourbon New Foundation laws, applied in the Crown of Aragon, had disempowered the urban oligarchies that had controlled municipalities since the thirteenth century. In cities such as Barcelona and Valencia, the monarchy appointed some of the town councilmen, while the *audiencia* appointed the rest. What is more, the Crown placed a *corregidor* (a high judicial and administrative official) at the head of each municipality. This administrative figure had long existed in Castilian municipalities as a civilian bureaucratic official. However, in the Crown of Aragon during the eighteenth century, 96 percent of them belonged to the military.[30] In the Americas, however, such councils continued to enjoy high levels of autonomy and to defend local interests, given that many of their members were elected from among the residents.

As long as the Spanish administration remained stable, these institutions—the *cabildos*, municipal and provincial militias, and new trade consulates (created between 1793 and 1795)—served as an effective bridge between local and imperial interests. However, when the imperial system began to break down, participating elite began to question their allegiances. When Napoleon invaded the Iberian Peninsula in 1808, sent the royal family into exile, and placed his brother José Bonaparte on the Spanish throne, things changed drastically. A constitutional convention convened in the southern city of Cádiz in 1809, opening up a whole new realm of possibilities for the reorganization of the empire. In America, the disintegration of the Spanish state meant that secession would be less costly. It was at this time that elites serving in key institutions began to weigh whether the benefits of remaining part of an empire in eclipse offset the costs, which incidentally had increased significantly during the last third of the eighteenth century.[31]

In the end, the story of the so-called end of the Spanish empire is well known. It featured the independence of the new republics in Spanish America by 1824 and the independence of Cuba and the ceding of Puerto Rico and the Philippines to the United States in 1898. All the same, this eclipse is arguably not over. The image of the Spanish empire, articulated by Gonzalo de Reparaz, still effectively illustrates Spain's long imperial retreat taking place over five centuries. Under this perspective, it is possible to interpret the continued vitality of secessionist movements in the twenty-first century—in Catalonia, the Basque country, and elsewhere—as part of this ongoing process. The current "asymmetric" structure of the Spanish state has its roots in the flexibility system of the imperial past. In short, it is possible that the circles will become progressively smaller. Neither the ethos nor the structure of the empire collapsed in 1824 or 1898.

Empires in Retreat

Spain and Portugal after the Napoleonic Wars

JOSEP M. FRADERA

THE FIRST SIGNIFICANT PERIOD of revolution and decolonization in modern European history, which took place from 1780 to 1830, was characterized, among other things, by two paradoxes. The first is that the long-standing Spanish and Portuguese colonial empires—pioneers of European ultramarine expansion—persevered within a new world order forged by the Napoleonic Wars. These two empires survived the first major round of American decolonization, which commenced with the secession of the thirteen North American colonies and concluded with the defeat of the Spanish royal armies in Peru in 1824. Upon their disintegration, these countries left not only a number of newly independent republics with vague frontiers but also two important, though precarious, monarchic empires: the successful Brazilian empire and the failed Iturbide empire in Mexico. The second paradox is that the survival of these old imperial systems during the Napoleonic Wars was essentially dependent on the military and financial might of the emerging British Empire. In exchange for its considerable military efforts, however, Great Britain exacted a price, which directly affected the political and economic interests of its Catholic allies and their capacity to embark on new imperial projects. These paradoxes give rise to an obvious question. How did Spain and Portugal not only survive as empires but also bolster their ambitions in a world dominated by their northern European rivals?

To begin to answer this question, it is first necessary to understand how British imperial hegemony affected other European countries with empires or imperial ambitions. On the one hand, it is evident that the rise of Great Britain radically curtailed the expansionist possibilities of Spain and Portugal; on the other hand, other northern European empires were able to expand their dominions. The Dutch increased their presence in Java and adjacent islands beginning in 1825, while the French began an aggressive empire project in Algeria in

1830 and in Senegal during the 1850s. By contrast, the Spanish and Portuguese empires shrunk following the independence of Brazil and the Spanish continental American republics between 1822 and 1824. In the ensuing decades, both countries sought to hold on to their remaining possessions. Spain maintained its sovereignty in Cuba and Puerto Rico in the Caribbean, in the Philippines in the South China Sea, and in a number of enclaves with vague borders in North Africa and the Gulf of Guinea. For its part, Portugal held on to its African possessions of Cape Verde, Angola and Mozambique, and enclaves in India, China, and Southeast Asia.[1]

To be sure, during the nineteenth century, Spain and Portugal managed to reposition themselves as smaller and less ambitious imperial powers within a broad British-led world order. For such purposes, it would be misleading to describe such empires as in "decline." Echoing Edward Gibbon, this expression gives the impression of an immovable system growing increasingly decrepit with the passing of time. Instead, the more neutral word *retreat* is preferred, since it does not carry such pejorative connotations. In short, even in the conflict-ridden world of nineteenth-century empire building, reorganization, misadventure, and abandonment, some retreats were more orderly and considered than others. As we shall see, Spain and Portugal—empires in retreat—needed to confront the same problems and came to share similar imperial dynamics as other imperial projects of the nineteenth century. Of course, this does not mean that they were devoid of peculiarities.

The Spanish and Portuguese empires managed to survive foreign invasion, civil wars between liberals and neoabsolutists, and aggressive competition from other empires. Explaining how this came about would be a book in itself. It would be necessary to examine and correlate a number of factors, which would go beyond the Spanish and Portuguese empires by carefully examining the changing strategic positions within a geopolitical order and a world economy of Britain and other rivals. It would also have to explore in depth the internal limits faced by Spain and Portugal, which confronted fiscal-military limitations, swings in public opinion, and institutional crises. In particular, slavery—the grand institution on which their empires were built—entered crises beginning in the late eighteenth century in spite of the wealth it generated. For its part, Spain was late in developing full-scale plantation slavery in the Antilles, although it came to be the economic pillar of the colonial system in the era following American independence. Maintaining this system, in an age of abolition, would be a major challenge. Of course, it is impossible to explain all this in such a short space, but it is possible to sketch the key characteristics of these empires in retreat.

To begin, it is helpful to outline the obvious. It would be a mistake to conflate territorial retreat (or lack of expansion) with full or complete decline. Following the independence of the Americas, statesmen in Spain and Portugal readjusted their outlooks and adapted to the trends of the times. The balance of power among world empires in the aftermath of the period 1780–1830 should not be analyzed first by charting the territorial advances and retreats of countries that shamelessly redrew the borders of the world, and second by labeling some of them as "ascending" and others as "declining." It is not a question of simply coloring a map red, blue, orange, green, and yellow. Rather, a more sophisticated analysis needs to examine how second-tier empires adapted to a new world order.[2] Of course, it would be a mistake to claim that Spanish and Portuguese nineteenth-century imperial reforms and endeavors were of the same caliber as those of Great Britain. To be sure, the Spanish and the Portuguese empires were unable to display the full gamut of imperial technologies to the extent of their more industrialized rivals. They did not aggressively link free trade, imperial expansion, and domestic industry. They did not boast such an impressive array of innovative financial mechanisms. Their systems of communication were not as sophisticated. They did not effectively channel migratory flows to the colonies for political purposes. Their military and technological might was limited. However, these countries did incorporate many innovations, albeit on a modest scale. The challenge, then, is to identify and measure the characteristics and ways in which these "empires in retreat" implemented reforms and continued sometimes ambitious imperial projects during the nineteenth century.

The Spanish and Portuguese empires faced challenges similar to those of the British Empire and its direct rivals. In the nineteenth century, a new imperial ideology congruent with liberalism began to take hold in which it was necessary to establish some form of political representation and extend citizenship to some people. It was also necessary to expand free trade and implement key reforms of governing institutions and tax-collection systems. All this needed to be articulated within the discursive framework of a "civilizing mission." What is more, many of these political, institutional, fiscal, and moral changes clashed with slavery. Hence, both Spain and Portugal had to come to terms with abolition. They formally abolished the slave trade during the 1830s and 1840s and shifted to a mixed system in which slaves coexisted with new laborers that came either as indentured servants or free immigrants from the metropole. To be sure, territorial retreat did not mean that Spain and Portugal failed to transform the fiscal-military basis and colonial ethos of their empires. The goal, then, is to chart how these empires navigated and renewed their ambitions during a period of imperial transition.

A Tale of Two Imperial Crises

In the latter months of 1807, Napoleonic troops invaded Iberia and soon thereafter installed José Bonaparte on the Spanish throne, triggering a disintegration of the Spanish and Portuguese states and a concomitant crisis in their empires.

Interestingly, these two monarchical states tumbled in different ways. Whereas the Portuguese court packed up and moved to Rio de Janeiro, the capital of its main overseas possession, Spain's Charles IV and Ferdinand VII shrouded themselves in dishonor by allowing the French to take them into custody.[3] In many respects, the destiny of the two monarchs had to do with Portugal's privileged relationship with Great Britain and Spain's historical alliance with France. As recently as 1801, France and Spain had united against Portugal in the so-called War of the Oranges.[4] Imperial rivalry between Spain and Portugal did not end with the Napoleonic offensive, despite the fact that both countries were allied against the French invasion. In 1809, Queen Charlotte, wife of King John VI of Portugal and sister of the Spanish king, attempted to create a private empire in the southern Andes and the Río de la Plata's Cisplatine region under Portuguese-Brazilian protection.[5] Meanwhile, the Spaniards were confident that they could recover the southern territories of the Brazilian frontier taken by Portugal following the Seven Years' War (1756–63).

The British were able to profit from the rivalry between the two countries. For example, on January 28, 1808, shortly after the French invasion of Iberia, diplomats secured the Carta Regia, opening Brazilian ports to British ships.[6] In fact, one of the reasons that Napoleon invaded Portugal was to obtain access to Portuguese ports in Europe and America. Although this attempt was unsuccessful and proved to be retrospectively disastrous, it demonstrates the extent to which the great powers vied over Portugal given its overseas presence. Once having gained access to Portuguese ports, Britain was able to impose a second, critical condition for the military and financial support of the House of Braganza. It inserted an additional clause in the trade agreement between the two countries, granting London the right to engage in the slave trade with the two African coasts. Had the British imposed abolition, the backbone of the Portuguese empire would have been broken.[7] However, this did not occur, and, against all odds, the Portuguese monarchs in Brazil proved unwilling to submit to the role of puppets. Neither during the reign of John VI nor in 1822 (when Portugal and Brazil separated under the same dynasty) did Britain succeed in imposing its will in Brazil. Rather, independent and monarchic Brazil proved surprisingly capable of forging its own way. It became the preeminent slave empire in continental America, even as Latin American wars of independence were spelling the end of slavery as an institution.

Events in Spain played out differently. As was the case of Portugal, the bulk of the Crown's territory was in America, and it might have been natural for the court and other political elites to gravitate there. However, unlike Portugal, a legitimate political authority remained in existence in Iberia and garnered massive public support during Spain's War of Independence (1808–13) against Napoleon. The Junta Central in Seville, the Regency, and the Cortes de Cádiz were able to fill the void left by the exile of monarchical authority, while local and provincial governing bodies (*juntas*) led the popular armed resistance against the invasion, known colloquially as the *guerrilla*. This created a situation in which the kingdom's central institutions in Seville and Cádiz exercised great symbolic power, while the provincial *juntas* and the various agencies in the Americas assumed real provisional power. The parallel existence of legitimate central and local authorities set the stage for the imperial crisis in the Americas from 1810 to 1824.

As was the case with Portugal, the British propped up the Spanish Bourbons' tottering empire across the Atlantic with ample military and financial resources. The strategic importance of Spain was every bit as crucial as that of Portugal. To state the obvious, Britain allied itself with Spain not only to counter Napoleon's continental advances but also to block French ambitions in Spanish possessions in the Americas. What is more, Spain's agonic experience during what Britain called the Peninsular War favored British interests. In the Americas, the British continued act as middlemen and quasi-legal smugglers in an empire that had never effectively enforced its trade monopoly. Still, Britain did not run roughshod over the Spanish. Diplomatic pressure failed to persuade the Spanish to open their ports to British ships, as Brazil had, or to make a formal commitment to the abolition of the slave trade. The powerful alliance of wealthy planters in Cuba and monopoly traders in Cádiz (Spain's leading port) successfully countered British attempts to push antislavery and free trade as a way to extend its interests in the Americas. In the end, Britain assumed control over Portuguese-Brazilian ports, maintained a dynastic presence on both sides of the Atlantic, and continued to profit from the Spanish empire in the Americas. All this compensated Britain, to some extent, for the loss of its North American possessions. The fate of Spain was different. The Spanish elite resisted imperial reform, leading to the disintegration of much of its empire.

THE HEYDAY OF IMPERIAL CONSTITUTIONS

To no one's surprise, neither the Spanish nor the Portuguese renounced their overseas empires during the Napoleonic Wars and subsequent conflicts. Statesmen in both countries attempted to forge a new imperial consensus by approving constitutions that were simultaneously liberal and imperial. The constitutional texts adopted in Cádiz (1812) and Lisbon (1822) shared many features and contained a similar structure. It is important to situate these august texts, so important to understanding the rise of independence movements in the Americas, within a comparative framework in constitutional history.

It is convenient to divide European liberal constitutions, adopted in the revolutionary period from 1780 to 1830, into imperial constitutions and constitutions with exceptional regimes. Imperial constitutions instituted systems of representation embracing all subjects in the monarchic empire, who were theoretically endowed with equal rights. In contrast, constitutions with exceptional regimes established a liberal system of representation and rights but did not extend it to overseas possessions. Indeed, very few constitutions merged nation and empire. In fact, it is not difficult to enumerate the ones that did: the U.S. Constitution of 1787 (the Northwest Ordinance inclusive), the French Constitution of 1793 (which never came into force), the French Constitution of 1795, the Spanish Constitution of 1812, and the Portuguese Constitution of 1822. In these cases, the unifying principle of representative liberalism replaced monarchical sovereignty. However, this first set of liberal constitutions, with the exception of the U.S. Constitution of 1787, proved fragile. In contrast, later and more durable constitutions mirrored the Napoleonic constitution of 1799. They were, in effect, dual constitutions, in which one regime governed the citizens of the nation and another governed the inhabitants of the overseas possessions.

Imperial constitutions aimed to reshape the metropolitan monarchy and resolve tensions in the empire. The offer of liberal representation and equal rights to the inhabitants of overseas territories was an inclusive covenant, which aimed to channel autonomous tendencies toward consensus. Tensions in the empire, of course, were not born solely out of the Napoleonic invasion. They began following the Seven Years' War as colonists protested against taxes resulting from the exorbitant cost of the conflict.[8] As might be expected, discussions about money inevitably led to more contentious debates about rights and political representation. In Brazil the Inconfidência Minera Conspiracy led to demands for major political changes with republican overtones.[9] The situation in the Spanish empire was somewhat different, even though Bourbon tax reforms also elicited responses from individuals of European descent, as well as a host of others: the creoles and mestizos of Quito and Bogota; the Quechua and Aymara peoples of the Andes; and, later, the Indian and mestizo peoples of central New Spain. However, unlike what took place in the Portuguese empire, protestors did not contemplate secession. Furthermore, such uprisings and parallel grassroots movements did not alter the overall imperial stability in either empire at the time.[10] All the same, they sufficiently affected public opinion so that the Napoleonic invasion became an apocalyptic dawn, causing so many people to perceive matters in a different light. For this reason, the Spanish constitutions of 1812 and 1822, mirroring French precedent, fervently proclaimed that all imperial territories belonged to a single legislative unit with the same laws applying to all subjects. Only by arriving at a new consensus would these vast political entities endure; in other words, old empires could only survive if statesmen implemented colonial reforms and established a single arena of representation.

In the Spanish case, the consensual abduction of the king, during the Napoleonic occupation, shifted the issue of sovereignty to a new political forum. Given the monarch's absence, legitimacy could only be exercised by the nation; the will of the nation, in turn, could only be legitimately expressed by subjects through political representation. Of course, the question was open as to the nature of such representation (individuals, communities, corporations) and as to who was considered a subject or citizen. To resolve these issues, the Regency summoned inhabitants of the empire to participate in an assembly, which would have the legitimacy and capacity to write a constitution enshrining principles applicable throughout the entire monarchy.[11] This constitution would, moreover, override any contravening laws contained in previous "constitutions" and the various legislative compilations applicable in the monarchy. Liberal principles, as embodied in the French and U.S. constitutions, would frame this new order and ensure the unity of the body politic. It could hardly be otherwise. After all, there were no previous domestic or imperial models that all the elites would agree represented the *constitución tradicional del reino* (the traditional constitution of the kingdom). The same logic operated in the Portuguese case with some exceptions. The main difference was that, from the outset, Portugal was one of the most unified and uniform monarchies in all of Europe.[12] The Portuguese king, in exile in Brazil, was far removed from the reform process, enabling William Beresford, the monarch's proconsul in Portugal, to decide on the fate of the metropolis. In 1820, liberals in Porto and Lisbon rose against the proconsulate, initiating the constitutional process. The foreign presence in Portugal and the remoteness of the monarch explain why the Cortes of 1820 had strongly liberal, nationalist, and imperial leanings. At the convention, Portuguese liberals successfully imposed their ideological preferences and adopted the Spanish Constitution of 1812.[13] This curious decision resulted from similarities between the two political processes and from the shared ideological perspectives among this heady generation of European liberals.

Framers of liberal and imperial constitutions began their projects cognizant that they faced three major challenges: first, they needed to establish rules for political representation; second, they had to define the scope of citizenship by erecting categories of inclusion and exclusion; and third, they were forced to resolve a plethora of local political contests, the most sensitive involving conflicts between colonial and metropolitan aspirations. Resolving these three issues proved immensely difficult. As Jeremy Bentham had warned (to those who were willing to listen), the fragility of these ambitious transoceanic constitutional projects stemmed precisely from the complexity of such matters. To understand the complexities facing the deputies of constitutional conventions in Spain and Portugal, it is helpful to address them one by one.

The first issue concerned the principle of equal representation and the nature of the electoral system. The Spanish attempted to institute an inclusive franchise based on the axiom of political equality. Driven by the need to forge the broadest possible consensus against Napoleon's occupying troops, constitutional framers agreed to employ (indirect) universal male suffrage. The Portuguese would also employ this open-ended formula in 1820. An inclusive voting base was deemed essential to win the support of the Latin Americans for a project that, from the outset, was viewed with deep mistrust. Despite the fact that there was broad agreement over this principle, deputies in both Spain and Portugal were aware that it harbored potential problems for the future. An underlying problem was the unreliability of the available population censuses. In Spain, these had been updated by the partial censuses recently published by Alexander von Humboldt, but they were still incomplete. In Portugal, the censuses were in worse shape. The uncertainty of the number of inhabitants in the empire raised reasonable doubts about whether it would be metropolitan or colonial representatives who would constitute a majority in the future parliament. This was a unique problem in constitutional history, one that the lawmakers of the French Revolution did not have to confront.

The second issue concerned the promise of equality. In Spanish America, the administrative bodies of the monarchy were in the hands of *peninsulares* (persons born in Europe) during the Napoleonic era. In spite of promises to the contrary, overseas inhabitants were never convinced that this situation would change, leading them to distance themselves from the constitutional project from the outset. The reliability of Spanish liberals on the issue of equality was also thrown into doubt by their decision to exclude free "colored" (black and mulatto) people from citizenship.[14] By excluding what amounted to one-third of the free American population, metropolitan deputies ensured that Spaniards would constitute a majority in future legislatures. The exclusion divided the American deputies, sparking heated debate in the constituent assembly in Cádiz. The majority of the American deputies wanted to include free colored people, but the Cubans and Spaniards favored excluding the so-called *castas pardas* (free blacks and mulattos). In the end, the latter position prevailed. The Constitution excluded the *castas pardas* from citizenship, a result that greatly undermined the credibility of the constitutional movement in the eyes of the Spanish American continental deputies and fomented independence movements across the Atlantic.

The Portuguese addressed equality differently. The Lisbon constituent assembly of 1820 awarded full citizenship to the free colored population. As stated in one of the projects submitted to the constitutional commission, distinguishing between "freed" (emancipated ex-slaves) and "free" was an insult to the sensibilities of any liberal. Pursuant to that logic, an ex-slave with a one-day-old letter of freedom would be a citizen (see title II, chap. 21). All the same, it is not surprising that the fine print undermined these valiant proclamations. In the articles devoted to the requirements for electoral participation, Portuguese constitutionalists restricted the citizenship rights of former slaves born in "foreign countries." As such, many such free blacks were given citizenship but deprived of voting rights. The Brazilian representatives in Lisbon were likely the ones who insisted on this provision, a camouflaged reference to *bozales* (slaves born in Africa) who had obtained freedom. All the same, it did not affect the rights of the numerous free colored people who were not *bozales*.[15] Not surprisingly, the restrictions on the citizenship of the *bozales* reappeared in both Portugal and Brazil even after this initial liberal phase had ended. The Portuguese Constitutional Charter of April 29, 1826, which had no effect in independent Brazil, also maintained this exclusion. What is more, even this exclusion was superfluous given that the Portuguese Constitution of 1822 (like the French Constitution of 1791) included a provision that restricted the franchise by requiring voters to demonstrate minimum yearly earnings. This effectively excluded all free people of color in addition to poor whites. In Brazil, the unapproved constitution of 1822 included a blanket provision extending citizenship to all free people, but the constitution of 1824 included the provision excluding *bozales*. Leading Brazilian historians have pointed out that it was paradoxical that a constitution designed to maintain slavery also incorporated free colored people in the imperial monarchy.[16] However, references to African origins effectively traced a demarcation line within the community of free people of color and between these and slaves.

The third issue confronting metropolitan and American deputies to the constituent assemblies in Cádiz and Lisbon concerned the form of state. In both countries, liberals agreed that the nation's future depended on the autonomy and authority of the Cortes (parliament) to impose reforms. In the case of Spain, the legislature was deemed sovereign, in the absence (but without the acquiescence) of a royal family held in opulent captivity in France.[17] In Portugal, the problem was more acute given that the Portuguese monarch was not held prisoner but had emigrated to Brazil along with the Royal Army under his own volition. The court never expressed a formal willingness to submit to the decisions of the constituent assembly, but played a complicated game of ambivalence. Given this lack of monarchical approval, liberals in both countries needed to find a way to ensure that they constituted a comfortable majority in the future Cortes and government bodies in order to implement sweeping legislative measures needed to establish a genuinely liberal society.[18] This generated heated debates between European and American deputies regarding the structure of the state and the administration of outlying areas. In the case of Spain, metropolitan deputies sought to ensure that the Cortes was the only legislative body that stood atop a chain of command that stretched from the center to the periphery. This would guarantee compliance with government decisions. They launched an ideological war against what was then contemptuously labeled "federalism." To Spain's metropolitan deputies, the U.S. model of legislative plurality was considered unworkable in the Hispanic world because it would inevitably lead to the disintegration of a historically tenuous political unity. This principle of unity was enshrined in the "Project for the Political and Economic Government of the Provinces" of the Spanish Cortes of 1813. For their part, Portuguese metropolitan deputies also rejected federalism using similar arguments.

Not surprisingly, colonials in both countries saw things differently. In Spanish America, colonial elites sought to defend the legislative powers of the provincial governments, which had blossomed during the Napoleonic Wars and remained in existence in many places thereafter. Only in 1822, when Spanish armies were already retreating from the Americas, and the possibility of reaching an agreement with American elites was patently impossible, did the Spanish contemplate the possibility of converting provincial governments into what autonomists had defended during the Napoleonic Wars. By then it was too late. In the case of Portugal, overseas representatives confronted the same obstacles.[19] Only with the tardy but energetic arrival of the deputies from São Paulo at the constituent assembly did the metropolitan government agree to negotiate. Again, it was too late. The response of the absent regent, Dom Pedro, to the Portuguese initiative to reconstruct the state according to a liberal agenda was to disobey the Cortes in Lisbon and proclaim himself the first emperor of Brazil in 1822.[20] The idea of a shared constitution had become a pipe dream. In any case, by 1823 both countries had regressed to neoabsolutism, putting such constitutional problems on hold.

When liberals again assumed power in both countries in the mid-1830s, their imperial outlooks had changed radically. The Spanish empire had been reduced to the two colonies of the West Indies (Cuba and Puerto Rico), the Philippine archipelago, and some minor enclaves in northern Africa and the Gulf of Guinea. With the effective independence of Brazil in late 1822, Portugal was left with colonies in Africa and Asia. It was also significant that the monarchical, slave-based Brazilian empire would maintain close ties with the African enclaves of the former metropolis, particularly Angola. As such, liberals in both countries were forced to adjust their expectations and strategies. For the Spanish, the goal was to retain what was left of the old empire and put an end to domestic conflicts. They accomplished this by means of a series of ambitious national and imperial reforms in the late 1830s and 1840s. By the late 1850s, politicians were so confident that they even launched new expansionist ventures in the Gulf of Guinea, Morocco, the Caribbean, and Vietnam. The Portuguese, meanwhile, needed to ensure the viability of an empire of scattered enclaves and to convert their vast African possessions into a modernized imperial order.

During the second third of the nineteenth century, these empires in retreat reconsidered their early liberal constitutional promises. From 1810 to 1830, the goal had been to forge a new consensus following collapse. In so doing, they had run up against serious difficulties, such as those generated by the aforementioned exclusion of the *castas pardas* from citizenship. For this reason, as both countries underwent revolutions from 1836 to 1840, liberals dispensed with the single-nation-empire principle and excluded the colonies from metropolitan politics. Metropolitans wished to ensure central legislative authority in all matters concerning the colonies by excluding the contentious ultramarine representatives from their parliaments. The Spanish and Portuguese constitutions of 1837 and 1838 emulated the Napoleonic model by including a provision stating that the colonies would not be governed by the constitution but by "special laws." In one fell swoop, the lawmaking mechanisms of colonies and metropolis were separated and metropolitan governments were freed from the scrutiny of the colonials. Overseas governors rarely had to respond to any authority that was not endorsed by the metropolis. What is more, the respective constitutions created legislative vacuums since nobody ever formally redacted a system of special laws. To repeat, the "promise" to approve special laws went unfulfilled. As a result, the metropolis governed overseas possessions with a firm political and military hand. In this respect, the governments of the Spanish and Portuguese—albeit with important differences between them—were no different than other European metropolitan governments. The historians C. A. Bayly and John Benyon, for example, have labeled similar arrangements in the British Empire as "proconsular." In French Algeria, the great military leader Thomas Bugeaud implemented a highly militarized and fiercely repressive version of colonial governance, the penal code of the metropolis notwithstanding.

Slavery and Imperial Political Economics

To understand the reconstruction of the Spanish and Portuguese empires in the nineteenth century, it is necessary to focus on the institution of slavery, which had a different history in the two empires. This difference can be appreciated by examining these empires at the midpoint of the nineteenth century. With regard to Spain, plantation-based slavery developed rapidly in Cuba after the slave revolt in Saint-Domingue (later Haiti) in 1791 and Haitian independence in 1804. For its part, Puerto Rico followed the Cuban path of plantation agriculture after 1820. By 1850, slavery had become the new bedrock of Spain's small but lucrative reconstructed empire. In Portugal, things were different. By 1850, Brazil was the center of the world's largest slave trade, but Brazil was no longer part of Portugal. In the African colonies, in contrast, the persistence of slavery hindered colonial reform.[21] Given the previous historical experiences of the two countries, this situation was paradoxical. The Portuguese empire had originally converted to slavery on a massive scale following the pepper crisis of the mid–seventeenth century, which made Portuguese Indian possessions significantly less valuable.[22] By the eighteenth century, the Portuguese empire was slave-based and American. The Spanish empire, meanwhile, was the only European empire in which slavery (and the slave plantation) was a minor institution, even though it had taken root in some outlying areas of the Antilles, Venezuela, New Granada, and the Peruvian coast. The loss of American continental possessions by both empires radically enhanced slavery's importance and altered the relationship between slavery and colonial development.

Just as Spain was making a dramatic withdrawal from the continent, Cuba's slave-operated sugar and coffee plantations brought fiscal salvation. Cuban money paid for the colonial administration and the army, most of which took refuge on the island after the political and military collapse of 1822–24.[23] By the late 1830s, sugar plantations had turned Cuba into one of the most productive colonies in the world, as the Duke of Wellington would remind Spanish ambassadors in London from time to time. Only Johannes Van den Bosch's Dutch Java was comparably profitable. Sugar not only generated enough wealth to maintain the colonial systems of Cuba and Puerto Rico, but it also provided much-needed resources for the Spanish treasury, which was hemorrhaging from the high cost of domestic civil war between liberals and absolutists. Indeed, Cuba (along with its appendage Puerto Rico) was the financial and economic engine of the monarchy. Although sugarcane suffered falling prices and slavery caused immense social problems, Cuba remained the fulcrum of the empire and the savior of the treasury. Cuban and Puerto Rican prosperity was underpinned by slave and contracted labor (usually *chinos de Manila*, Chinese immigrant workers) on a scale unprecedented in the history of the Spanish empire.[24]

In the Philippines, the situation was similar. There coerced (rather than slave) labor fueled the massive expansion of tobacco, abaca, and coffee production on the island of Luzon, and, after 1850, in the Visayan Islands. The establishment of a tobacco monopoly in 1782 was the key to the fiscal reform of the Philippines. This innovation mirrored that which already existed in New Spain (later Mexico). Massive profits enabled the Spanish administration to survive and finance political and military reform in the archipelago, even as the continental American empire foundered.[25] Tobacco revenues allowed the Spanish to expand into tribal mountain lands and the islands of the Islamic south and helped maintain other Pacific enclaves. When benevolent reformers in Spain questioned the morality of this cruel form of coerced labor, defenders of the system pointed to similar practices in Dutch Java and Madura and the forced labor of convicts in New South Wales and Van Diemen's Land (Tasmania).

Spain, though, constructed a modern slave and coerced-labor empire with substantial risks. In the aftermath of the Napoleonic Wars, the emerging British Empire and the international abolitionist movement considered the maintenance of slavery nothing less than a casus belli. The British ambassador to recalcitrant Spain, Henry Wellesley—brother of the general who was then fighting against the Napoleon on the peninsula and brother of the onetime foreign secretary—was unable to force the deputies to the constituent assembly in Cádiz to abolish the slave trade.[26] Cuban planters, generals, and colonial administrators wielded great influence in Spain, exerting pressure on the metropolis by stressing the financial importance of Cuba and the sugar industry. In 1814, the absolutist monarchy was restored in Spain, and in 1817 Ferdinand VII signed a treaty with Great Britain abolishing the slave trade. However, neither absolutists nor the liberal politicians who governed from 1820 to 1823 complied with the treaty. This commonality of interests with respect to slavery among ideological enemies was indicative of the immense weight of Cuban sugar interests in Spanish politics. In 1836, liberals definitively came to power in Spain, but compliance was not forthcoming. Refusal to comply with treaties abolishing the slave trade was a hallmark of Spanish foreign and colonial policy right up to the time of the American Civil War. British governments often used a rather vague abolitionist tone, which vacillated from one government to another, facilitating Spanish interests.

The fierce defense of slavery in the Spanish West Indies has to be understood within the context of Spain's Atlantic political economy. Following the collapse of the continental empire, slave labor became the cornerstone of Spain's overseas possessions. Cuba and Puerto Rico used slave labor on a scale equivalent to that of the southern United States and Brazil. What is more, slave labor also generated other income. Cuban exports turned the island into a massive trading platform for the Americas. "Triangular" trade routes included metropolitan, African, and Cuban ports in addition to a host of others in the Americas. Profits from Cuban sugar brought New Orleans and Mobile cotton to Barcelona, food from Río de la Plata to the West Indian slave communities, and numerous goods from Mexican and Caribbean ports to the world. Cuba also attracted new flows of migrants from the Iberian Peninsula. This web of connections sustained the merchant navy and justified the high cost of a fleet of warships. In 1820, Spanish liberals sought to bring Spain and the West Indies under a single tariff regime to rationalize this emerging political economy. The Cuban planters found this unacceptable. Tariffs on exports were so high that Cubans were forced to sell their sugar to Spaniards, which, in effect, established Spaniards as brokers of Cuban sugar in international markets. Over the following two decades (1820–40), Spanish politicians and Cuban interests engaged in ongoing negotiations. In the end, the metropolis allowed planters the liberty to export directly to the large export markets of Great Britain and the United States (and whoever else they chose) in exchange for a colonial covenant that promised hefty tax revenues for Spain by taxing imports to Cuba rather than exports.[27]

The Spanish army in Cuba protected this great pyramid of power, built on the resources generated by the slave trade and sugar exports, as well as trade and shipping. Once politicians had consolidated this fiscal-military colonial system, they launched expansionist endeavors in former colonies (Chile and Peru, Mexico, and Santo Domingo) and traditional scenarios of imperialist aggression (Morocco and the kingdom of Annam), beginning in the late 1850s.

Whereas the slave trade was central to Spain's imperial political economy, this was not the case for Portugal. The maintenance of the slave trade raised a host of problems. The flow of slaves from the colonies in Africa to its former colony in Brazil threatened Portugal's future as an imperial entity.[28] In the eighteenth century, Brazil had essentially developed into a submetropolis," as Santos and other ports sent goods such as *cachaça* (a fermented sugarcane liquor) to East Africa in exchange for slaves. The continuity of the slave trade prolonged Portugal's African colonies' traditional dependence on Brazil and empowered slave traders in the hinterland.[29] The problem was that the slave trade placed Portugal in a very delicate position vis-à-vis Britain, given that this supremely liberal, Protestant, and abolitionist empire was poised to penetrate the two African coasts. Portugal had formally complied with British rules since the 1810 agreement, including clauses on trade liberalization and slave-trade abolition (which Wellesley had unsuccessfully attempted to impose on the Spanish).[30] Still, despite efforts to the contrary, the slave trade persisted and the British continued to pressure the Portuguese to eliminate it. For their part, the Portuguese refused to accept the unilateral Palmerston Act of 1839, since they considered this an intolerable violation of their national sovereignty.[31] They did, however, come to an agreement with Britain the following year. In 1842, the Portuguese government signed a treaty recognizing the slave trade as equivalent to piracy. In the ensuing decade, the Portuguese implemented internal colonization projects centered around non-slave-based plantation agriculture. Results, though, were mixed. Only in Angola did such enterprises prove somewhat viable.

Lisbon liberals faced major difficulties in making their colonial system compliant with these international abolitionist norms. Africa was an extremely difficult, brutal place in which to try to enforce such objectives, featuring a number of actors with questionable morals who could not be easily brought under the authority of civil governors. Difficulties also stemmed from Portugal's relationship with Brazil. Unlike Spain's rupture with its colonies, Brazilian independence did not represent such a trauma. Northern Portugal was a major supplier of wines and foods to its former colony and was the point of departure for numerous Portuguese migrants and traders, the lifeblood of the economic nexus between the two countries. In southern Brazil, the importation of slaves continued, peaking at over fifty thousand Africans per year in the period 1846–49.[32] For Portugal, the inability to suppress the traffic in slaves signaled the weakness of its political authority. In the end, despite political intentions to the contrary, the slave trade was a defining feature of its political economy and its relationship with the African colonies. Liberal *setembrista* and *cabralista* governments of the 1830s and 1840s expressed the desire to convert the huge African colonies into what the Marquês de Sá da Bandeira revealingly called *os novos Brasis* (new Brazils) without slavery. Nothing comparable happened in Cuba until the defeat of the southern slave states in the U.S. Civil War firmly put the slave trade and abolitionism on the agenda in the Spanish Caribbean.

Settlement and agriculture without slaves required financial resources and administrative penetration that the Portuguese government was unable to provide. Although slavery was formally abolished in 1858, it took some time for abolition to become effective. Initially, Portugal only had the capacity to implement its nonslave policy in the Angolan sugar and coffee plantations along the coast. It took an additional twenty-five years for abolition be enforced in the hinterlands. Attempts to develop new economic sectors based on salt, millet, sugar, and coffee in Cape Verde led to episodes of famine.[33] What is more, the working conditions of laborers in the new agricultural plantations, at a great physical and political distance from Lisbon, were pathetically reminiscent of slavery.

How to convert loosely controlled possessions in the hinterlands into efficiently governed colonial dominions was another major issue faced by the Portuguese. To do this, they had to find an alternative to the labor exports coming from what Martin A. Klein has termed African "predatory states."[34] They also encountered major difficulties with the so-called nationalization of the *prazos da Coroa*, large agricultural estates in Mozambique, located between the hinterland and the coastal world of the trade in human flesh.[35] The *prazeiros* (estate holders) were Zambezi *mestiços* (of mixed descent) holding heritable leases, remote descendants of the initial beneficiaries of large tracts of Crown land. They were effectively independent, rarely obeying colonial governors appointed by Lisbon. The Portuguese empire, however, needed to confront these challenges in order to survive. The task was particularly daunting in Mozambique, where there was no properly constituted authority and where the slave route between the Muslim north and the Boer states to the south remained active in the age of abolition.

LESSONS OF AN "ORDERLY" WITHDRAWAL

The dismembered Spanish and Portuguese empires, then, followed pathways that shared some characteristics but also contained many peculiarities. Both empires underwent an "imperial transition" during the period inaugurated by the wars and conflicts of the eighteenth century. However, this transition did not occur in the strict sense of the word—a replacement and displacement of one empire by another. Instead, this transition could be described as an "orderly"— but by no means premeditated—withdrawal that began with the revolutions of the 1820s and did not end until postwar Spanish and Portuguese decolonization of 1898 and of the 1950s, 1960s, and 1970s. In short, "decolonization" was a long, drawn-out process of unintentional but comparatively orderly retreat, which consisted of phases of defeat, losses and withdrawal, successful internal reform, and failed expansion. It is widely held that an imperial transition means that a retreating empire plays a small role in a new world order. However, it is perhaps necessary to shift to a more flexible framework. In the case of Spain and Portugal, both countries transformed their imperial systems following the massive loss of territory, adapting to a new century characterized by new imperial technologies and ideologies and fierce competition between empires. Indeed, general narratives of world history have inadequately explained the transformation of the Spanish and Portuguese empires. They have assumed that imperial retreat is synonymous with absence or the inability to adapt and assess. However, it is necessary to analyze the changes in colonial policy of these empires in a more sophisticated manner by adopting a comparative method that goes beyond the limits of purely national histories. The ruthless application of the perception of *decline* to the Spanish and Portuguese empires conveys the notion that nothing of relevance occurred in them between the sixteenth and twentieth centuries.

The history of the Philippines demonstrates why such assumptions are laden with problems. In the Philippines, Spain changed its colonial policy three times between the second half of the eighteenth century and 1898, when the islands fell under American control.[36] The first took place in the 1780s, when colonial reformers introduced military reinforcement, taxation, and trade-reform formulas, previously tested on the American continent. The solution was to form a chartered company for this archipelago on the South China Sea. By so doing, they broke Spain's fiscal dependence on the Manila Galleon, which sailed once a year from Acapulco to Manila, loaded with silver.[37] The second change occurred in the 1830s, when the Spanish government applied new taxation models to the entire archipelago, which allowed foreign trading and banking companies to penetrate the islands and the Spanish treasury to share in their profits. This opened Philippine ports to foreign trade and led to the licensing of European and American companies. The third change took place in the 1880s, when Spaniards attempted to promote greater participation of Spanish capital in the archipelago. It included laws widening the tax base, deregulating state monopolies, and favoring Spanish exporters. Given the above, two observations can be made. First, without such changes, Spain would have lost the Philippines in the early nineteenth century along with much of continental America. Second, Spanish governments recognized that it was preferable to open up the Philippines to foreign interests (British, French, and American) rather than persist with an unworkable protectionist system. Ultimately, Spain could not afford to maintain its old monopolistic practices. Instead, it joined other European partners in a game of mutual collaboration and rivalry in various areas of the globe. Following Ronald Robinson and John Gallagher, many historians have claimed that "free-trade imperialism" effectively expanded Great Britain's "informal empire" even in dominions that were not colored red on the map. However, the expression "informal imperialism," which presupposes a bilateral and unequal relationship, does not effectively explain the process by which Spanish and Portuguese territories and former colonies adapted to a new imperial constellation and shared in the exploitation of their resources with other imperial powers.

The imperial transition that took place from 1780 to 1830 has to be understood from a framework that analyzes the complex relationship between retreating colonial powers, ascending colonial powers, and the territories themselves. The Spanish and Portuguese empires did not drop out of the imperial game. They retreated geographically, but they did so while adjusting and modifying their fiscal, military, administrative, and constitutional models to maintain possession of the territories they held. All the same, many historians treat the Spanish and Portuguese empires as fifteenth- and sixteenth-century pioneers but then proceed to write them out of the subsequent narrative. They have neglected to pay attention to the history of these empires in the period that follows the Napoleonic Wars and the revolutions for Spanish American independence. Describing a dual process of collapse and orderly withdrawal is not easy. Nonetheless, the history of the Spanish and Portuguese empires in the postrevolutionary period is a story about how well-established imperial traditions and colonial practices survived in a world of changing rules, practices, and justifications. Spain's empire collapsed in many parts. In those areas under direct control, or indirect influence, the Spanish retrenched their positions, adjusted their strategic objectives, and adapted to colonial trends. In pursuing stability, the pendulum swung between failure and success—just as it did for other empires. Imperialism should not be viewed, then, as a rat race between empires with an exclusive focus on winners. We should, rather, consider the "new imperialism" of the nineteenth century as an effort by Europeans—later joined by Asian and U.S. latecomers—aimed at subjugating populations of other continents and forming new colonial societies where none existed before. Conflict and collaboration between empires were inevitable and essential parts of the process.

Under this perspective, we need to reconsider continuities between colonial and postcolonial historical experiences in the South Atlantic, a part of the world that experienced rapid development in the nineteenth century. While this area of the world was not the industrial heartland of Europe—which set the technological and financial threshold for expansionary capacities—the South Atlantic certainly did not remain on the sidelines. The Spanish and Portuguese empires were part of a (possibly) second-order European, African, and American wave of development, which had a ripple effect on the Spanish Philippines and Portuguese enclaves in India, China, and Southeast Asia. In many respects, imperial transformations included many classical features of nineteenth-century colonialism. Connections between Brazil and the West Indies prolonged slavery and forced labor in the Portuguese empire, while the profitability of the sugarcane industry in Cuba and Puerto Rico fueled it in the Spanish one. Both countries expanded into uncolonized territories. Portugal penetrated the African hinterland, while Spain extended its hegemony in the Visayas, Mindanao, and the Sulu islands of the Philippines. Both sought to channel migration flows within their imperial possessions, sometimes successfully and other times not. And, finally, both adjusted their imperial models to patterns of consumption, communication, and investment. Parallel to what John Darwin has astutely described as the "Eurasian revolution" was a distinctive Atlantic revolution in which the Spanish and Portuguese empires in retreat played a significant role.[38] Spanish and Portuguese colonial policy had an extraordinary impact on the Asians and Africans who were massively incorporated into the West Indian plantation economy and exploited in situ. This is the major issue in nineteenth-century European colonial history.

To explain the survival of the Spanish and Portuguese empires, it is necessary to trace how they adapted to trends and changes, especially with respect to the transformation of political institutions and the regulation of trade. Also critical to survival was how these countries employed native labor. This involved various species of oppressors (state monopolies, private planters) and oppressed (outright slaves, forced and coerced servants). The Spanish and Portuguese empires differed. In the Spanish empire, African slavery was a minor institution due to the availability of coerced Amerindian labor during the colonial period; however, in the nineteenth century slave and indentured labor plantations became a defining feature of the West Indies much like forced labor became so in the Philippines. In Portugal, the reverse occurred. The Portuguese were major players in the slave trade and the development of plantation economies in the seventeenth and eighteenth centuries but then moved slowly toward abolition in the nineteenth. In the end, various features characterized the Spanish and Portuguese empires: liberal institutions; special colonial juridical regimes; highly centralized political and military apparatuses; deregulated trade; mixtures of slave, indentured, coerced, and free-peasant labor; and the presence of strategic migratory flows from the metropole to the colonies. When such characteristics are enumerated and analyzed, they surprise no historian of major imperial powers. There is nothing new under the sun, or, at least, under the cheerless sun of the imperial nineteenth-century tropics.

The trajectory of the Spanish and Portuguese empires, like other empires, followed a variety of well-engineered formulas to ensure survival. Although these empires inherited centuries-old traditions of government, they did not remain anchored in tradition. Diminished political authority was offset by a remarkable ability to develop political economies that admitted negotiation and shared ownership of the fruits of empire among various actors. In this way, both countries avoided conflicts (and hence disaster) with more industrialized world powers.

Both the Spanish and the Portuguese deregulated previous monopolistic practices, opened colonial ports to foreign navies, admitted foreign financial interests within their territories, and allowed free outward migration. Humanitarian concerns featured little in domestic politics, allowing politicians to maintain slavery and slave trafficking in their colonies for a few decades longer than elsewhere.[39] By so doing, they were able to conserve a partially protected market, which provided reformers time to convert their remaining colonies into outlets for migration, destinations for civil and military personnel, and points of support for their merchant navies. Neither the British nor other rivals were able to impose free trade and abolition until well into the nineteenth century. The Spanish and Portuguese were able to take advantage of interimperial rivalries, especially in the Caribbean where a balance of power between European countries and the United States (wielding the Monroe Doctrine) led to relative stability in the nineteenth century. Ultimately, empires had little choice but to remain and reform. Although this was a formidable challenge, withdrawal would have given rise to even greater problems. Not only would rapid withdrawal have caused domestic problems among economic actors and patriots, not only would it have caused Spain and Portugal to lose massive power in geopolitical arenas, but it could have caused even more traumatic and violent situations in colonies. Various European powers would discover the risks of rapid withdrawal in the aftermath of World War II. Comparatively, Spanish and Portuguese retreat was a case of "orderly" and extended withdrawal.

For all these reasons, it is not possible to write the history of empires between 1780 and 1850 by referring exclusively to developments within the colonies themselves. Nor is it possible to focus exclusively on the great powers. We also need to assess the complex parallels and intersections among metropoles, colonies, and imperial rivals. The history of empires in retreat is equally as important as the history of expansionist empires; both continued to participate in a geopolitical contest for domination over other societies. These developments are part of the same history, which should be examined as a whole.

Imperial Ambitions in an Era of Decline

Micromilitarism and the Eclipse of the
Spanish Empire, 1858–1923

STEPHEN JACOBSON

SCHOLARS OF WORLD HISTORY have taken great interest in the rise of the Spanish empire but have paid scant attention to its eclipse. Discovery, conquest, and colonization are central themes in what has been called the "rise of the West," "the European miracle," or the "great divergence." After the colonization of Latin America is recounted in many histories, Spain disappears from the narrative.[1] Its decline is often assumed to be a chronicle of a death foretold, the return of an impoverished and disjointed country to its original position.[2] The end of the empire can be summarized rather succinctly. The Napoleonic occupation of Iberia (1808–13) caused the state to disintegrate, spurring revolutionary movements in the Americas. By 1824, a series of continental Spanish American nations had been born, and Spain had also forfeited its North American territories. Following defeat in the Spanish-American War of 1898, Spain ceded Puerto Rico, the Philippines, and a number of small Pacific islands to the United States, while Cuba became nominally independent. In 1956, France and Spain recognized Moroccan independence (save the Spanish cities of Ceuta and Melilla). In 1968, Equatorial Guinea, in western Africa, also broke free of its colonial shackles, definitively ending the Spanish empire after nearly five hundred years.

One of the principal reasons that so little attention has been paid to this eclipse is that the long duration of the Spanish empire is deemed to have run against the grain of modernity. In ordinary historical conversation, "decolonization" (loss of colonies) is understood to have taken place in the aftermath of World War II when practically all of Europe's overseas colonies gained independence and European states ceded their informal, and in some cases formal, empires and global influence to the United States and the Soviet Union. This postwar imperial transition saw the United States take over as the hegemonic power in key areas of the globe from Japan to Indochina, from the Middle East to Latin America. The Soviet Union inherited much of the Nazi empire in Eastern Europe and developed its own elsewhere. From the Cold War until today, U.S. imperial power has become increasingly diffuse, with few governors on the ground but many in the air. Its immense military budget endows it with a greater "hard power" advantage than any empire has enjoyed since Rome. Hollywood studies, fast-food chains, multinationals, Google and Facebook transmit soft power around the globe with much greater speed and swath than the pulpit and confessional of the Spanish priest. Under this narrative of modernity (or even postmodernity), the decline of Spain, an enigma from the past, appears hardly relevant.

There are good reasons, though, for abandoning this vision of Spanish exceptionalism. Shifts in world power taking place in the twenty-first century point to the ongoing decline of the United States as an empire. The rise of productive capacities in countries such as China, India, and Brazil will lead to an expansion of military might, economic clout, and diplomatic influence. The slow eclipse of the United States should turn the study of Spain into an increasingly topical subject. It is unlikely that British, French, Dutch, and Belgian decolonization—triggered by World War II, the dawning of the nuclear age, and the onslaught of the Cold War—will forever serve as the paradigmatic point of reference. Viewed from the perspective of U.S. decline, the history of Spain's long—but by no means unidirectional—imperial recessional appears more typical than exceptional.

This essay focuses on one aspect of this eclipse: micromilitarism. In a bestselling book, Emmanuel Todd argued that one of the telltale signs of the decline of the United States is "theatrical micromilitarism."[3] As described by Todd, military campaigns since the Vietnam War have been directed against weak countries, such as Grenada, Panama, Somalia, Iraq, and Afghanistan, where planners foresaw quick wars and easy victories with few domestic casualties. Their purpose was, among other reasons, to showcase the United States' vast military superiority, and to consolidate and expand key zones of influence amid economic, political, and cultural decadence. Things, of course, did not always go as planned, as sudden invasions often gave rise to guerrilla resistance, which could often outlast and oust occupiers. Todd's analytical framework can be applied elsewhere. European postwar decolonization featured numerous micromilitary displays of deadly imperial power—bombardments, torture, assassinations, and proxy wars— that took greater tolls on civilian populations than on metropolitan armies. Such actions were often followed by resistance, escalation, third-party diplomatic intervention, and withdrawal. The Suez Crisis of 1956 was exemplary of such micromilitary debacles. In this pivotal exercise of misplaced imperial hubris, French and British statesmen deployed troops in a desperate and astonishing attempt to reassert their informal empire in Egypt before being curtly asked to leave by the United States. Only after Suez did French and British leaders adjust their foreign policies to geopolitical realities and accept a reduced role within global politics.

Spain's imperial retreat was a precursor for the fate of other European empires. Like the others, it was not a linear history of recession and withdrawal but featured a number of campaigns in which political and military leaders sought to expand influence and add territory and were pulled into new theaters by the inertia of the empire itself. In other words, the decline of the empire was characterized not only by the loss of colonies but also by failed attempts to join more powerful countries in a new "empire project."[4]

This era of Spanish micromilitarism can be divided into two phases. The first took place from 1858 to 1866, when Madrid carried out actions in Vietnam, Morocco, Santo Domingo, Mexico, and along the Pacific coast of Chile and Peru. Taken together, these invasions, occupations, annexations, blockades, and bombardments were equivalent to Spain's Suez, hubristic episodes foreshadowing the end of its global empire. The second phase took place in Morocco beginning in 1893 and lasted until the outbreak of the Rif War (1919–26), the first native-led war of independence in Africa and a major "macromilitary" conflict. In the end, Spain succeeded in securing a small "backdoor" empire, which endowed it with a limited presence in international affairs commensurate with its status as a lesser, though not completely forgotten, global player.

For the sake of clarity, it is not being argued that the decline of world empires can be understood by examining micromilitarism alone. In the case of Spain, major (macromilitary) conflicts followed these micromilitary adventures. In the aftermath of the failed expansionism of the late 1850s and 1860s, Spain fought two devastating wars in Cuba: the Ten Years' War (1868–78) and the Cuban War (1895–98). In 1896, this latter conflict spread to the Philippines; in 1898, it became the Spanish-American War. These wars differed from previous nineteenth-century campaigns in scale and objectives. They did not aim to add territory or boost international influence but sought to preserve remaining colonies. During the Ten Years' War, Spain sent 180,000 soldiers to Cuba, over half of whom died. During the Cuban War, Spain shipped more than 200,000 men to the island and suffered an excess of 45,000 deaths. In addition, some 170,000 Cubans perished in concentration camps, approximately 10 percent of the population, a proportion similar to Russian losses in World War II.[5] In the case of Morocco, limited campaigns likewise gave way to a prolonged and costly war in the 1920s. The relationship of these major wars of independence—the two Cuban wars and the Rif War—to the end of Spain's formal empire is evident. The focus on micromilitarism, in contrast, provides an additional and often overlooked piece to the puzzle. Finally, it should be underscored that it is not being claimed that the eclipse of all empires corresponds to a similar timeline or sequence. Rather, the point is to examine pivotal episodes of micromilitary adventurism in order to gain an additional perspective on comparative imperial eclipses and transitions.

THE FIRST WAVE OF MICROMILITARISM (1858–66)

Before beginning the analysis, it is necessary to dispel some myths. It is often assumed that Spain's decline as an imperial power paralleled its decline as a world power. This, however, is false. Rather, statesmen and legislators reformed the fiscal and military foundations of state and empire in the late eighteenth and early nineteenth centuries and by so doing, halted a period of decadence. The decline of Spain as a world power did not trigger a parallel decline of the empire. At the Congress of Vienna (1815), Spain formally lost its status as a "great power" on being excluded from the Council of Europe. Yet the country maintained a global presence even after it had lost its continental American colonies by 1824. In the mid–nineteenth century, Spain still governed the second or third most extensive and profitable empire in the world alongside Britain and Holland. The jewel of the crown, or the "pearl of the Antilles" as it was called, was Cuba, where slave plantations produced 70 percent of the world's sugarcane supply by the 1870s. Between 1816 and 1867, almost six hundred thousand slaves arrived in Cuba, roughly equivalent to the total number shipped to the United States throughout the trade's history.[6]

During the first two-thirds of the nineteenth century, the history of the Spanish empire reads much like that of Britain or France. Spain lost most of its American colonies in the late eighteenth and early nineteenth centuries. Yet defeat did not usher in a crisis of conscience or a national humiliation. Rather, Spanish, British, and French liberals and republicans attributed the success of American independence to the ideological and military failings of absolutism. In the nineteenth century, these countries and others tightened their grip on their existing territories and renewed overseas expansionist activity. To be sure, the Spanish empire bristled with peculiarities. The captain generals ruled the colonies with uncommon dictatorial powers; colonial subjects did not possess basic rights, nor could their grievances be expressed in any sort of mock representational body.[7] The persistence of slavery into the 1880s distinguished Spain's Caribbean colonies from those of other European powers, stifling the emergence of a convincing ideology of tutelage or civilization as existed elsewhere. Still, the profitable political economy of slavery in Cuba and Puerto Rico strengthened the foundations of empire.[8] For much of the century, slavery was common in the wider southern and mid-Atlantic regions—present in Brazil, Cuba, Puerto Rico, and the southern United States. Slavery was as terrible for its victims as it was unexceptional for its perpetrators.

In the mid–nineteenth century, Spaniards did not perceive themselves as living in an era of decline. Rather, the presence of the empire—although it was never called that—in many areas of metropolitan life was increasing. Nowhere was this more apparent than in Barcelona, Spain's fastest-growing urban area and the nucleus of its industrial heartland, Catalonia. During the mid–eighteenth century, foreign commerce had been tied into European markets. However, by the mid–nineteenth century, activity had shifted toward the colonies, the former colonies, and the cotton-exporting ports of Brazil and North America, accessed through the colonies.[9] A typical trade route was one in which a ship left Barcelona with wines, liqueurs, and finished goods. Often it carried little cargo given that its first stop was the west coast of Africa where it boarded slaves.[10] Sometimes it went directly to the Río de la Plata region, picking up beef jerky used to feed slaves in Brazil or Cuba. This ship would frequently proceed to Cuba, where it would exchange its cargo for sugar to be delivered to New Orleans, Charleston, and Mobile. It would return with American cotton to feed the looms of Catalonia's textile industry, one of Europe's largest.[11] The Antilles were not the only trading partners. Ships regularly departed to other countries or colonies, including the Philippines. Spanish investors, aware of the value of Asian commerce, were major purchasers of shares in the Suez Canal Company in 1858.[12] Barcelona was not the only overseas link. Santander, Bilbao, and smaller ports on the Cantabrian coast, in addition to other coastal cities, plied similar "triangular" or "quadrangular" trade routes.

The most conspicuous representative of the empire within social life was the *indiano*, equivalent to the British nabob. This nouveau riche returned to the metropole determined to make an impact on high society. One of the most famous was Antonio López, a poor peasant from the province of Santander, who emigrated to Cuba as a young man and became a wealthy merchant and slaver. In the 1850s, he settled in Barcelona, where he obtained the title Marquis de Comillas and founded the Transatlantic Steamship Company, the Hispano-Colonial Bank, and the Philippines Tobacco Company.[13] Spain was littered with numerous *indianos*, from the ostentatiously wealthy to members of the middle class, in much the same way the colonies and former colonies remained populated with men and women who had emigrated in search of sustenance, profit, adventure, fulfillment, and power. In the mid–nineteenth century, many of these traders, slavers, coolie traffickers, missionaries, merchant bankers, settlers, diplomats, and soldiers would seek to gain the ear of the government. These were the "men on the spot," the lifeblood of renewed European imperial ambitions.

The empire was not only present in economic and social life. It returned to the center of Spanish political life in 1858 when General Leopoldo O'Donnell and his Liberal Union Party won elections and assumed the reins of state. The party comprised politicians and army officers previously associated with the leftist progressives and the rightist moderates, who came to power as a "national government" committed to overcoming rivalries, pursuing economic development, and raising the international prestige of a country devastated by civil war for much of the first half of the century. O'Donnell had been captain general of Cuba from 1844 to 1848, a period in which the Cuban sugar industry continued its massive expansion due to the comparative edge gained through slave labor despite the fall in sugar prices. Along with a number of other generals involved in the Liberal Union, he was intimately connected to networks of Cuban plantation owners and slavers.[14] This observation is no mere anecdote. It would be difficult, if not impossible, to find another nineteenth-century head of state anywhere in the world who had been a colonial governor. The rise of O'Donnell begs the question of whether Spain was governing the empire or the empire was governing it. It is probable that Cuban plantation owners influenced metropolitan politics to a greater extent than any colonial lobby in any other European country at the time.

Unionists launched Spain on a new empire project with bravura and initial success.[15] In September 1858, a Franco-Hispanic expeditionary force of some two thousand men, largely recruited from the Philippines, landed in Tourane, inaugurating the maiden European invasion of Vietnam. The most successful campaign came just a year later. In October 1859, Spain declared war on Morocco, and by April 1860 the sultan had surrendered. The "War of Africa" was a short but brutal conflict against an ancient enemy, the successor state of the Islamic medieval kingdom of Al-Andalus. Led into battle by O'Donnell himself, troops were sent off and welcomed home with parades, receptions, and great fanfare. The third micromilitaristic enterprise took place a year after this victory when nationalist fervor, and belief in renewed imperial ambitions, was at its height. The government agreed to annex the Dominican Republic, accepting a petition from its president who feared an imminent Haitian invasion. Spain initially sent a few thousand troops together with judicial and administrative personnel. In July 1861, a small fleet sailed into the harbor of Port-au-Prince, threatened bombardment, exacted a small reparation (U.S.$200,000), and dissuaded the Haitians from mounting an attack.

Then came the highest-profile campaign—the invasion of Mexico. In October 1861, Spain, France, and Britain landed on the Yucatan, taking advantage of a vacuum of power in the Gulf of Mexico created by the outbreak of the Civil War in the United States. By the autumn of 1861, the Liberal Union had gone a long way in recovering international prestige. Amid economic growth and a railway boom, Spain had augmented its influence around the globe. Its diplomats had persuaded France and were pressuring Britain for entry into the Council of Europe.[16] Even to skeptical observers, Spain was a rising power with armies and navies in the South China Sea, North Africa, and the Caribbean.

In 1862, however, this project began to go pear shaped. In April, General Juan Prim, without consulting Madrid, took the controversial decision to withdraw

BATALLA DE TETUAN

Spanish micromilitarism in the age of new imperialism is shown in this etching, *The Battle of Tetuán* (1860), depicting fighting in Morocco featuring General Juan Prim in the center mounted on a horse. (drawing by Manuel Moliné [1833–1901], image courtesy of Arxiu Històric de la Ciutat, Barcelona)

the Army of the Antilles after full-scale war had broken out between France and Mexico. Like the British, he refused to support the move by France's Second Empire to convert Mexico into a puppet state by placing Archduke Ferdinand Maximilian on the throne. Even though the dismal French fate in Mexico attested to the wisdom of this decision, it entailed serious consequences. As a manner of retribution, France's Second Empire froze Spain out of key diplomatic negotiations in Vietnam. In June 1862, Spain begrudgingly signed a treaty with France and Vietnam in which it received no territorial concessions despite its considerable support for France during multiple campaigns, including access to the Philippines for manpower and supplies. As a result, Spain lost its opportunity to develop a trade route into China. This diplomatic fiasco was followed by a greater problem.

In 1863, Dominican rebels rose up, causing the government to pour in serious resources, eventually leading Spanish public opinion to turn sour as the war dragged on and the death toll and bills mounted. At the height of the conflict, Spain deployed some twenty-five thousand troops, consisting of mostly Cubans and Puerto Ricans, to pacify a local population only ten times the size. The human costs were heavy: the Army of the Antilles, ordinarily stationed in Cuban and Puerto Rico, may have lost more than twenty-seven thousand men.[17] Once this modest undertaking turned into a guerrilla war requiring serious outlays of money and men, Spain withdrew in 1865. With the end of the U.S. Civil War, the Army of the Antilles returned to Cuba and Puerto Rico to rebuild their defenses in case of a U.S. attack.[18]

The final sign that Spain's expansionist endeavors had been overambitious, if not delusional, was the bombastically named "War of the Pacific" (1864–66). In an attempt to emulate Britain, Spain mounted a form of gunboat diplomacy along the coasts of Chile and Peru. The unstated goal was to "negotiate" favorable trade agreements or even to lend support to small monarchist factions within these republics, which may have looked on a Bourbon pretender with favor. It is likely that the stimulus came from the positive results of gunboat diplomacy Madrid had achieved in Haiti in 1861. Initially, Spain had some success in this game of extortion and blackmail, introduced most brilliantly by Britain during the Opium wars and repeated with success in South America. Spain seized the Chincha Islands, a source of the valuable commodity of guano; it returned them to Peru after receiving a hefty sum in reparations and negotiating the outlines of a future trade agreement to be signed in Madrid. The war, though, ended badly. Spain attempted to repeat this script in Chile, to no avail. A decimated Spanish fleet hobbled home in 1866 after bombing the ports of Callao and Valparaíso. Chased out of the Pacific by Chilean and renewed Peruvian resistance, and pressured to leave by British and U.S. diplomats, Spain lost the War of the Pacific.[19]

By 1866, overseas expansionist experiments had come to a close. Spain had retreated from theaters in Southeast Asia, the Caribbean, and the Pacific. If the French invasion of Vietnam had opened opportunities in Southeast Asia, then Spain's sudden withdrawal from Mexico put an end to such Franco-Hispanic cooperation. If the descent of the United States into civil war in 1861 had presented opportunities in the Caribbean, then peace in 1865 had closed them. Only in North Africa could the Spanish claim victory on signing the Treaty of Wad-Ras. The government reported spending some 200 million reales (U.S. $6.1 million) on the War of Africa, while receiving double the amount in reparations. Thereafter, Spain intervened in Moroccan customs administration, hence developing an "informal empire" that would provide a gateway for formal empire in the early twentieth century. Still, monetary gains came at a high price. Spain lost some eight thousand soldiers in a few months, the majority to disease.[20] The British managed the war from diplomatic posts, forcing Spain to return the captured city of Tetuán. Aside from a few small enclaves surrounding the Spanish cities of Ceuta and Melilla, Spain acquired no new territory. In 1866, the Liberal Union set into motion the propaganda machine it had used so effectively in the War of Africa by receiving the "heroes of Callao" with a bombastic welcome-home parade. In 1910, a central plaza in Madrid was named Callao once the gravity of the loss had been disremembered. In 1866, however, few were fooled, despite celebrations to the contrary.

DOMESTIC "BLOWBACK"

As is often the case, imperial folly boomeranged back on the metropole. The state of Queen Isabel II—a hybrid of conservative constitutionalism, Bonapartist administrative centralization, liberal economic policies, and old-regime-style royal gluttony—came to an end. In 1866, the Spanish stock market crashed due to a number of factors: spiraling government debt; plunging railway shares; and a worldwide economic crisis caused by the U.S. Civil War, which had sent cotton prices soaring. The high cost of military misadventure contributed mightily to the crisis. The treasury had received 766,722,902 reales (U.S.$29,902,193) from the sale of church and communal lands in 1855 and 1856, a windfall that allowed the government to launch such endeavors.[21] However, the health of the books quickly deteriorated. By 1860, 20 percent of the state's budget was dedicated to debt-service payments.[22] The full cost of the annexation of Santo Domingo possibly ran up a bill of U.S.$25 million, more than twice the amount the government claimed to have "earned" from the invasion of Morocco. Military operations in Mexico and the Dominican Republic alone came to 14 million pesos (U.S.$11 million).[23] The War of the Pacific was also expensive. Even though Spain exacted U.S.$3 million in cash reparations from Peru, by 1865 the estimated cost of keeping the fleet in the Pacific was around U.S.$6 million per year.[24] In 1866, the Liberal Union definitively fell from power and disappeared from the political map, but the economy hardly improved. Economic and imperial disaster ushered in the Revolution of 1868. Queen Isabel II fled into exile. In 1868, war broke out in eastern Cuba, igniting what would become known as the Ten Years' War.

Illustrative of the consequences of imperial "blowback" was the story of General Juan Prim and successor generals who continued to dominate domestic political life for much of the ensuing decade. Born into a humble family, Prim had been captain general of Puerto Rico and was the hero of the conquest of Tetuán during the War of Africa. As the commander of working-class volunteer troops, he had forged a reputation—in contrast to the more patrician O'Donnell—as a democratic friend of the ordinary man. He was also the commander of the Spanish troops in Mexico who, after being accused of posturing for the Mexican throne, had taken the controversial decision to abandon the expedition. He then returned to Spain where he orchestrated the Revolution of 1868. In an attempt to convert himself into a Spanish Garibaldi, he turned kingmaker by installing the House of Savoy in Spain. His role as the sword behind the throne ended in 1870, when he fell victim to an assassin's bullet. Who ordered the murder remains a mystery, but likely suspects include Cuban slaveholders fearful that he might definitively abolish slavery.[25] Another suspect was General

Francisco Serrano, Prim's chief rival and a colleague of Leopoldo O'Donnell, who had publicly opposed Prim's decision to quit Mexico. As captain general of Cuba from 1859 to 1862, Serrano was also a major player in the Liberal Union's world of sugar and slaves. For his part, Serrano—who also fashioned himself a democrat—was regent of Spain in 1869–70 and became president in 1874 after the First Republic (1873) had fallen to a military coup. He, in turn, was deposed by General Arsenio Martínez Campos in December 1874, a veteran of campaigns in Morocco, Mexico, and Cuba. This cycle of "liberal" Bonapartist dictatorships

King Amadeo I swears to uphold Spain's liberal constitution before the body of General Juan Prim, the hero of the War of Africa and the progressive leader of the Revolution of 1868, who was assassinated in Madrid, December 1870. This is a detail of an etching of a painting done soon after the actual event by Antonio Gisbert Pérez, then director of the Museo del Prado in Madrid and a personal friend of both the king and general. (Biblioteca Nacional de España)

by imperial generals ended with the restoration of the Bourbons to the Spanish throne in 1876 and the removal of the military from politics.

Historians have identified various motivating factors driving this imperial zeal. To some, General O'Donnell's errant decision to follow France's Second Empire, and indeed to emulate the figure of Napoleon III, was the chief cause of military misadventure. According to this version, French diplomats seduced and dragged Spain into conflicts in Southeast Asia, North Africa, and the Caribbean, with the goal of counteracting British ambitions in these same areas. To others, the Liberal Union's "imperial dreams" were a cynical attempt to boost domestic patriotism by winning easy wars designed to raise the prestige of the army, which had not celebrated a victory against a foreign enemy since the age of Napoleon. To others, the campaigns were cast with economic interests in mind. Under this interpretation, the overriding goal in Southeast Asia, the Dominican Republic, and Mexico was to ensure a steady supply of slave and indentured labor to the Cuban sugar industry, the central axis around which the colonial system revolved.[26] Experts have calculated that during the 1850s and 1860s approximately 140,000 "Chinese" coolies disembarked in Cuban ports, mostly from French and Spanish vessels. In addition, some 60,000 Africans arrived in Cuba from 1856 to 1860.[27] The government had a direct interest in keeping the sugar industry buoyant. In 1860, monetary transfers to Spain were at their high-water mark, with Cuban customs sending some 5,372,205 pesos (U.S.$4.22 million) in cash to the treasury.[28]

These explanations are helpful, but they also give the impression that domestic and diplomatic considerations were paramount. By turning to comparative history, two further observations come to light. In the first place, Spanish politicians and military officers responded to stimuli emitted by the same actors then influencing other world powers. Spain's large territorial holdings in the South China Sea and the Caribbean, and its status as a former empire in Spanish America, meant that there were many "men on the spot" who eyed opportunities and pressured Madrid to take action. After all, it was not difficult to find a "violation" of international law that could be used to demand retribution or justify an invasion. In the case of Vietnam, the murder of Dominican missionaries in Tonkin provided grounds for a Franco-Hispanic reprisal. In Morocco, propagandists decried vandalism (including the desecration of the flag) and small attacks around the Spanish cities of Ceuta and Melilla. In Mexico, the three intervening countries sought to reverse the Juárez government decision to suspend debt obligations to foreigners. The spark that ignited the War of the Pacific was the treatment of a number of poor Basque agricultural workers accused of murder in Peru. Although all such casus belli were no more than pretexts, they evidenced the activities of a plethora of men on the spot engaged in spreading the gospel, seeking sustenance, stirring up trouble, soliciting help, peddling influence, and searching for profits. Ultimately, Spanish micromilitarism was not designed from Madrid solely in response to domestic developments. It was the inertia of the empire itself that pulled the state into new and old theaters.

Cuban planters were the most influential men on the spot. They had the government's ear and contributed heavily to military campaigns to further their economic interests, ensure the security of the island, and provide a steady stream of slave and indentured labor. However, a host of other voices made themselves heard. In Southeast Asia, military men, commercial houses, and missionaries in Macao, Manila, and Vietnam constantly pressured Madrid to implement more aggressive policies.[29] In the decades preceding the invasion of Mexico, a clutch of creditors—many with shady pasts, dubious commercial interests, and bogus claims to Spanish citizenship—lobbied the Foreign Office in furtherance of their cause.[30] In the Gulf of Guinea, where Spain was beginning to establish its last colonial enclave in the 1860s, missionaries promoted the production of palm oil, an export notoriously used as a front for the slave trade.[31] In the War of the Pacific, the key diplomatic actor was a histrionic man named Eusebio Salazar y Mazaredo. As the official representative for what had initially been a "scientific expedition," he provoked a serious diplomatic incident with Peru by essentially asserting that Spain had never recognized its independence. According to one Spanish admiral, his megalomaniacal fantasy was to seize the Chincha Islands as a way of purchasing Gibraltar from Britain.[32] After abandoning the Pacific fleet, Salazar ratcheted up tensions by claiming to have been the target of a series of foiled assassination attempts by Peruvian agents in Callao and Panama. To the astonishment of many, the Spanish government pushed these fantastic claims, in addition to the case of the Basque prisoners, as a justification for war.[33] With respect to the Dominican Republic, it is easy to imagine various men on the spot, pressuring General Pedro Santana to petition for reincorporation.

The second observation derived from this comparative history is that Spain followed the path of other European powers by attempting to develop what Ronald Robinson and John Gallagher famously labeled "informal empire."[34] Although this term was initially employed for Britain's "free-trade" version, it has come to describe a plethora of mid-nineteenth-century arrangements in which countries avoided outright colonization but exercised influence through a variety of means: loans, gunboat diplomacy, client states, control of the treasury and customs, and the imposition of commercially advantageous treaties.[35] In the case of Spanish expansionism, outright colonization followed by massive immigration—the old colonial model—was only vaguely contemplated in Santo Domingo. In other cases, informal empire was the goal. In Indochina, politicians mulled over providing military support to an independent client state in the region of Tonkin. In Morocco, Spain intervened for decades in the treasury in order to exact reparations. In Mexico, the three powers, on landing, immediately seized the customs house in Veracruz and began shaving off import duties to be credited against outstanding debts. For its part, Spain tried to place a Bourbon on the Mexican throne only to be thwarted by France, which preferred a Hapsburg. Military intervention in Indochina, Mexico, Morocco, Chile, and Peru had the goal of imposing favorable treaties of friendship, commerce, and reparations. Only in Morocco was Spain successful.

These explanations also shed light on British and French tolerance for Spanish bravura. Men on the ground loyal to these countries perceived that they had much to gain by collaborating or simply waiting to see what the Spanish stirred up. In Indochina, France was aided by considerable Spanish help, but, in other instances, Britain profited. In Morocco, the sultan turned to the City of London (as well as other investors) to help pay reparations.[36] During the War of the Pacific, South American countries put in orders with British shipbuilders to build navies needed to repel the Spanish fleet.[37] After the war, the Chilean government convinced the Baring Brothers and other British lenders to provide funds for rebuilding the port of Valparaíso.[38] This initial flurry of loans inaugurated an era of continued fiscal collaboration between Chile and Britain. As a result, Chile fell into line behind Argentina, Uruguay, and other countries. Britain continued to expand its informal empire in Latin America as Spain retreated, a trend that helps explain London's tolerance for Madrid's recklessness. The British could wait to occupy areas that Spain had opened but could not fill.[39]

Comparative history, then, helps us to understand this micromilitarism. Ultimately, Spain was caught in a transition in which established empires, such as Britain's, and new pretenders, such as France and the United States, constructed an informal empire through diplomacy, invasions, threats of force, blockades, and extortion. In concert with global events, Spain lurched toward expansion, pulled by men on the spot and pushed by domestic optimism, nationalism, and the promise of riches. On one level, politicians learned the lessons of others: that profits would rarely fall directly into state coffers and overseas military expeditions could boost as much as damage the reputation of a government. On another level, Spain failed to navigate the transition into informal empire due to material limitations. Any measure of "development"—kilometers of railway, the size of the economy, customs revenues, the size of the navy—suggests that Spain did not have the resources either to compete with European rivals or to carry out complicated campaigns in territories outside of its established colonies.[40] Spain became bogged down and was nudged out of theaters where it could not pacify domestic resistance or resist diplomatic pressure. In the end, micromilitaristic endeavors—followed by debacle, escalation, and retreat—were a definitive sign that Spain had ceded initiative to other powers within its historic zones of influence.

Spain in Morocco (1893–1926)

Twentieth-century military operations in Morocco shared some things in common with these earlier wars. If the independence of the Spanish American colonies by 1824 was the backdrop to efforts to open new overseas theaters, then the loss of Cuba, Puerto Rico, the Philippines, and the Pacific islands in the Spanish-American War of 1898 motivated politicians and generals to erect a "backdoor empire" in Morocco. Paralleling the earlier project of the Liberal Union, the Moroccan campaigns were part of another global transition in imperial strategies. Beginning with the Conference of Berlin (1885), European countries turned many zones of "informal" into "formal" empires, their ambitions furthered by murderous technological advances in weaponry. In effect, Spain joined the scramble for Africa. From 1893 to 1926, it expanded from its enclaves of Ceuta and Melilla, establishing a protectorate that stretched along the Mediterranean and north Atlantic coast of Morocco. The larger (and less rebellious) French Protectorate covered the great majority of the country, including most of the Atlantic coast, the capital of Marrakech, and the holy city of Fez. The Rif War (1919–26) was the name given to the Franco-Hispanic quashing of the Jibala tribes, which, led by Abd el-Krim, rebelled against the Spanish occupation and the sultan's forfeiture of sovereignty, and declared independence for the Rif region in 1921. This was the first native-led armed independence movement in Africa.

Another parallel was that Spanish military actions in Morocco gradually escalated from small campaigns into a full-scale war. This trend was similar to events in Latin America during the 1860s. The invasion of the Yucatán Peninsula in 1861, the occupation of the Dominican Republic (1861–65), and the War of the Pacific (1864–66) can be viewed as precursors to the prolonged dedication of serious levels of troops during the Ten Years' War (1868–78) in Cuba. With regard to Morocco, Spanish statesmen initially hoped that modest military incursions could protect their interests and enforce "agreements" with local tribal leaders. For a while, this strategy yielded results. In 1893, the army defended Melilla with a few additional troops while suffering a small number of casualties. In July of 1909, the government issued another extraordinary call-up to defend mining and railway installations outside Melilla after a contingent of troops had suffered a humiliating defeat at the Battle of the Wolf Ravine. Although this triggered a violent anticlerical revolt in Barcelona, the conduct of the war was much less problematic. Spain poured in forty-two thousand troops, who accomplished their objectives by November. With the signing of the Treaty of Fez (1912), Spain gained a "protectorate" in northern Morocco, with its capital in Tetuán, at a relatively low cost.

By the 1920s, however, Spain had become immersed in a complicated war against Rif rebels. Spain escalated troop levels significantly after its thinly stretched army lost between 8,000 and 12,000 lives at the Battle of Annual in July 1921. Any measurement—duration, troops, or civilian casualties—indicate that Morocco turned into a "macromilitary" enterprise. In March 1922, a government minister reported having sent 160,000 men into Morocco and having spent some 700 million pesetas (U.S.$110 million) since the debacle at Annual. In 1924, General Primo de Rivera, who had come to power in a military coup in 1923, reported 125,000 soldiers deployed in Morocco. From August to mid-October 1924, a period of intense fighting, Spanish casualties numbered between 12,000 and 18,000. The key invasion—the landing in Al Hoceima Bay on September 8, 1925—featured the arrival of 18,000 troops, 160 airplanes, and a tank squadron in a fairly sophisticated amphibious landing. The ensuing Hispano-French land offensive numbered 90,000 men (with more in the rearguard), complemented by light tanks and aircraft, chasing a Rif army of 20,000. One source calculated that factories in Madrid and Melilla produced 400 metric tons of mustard gas between 1923 and the third quarter of 1925, which was used in the production of tens of thousands of 2.5 to 25 kilogram bombs, causing an incalculable number of deaths, indescribable human suffering, and escalated cancer rates.[41]

Reflecting Spain's advanced technology in the Rif War, Renault FT-17 tanks were used against Berber guerrillas in Morocco from 1922 to 1926, participating in the world's first amphibious tank landing at Al Hoceima Bay. These tanks protected a convoy near the town of Tafersit during Spanish Foreign Legion operations to lift a siege on Tizzi Asa in June 1923. (Jesus Dapena for the Cipriano Briz Collection)

As was the case with the Liberal Union, overseas debacles boomeranged back on the metropole in the form of military dictatorships. In the 1860s, imperial generals had broadly liberal and even democratic ideas at home, proving grudgingly amenable to working with and turning power over to constitutionalist regimes. This was not the case in the 1920s when fascism (as opposed to liberalism) was on the rise. The Rif War had converted the Army of Africa into a hardened fighting force with racist and right-wing convictions. Significantly, both of Spain's twentieth-century military dictatorships had roots in Morocco. One of the major reasons behind the fall of the liberal-constitutionalist, though oligarchic, Restoration Monarchy (1876–1923) was a string of military disasters that discredited the regime and set the stage for the dictatorship of Miguel de Primo de Rivera (1923–29). Although the general did not have African experience himself, he gained support for his coup among officers and draft-eligible classes by pledging to end the unpopular war. He kept this promise by sacrificing more lives and limbs, soliciting the aid of France, and deploying chemical weapons against civilians. Even after the pacification of the protectorate in 1926, Morocco cast a shadow over the metropole. In June of 1936, the Army of Africa crossed the Strait of Gibraltar, invaded Spain, plodded its way up the peninsula, and caused the government of the Second Republic (1931–36) to abandon Madrid. Led by General Francisco Franco, who came to prominence as a capable leader of the Spanish Foreign Legion during the Rif War, the army was the decisive ground force in the Spanish Civil War (1936–39). Franco's thirty-six-year dictatorship (1939–75), in many respects, had its origins in Morocco.[42]

Metropolitan stimuli and interests in Morocco can be analyzed by examining the same factors that provoked the wave of expansionism of the mid–nineteenth century. Nationalism, for one thing, was no longer a major factor. Unlike the War of Africa (1859–60), the twentieth-century campaigns were, with few exceptions, unpopular. All the same, other factors remained relevant. Spain was equally, if not more, dependent on France in the twentieth century. The French carved out the protectorate for the Spanish by controlling negotiations with the sultan and other European powers leading to the Treaty of Fez. Afterward the French continued to mediate negotiations between the Spanish and the sultan. In the Rif War, the French intervention in 1924 was the deciding factor in a victory that otherwise would have probably eluded the Spaniards. Economic motives were also paramount. The largest corporation in Morocco was the Spanish Company of the Mines of the Rif, which consisted of a mixture of French, Spanish (mostly Catalan and Basque), and German investors. With capital of 10 million pesetas (U.S.$1.56 million) in 1910, it exploited iron ore deposits in the mountains outside Melilla, sending the lion's share of its exports to Britain and Germany. Mining companies were also the chief promoters of the railways and were in constant contact with local tribal leaders, negotiating iron extraction and railway construction rights. Commercial, shipping, telephone, and electric ventures in Melilla and the international (French-dominated) city of Tangier also penetrated the hinterlands, eager to do business with cities in the French protectorate by planning a railway from Tangier to Fez. These and other companies caused the mushrooming of various men on the spot who solicited the support of the Spanish army to pacify the protectorate and intimidate tribal leaders.[43]

Economic interests, however important, were not the driving force. After all, the hundreds of millions of pesetas spent in military actions greatly outweighed the tens of millions in investment. The state—led by the army and the politicians—was the chief promoter. Following the loss of the colonies in 1898, army officers pressured politicians to grant them a new role overseas by expanding Spain's ambitions in Morocco. This did not mean that soldiers lined up to fight in the most inhospitable of terrains. Rather, top brass used the war to pressure politicians for an increased budget, much of it used on the salaries of the officer corps, the most bloated in Europe.[44] Politicians and diplomats, many of whom by the 1920s were also in the army, or connected to it through family, friends, and shared interests, were eager to pursue military objectives. Just as postwar British decolonization after Suez was carried out to maintain a "world role," Morocco also gave Spain a card to play.[45] The Treaty of Fez—negotiated between Spain, France, Germany, and the sultan in 1912—was the first such opportunity. Thereafter Spanish diplomats kept themselves busy with the Moroccan question in Tangier, Marrakech, Paris, Berlin, Rome, and London.

This quest to maintain an international role was not a quixotic exercise in diplomatic imagination. The small stretch of Mediterranean territory across the Strait of Gibraltar was of critical strategic significance. What is more, Morocco's international cities bristled with consuls, emissaries, middlemen, businessmen, and other imperial opportunists representing or seeking to represent various political and economic interests—a milieu later romanticized in the Hollywood film *Casablanca* (1942). In June 1936, key conversations took place between Franco and Benito Mussolini's diplomats stationed in Tangier over the transportation of the Army of Africa to the mainland. Indeed, if the Italians had not flown the army to Spain, the Spanish Republic might have succeeded in quashing the uprising before it could gather momentum. These negotiations were among the most important steps in convincing Italy and Germany to back Franco with ground support and airpower in the Spanish Civil War.[46] In October 1940, Adolf Hitler traveled to Hendaye to discuss Spanish participation in World War II. Having already occupied Tangier in June, Franco demanded the French protectorate of Morocco and its Algerian province of Oran (over which Spain asserted some vague historic claims) as a precondition. However, Hitler did not want conflict with Vichy France, and hence no agreement was reached.[47] Although there were other reasons for this outcome, Franco was the only head of state able to negotiate and avoid a German occupation. Its backdoor empire in Morocco had given Spain some leverage within the sweep of global events.

CONCLUSION

The history of Spain's imperial eclipse should now appear more recognizable than the assumption that decline was a linear process of ongoing retreat over several centuries. In the case of Spain and other countries, decolonization obviously featured the loss of colonies, the most notable of which took place in 1823 and 1898. However, it also included a litany of micromilitaristic expansionist endeavors bearing mixed results. Countries with imperial pasts, with links to many ambitious men on the spot, do not just shrink in reasoned concert with fiscal-military realities. Rather, both competent and bungling statesmen start, join, and get cajoled into deploying troops for a number of reasons—diplomatic, economic, and nationalistic. In such periods of imperial eclipse and transition, rising empires occupy spaces that declining ones open and cannot fill. In the case of limited success, lesser powers can succeed in securing small backdoor empires that afford them a minor role in world affairs. In many cases, "blowback" takes the form of an enlarged presence of the military in metropolitan life. As is obvious, militarism never appears so "micro" to soldiers and civilians who face the bullets and bombs or who fall victim to disease. With these generalizations in mind, one might ask whether the Persian Gulf represents Washington's high-tech backdoor empire in what is shaping up to be its age of decline.

The purpose of this exercise has not been merely to demand a space for Spain—its "seat at the table," so to speak—in studies of comparative decolonization. It has also been to use the case of Spain to shed light on a more general phenomenon. To be sure, the eclipse of its empire is not a process in which the metropole sheds colonies in neat proportion to fiscal-military realities. Rather, statesmen and generals promote overseas expansionist enterprises only to be confronted by economic and geopolitical limitations. In the end, Spain was caught in an imperial transition, in which Britain, France, and the United States were in the process of occupying its zones of influence. In the aftermath of World War II, other European powers would undergo a similar process, forced to cede territory and influence to the United States and the Soviet Union. Imperial eclipses, dawns, and transitions are drawn out, deadly, and complicated. They are not unidirectional, nor do they resemble a downward spiral. The message in Thomas Cole's famous painting reproduced in the first pages of this volume—featuring a romanticized version of the onslaught of fiscal-military disaster—represents the exception rather than the rule.

"The Empire Is No Longer a Social Unit"

Declining Imperial Expectations and Transatlantic Crises in Metropolitan Spain, 1859–1909

ALBERT GARCIA BALAÑÀ

TOWARD THE END OF 1859, four armed companies of "Catalan Volunteers" departed Barcelona bound for Morocco. Recruited and financed by the provincial deputation, their objective was to join the military offensive that Spain had launched against the sultanate in October as a response to border skirmishes in Ceuta, a city in North Africa that had been under Spanish sovereignty since the sixteenth century. The "War of Africa," as it came to be called, was a short conflict, lasting from October 1859 to April 1860, that marked the first chapter in Spain's modest colonial dominion over the northern part of Morocco. The outcome of the conflict also demonstrated how Britain and France would exercise a tutelary role over Spain's colonial ambitions, restraining Madrid's sphere of action in northern Africa, the Caribbean, and the Pacific in coming decades. During this short war, Spanish forces conquered Tetuán, but Britain required the city's return after the armistice. During the peace negotiations, Britain, without firing a shot, shared in Spain's right of intervention in Moroccan customs to exact reparations and also became the sultanate's major creditor after the war. Consequently, Spain's chief gains from its victory were neither financial nor territorial. As clearly illustrated by events in Barcelona during the winter of 1859–60, the country's real achievement was on home front.

Enthusiasm for the war permeated all social levels of the city. Not only was there broad agreement over the reasons for engagement, but there was nearly unanimous support for the monarchical liberal government of General Leopoldo O'Donnell, who was then convincingly posturing as a Spanish Napoleon III. Upon publication of the recruitment announcement for the Catalan Volunteers, the five hundred civilian positions were quickly filled. Many such volunteers and their supporters came from popular, radical sectors of Barcelona society, including democrats and republicans who had long been opponents of the liberal governments of the Bourbon monarchy under Queen Isabel II. The *Times* of London's war correspondent in Morocco, Frederick Hardman, was impressed by such intense imperialist patriotism, which bridged ideological divides. He observed that when the volunteers arrived in Morocco, they were welcomed by O'Donnell with "the band playing the [royalist] *Marcha Real*"; upon departing, they were sent off to the lively revolutionary songs of "Riego's hymn and other Liberal melodies."[1]

Fifty years later, in the summer of 1909, Spain embarked on another war in Morocco, and the city of Barcelona again captured the headlines. Yet much had changed since 1859. In July 1909, there were no civilian volunteers preparing to embark in the port. Instead, the government had to call up reservists to be sent to the Spanish city of Melilla in northern Morocco to fight the armed *kabilas* of the Rif region. This order sparked greater turmoil than the city had witnessed for more than half a century. On Monday, July 26, Barcelona awoke to a crippling general strike. Led by trade unions and republican groups, the protest spread into the hinterland of Barcelona, then the largest urban and industrial region in Spain. A wave of social strife and violence washed over the city, until the arrival of troops from outside the area crushed the rebellion on Saturday, July 31. Even for radicalized turn-of-the-century Barcelona, the extent of the violence in this "Tragic Week" of 1909 was astonishing. Rebels destroyed at least fifty-two churches and religious buildings and tore up over six thousand square meters of pavement to build barricades. At least one hundred civilians died in the course of street fighting. In its aftermath, the army brought more than seventeen hundred people before military courts, of whom seventeen were sentenced to death and five finally executed. To be sure, the causes of such widespread discontent were multifarious and deeply rooted.[2] Still, we must ask why this new military campaign against the sultanate, which could have stirred, as in 1859, popular enthusiasm for African conquests, instead sparked such violent opposition in 1909.

What had changed since 1859? Had defeat in the Spanish-American War of 1898 inculcated a sense of decline so profound that the public found further imperial adventures repugnant? Had the weakness of Spain during the Algeciras Conference of 1906 made it clear that expansionist efforts in Morocco would be limited by the great powers? Or had the principal changes taken place within society itself? As we will see, the difference between 1859 and 1909 was due to both social and geopolitical factors. What is undeniable, though, is that many in Barcelona—as in the rest of Spain—had lost their enthusiasm for imperial projects.

It might be tempting to explain this change—from enthusiasm to revulsion— by simply referring to various episodes of colonial crisis over two generations, in which Spain suffered one humiliation after another on the battlefield and at the negotiating table. The troubled situation of Spain's Caribbean colonies accounted for a string of overseas disasters, which hamstrung Madrid's pretensions in Africa and ushered in a withdrawal from the Pacific. But a mere list of military defeats and retreats is not sufficient. Rather, it is necessary to identify precisely what were the "imperial expectations" of metropolitan groups in 1859 and trace how such expectations were modified by colonial crises, overseas military adventures, and their metropolitan impact. Through this process, it will become evident that waning imperial expectations across a wide social spectrum in places such as Barcelona were a cause as much as a consequence of the collapse, not the eclipse, of the Spanish empire at century's end.

An explanation of why broad sectors of society lost interest in the colonies should not focus solely on the Spanish-American War of 1898. Spain's ultimate defeat by the United States in the Caribbean and Pacific does not provide a full explanation. By examining events in Barcelona, Spain's most industrialized city, it is evident that the decline in imperial enthusiasm had been a long time in the making. After the patriotic celebrations surrounding the send-off and welcome home of the Catalan Volunteers in 1859, they reappeared ten years later in 1869. This time the volunteers left to fight in what would come to be known as the First Cuban War or the Ten Years' War (1868–78). More than thirty-five hundred Catalan Volunteers enlisted and set sail for Cuba, accounting for over 10 percent of all metropolitan forces sent in 1869. Members of the city's economic and institutional elite launched the recruitment drive, and again it was a resounding success. In fact, the number of volunteers was three times greater than the number of soldiers that the ministry conscripted for the same campaign in the province of Barcelona the same year.[3] Even the republican press, which opposed an exclusive military response to the Cuban uprising, gave its initial, albeit qualified, support. In an article published in Seville, the young Cuban nationalist José Martí, exiled in Spain since 1871, referred to the "republican Catalan Volunteers," a turn of phrase evocative of the popular and democratic sectors filling their ranks.[4]

Given such precedents in 1859 and 1869, one might think that the same script could be repeated in the next major conflict, the Second Cuban War, which began in 1895. Although few thought this uprising was any worse than previous ones, not a single battalion of Catalan Volunteers sailed from Barcelona. In one generation, matters changed markedly. Clearly, even before the collapse of the Spanish empire in 1898, enthusiasm for overseas adventures had waned. So what had changed in cities such as Barcelona between the 1860s and the 1890s that caused so many to lower their "imperial expectations"?

METROPOLITAN MIGRATION AND IMPERIAL DECLINE

One way to approach this question is to examine emigration to the colonies, since these patterns can shed light on such imperial expectations. In fact, many young men of modest means and commercial ambition had used enlistment for free passage and eventual emigration to Cuba in 1869. In March of that year, one of the promoters of the volunteer militias wrote to Víctor Balaguer, a future colonial minister, saying, "In the hope of going to Cuba almost all have left the positions they occupied [in Catalonia], and many of them expect to find good positions there once the campaign has ended."[5] In the eyes of such volunteers, Cuba was not so much a destination for mercenaries as a labor market with a potential for rapid promotion. One study found that, among almost a thousand Catalan Volunteers, 66 percent described themselves as artisans and tradesmen, skilled workers likely to find colonial employment; in contrast, scarcely 15 percent described themselves as peasants or day laborers.[6] These statistics were part of a broader trend that began with the loss of Latin America and the subsequent administrative reorganization of Cuba and Puerto Rico. Beginning in the 1810s and 1820s, Catalans began to migrate to the Spanish Caribbean, creating a true diaspora. While Catalans constituted 11 percent of Spain's population in 1860, they represented almost 16 percent of the seventy thousand peninsular emigrants in Cuba.[7] Since Barcelona was the center of one of Europe's most industrialized regions, the ambitions of these emigrants are quite revealing.

Catalan migrants were usually young men from coastal and urban areas of commercial or artisan backgrounds; they expected good opportunities in Cuba and ordinarily planned to return home in ten to fifteen years. Active and latent family and community networks were the links in diasporic chains, facilitating the arrival of unmarried brothers, relatives, and acquaintances. It was essentially a diaspora of commerce, a regional network that promoted new Atlantic trade flows whose epicenters were in the Spanish Caribbean and key Catalan industrial areas.[8] In 1843, 33 percent of the more than thirteen hundred merchants registered in Havana were born in Catalonia (compared to only 11 percent on the whole island). Between 1850 and 1865, 65 percent of new metropolitan traders registered in Santiago de Cuba—where creole traders were a minority, as in Havana—were of Catalan birth.[9]

In the 1870s and 1880s, however, these strong migratory links would weaken significantly. In 1860–61, 72 percent of Catalan migrants to the Americas settled in Cuba and Puerto Rico. From 1885 to 1890, by contrast, this figure dropped to 26 percent as Argentina and Uruguay became the destination for almost 60 percent of Catalan migrants to the Americas.[10] To be sure, the empire became a less attractive destination than the former empire.

The percentages of migrants to the colonies and ex-colonies were not the only things that changed. So did the sociological profile of migrants. Those from the overwhelmingly rural provinces of Tarragona and Lleida rose from only 4.5 percent of Catalan migrants in 1861 to 24 percent in 1889. In a like manner, the number of peasants (as opposed to the number of skilled workers) embarking from Barcelona also increased dramatically.[11] Although the Catalan migration rate rose slightly between 1860 and 1890, it remained notably lower than the equivalent figure for all of Spain—a marked contrast to the situation at the beginning of the 1860s.[12] This reflected a shift in the way Spaniards viewed Cuba. While the island had attracted 73 percent of all Spanish migrants across the Atlantic in 1861–62, between 1880 and 1890 this figure dropped to only 38 percent of the 420,000 people who migrated to the Americas, about the same as those who went to Argentina.[13] In short, migrants no longer preferred the colonies.

Although colonial Cuba was no longer the exclusive destination for Spanish emigrants, migration flows did not stagnate. In the early 1860s, some ten thousand migrants arrived on the island per year; during the 1870s and 1880s, the annual numbers would fluctuate between twelve and twenty thousand.[14] At first glance, the increasing numbers might be interpreted as representing increasing enthusiasm. However, it is not only necessary to look at numbers but also at percentages (as above) and profiles. The profiles of emigrants, in fact, were not only influenced by the attractiveness of other destinations in the Atlantic but also by developments in the colony itself. In the early 1860s, Cuba's skilled labor market was highly structured, consisting of slaves and free blacks, a majority of white islanders, and influential regional networks of metropolitan migrants that could provide skilled work for newcomers. Yet this racial and ethnical ordering of the labor market would change in the following decades due to the First Cuban War and its aftermath. As a result of the war, many slaves and Chinese indentured servants became liberated, especially in the eastern part of the island. In addition, the war deepened divisions between white islanders and peninsulars in the west. The net effect of these developments on the labor market was that after the war skilled labor migrants found it more difficult to find a position with prospects of rapid promotion.

To illustrate this point, it is helpful to focus on the the six years following 1886, a period that featured the greatest civilian migration in Cuba's history. While fourteen thousand migrants arrived on the island in 1886, this number doubled to over twenty-eight thousand as preindependence migration peaked in 1892.[15] Again, such numbers can be deceiving. Recent research has shown that immigration companies linked to plantation owners recruited and shipped many of these migrants, who were largely peasants from the Canary Islands and Galicia bound for the sugar harvest. Much of this was seasonal or "swallow migration" since many laborers returned home in a matter of months. In 1892, one of these companies, the Sociedad Protectora del Trabajo Español en las Posesiones de Ultramar, was responsible for over four thousand migrants, representing 15 percent of the annual total.[16]

How should this migration be interpreted? First, it is evident that the presence of this peasant migration showed Spain's decline in the Caribbean. The definitive end of Cuban slavery in 1886, a decade after the rebellion by creoles and blacks during the Ten Years' War, led planters to pursue white "Spanish" workers.

Second, the arrival of so many temporary migrants was a short-term victory for pro-Spanish plantation owners, who were more interested in a seasonal over-supply of landless labor than in forming a potential landowner class. Third, colonial Cuba simply became less attractive to urban, artisan, and skilled-labor migrants like the Catalans. Consequently, between 1885 and 1890, six of every ten transatlantic passengers leaving Barcelona were bound for the Río de la Plata region, while just over two of every ten headed for Cuba. Indeed, studies of the growing Catalan community in Buenos Aires during the 1880s and 1890s have demonstrated that new arrivals had characteristics similar to those of migrants coming to Cuba in earlier decades. Catalans in Buenos Aires tended to consist of skilled labor from urban areas; took advantage of familial and regional migration chains always active but never saturated; upon arrival, they inserted themselves in employment- and association-based networks; and, on settling, experienced rapid social ascent before 1900.[17] In a report of 1882, the Argentine consul in Barcelona observed, "The push for Catalans is the desire to make fortunes rather than the need to placate hunger."[18]

From a comparative perspective, it should be underscored that migration to areas outside the empire was not a clear indicator of the end of the empire. Migrants leaving Great Britain did not emigrate overwhelmingly to the territories of the Commonwealth and the empire until the first decade of the twentieth century.[19] What distinguishes the Spanish from the British case is that its lesser-qualified migrants went to imperial destinations (e.g., peasants and conscripts to Cuba in the 1880s and 1890s), while those more qualified chose destinations outside Madrid's control (e.g., Catalan artisans to Argentina in the 1880s and 1890s).

The dwindling interest in the empire among qualified workers was mainly, though not exclusively, a consequence of the metropole's growing weakness in the colonies. As the urban labor market in Cuba faded in the 1880s, Madrid proved unable to open alternative attractive destinations, however modest, in Spain's African and Asian territories. Although Madrid had planned, back in the 1860s, to establish civilian colonies in its small Gulf of Guinea possessions, by the 1880s the Colonial Office abandoned these plans in favor of Catholic missions in consonance with the "Principle of Effectivity," as famously articulated at the Conference of Berlin of 1884–85.[20] The 1880s and early 1890s, therefore, witnessed the dawning of imperial biopolicies that could have attracted the more dynamic metropolitan working classes to the colonies. Such potential migrants proved reluctant to participate in the "re-Hispanization" of Cuba or in the few and relatively unsuccessful projects to promote emigration to West African colonial sites. By 1900, just twenty-four thousand Spaniards were living in the North African territories, and barely five hundred "whites" had settled on the Spanish-Guinean island of Fernando Poo (compared to over eighteen thousand "continental Negroes" and the indigenous Bubi people).[21] By contrast, over two hundred thousand Spaniards were then living in French Algeria, half of whom were recently naturalized. Indeed, French Algeria, rather than Spanish Africa, had become the destination for at least three hundred thousand Spanish migrants since 1882.[22] In sum, migration patterns demonstrate declining imperial enthusiasm well before the loss of colonies in 1898.

IMPERIAL DECLINE AND METROPOLITAN COUNTERREVOLUTION

The decline of the Spanish empire in the last third of the nineteenth century had a significant military dimension. During the First Cuban War more than 175,000 armed men crossed the Atlantic to Cuba where they joined the almost 60,000 civilian volunteers there in 1871. During the Second Cuban War of 1895–1898, another 220,000 soldiers sailed to Cuba, yielding a total of more than 500,000 arrivals for the period 1868 to 1898.[23] Other colonial expeditions on this scale were uncommon until 1899, when Britain recruited 450,000 men throughout its empire for the South African War. The Spanish military campaigns in Morocco before the establishment of the Spanish protectorate in 1912 were smaller but still substantial: some 48,000 men were dispatched to Ceuta during the 1859–60 War of Africa; and some 42,000 troops were mobilized for the 1909 campaign in the Rif, with 20,000 remaining in Africa to occupy part of the future protectorate.[24] These contingents and their scant results may be interpreted as evidence of Madrid's growing weakness overseas. However, it is possible to observe an equally striking phenomenon. By comparing troop mobilizations in 1859 and 1869 with those of 1895 and 1909 in Barcelona, it becomes apparent that major shifts had occurred in recruitment for overseas military service and popular enthusiasm about the benefits of empire. Paralleling hopes of promotion through imperial migration, this shift was the outcome of a continuously changing alchemy between colonial and metropolitan crises.

The Catalan Volunteers sent to Morocco in 1859–60, like those who went to Cuba in 1869, were quite different from the *quintos* or conscript troops. Not only were the former volunteers, but they also had distinct conditions of service. The volunteers wore different uniforms, had civilian officers, and were assigned to different and generally less dangerous positions at the front. From 1869 to 1871 in Cuba, for example, the chief task of the Catalan contingent was to defend the loyalist rear guard. Such distinctions were loaded with symbolic import, particularly since the volunteers cloaked themselves in the symbols of the Spanish National Militia of the 1830s to the 1860s.[25]

These militias had their roots in the famous guerrilla resistance during the war against Napoleon and in civil wars against absolutists during the 1820s and 1830s. They were not only an armed civilian defense institution but they also served as strong urban associations with democratic beliefs, harbingers of the age of mass politics. Spain's political parties, however, had different, though not always favorable, opinions about the usefulness of the National Militia. The Moderados, the most conservative of the liberal parties, viewed it with suspicion and disdain; when in government, they dissolved it time and time again in 1844, 1856, and 1874. By contrast, the Progresistas, the more inclusive of Spain's two liberal parties, reestablished the National Militia on coming to power in 1854 and 1868. Radical republicans, the group the farthest to the left, provided unconditional support. In urban Catalonia, as in Madrid, the militias were shrouded in a democratic political culture, synonymous with an armed civilian camaraderie. Militiamen took pride in their autonomy from the command of a closed and increasingly patrician army. They expected that service would bring material and symbolic rewards. While militias were voluntary, the army consisted of conscripts unable to purchase exemptions.[26] For this reason, few readers were surprised when, in April of 1869, an article in the republican press showered praise on the Catalan Volunteers sailing for Cuba while condemning the *quintos* (recruits) bound for the same destination.[27]

The success in the recruitment drives for the Catalan Volunteers in 1859–60 and 1869 cannot be understood without recognizing their militialike visibility— a visibility far greater than their numbers warranted. The Catalan Volunteers were like an urban militia mobilized to fight overseas. Thus, in 1860 the most important prorepublican opponent of the O'Donnell government published this tribute to the africanist militia in Barcelona: "The middle class and, above all, the proletarian classes have on this occasion shown their great patriotism.... While [the neo-Catholics] believed that the war against the Mohammedans would rekindle dead fanaticism [and] old historical traditions presumably favorable to their interests, these modern absolutists have encountered a liberal spirit so closely bound to the sentiment of patriotism that they have been unable to avoid the conclusion that fatherland and liberty are now and forever synonymous."[28]

Just as the liberal imperialism stoked by the Crimean War (1853–56) encouraged British radicals to support Garibaldi through the British Legion, so the War of Africa, combined with the republican spirit of the Catalan Volunteers, was instrumental in promoting the more modest Legión Ibérica. A hundred volunteers returned from Morocco and then set sail for Genoa in September 1860 to join their Italian comrades.[29] This association of popular political activism with overseas adventure continued even after the Catalan Volunteers had departed for Cuba in 1869. The working-class press of Barcelona praised these ordinary armed men serving as civilian volunteers in pro-Spanish Cuba ("for the worker now possesses a rifle"), depicting a loyalist scenario in which military authority would not go unchallenged.[30]

In the autumn of 1868, a military *pronunciamiento* lent momentum to an anti-Bourbon revolution that resulted in the permanent exile of Queen Isabel II from Spain. Although no one realized it at the time, this marked the beginning of the end for the National Militia. During a period of rather unstable democratic governments, known as the Democratic Sexennium (1868–74), the right of civilians to take up arms and form urban battalions became hotly contested. The question was, furthermore, bound up in debates over universal male suffrage, freedom of association, and the free press. The city of Barcelona was once again, as in the 1840s and 1850s, the main site of this conflict. Considerable numbers of artisans and workers demonstrated against conscription in the spring of 1869. At that time, the National Militia, abolished in 1856, was in effect reestablished under a different name, rebaptizing itself as the Voluntarios de la Libertad. The response of the government was to control and weaken this militia, since it had become a vehicle for spreading republicanism among the lower classes. In the autumn of 1869, tensions exploded. Working-class battalions of the National Militia raised barricades and faced down the army. Similar struggles occurred in other cities, then recurred in Barcelona in 1870 and again during the short-lived First Republic of 1873.[31] The collapse of the republican bloc in 1873 opened the way for a praetorian Restoration in 1874 and, a year later, the return of the Bourbon monarchy in the person of young King Alfonso XII. The restrictive 1876 Constitution dissolved the National Militia once and for all. Two years later the electoral law restricted voting to just 15 percent of the male population over twenty years old (only about 800,000 to 950,000 voters from 1879 to 1890), a marked contrast to the universal male suffrage in the constitutions of 1869 and 1873.

The Bourbon Restoration also saw the reorganization of the *quinta*, a discriminatory system of conscription. Previously, one in five men (hence the name *quinta*, "one-fifth") eligible for military service would be conscripted by lottery. However, since the First Cuban War (1868–78) was still raging, the conservative government gradually upped this figure from 20 to a whopping 60 percent. This, however, did not mean that everyone was at risk of being drafted. Rather, recruits could pay a redemption fee or buy a "substitute" (if one's name came up), a policy that obviously had the effect of discriminating in favor of the middle classes and rich and against workers. As everyone knew, this system served as a despised form of indirect taxation. By overrecruiting, the treasury was able to replenish shortfalls aggravated by the war. State revenues collected through redemption fees in the 1894–95 budget amounted to nine million pesetas. Following the outbreak of the Second Cuban War in 1895–96, this figure rose to thirty million pesetas and year later rose to forty-two million.[32] Apart from this indirect tax, the state financed the war by inflating the currency and, above all, issuing debt with attractive interest rates to large investors. By the end of 1898, state debts were almost equal to Spain's annual gross domestic product.[33]

This dismal fiscal picture was made even more ugly by the fact that the *quinta* was essentially a "blood tax." A redemption could cost up to 2,500 pesetas, equal to the annual income of a family of skilled industrial workers in Barcelona around 1900. For those innumerable families that could not raise that payment, often those with multiple boys of draftable age, it was plainly an unfair burden paid in blood. After all, conscription into the Spanish colonial wars of the late empire was nearly a death sentence. In the First Cuban War (1868–78), approximately half of the 150,000 soldiers were dead by 1878. Only 10 percent of these perished in battle or as a result of wounds; the other 90 percent died from fevers or from appalling health and material conditions.[34] In 1895–96, the first year of the Second Cuban War, four out of every five *quintos* who died succumbed to "tropical diseases."[35] The high domestic costs of such squalid colonial militarism were a result of the political dominance of the upper classes after the counterrevolution that brought the Bourbon Restoration of the Spanish throne in 1875. It comes as no surprise, then, that social classes subject to conscription were no longer enthusiastic about empire.

This is not to say that expressions of mass patriotism had ceased to exist. Patriotic demonstrations occurred in 1885 during a now forgotten dispute with Germany over the sovereignty of the Caroline Islands in the Pacific. They recurred at the outbreak of the Second Cuban War in 1895 and again when the United States sided with the Cuban rebels in 1898. All the same, such periodic expressions of patriotism should not obscure the fact that a great transformation had taken place since the early 1860s. Simply put, by 1895 nobody in Barcelona was volunteering to fight in Cuba. All in all, metropolitan policies affecting overseas colonial territories had spawned more grievances than enthusiasm among the working classes, particularly in industrial cities like Barcelona. Of course, this change can also be attributed to the birth of new internationalist and semipacifist urban political cultures (anarchism, socialism, anti-imperialism) in industrial cities throughout all of Europe. In the case of Spain, however, these grievances stemmed, more precisely, from the combination of metropolitan counterrevolution and imperial decline.

Two examples serve to illustrate the depth of this change. Discriminatory conscription practices and high mortality in the Second Cuban War forced many republican leaders to reformulate (but not abandon) their patriotic resolve to defend Spanish sovereignty over Cuba. In the summer of 1896, they demanded that "Everyone must go, rich and poor alike!" However, this stance paved the way for antimilitarist, anti-imperialist, metropolitan political groups to come to the fore. The socialists of the embryonic PSOE (Spanish Socialist Workers' Party), which had won a scant fourteen thousand votes in the 1896 elections, united over one hundred thousand people in their 1897 anti-conscription campaign under the slogan "All or none!" Although this may look like a republican slogan, they were actually demanding that nobody go.[36] At the same time, growing numbers of anarchist activists in Barcelona were linked to European associations supporting Cuban, Puerto Rican, and even Filipino nationalists. A story of "anarchism and anti-colonial imagination," narrated by the historian Benedict Anderson, was based on a forced but fraternal encounter in Barcelona's Montjuïc prison in the autumn of 1896. There the Filipino leader José Rizal and the Cuban expatriate Fernando Tarrida del Mármol, who was soon to become one of José Martí's men in Europe, found themselves jailed among local anarchists then being detained and tortured.[37]

While mass political culture was growing increasingly opposed to the oligarchic state and its colonial misadventures, many draftees weighed their options. Resistance to military conscription for the Second Cuban War illustrates this trend. The number of deserters and draft evaders doubled between 1895 and 1898 (from 2.5 to 5 percent of those enlisted); moreover, they were much more numerous in the coastal and border regions of the north (approaching 14 percent in Galicia) and the east, including Catalonia. The reason, of course, was that it was easier to escape abroad from these regions. Some fugitives found refuge in France, but, revealingly, a great number fled to the Latin America republics, which had been the destination of the more dynamic communities of Spanish migrants since the 1880s.[38]

CONCLUSION

C. A. Bayly has argued that it is impossible to explain the rapid imperial expansionism from 1870 to 1914 without paying close attention to the nation-building process at home. The state undertook novel functions and established new loyalties, fostering a "more strident European nationalism." This patriotic spirit, paired with intensified international rivalries, led to a jingoistic enthusiasm for imperial projects.[39] Catherine Hall, Antoinette Burton, and others have explored various cultural expressions, ranging from literature to song, to show how the public offered massive support for the British Empire during the decades before the Great War. With the spread of a "civilizing" discourse from the 1860s onward, imperial expectations served to reify cultural, racial, and gender distinctions, as working-class white males clamored for the vote by emphasizing their political fitness in contrast to imperial "others"—women, blacks, Orientals. This discourse proved decisive in the demand for democratic reforms in both the British metropole, winning passage of the Reform Acts of 1867 and 1884–85, and its dominions.[40]

The Spanish case was not only unique because of its then exceptionally strong anticolonial nationalisms, particularly over Cuba, but also because its statesmen found it extremely difficult to reactivate the interclass allegiances and alliances so crucial to earlier imperial expeditions. After 1868–74, each and every colonial crisis was accompanied by the threat of a greater metropolitan upheaval—not only because defense of the Caribbean colonies involved the serious risk of life and limb but also because working-class and industrial Spain had long experienced declining imperial expectations.

In the early 1860s, radical liberals and even republicans had shown both optimism and enthusiasm toward overseas expeditions. In 1860, the Catalan Volunteers embarked amid a grand send-off to fight an expansionist war against the Moroccans, later described as a "race of slaves" in the lyrics of the worker-musician and republican leader J. A. Clavé.[41] These declarations of working-class political pride directed against a racial "other" and social inferior resurfaced in 1869 when the volunteers went to fight the largely African rebellion in Cuba.[42] These reactions are reminiscent of how British radicals popularized their message in the wake of Jamaica's Morant Bay rebellion in 1865. In this case, British working-class organizers used racial and imperial categories to distinguish between free colonial blacks (denied the vote in Jamaica) and themselves, working whites who deserved the franchise and other political rights.[43] In the 1860s, Spanish republicans and liberal progressives were pushing in similar directions.

By 1893, however, Spanish republicans had given up the hope of being able to profit domestically from imperial policies directed against African populations. In 1893, the republican press, motivated by the outbreak of the emphatic "Margallo War" against the tribes of northern Morocco, reminisced about earlier enthusiastic volunteerism for Africa in 1859–60. However, their purpose was not to attempt to stoke the fires of past patriotic glories. Rather, it was to highlight the halfhearted response of contemporary readers and their complete lack of interest in the embarkation of the artillery. The military difficulties of the conscript army (with little Catalan presence) and imperial Germany's watchfulness led to imperial ruminations that contrasted sharply with those of 1859–60. By 1893, many were already well aware that the great powers would always limit Spain's "peaceful penetration" in Morocco. In December, an editorial in Barcelona's leading republican newspaper, *El Diluvio*, captured the gloom: "The empire is no longer alive, the empire is no more than a shadow, the empire is no longer a social unit. . . , the empire languishes in corruption, in feebleness, in the ferociousness of a dominion without morality."[44]

PART 3

Imperial Transitions in Latin America and the Philippines

"Commercial Might versus Divine Right: The Morgan Trust King Brings Dismay to the Old Kings of Europe." (*Puck*, May 21, 1902, Library of Congress Prints and Photographs Division)

Facing South

How Latin America Socialized United States Diplomacy

GREG GRANDIN

IN THE DEBATES OVER American exceptionalism and what is distinct about the United States, little attention has been paid to one variable that can, at least in relation to its global ascendance, unambiguously be called unique: its relationship with Latin America. "South America will be to North America," the *North American Review* wrote in 1821, "what Asia and Africa are to Europe."[1] Not quite. Other capitalist world powers—France, Holland, and Great Britain—tended to rule over culturally and religiously distinct peoples in Africa, Asia, and the Middle East. The Anglo-Saxon settlers who colonized North America, by contrast, viewed Iberian America not as an epistemic "other" but as competitor in a fight to define a set of nominally shared but actually contested ideas and political forms: Christianity, republicanism, liberalism, democracy, sovereignty, rights, and, above all, the very idea of America.

After the republican revolutions of the late eighteenth and early nineteenth centuries, the relationship between the United States and the new nations of Spanish America developed a contentious ideological intimacy, unmatched by other hegemon-periphery relations. The content of the critique has remained consistent: the United States has consistently attempted to contain what its captains thought to be the excesses of Latin American republicanism/liberalism, while Latin American nationalists have consistently pointed out the gap that separates U.S. republican/democratic ideals from its superpower actions. In the Americas, extended space and time distilled European ideological conflicts and contradictions into purer essences, unprecedented in their generative force, providing form and content to the United States' system of post–World War II informal empire and the de facto international rights regime that grounded it.

EXTENDING OUR RESEARCHES

Even before Jamestown and the Puritan settlement of New England, the Elizabethan imagination was fired, and sharpened, in relation to Spain. Watching uneasily as conquistadores incorporated the great Aztec, Maya, and Inca civilizations into Spain's dominion, Great Britain defined its emerging notions of freedom, rights, and imperial aspirations in opposition to the belief that the Spanish were particularly cruel, oppressive, and warlike—a set of ideas that later collectively came to be known as the "Black Legend." In the late 1500s, London historian Richard Hakluyt condemned "the Spaniard" as "the scourge of the world. . . . Ravisher of virgins and wives" and even voiced what could be the first call for humanitarian intervention in the name of protoliberalism, predicting that Native Americans would rise up and overthrow their papist yoke were Britain to offer them encouragement. In the Americas, this Anglo and Spanish ideological rivalry, secularized as Christian schism and the Black Legend, gave way to the age of revolutions, helping U.S. politicians and intellectuals define their exceptional republicanism, especially when it came to ideas concerning race, property rights, citizenship, and law within a context of ceaseless territorial and market expansion.

Before turning to the rivalry itself, I want first to draw from two scholars, Louis Hartz and Michael Rogin, whose work is, I believe, indispensable in probing the fundamentals of American exceptionalism. The shortcomings of Hartz's 1955 *The Liberal Tradition in America*—particularly its argument that what made the United States exceptional was its lack of feudalism—are well rehearsed. Yet one does not have to accept Hartz's argument to appreciate the prominence of Lockean individualism in formulations of American exceptionalism. And those who consider Hartz a proponent of liberal consensus history miss the rampage that he says lies just below the surface of superficial accord, the easy way "innocence" yields to conformity and then slides into domestic repression: absent an ancien régime to fight against, with no aristocracy promoting the "virtues of a public spirited paternalism" nor a threatening socialist or proletarian movement offering alternatives for how to organize society, U.S. liberalism, Hartz argued, was never compelled to move beyond its Lockean adolescence. Since all conflict, from the left or the right, took place within the "implicit moral limits of the liberal tradition," the result is an "innocent" liberalism that "forgets the context" in which it was created "and elevates it own fragmentary ethic into a psychic absolute." Thus U.S. liberalism's absolute "moral unanimity" blinded itself to itself, generating an "irrational," or "mass Lockianism," a "hysteria" founded on the repression of perceived threats, "which no other nation in the West has really been able to understand."[2]

Two decades later the political theorist Michael Rogin built on Hartz's argument in his study of Andrew Jackson, arguing that what gave U.S. liberalism its cutting distinction is that it was forged not in a fight against feudalism or revolutionary socialism but against Native Americans.[3] Race violence, Rogin wrote, helped maintain, for a time, sectional unity; the expropriation of indigenous land capitalized the Jacksonian market revolution. But more important was the way extended Indian wars, which began in full with the 1830 Removal Act, allowed Jacksonian nationalism to reconfigure patriarchy on a broader, abstract level, even as commercial expansion was disintegrating the actual productive family unit. The social and psychic dissolution generated by market relations was stemmed by projecting an ideal of a bounded, disciplined, self-restrained, reasoning, and propertied male self against an enemy imagined to be wild, unbridled, propertyless, and unreasonable. Indians were identified as children, whites as fathers, and eliminationist war, later called genocide, was analogized as "growing up." "Barbarism is to civilization," Rogin quoted Francis Parkman's 1855 *History of the Conspiracy of Pontiac*, "as childhood is to maturity." Rogin finds in Jackson's Indian wars a perfect circle of cause and effect whereby Jackson's violent expropriation of Native American land, both as general and as president, jump-started the speculative capitalism that defined his age. This in turn both accelerated the commercial relations that corroded republican virtue (along with patriarchal authority) and created the two "monsters that Jacksonian politics sought to slay": the "mother" bank and Indians. "Jacksonian Democracy," Rogin wrote, "defined itself against enemies Jackson's primitive accumulation helped bring into being."[4] Put another way, concrete violence hastened abstract violence, which was healed by more concrete violence, creating a perpetual feedback loop that, for Rogin, building on Hartz's observations on the inability of U.S. liberalism to evolve, helps explain the inescapability of race, and of the recurring tendency of racial demonization, in American culture.

To illustrate the centrality of race in the formation of U.S. nationalism, Rogin quoted James Madison's admission that "next to the case of the black race within our bosom, that of the red on our borders is the problem most baffling to the policy of our country." I would like here to further extend Rogin's extension of Hartz and add another color to the code that helps decipher American exceptionalism: the multihued brown to the south. This Madison quotation has been, following Rogin, frequently cited in much contemporary scholarship on race and U.S. nationalism. But so far no one has noticed what comes next in the original text, where Madison suggests that the best way of "estimating the susceptibilities of the Indian character, and devising the treatment best suited to it," would be to study "the red race in the regions south of us." The former president was aware of deliberations then taking place in Spanish America over the question of citizenship. His letter was composed in February, a few months before the ratification of Bolivia's republican constitution, which formally declared Indians and slaves to be citizens. At that point, the U.S. Congress had been debating, for over a year, whether it would send delegates to Simón Bolívar's Panama Congress, which would convene at the end of 1826 and have on its agenda a discussion of how best to abolish slavery throughout the Americas. And Madison thought that the United States could learn about how the new nations of America attended to the issue of the relationship of race and citizenship, especially in relation to Native Americans. "Examples have there been furnished," he wrote of South American Indians, "of gradations from the most savage state to the advanced ones in Mexico and Peru."

> The descendents of these last, though retaining their physical features, are understood to constitute an integral part of the organized population. But we have not sufficiently extended our researches to their precise condition, political, legal, social, intellectual, moral; and with respect to the inferior tribes adjoining a white population, or comprehended within its limits, their actual condition, and the policy influencing it, is still less known to us.[5]

Similarly, a *North American Review* essay published two years earlier imagining future U.S. relations with Spanish America—cited above and written by the *Review*'s editor, Edward Everett, a professor of Greek literature at Harvard and Unitarian pastor—engaged in an extensive discussion, pointedly more pessimistic than Madison's, of how the new Spanish American nations were incorporating "Indians civilized or un-reclaimed, in different degrees of mixed blood and of Africans and their descendants, or negroes and mulattoes." After listing various racial permutations recognized under Spanish colonialism—*mestizo, quarteroon, puchuela*, and so forth—Everett concluded that he could not "see upon what principles of human nature any high national spirit, or even any ordinary political concert can exist under such heterogeneous and odious confusions of Spanish bigotry and indolence, with savage barbarity and African stupidity."[6] Republican Spanish America, then, served in a role similar to the one Rogin attributes to race, allowing U.S. policy makers and intellectuals to measure and outfit their own assumptions related to republican citizenship, governance, and international law—as well as the implicit ideas of property rights that underwrote these assumptions.

From 1818 to 1848, U.S. territorial expansion into Spanish Florida and Louisiana, Texas, and Mexico (and projected expansion into the Caribbean) helped intensify both Native American eliminationist war and chattel slavery, leading to deepening debate over the same race and citizenship issues that vexed Madison. Territorial expansion into Spanish and Spanish American lands in turn produced military tactics and legal arguments that, as Brian Loveman has recently detailed, continue to shape U.S. diplomacy to this day.[7] Then came the Mexican War, which Rogin defined as the "American 1848" for performing an ideological function inverse to what contemporary social revolutions did for Europe. In

Europe, the great social revolutions of 1848 exploded the tension within political liberalism—between civil society and the state, private property and public virtue, bourgeois and citizen—to reveal the exploitation of daily life. In the United States, by contrast, expansion and war allowed these tensions to remain muted.[8] The fallout from the Mexican War, by accelerating the sectional crisis, did eventually reveal the United States' own "social question" in the bloody Civil War, yet only spasmodically so, as ongoing movement outward allowed for its continued deflection. Rogin's case for the centrality of the Mexican War in prolonging, and thus hardening, an extreme individual liberalism could go further: in a way, Latin America has served as something like the United States' perpetual anti-1848. The region's seemingly chronic political violence, as well as recurrent efforts, running from Hispanic republicanism to populism and socialism, to use the state to enforce virtue, served as the shadow side of Lockean exceptionalism, a warning of what might lie ahead if the firewall separating privatized civil society from public, political power is not maintained.

It was after the Mexican War when the United States' exemplary exceptionalism—the idea that the country could serve as a model to be emulated but would largely restrain itself from imposing that model on other nations—began to transform into what might be called actionable exceptionalism, that is, direct intervention to remake the politics and economics of other nations.[9] As early as 1820, Henry Clay predicted that "in relation to South America the people of the United States will occupy the same position as the people of New England do to the rest of the United States. Our enterprise, industry, and habits of economy, will give us the advantage in any competition which South American may sustain with us."[10] So Mexico, in the decades after Appomattox, became Washington and New York's first sustained nation-building project, an endeavor that would continue after 1898 in Cuba, Haiti, the Dominican Republic, Nicaragua, and Panama.[11] With the frontier closed, and the trope of maturity/immaturity that Rogin identified as being imposed on stateless, "property-less" Indians no longer made vital by war, Latin American nations became the new irresponsibles, their "immaturity" used to justify serial Caribbean and Central American interventions.[12]

Yet whereas competition in the economic sphere was as one sided as Clay imagined, Latin America proved to be much better matched in the ideological arena, containing, for a time, the "irrational Lockeanism" identified by Hartz and Rogin, which, however powerful a creed when it came to accumulating capital and propelling territorial expansion, was too volatile to underpin the kind of world power the United States would become in the twentieth century.

LIBERAL TRADITIONS IN THE AMERICAS

"I hate the dons; I would delight to see Mexico reduced," wrote Andrew Jackson, congealing two centuries of Black Legend thought to explain his involvement in

Aaron Burr's failed 1806 effort to break Mexico from Spain.[13] But just seven years later Thomas Jefferson issued the first full expression of what Arthur P. Whitaker has called the Western Hemisphere idea, stating that the Americas have a common and "separate system of interests, which must not be subordinated to those of Europe."[14] Recently, comparative histories of the Americas have identified "ambivalence," rather than simple "Hispanophobia," as giving shape to the Black Legend, which would help to explain the seemingly easy progression from the kind of opinions expressed by Jackson in 1806 to those of Jefferson in 1813. Anglo settlers might have defined themselves against the cruel, avaricious, superstitious papists, yet they admired their resolve and daring, the quick way they subjugated a continent and raised an empire. Historians tend to locate the source of this "ambivalence" in imperial competition between Spain and England, intensified after U.S. independence by the threat of European restoration, which led statesmen like Jefferson to imagine common cause with American nations despite his belief that centuries of Spanish rule "have enchained their mind, have kept them in the ignorance of children, and as incapable of self-government as children."[15]

But the ideological sources of this attraction/repulsion also need to be specified and grounded in the social experience that distinguished Spanish and Anglo colonialism in the Americas: fundamentally, it comprised, by the early nineteenth century, distinct republican and liberal traditions, each with discrete conceptions of citizenship, sovereignty, and international law.[16]

By the time of their respective revolutions, both U.S. and Spanish American independence politicians and intellectuals shared an aterritorial, natural-rights notion of sovereignty—rooted in the idea that the Americas represented a rejuvenating force in world history. But two key differences distinguished Spanish from Anglo republicanism.

First, in terms of domestic governance, Spanish Americans emphasized the active role of the state in promoting virtuous citizenship, an activism that contrasted with both Lockean ideas that privileged individual rights and Madisonian restraints that imagined the state serving primarily as a protective shield around an independent, commercial civil society. Spanish American independence leaders, in contrast, envisioned a much more active role for government institutions in creating the public good. In his study of Spanish imperialism and political theory, Anthony Pagden, for instance, writes that Simón Bolívar appreciated the vitality of the kind of civil society that drove the federal expansion of the United States but did not believe the conditions for it existed in Spanish America. Republican liberty in Spanish America, thought Bolívar, could not be cultivated by procedural institutions protecting inherent rights (much less property rights) but by a strong executive presiding over a moral state that would "make men good, and consequently happy." The goal of constituted societies was, Bolívar wrote, to produce "the greatest possible sum of happiness, the greatest social security, and the highest degree of political stability."[17] Pagden characterizes Bolívar's political thought as a muddled amalgam of what Benjamin Constant, nearly Bolívar's contemporary, called ancient and modern liberty. In the modern variety, the self-interest of private man exists independently in civil society, generating, or at least in balance with, the virtues of public citizen; in the ancient strain, private interest is subordinated to public good.[18]

This distinction between Anglo and Spanish American republicanism was summed up succinctly by Francisco de Miranda, during his 1784 tour of New England, when he asked Samuel Adams how a democracy like that of the United States, founded in the name of virtue, could have a constitution that takes no positive action to enforce virtue. All power, Miranda noted, seemed to be "given to property," which, as all good republicans know, is the "poison" of virtue.[19] Miranda did not record Adams's response, but something of an answer can be found in Edward Everett's essay. In it he used Spanish America, with its "corrupt and mixed race of various shades and sorts," its feudal institutions, seigniories, and population divided into a "wealthy aristocracy and a needy peasantry," to draw a distinction between "political liberty"—by which Everett meant formal independence from European empires—and "social and civil liberty," meaning a constituted civil society of free, property-bearing individuals. If one did not have social and civil liberty, he argued, then the "question of independence of a foreign crown is one of little moment." When intellectuals like Everett looked south, they saw not a kindred republicanism on the march but a dangerous migration of ideas associated with the out-of-control French Revolution. It was Everett, not Tocqueville or the later coiners of American exceptionalism, who explicitly identified the United States as unique in its privileging of privatized civil society, in contrast to Spanish America: "We, in North America, succeeded in achieving our political independence, because we had already the social and civil liberty, which is its best foundation."[20]

Some intellectual historians have identified the influence of Catholic monism in the development of early Spanish American republicanism, which drew less from John Locke than from Saint Thomas Aquinas. Thomism did not allow for a separation between private interests and the public good and most definitely did not allow for the idea, central to Locke, that the latter would be generated by the former.[21] Yet whatever the philosophical origins of this distinction between Anglo Lockeanism and Hispanic Thomism, it was also deeply rooted in the social history that distinguished British from Spanish colonialism in the Americas as related to the subjugation of Native Americans.

In the history of Spanish America, the genocide was front-loaded, with the catastrophic violence of the conquest forcing a revitalization of rational natural law theory—which was indeed associated primarily with Thomas Aquinas and today identified by many legal theorists as the foundation of the modern human rights movement—by sixteenth-century Spanish theologians and priests concerning the souls and minds of Indians.[22] These debates were followed by the creation of a highly centralized colonial state, in which Native Americans played a primary function in the construction of Hispanic modernity. After independence, of course, race-based hierarchies, primarily enforced through economics and politics, continued. Ideology furthered exploitation, as notions of progress, honor, and hygiene were used to exclude large numbers of people from the protections and rights afforded to citizens. But unlike the rigid, formally exclusive racialism at play in the United States, race thinking in Latin America made possible imagined notions of what Madison called "adjoining" or "comprehended" citizenship. They also, through the nineteenth and twentieth centuries, produced powerful countervailing radical republican and democratic movements and ideologies, such as the antiracist nationalism of Cuba's late-nineteenth-century independence movement.[23]

By contrast, in Anglo North America, notwithstanding the race wars and massacres that accompanied initial settlement, the sustained assault against Native Americans was largely back-loaded, taking place mostly in the nineteenth century. In Spanish America, debates about how best to turn Indians into citizens, however hypocritical and premised on cultural erasure, played a central role in the formation of nineteenth-century republican nationalism; in the United States, eliminationism underwrote its nationalism. Acknowledging the ideological centrality of frontier violence in generating and regenerating nationalism, Indians themselves were *relatively* peripheral to the Anglo colonial project, at least compared to the keystone role they played in Spanish colonialism.[24] As such, the kind of moral debates that took place in the early sixteenth century immediately following the Spanish conquest associated with Bartolomé de las Casas and the scholars affiliated with the Universidad de Salamanca—part of the renewal of rational natural-law theories mentioned above—were avoided. There was often outrage, and frequent calls for reform, yet the repression of Native Americans under British rule did not prompt the kind of wholesale legal and philosophical reflection it did in Spain.

Anglo violence against Native Americans did generate political argument and legal revision, but nearly exclusively in negative form—that is, how to justify it.[25] In the realm of domestic law, for instance, dispossession of Native Americans contributed to Lockean principles of property rights, which, once formulated, were then applied to further dispossession, contributing to the "Americanization of the law of real property."[26] In the intellectual sphere, both Thomas Jefferson and Simón Bolívar believed that they inherited their respective Indian problems from Old World colonialism. Yet it is one thing to advocate, as Bolívar did, for a righteous state that could overcome the dead weight of Spain and transform Indians into citizens; it is quite another to blame London, as did Jefferson, for inciting Indians to "take up the hatchet against us," which "will oblige us now to pursue them to extermination."[27] That Jefferson made these remarks in the same 1813 letter where he enunciated the "Western Hemisphere Idea" underscores how the realization of the New World and the break with the old was imagined in relation to the destruction of Native Americans. Moreover, by offsetting republicanism against the cupidity and "two-penny interest" that motivated the British to incite the Indians, this letter highlights the way Anglo New World virtue, based on the pursuit of individual interests and absent the kind of proactive vision Miranda asked about, was generated nearly exclusively in negative terms by the suppression of perceived enemies.

Latin America, as we have seen, developed a decidedly activist vision of what virtue should entail, embodied in a series of postindependence constitutions that drew from both the Anglo and French rights tradition, trying to balance individual protections with an interventionist government charged with, in Bolívar's words, making "men good." In practice, of course, that balance was not achieved, and, during the Cold War and after, political scientists and some intellectual historians focused on the negative consequences of enforced virtue. It was this desire to restore a shattered unity, a corporate sense of social holism, whether under the banner of populism, socialism, or conservative authoritarianism, they argued, that was responsible for the region's chronic reversion to instability and political violence. But the very philosophical tradition that Pagden and others have described as a muddled mix of ancient and modern republicanism can be credited with giving rise to modern notions of social and economic rights. In other words, Latin America, infamous for its revolutionaries, reactionaries, and state-executed violence, also deserves credit for helping to invent modern social democracy. Mexico's 1917 constitution was the world's first fully conceived social-democratic constitution, predating similar charters in Europe and India. It guaranteed not just individual freedoms but the right to education, health care, welfare, and labor rights. In the decades that followed, nearly every country in the region adopted similar charters. Likewise, most of the social rights that were enshrined in the 1948 United Nations Declaration of Human Rights came from Latin America.[28]

The second, and related, difference distinguishing Anglo from Spanish republicanism concerns international law. The United States was born expanding, a fact its early leaders and intellectuals were fully aware of and theorized about. Lockean notions of dominion justified the drive west while Madisonian ideas of federal expansion diluted the factional passions that arise from a civil society founded on those property rights.[29] Spanish American republics, in contrast, accepted colonial administrative borders as the limits of the new nation-states and were conceived into confederation at the time of independence. In a series of international conferences—in Panama in 1826, Mexico in 1831, 1838, and 1840, Lima in 1847–48, Santiago in 1856, and Lima again in 1864–65—regional diplomats and jurists formalized a legal doctrine unprecedented in the accepted international law of the time—*uti possidetis*—which recognized existing international borders, thus proscribing, in principle if not always in fact, war in the name of territorial aggrandizement.

What emerged, then, in Spanish America and the United States were almost mirror-opposite frameworks when it came to domestic governance and international law. Put crudely, Latin America advanced a *relative* ideal of individual rights, balanced against the common good, and an *absolute* ideal of national sovereignty. Conversely in the United States, individual rights, as much as possible, were considered absolute while, increasingly after the Civil War, only a "morally good" nation could be sovereign. What was judged moral changed according to the circumstance: at times it meant the ability to exercise effective control of a population and territory; at other times it mean meant democratic or procedural legitimacy— with Washington determining which of these two criteria to invoke based on what best protected foreign private property. In either case, the United States reserved the right, often invoking its own sense of exceptionalism, to be the judge. As Secretary of State Richard Olney put it 1895, "The people of the United States have a vital interest in the cause of popular self-government. . . . They have realized and exemplified its beneficent operation by a career unexampled in point of national greatness or individual felicity. They believe . . . that civilization must either advance or retrograde accordingly as its supremacy is extended or curtailed."[30]

THE SOVEREIGNTY–SOCIAL RIGHTS COMPLEX, OR, DIALECTICS OF THE MONROE DOCTRINE

The history by which Latin America forced the United States to accept the basic principles of what I have elsewhere called its "sovereignty–social rights complex"—and what by the end of the nineteenth century Latin American jurists and diplomats had begun to call American International Law—is often narrated as a litany of outrages, of U.S. freebooting, interventions, counterinsurgencies, gunboat and dollar diplomacy, and pre–Cold War coups in Texas, Nicaragua, Mexico, Cuba, Puerto Rico, Panama, the Caribbean, and Central America.[31] But threading through this narrative of expansion is a slow yet steady revision of the fundamentals of international law, which served both to restrain U.S. power—which contained its own "intervention–individual rights complex"—and to make it more effective.

Immediately after James Monroe declared the Americas off-limits to European intervention in 1823, Spanish American jurists and politicians attempted to incorporate the Monroe Doctrine into their emerging multilateral framework, including their antecedent affirmation of *uti possidetis*. In 1825, Brazil recognized the Monroe Doctrine; a year earlier, Colombia had invoked it, asking for Washington's help against what it feared were designs by France and Spain on its territory; and in 1826, Argentina likewise cited the Monroe Doctrine and asked for U.S. aid in a conflict with Brazil, arguing that since Brazil was still tied to Portugal it constituted a European power. And in 1826, Bolívar invited the United States to attend the Panama Congress to "proclaim" the Monroe Doctrine and discuss how to abolish slavery.[32]

The United States refused these specific requests for aid and resisted all efforts by Spanish Americans to define the Monroe Doctrine as international law or to read the doctrine normatively, in a way, say, that would imply the end of American slavery or suggest a revision in international law. Through the nineteenth and early twentieth centuries, presidents, secretaries of state, and politicians would expand its interpretation, in purely nationalist terms, to justify territorial expansion and unilateral policing. American exceptionalism aside, when it came to retaining the great power right to intervene in the affairs of other nations to protect its interests, the United States repeatedly deflected calls that it conform to what Latin Americans understood to be a specific "American" multilateralism. "I object to the term 'American International Law,'" wrote Washington's envoy, William Henry Trescot, following 1889's inaugural Pan-American Conference where Latin American delegates passed a number of resolutions attempting to standardize their ideas, including the adoption of arbitration to settle regional disputes as a "principle of American International Law."[33] To the degree that U.S. statesmen did call for the Monroe Doctrine to be entered into the "admitted canon of international law," as Secretary of State Olney did in the case of the Venezuela-British dispute, it was to confirm the United States' privilege and right to intervene "whenever what is done or proposed by any of the parties primarily concerned is a serious and direct menace to [the United States'] own integrity, tranquility or welfare."[34]

Still, even as regional nationalists began to talk about "two Americas," separating their "Latin" America from rapacious, filibustering, warmongering, slave-trading "Saxon" America, Spanish American jurists persisted in their efforts to "mutualize" the Monroe Doctrine and have it recognized as international law.[35] This tension led the Chilean jurist Alejandro Alvarez, a leading theorist of American International Law, to make the Hegelian observation in 1909 that the roots of twentieth-century multilateralism are to be found in Monroe's nineteenth-century unilateralism. Alvarez believed the doctrine to be evolving in two distinct realms: *politics*, where Washington's preponderant power allowed it to interpret the doctrine according to its own interests; and *law*, which, while initially dependent on U.S. unilateralism, would eventually transcend that dependence and become international jurisprudence.

On recognizing that solidarity of interests as to the continuance of their independence existed between the states of America, Monroe did not do more than serve as an echo of the sentiment that then predominated in all the republics. . . . In this sense, it may be said . . . that the Monroe Doctrine is neither *doctrine* nor *of Monroe*. But that which constitutes its undeniable merit . . . is that such an exact synthetic statement of the destinies of America should have been given thus early . . . by a people whose increasing power would not permit the rest of the world to regard that statement as merely utopian. It was this that enabled America . . . to give to its foreign policies a safe norm instead of vague ideas then existent on these subjects. In this sense the Monroe Doctrine is *doctrine* and is *of Monroe*.

But for American International Law to become universalized, he argued, "we must first of all do away with the term Monroe Doctrine, while preserving its ideas."[36]

This proved to be more difficult than hoped, although Alvarez, a great admirer of President Woodrow Wilson, did have hope that post–World War I reconstruction would provide the opportunity to bring about this revolution in international law. Wilson himself, in the run-up to Paris in 1919, often admitted that norms and practices worked out within the Western Hemisphere did indeed inspire much of what he hoped to accomplish at Versailles, proposing that "nations should . . . adopt the doctrine of President Monroe as the doctrine of the world." Here, then, is a crystalline example of Alvarez's point that liberal internationalism was a synthesis of U.S. power and Spanish American ideas, with Wilson taking the principles associated with the American International Law movement—nonaggression, arbitration, territorial sovereignty, mutual defense, and the belief that common interests (as opposed to "competitions of power") should form the basis of international agreement—and attributing them to the "timeless wisdom of the Founding Fathers."[37] Latin America's importance in generating Wilsonian liberal internationalism is likewise revealed by the incorporation of the spirit of the doctrine *uti possidetis* into Article 10 of the League of Nations' Covenant. And the league itself—Wilson's famous fourteenth point— was directly modeled on the Pan-American conferences in which the United States had been participating since 1889 and Spanish Americans had been convening since 1826. The point is not merely to credit Latin America's unacknowledged contribution to liberal internationalism but to reveal the region's role as the missing, mediating link in the process—which has long confounded critical scholars concerned with the endurance of American exceptionalism—through which the U.S. presents its particular values as the world's values.

The league's charter did include a specific reference to the Monroe Doctrine. Yet this had less to do with "universalizing" the doctrine than with Wilson trying to appease nationalists in the Senate who were afraid of losing regional privilege. Of course it did not, but it did alienate supporters in Latin America, who read the article as investing the United States with "mandatory" powers within the Western Hemisphere, similar those granted the United Kingdom in the Middle

East. Many of the delegates resented being marginalized from the conference proceedings. "I find that they have been left alone too much . . . and have been having Latin American Conferences among themselves," observed a State Department official, perhaps unaware of the historical resonance of his remarks describing diplomats and jurists who were indeed used to holding their own counsels. They continued the conversation in subsequent Pan-American conferences, persistent in their demands that Washington concede what now had become the overriding point of American International Law: an acknowledgment of the absolute right of sovereignty of all nations. In practical terms, this meant one thing: Washington—then bogged down in a series of occupations and counterinsurgencies in the Caribbean—would have to renounce the right of intervention, something it continued to resist doing through the 1920s.

If the discussion of the Monroe Doctrine at the Paris Peace Conference signaled the limits of Washington's willingness to recognize territorial sovereignty as a universal norm, the arrival of an uninvited guest from Mexico, Alberto Pani, highlighted its steadfast hostility toward the region's emerging social-rights regime. Pani was sent by Mexican president Venustiano Carranza to observe the peace conference, although Mexico, neutral during the war and thought to be pro-German, had not been invited to the talks. Relations between Mexico and the United States, bad due to the latter's heavy-handed interventions in the former's affairs, had grown worse with the ratification of Mexico's 1917 Constitution, which not only guaranteed social rights but authorized the nationalization of land and mineral resources in the name of the public interest. The constitution's Article 27 could be read as a direct refutation of Lockean notions of property rights, and its many critics in the United States believed that it represented a fundamental threat to international law, instituting a "system of property which denies all principles of justice."[38] The evolution of U.S. property law is complex, and by the early twentieth century it went well beyond Locke to incorporate the principle that public interest could mitigate inalienable rights. Yet many legal theorists who accepted this principle still thought the Mexican constitution heretical because it pushed "the spirit of this modern theory of property rights" further, explicitly stating that "private property is a privilege created by the nation." And many feared that the Mexican Constitution, if legitimated, would lead other countries to a similar conclusion, thus threatening "certain hard to define but nevertheless well-internationally recognized vested individual rights."[39] Carranza also pushed for the principle of absolute nonintervention and "the ideas of the new Mexican constitution" adopted within the canon of international law.[40] Though unsuccessful, the attempt allows for a more complex interpretation of the Paris Peace Conference beyond a clash between Soviet Marxism and Wilsonian liberal internationalism. In many ways, the 1910 Mexican Revolution offered a more subtle subversion of the interstate system than what was achieved by the frontal challenge offered by Leninism, since it based its challenge to property rights within the terms of political liberalism, rather than rejecting those terms outright. In the years to come, similar social rights would be incorporated into every Latin American constitution, while Article 27's definition of property would indeed migrate into other Latin American charters and domestic law, later serving as the central legal instrument of import-substitution developmentalism.

The United States adamantly resisted Latin America's sovereignty–social rights complex, until it faced strong regional opposition to its Caribbean basin militarism and a shortfall of power caused by the contraction of the Great Depression. In retrospect, the extemporaneous agreement of Franklin Delano Roosevelt's secretary of state, Cordell Hull, at the 1933 Montevideo Pan-American Conference to the demands of Latin American countries that Washington give up its right to intervene in their internal affairs must be considered one of the most unambiguously successful foreign policy initiatives the United States has ever undertaken. Facing militarists, fascists, and imperialists in Europe and Asia, Latin America provided key economic and political shelter to the fledging New Deal coalition.[41] For a moment, it seemed that the United States would turn not inward but southward: in 1936, Roosevelt described the Western Hemisphere a "happy valley" in a world of mountainous troubles and called for the ideal of the withered League of Nations to be revived in a "League of Americas."[42]

But the Good Neighbor Policy—a phrase that hides more than it reveals, presenting Washington's long-resisted acceptance of the terms of American International Law as a U.S. initiative—provided a template for revived globalism, allowing for the construction of the four pillars of Washington's post–World War II diplomacy: (1) an acceptance of national sovereignty; (2) a way of managing that acceptance through a new array of multilateral institutions and agreements; (3) the recognition of social rights (including the right of developing countries to regulate foreign investment and property), which gave Washington an important moral weapon in the coming Cold War; and (4) a regional alliance system. On this last point, Latin America served as a model for other such alliances in two ways. First, the North American Treaty Organization (NATO) and similar mutual defense treaties were based directly on the 1949 Rio Pact. Second, the relationship of the Organization of American States (OAS) and the United Nations provided an example of how Washington could tack between "regional" and "universal" treaty obligations as needed. By 1943, Roosevelt was holding up the "illustration of the republics of this continent" as a model for postwar reconstruction. Latin America's containment of the United States was historically consequential, leading to the creation of a multilateral order that allowed Washington to accumulate unprecedented global power.

But it was always tentative and, in retrospect, short-lived. By the 1980s, with the ascendance of the New Right to governance in the United States, Ronald

Reagan was again invoking the Monroe Doctrine in its most interventionist form. And just as Latin America played a central role in the consolidation of multilateralism, the region—in Grenada, Nicaragua, and Panama—would be where it was first rolled back, paving the way for the neoconservatism of George W. Bush, whereby Washington again claimed the right to intervene unilaterally in the affairs of another country, not just defensively but because it deemed the quality of its sovereignty unworthy of recognition.

The 1989 invasion of Panama was a turning point in this process. Sounding a lot like Secretary of State Richard Olney in 1895, Luigi Einaudi, George H. W. Bush's ambassador to the Organization of American States, told twenty OAS representatives, who had just *unanimously* condemned the invasion, that the United States had acted because "today, we are . . . living in historic times, a time when a great principle is spreading across the world like wild fire. That principle, as we all know, is the revolutionary idea that people, not governments, are sovereign."[43] Concurrent with this dilution of sovereignty was an attempt to disentwine social and political rights. In the decade prior to the invasion of Panama, Ronald Reagan embraced the rhetoric of human rights in order to reinvest U.S. military power with moral authority. Yet this embrace came with an important caveat. "All too often," said Richard Allen, Reagan's national security adviser, in 1981, "we assume that everyone means the same thing by human rights." Yet when the United States talked about human rights, Allen stated, it meant strictly the defense of "life, liberty, and property" and not "economic and social rights." The expansion of human rights into the social realm, he went on, constituted a "dilution and distortion of the original and proper meaning of human rights."[44] That same year, Elliott Abrams, Reagan's assistant secretary of state for human rights, drafted an influential memo, often cited as key in Reagan's efforts to once again define the Cold War as a righteous fight. After announcing that "our struggle is for political liberty" and in defense of "human rights," Abrams nonetheless felt that the latter expression was too tainted by issues related to economic justice. He suggested a rebranding: "We should move away from 'human rights' as a term, and begin to speak of 'political rights' and 'civil liberties.' We can move on a name change at another time."[45]

Neoliberalism—known in the United States by the unintentionally apt Hartzian phrase "the Washington Consensus"—needs, then, to be seen as more than an effort to impose economic structural adjustment; it was a project of moral adjustment centuries in the making. That bid, as events over the last decade in Latin America and the United States have demonstrated, has failed. "A dialectical process," to close with a quotation from Louis Hartz, is still "at work, evil eliciting the challenge of a conscious good, so that in difficult moments progress is made. The outcome of the battle between intensified 'Americanism' and new enlightenment is still an open question."[46]

"Alliance Imperialism" and Anglo-American Power after 1898

The Origins of Open-Door Internationalism

COURTNEY JOHNSON

AMONG THE HISTORIC CHANGES that accompanied the rise of U.S. imperialism circa 1900, scholars have tended to treat the sudden improvement in social and diplomatic relations—the so-called great rapprochement—between the British Empire and the United States with something akin to benign neglect.[1] While many historians have chronicled the various diplomatic, cultural, political, and military dimensions of Anglo-American relations, few have grasped a larger, enduring pattern in this "special relationship." Careful examination of the emergence, growth, and impact of Anglo-American realignment, however, reveals that the course followed by Washington in its ascent to a predominant place in world affairs did not flow spontaneously from its defeat of the Spanish navy in the summer of 1898, nor was it simply a natural manifestation of internal conditions in American society. Rather, viewed over a span of decades, what comes into view is a pattern of implicit Anglo-American strategic cooperation on two decisive endeavors. First, the United States shared with the British Empire a global grand strategy of joint guardianship over the world's oceans. Second, the two powers jointly sponsored an emerging system of international legal authority capable of restraining alterations in the territorial status quo.

Starting in the 1890s, British imperial policy makers and elites initiated this partnership with their American counterparts to protect their maritime empire, then at its zenith, from encroachment by ascendant rivals like Germany and Russia. American elites, in turn, welcomed a silent partnership with Britain as a way to secure a place among the great powers and a share in global markets. Or, as Cecil Rhodes, one of the earliest backers of an Anglo-American reunion, put it in a letter to the publisher W.T. Stead, "Fancy the charm to young America, just coming on and dissatisfied—for they have filled up their own country and do not know what to tackle next—to share in a scheme to take the government of the whole world!"[2]

In the context of imperial alliances among the great powers at the turn of the twentieth century, this realignment in Anglo-American relations was unique. Unlike traditional treaty-based alliances, this Anglo-American entente was not solely the work of diplomats and statesmen but involved an international social, public relations, and institutional network built around the increasing integration of a transatlantic elite committed to the preservation of an enduring Anglo-American world order. To a surprising degree, then, the course of U.S. foreign relations in the twentieth century, including its hegemonic role in the Western Hemisphere and as a power broker in the Pacific, was premised on a naval pact—a veritable Treaty of Tordesillas for the twentieth century—in which each partner focused its activities on its half of the globe. This arrangement allowed the reconcentration of British naval forces in the Indian Ocean and the eastern Atlantic and extended the reach of America's reinvigorated Monroe Doctrine from the Western Hemisphere across the Pacific to China's open door.

I have termed this change in Anglo-American relations "alliance imperialism" following a term—*alliance capitalism*—developed by business scholars to describe intercorporate strategic relations among otherwise competitive multinational firms in the post–Cold War era.[3] Multinational firms that engage in alliance capitalism might cooperate with rival companies in developing mutually beneficial technologies or in safeguarding their economic sector against perceived threats; yet they are also careful to maintain their public autonomy as competitors. Similarly, the informal nature of Anglo-American alliance imperialism allowed broad strategic cooperation while preserving independence of action. Among the features that distinguish alliance imperialism from the anarchic system of great power diplomacy that it supplanted was its commitment to the preservation of the global territorial status quo.

Unlike the "secret diplomacy" among the imperial powers from 1882 to 1914, with alliances publicly proclaimed but treaty obligations often concealed from non-contracting parties, Anglo-American alliance imperialism entailed an informal, even unacknowledged, cooperation through an elaborate entente while maintaining an apparent independence of action so as to avoid disrupting the existing balance of power among rival empires. Alliance imperialism, then, refers simultaneously to an implicit set of shared geopolitical goals (Anglo-American hegemony in world affairs); to a coordinated methodology of pursuing those goals (strategic military cooperation, public relations, and international jurisprudence); and, finally, to an expanding network of people, associations and institutions dedicated to these objectives (e.g., the Pan-American Union and the Permanent Court of Arbitration).

This grand strategy proceeded in stages and rested on personal relations. First, political elites in New York and London pushed a political rapprochement through a presumed Anglo-Saxon cultural identity, and, second, an entente between

Washington's new imperial strategists and important Latin American elites developed lasting relationships, and thereby set the foundation for wider U.S. influence in the former Spanish empire. Through this latter process, Washington largely succeeded in convincing Latin American leaders to trade the revanchist cultural politics of global Hispanism for a seat at the international table via the U.S.-led Pan-American Union and the emerging international institutions at The Hague. Yet even as these Latin American leaders adapted to their new status as Washington's subordinate elites, they were maneuvering successfully, within a changing geopolitics, to safeguard the sovereignty of their respective nations and make their mark on an emerging international system. But in doing so they lent crucial legitimacy to the emerging international order promoted by Anglo-American alliance imperialists.

The following sections describe the development of the transatlantic network and how U.S. policy makers harnessed inter-elite relationships to advance Washington's international and regional leadership. By focusing on several representative figures whose work had a decisive impact on its emergence in the early twentieth century, we can highlight some of the critical phases in the development of alliance imperialism. As this Anglo-American entente evolved, the influential British geographer Halford J. Mackinder articulated a geopolitical strategy for sustaining the empire through such alliances. As a seasoned reformer and well-connected public relations pioneer, famed journalist W. T. Stead, together with his American protégé Albert Shaw, played a lead role in laying the social and intellectual groundwork for Anglo-American cooperation through a sustained public relations campaign in newspapers, books, public speaking tours, and civic events beginning in the early 1890s and continuing up to Stead's death in 1912 aboard the ill-fated *Titanic*. In a succeeding consummation phase, Secretary of State John Hay leveraged the alliance imperialism network to establish U.S. title to an archipelago of strategic outposts that laid the diplomatic foundations for American diplomacy beyond the Western Hemisphere—a canon of foreign policy principles that I term "Open-Door internationalism." As the alliance firmed, Elihu Root, Hay's successor, was the person most directly responsible for the revitalization of the Pan-American movement and for bringing Latin American elites firmly into Washington's sphere of influence. Through the Pan-American Union, Root presided over formation of the internationalist institutions in the Western Hemisphere on which alliance imperialism could justify integrating the Monroe Doctrine and the Open Door into a growing body of international legal norms.

ALLIANCE IMPERIALISM AND BRITISH DECLINE

As early as the 1880s, at the zenith of their global power, British imperial strategists anticipated challenges to their empire as rapidly industrializing nations in

North America, Europe, and Asia began to build modern navies that could contest England's control of the seas. The completion of transcontinental railways in the United States (1869), Canada (1885), and Asia (1898), as well as a transisthmian canal in Central America (1914), promised to join the densely populated Atlantic seaboard with the Pacific littoral where Russian and American commerce could counter the established advantages of British sea power. Simultaneously, the naval prowess of a powerful and belligerent Germany took center stage as the most immediate threat to British sea supremacy in the Atlantic. Influenced by Captain Alfred Thayer Mahan's concept of a "new navalism," British strategists believed sea supremacy was paramount not only for the maintenance of the commercial and political imperialism at the heart of the "British way of life" but to the survival of England itself.

Amid these challenges, London began a policy of risk reduction by enlisting the Dominion of Canada and the other self-governing settler colonies to share its imperial burden in exchange for greater political autonomy. Simultaneously, Britain abandoned its traditional posture of "splendid isolation" from European affairs and brokered conciliatory resolutions with its major geopolitical rivals— Russia in Central Asia, Germany in Africa, and France in Egypt. In keeping with its policy of risk and resource consolidation, British imperialists sought improved relations with the United States, beginning in 1898, by lending crucial diplomatic support to America in its war against Spain.

Geostrategically, the implicit cooperation of alliance imperialism facilitated the British navy's effective evacuation of the Western Hemisphere and Pacific after the 1890s. With their hard-won victories in the Philippines and South Africa by 1902 adding to an already formidable naval strength, the Anglo-American powers effectively controlled all the world's key maritime choke points. For Britain, naval cooperation with America was the necessary backdrop to its formal alliance system, which included the Anglo-Japanese treaty of 1902, the Entente Cordiale with France, the resolution of Anglo-Russian claims in Central Asia, and the reduction of Anglo-German friction in East Africa. Under this Anglo-American entente, London ceded commercial and political authority in the Western Hemisphere while retaining a free hand in Africa, Europe, and Asia. Paul Kennedy obliquely characterizes this as a strategy "disguised under the term 'Anglo-American rapprochement.'"[4]

Although Washington and London quickly established a mutually beneficial partnership, supported in part by a shared cultural and ethnic heritage, this diplomatic rapprochement was also driven by a strategic calculus. When Britain supported the United States in its war against continental rival Spain, Americans reciprocated with a wave of goodwill for Britain and a welling enthusiasm for the Anglo-Saxon imperial mission. After 1898, Washington shifted its diplomacy away from island conquests toward building a global balance of power that avoided armed conflict through a new system of binding international governance and a special relationship with England, the world's preeminent power.

Beyond providing key diplomatic support to the United States in its war with Spain, alliance imperialism played a decisive role in three overlapping spheres of U.S. foreign policy. First, the new rapprochement cleared the way for resolution of outstanding territorial disputes in North America between the British Empire and the United States in a way surprisingly deferential to American claims. Next, British support for the reassertion of the Monroe Doctrine and its institutionalization through a revitalized Pan-American movement effectively precluded European expansion in the Western Hemisphere. Finally, Anglo-American collaboration in the development of a new system of international law to govern interstate relations via arbitration rather than armed conflict led to the virtual institutionalization of the Monroe Doctrine within the emerging international order.

After a long-term decline of its informal empire in Latin America, London conceded Washington a de facto hegemony over the Americas and the Pacific, thus recognizing the Monroe Doctrine, which had long been a point of contention between the two nations. To remove long-standing irritants in their bilateral relations in North America, Washington negotiated a series of treaties with London that were generally advantageous to U.S. interests: notably, the Hay-Pauncefote Treaty (1901), setting rules for the Panama Canal as an international waterway administered by the United States; acquiescence to U.S. demands for arbitration in the Venezuela debt crisis (1902); the Alaska Boundary Tribunal (1903), demarcating the international border between Alaska and Canada; and the North Atlantic Fisheries Dispute (1910), resolved through arbitration at The Hague. In each of these cases, the hallmark of the negotiations was a remarkable British respect for American claims, and common zeal by both the United States and Britain to avail themselves of the Hague Court.

HALFORD MACKINDER: LOOKING BACKWARD, 1919–1898

As these geopolitical shifts took form in the years before World War I, British geographer and imperial strategist Halford J. Mackinder articulated, with theoretical acuity, the foundational importance of an Anglo-American alliance in preserving Britain's waning control over the sea-lanes surrounding the Eurasian landmass. In an article written for the *Geographical Journal* in 1904, he argued for a British grand strategy that would preserve the political and economic benefits of its sea superiority against the naval expansion of two continental rivals (Russia and Germany) through strategic imperial contraction involving cooperation with a former rival (France) and emerging regional naval powers (Japan and the United States). Mackinder was thus one of the first British imperialists to articulate publicly that London alone could no longer maintain its global naval supremacy.[5]

In his postwar masterwork on geopolitics, *Democratic Ideals and Reality* (1919), Mackinder asserted that the Great War had been a "straight duel between land-power and sea-power" for control of that contiguous landmass of Europe, Asia, and Africa that he called the "World Island." Looking backward from 1919, Mackinder saw that the opening salvos of the Great War between Allied sea power and Central land power stretched back more than two decades to "three great victories won by the British fleet without the firing of a gun." In each case, British sea power had neutralized the ability of a rival to deploy its naval forces in a decisive imperial conflict. The first such victory, Mackinder explains, "was at Manila, in the Pacific Ocean, when a German squadron threatened to . . . protect a Spanish squadron, which was being defeated by an American squadron, and a British squadron stood by the Americans." In words that have no meaning apart from the informal rubric of Anglo-American alliance imperialism, Mackinder asserted that Manila Bay was "a first step taken towards the reconciliation of British and American hearts. Moreover, the Monroe Doctrine was upheld in regard to South America."[6]

In his prescription for maintaining a peaceful postwar order, Mackinder acknowledged the de facto nature of Anglo-American cooperation when he argued that "the American Republic and the British Empire should work together as World Trustees for the peace of the Ocean." Yet, he noted, this alliance "would amount merely to a regularization of existing facts."[7] The "existing facts" to which he alluded were the known particulars of alliance imperialism, since the British political elite had been working with their transatlantic counterparts in New York and Washington to make this de facto joint trusteeship over every globally strategic sea lane a defining feature of twentieth-century geopolitics.

William T. Stead: Alliance Imperialism before 1898

Before the "existing facts" of Anglo-American cooperation began to take shape after 1898, the intellectual and social groundwork for rapprochement was laid in the periodical press on both sides of the Atlantic. During the 1890s, in part through a growing transatlantic integration of the press, particularly via influential monthly journals, a campaign aimed at shaping elite opinion about America's role in world affairs and combating traditional anti-British feeling began to make its mark. The preferred format for these journals, modeled on the success of William T. Stead's English and American editions of his *Review of Reviews*, was a thematic smorgasbord of current opinion drawn from leading periodicals across the world. In this endeavor, Stead was an exemplar of transatlantic integration of public opinion and became a veritable apostle of Anglo-American reunion.

Intentionally or not, British opinion dominated these reviews through the sheer volume of the British press. A similar structural bias advanced British influence over the international reportage in U.S. daily newspapers. The absence of American correspondents at international conflicts in Africa and Asia, Reuters' worldwide news cartel, and British control of global telegraph cables combined to make U.S. newspapers dependent on British journalists. Consequently, in 1900 American readers often saw the world through British eyes, creating an implicit cultural empathy that eroded the country's collective memory of earlier strife.

In the 1890s, public discussion of an alliance became common to media on both sides of the Atlantic. Stead, through his publications and personal contacts, was perhaps the most public advocate of alliance imperialism, and his *Review of Reviews* was among the first commercial publications to have English and American editions. His advocacy for Anglo-American reunion in this early period was tempered by an understanding of the obstacles faced by its proponents and a respect for the long-range planning required to bring it forth. For example, Sir George Grey, a long-serving colonial governor, proposed in 1891 that Washington and Westminster come to a "standing agreement" through an Anglo-American Council so that "whenever any subject affecting us both arises, or when there is any question affecting the well-being of the world generally, we shall meet in conference and decide upon common action." Acknowledging the political limits of Anglo-American cooperation, Grey suggested that this council would come "quietly into action when there was cause" and then disappear "for the time when it had done its work."[8] With his sensitivity to the complexity of the U.S. position toward Britain, Stead rejected Grey's suggestion as unnecessarily visible, favoring instead transatlantic cultural projects and steady political evolution as a more lasting foundation for this alliance.[9]

In effecting this rapprochement, Stead cultivated some very influential allies across the English-speaking world. Among them, perhaps the earliest and most consequential ally in Stead's campaign was Cecil Rhodes who, like Stead, considered "as his common fatherland, the great English-speaking community which includes both the United States and the British Empire."[10] Although the two men later broke over the Boer War, Stead found in Rhodes a like-minded patron for his vision of an Anglo-American cultural and political reunion. So much so that Rhodes entrusted Stead with his immense personal fortune as executor of one of Rhodes's early wills. Indeed, after meeting Rhodes in 1889, Stead wrote to his wife: "Rhodes is my man. He is full of a far more gorgeous idea in connection with the paper than even I have had. I cannot tell you his scheme, because it is too secret. But it involves millions. . . . He expects to own, before he dies, four to five millions, all of which he will leave to carry out the scheme of which the paper is an integral part. . . . His ideas are federation, expansion and consolidation of the Empire."[11]

Soon after meeting Rhodes, Stead left the *Pall Mall Gazette* to found the London-based *Review of Reviews* in 1891. Shortly thereafter he helped create both the *American Review of Reviews* in New York and the *Review of Reviews for*

Australasia in Melbourne, thus making Stead a true pioneer of global publishing. His magazines were steeped in the internationalist thematics that would form the core of a lasting Anglo-American world order whose future he also prophesied in his best-selling books, *The United States of Europe* (1899) and *The Americanization of the World* (1902).

JOHN HAY: OPEN-DOOR INTERNATIONALISM, 1898–1904

The first U.S. implementation of alliance imperialism was starkly visible in the contrast between Open-Door diplomacy in China and the military subjugation of the Philippines. In the years after 1898, U.S. foreign policy moved tacitly away from the further acquisition of formal overseas colonies toward a more supple policy of "informal empire." This diplomatic shift was inaugurated in 1900 by John Hay's "Open Door Notes" concerning China, and soon became one of the pillars of alliance imperialism, distinguishable from traditional European imperial treaties that Washington had long rejected as "entangling alliances."

Having secured, diplomatically at least, its claim to a strategic archipelago stretching from Puerto Rico to Manila, the United States began exercising a restraining hand in checking the expansionist ambitions of other powers in the Western Hemisphere and the Asia-Pacific region. While advocating the avoidance of armed conflict through a new system of binding international arbitration, Washington began to more forcefully arrogate to itself the role of guarantor of peace and territorial status quo in the Americas and the Pacific. When Secretary Hay sought an informal understanding with imperial powers interested in the "China market" through the circulation of his Open Door Notes, he was, in effect, presenting as American policy what had been a long-standing objective of British policy in the Far East. Eschewing a formal treaty, the United States successfully gained tacit international acquiescence to the two aims outlined in the circular—equal access to Chinese markets for all powers and the maintenance of China's territorial status quo—which became hallmarks of more expansive American efforts to forge a lasting international order that I have termed "open-door internationalism." Hay's initiative in China was further cemented through America's enthusiastic participation in the military campaign against the so-called Boxer rebellion and in the First Hague Convention of 1899. These diplomatic initiatives represent an important qualitative shift in the rhetoric and practice of U.S. foreign policy after the expansionism of 1898 as the United States threw its weight behind the creation of a regime of international law in its relations with its two principal diplomatic partners: Britain and the Latin American republics.[12]

From the outset, a formal alliance between the United States and the British Empire confronted formidable domestic and diplomatic obstacles, making the alliance that emerged necessarily implicit—a political imperative understood by both players. Traditional anti-British sentiment remained strong in the United

States, aggravated by Irish American anger over British policies in Ireland, lingering suspicion of British meddling in the Civil War, and, of course, the War of 1812. Similarly, America's isolationism eschewed "entangling alliances," rendering public acceptance and formal ratification of an alliance treaty between the United States and its former metropole untenable. Perhaps more important was the impact that any formal alliance between the two nations would have on balance-of-power rivalries among the great powers.

It fell to the Anglophile network within America's eastern Republican elite and Britain's diplomats to create support for an Anglo-American community of interests. Britain's point men in this process were three skilled ambassadors to Washington: Julian Pauncefote (1889–1902), James Bryce (1907–13), and Lord Grey of Fallodon (1919–20). America's architects were John Hay, secretary of state and former ambassador to Britain (1897–98) and Joseph Choate (ambassador, 1899–1905), both backed by the New York Republican establishment. Ambassador Pauncefote was, like his counterpart Secretary Hay, responsible for smoothing diplomatic relations in the Western Hemisphere between the United States and Britain. Pauncefote's successor was James Bryce, who had lived for an extended period in the United States while preparing his much-admired book *American Commonwealth* (1888). Once back in England, it was Bryce who, following the initiative of W. T. Stead, launched the Anglo-American Committee of London, which resolved in 1898 "that every effort should be made in the interests of civilization and peace to secure the most cordial and constant cooperation on the part of the two nations."[13] With the formation of a Liberal government in 1904, Bryce was named British ambassador to Washington, where he worked to foster the aims of alliance imperialism. Bryce's address to the Pilgrims Society of New York, which had a corresponding organization in London, was the first in a long-standing tradition that made this private venue the first port of call for British ambassadors or visiting dignitaries.

The cooperative tone of Anglo-American relations during Hay's earlier tenure encouraged political rumors of a secret U.S.-British treaty, something the secretary stridently denied in public. Privately, though, Hay reassured the British government that his public statements were only meant to "refute the Democratic platform's charge that we have made 'a secret alliance with England.' This charge was having a serious effect on our Germans and it had to be denied. The fact is, a treaty of alliance is impossible. It could never get through the Senate." Yet Hay would still hold firm to his conviction "that the one indispensable feature of our foreign policy should be a friendly understanding with England. But an alliance must remain, in the present state of things, an unattainable dream."[14] While a formal military alliance was, as Hay indicated, impossible, Britain and America could, through the skilled leadership of his successor, Elihu Root, cooperate successfully in the diplomatic arena.

Elihu Root: Architect of Power, 1905–1910

If Secretary Hay conducted the cultural rapprochement, then Elihu Root consummated the courtship by forging a close working alliance with British and Latin American elites over the next fifteen years. As secretary of war (1899–1904), secretary of state (1905–9), U.S. senator from New York (1909–15), and roving U.S. envoy (to revolutionary Russia, the Permanent Court of International Justice, and the Washington Naval Conference), Root was foremost among the architects who constructed Washington's imperial machinery. More important, he helped orient the raison d'être of American foreign policy toward a form of supranational governance we now call the international community. To this end, Root was seminal in the development of key foreign policy institutions capable of managing America's growing international commitments—including the Pan-American Union, the Carnegie Endowment for International Peace, the American Society for International Law, and the Council on Foreign Relations.

In large part through the support of his friend and client Andrew Carnegie, Root also worked to place the New York Republican establishment at the core of the national and global peace movement. In support of this strategy, Root executed Carnegie's philanthropic endeavors, which funded construction of the Peace Palace at The Hague (1903–13) and championed the elimination of war among the great powers. The conceptual cornerstone of the process was the idea that a Permanent Court of Arbitration at The Hague (established in 1899) would be the first step toward this goal. This policy sought to remove the primary incentive for warfare—territorial aggrandizement—through the diplomatic doctrine of status quo ante first promoted in Hay's Open Door Notes.

Alliance imperialism also facilitated resolution of serious international disputes in Latin America. When the Venezuela debt crisis erupted in 1902, Washington asserted the right of military intervention in the internal affairs of American nations under the Roosevelt Corollary to the Monroe Doctrine, threatening France, Germany, and England if they attempted to collect debts in Caracas through force. In response to this crisis, the Argentinean minister of foreign affairs, Luis María Drago, asserted that delinquent debts owed by any national government in the Americas to citizens of foreign nations could not be collected by armed coercion. In the end, Washington referred the conflict to the Permanent International Court of Arbitration at The Hague where it became the first major international dispute so resolved.

Significantly, Washington adopted the Drago Doctrine as a central facet of U.S. foreign policy in 1906–7. At the Rio de Janeiro conference of Latin American nations in 1906, Secretary of State Root incorporated Drago's principle as the foundation for inter-American relations through status quo ante, arbitration, and nonintervention in a nation's internal affairs—a soft-power approach referred to as the Root Doctrine.[15] When the American delegation presented a repackaged Drago Doctrine at The Hague Peace Conference in 1907, they argued for a system of neutral arbitration to supplant brute force as the only way to fairly settle debt collection. In effect, Root deftly deployed a Latin American diplomatic principle to establish the legal validity of a revitalized Monroe Doctrine—otherwise unacceptable within the rubric of international law—and thus made Latin American leaders complicit in their own subordination.

LATIN AMERICAN CULTURAL DIPLOMACY

In the Americas, where U.S. interests were more starkly set out in a vigorous reassertion of the Monroe Doctrine, a parallel shift from hard- to soft-power tactics was also apparent in the Theodore Roosevelt administration's response to a wave of anti-American Pan-Hispanism after 1898. In the aftermath of its wrenching defeat and the rupture of its strategic alliance with London, Madrid promoted a compensatory cultural empire of Hispanism to preserve and defend the linguistic and cultural coherence of the Spanish-speaking world. The newly animated Pan-Hispanist project gained an unexpected potency among intellectuals across the Spanish-speaking world since Madrid no longer threatened their independence, allowing them to identify with Spain and express a rising resentment toward Anglo-Saxon nations.

Within the Hispanist movement, Uruguayan writer José Enrique Rodó most influentially articulated this incipient anti-Yankee sentiment in his 1900 essay *Ariel*. Rodó framed the Yankee threat through reinterpretation of Shakespeare's *The Tempest* in which a barbarous horde of Anglo-Saxon Calibans from the north threatened Ariel, the heir of Latin idealism. The "big stick" policies of the Roosevelt Corollary, most visibly enforced in Panama in 1904, led the normally politically quiescent Nicaraguan poet Rubén Darío to write a jeremiad against Roosevelt, demanding, "Will we be delivered up to savage barbarians? / Will so many millions of us speak English?" The post-1898 Pan-Hispanist movement, labeled Arielism, swept the Americas, spread across the Atlantic to Spain, and traveled to the Philippines. In Spain, Arielism was warmly received by a dispirited Spanish intelligentsia, whose members had labored tirelessly but unsuccessfully for decades to recover the Americas as a sphere of Spanish economic and cultural influence—a thinly veiled effort at imperial regeneration.

American elites moved quickly to disarm political Pan-Hispanism, which had gained exceptional influence in Latin America after 1898. Secretary Root quickly circumvented this threat through a savvy policy innovation that resuscitated the Pan-American movement. When he attended the 1906 Pan-American Congress in Rio de Janeiro, Root solemnly professed that the United States would defend the sovereign rights of all American states. His visit and subsequent tour of Spanish American capitals aboard a U.S. gunboat was so successful in winning the proverbial hearts and minds that Rubén Darío himself wrote an ode to the

American eagle, praising the United States for its hemispheric leadership: "Come, magic eagle with the great and strong wings / To extend over the South your great continental shade."

Upon returning from his tour, Root and other policy makers continued to engage Spanish America, proclaiming a new doctrine—which he styled "the true Monroe Doctrine"—of kindly consideration and honorable obligation to fulfill the destiny common to the peoples of the Western world.[16] In an address to congress after Root's return, President Roosevelt attempted to quell fears of impending U.S. dominion over Latin America: "It was part of Secretary Root's mission to dispel this unfounded impression, and there is just cause to believe that he has succeeded. In an address to the Third Conference at Rio on the thirty-first of July . . . he said: 'We wish for no victories but those of peace; for no territory except our own; for no sovereignty except the sovereignty over ourselves. . . . We neither claim nor desire any rights or privileges or powers that we do not freely concede to every American republic.'"[17] But, while Root's immediate need was the reversal of anti-Americanism, his long-range diplomatic and geopolitical goals focused ultimately on the institutional framework for an emerging international order centered in The Hague.

At this time, Root was more than just the U.S. secretary of state. He was also the chairman of Andrew Carnegie's network of philanthropic foundations and, as such, was at the heart of national and international efforts to promote the Permanent Court in The Hague as a body capable of enforcing international law. In this process, Root's new alliance with the Latin American republics and advocacy of the Drago Doctrine were seminal. Indeed, at a meeting of the National Arbitration and Peace Congress held in April 1907 at New York's Carnegie Hall as a send off for the U.S. delegation to the Second Hague Conference, both Carnegie and Root gave speeches advocating that the United States assume the leadership of this international movement. The basis for the formulation of the Root Doctrine was, for its day, farsighted indeed, for it meant persuading an emerging international community to accept as a fact (if not a canon of international law) the U.S. Monroe Doctrine as a settled matter. For this strategy to work, Root needed the Latin American republics as a voting bloc at The Hague where they would give a diplomatic impression of agreement with the new doctrine and act as clients of a hegemonic United States—allied with the British Empire—in pressing for an enforceable international peace.

It is worth noting that Root's endeavors paid long-term geopolitical dividends. The gradual hegemony of alliance imperialism accounts, in large measure, for the sudden evaporation, circa 1916, of liberal Pan-Hispanism in the Americas, Spain, and the Philippines. Many former Arielists and Pan-Hispanists began to cultivate ties with the emerging Pan-American-inspired field of Hispanic and Latin American studies in the United States.

The career of Rafael Altamira, a Spanish social scientist and jurist, and later a prominent proponent of Washington's Pan-American Union, is a clear example of such diplomatic dividends. In the aftermath 1898, he became a leading advocate of Spain's need for national regeneration. After 1906, however, Altamira, like his friend the literary scholar Federico de Onís, began cooperating within the cultural and political framework of the Pan-American Union to promote Hispanism in the United States. Altamira published articles regularly in the *Hispanic American Historical Review, Hispania, Inter-America,* and other U.S.-based periodicals. Moreover, his *History of the Spanish People* became the standard textbook for an emerging Hispanic studies curriculum in U.S. universities. Like Onís, Nicholas Murray Butler, Elihu Root, and others in this network, Altamira was a member of the Advisory Board of the Hispanic Society of America and promoted what Columbia University Hispanic studies professor William R. Shepherd—leader of the first working group on Latin America at the Council on Foreign Relations—called the "triangular friendship/amistad triangular."[18] Two years after Root led the U.S. delegation to the Washington conference that organized the Permanent Court of International Justice in 1920, Altamira was appointed a founding justice on this tribunal, which operated under the auspices of the League of Nations—a project to which Root had also devoted much of his intellectual energy.

Root's capacity to capture the support of Latin American elites, U.S. academic specialists, Hispanic literati, and American public opinion within the matrix of a new internationalist order is certainly impressive. In his merger of informal empire within an emerging system of international relations, Root's significance brings to mind the diplomacy of his lineal predecessor, Lord Palmerston of London, who built an earlier, if less refined, system of informal empire for the United Kingdom in the mid–nineteenth century. But to focus on Root's seeming brilliance obscures his significance. From Washington's perspective, the genius of his geopolitical system was that it both advanced and effaced Washington's role, as well as his own stature as its plenipotentiary. By promoting Washington's power as primus inter pares, cloaking national interest in cultural amity, and advancing his agenda through allies, both peer and subordinate, Root's system fashioned a form of global power through a paradoxical reliance on empowered surrogates. By exercising its power indirectly through allies, whether in its informal empire in Latin America or its formal Philippine colony, Washington's alliance imperialism thus rested, above all, on its relations with a transnational network of subordinate elites.

To contextualize this latter term and strip it of its derogatory connotation, we need to emphasize that these subordinate elites demonstrated an impressive acuity in furthering their own aims within this changing imperial system. At an analytical level, these events point to the central role of such elites in the processes of both formal and informal empire. In the still colonized areas of Puerto Rico, the Philippines, and Cuba, subordinate elites quickly learned to play politics within the U.S. imperium with skill, although their ambit of movement was limited. In the Latin republics, newly subordinated elites developed an acute sense of the internationalist ambitions of their emerging imperial overlords and demonstrated an equally sensitive grasp of shifting global geopolitics. At critical junctures, they drew on all of the above to produce visionary leaders who, at times, succeeded in redesigning the broad frame of global diplomacy in service of their perceived interests, creating part of the new international system that Washington would adopt.

By soliciting the support of well-known Spanish Hispanists, Washington slowly courted support for U.S. hemispheric leadership, contributing to a shift from competition to eventual collaboration with the Latin American republics by the time the United States entered the European war in 1917. These moves led to the formation of that "triangular friendship" that effectively enfolded Latin America's Pan-Hispanists into Washington's Pan-American project.

CONCLUSION

The reality of alliance imperialism, rumored but never confirmed or formalized even in secret, provides the key to understanding not only U.S.-British relations between the Spanish-American War and the end of World War I, but also a continuing pattern in the longer arc of U.S. foreign policy throughout the twentieth century. As we have seen, this global geopolitical shift rested at the intersection of two transnational cultural movements, Anglophone amity among transatlantic elites in New York and London as well as Pan-American ties between Washington and the subordinate elites of Latin America and the Philippines. These cultural movements, in turn, forged close working relations with peer elites in the United Kingdom and subordinate elites in Latin America that would prove characteristic of a distinctive global statecraft as Washington's power expanded steadily throughout the twentieth century.

Pro-imperialist Nationalists at the End of Spain's Caribbean Empire

FRANCISCO A. SCARANO

BETWEEN THE OUTBREAK OF anticolonial revolutions across Spanish America in 1810 and the Spanish-Cuban-American War of 1898, powerful monarchist minorities that had long guarded the privileges of Spain and its peninsular-born merchants, clergy, and officials in the Hispanic colonies of the Caribbean (Cuba, Santo Domingo, and Puerto Rico) were challenged by robust nationalist movements favoring either sovereignty exercised in situ or performed from a distant imperial capital. Beginning with the Spanish American independence wars, separatists in these islands advocating independence locked horns with so-called assimilationists, who wanted fully enfranchised incorporation into the reigning metropole, Spain, and "annexationists," who favored a union with the aspiring hegemon, the United States. In the long history of the Spanish American empire, only these three island nations experienced this extraordinary array of nationalist options, one that could only emerge when national projects had matured in both Europe and the Americas and nationhood itself had become a normative political form in the Atlantic world.

Over time, and to varying degrees within these islands, the contest between the two leading forms of Spanish Caribbean nationalism (separatism or self-governing status) tilted toward those who favored total separation.[1] By century's end, Dominicans had established an incipient republic; insurgent Cubans had come within reach of republican independence just before U.S. troops invaded, allegedly on their behalf; and most Puerto Ricans had thrown their support behind an autonomous project that inched them closer to independence under a diminished Spanish sovereignty.

However, the U.S. invasion of 1898 outmaneuvered these nationalists (separatists or autonomists) in Spanish-controlled Cuba and Puerto Rico, forging nations that took colonial or neocolonial form under Washington's hegemony. At the same time, the liberal forces most willing to collaborate with the new imperialists, *pro-imperialist nationalists* according to Lillian Guerra, facilitated the transition from Spanish to U.S. dominion, which was the main overall result of the Spanish-Cuban-American War of 1898.[2] This essay explores the distinct ways in which, at the end of Spain's Caribbean empire, pro-imperialist nationalists positioned themselves to perform this neocolonial role in Cuba and Puerto Rico, the two most similar and synchronous cases. An argument for including the Dominican Republic in this comparison could be advanced, as pro-imperialist tendencies were woven through nationalist projects there for much of the nineteenth century. Maintaining the comparison between the two Spanish dependencies that quickly fell under colonial or neocolonial U.S. rule is important, however, because it allows us to observe a similar array of political forces as they played through a set of circumstances marked, in one case, by partisan electoral politics (Puerto Rico) and, in the other, by anticolonial insurrection (Cuba).

Political traditions, economic interests, social contexts, and historical conjunctures established the Cuban collaborators as the moderators and main beneficiaries of a neocolonial republic and their Puerto Rican counterparts as staunch supporters, albeit perennially frustrated, of eventual U.S. statehood. During the nineteenth century, conflicts of race, class, and gender fundamentally shaped many of these traditions, interests, and contexts. The confluence of these tensions and the U.S. imperial thrust of 1898 shaped a variety of Spanish Caribbean nationalist responses, not the least of which were of the collaborationist or pro-imperialist sort.

These two cases provide an exemplary study, then, in how and why imperial and native classes collaborated at the start of a formal relationship that combined subordination to an imperial power and conditional consent from below. As the introductory essay in this volume suggests, empires of all kinds and eras succeeded because they deftly marshaled the collaboration of native elites by forming a mutually beneficial coalition, usually to dominate the colony's resources and workers. Since native elites were factionalized themselves, and often subordinate to other elites (as in the Spanish Caribbean case), the opportunity to forge an alliance with a powerful imperium presented a competitive advantage in local power struggles.

In the case of modern empires of the liberal nineteenth and twentieth centuries, collaboration also included the likelihood of inclusion or at least preferential treatment in lucrative capitalist markets, as well as increased political participation. The first of these attractions was, of course, a key element. Secure access to markets proved particularly valuable for producers of commodities when the world market functionally ceased to exist, replaced by trading blocs attached to imperial economies—veritable imperial spaces for the preferential exchange of strategic raw materials or commodities. This was the case, acutely so, when beet sugar production rose in the cold climates of Central and Eastern Europe in the second half of the nineteenth century, powerfully affecting the most important tropical commodity, sugar. The less regulated marketing relationships of the old economic order dissolved under the weight of this competition, replaced by preferential or exclusive—and *intra-imperial*—marketing partnerships.[3]

In the aftermath of this wrenching change, elites in sugar-producing countries or aspiring nation-states saw their prosperity intricately bound to such preferential market access. They understood correctly that their newly forged imperial relationship implied subordination to the power centers that controlled those novel trading blocs, whose geographic boundaries, as I have noted, were coterminous with those of empires themselves—particularly in the cases of Britain and later the United States. Since the search for such preferential market access was a key to their (and Spain's) foreign relations for nearly a century, Cuba and Puerto Rico illuminate this modern imperial accommodation amid a rising tide of nationalist affirmation.

The pact of domination and subservience that describes U.S.-Cuban and U.S.-Puerto Rican relations was more complex than this, however. Besides the elites who controlled key commodities, certain nonelite groups, such as women of the popular classes and some organized workers, identified with the United States, especially with the legal protections or organizations that advanced their collective interests. These groups, some better organized than others, realized that they were unlikely to find such beneficial legal advances, institutional protection, or political alliances in the old metropole or even, they thought, in a newly founded nation-state led by the local bourgeoisie.[4]

In short, during the transition from Spanish to U.S. control an array of elite and nonelite groups accommodated to the novel imperial climate for economic or political expediency, as well as for reasons that can only be understood in the context of a long history of internal social strife. Struggles of this sort, connected as they were to international currents of capitalist development and racial thought, were deeply stamped in the political cultures of Cuba and Puerto Rico. As some historians have argued, in the confusing and, for some, exhilarating circumstances of 1898, a putative "lack of clarity" about U.S. intentions contributed to these groups' collaborationist bent.[5] But that confusion needs to be understood precisely as the end product of a long history of elites' perception of U.S. society through the prism of their own racially tinged ambivalence toward the native working classes. We now turn to the historical processes through which such ambivalence was constructed.

THE STRUGGLE FOR NATIONS WITH AND WITHOUT NATION-STATES

Recent historiography about the 1898 transition in Cuba and Puerto Rico has demonstrated the complex nature of Spanish Caribbean nationalisms and how this complexity played into the establishment of U.S. authority.[6] Unlike in the Philippines, the Americans did not have to fight a brutal war of colonial domination in Cuba or Puerto Rico, although they dealt with varying degrees of resistance. The "new empire" thus became ensconced in the political systems of these occupied nations with relative ease.[7] In order to do so, it relied heavily on local actors willing to collaborate with the new rulers and took advantage of numerous opportunities to justify the occupiers' presence.[8] While those native actors were not necessarily in favor of assimilation to the new metropolitan power (although some were), many saw national construction via collaboration as a desirable outcome. During the Spanish-Cuban-American War's centennial in 1998, revisionist literature grew in size and complexity, especially among scholars in Spain and its former colonies, with certain works challenging the one-sided narrative of U.S. dominion, developing counternarratives of complex negotiations on the ground that featured local protagonists, including those who stood against the new subordination but were willing to collaborate tactically in order to break up the old Spanish order.[9]

These new approaches offer a more nuanced understanding of the deep racial and class fissures that existed in these societies, and how struggles arising from these schisms influenced events on the ground, especially during the chaotic first phases of foreign occupation and rule. Ada Ferrer's work exemplifies some of the most compelling revisionism, reexamining the Cuban independence struggle between 1868 and 1898 to argue that the movement harbored its own betrayal, one born largely of contested racial and class origins. The first two Cuban wars against Spain (the Ten Years' War of 1868–78 and the Guerra Chiquita of 1879–80) saw large numbers of Afro-Cubans, predominantly from the eastern region, joining the rebel forces. Many rose in their ranks to high-level commanding positions and made racial equity one of their leading causes. But as larger contingents of bourgeois whites from the western regions began to join the independence army during the final war (1895–98), the movement turned more socially conservative and racially exclusive. Thus, when the U.S. troops intervened in the insurgency, the rebel army contained within it a powerful element that favored collusion with Yankees and disempowerment of Afro-Cubans. The stage was set, then, for the more conservative members of the Cuba Libre camp—pro-imperialist nationalists in Guerra's term—to reap the rewards of their whiteness and the privileges of their class, turning the independence movement away from subaltern vindication. For these pro-imperialist nationalists, collaboration with the United States was a necessary condition for their access to power in the new republic.[10]

A rightward turn that embraced collaboration also took place in Puerto Rico, where, in contrast to U.S. designs on Cuba, the new masters planned to build a strategic colonial possession all along.[11] With no anticolonial insurgency to radicalize its liberals, in the final third of the nineteenth century politically active Puerto Ricans embraced *autonomía*, a political status that would grant them internal self-rule with considerable negotiating room in international affairs, while remaining under the Spanish Crown's sovereignty. Whereas in Cuba autonomy was the political emblem of a minority of liberals, in Puerto Rico it was a status embraced by the majority. As the century came to a close, moreover, *autonomismo* was a growing political movement that represented a break with the liberal desideratum of complete assimilation into, or integration with, the peninsular political system—the preference among liberal Puerto Ricans until 1868. But as U.S. forces booted the Spanish army from the island in the fall of 1898, autonomists of all stripes moved to embrace the new imperialists; some adopted an "unconditional" stance favoring the United States, while others demanding reforms ultimately became disillusioned opponents of the territorial status granted by the Foraker Act of 1900. Unquestionably, however, both autonomist factions were in the collaborationist camp, counted among those who expedited the passage from Spanish to American imperial rule.[12]

That Cuban and Puerto Rican nationalists collaborated with the agents of an ascendant imperial power—one that heralded its democratic aspirations and open political system—is hardly a surprising conclusion. It is almost universally agreed that modern imperialisms need local collaboration, both to provide legitimacy and to help perform the nuts-and-bolts functions of establishing foreign rule. But how this collaboration shaped up, what its precise consequences were, and what this all means for peripheral nation building in the long run are open questions requiring a fine-grained analysis of background, context, and circumstance. Generalizations about both the imperial agents and those local residents who join hands with them are often hollow and do not provide much-needed detail. To address these questions, in the remainder of this essay I examine the manner in which a long history of pro-imperialist nationalism, including a pronounced strand of annexationism, facilitated the willing collaboration that many local actors lent to the invading U.S. forces. The long-term, comparative analysis of these two types of pro-imperialist nationalism helps to shine a bright light on the channels through which such actors conducted their work, and the contingent manner in which imperial actors incorporated such collaboration into the work of empire building.[13]

THE MAKING OF MULTIPLE NATIONALISMS

After losing its continental empire in 1825, Spain hardened its grip on Cuba and Puerto Rico, two colonies where the crisis of Spanish American independence (1810–25) had prompted an incipient nationalism. Across the islands' landscape, the 1810s and 1820s saw multiple expressions of both outright anti-imperialist nationalism or separatism and a milder, reform-oriented proto-nationalism, which sought to balance the celebration of cultural difference with the maintenance of Spanish sovereignty.[14]

In the Caribbean, however, the arousal of creole nationalism clashed with entrenched interests for whom loyalty to Spain was imperative: a militaristic culture where imperial service conferred privilege and status; and a sprouting plantation society whose most powerful figures, planters and merchants, were reveling in the wealth recently created on the backs of an unprecedented number of enslaved Africans. These factors proved potent inducements for these islands' creole elites to remain loyal to Spain, though not without wresting new privileges from a weakened metropole. Based on this transaction, by 1818 Spain had dismantled its ancient mercantilist restrictions on commerce with foreign ports and immigration of foreigners and constructed its relationship with the Caribbean colonies on the basis of a new colonial contract. Because of the liberal intent of many of its provisions, such as the adoption of policies to promote colonial capitalism, I prefer to call this agreement between Spain and the colonial elites the Liberal Pact.[15] The metropole's commitment to the continued importation of African slaves proved to be the crucial leverage it needed to maintain colonial control of suddenly self-assured Cubans and Puerto Ricans. In the process, as José A. Piqueras notes, Cuban elites "managed to nationalize decision-making without breaking the Empire."[16]

From its inception in the late 1810s, the Liberal Pact involved an intractable conflict between Spanish, American, and colonial objectives and interests. With the Cuban and Puerto Rican colonials loyal for the time being, Madrid enhanced its ability to control and divert tax and tariff receipts, which by mid-century were providing as much revenue as the entire American empire had supplied at the outbreak of the independence wars.[17] But this prosperity translated into a groundswell of self-awareness for the colonial elites who increasingly conceived of their cultural and economic interests as different from those of most peninsular elites. In both islands this consciousness manifested itself in multiple ways, from nativist literature and other cultural expressions to political movements that sought to declare independence from Spain—or, significantly, annexation to the United States. It also translated into a growing suspicion that Spain, caught between an abolitionist Great Britain and an expansionist United States, both of which had designs on Cuba, could not preserve the status quo. The suspicion was strongest in Cuba, where the plantation economy and population of African descent were growing at a breakneck pace.

In Cuba the contradictions contained within the Liberal Pact emerged forcefully in the 1830s, due in part to the heavy-handed Spanish governor-general, Captain-General Miguel Tacón, and a growing racial rift. Tacón's years in the governor-generalship were marked by a feverish pursuit of colonial modernization, ruthless repression of all signs of discontent with Spanish rule or the colonial social (slavery) system, and attempts to control British-led activities to end the slave trade. The severity displayed by colonial authorities touched a raw nerve with many liberal creoles and alienated many of them from Spain, but the structural changes the island was undergoing were more consequential in the long run.

As sugarcane cultivation spread east-southeast, from Havana to Matanzas, Trinidad, and elsewhere, and hundreds of thousands of enslaved Africans arrived illegally, the slave population grew rapidly, from 199,145 in 1817 (36 percent of the total) to 436,495 in 1841 (43 percent). This was accompanied by moderate growth of the free colored group, which represented another 21 and 15 percent of the Cuban population, respectively.[18] By the latter date, Cuba had become a slave society—not just a society with slaves—whose security and prosperity depended on the maintenance of internal order.[19] The enslaved workers challenged this order, as did the international abolitionist campaigns spearheaded by Great Britain; as a result, the situation on the island grew tense, spilling over into real and imagined conspiracies such as the bloodily repressed La Escalera (1843–44).[20]

The specter of a Cuba where persons of African descent would hold considerable sway was a potent inducement for some Cuban nationalists to disavow the formation of an independent nation-state and seek the security and civilizational guarantees of U.S. protection.[21] Intensifying this relationship were expansionist, proslavery Americans, from businessman John A. Quitman to President Franklin Pierce, who explored invasion and purchase of the island. All of these annexationist schemes involved Cuban collusion and active participation. In fact, Cuban sentiment in favor of incorporation into America continued even after the U.S. Civil War (1861–65) and at least through the early phases of the Ten Years' War against Spain (1868–78).[22]

This well-known Cuba-U.S. dance underscores a key point about Spanish Caribbean collaboration with the United States: from the beginning, annexation schemes involved a kind of *utilitarian nationalism* whose strategic aims were social and racial, and for whose supporters cooperation with a culturally distinct foreign outsider was a necessary step in the perpetuation of a particular socioracial system.

For this nationalism, the ultimate objective was slavocracy and/or racial domination; the means was the reconstruction of the former Spanish colony as part of the larger American republic, with an implicit exercise of sovereignty through federal statehood. In this instance, nationalism had much less to do with culture and ethnicity than with race and class, although annexationists hoped U.S. statehood would safeguard a social system based on slavery *and* somehow also protect the Cubans' cultural and linguistic distinctiveness (how this would happen was never clear). Unlike contemporaneous European nationalists, annexationist Cubans did not exclusively align their country's dominant Hispanic culture and ethnicity with a corresponding nation-state.

Two of the three major nationalisms—separatism to prevent Africanization and annexationism to cement the racial order—were predicated on maintaining

or even enhancing racial domination. Both the racist version of Cuban separatism, to which the early nationalist theorist José Antonio Saco subscribed, and
the more consistent and longer-lasting strand of racist annexationism drew their
strength from the defense of the slave regime per se and, more broadly, the racial
system that legal enslavement represented. The fear that Spain could not prevent
Africanization, or alternatively, that only a greater state power (i.e., the United
States) could keep the *raza de color* properly subordinated drove many Cubans
to embrace such a view.[23] Although one faction advocated a society dominated
by a majority of whites and the other a society of whites dominating a large subservient Afro-Cuban sector, both nationalisms turned on a view of Cuban racial
composition and social order hinged on white supremacy. These were strands
of the same sort of nationalism, which, following Guerra's nomenclature, one
might call "racist utilitarian nationalism"—an antecedent of the pro-imperialist
nationalism that prevailed among some members of the insurgent leadership at
the end of the nineteenth century.

In both Spanish Caribbean colonies, especially in the second half of the nineteenth century, there developed progressive movements that pursued a profound
social and racial transformation through the creation of independent nation-
states. The three-decade-long Cuban insurrection against Spain, from 1868 to
1898, constituted by far the most important of these. Scholars have documented
how the movement for Cuba Libre was a broad tent that included all sorts of
nationalists, including "pro-imperialist" ones who were driven by racial fear of
the masses even though they were hoping for a sovereign, republican outcome to
their struggle. In the final push toward independence from 1897 to 1899, more
conservative (and whiter) recruits from the "pro-imperialist nationalist" camp
rose through the ranks of the movement, achieving commanding positions. The
arrival of U.S. troops on the island coincided, then, with a socially conservative
upturn within a movement that, under its deceased mythical leader José Martí,
had countenanced the notion of a *raceless Cuba*—with all the contradictions
and problems the concept implies—and adopted a program for the anticipated
republic that would redistribute land and accord citizenship rights to those who
lacked them. Because so many of the poorest members of the rebel group were
also dark skinned, these redistributive and enabling policies contained the seeds
of an unprecedented empowerment of Afro-Cubans.[24]

If the some of the most influential of Cuba's nationalist forces were turning
more conservative (and ultimately pro-American) as the final war pushed to its
unexpected denouement, the situation in Puerto Rico displayed both interesting
parallels and substantive differences. The resemblance between the two islands
hinges on the strong development after 1868 of overlapping forms of revolutionary and popular nationalisms. As in Cuba, separatism emerged in Puerto Rico
in the second half of the nineteenth century as a socially radical movement, driven

by abolitionism even more than in Cuba. Revolutionary and popular nationalisms jointly had their finest hour during the failed 1868 Lares revolt against Spain—a clear example of cooperation between the two strands of separatism.[25] However, Spanish forces quickly repressed the Puerto Rican insurgency, which did not gather traction as it did on the battlefields in eastern Cuba, thereby preventing an escalation into outright war.

In the aftermath of the Lares revolt, by contrast, Puerto Rican independence-minded nationalists were repressed and many of the movement's leaders exiled. Some, like Ramón E. Betances, a revolutionary physician who aided rebels from his home in Paris, remained for the balance of their lives committed revolutionaries.[26] Numerous others, like José Julio Henna and Roberto H. Todd, cooperated with the Cuban effort from exile in the United States. But as events unfolded during the Spanish-Cuban-American War and in its immediate aftermath, they upgraded their collaboration with the invading U.S. troops, sharing intelligence about the Spanish defenses, assisting during the invasion, and eventually serving as intermediaries with and facilitators of the new military occupation government.

A different, reformist nationalism gained the political upper hand in Puerto Rico after 1868: *autonomismo*. Whereas in Cuba revolutionary nationalists pursued national independence through armed insurgency, in Puerto Rico the autonomists sought local self-government via the electoral system. Although they did not seek outright separation from Spain, the autonomists deserve to be called nationalists for several reasons. First, they did not rule out independence in some indeterminate future. In their view, the large majority of peasants (*jíbaros*) were not *yet* ready for full sovereignty, but once they underwent a period of civilizing reforms, they could constitute a democratic polity under the leadership of the landed gentry (*hacendados*). Second, the autonomists, like the separatists, believed that a Puerto Rican ethnicity had taken shape that was sufficiently different from those of the metropole to deserve a system of self-government. For some of these autonomists, especially the earliest ideologues of autonomism in the 1870s, the eventual goal was the attainment of a status similar to what Great Britain had granted Canada in 1867, a status that could ultimately lead to independence.[27]

By the mid-1890s, as electoral rules continued to favor a tiny minority of pro-monarchical conservatives, other autonomist leaders, like the pragmatist (*posibilista*) Luis Muñoz Rivera, essentially grew frustrated with the pace of progress. He grabbed what he could get, however he could get it, even if what Spain ultimately granted fell short of the original goal or if it involved fusing the Puerto Rican Autonomist Party with a conservative peninsular party (Práxedes Mateo Sagasta's Liberal Party). In November, 1897, to Muñoz Rivera's delight, but in reality on account of the strength of the Cuban insurgency, Spain was forced to grant autonomy to Puerto Rico in anticipation of a similar grant to Cuba.

Although it was an arresting distinction between the two islands, the lack of a broad, cross-class anti-imperialist nationalist movement with a long fighting resume was not the sole difference between them—or even the most important. One needs to remember that a significant Puerto Rican separatist contingent collaborated with the Cuban rebels in New York through the Cuban Revolutionary Party, and that many from this group and from Puerto Rico itself went to Cuba to fight on the side of the rebels, especially during the decisive last years of the liberation war, sacrificing their lives in the military campaigns of the *manigua*, or tropical jungle. It was a tenet of Cuban revolutionary ideology in the 1890s that once Cuba had been liberated the effort would turn to the unfinished task: the liberation of Puerto Rico.

There is no question that the alliance of revolutionary and popular nationalists in Cuba portended a more radical force than anything else seen in the Caribbean since the days of Toussaint Louverture and his army of self-liberated Haitian slaves during the late eighteenth and early nineteenth centuries. By the time they had fought several wars of national liberation, key Cuban revolutionary nationalists had become, on the whole, bolder and more socially progressive than their Puerto Rican counterparts. Slave emancipation fused with the cause of Cuba Libre during the Ten Years' War and the Guerra Chiquita, lending the Cuban rebel movement significantly larger input from the popular classes, including people of African descent. But in a curious twist, the pro-imperialist nationalists and collaborationists were distinctly more conservative, and of higher socioeconomic extraction, among the Cubans than among the Puerto Ricans. Since the comparative story of how these forces were set up by the events of 1898–1900 to collaborate with the invaders, influencing the course of colonial and neocolonial construction, remains untold, it is worth delineating some of its main contours here.

Collaborations Were Not All Alike

In examining the nature of Cuban collaboration with the U.S. imperial project in the late nineteenth century, Jorge I. Domínguez observes that not all collaborations were alike; in fact, some were meant to be transitory and supportive of a revolutionary outcome while others were not. The uncertainty and ambiguity of events during the first U.S. occupation of Cuba (1898–1902) profoundly unsettled the matrix of collaboration versus confrontation, such that the ideological and tactical certainties of Cuban nationalists were shuffled and rearranged. The key variable, in Domínguez's case, was whether the local actors perceived the foreign military presence to have a limited or open-ended purpose. In Cuba collaboration was principally a means toward a greater end: national independence.[28]

The underlying assumption in this typology of collaborations is that the Cuban insurgencies of the last third of the nineteenth century had turned almost all pro-imperialist nationalists into advocates of some form of Cuba Libre. At stake in the debates among the various nationalist factions was not independence as such but what kind of independence and for whose ultimate well-being. Stalwart conservatives like Tomás Estrada Palma, as enamored of U.S. lifeways as anybody among the Americans' interlocutors in Cuba, agreed with this eventuality and struggled to bring it to fruition. The devil was in the details of a republican polity, however, and even revolutionary nationalists like Máximo Gómez, commander in chief of the Liberation army, agreed to terms that disenfranchised many poor and black Cubans who had valiantly fought to bring about the republic—all because it would convince the American occupiers that the republic would possess civic virtue and lead toward the construction of a civilized nation.[29] The wars, the enormous sacrifices, had pushed pro-imperialist nationalists decisively into the camp of believers in national independence.

This was not the case in Puerto Rico. Within the Autonomist Party (1887–95), a rift widened between believers in *posibilismo*, such as Muñoz Rivera, and those who, following the Afro–Puerto Rican doctor José Celso Barbosa, argued from a socially progressive stance that supported an alliance with a republic rather than a monarchy and opposed merging into a Spanish political organization for the sake of attaining a grant of autonomy. As Angel G. Quintero Rivera and others have pointed out, class differences animated this schism: the *muñocistas* stood for the interests of the landowning *hacendados* while the *barbocistas* clearly represented an artisanal sector that was fast becoming proletarianized, and indeed had begun to organize the first labor organizations on the island.[30]

The conflict between these two camps turned especially noxious after the U.S. invasion. Both factions initially supported federal statehood for Puerto Rico; in the terms of our discussion, they became pro-imperialist and annexationist nationalists. But events soon showed that not all statehood proponents were alike, as the *muñocista* faction (now members of the Federal Party, founded in 1899) withdrew its unconditional support for statehood when the U.S. Congress handed down the terms of the colonial relationship. The *barbocistas*, since 1899 organized as the Republican Party of Puerto Rico, continued to lend support to the idea of constituting the Puerto Rican nation by fusing it into the United States as a state, even after the Americans' colonial intentions became clear. Throughout the early years of the new colonial arrangement, the *republicanos* helped legitimize the U.S. colonial regime while providing it with administrative cadres and an unconditionally engaged group of locals, some of whom belonged to a rising labor movement.

Significant comparative lessons about subaltern collaboration with a rising imperial power may be drawn from this contrast of two closely comparable cases. In Cuba, the pro-imperialist nationalists worked within the strictures of a new republican order to neutralize the aspirations of poorer and darker citizens. They took advantage of the trust the Americans placed in them to shape the republic according to their interests, which corresponded to what they perceived to be consonant with the hegemon's expectations of civilization and political maturity. In Puerto Rico, those who had constituted the more socially progressive wing of the reformist nationalists (i.e., the autonomists) used the sudden transformation of the political system after 1898 to politically neutralize their opponents, a conflict many saw (and rightly so) in terms of class and racial struggle. The strongest collaborators with the U.S. regime essentially bartered their oft-articulated and well-calibrated national aspirations, even as Washington exposed its raw colonial intentions, for a chance to ally themselves with imperial power against their class enemies— an opposition that drew inspiration also from the unspoken, but barely hidden, racial conflicts that plagued Puerto Rican society in early twentieth century.[31]

In sketching the history of pro-imperialist nationalisms in two former Spanish Caribbean societies up to 1898, this essay suggests that collaboration can be shaped by forces deeply rooted in a country's past and thus not easy to predict or control. As in Cuba and Puerto Rico, contradictions lay deep inside the subaltern society, with fissures of race and class revealing past struggles for internal hegemony and external control—struggles that can give rise to "societies structured in dominance."[32] Cuba and Puerto Rico became ever more structured in dominance when thrust into the cauldron of world commodity markets in the nineteenth century, enduring a new regime of force and authority—including new inflictions of slavocratic power on a rising population of slaves and free people of color, liberal-inspired coercion of peasants and workers whose lives were not yet regimented according to the standards of the capitalist marketplace, and dictatorial military governments. Impositions like these aggravated preexisting conflicts through a series of concrete actions that turned the patrimonial (Spanish) colonialism of old into a modern, even liberal regime crisscrossed by ambiguities and inconsistencies.[33]

Such concessions included an agreement between island elites and the Spanish metropole to maintain an internal order threatened after 1810 by slavery, labor coercion, and separatist movements; a renaissance in the importation of enslaved Africans, with its insidious corollary of antiblack racism; a colonial legal system that accorded a bevy of privileges to the peninsular born and kept the native born subordinated; and intricate institutional, juridical, and ideological frameworks that codified all of these forms of subordination. The kaleidoscopic pro-imperialist nationalisms that welcomed or even embraced the United States during its incursions into Cuba and Puerto Rico in 1898 were certainly the product of those fissures. But they were also the result of the sheer alignment of economic interests— the search for new markets or new partners in trade and investment—and, for that matter, of the idealistic attraction of a freer, republican way of life that many believed would be realized under the U.S. flag.

Imperial Transition
in the Philippines

The Making of a Colonial Discourse about Spanish Rule

MARÍA DOLORES ELIZALDE

ONE OF THE MORE IMPORTANT questions within the literature on imperial transitions concerns the role of international opinion. One interesting place to study this phenomenon is the Philippines, which experienced such a transition in 1898 when the United States replaced Spain as the metropolitan power following the Spanish-American War. As is well known, imperial powers everywhere justified their sovereignty by claiming they exercised a tutelary role over native inhabitants who had not yet reached a point where they could govern themselves properly. For this reason, so the argument went, colonial governors needed to teach native inhabitants how to construct institutions that would guarantee respect for human dignity and the rule of law, and how to implement policies that would foster technological and economic progress. Many among the native elite, of course, debunked this so-called civilizing mission, exposing such arguments as false, self-serving, and racist.

Less explored, however, are instances when rival imperial powers questioned the fitness of the tutor as well as the student. This, in fact, is what occurred in the Philippines when U.S. propagandists used so-called empirical information contained in reports and accounts written by critics of Spanish rule in the decades before 1898. The authors of such reports were not on a stated mission of spreading propaganda aimed at provoking a transfer of imperial governance. Yet these texts did serve to portray the Spaniards as poor teachers and the Filipinos as unschooled children. They proved to be a useful tool for American officials, and a jingoist press, seeking to justify a transfer of imperial sovereignty.

On examining such reports, it is not difficult to discern the motivations of the authors, who were overwhelmingly concerned with exploiting economic and political opportunities while commenting on the history of Spanish colonial rule or misrule. What is also striking is the extent to which they ignored the reforms of Spanish authorities, who, throughout the nineteenth century, were engaged in ceaseless attempts to devise a colonial model to bolster their weakening sovereignty over the islands. These reforms had mixed success, but they did reorder the fiscal, administrative, and military basis of colonial rule over the Philippines. All the same, most authors did not evaluate the efficacy of such reforms but instead portrayed Spain as a decadent power caught in the tentacles of a tradition-bound colonial rule inherited from the ages of exploration, colonization, and Counter-Reformation, oblivious to contemporary notions of proper imperial governance. Such reports did not cause the end of Spanish hegemony, but, as we shall see, they did influence the form it would take.

An Empire in Transition and in the Throes of Redefinition

Before addressing the hyperbolic images spread by the reports, it is helpful to summarize the realities of Spanish rule, which, though far from enlightened, certainly evoke parallels with other forms of colonial rule at the time. In the nineteenth century, Spain was an empire undergoing reform, with governing officials constantly engaged in an effort to reorganize the fiscal and administrative organization of the colonies.

With respect to the Philippines, the need for such a transformation had been clear since the mid–eighteenth century. The British occupation of Manila during the Seven Years' War in 1763 showed the world what many familiar with the situation had long known: Spain lacked the money and resources to defend the colony. In the early nineteenth century, Spain's hegemony faced another major challenge. The independence of the continental American countries ended Manila's close relations with New Spain sustained across the Pacific. The voyages of the Manila Galleon, the backbone of the Philippine economy, came to close. The galleon had sailed at least once a year from 1593 to 1825 between Acapulco and Manila loaded with Mexican silver, which was then used to purchase Asian products to be reexported to the rest of the world. For many years, this trade assured Manila's place as a major Asian center of commerce and an entrepôt between America and Europe.[1] With the end of the galleon, it was by no means a foregone conclusion that Spain would be able retain the Philippines. However, sweeping reforms undertaken by the Bourbons in the closing decades of the eighteenth century were successful enough to withstand the domino effect of the independence of much of Spanish America. These innovations strengthened administration, created new colonial institutions, and fostered a move to a new economy based on state monopolies over the production and sale of tobacco and indigenous alcohols. Combined with the taxes paid by the inhabitants, these monopolies enabled the colony to remain financially viable.[2]

By the early nineteenth century, however, authorities had become conscious that another fiscal and administrative overhaul was needed. From the outset, there were some doubters. Many believed that Spanish rule was not flexible enough to adjust to the rapidly changing circumstances in Asia and the Pacific, an increasingly important theater for European expansion. Shifting trends of international trade, a growing demand for tropical products, and raw geopolitics caused rival powers to eye the archipelago. Moreover, Spanish rule faced internal problems, including the high cost of maintaining the tobacco and alcohol monopolies and the growing strength of diverse opposition groups of Filipinos who protested against fiscal and administrative burdens. Although a number of discordant voices recommended abandoning the islands in view of the high cost, few Spanish authorities entertained the notion. They did not want to abandon the Philippines, an outcome that would affect other possessions in Micronesia: the Marianas (including the valuable island of Guam), the Caroline Islands, and Palau. To be sure, Spain was loath to retreat from Asia and the Pacific, a complex and interrelated network of islands to which it had dedicated serious military and civilian resources since the sixteenth century. By the nineteenth century, authorities were engaged in an ongoing pursuit to find a workable fiscal-administrative model that would ensure sovereignty and maintain a system of governance acceptable inside and outside the Philippine colony.

Beginning in the early nineteenth century, the Spanish government sought to meet these challenges by centralizing power, and, by so doing, it handed direct control over the levers of government to its governor-general. This meant obviating many of the powers delegated to local elites who had been responsible for the political, economic, and social organization of the Filipino people. It also entailed an increase in direct rule over the population. Such measures brought tensions. The old model of delegated or decentralized authority had allowed for a certain balance of power in the islands and had provided space for multiple actors. The Filipino elites not only witnessed the dismantling of this system, but they also realized that they would not be granted Spanish citizenship. In the midst of a liberal era, instead of enjoying enhanced political participation, they actually lost rights and privileges. Though hardly unique in the colonial world, such reforms spurred protest movements, which were harshly repressed, until many Filipinos became convinced that they would never fulfill their goals through peaceful negotiation and hence took up armed struggle. As a result, continuous colonial reforms created a widening divide between the imperial system and local elites.[3]

Another powerful group seriously affected by the decision to increase the authority of the governor-general was the religious orders, which included Augustinians, Franciscans, Jesuits, Dominicans, and Recollects. Since the sixteenth century, they had been an essential cog in the colonial wheel, entrusted with the task of Christianizing the islands. They were practically the only organizations with a presence in most of the islands. Familiar with local languages, they had long acted as conduits through which Spanish authorities could establish a dialogue with the population. Their role as representatives and intermediaries complemented their evangelizing duties, justifying their presence in the archipelago. They were also responsible for education and were involved in Philippine economic life. In short, they occupied a central place within the colonial constellation. They also proved to be a serious problem for Spanish authorities, who, throughout the nineteenth century, sought to limit their traditional autonomy.

In addition to native elites and the religious orders, Spanish authorities also restricted the autonomy of provincial officials in an attempt to curb abuse and ensure that taxes reached their destination. Rationalizing colonial administration required an end to old practices. This sparked an intense but relatively silent struggle for power among various competing sectors.

To be sure, many Spaniards were conscious of the need to introduce reforms in the archipelago.[4] Such individuals included a number of administrative authorities, a few insightful politicians, and a handful of others preoccupied with promoting economic growth rather than perpetuating elite privilege. Still, progress was not easy. Influential voices of reason made themselves heard, plans were drawn up, and piecemeal reforms were introduced. All the same, governing circles were characterized and hamstrung by the persistence of a generalized and amorphous but debilitating fear of change. Broad sectors of colonial society opposed any talk of reform, viewing plans with deep suspicion and often outright antagonism. Opponents included conservative politicians and military officers, members of religious orders, and a plethora of entrenched individuals, who, for one reason or another, favored maintenance of the status quo. As a result, the nineteenth century was a period of constant struggle between reformists and antireformists, between reaction and progress. The reform measures that emerged from this divisive political process were clearly insufficient to meet the multiple challenges facing the Spanish Philippines.

Political reforms were not the only reason that local elites grew hostile to colonial authorities. Economic circumstances also weighed heavily. Over the course of the nineteenth century, the Philippines also experienced a major transition. A closed imperial mercantilist system characterized by reliance on the Manila Galleon and fiercely controlled monopolies in trade, tobacco, and alcohol was transformed into a new imperial space open to free trade. Foreign penetration grew stronger. Rising demand for tropical goods created an export-oriented economy focused on sugar, tobacco, and Manila hemp. Colonial authorities were not the only ones responsible for this transformation; rather, new Filipino landowning elites as well as foreign traders and investors played important roles. This caused a realignment of power. Since Spain was not a principal export market for Philippine products, native economic elites were often closely allied with foreign recipients of such trade, which caused their interests to clash frequently with those of the metropole. In the closing years of the century, the government attempted to restrain such foreign interests by erecting protectionist walls. Although this prompted an influx of Spanish enterprise, capital, and imports, it logically created impediments to trade with foreign partners. The end result was that local elites continued to view Spain as an obstacle. Other colonial reforms, especially those having to do with taxation, exacerbated tensions.

In retrospect, it is easy to judge colonial reforms harshly, especially given their effects on the native elite. All the same, it must be realized that Spanish options were limited. These measures represented a concerted effort on the part of authorities to maintain Spain's presence in the Philippines, which was the center of the Spanish empire in Asia. As we shall see, however, critics did not address the efficacy such reforms but tended to stress a different image of imperial rule.

ACCOUNTS OF THE PHILIPPINES AND DIAGNOSIS OF A COLONIAL MODEL

Spain was not the only country attempting to assert an increased presence in the Philippines. Great powers with rising colonial ambitions in the Pacific and the South China Sea grew increasingly interested in future possibilities. From a strategic perspective, the archipelago faced the China coast and was located at the crossroads of several major transoceanic shipping lanes. From an economic perspective, a burgeoning demand for tropical exports attracted traders, investors, and travelers. Investment was needed for the production and export of sugar, Manila hemp, tobacco, coffee, and other goods. Not to be forgotten, Filipino consumers were an increasingly attractive market for Western manufacturers. For enterprise to prosper, it was necessary to undertake improvements in infrastructure and communications, which in turn provoked rival imperial aspirations. At first, foreigners limited their activities to commerce, investment, and the exploration of possibilities. By the end of the nineteenth century, however, low-level penetration was giving way to outright expansionist ambitions in various parts of the archipelago, thus representing a growing threat to Spain's geopolitical position.

The foreign residents and visitors responsible for writing and circulating reports were eager to publicize the fact that the islands were open to foreign investment and offered vast, previously underexploited opportunities. Many of these writings were essentially guidebooks surveying various aspects of the Philippines and offering advice on how best to operate. At the same time, many included an analysis of Spanish colonial rule that revealed as much about foreign ambitions as it did about the nature of that rule. Of course, the reports were not part of a propaganda campaign directed from some sort of government agency bent on undermining Spanish sovereignty. However, the authors did represent specific foreign interests who believed that Spanish rule represented an obstacle rather than a catalyst for the economic development of the islands.

Most such writings by European travelers and officials identified a number of common features inherent in the Spanish administration. Taken as a whole, they painted an image of Spanish colonial rule as a continuation of the original settlement patterns of the sixteenth century. According to the British envoy John Bowring, the Spanish were primarily motivated by the quest to conquer and evangelize. As a result, a small number of soldiers and priests administered the colony. In particular, the religious orders, entrusted with evangelizing the natives, were said to hold immense power.[5] The French traveler Jean Baptiste Mallat also insisted that Spanish colonization lacked any overarching economic motivations. The Spaniards were portrayed as being uninterested in developing or exploiting the islands' immense natural resources.[6]

This depiction was not true, even with respect to the sixteenth century. As was the case with all empires, economic motivations went a long way in explaining the history of Spanish colonialism. One of the primary purposes of initial Spanish expansionist efforts in Southeast Asia was to penetrate the lucrative spice and precious metals market. This quest did not bear fruit given that the Philippines did not yield the same products as Indonesia or India. And although it was a long time before the Spanish fastened upon a viable economic system, Spanish authorities were always conscious that the islands must be profitable to sustain the evangelical project and cover the costs of colonization. By the nineteenth century, however, it was abundantly clear that the mechanism that was eventually devised—the Manila Galleon—though profitable for many, had done little to develop the islands. For centuries, the galleon had ensured that the Philippines remained fiscally viable. However, the creation of a buoyant brokerage economy between Asia and America left the islands largely undeveloped. This was problematic given that the internal economy was essential to supply the food, commodities, and labor necessary for overseas trade. In short, underdevelopment was not due to a lack of interest in profit and fiscal viability but to the peculiarities of an economic system revolving around the galleon trade.

In any case, foreign observers judged that Spanish colonial governance in the Philippines was obsolete, given that it was founded on goals, practices, and institutions that may have worked well in the sixteenth or seventeenth centuries but were unsuited to nineteenth-century conceptions of imperial rule. Reports ignored Spanish reforms and efforts to modernize the colonial administration and instead painted a monolithic picture of an antiquated administration, burdened by centuries of bad practices and rife with abuse and corruption. Ill-defined policies, few resources, and the absence of guidelines necessary for economic development were all said to characterize Spanish rule. Recommendations included redefining the functions of colonial authorities, who should be provided with specific training as overseas administrators. Another suggestion from the British official Bowring was to further strengthen the powers of the governor-general, who should be given greater independence and more ample decision-making capacity. Ideally, he should be "surrounded by a council composed of the best qualified advisers."[7]

British accounts, in particular, focused on the need to remedy the perennial lack of training among Spanish officials, their poor sense of vocation, and their paucity of stimuli. Reports noted that officials regarded a posting in the Philippines as a mere step in a career, often compulsory and usually unwanted, in which they simply hoped to survive unscathed rather than seeking to make a difference. This constant shuffling meant that officials rarely became familiar with the archipelago. By the time an official had acquired a modicum of local knowledge, it was time to move on. Unlike English and Dutch colonials who were "especially educated and instructed for their difficult mission," reported the German ethnographer Fedor Jagor in 1874, the Spanish administration was characterized by uninterested colonial officials, frequent changes in decisive positions, and fluctuating policies and guidelines.[8] Many foreign observers drew attention to the fact that the Spanish did not have full control over the entire archipelago, possessing neither dominion nor surveillance over vast territories. This promoted the proliferation of loopholes, opening up a world of possibilities for semilegal agents. Their activities were never sanctioned, but they were hardly secret—the Spanish scarcely had the means to stop them.[9]

Another omnipresent theme was the ambivalent status of the religious orders. Most writers believed that the religious played too large a role in the colonial machinery, attributing their prominence to original settlement patterns and the perennial shortage of competent civil servants. Such depictions by Bowring and John Foreman were not uniformly critical. Many authors praised the clergy for their work as interlocutors and mediators. They also acknowledged their laudatory role in educating the inhabitants.[10] All the same, they considered the relationship between colonizers and colonized unduly religious, which complicated governance. Some religious had become too deeply involved in the economy, creating numerous conflicts of interest. Given that they also had their hands on the levers of power, they found themselves in frequent conflict with secular officials. Taken as a whole, foreign observers were well aware of the frequent clashes and the divergence of interests between the political and spiritual authorities. Most reasoned that the state should tightly control the missionaries and keep them out of governance and administration.[11]

The authors of these accounts and reports also paid special attention to the world of the Filipinos. They were interested on the way in which local elites had become integrated in the colonial system, acting as delegates of the governor-general on appointment as *gobernadorcillos* (high officials) of their villages. They looked favorably on the way such elites retained their functions as organizers of the public lives of their subjects while ensuring compliance with colonial rules and laws. They noted that this system allowed for the maintenance of local customs, so necessary for legitimacy, order, and efficiency. Moreover, the fact that such elites were granted the privileged legal status of *principalías* (local authorities who governed a district) made them more accepting of the colonial system. However, the reports were also critical. By respecting the social organizations and even the language of the Filipinos, the Spanish, said the British envoy Bowring, had lost an opportunity to assimilate Filipino elites into Western culture.[12] Spain had never made westernization attractive as a vehicle through which the population could have aspired to increasing education and affluence.

The inability of the Spaniards to inculcate Western values and ambitions in the population provided observers an opportunity to highlight Filipino backwardness. The most frequently recurring image is one of primitive tribes, racial distinctions, savage customs, and lazy workers. What is more, the Spanish had failed as a colonial power to undertake a tutelary mission and hence help these peoples achieve a desirable measure of progress. These writers continually stressed the need for initiating a process of tutelage in which the Filipinos would eventually become capable of self-government. Given proper guidance from a "superior" nation, natives would be led down the road of civilization. All in all, such images presented indigenous peoples as unschooled children and Spaniards as inadequate teachers. As such, these writings interwove two levels of "orientalist" discourse. The first emphasized the inability of the Filipinos to govern themselves, while the other focused on the incompetence of the Spaniards (a "Hispanist" version of orientalism) to govern anybody except possibly themselves.[13]

Such images continued until the eve of American rule. During the 1890s, the British writer John Foreman described Spanish colonial authorities as lacking initiative; their laziness denied the Philippines the possibility of reaching its potential. "Few improvements appear to have been made in the provinces by initiative of the local Governors, nor did they seem to take any special interest in commercial and agricultural advancement," wrote Foreman. "If a bridge broke down, so it remained for years."[14] Spanish rule reeked of "the spirit of Caesarism," creating unbridgeable divisions between the colonizers and the colonized.[15] In his book's second edition in 1899, he added, "One cannot help feeling pity for the Spanish nation, which has let the Pearl of the Orient slip out its fingers through culpable and stubborn mismanagement, after repeated warning and similar experiences in other quarters of the globe." As such, Foreman posed the possibility that a change in colonial administration would be beneficial to Filipinos and foreign interests alike: "The intelligent world will watch with considerable interest the development of Philippines Home Rule under American auspices, and expect America to substitute a better government."[16]

USE OF CONSTRUCTED IMAGES DURING
IMPERIAL TRANSITION

The popularity of these writings among foreigners living, or taking an interest in, the Philippines meant that almost everyone was aware of the urgency of reform. The consensus was that Spain was an empire in flux with such critical problems that the choice was between collapse or renewal. Yet, until the very end of the nineteenth century, few openly questioned Spanish sovereignty. Like the British consul Bowring, the goal was to encourage the Spanish (or foreign powers to pressure the Spanish) to bring stability and open up opportunities. The debate over a possible change of hands in the colonial administration only came into the open at the close of the century.

Two events caused this situation to change drastically: the Philippine Revolution of 1896 and the Spanish-American War of 1898. During the revolution, Filipinos from diverse sectors of society rose against the Spanish, initiating a movement for independence, the first of its kind in Asia. Philippine rebels justified their actions by emphasizing a number of factors recognizable to international opinion: colonial misrule; the legacy of Spanish intransigence, abuse and injustice; and the large governing and economic roles given to the religious orders. The great powers acknowledged the validity of such claims but did not come out in support of independence. After all, virtually every major power had its own empire and was aware of the risks of fueling similar movements in its possessions. Only a very few groups in European countries trumpeted Filipino self-government. Rather than supporting the rebels, foreign governments stressed the need for a change in colonial administration, thus leaving the field clear for another power or powers to intervene. From the start, the intention was not to put an end to colonial rule, nor to create an independent state, but to orchestrate a transition between empires.

The outbreak of the Spanish-American War proved to be the decisive factor in the end of Spain's Asian empire. In the summer and autumn of 1898, before the future of the Spanish archipelagos in the Pacific had become clear, European powers began to show their true intentions, spreading all kinds of rumors and engaging in secret negotiations over the future of the Philippines and the islands of Micronesia. The expansionist ambitions of the powers became a real threat to Spanish sovereignty over those territories.

During these months of uncertainty, journalists, propagandists, and government officials began to see the need to introduce the notion of a possible annexation of the Philippines to the American public.[17] To frame their arguments, they dusted off old images of colonial misrule contained in decades-old reports and descriptions: Spanish administration was inefficient, abusive, and corrupt; Spaniards lacked the economic motivations and technological know-how needed for development; the excessive interference of the religious orders stymied any

President William McKinley watches as French ambassador Pierre Paul Cambon signs the Peace Protocol on behalf of Spain, ending the Spanish-American War in August 1898. (Library of Congress Prints and Photographs Division)

reform efforts. The criticism of Spanish rule in Cuba was thus extended to the Philippines.[18] The so-called Black Legend—identifying Spain with absolute monarchy, the Inquisition, and the cruelty of the New World conquest—was broadcast to an American public well acquainted with such stereotypes. Imperial Spain of the Counter-Reformation was said to persist in modern times; hence any Spanish colonial regime was synonymous with absolutist policies, military arbitrariness, religious intransigence, despotism, brutality, and corruption. Propagandists and their readers reasoned that the best thing to do was to take advantage of the war against Spain in Cuba to free the Filipinos from such a noxious regime.[19]

The propaganda campaign also included descriptions of and remedies for the Filipinos. It was necessary to justify the U.S. policy of choosing to ignore Filipino demands for independence by propagating images of savage and backward tribes characterized by a lack of political and social maturity. Filipinos were depicted as unschooled children, a people in need of a more mature nation to tutor them in the advantages of democratic institutions and to lead them down the road to eventual self-government following a period of guardianship.[20] And who better to fulfill that mission than the United States?

CONCLUSION: IMPERIAL TRANSITION IN THE PHILIPPINES

The imperial transition from Spain to the United States raises two key questions. Why did Spanish hegemony in the Philippines grow weak? Why did the Philippines undergo an imperial transition?

With respect to the first question, it must be noted that Spain's weakness as an imperial power stemmed from problems present in the metropolis. Nineteenth-century Spain was characterized by a succession of weak political regimes and a number of internally debilitating civil wars. Given chronic political instability and fiscal problems, statesmen did not devote the requisite attention to the Philippines nor did they direct enough investment into the islands. Moreover, Spain had insufficient economic resources to reform the colonial administration and also lacked a well-equipped navy and army. Its international influence was modest and its alliances with the great powers tenuous.[21] All these factors prevented Spain from carrying out ambitious reforms. On the most fundamental level, Spain, as noted elsewhere in this volume, lacked the attributes needed to possess a "successful" or effective empire: sufficient finance, effective administration, strong local and international alliances, and an advanced military.[22]

These problems were not only domestic. The Spanish colonial administration failed to evolve, modernize, and keep pace with changing circumstances. Imperial administrators never really understood the profound nature of the ways Filipino society was evolving during the century and proved incapable of integrating Filipinos into the colonial system. These failures were so manifest that Spaniards could not even satisfy minimal demands. During Spain's first constitutional convention, known as the Cortes de Cádiz (1809–13), held during the Napoleonic Wars, deputies were well aware of the problems in the colonies and engaged in discussions concerning the legal status of their inhabitants. At this point, Filipinos were still loyal to the colonial regime. By the end of the century, however, little progress had been made and the loyalty of Filipino elites had evaporated.

Changes in Philippine society itself were another factor. From an economic perspective, the interests of Filipino and Spanish metropolitan elites were at odds with one another. The growing export-oriented agricultural economy was not controlled by Spaniards. Since Spain was not the preferred market for Philippine exports, native economic elites and foreign traders and investors forged lasting relationships, creating obstacles for the plans of colonial administrators. From a political perspective, Philippine society was itself dynamic, producing leaders with coherent proposals that Spain ignored at its peril. Various groups called for a new political order, more rights, an end to inequality with peninsular Spaniards, greater access to economic opportunities, and greater power to decide on their own future. The failure of authorities to acknowledge these aspirations led Filipino nationalists first to rebel and later to commence a struggle for independence.

International developments were a final factor. As the great powers grew interested in Asia and the Pacific, Spain's position as a colonial administrator became suspect. With the British present in India, the French in Vietnam, and the Dutch in Indonesia—and given that neither Germany nor Japan was sufficiently strong to counter American ambitions—the United States was a logical choice as a successor empire to maintain a certain balance of power in Asia. It was then simply a matter of awaiting the right opportunity, and the chance came with the Spanish-American War.

All in all, these factors signaled an end of Spanish hegemony in the Philippines. Spain lacked the wherewithal to defend its empire against an external threat given the seriousness of its internal problems. Its statesmen and administrators were incapable of arriving at the solutions necessary for a successful colonial policy reflective of an organized metropolitan power. A widening and unsolvable political and economic rift developed with local elites who established foreign contacts and alliances outside of colonial rule. A dynamic Filipino nationalist movement dedicated to independence emerged. Spain faced the serious external threats of foreign penetration and outright American intervention while bereft of reliable allies. By the end of the nineteenth century, Spain had little chance of retaining its hold on the Philippines and was forced, ultimately by its military defeat in Cuba, to bring an end to a colonial relationship that had lasted more than three centuries.

The answer to the second question (why the Philippines underwent an imperial transition as opposed to taking the path to independence) is linked to international public opinion. Although it became clear that the colonial relationship between Spaniards and Filipinos would eventually have come to an end, the nature of this break was by no means a foregone conclusion. One possible outcome could have been an easing of the colonial relationship in a way that allowed Filipinos increased autonomy and eventual independence without foreign interference. However, it is here that international public opinion weighed heavily. In the absence of writings containing tales about the malevolence of Spanish rule, a different outcome might have been possible. However, any possibility that Spain and the Philippines might have developed a stable postcolonial relationship was seriously hindered by exaggerated images touted by a jingoistic American press and a U.S. administration seeking to justify its imperial ambitions in the Pacific. Spain had failed in its tutelary mission, hence a different tutor was needed.

The Broken Image

The Spanish Empire in the United States after 1898

CHRISTOPHER SCHMIDT-NOWARA

THE "SPLENDID LITTLE WAR" of 1898 engendered new attitudes toward overseas empire in the United States, some critical, others celebratory. One aspect of this ideological transformation was a reconsideration of the history of the Spanish empire. As Iván Jaksić, Richard Kagan, and Mike Wallace have demonstrated, there was a deep distrust of Spain dating back to colonial times. In the nineteenth century, American historians such as William Hickling Prescott and George Ticknor dwelled at length on Spain and its global empire to draw lessons about church and state, religious freedom, democracy, and free enterprise. In their view, imperial Spain was the antithesis of the United States; it was a global empire quickly undone by religious bigotry, monopoly, and despotism.[1]

While these updated versions of the Black Legend remained alive and well, victory and annexation also transformed perceptions of the Spanish empire. Americans went beyond trumpeting their victory over a longtime foe by appropriating the symbols, heroes, and history of the deposed empire and making them their own. Cortés, Coronado, and other conquistadores were not only banditti but also pioneers, the first Europeans to implant civilization in the New World, including the United States. In other words, after 1898, many Americans came to see Spain not as antithesis but as predecessor in the kind of "metamorphosis" emphasized by this volume's editors. Although Rome and Britain were unavoidable points of reference for the emerging imperial order, Spain also loomed large in the United States because of the annexation of Spanish colonies—Puerto Rico, the Philippines, and Guam—and because of the footprint, at times faint, that Spanish conquerors, priests, and settlers had left from Florida to California, places where the friar's robe and the soldier's helmet fit as comfortably as the Roman tunic.[2]

This essay will explore American acts of imitation and affiliation with the Spanish empire in the aftermath of the war with Spain and during the expansion of U.S. influence in the Caribbean, Pacific, and Central America. Drawing on archival records in Spain's Ministry of Foreign Affairs, the Royal Palace, and the personal archive of the prominent U.S. Hispanist Charles Fletcher Lummis, it will discuss how municipal governments, civic groups, and historians in the southwestern United States solicited Spanish participation in public acts that commemorated local origins in the Spanish imperial past. By examining the crafting of a historical lineage grounded in the Spanish conquests, this essay will argue that Americans sought to comprehend and justify imperial expansion by endowing it with a venerable past that demonstrated continuity, not rupture.

Prescott's Paradigm

In his magisterial introduction to the new collection on *Nueva York*, about the city's changing relationship with the Spanish-speaking world over the centuries, Mike Wallace summarizes the strong Dutch, British, and early American aversion to the fearsome, and later despised, imperial rival, Spain: "New York was an anti-Spanish city, its front door signposted, figuratively speaking, 'No Spaniards—or Catholics—Need apply.'"[3] Gotham's rejection and sense of difference was widely shared by U.S. elites in the nineteenth century, as several recent studies have shown. Richard Kagan has spoken of "Prescott's Paradigm" as a means of encapsulating such attitudes.[4] The reference is to William Hicking Prescott, the mid-nineteenth-century Bostonian who penned internationally applauded historical narratives of the reign of Ferdinand and Isabel and the conquests of Mexico and Peru. Though admiring in many ways, these histories also contrasted imperial Spain with the United States, as Prescott sought to spell out the failings of the former and the strengths of the latter. As Prescott and other U.S. Hispanists saw it, Spain had rocketed to global power between the late fifteenth and late sixteenth centuries but then succumbed just as quickly, undermined from within by absolutism, religious and intellectual intolerance, as well as a weak entrepreneurial spirit. They believed that their own country could avoid these pitfalls because of its religious freedom, constitutional government, and dynamic economy. These lessons and contrasts had remarkable staying power and resistance to empirical research in the nineteenth century, as Iván Jaksić has concluded in his authoritative study of U.S. Hispanism: "The assumptions about the Spanish empire proved to be resilient, and remained in place despite the massive documentation that was now standard and commonplace among American historians. In the court of history, Spain was declared guilty in absentia; no mitigating evidence was acceptable."[5]

These assumptions were telling because Americans in the mid–nineteenth century found themselves following in the footsteps of Hernán Cortés when the United States went to war with Mexico in 1846. Prescott's military friends reported to him the popularity of his *The Conquest of Mexico* among American soldiers and sailors.[6] Thus, while Prescott and other major Hispanists, like his close friend George Ticknor, the Harvard professor of Spanish literature, sought to inscribe difference in their histories of Spain, they nonetheless admitted, perhaps unintentionally, that there was a "broken image" of their own country in that of Spain and its former colonies as the United States confronted colonial legacies in North America and incorporated the territories of Spain and Mexico. Perhaps Spain was less different than they hoped.[7]

IMPERIAL TRANSITIONS AND LOCAL COMMEMORATIONS

The broken image of Spain and American empire became more coherent after 1898 as Americans reconsidered Spanish legacies in light of their country's resounding victory and subsequent overseas expansion into the Caribbean and Pacific colonies of the erstwhile antagonist. Many came to see Spain not as the eternal enemy but as the wellspring of U.S. global power. The first three decades of the twentieth century witnessed widespread commemorations of Spanish origins in the United States, not only in the cultural and financial capitals of the East Coast but also in those more marginal places once settled by Spaniards stretching from Florida to California, what Herbert Eugene Bolton dubbed the Spanish Borderlands.[8]

This appropriation is especially evident when seen from the perspective of the Spanish archives, as Spanish dignitaries received frequent pleas to take part in celebrations in places like Palm Springs, San Antonio, and Los Angeles. Immediately after 1898, hard feelings from the war influenced official Spanish attitudes. For example, in 1900, the Spanish representative in Washington sent a terse note to the mayor of Chicago, turning down his invitation to participate in festivities marking the second anniversary of the Battle of Manila, which he considered "an insult."[9] A few months later, however, the Spanish minister was in Chicago, hosted by the Grand Army of the Republic for its annual gathering. While he still expressed some reservations in his note to Madrid, he also commented on the apparent goodwill of the Americans: "My attendance at those festivities gave rise to repeated demonstrations of sympathy for Spain. In this occasion and on others I have observed that there is an effort here to make clear that any kind of resentment has passed and that they want to consider Spain as a country with which they maintain the most cordial relations."[10]

This surprising spirit of cooperation and kinship became the norm as Spanish diplomats figured prominently in numerous festivities in the years to come. These included a dinner hosted at the Gridiron Club in Washington during which the members reenacted the reception of Columbus by Ferdinand and Isabel for the benefit of their Spanish guest and the commemoration of Gaspar de Portolá's founding of San Francisco, for which the Spanish minister, the Marquis of Villalobar, made the cross-country train trip in 1909.[11]

Invitations and acts of homage continued to arrive from numerous groups and governments. The federal government bent over backward to lure Spanish participation in the opening of the Panama Canal in 1914, while San Francisco wined and dined Spanish officials, including the king's envoy, so that Spain would take a central role in the Panama-Pacific Exhibition of 1915 (both efforts failed). Florida, Texas, and Southern California also got in on the act. Alfonso XIII received tribute from Floridians traveling to Spain for the reburial of Pedro Menédez de Avilés, the first Spanish governor of Florida. He also received a plea to come to Palm Springs to preside over the laying of the cornerstone of a Catholic church modeled after the León cathedral and an invitation to take part in celebrations marking the founding of Saint Augustine. The Spanish minister in Washington, Juan Riaño, did travel to Palm Springs where he told the large crowd that the architecture and physical surroundings "make it difficult for me to realize that I am not in my native land."[12] In Texas, a Catholic organization asked Alfonso XIII to come to San Antonio for the bicentennial celebration, while President Rufus B. KleinSmid invited him to join in the fiftieth anniversary events of the University of Southern California.[13]

Events in Southern California during the celebrations of the Panama Canal reveal some Americans' new commitment to crafting and trumpeting Spanish origins.[14] When traveling as an unofficial representative to the 1915 San Francisco (Panama-Pacific International Exposition) and San Diego (Panama-California Exposition) fairs marking the opening of the Panama Canal, the Spanish consul based in San Francisco, the Count of Valle Sálazar, informed Madrid that the organizers and architects imitated Spanish architectural styles and used Spanish place-names. Local supporters also recalled their remote, even imaginary, Spanish antecedents, as he discovered when he was feted by a group called the Order of Panama, whose Anglo members greeted one another as "Compañero," possibly the only word of Spanish they knew. He also met the historian Charles Fletcher Lummis, who was beloved in Spain: "I had the pleasure of meeting Dr. Charles F. Lummis in San Diego. He is the author of various works of research related to the history of Spain in America, including the notable book 'The Spanish Pioneers' in which he eulogizes the immortal discoverers. He feels a profound veneration for our homeland."[15]

Lummis, a New Englander and Harvard man who took up journalism in Los Angeles in the 1880s, was a key figure in reviving the Spanish empire in the American Southwest. At the end of the nineteenth century, he established his fame as perhaps the leading North American scholar of the early Spanish empire. His particular emphasis was on the U.S. Southwest, although he also led archaeological expeditions to Central American and Peru, where he gathered pieces for the collection of Los Angeles's Southwest Museum. Among his early works was the study of the Spanish conquerors mentioned by the Spanish consul. The title of his book *The Spanish Pioneers* was significant as it linked Cortés, Coronado, and Oñate to the Anglo (or "Saxon-Americans" as Lummis called them) settlers of the American Southwest.[16] A similar connection was made in the 1920s by Bolton, who spoke of "Spanish pathfinders and pioneers."[17] Lummis's sketches of the contemporary Southwest were also influential in defining Spanish legacies at work in the United States, especially his accounts of northern New Mexico, which he portrayed as the most perfect embodiment of Spanish colonial culture.[18]

The Spanish expatriate J. C. Cebrián, who lived for many years in San Francisco, promoted the translation and republication of *The Spanish Pioneers* in Spain. The 1916 edition was graced with an introduction by the leading Spanish historian of the era, Rafael Altamira, an ardent champion of renewed ties between Spain and the Americas after the debacle of 1898. For the Spanish public, Altamira made explicit what was latent in Lummis's account: that the North Americans of his day were the new conquistadores, spiritual descendants of the Spaniards of the sixteenth century. The Americans admired the Spaniards because, like them, they overcame great physical suffering and demonstrated courage and heroism in their westward expansion and settlement: "[T]hese qualities of the Yankee people (*pueblo yanki*) . . . are the very ones that shone so brightly in our own 'Discoverers' and 'Conquerors.' The North American admiration for us is thus legitimate."[19]

Lummis promoted this act of affiliation in his collaboration with the compañeros of the Order of Panama. Founded to promote San Diego's role in the celebration of the Panama Canal opening, the order also dedicated itself to erecting monuments that linked the city to major currents of world history. These monuments included one to Juan Rodríguez Cabrillo, the first European to land in what became San Diego in 1542, and to the friar Junípero Serrá, who established the California missions in the eighteenth century. The compañeros of the order were businessmen; the company letterhead of one of the founders, the wealthy real estate developer D. C. Collier, read "Profit Follows the Flag." For history, they sought out Lummis. In 1913, a member of the order asked him to provide the historical justification for its proposed Cabrillo monument.

> To this end would you not furnish as early as convenient,
>   a. A brief romantic narrative of Cabrillo;
>   b. Historical outline of the discovery of California;
>   c. Why Pt. Loma is a fitting site for such a monument;
>   d. International reasons for such a project.
> Now, dear Mr. Lummis, we realize this is asking a great deal of you, but we realize that you are the most fit man to outline such a proposition for the Pacific coast, and besides we will repay your kindness in many ways if you will but favor us with a visit so that we may confer the Honorary degree in the Order of Panama

which was unanimously voted you some time ago. You will find this one of the most enthusiastic organizations in America, the purposes of which are constantly broadening, and it is our sincere opinion that it will become of international fame ere long.[20]

Lummis commended the order on its selection of a fitting name and for gesturing to the Spanish past. However, he urged on the order a new nomenclature, which, after consideration, he borrowed from the imperial councils of Charles V. In the *Recopilación de las Leyes de Indias* he found the decree by which the emperor created the Consejo Real de Indias. He sent a translated copy to San Diego and explained why this council was so appropriate a model: it was established in 1542, the same year as Cabrillo's landing; it enjoyed supreme authority over the Indies; and, as a secular, governing body, its nomenclature, which he carefully broke down, was more fitting than terms borrowed from the Spanish military or church.[21]

The Order of Panama met Lummis's recommendations with enthusiasm, adopting as its own the titles and structure of the Consejo Real de Indias. Its highest officers, on Lummis's prompting, called themselves collectively "hidalgos." Lummis's promotion of the Spanish imperial past pleased not just the boosters of San Diego. In 1915, the Spanish monarchy bestowed on him its highest honor for foreigners; he was made a Knight Commander of the Royal Order of Isabel la Católica.[22]

The Broken Image Made Whole

What do the Order of Panama and the Hispanism of Lummis tell us about the eclipse of Spain's empire and the ascent of America's? They show that an imperial metamorphosis was under way in the United States. After 1898 the Spanish legacies in the United States, even if vestigial at best, as in San Diego, provided local boosters with the language of global empire. The compañeros of the Order of Panama were concerned with making San Diego into a tourist destination, restoring order during a period of civil strife (both in the city and across the border in Mexico), developing real estate, and celebrating the global prominence of their city and state.[23] The Spanish imperial past—embodied in Cabrillo, Serrá, and, through Lummis's flight of fancy, the Council of the Indies—offered the materials for representing this simultaneously global and local present. Moreover, the enthusiastic appropriation of Spanish history by the Order of Panama, and other groups like it in the one-time Spanish Borderlands, indicates that Americans were carrying out the ideological work of empire far beyond the elite circles of Washington and New York or the military bases around the Pacific and Caribbean. Empire was indeed becoming a way of life as the broken image of Spain became whole in the early twentieth century.

Lummis was no less of a booster and hustler than were the Babbitt-like businessmen in the Order of Panama, but as a newspaperman, writer, collector, and historian he was less concerned than they with markets and zoning boundaries. Nonetheless, like the Order of Panama, Lummis explicitly linked the history of the United States to the Spanish imperial past, a historical vision that differed from that sketched by Prescott and others in the nineteenth century, even though they at times implied some connection given the reach of U.S. power in the Hispanic world even before 1898. Lummis, a friend of Theodore Roosevelt, was keenly aware that the United States' new global reach, from his own Southwest to the Caribbean and the Pacific, was built on the ruins of the Spanish colonial world that he travestied for the Order of Panama. For North Americans in the twentieth century, Spain had become more than the historical opponent whose function was to provide negative lessons on the fate of religiously inspired empires. It was now also the predecessor and model for a new breed of conquistadores, entrepreneurs, and missionaries.

PART 4

BRITISH GLOBAL DOMINION
AND DECLINE

Lieutenant William Alexander Kerr of the Twenty-Fourth [Bombay] Regiment Native Infantry winning the Victoria Cross during the Indian Mutiny against British rule, July 1857. (National Army Museum, United Kingdom)

Information and Intelligence in the Mid-Nineteenth-Century Crisis in the British Empire

TONY BALLANTYNE

PRODUCING, CONTROLLING, AND ORDERING knowledge was at the heart of British colonialism during the nineteenth century. Recent scholarship on Britain's Victorian empire has suggested that colonial knowledge was central in enabling, justifying, and naturalizing British empire building.[1] While these cultural readings of Britain's global reach have illuminated how colonial discourses produced and reshaped various forms of cultural difference, they have been less successful in tracing the connections between discourse and practice. This essay attempts to reconnect a cultural reading of British colonialism with a careful consideration of the place of communication in the empire's political economy. In particular, it seeks to explore some key questions about the role of knowledge and communication in enabling the assertion of British colonial authority. What was the significance of information in rebellions against British rule? What role did intelligence gathering and information flows play in the suppression of these revolts? And what strategies allowed colonial states to reassert their paramountcy? These are important questions for historians who seek to understand the significances of the long sequence of uprisings, rebellions, and wars that shook the British Empire in the middle of the nineteenth century. This essay focuses particularly on the Indian rebellion (1857–58) and the New Zealand wars (1860–72), using these two sustained struggles, both deep-rooted rebellions that dismantled British sovereignty for extended periods, to examine the ability of imperial systems to reinvent themselves during and after times of crisis.

This crisis that shook the mid-Victorian British Empire reminds us that the management of cross-cultural engagements was central to the rise and fall of *all* empires. More specifically, the British preoccupation with the "native mind"— which required an understanding of language, culture, and history—charted in this essay can be productively read against the almost antithetical strategies at the heart of U.S. empire building, outlined in Alfred W. McCoy's examination of American imperial data management and information infrastructure in this volume.

The key starting point for such analysis is C. A. Bayly's landmark study of intelligence gathering and social communication in colonial India, *Empire and Information.* He suggested that the transformation of the British East India Company into a colonial power was dependent on the ability of its agents to access and reshape the complex forms of social communication that had developed in the courts and bazaars of Mughal north India. As colonial rule matured and the political terrain of both India and Britain shifted, the company increasingly attempted to "improve" Indian knowledge traditions, foster new forms of Western learning in India, and engage scribal experts and traditional authorities in debate over the nature of knowledge. These innovations, Bayly suggested, were reworked by various Indian scholars and social groupings, and the massive uprising against British rule in 1857–58 laid bare the gap that had developed between the colonial state and its subjects.[2]

This essay not only explores these connections between knowledge and authority, but it also reflects on the place of such communication within the broader cultural landscape of empire. One of the key concerns of the "new imperial history" has been the ways in which cultural difference encoded the political order, what Partha Chatterjee famously termed the "rule of colonial difference."[3] Much recent work on the British Empire has suggested that race came to occupy a central position in imperial politics and culture in the middle of the nineteenth century, as colonial officials, the military, and expatriates reacted to a sequence of colonial crises by asserting the primacy of racial hierarchies in explaining both the imperial order and the nature of colonized peoples.[4] The ascendancy of race has also been posited in intellectual histories of the Victorian era that have also emphasized the centrality of biological race in ordering both scientific and popular British views of the world in the wake of the colonial conflicts of the 1850s and 1860s.[5] This interpretation has been refreshed by more recent work by postcolonial scholars like Robert Young, who have asserted that heated mid-nineteenth-century debates over race and hybridity were fed by the pressures of colonial authority and events like the "Mutiny" in India.[6]

The first part of this essay examines the connections between colonial information systems and the eruption of armed anticolonial struggles, followed by a brief assessment of the place of intelligence gathering and knowledge control in the suppression of rebellions in both India and New Zealand. I then sketch the ways in which new colonial knowledge orders were elaborated as colonial authority was reconstructed. The essay concludes with some broader reflections, highlighting the persistence of colonial "information panics" and the ways in which "religion" in fact stood near the heart of anticolonial rebellion and the efforts of colonial officials to know the "native mind."

CULTURAL KNOWLEDGE AND DOMINANCE IN INDIA

What was the connection between the colonial information order and the rebellion against British rule in India during the Mutiny of 1857–58? Essentially, Bayly's thesis is that the growing distance between the colonial rulers and Indian society created a set of cultural barriers that restricted flows of knowledge to state functionaries, allowing social space in which rebellion could develop. The rebellion itself brought together disparate elements of the social order—mutinous sepoys, dispossessed elites, disgruntled urban artisans, caste Hindus anxious about company policy, and Wahhabi-inspired jihadis—into a common struggle galvanized by the mobilizing power of religious idioms, dreams of millenarian renewal, and a series of inchoate patriotisms.

If we are to understand how the colonial information order enabled the insurrection to take hold and assess its role in shaping the British response, we need to briefly map the development of that order. Following its assumption of responsibilities of governance as the *diwan* (the authority responsible for the collection of taxation revenue) of Bengal, Bihar, and Orissa in 1765, the British East India Company worked hard to clothe its authority in the institutions and conventions of Mughal rule.[7] As its power was consolidated and extended, the company drew on some of the complex knowledge systems that had underwritten Mughal authority, which it used to maximize revenue flows, monitor the movements of its rivals, and secure the stability of the economic and social order. Wherever possible, the British inserted themselves into local knowledge networks, attempting to turn local spies and runners to their service, and drawing on the complex system of political information produced through the offices of *akhbar nawis* (news writers installed at courts).[8] Before 1800, the company was also able to access some significant reservoirs of "affective knowledge" through the intimate relationships that many company officials and military figures established with Indian women. These dried up, however, as a consequence of the legal and social pressures arising from a new rhetoric of imperial loyalty and racial superiority that took root in the 1790s.[9] As this affective knowledge was lost, company officials produced a new body of empirical colonial knowledge about contemporary social and economic organization, as well as about influential textual and historical traditions.[10] Company officials placed less trust in the human intelligence they gleaned from local runners, policemen, and informants as they placed growing emphasis on the value of direct observation, the surveillance of the output of vernacular presses, and the power of statistics to represent the society they ruled over.[11] At the same time, the state worked hard to police knowledge flows by restricting the flow of both strategic information and "opinion" *out* of the military establishment and bureaucracy.[12]

While these reorientations in colonial knowledge distanced the East India Company's state from Indian communities within its dominion, they are insufficient

as an explanation for the outbreak of the Mutiny in May 1857 or its development into a large-scale rebellion. The immediate cause of the Mutiny lay in the
changing conditions of service in the company's Bengal army, but there was also
widespread disaffection with colonial rule, which enabled the sepoys to form
connections with a range of other groups. Key factors here were the aggressive
territorial expansion of the company (made clear in the conquest of Punjab and
the annexation of Awadh) and its willingness to interfere in "domestic" matters
such as marriage law, which produced a growing sense that the company was
intent on the propagation of Christianity. In the midst of swirling rumors and in
the wake of several small mutinies, the Third Bengal Light Cavalry, stationed at
Meerut, mutinied on May 10, 1857. This was the catalyst for a large-scale uprising. The soldiers were quickly joined by Indian sepoys from the Eleventh Bengal
Native Infantry and various bazaar *goondas* (ruffians) who marched to Delhi and
took control of the old Mughal capital. News of this success spread swiftly, triggering uprisings across the Gangetic Valley and drawing significant numbers of
men from across South Asia to Delhi.[13] The rebels themselves looked for support
over long distances, sending emissaries to Persia and Russia.[14] Given the depth
and range of the revolt, it took the British until June 1858 to reassert their authority over North India.

As company forces attempted to reestablish control, a heated interpretative
battle broke out over the nature of the rebellion. Was it merely a military mutiny?
Was it the product of a conspiracy? Had Muslims planned and coordinated the
uprising? Was it essentially a protest against Christianization by disgruntled
Brahman? Many of these arguments underlined the gap in knowledge and sentiment that separated the company from Indian society. Some argued that this gap
was the product of British attempts to reform and civilize India, while others
suggested that this chasm could only be bridged by the Christianization of Indian
society. But it was clear to most British that the rebellion represented a failure to
understand the native mind.

In the wake of the rebellion, the administrator and historian Sir John Kaye
reflected, "We know little of Native Indian society beyond its merest externals,
the colour of the people's skins, the form of their garments, the outer aspects of
their houses." While the British could sense the power of indigenous connections
and communication, Kaye suggested they were outside these networks and their
authority was therefore precarious, writing that "there is a certain description of
news, which travels from one station to another with a rapidity almost electric."[15]
Kaye's stress on the company's failure to infiltrate local networks must be placed
alongside the substantial evidence suggesting that a complex mix of economic,
social, political, and religious factors set the tinder that the mutiny at Meerut
ignited. But the inability of the British to either foresee the likelihood of large-scale
civil rebellion or interpret the religious idioms that fueled much of the disaffection

meant that the company's establishment was blindsided by the revolt. Not knowing the native mind almost cost Britain its control over India.

War in New Zealand

Given the important ways in which precolonial knowledge experts and traditions shaped the colonial order, it is hardly surprising that colonial knowledge took a different shape in New Zealand.[16] The commonality of *te reo Maori* as a shared language and the fundamental cultural continuities between tribes meant that colonial officials in New Zealand were not confronted by the range of complexities that characterized South Asia's polyglot cultures, profound regional variations, and highly variegated social organization. The smaller scale of both Maori and colonial society in New Zealand meant that high-ranking colonial administrators and Maori leaders were in frequent and direct contact, whereas in South Asia the state's bureaucratic machinery was increasingly complex and relationships with indigenous states were mediated by the more complicated processes and institutions of the colonial state.

In New Zealand during the 1850s, the pressing question was how the state should enact its authority, especially in the central North Island where over five-sixths of the land remained in Maori hands. Here colonists were hemmed in on coastal bridgeheads, and both civil authorities and military leaders had very limited knowledge of the wooded and hilly interior. In the mid-1850s, colonists placed increased pressure on the governor to apply British law in "Maori districts" even though section 71 of the 1852 Constitution Act allowed for the governor to identify specific districts where Maori practices and customs could be maintained. Governor George Grey appointed resident magistrates to oversee the implementation of British law in several parts of the North Island and his successor, Governor Gore Browne, reluctantly followed this path, appointing F. D. Fenton to act as a traveling magistrate in Waikato. Fenton's presence in the Waikato area evoked considerable hostility and was an important catalyst for the proclamation of Potatau Te Wherowhero as the Maori "king" in 1857.[17] This pantribal Kingitanga (King Movement) attempted to maintain control of Maori-owned land and assert the authority of a king elected from a confederation of North Island tribes. The hope of the movement was that this king would be able to stand on equal footing with the Queen of England.

Many colonial politicians argued that the governor's weakness had allowed the emergence of Kingitanga, which they saw as a serious challenge to the sovereignty of the Crown. For Governor Browne, Kingitanga reflected the larger reality that British law continued to hold little sway in Maori-dominated districts where it was, he reflected in 1860, a "dead letter."[18] By that stage he felt that Maori challenges to the sovereignty of the governor and Crown could no longer be tolerated. Browne hoped that a single "sharp lesson" from the army would crush resistance to the Crown's sovereignty, but armed intervention in 1860 triggered a thirteen-year sequence of conflicts, campaigns, and insurrections through the central North Island.[19] The resulting wars in Taranaki (1860–61, 1863–66) and Waikato (1863–64), the search for Kereopa (1865–71), and the campaigns against the prophets Titokowaru (1868–69) and Te Kooti (1868–72) reflected the colonial state's commitment to crushing any explicit challenge to its authority.

But the path to the actual outbreak of war in 1860 was quite slow, unlike the eruption of the rebellion in India. During the 1850s the governor and his agents engaged with Maori leaders on a sustained basis. Meetings, conferences, the exchange of letters, Maori-language newspapers, and communication through missionaries and the Anglican church brought tribal chiefs, influential leaders in the native church, and key figures in Kingitanga into dialogue with the state. But by the end of 1850s it seemed that these engagements were unable to direct Maori thought and action.[20] Channels of cross-cultural communication were attenuated when Browne resolved to go to war in Taranaki in 1860. This closed off some important church and humanitarian networks that could have provided the state with detailed information on indigenous sentiment.[21] Kingitanga leaders also limited communication and the free flow of people, goods, and information. They refused to open their lands to road building in 1861. Without these routes it was very difficult to move large numbers of soldiers and artillery into the Waikato, and this effectively delayed the state's invasion of the region by six months. Kingitanga also imposed an *aukati* (boundary line) to separate the king's lands from those areas where the writ of colonial law was recognized. Even after the conclusion of the Waikato war, this was maintained with the aim of preventing military raids, controlling colonists entering the king's domain, stopping the flow of goods, and preventing the construction of public works schemes. This was forcefully policed: colonists who transgressed the *aukati* without permission were liable to be killed.[22]

Despite this understandable assertion of Maori authority, colonial officials and newspapers generally saw Kingitanga as a threat to their sovereignty, a movement whose aims and language were both comprehensible and a fundamental challenge to the colonial project.[23] Not only were the language and symbols of Kingitanga clearly Christian, but it was also possible to communicate with Kingitanga leaders directly or through church figures such as the Anglican bishop George Selwyn. Conversely, the prophet-warriors who led their followers into guerrilla campaigns against the state—such as Kereopa, Te Kooti, or Titokowaru— were much more difficult for the state to engage. To colonial officials their teachings were garbled and cryptic, they were excessive and fanatical, they disappeared into the bush and hills, and they made their homes beyond the reach of colonial power. They did not attend conferences with the governor, they did not communicate in any regular way, and their blend of religion and violence was a potent threat to the colonial order. For many colonists their actions were a reenactment of the worst atrocities of the rebellion in India. In 1869, for example, Sir Edward Stafford, a colonial politician renowned for his moderate pragmatism, suggested that in Te Kooti's actions "[e]very atrocity of the Sepoy rebellion had been paralleled and outdone in the raids, burnings, violations, tortures and cannibalism of the last nine months in New Zealand, and with less provocation or excuse."[24]

COLONIAL KNOWLEDGE AND PACIFICATION

How were these anticolonial movements suppressed? In India, the pacification of the revolt was only possible because it remained contained to central portions of North India. The Bombay Presidency in the west and the Madras Presidency in the south remained calm, as did key princely states such as Kashmir, Hyderabad, and Mysore. Most important, in Punjab powerful Sikh princes supported the company and the company also mobilized large numbers of Punjabi troops, in part by stoking their animosity toward the rebellious sepoys from the plains and Bengal. Pacification was also made easier because the rebels never succeeded in clearing all local opponents and British functionaries from the lands over which they asserted dominance. There was no equivalent to an *aukati* (boundary), and this meant that in key locations, such as the area just to the west of Delhi, the British were able to hold on to some strategic positions and military capacity.[25] Even though ideas about restoring the old Mughal order had wide currency, the leaders of the various strands of rebellion struggled to develop any coherent and cohesive ideology once they had succeeded in gaining control of key cities and military outposts.[26] Their inability to either restore a functioning re-creation of Mughal governance or articulate another unifying vision of the political future alienated support. Rebel leaders also struggled to maintain communication lines, secure reliable food supplies, provide sufficient powder and weapons, and ensure that basic needs, such as sanitation, were maintained in areas under their control, undercutting popular support and eroding the morale of rebel forces. These logistical failures were one important context for the increased flow of information to the British, as spies and informants gave British officers information about the state of rebel forces that proved valuable in the planning of counterattacks against sepoys weakened by hunger and desertion. The company was also greatly assisted by its fledgling telegraph network: even though only a limited number of trunk lines were in operation, they allowed intelligence to be transmitted at great speed and enabled the coordination of the British pacification campaign. The broader resources of the imperial system were also significant: an expeditionary force en route to China was quickly diverted to India; and colonial governors, especially George Grey in the Cape Colony, pledged resources to enable of reassertion of British paramountcy.[27]

The key feature of the suppression of the revolt in India was the unrestrained retribution visited on sepoys and their supporters by the company's armies.

While many rebel soldiers and their peasant supporters were killed in combat, tens of thousands of others were subject to summary execution—hung, shot, or blown to pieces by cannons—in a relentless display of military power and imperial rage. In this campaign detailed information about the actions and loyalties of suspected rebels was seen as being of little value: there was to be no time for legal hearings and weighing evidence. Judgment was swift, and punishment was brutal and final.

The rebellion was not only crushed by the massive and often indiscriminate deployment of state-sanctioned violence, but it was also pacified through the penal system. The old Mughal emperor Bahadur Shah, who had been restored as the figurehead of the uprising, was found guilty of treason by a military commission and exiled to Rangoon where he died in 1862; twenty-six members of his family had been executed by that stage, and another thirteen were imprisoned in Agra. This excision of the Mughal royal family could not be simply justified on the grounds of its role in the rebellion but instead was motivated by the desire to smash the symbolic freight of the emperorship.[28] Bahadur Shah was not the only exile: the chief destination for exiled rebels was the Andaman Islands, which the British swiftly converted into a penal colony. The transportation of the convicted mutineers and rebels effectively expelled them permanently from the Indian body politic, a strategy that was designed to minimize potential disruption to colonial authority in the future while also placing these rank-and-file insurgents in an environment where they could be reformed in isolation far from political "agitators."[29]

The pacification of Maori antistate movements was less explosive and vehement. Whereas in India colonial forces were confronting concentrations of rebels in the towns of the Gangetic Plain, in New Zealand the foe was smaller, more nimble, and aided by its superior knowledge of a complex and difficult topography of broken hill chains and dense bush. The state relied on three key strategies to overcome these challenges. The first was, of course, military suppression. James Belich's work had detailed the difficulties of this process, demonstrating that Kingitanga soldiers and bands of fighting men attached to warrior-prophets were difficult opponents for the state to overcome. In some significant engagements, strategic innovations and deep knowledge of the terrain allowed Maori forces to outthink and outfight British and colonial troops.[30] Some conflicts were inconclusive, and some others resulted in victories for the state forces that were symbolic rather than substantive. The first war in Taranaki ultimately ended in a stalemate. While the invasion of the Waikato opened up some land for colonial settlement, this was more the consequence of punitive legislation than military action, as General Duncan Cameron was unable to deliver a "decisive blow" on the battlefield. Later efforts to capture the warrior-prophets Kereopa, Te Kooti, and Titokowaru proved to be frustrating. Kereopa was only placed in custody when his Tuhoe protectors gave him up, and Te Kooti proved even more elusive. State forces did not capture him, and ultimately, in 1883, he made a public pledge of peace and in return received a pardon from the native minister. Titokowaru's ability as a military leader and his fearsome reputation were such that the areas of Taranaki he controlled in the 1870s were essentially autonomous. He was finally captured in 1881 but spent only eight months in prison.

In executing these campaigns the state was heavily reliant on Maori knowl- edge and military resources. Even though British governors drew on contingents of troops from Australia, India, and Britain, Maori assistance was more impor- tant as it allowed state soldiers to be deployed with greater precision. By 1863 it was clear that weakness in the communication systems supporting colonial forces was hampering the ability of the army to locate, engage, and defeat rebel forces.[31] The value of local knowledge was made clear in 1864, when colonial forces cap- tured the key Kingitanga fortification at Rangiaowhia. This success was largely due to two mixed-race guides, James Edwards and John Gage, who had lived in the region before the war and furnished General Cameron with information that enabled the colonial army to outflank the defenses of the Kingitanga army and capture the pivotal element in the Paterangi line of fortifications.[32]

In later campaigns a range of Maori groups that the state saw as "loyalists" or "Queenites" supported the colonial forces. In fact, as Monty Soutar has shown, these groups were primarily acting within tribal or subtribal interests. Some Ngati Porou *hapu* (subtribal groups), for example, fought alongside state forces against the followers of the prophet Te Ua, a powerful threat to tribal autonomy.[33] The assistance of such groups allowed the state to quickly access rich pools of knowl- edge about the landscape, as well as the genealogical connections and political dispositions of the groups that supported the prophets. Even when only a small number of Maori were prepared into enter battle alongside colonial soldiers, significant flows of intelligence and rumors came to the government and mili- tary units from chiefs sympathetic to the Crown's goals.[34] Conversely, prophet- warriors like Te Kooti strove to restrict information flows. One of his first acts after assuming the mantle of leadership was to order the drowning of his uncle Te Warihi whom he suspected of being a spy and informant.[35]

The state's drive to suppress rebellion also rested on the use of land confisca- tions as a punitive weapon against communities that had resisted the queen's sovereignty. Under the terms of the New Zealand Settlements Act (1863), "rebel tribes" in Taranaki, Waikato, and the Bay of Plenty had large swathes of their land confiscated (*raupatu*). This law was the basis for an increasingly expansive legal apparatus that effectively allowed the state to undercut the territorial foun- dations and economic base of many Maori communities. Colonists saw *raupatu* as justified by British precedents, especially its historical use in Scotland, in the confiscations that underwrote the English plantations in Ireland, and in East

India Company policies in India.[36] Of course, *raupatu* also enabled the rapid extension of colonization through the extension of white settlement, which ultimately proved to be the most powerful engine for securing colonial domination.

A purging of the body politic through the legal and penal systems was also central to the suppression of the rebellion. State powers were amplified through the Suppression of Rebellion Act (1863), which extended the powers of the governor, suspended habeas corpus, and established Courts Martial, which were empowered to pass death sentences and sentences of penal servitude. Harsh punishments were frequently handed down to rebels during the 1860s, but in comparative terms the death penalty was not applied broadly, even though Kereopa was executed for the murder of the missionary Carl Sylvius Völkner.[37] A more important component of the judicial pacification was the sentencing of prisoners to locations distant from the seat of insurrection. From the late 1860s, some Waikato and Taranaki Maori were sent to serve their sentences in the southern city of Dunedin. But the most important site for this penal exile was the Chatham Islands, five hundred miles off the east coast of the South Island. Groups of prisoners were sent there in the mid-1860s, including Te Kooti (after his second arrest for allegedly being a Hauhau spy). Te Kooti's incarceration, however, was a spectacular failure. It was during his exile that he first received revelations from the "Spirit of God." Assuming the mantle of prophethood, he led the daring escape of 298 prisoners onboard the *Rifleman*. Within two weeks of his return to the North Island, Te Kooti defeated colonial forces at Paparatu, confirming his distinctive mix of military prowess and prophetic foresight.

In both colonies, pacification and reconstruction shaded into each other. But it is important to note that there were significant commonalities in the longer-term project of reconstructing colonial governance in New Zealand and India. Most important, new efforts were made to incorporate local populations into the functioning of the state and to build "loyalty." The Government of India Act (1858) formally transferred the East India Company's authority in India to the British Crown. A new department was created in the British government, the India Office, to ensure metropolitan oversight of India. Much greater emphasis was placed on the role of the Crown in governance: key proclamations were issued in Queen Victoria's name, and new stress was placed on her personal investment in India. On the ground in the colony, a program of government reform was launched. This had two key elements: first, prerebellion policies of westernization were abandoned; and second, the state incorporated larger numbers of South Asians into its service and some low-level places were opened up for Indians in the machinery of local government. These moves were designed to reconcile important social constituencies to colonial rule, to give the state some new mechanisms through which to shape native opinion, and to create a safety valve for Indian political aspirations. The military was also reorganized, with recruitment increasingly redirected to Nepal and especially Punjab. The rapid Punjabization of the army from the 1860s on reflected the points of recognition that Britons were able to identity in Punjabi and especially Sikh culture, but it also reflected the widespread belief that the loyalty of the Sikhs had "saved" British India.[38] This military reorganization created an important template for imperial security: Sikh soldiers and policemen served extensively outside India and became an important embodiment of imperial power.[39] Finally, the new Crown Raj sought to shore up its connections with important traditional magnates and maharajas even as it used various forms of indirect influence to encourage the princely states to adapt to some of the conventions of the "modern" order.[40]

In New Zealand, the state sought to fashion similar connections to reanchor its authority. The Maori Representation Act (1867) allowed for the creation of four seats reserved for Maori voters to elect Maori representatives to Parliament. All Maori men over the age of twenty-one were enfranchised with the exception of those who had been charged or convicted for "any treason felony or infamous offence."[41] Early Maori members of the House of Representatives were usually chiefs who had supported the state during the war, and the act was thus an important mechanism for cementing ties between the state and its Maori allies.[42] At the same time, it ruptured the separation of Maori and settler politics. "Native affairs" were no longer the domain of the governor and his "protectors of aborigines": Maori now had the ability to directly contest and shape legislation.[43]

Just as the waging of war drove the emergence of centralized states in Europe during the long eighteenth century, the wars of the 1860s were also an important impetus toward the centralization of power in New Zealand.[44] In 1870, the colonial treasurer, Julius Vogel, launched an ambitious new program of state-driven development. His plan for government-assisted migration fundamentally transformed the demographic, economic, and political face of New Zealand. Of course, large flows of assisted migrants fundamentally recalibrated the relationships between Maori and colonists; these state-sponsored colonists joined with various other migratory flows to effectively "swamp" the Maori.[45] Demography became a key buttress of state dominance.

The other plank of Vogel's developmental scheme—roads and railways— echoed post-1857 initiatives in India. In both contexts, transportation and communication were seen as vital to the improvement of the economy. But more extensive and better-quality networks also would allow the state to move resources and troops more efficiently if rebellion were to recur. In New Zealand, new roads allowed white settlement to be extended into areas previously controlled by Maori, and there was hope that these routes, together with the pull of the market, would help to lace Maori more firmly into colonial life. In India, the Crown Raj rapidly extended the telegraph network from the late 1850s on.

The British invested heavily in the railway network as well, and it was rapidly extended in the 1860s and 1870s; it functioned as the "hard backbone" of the Crown Raj, shaping the organization of military resources and standing as a potent symbol of British power.[46]

CONCLUSION

In sketching these processes of imperial reconstruction, this essay has traversed a range of dynamics that have little direct connection to colonial knowledge. This has been a deliberate strategy to produce a contextualized reading of the place of information and opinion in the creation of colonial authority. Recent work has tended to either treat colonial knowledge as an independent variable or reduce state functions to the creation and policing of knowledge flows. But in the British Empire information is best thought of as a prominent and recurring thread within the larger fabric of these reconstructed colonial political economies: it cannot alone explain the nature of colonial rule, but the pattern of that rule cannot be comprehended with recognizing its prominence.

While the cluster of rebellions and small wars in the middle decades of the nineteenth century undoubtedly constituted a very real crisis for the empire, resistance, mutiny, and rebellion were constant parts of colonialism. In New Zealand, of course, there had been open war in the 1840s, as well as a later series of minor prophetic leaders who openly challenged the legitimacy of colonial rule. During the first half of the nineteenth century, riots, small-scale rebellions, and warfare molded the extension of the company's territorial sovereignty in South Asia. These were central in giving shape to the state and the limits of its power. Against this backdrop, it is best to see these larger conflicts as broader and more deeply rooted manifestations of the open contestation central to the birth of these colonial orders. This is an important point to underline in the context of British imperial historiography as it frequently offers a kind of steady, gradualist, and even teleological narrative of "imperial expansion." Here we can perhaps to begin to see one of the very significant features of colonial knowledge production: it did not simply solidify colonial dominance through enumeration and the hardening of cultural categories, but rather it was an element that was integral to a range of practices that secured and reproduced the dominance of the state. More than abstract ideology, the processes of war making, pacification, and counterinsurgency defined the contours of the colonial state.

What is actually discernible in the 1860s and 1870s is not so much simple racialization, but rather a deepening and broadening preoccupation with difference. While the new biology inserted a potent series of arguments into debates over human variation, these ideas were jostled by and interacted with a host of other explanatory schema and interpretative preoccupations. Rank, class, nationality, religion, ethnicity, language, and economic systems were all identified as important ways of accessing the nature of human variation and explaining historical development. Even as particular scholars and disciplinary traditions prioritized specific categories of difference, these variables rarely emerged as discreet and entirely self-contained: religion might be racialized, language could be seen as a guide to racial history, or economic systems were thought to be the product of religious values. Each endeavor was, however, deeply concerned with explaining difference, a project that seemed more urgent than ever as a consequence of these attempts of colonized peoples to throw off British rule.

These conflicts, I have suggested, raised the problem of the "native mind," a term that was imperial shorthand for the content of the intellectual traditions of the colonized, their religious movements, the idioms through which their ideas were articulated, and indigenous processes of communication. In both India and New Zealand, the native mind was a discursive product of colonial anxieties about the limits of British understandings of local knowledge traditions. In both contexts, Indian and Maori, newspaper stories, political debate, and ethnographic texts produced an image of the native mind that was deeply contradictory. While it was the most important gateway to colonial improvement, Western cultural forces found it generally impenetrable. At the same time, colonists believed the vernacular press, popular rumors, and native gossip easily swayed native opinion. But even if it was fickle, and thus quickly influenced by snatches of conversation, its patterns and preoccupations were believed to be deeply ingrained. Most important, the native mind was understood to be prone to superstition and excesses of religious enthusiasm; in its unimproved form it was not disciplined or rational.

This is why the colonial "information panics"—moments of crisis in which imperial officials worried about the depth, quality, and accuracy of the knowledge they possessed about the colonized—were so often focused on native religious movements during the final third of the nineteenth century. These panics, whether they were over the threat that *sadhus* (religious mendicants) posed to civil society in British India or the teachings of Maori prophetic leaders, remind us that crisis was a persistent and integral feature of the colonial order. Although apologists for empire, in the Victorian period and today, frequently suggested that imperial intrusion could transform turbulent frontiers, create political stability, and enable progressive reform, modern colonialism has consistently precipitated and fed on conflict. Insurgencies, rebellions, and wars certainly challenged imperial authority, but they also were engines that propelled the growth of colonial states, energized the creation of new regimes of surveillance and control, and frequently resulted in the emergence of more durable and potent forms of colonial authority.

The Fin de Siècles of Great Britain and the United States

Comparing Two Declining Phases of Global Capitalist Hegemony

KELVIN SANTIAGO-VALLES

FOLLOWING THE THEMATIC AGENDA of this volume's introduction, the present essay strives to rise above the narrative details of a single empire to instead identify the general features of imperial decline and global governance, albeit within the capitalist world-system. Yet in critical dialogue with most of the other essays in this collection, I argue that core (imperialist) countries—regardless of their direct participation in military expansionism and formal colonialism—develop by exploiting and dominating peripheral peoples. Imperialism is an inherent attribute of the capitalist world-order: it is a constitutive feature of a globally unequal interstate system. Rather than seeing imperial decline as synonymous with formal decolonization, for me global leadership among all the imperialist states has shifted cyclically via the rise and fall of various hegemons.[1] Their decline begins, says Arrighi, with a hegemonic crisis through "the intensification of interstate and inter-enterprise competition; the escalation of social conflicts; and the interstitial emergence of new configurations of power." The ensuing hegemonic breakdown "temporarily inflate[s] the power of the declining hegemonic state," which then "reaps the benefits of its leadership . . . [via] privileged access to . . . world financial markets." Ultimately, "even a small disturbance can tilt the balance in favor of the forces . . . undermining the already precarious stability of existing structures. . . . [Long periods of] systemic chaos set in."[2]

During the declining phase of these hegemonic cycles the leading capitalist states preside over the upsurge of new forms of knowledge, data retrieval, and social regulation. These mechanisms have been deployed to manage social conflicts, as well as to reduce the costs of socioeconomic production and reproduction. This essay examines the large-scale structures shaping the distinctive informational and regulatory modes central to imperialist domination during the fin de siècles of British global hegemony (1873–1914) and U.S. global hegemony (mid-1970s to the present). Such modes merged the panoptic inspection practices (data collection, surveillance, disciplinary procedures) characterizing each imperial leader's protracted collapse with biopolitics.[3] The latter term refers to the "entire series of interventions and *regulatory controls*" over populations but "biologically transcribed" and "articulated with European policies of colonization," in this case throughout the declining phase of hegemonic cycles.[4] Indeed, as Foucault has argued, "It is . . . at this point that racism intervenes" as biopower introduces "the break between what must live and what must die" or between basic welfare versus the wretched of the earth. This is why I am conceptualizing the articulation of panopticism and biopolitics (whether during waning global hegemonies or during their ascent) as global-racial regimes integral to capitalism's *longue durée*—qua Braudelian world-historical structures.[5]

THE BRITISH FIN DE SIÈCLE

Given the parameters of this volume, I will not closely examine the decisive role of the financial sector during the downward stage of the fifty-year-plus cycles (Kondratieff waves) of global economic prosperity and contraction but will instead focus on other crucial features of all leading core states during their decline within the interstate imperialist network.[6] Great Britain's waning hegemony on a world scale was characterized by the desperate proliferation of globally trendsetting ways of containing and disciplining labor and subaltern populations. These emergent social-regulatory forms and dominant knowledges arose in the midst of a no less desperate interenterprise and interimperialist competition for the new markets, natural resources, and cheap labor that would guarantee continuing capital accumulation.

One key imperialist reinforcement during the British fin de siècle was the civilizing missions oriented by social Darwinism and eugenics, which understood "civilized" societies to be composed of reputable citizens exercising self-control over their baser instincts against the allegedly atavistic elements threatening the social order. The key was understanding what these primitive elements were ethnobiologically, from Euro-descended criminals and laborers to the "lesser races" at home and abroad.[7] The other side of this same (imperialist) global-racial regime was the series of biopolitical measures creating and maintaining exploited and/or oppressed populations as identifiable-manageable bodies. During 1870–1920 the latter measures included globally reducing legal slavery but continuing to use other forms of racialized forced labor, plus a spike in genocidal famines and pogroms worldwide.[8] Rising factory Taylorism and Fordism also impacted core laborers, who won greater political and trade-union rights, versus persistent social-political restrictions on "subject peoples."[9] These panoptic and biopolitical mechanisms enabled one of the most significant ethnoracialized, socioeconomic polarizations within the history of the global labor force—a social order

W. E. B. DuBois called "the new colonialism," centered on "the exploitation of backward races under the political domination of" the West.[10] Such socioregulatory measures also included positivist, formal-colonial, criminal-justice procedures with a growing split between the uneven decline of "levying violence" and spectacles of punishment, mostly for core populations.[11] Yet penal servitude, exemplary punishments, and generalized surveillance persisted for the "backward races." (See the essay in this volume by Ballantyne and the final essay by McCoy for elaboration.)[12]

On the other hand, the imperialist arts of domination integral to the British fin de siècle generated global waves of resistance, especially within colonial contexts—including the last Asante, Zulu, and Matabele wars against the British in Africa, Southeast Asian social banditry revolts, the Tukolor/Dahomey wars against the French, anti-Belgian attacks and social banditry in the eastern Congo, riots and social unrest that swept the British Caribbean, and Thuggee and Dacoit social banditry in northern India. Against Spain, one can cite the Filipino Cavite Mutiny, Katipunan insurrection, Cuban wars of independence, and Moroccan insurgencies (see the essays in this volume by Garcia Balañà and Scarano); against U.S. domination, the last Indian wars and the Filipino guerrillas (see the essay by Johnson and the final essay by McCoy); and against Western interests in general, the peasant and urban poor assaults, riots, Luddite attacks, and secret society revolts across China in the lead-up to the Boxer Rebellion.[13]

This global wave of social unrest against the new panoptic and biopolitical mechanisms impacted the entire British-ruled world-system by increasing Western expenses for pacification, labor control, and political rule insofar as they obstructed access to new global markets, raw materials, and cheaper labor. Such anticolonial resistances accelerated interimperialist competition and interenterprise strife, thus stalling economic recovery worldwide during the great depression of 1875–96 at the dawn of the Second Industrial Revolution.[14] The interimperialist rivalry augmented by these anticolonial resistances and the new rush to industrialize led to an arms race and military adventurism among the world powers. (See the essays in this volume by Jacobson and Garcia Balañà.) However, the socioeconomic burden of these ballooning imperial war budgets and mass industrialization increasingly fell, in part, on the restless laborers in the overseas colonies and spheres of influence, inciting full-fledged peasant wars in China, Mexico, Rwanda, and elsewhere.[15]

The rebellion across Puerto Rico's countryside is one of the lesser-known examples of these turn-of-the-century peasant wars, in this case when the United States invaded that island as part of the Spanish-Cuban-Philippine-American War. During late 1898 and early 1899, insurgent bands (averaging 150 to 200 strong) of armed destitute peasants attacked the mostly Spaniard large landowners (*hacendados*) and their families, burning and looting haciendas and warehouses and distributing the proceeds among the raiders. The remnants of the Spanish army and constabulary (the Guardia Civil) were unable to suppress this agrarian uprising, which eventually was crushed by the U.S. Army.[16] Not surprisingly, this *jacquerie* impacted local patricians on this island—Spanish and creole—contributing to their transformation into more willing subordinate-elite collaborators with the new U.S. colonizers. (See the essay in this volume by Scarano; on other subordinate elites, see the essays by Barton, Raben, and Anderson and Pols.) The peasant war in Puerto Rico also illustrates some of the continuities between mass resistances to social regulation and exploitation under flagging core segments of the capitalist interstate system (Spanish imperialism) and such resistances under the reign of ascendant core states (U.S. imperialism) during an era of global-hegemonic transition. We thus gain a much fuller sense of imperial rise and decline, avoiding one-dimensional analyses that might otherwise result from an exclusive focus on ruling sectors as the sole shapers of world history.

But the burden of growing imperial-military expenses and mass industrialization also tended to weigh down the working classes within core countries and older empires (e.g., the czarist and Ottoman realms). In both instances, this burden created extremely unstable imperialist national alliances. On the one hand, it cemented working-class patriotic fervor for [short-term] armed conflicts, as in the U.S. "splendid little war" of 1898. On the other hand, financing the weapons buildup compressed real wages and, together with breakneck industrialization, deteriorated real living conditions and led to mass strikes and labor uprisings during 1890–1914 in Great Britain, France, Germany, the United States, and Russia.[17] This entire confluence of factors eventually accelerated the collapse of British global hegemony, resulting in a long chain of global interimperial conflicts. Or, as Winston Churchill narrated it, World War II turned into "a continuation of the story of the First World War," which "together cover an account of another Thirty Years War" (1914–45).[18] At the center of this sequence of worldwide conflagrations was the contest between Germany and the United States concerning which up-and-coming world leader would inherit the British mantle, an outcome that inaugurated a new world order exemplified by the United Nations and Bretton Woods financial system.

The U.S. Fin de Siècle

The specific received knowledges of the U.S. fin de siècle have reproduced certain aspects of its British counterpart, including the resurgence of biologistic positivism based on parasitological perspectives transforming certain citizens into denizens. Social relations once again began to be understood as a host-parasite relationship, involving the permanent quest for (non-Western) vectors of infection.[19] These structures of knowledge first resurfaced in mid-1960s theories on

the "culture of poverty," later flourishing world-systemically from the late 1970s
to the present as sociobiology, the biopsychologies of race, and "underclass" theories.[20] Others included "Afro-pessimism," third-world "cultures-of-violence,"
"Islamic fanaticism," and other "breeding grounds for global terrorism."[21]

The economic-neoliberal aspects of the U.S. fin de siècle's global-racial regime
became the structural response to the long-term downturn in the world-economy,
a protracted descent that began in 1967–73 and continues to the present day.
This response has been characterized also by interenterprise and interimperialist attempts to corner new global markets and cheaper sources of labor. But,
starkly unlike the British fin de siècle, such efforts during the present era have
also entailed a desperate rush to procure new advanced technologies and especially to monopolize and privatize no longer plentiful resources and consumption items (from hydrocarbons to water) located in highly contested peripheral
and semiperipheral regions of the world. This confluence of forces has led to
several pivotal processes framing the U.S. fin de siècle.

Beginning with the resource wars of the last forty years and continuing into
the foreseeable future, the militarism and concomitant arms race of the Second
Cold War (1979–85) up to the "Global War on Terror" have meant the uninterrupted politico-economic and military defiance of key semiperipheral state
elites (e.g., Russian, Chinese, Iranian, Venezuelan, Indian, Syrian, and Brazilian)
to the bloc comprised of the United States, Israel, the European Union (EU),
and members of the North Atlantic Treaty Organization (NATO).[22] Such developments, in turn, have strengthened, from the 1970s onward, the global trend
toward authoritarian statism and restricted citizen rights. In the current world-
economic downturn, these resource wars and militarism overlap with the limits
of the interimperialist and interenterprise tendency to externalize the ecological
costs of capitalist accumulation. Core states face serious constraints in repairing
the damage of corporate pollution, while major corporations resist having their
profits encroached upon. Both prefer to continue exporting their industrial
waste and ecodegrading industries to the third world but encounter growing
political, economic, and/or military resistance from peripheral and semiperipheral state elites and populations.[23]

Such is the relentless social instability that core states have been attempting
to manage and domesticate, through the five measures discussed below, so as to
guarantee unfettered capital accumulation and imperialist forms of global domination by reducing the costs of production and social reproduction. At this level,
too, the panopticism/biopolitics of the U.S. fin de siècle recuperated yet transformed other aspects of the British fin de siècle. This replication began with the
economic-neoliberal (albeit uneven) dismantling of government social provisions, now replaced with privatization, structural-adjustment austerities, and/or
"free trade" pacts. Recalling British era economic liberalism and poor laws, we

now have the neo-Malthusian and neo-Victorian reintroduction of the capitalist "work ethic," the refeminization and reinfantilization of poverty, the erosion of trade union rights, and the massive deruralization of the world.[24] Second, there is the neo-social-Darwinian resurgence of the most despotic forms of work, disproportionately focusing on today's "lesser races" with the rising tide of migrant (former peasant) and displaced laborers being the hardest hit through measures from informal slavery to highly coerced wage labor, combined with massive agricultural pauperization.[25] Next, the urban visions of Georges Haussmann have been resuscitated as increasing gentrification, gated communities, homelessness, aggressive containment of ghetto populations, and massive globalization of slums. (See McCoy's introduction to this volume.)[26]

Moreover, many of the latter forms overlap with the neo-eugenic spread of neoliberal criminal-justice measures, again disproportionately targeting ethno-racially depreciated global labor and/or alleged global terrorism, including extensive surveillance and exceedingly invasive, high-tech information retrieval (see the final essay in this volume by McCoy); generalized policing and formalized racial profiling; more severe sentencing and confinement; massive persecution, detention, and deportation of immigrants; greater extracarceral supervision (parole, probation); and both formal and extrajudicial executions, torture, and beatings by government agents, state paramilitary groups, mercenaries, and warlord armies. Such measures also overlap with restrictions on abortion, women's social mobility, and same-sex practices, plus an amplification of state and/or clerical-religious tolerance and redirection of domestic violence, honor killings, and "crimes of passion."[27]

Finally, there are the echoes of the "scramble for Africa" in the globalization of local conflicts, disaster profiteering, resource wars, and again the so-called wars against international terrorism, targeting peripheral/semiperipheral populations, notably, civil and/or regional wars in Northern Ireland, Africa, Latin America, the Levant, the Maghreb, the Persian Gulf, Central Asia, South Asia, Southeast Asia, and the Balkans, plus corporate profiteering from the 1980s Sahel drought, 1990s South Asian floods, the 2004 Indian Ocean tsunami, and the 2010 Haitian earthquake, and their core-country equivalents (e.g., ghetto gang wars, Hurricane Katrina). Practically all such events function as the imperial monopolization of key commodities, population control, arms-sales profits, redirecting popular unrest, creating or reproducing cheap labor among refugees and the internally displaced, and rerouting labor toward formally outlawed extraction and production (e.g., "blood diamonds," opium poppies, and cocaine) and/or outlawed sales (e.g., the illegal drug trade, gunrunning, stolen car parts, and/or human trafficking in the global slums).[28]

Nevertheless, the U.S. fin de siècle simultaneously provoked its own global waves of resistance to this era's panoptic and biopolitical mechanisms, particularly riots against the International Monetary Fund (IMF) and food riots and/or the antiausterity mobilizations of the late 1970s to 2011 sweeping most of the third world and even some Western countries such as Greece, France, the United Kingdom, Spain, and the United States.[29] Since the 1990s, these protests have merged with global prodemocracy movements against privatization, "free trade" policies, corruption, high unemployment, and state repression. Such movements have included civil disobedience (versus the World Trade Organization, IMF, World Bank, G-8, and World Economic Forum) and armed resistance (notably, the Zapatistas, the Movement for the Emancipation of the Niger Delta, and certain Islamist groups), as well as international assemblies (e.g., the World Social Forum) and massive antiauthoritarian revolts such as the 2009–11 resurgence in the Arab region and the Persian Gulf. These uprisings and mass protests have overlapped with broader social activism against labor servitude and global enclosures, including antislavery campaigns against Florida's agribusinesses, social-movement trade unionism, the Brazilian landless people's movement, *Via Campesina*'s battle against debt peonage, and village women's campaigns against sexual trafficking in Southeast Asia.[30]

Such has also been the case of the struggles against neoliberal penality and civil rights restrictions, manifest in the prison uprisings and inmate protests across the United States, Canada, Latin America, the Arab region, and South Asia and East Asia from 1993 to 2011; mass movements for immigrant rights and against repressive legislation and police brutality in the United States and EU; the popular mobilizations and armed defense of dispossessed communities from Colombia to Palestine; and anti-sexual-exploitation and pro-reproductive-rights campaigns among poor women from El Salvador to Nigeria to Egypt.[31] Corollary challenges have emerged to social-racial segregation, dispossession, corporate pillage, and military expansionism, producing the ghetto riots in the United States, United Kingdom, and France between 1980 and 2011; the grassroots movements against evictions (1975–2010) from Mexico City and Cape Town to Chicago and East Jerusalem; and popular struggles related to natural resource wars from Bolivia to India to the Gulf of Mexico; as well as the regional and international challenges (nonviolent and armed) to post -9/11 U.S.-U.K.-NATO-Israeli interventionism and military aggression.[32]

CONCLUSIONS

This essay has tried to show why comparing the decline of British and U.S. global hegemonies needs to be done not only in the historical long-term. Such comparisons are more fruitfully framed in relation to the ethnoracially structured, panoptic, and biopolitical mechanisms that manage social conflicts and interstate/interenterprise competition. In other words, these comparisons involve world historically contrasting and relating each era's global-racial regime. This essay has also demonstrated how the declining phases of both of these global hege-monies are not merely similar but rather represent cyclical, larger-scale con-nections and resonances over world–capitalism's *longue durée*. In terms of the widening ethnoracialized gap within global labor, the British fin de siècle's not only laid the groundwork for the even greater, worldwide colonialism and labor force bifurcation of the U.S. fin de siècle. As this essay shows, the British fin de siècle's panoptic and biopolitical mechanisms also have been resurrected, sys-tematized, and implemented more brutally during the U.S. fin de siècle.

The ethnoracial socioeconomic polarization inherent to the U.S. fin de siècle has not merely generated this global wave of social unrest. This precariousness also renders peripheral regions increasingly dangerous for transnational-corporate investment. Third world poverty will expand exponentially, generating even more social strife and larger migratory waves from deprived regions to the core countries. The ensuing cycle of deruralization will inevitably shift the social-reproduction expenses of these displaced peasants to the urban administrations and informal economies—thus, further inflating the cost of global labor at rela-tively higher levels than during British fin de siècle. This growing immigrant laboring population, on the one hand, will add to the already existing social-political pressures and cultural complexity within core states as they face demands on their ever shrinking social-service provisions and citizens' rights. On the other hand, the immigrant wave toward rich countries will complicate the core states' capacity to address political-economic (and military) challenges to imperialist militarism, resource wars, and ecodegradation from peripheral and semiperiph-eral governments, elites, and populations. All of these factors spell additional internal and external instability within interimperialist and interenterprise cir-cles and, hence, additional competition among them.[33]

Likewise, the greater extension and brutality of the U.S. fin de siècle's panop-tic/biopolitical measures might help us to better understand this declining hege-mon's unending colonial wars and related social contradictions. The wider reach, social depth, and greater heterogeneity of the ongoing social conflict could account for this tide's tenacity, longer duration, and proliferation. In turn, the rising cor-porate and state costs of—and limits to—containing and managing this social conflict worldwide might help explain why, in contrast to the British fin de siècle's relatively short-lived great depression (1875–96), the long-term world-economic decline of 1967–73 that opened the U.S. fin de siècle has lasted twice as long, stalling recovery worldwide, with no clear long-term recuperation in sight. In the meantime, to an extent that exceeds even the British fin de siècle, we may be "entering a [long] period of systemic chaos characterized by widespread social upheavals, state breakdowns, and dysfunctional violence."[34]

True, the existing social conflicts and the rise of new state contenders to world leadership (the EU and Northeast Asia) suggest upcoming realignments between the core empires and some leading semiperipheral states (i.e., U.S.-Japan-China versus EU-Russia or U.S.-EU-Japan versus Russia-China). These emerging alignments will, in turn, face continuing challenges from other key semiperipheral state elites (Iranian, Syrian, Venezuelan, Brazilian, and Indian, as well as Iraqi and Libyan) and anticore resistance by third world populations. In contrast to the British fin de siècle, the greater complexity of these social conflicts and the absence of any clear-cut, short-term (military) interimperialist competition obscure the outcome of the U.S. fin de siècle. On the one hand, there could emerge an ultimate resolution to this hegemonic transition with the end of its systemic chaos and the rise of a new imperialist hegemony within the capitalist world-system. On the other hand, there is the likelihood of a complex transition to a qualitatively new and different world-system altogether, one that could be noncapitalist, though not necessarily any more equitable.[35]

The Geopolitics of Decolonization

JOHN DARWIN

THE CAUSES OF DECOLONIZATION have long been the subject of historical controversy. The relative contributions of the three "usual suspects"—colonial nationalism, domestic political change, and the post-1945 transformation in world politics—all have their partisans. Nor is it obvious that any one formula can be successfully applied to the wide variety of cases that the historian must consider. The argument here is that the world order demolished by decolonization had required the existence of certain geopolitical conditions, which gradually collapsed (though at unpredictable speeds) after 1940–42. On the "space" this created, the three agents of change acted with variable force as time, place, and sequence exerted their influence.

THE IMPERIAL WORLD ORDER CIRCA 1840–1942

Decolonization was a process but also a geopolitical event. It can best be defined as the unraveling of a complex imperial world order. The key features of that order extended beyond the parceling up of much of the world into the colonial domains of the imperial powers, a group that included, by the late nineteenth century, Britain, France, Russia, Germany, the United States, and Japan, as well as the smaller fry: the Netherlands (a colonial "giant"), Belgium (although the Congo was until 1908 the personal property of the king), Spain (in 1898 on the verge of losing Cuba and the Philippines), Portugal, Italy, and Denmark—the possessor of Iceland and Greenland. Second, these "formal" empires also had a larger penumbra: the zones of informal influence where the commercial and diplomatic leverage of the great powers (Britain most of all) was exerted through the presence of banks, railway companies, and merchant houses (as in Latin America); a "temporary occupation" (as in Egypt); or the apparatus of extraterritorial privilege most strikingly visible in the "settlements" and "concessions" granted by China under the "unequal treaties" of 1842 and 1858–60.[1] It was this Machiavellian flexibility that brought South and Central America firmly into the sphere of this global colonialism. Third, the legitimacy of colonial authority and the right of intervention to protect persons and property were upheld by the contemporary norms of the law of nations. These laid down that those states or polities that fell short of the "standard of civilization" could not enjoy the full sovereignty to which "civilized" nations were entitled.[2] Fourth, it was considered a fact of life, and to all intents an unalterable one, that the world beyond Europe and its North American annex would remain technologically backward for an indefinite time (except where Europeans had settled) and thus dependent on Europe for advanced skills and capital. Economic sovereignty was thus beyond its reach. Fifth, the imperial world order also embodied a cultural assumption: that however exotic or charming, non-European cultures were so many dead ends. They lacked the vital ingredients that had enabled (some) Europeans to achieve "moral and material progress" (the title of the Government of India's annual report). They failed the test of "social efficiency"—in the words of the leading social Darwinist of the age.[3] Finally, that order had a demographic dimension. It favored the torrent of European emigration to the extra-European world and acknowledged its claims on the lands of indigenous peoples. But it treated the movement of non-Europeans as entirely subservient to imperial purposes and sanctioned their exclusion from the tracts to be designated as "white men's countries"—of which the greatest by far was the United States.

The full realization of this matrix of practices was delayed until the later nineteenth century. It was really the product of three world-shaping pressures and their close interaction. The first was the economic and cultural expansion of Europe, which accelerated sharply after circa 1870. With the rapid extension of the railway, the steamship, and the telegraph beyond the Atlantic basin, vast new regions of the Afro-Asian world now fell within range of European commerce, information, ideas—and armies. The great British bastion in India became more than ever the springboard for the commercial conquest of Asia, and, if necessary, for its coercion as well. The second was the response in many Afro-Asian societies to the subversive effects of this tentacular growth. Torn between the desire to resist and the desire to exploit new techniques and ideas, tempted to borrow and (sometimes) condemned to default, or beached by the changes in long-distance trade, many lurched into crisis. This merely served to confirm their "unfitness" for sovereignty, and the "need" for external control, while simultaneously rotting their means of resistance. The result was a "scramble"—in the Pacific and Southeast Asia, as well as Africa. But—and the reservation is vital—it was an orderly scramble in which no blood was shed between the European powers. For the third critical element in this emerging world order was the concert in Europe.[4] Far from pursuing their Afro-Asian ambitions with reckless abandon (the myth to which too many historians adhere), the great powers in Europe were keenly aware that controlling their multiethnic dominions at home dictated an essentially conservative policy abroad: a general war *within* Europe for some acres of African bush was not to be thought of. Instead, despite the jostling and crowing of their "men on the spot," and the yelping of "patriots" and publicists, European statesmen preferred to settle their differences in the smoke-filled rooms of the "old diplomacy." The geopolitical conditions for Europe's imperial preeminence thus lay in the broadly "passive" state of East Asia (before ca. 1900) and in the special conjuncture of power relations within Europe itself.

Yet in important respects, the late-nineteenth-century world order was both brittle and fragile. It rested in part on the shrewdness and judgment of European statesmen, and their skill in the management of domestic constituencies. Dynastic ambition and dynastic prestige (among Hohenzollerns, Hapsburgs and Romanovs) were the jokers in their diplomatic pack: they might be played at an inopportune moment. More serious, perhaps, was the fact that the partition of the world was far from complete. The Europeans had partitioned where partition was easy—in Africa above all, where the stakes were so low. Where it mattered much more, and the stakes were sky-high—as in the Ottoman Empire or China—a waiting game was preferred. In East Asia that permitted the growth of a powerful new claimant, at best deeply resentful of European influence. Most serious of all, where an agreed partition was of crucial importance to the peace of Europe, in the ex-Ottoman Balkans, a war of diplomatic maneuver was fought. Neither Russia nor Austria-Hungary (and its German "protector") could tolerate a solution that yielded decisive geostrategic advantage to the other in what was expected to be the endgame of Ottoman rule in Southeast Europe, Asia Minor, and at the Straits (the Dardanelles and the Bosphorus). Indeed, it was from there, of course, and not from their rivalries elsewhere in the world, that the chain reaction began that demolished—eventually—the imperial world order.

It is conventional to see World War I as the calamity from which Europe's central place in the world could never recover. Up to a point, that is true. The spread of the war to the Middle East, the high seas, Africa, and (briefly) the Pacific wrecked the tacit understanding of the prewar era that no large-scale transfers of territory should occur without great power agreement.[5] At the end of the war, the Germans were expelled from the colonial club, and, by losing their navy, from the club of world powers. The Ottoman Empire in Asia was shared between Britain and France. The old ruling principle of the imperial world order, that all the great powers had a vested interest in its existence, no longer held good. For Russia, like Germany, was a loser power, although its largest "lost colony"—Poland—was in Europe. Perhaps, more to the point, its Bolshevik leaders fiercely repudiated "capitalist imperialism" and affirmed solidarity with the subject "toilers of the East." Meanwhile, the weight of American power, at its height in 1918–19, ensured that the Wilsonian ideology of self-determination for "nations" (a somewhat nebulous category) as the key to world peace commanded a respectful hearing in high places and an enthusiastic welcome among those who believed that its scope would be extended to them. And although Britain and France made sure that the "mandate" idea of international supervision should only apply to their new acquisitions, its language crept into their colonial theory and practice.[6] It was in East Asia, however, that the challenge to imperialism went furthest. Amid a surge of Chinese national consciousness, all the great powers (including Japan) had acknowledged by 1922 that the apparatus of "informal imperialism"—the treaty ports and concessions—must be dismantled and the unequal treaties revised.[7] Altogether, these changes signaled a profound shift, not least in the ideological premises that had sustained the pre-1914 order.

Yet, despite the symptoms of general collapse which deeply alarmed many imperial-minded observers, when the dust had settled much of the landscape of empire remained intact. The Locarno treaties of 1925 seemed to promise that the storm center of world politics had now calmed down and that the Germans had accepted their postwar condition. In India and the Middle East, the British succeeded in dampening the nationalist excitement that seemed so threatening between 1919 and 1922. There was little sign that colonial rule was under pressure in Africa south of the Sahara: indeed, in the settler countries, the initiative still seemed to lie with the colonizers. The main exception to this rule could be found in China. Here, certainly, the force of Chinese demands to reclaim the sovereignty that the unequal treaties denied now seemed irresistible. Faced with violent demonstrations in Shanghai and the boycott of Hong Kong, the British caved in.[8] In the "Christmas memorandum" of December 1926, the policy of "rendition"—the progressive abandonment of extraterritorial privilege—was laid down. The following year the concession at Hankow was given up under the Chen-O'Malley agreement of 1927. But, as it turned out, the sun had not set on this enclave empire.

In fact, the 1930s were to witness a violent new phase in the history of imperialism. The Japanese occupation of Manchuria, tacitly accepted by Britain, France, and the United States, exploited the growing internal struggle in China between nationalists and communists. The nationalist regime, under pressure from two sides, abandoned the effort to evict the foreign concessions, preferring instead to solicit the diplomatic support of the British. In 1934–35, the Italian campaign to subjugate Ethiopia set off a major diplomatic crisis in Europe. But Anglo-French disagreement, as well as British misgivings about the naval and military costs of a war against Italy in the Mediterranean, ensured that the international response was vacillating and ineffectual. Lurking behind the calculations in London and Paris was a growing geostrategic anxiety. For both, Hitler's evident determination to throw off the shackles of Versailles and restore Germany as a great power, threatened the whole European settlement on which their safety in Europe and beyond seemed to rest. For the British in particular, conviction that a naval war against Japan had become increasingly likely, and must be prepared for, made the risks of Mediterranean war—and the probable loss of several capital ships—an unacceptable prospect.[9] But caught between the need to denounce the Italian aggression and the impossibility of doing anything about it, the British got the worst of both worlds: the alignment of Germany and Italy, and then of Japan, as "revisionist powers."

The late 1930s thus saw a new age of imperialism that was much more unstable and internally riven than in the earlier phase of the 1880s and 1890s. Indeed, the contrasts are dramatic. Then the major (would-be) colonial powers were restrained by their fear of a convulsion in Europe and by a sense of common commitment to the imperial order. Moreover, the "concert" ethos in Europe and the keen sense of balance between the major European powers were a powerful constraint on "rogue" imperialism by any one power. In the 1930s, however, all these restraints were marked by their absence. The economic depression made the case for autarkic trade zones compelling, especially for the Germans and Japanese, who feared exclusion by the "white" powers.[10] Second, the regimes in power in the "have-not" countries regarded the international system with loathing and contempt and longed to pull it down. They acknowledged no limits to their imperial ambitions. Third, the means to assemble a coalition against them were painfully lacking. The two "old colonial powers," Britain and France, were divided by suspicion. Their most promising partner, the United States, moved deeper into diplomatic detachment as the 1930s progressed. The Soviet Union, the most powerful check on German aggression in Europe, regarded the Western powers as ideological enemies, and the mistrust was reciprocated. Fourth, the pall of ideological conflict that hung over Europe erased the conditions in which the great powers had once been able to settle their differences through the courtly ambiguities of the old diplomacy. Finally, there was, perhaps, in British leaders especially, an insular blindness. Removed as they were from the ethnic and ideological battlegrounds of Europe, and still deeply attached to a form of liberal internationalism, they failed to grasp the revolutionary logic that guided their enemies until it was too late.[11]

The result in 1939–40 was that the two great colonial powers, Britain and France, lacked the military strength and diplomatic resources to defend the imperial world order they had played such a large part in constructing. Instead they encountered a geopolitical disaster of exceptional magnitude. Without a real ally in Europe (the Soviet Union having reached an accord with Hitler), they faced the German Blitzkrieg. They might have expected an inconclusive war of position as in 1914–15. Instead Hitler's conquest of France set off the implosion of the whole system of empire. It unleashed the Italian invasion of Egypt and threatened to break the British Empire in half. It encouraged the Japanese—who had occupied French Indochina—to make their fatal advance into Southeast Asia. It drove the British into financial dependence on the United States. With the Japanese capture of Singapore in February 1942 (the strategic consequence of British defeat in Europe), growing political unrest in India, and (by July 1942) a German-Italian army poised to capture Cairo, the prestige and ideology, as well as the actual territoriality, of the old imperial order were on the ropes. Its chances of survival in recognizable form were surely remote.

THE GEOPOLITICS OF SURVIVAL

It was the astonishing outcome of the war in both Europe and Asia that reversed that assumption, though never completely. The two guarantors of the prewar imperial order emerged as victor powers—of a sort. The British regained all their lost territory. Indeed, they consolidated their hegemonic position in Egypt and the Arab Middle East, at least in military terms. With their large air force, army, and navy, they were the most powerful state in Western Europe. France, too, was restored to its colonial domain, though somewhat equivocally. In Syria, Lebanon, and Indochina, this was partly through the efforts of others, and the corrosive effects of the war had badly damaged their political grip.

But if the superstructure of imperial power had been revived, both France and Britain had been badly holed below the waterline. France's economy, still heavily rural, had been wrecked by the occupation and the effects of battle. The British, in the desperate lone struggle of 1940–41, had liquidated much of their portfolio of overseas assets, especially in dollars, and had piled up huge debts—including a large sterling debt to their colony India for military services. Much of their prewar commercial empire—to which they had sent exports and from which they drew profits—had slipped from their grasp. They faced, meanwhile, an enormous bill, in hard currency (i.e., dollars) to replenish the capital goods on which their industrial economy depended and to meet the need for food and other materials for a home population exhausted by six years of privation.[12]

The problem went deeper than that. The "real" British Empire was only founded in part on the exertion of sovereignty. That was best seen in India, where the British preserved through the interwar turbulence the critical power to raise and deploy an Indian army for imperial purposes (partly) at India's expense. But India was an exception. London's empire of commerce, managed from the City, was by its nature a collaborative affair that depended on mutual self-interest and the state of the global economy. The third source of power, often overlooked by historians for whom "empire" is a matter of drum, trumpet, and pith helmet, was the continued allegiance of the "white dominions": Canada, Australia, New Zealand, and South Africa. The dominions contributed at least a million men to the imperial war effort in 1914–18 and at their own expense. They did so again in World War II. Their motive was partly a strong sense of race loyalty (though not among Afrikaners or French Canadians) and partly apprehension over what a British defeat would mean for their own independence. But in the World War II, unlike the first, their sense of strategic dependence came under severe strain. Britain's continental disaster in June 1940 persuaded Canada to commit itself to a permanent alliance with the United States—a seismic reorientation of its external allegiance. The fall of Singapore and the threat from its "Near North" pulled Australia (and tacitly New Zealand) in a similar direction. Only South Africa—the least loyal of the four—retained its sense of geostrategic dependence, though sharply qualified by much Afrikaner resentment at being dragged once again into a "British" war against "foes" for whom they felt little antipathy.[13]

A realistic analysis, then, might have raised many questions over how far the victory the British had won could enable the recovery of their prewar position and the world order it needed. They could no longer assume first claim on the strategic commitments of the white dominions. Their vast reserve of overseas assets had melted away. And it soon became clear that their hopes of shaping India's postwar independence—to which they had committed themselves in the desperate circumstances of 1942—to suit their imperial design were founded on sand. They wanted a united India, a single Indian army, and a self-governing India that would still be part of their system of "imperial defense." Notoriously, they failed on all counts. India's postwar turbulence (both political and communal), their own economic exhaustion, and the impossibility of sending an army to buttress their rule enforced the rapid surrender that led to independence by partition. It was a geopolitical revolution. After 1947, the British could no longer rely on the deployment of Indian manpower and resources to underwrite their interests in Southeast Asia and the Middle East. Yet, we will see, they were extremely reluctant to abandon those interests: indeed, they came to see them as more important than ever.

The British dilemma was shared in different ways by all the old colonial powers in Europe, great and small. There was, on the one hand, a grudging acceptance that the ideological "fallout" of the war had demolished much of the remaining legitimacy of colonialism as a permanent condition. Loud rhetorical blasts from Washington, and the long-standing hostility of the anti-imperialist imperialists in Moscow, made it clear that the new "superpowers" would be deeply antagonistic to the "old colonialism." But, on the other hand, governments in Lisbon, Brussels, and The Hague, as well as in London or Paris, were unwilling to enrage their supporters with a timid withdrawal or—more to the point—to forgo the economic resources that their empires still offered.[14] Indeed, in the immediate postwar conditions, access to produce in colonial economies, whose price could be set below the world market price and could be paid in "soft" money, was far more valuable than it had been before 1939. In the case of the French, the bitter taste of defeat in June 1940 added an extra dimension. Restoring France's fragile claim to be a great power meant retaining its empire, and not just for prestige. Its

African empire had been the last ditch of French independence in wartime, and African soldiery had been and remained a critical part of France's military power. The British discovered a yet deeper imperative.

In the aftermath of the war, the most acute source of anxiety for governments in London and Paris turned on the European settlement. They mistrusted Russian intentions and were deeply uncertain how much they could hope for American help if Russia moved deeper into Central Europe. British grand strategy had to take account of the fact that its prime means of deterrence—its huge bomber force—could be not be deployed against Russian industrial power from bases in Western Europe: the distance was too great. The exotic solution to this strategic dilemma lay in the Middle East. It was from there that they planned to dispatch their bomber force to South Russia. Together with access to oil, and the need to command the air and sea routes to the East, it made an irresistible case for maintaining their grip on the region's military assets, most of all on their huge wartime base in the Suez Canal Zone.[15] Although their mandate in Palestine was destroyed by Jewish terrorism in 1948, they remained just as determined to be Iraq's great power protector, to exclude other powers from the Persian Gulf, and to force Egypt to sign a new military alliance as the price of shrinking their visible presence in the country.

Thus a strange reassertion of imperial motives and claims followed the end of the war, including the reoccupation of lost colonial domains by the British, French, and Dutch. Of course, this was only made possible by two great geopolitical facts. The first was the acquiescence, first passive then active, of the United States. As is now widely known, American foreign policy underwent a profound transformation toward the end of the war. The dislike for the European empires, seen (the British especially) as the barrier to their economic expansion, was gradually replaced by ever deeper disquiet at the breathtaking transformation in Russian military power.[16] As the prospect that America would become, much more completely than in 1919, the arbiter of world politics began to recede, and the scope of Soviet ambitions became clearer, American priorities changed. The demolition of Europe's colonial regimes now played second fiddle to counterbalancing Soviet Russia's power in Europe and the Middle East. Western Europe's economic recovery and its precarious stability were not to be risked by dispossessing them of their colonies. The British in the Middle East became a valuable buffer when American military power had yet to begin its great postwar expansion. The threat of communism in East and Southeast Asia turned the colonial regimes there into necessary auxiliaries. The result was American willingness to underwrite not only the economic recovery of their European allies—as they became in 1948–49—but their colonial commitments as well.

The second great fact was the relative caution of Soviet world policy. Stalin's priority (despite his adventurism in Korea) lay in Europe. Despite much huffing and puffing, there was no forward movement in the Middle East. Nor was the Soviet Union then able to exert much influence (except through propaganda) in Africa and Southeast Asia. Despite British unease, it made no effort to exploit the partition of India or the first India-Pakistan conflict over Kashmir. The colonial empires survived in part because of this curious geopolitical vacuum. The imperial world order lived on in this shadowy form. As a result, the full costs of empire were, for the moment, almost hidden from view. And those political movements that had hoped to exploit the effects of the war to extract independence from their colonial masters found little support, material or psychological, in the international sphere. But by the mid-1950s, this was about to change.

THE IMPERIAL ENDGAME

In reality, of course, the imperial world was already breaking apart. India, by now a republic, had remained a Commonwealth member, but on its own terms. Jawaharlal Nehru was determined that it should not be drawn into the Western Alliance, nor be complicit in the retention of empires. The triumph of Mao Zedong in China ensured that Asia's other great state would be an active opponent of European colonialism. In what became Indonesia, the Dutch effort to revive their prewar control had foundered on American opposition to the repression of a nationalist movement that Washington judged a valuable ally against the spread of communism. In the Middle East, where British prestige had been eroded by their hasty exit from Palestine and the betrayal of its Arabs, Iran had inflicted a further humiliation by forcing the Anglo-Iranian Oil Company's abandonment of its great Abadan refinery installation.[17] And in Egypt, the head and center of their regional sway, the British faced by the early 1950s an opposition so widespread as to turn their retention of the Canal Zone into a strategic albatross. The eighty thousand men they had there, one British mandarin said drily, were simply engaged in defending themselves. Their withdrawal under the Suez Agreement of 1954 marked, to an extent that soon became clear, the end of Britain's "moment" across most of the Arab Middle East.[18] In that same year, the fall of Dien Bien Phu, with its large colonial army, destroyed the French political will to continue the struggle to keep Indochina as a part of overseas France.

Behind this redrawing of the old colonial maps lay a further large shift in geopolitical dynamics. The war in Korea (1950–53) was a turning point. It drew the United States much more completely than before into intervention in East Asia against the communist threat. When French resistance collapsed, American support was critical in sustaining a noncommunist South Vietnam amid the wreck of French rule.[19] But elsewhere in the world, the strain of rearming for a conflict in Asia made Washington reluctant to back the old order against its local opponents. Egyptian leaders understood this and used it relentlessly to wear down British demands for continued control of the Canal Zone.[20] By the time of the 1954 agreement, it was clear that American support and its promise of aid were the critical factors that were shaping the outcome. In 1955, the conference at Bandung signaled the emergence of a "nonaligned movement," the informal agreement of India, China, Indonesia, and Egypt, among others, to pull down what remained of the imperial order. Perhaps encouraged by this (and a growing rivalry with China), Soviet foreign policy, now under Nikita Khrushchev's energetic new management, became considerably more venturesome. In 1955, the supply of arms to Colonel Gamal Abdel Nasser—breaking a Western embargo— showed that the Soviet Union was now willing to compete for world influence in zones previously left to the West. When Nasser made a bold move to assert his complete independence by nationalizing the canal, American reluctance to see him destroyed by an Anglo-French expedition turned his astonishing gamble into a no less astonishing triumph. The wider implications of this soon became clear. From 1956 on, the United States and Russia were engaged in a global competition for influence in the ex-colonial world. For the United States in particular, there was now little merit in prolonging colonialism (and reaping the ideological obloquy) when its fall seemed only a matter of time. Worse still, it appeared, the longer the delay in coming to terms with colonialism's "nationalist" successors, the more likely it was that they would turn in frustration and anger to America's rival. Empires must die if the Cold War was to be won.

It would be a mistake to suppose that this geopolitical pressure was exerted on a rigid and unchanging colonial system. In what remained of their empires in Africa, Southeast Asia, the Caribbean, and the Pacific, the colonial powers could not escape the political and ideological impact of Asian and Middle Eastern events. They faced varying levels of local resistance from full-scale rebellions in Algeria, Malaya, and Kenya to mass political movements (as in Ghana/Gold Coast) to milder demands for representative government. What made this resistance so hard to contain was that the old levers of rule were now much less effective. Colonial states were past masters in managing divided and disparate communities: "They divide, and we rule" was the ironic mantra of this. Devolving political power to very local elites, discouraging lateral links between different districts, and avoiding colonial initiatives that might rally more general opposition were the nostrums of policy under "indirect rule."

But after 1945, for reasons we have seen, orders from London and Paris forced an abrupt reverse course. If colonial economies were to serve the metropole's interests, they had to be dragged into commercial modernity as quickly as possible. That meant more taxation, more centralization, and an activist state whose grasping, governing hand would reach down far deeper into rural society. The result, in retrospect, seems highly predictable. Faced with this aggressive forward movement by the colonial state, colonial communities made common cause. The vacuous rhetoric of café politicians acquired novel force. Parties and movements proliferated. Rural unrest—the real threat to colonialism—grew wider and deeper. Colonial states quickly discovered that their security "apparatus" was grossly deficient in manpower, equipment, and intelligence.[21] Their masters at home began (more slowly) to realize that if colonial rule was to survive it would demand much more resources than they were willing to give. Not only that. If restoring effective control meant even short-term repression, the cost at home might be high; in the international sphere where Cold War competition prevailed, it would be astronomical.

This would have mattered somewhat less if the chief colonial powers had adopted what might be called the Portuguese attitude. Portugal (as a member of the North Atlantic Treaty Organization) could be confident of America's support for its external security. It had nothing to gain from competing for influence elsewhere in the world, and no ambitions to world power. Its main African territories were shielded strategically by the two "settler" states of south-central Africa. But for Britain and France, the stakes were much higher. The British especially, even after the disaster of Suez, were determined to assert as far as they could the status of parity in the Western Alliance, attending "summit conferences" as an equal party not a junior partner.[22] The price of ambition was the enjoyment of influence, in this case over a supportive, if not loyal, Commonwealth composed increasingly of Afro-Asian states. These were to be bound to Britain by shared political values, a measure of aid, the promise of help, and a personal bond

Egyptian tanks and vehicles damaged by Israeli forces in the Sinai during the Suez Crisis, 1956. (U.S. Army Heritage and Education Center)

between their new political rulers and the "statesmen" in London who had eased their path into power. The alternative route, once resistance appeared, of endless "emergencies" and costly repression, had little appeal. Indeed, by 1960 it seemed a dead end of humiliation and impotence.

CONCLUSION

In this way, and for fundamentally geopolitical reasons, the pre-1914 consensus that empire was necessary was replaced by a no less powerful consensus that it was outdated, repressive, and dangerous. Needless to say, the optimistic prospectus on which winding up empire became the political orthodoxy was soon belied in reality. The "empire" of influence that was imagined in Whitehall shriveled all too quickly. Nor was the imperial order to be as smoothly and quickly dismantled as might have been hoped. It survived in Angola, Mozambique, and Rhodesia (Zimbabwe) well into the 1970s and in its local mutation in South Africa into the 1990s. The successor states that replaced it bore the marks of their hasty invention, of the bitter divisions between rival inheritors and the eagerness of superpower "sponsors" to arm their clients to the teeth. Nor, of course, were all empires wound up by the mid-1970s. The Soviet empire staggered on into the late 1980s. Its eventual collapse, however, followed a curiously similar course to that of the others. To ease the crushing burden of geopolitical competition, the "modernizer" Mikhail Gorbachev sought to galvanize the "colonial" economies of the Soviet domain. He searched for new allies in his European "empire" and conceded more freedoms. But, like the French and the British, he lost control of the process: the ratchet of change slipped out of his hands. Hoping, like them, to turn his empire of rule into an empire of influence, he discovered, like them, that "informal" empires are just as costly to master and require a dynamic center: commercially, ideologically, culturally.[23] His successors were left with the rump of an empire, but one that may yet prove a considerable inheritance.

Decolonization was one of the founding processes of the contemporary world, which would be unrecognizable without it. The argument here is that it was profoundly shaped by the geopolitical traumas of World War II and its forty-year aftermath. Its cultural and demographic dimensions have yet fully to unfold. The impact on them of globalization (the second "founding" process) has yet to be realized. Decolonization remains a work in progress. Nor, perhaps, should we conclude too hastily that the age of empires is over. From the 1950s to the 1970s, it could even be argued, decolonization masked the transition from old empires to new: the superpower empires based on new combinations of influence and control. One mighty empire of rule survives to this day. And since wealth and power are (and always will be) distributed so unevenly over the world, the urge to empire (sometimes restrained, sometimes unleashed) is unlikely ever to vanish completely.

PART 5

Complexities and Contradictions of French Decolonization

French General Henri Delteil signing truce documents at Geneva ending hostilities
between the French and the Democratic People's Republic of Vietnam, July 28, 1954.
(Library of Congress Prints and Photographs Division)

The Absent Empire

The Colonies in French Constitutions

EMMANUELLE SAADA

England is an Empire; Germany, a country—a race, France is a person.
—JULES MICHELET, *Tableau de la France*, 1833

THE PAST FIFTEEN YEARS have witnessed a profusion of publications with the words *France* (or *French*) and *empire* in their titles. With some notable exceptions, these works attempt to identify what was "imperial" about France at various points in its history.[1] They tend to use the word *empire* in a very casual way—often as synonymous with one or more "colonies."[2] But, as the Jules Michelet quote that begins this essay suggests, this now frequent juxtaposition of words had very little purchase for most of the nineteenth and twentieth centuries.[3] The goal of this essay is to explore this significant absence—the missing concept of "empire" in French political culture—and how it may have impacted the process of decolonization. It will do so by focusing mostly on the constitutional history of the "French colonial empire." While constitutional texts have a long and rich history dating back to 1791, very few of them defined the concept of empire or even mentioned it. When they did, it was typically to establish a very strong separation between France and its overseas territories and to indicate that the constitution did not apply to the latter. Here they followed the "principle of colonial specialty" or exception (*le principe de spécialité coloniale*), according to which France per se and its colonies were under different legal regimes and "special laws" applied to the latter.

This double absence from political discourse and constitutional texts, I believe, raises some questions about use of the category "empire" by historians. To what extent did it matter that the French state did not "think like an empire"? And how to interpret the absence of a formal inscription of empire in French constitutional texts? Did that make it less "real"? Did this absence of constitutional recognition impact colonial projects in the *longue durée,* as well as the process of decolonization?

These questions call for a truly comparative study of the different valences of the term *empire*, especially in French and British constitutional histories, rather than the short account I can provide here. In addition, the subfields of constitutional and colonial history have yet to meet in the French case—in contrast to the rich tradition of scholarship on this point in the British and American cases.[4] So, this essay cannot pretend to answer all these questions and has a more modest aim: it will describe the political and constitutional trajectory of the term *empire* in the French case and suggest two hypotheses about its impact on the "eclipse" of the French empire. First, the absence of an imperial constitutional tradition left a large space for experimentation after World War II, at a moment when international and national political changes pressed for a reinvention of colonial politics. One of the options on the table was that of what one might call a "noncolonial empire"—a more egalitarian federation.[5] This project failed, but it could have become one of the "metamorphoses" evoked by Alfred McCoy in the introduction to this volume. Second, in the *longue durée* of French imperialism, legal exception led to the construction of a relatively autonomous sphere of colonial politics, quite untouched by democratic principles. All too often this sphere reproduced itself after the end of French formal sovereignty, especially in West Africa. To some extent, the deep-seated denial of empire facilitated continued imperial domination beyond decolonization.

An Empire without a Name

The language and representation of empire have been relatively absent in France for most the nineteenth and twentieth centuries. Here I am not making a claim, à la Bernard Porter, about the low "impact" of colonial projects on metropolitan economy, society, politics, and culture.[6] A large body of historical work now exists that convincingly points to the contrary, especially for the long twentieth century, starting in the 1880s. The ideological and economic dimensions of this "feedback effect" have been the object of French historians' attention for quite some time.[7] An abundance of more recent research has made clear that after 1830 French culture—both "high" and "popular"—was impacted by colonization.[8] These effects reached the heart of "everyday life" in France, even in the rural working classes.[9]

In addition to this colonial "impact" literature, the imperial nature of France has also been the object of recent historiography that focuses on the ensemble formed by colonies and metropole. If, following Frederick Cooper and Jane Burbank, we take empires to be "large political units, expansionist or with a memory of power expanded over space, polities that maintain distinction and hierarchy as they incorporate new people," then, undeniably, France, at least for most of the nineteenth and twentieth centuries, was one.[10] One concrete aspect of this reality is that important political debates about inclusion and exclusion happened at the imperial level. This was true during the Revolution, which was "imperialized" by the uprising of slaves; at the end of the nineteenth century, when the definition of French nationality and its intersection with French culture were debated in several colonies; and after World War II, when the distributive practices of the welfare state were as much discussed in Dakar as they were in Paris and Marseilles.[11]

But the distinctive character of this "unit," its subjective and objective degree of coherence, needs closer examination in the light of the relative absence of any clear framework within France or the colonies for understanding imperial relations as a singular political entity or project. In this short essay, I argue that France (or rather its elites) did not think of itself as an empire, in the usual terms, until the late 1930s and even the 1940s. For most of the period, the actors responsible for the conquest and administration of the "second French colonial empire," to use the typical formulation, had in mind primarily the bilateral relations between France and its colonies, not a unified (albeit heterogeneous) empire.[12] This fragmentation is arguably a common feature of all empires but is perhaps more pronounced in the French case. It has deep roots in French constitutionalism dating back to 1791—namely, the principle of the "unity and indivisibility of the Republic," and one of its principal consequences was the separation between metropole and colonies.

In the nineteenth century, the word *empire* was remarkably absent from French political discourse. The signal event of French empire building—the conquest of Algeria—opened a debate on the usefulness and methods of colonization more than a "turn to empire."[13] Alexis de Tocqueville, reflecting in the 1830s and 1840s on the presence of France in Algeria, did not see it in any way as the launching pad for a new "colonial empire" and did not mention other French possessions in his writing. For most of the nineteenth century, for the French political elite, *"l'empire, c'est les autres."* Its contemporary usage referred mostly to the regimes of Napoleon I and III—and, less frequently, to the absolute monarchy of the ancien régime—obviously a very negative association for the politicians of the Third Republic.[14] Its historical evocation referred mainly to the Roman Empire and the later Holy Roman Empire—two central models for Napoleon's continental empire.

The term was also used to contrast France with its national rivals: first Britain and, after 1871, Germany, which became a nation by proclaiming itself an empire at Versailles, on the ruins of the Napoleonic imperial dream. The strong association of "empire" with Germany is best illustrated by the writings of French legal theorists who were proposing a new theory of the state and state sovereignty at the turn of the century. One of the last but most important members of this cohort, Raymond Carré de Malberg, published his first scholarly article in 1913, entitled "The Legal Condition of Alsace and Lorraine within the German Empire."[15] In his major work, a two-volume *General Theory of the State*, he devoted long passages to the concept of empire but related it exclusively to continental Germany.[16]

In the late nineteenth century, while France was dramatically expanding its "colonial domain," the descriptive term in political debates was usually *les colonies*. The word *empire* is virtually absent from the heated parliamentary debates of July and December 1885, during which the financing of the conquest of Madagascar and Indochina was discussed. In those debates, while Jules Ferry articulated the colonial doctrine of the Republic under the attack from both right and left, participants compared the situations of several other territories, whose conquest was either projected or a fait accompli—in particular Algeria, Tunisia, and Equatorial Africa. One could see here "only" a question of semantics and decide that *the colonies* in plural was, after all, conceptually synonymous with *empire*. Yet the lines of fracture within the "colonial domain" are too deep to support this thesis.

First, there were no "imperial institutions" encompassing all territories under French domination. The "empire" was fragmented into territories of very different legal and administrative status. At the "highest" point of expansion, *colonies* were those inherited from the ancien régime in the Caribbean, the west coast of Africa, the Indian Ocean, Saint-Pierre-et-Miquelon, the Kerguelen Islands, and the coasts of India. *Possessions* were territories acquired during the nineteenth and twentieth centuries, notably the Comoros Islands, New Caledonia, Cochinchina, Tahiti, Madagascar, French West Africa, and French East Africa. They also consisted of *protectorates* in which a very low level of local sovereignty had been maintained (Cambodia, Annam, Tonkin, Laos, Tunisia, and Morocco). Finally, after World War I, the League of Nations awarded *mandates* (Syria, Lebanon, Togo, and Cameroon). To these one should add the particular cases of New Hebrides, an Anglo-French condominium since 1906, and Algeria, which was divided into three French departments in 1848 but administered by a governor-general, as in the colonies.

Another, possibly deeper fracture within the empire was the difference between colonies in which the entire population acquired political rights and representation in the French parliament in 1848 (the "old colonies" of the ancien régime, including Guadeloupe, Martinique, Réunion, Guiana, and French territories on the coasts of Senegal and India) versus all the other territories situated in Africa, Asia, and the Pacific where natives had diminished political and civil rights.

A "Ministry of Colonies" was created in 1894 to administer the increasingly complex relationships between colonies and metropole. Even here, however, authority remained fragmented: the Ministry of Colonies had no jurisdiction over Algeria or the protectorates. The latter were the province of the Ministry of Foreign Affairs, as the mandates would be after 1920. These geographical lines of division were also reproduced *within* the ministry of colonies: from 1894 and 1920, it was organized into autonomous departments, each devoted to a region of the "empire." The same was true of the High Colonial Council, a mixed body of elected representatives and nominated experts, which advised the ministry on matters of colonial legislation. Until 1920, it was organized in four groups, representing the four main regions in which France had possessions.

Finally, the École coloniale, the training school for colonial administrators, was also divided along regional lines. It was founded in 1888 with an Indochinese training section, to which African and North African sections were added, respectively, in 1892 and 1914. Only two transversal sections existed: one to train colonial judges (created in 1905) and another to train labor inspectors for the overseas territories.[17] These divisions, justified by the difficulty of teaching local languages and cultures, resulted in a relative lack of mobility for French colonial officials, particularly middle-level administrators, from one region of the empire to the other and, consequently, in limitations on the circulation of representations and practices from one point of the empire to the other. Governors' positions were more political and required less local knowledge. Joseph Galieni, Hubert Lyautey, Joost Van Vollenhoven, and Jules Brévié, were all top colonial officials whose careers took them from Asia to Africa and back.

Obviously these characteristics were not unique to the French case: layered sovereignty has been a common characteristic of all empires, since "the concept of empire presumes that different peoples within the polity would be governed differently."[18] In the late nineteenth century, Britain's imperial mode of governance was predicated on this fragmentation: the Colonial Office never had responsibility for India, which was under the authority of the India Office, while certain informal protectorates, such as Egypt, were dealt with by the Foreign Office. Nevertheless, while it may be that all modern empires were in one way or the other "fractured," some were more so than others. A comparative approach would be necessary to understand the nature and depth of these divisions, and the density of the circuits that established continuity.

Only in the 1930s did the notion of empire as a coherent unit enter into more frequent usage in political parlance. But then again, the word was used primarily to decry the lack of "imperial consciousness" among the French population. In 1933, an important academic journal, *L'Afrique française*, noted that the success of the international colonial exhibit of 1931 did not translate into a public awareness of empire. In its pages, George Hardy, then director of the École coloniale, denied that "the majority of the French people are aware of the solidarity between France and its colonies. Have we gotten used to thinking like an empire (*penser impérialement*)? Certainly not!"[19] In 1936, a high-ranking staff member of the Ministry of Colonies, Gaston Pelletier, and a journalist, Louis Roubaud, published with some success a book entitled *Colonies or Empire?* They denounced the lack of "imperial conscience" in all matters and answered the question posed in the title by claiming, "Empire! It is finally time! Imperial France, go to work!"[20] That same year, commenting on the trains sent around France to exhibit the riches of empire throughout the country, the writer Maurice Martin Du Gard noted, "[T]he word 'empire' is suspect and the thing indifferent. For most people, it evokes I don't know what tendentious idea of conquest and subjection." And the Blum government rejected the word *empire* in favor of *Overseas France* when it renamed a number of its institutions, including the École coloniale.[21]

In the end, it may well be that only when directly faced with the Nazi threat did the French elite become aware of the country's status as an empire (as Charles-Robert Ageron has noted).[22] Out of this crisis came the "doctrine of salvation through empire" (*le salut par l'Empire*). The notion was central to the appeal of Charles de Gaulle in June 1940, who argued that free France had the "empire behind her"—a major basis for France's hope. The Vichy regime also used the notion like no other government before and created many institutions to promote the "imperial idea." Philippe Pétain and his affiliates even thought about clarifying in the new constitution that "the French State is the French Empire" (*l'Etat français est l'Empire français*). The years between 1940 and 1944 saw a boomlet in books with *empire* in their titles—among them *The French Empire* by René Maunier.[23] A prominent figure of the colonial sciences and the holder of the chair in "colonial sociology" at the Paris Law School since 1926, Maunier had published many books examining the "colonial" in the 1920s and 1930s but had never written on empire per se.

So France, especially as a Republic, might have been imperial in practice, but French elites consistently rejected the concept—and consistently structured the administration of empire around that contradiction.[24] To borrow from a completely different analytical framework, one could say that France was an empire "in itself" but not "for itself." As mentioned earlier, the reasons for this reluctance derived from the negative associations of the word *empire* with the Napoleonic regimes and France's rivals, Britain and Germany. But more deeply, it can be explained by the difficulty of thinking about the colonial domain as a coherent, if heterogeneous, unit. In the French political imagination since the Revolution, the Republic is "one and indivisible"—the colonies are seen as additions to this unit, not integral parts of it. This fragmentation is reflected in the French historiography of colonialism, which, since the late nineteenth century, has been divided into studies of French colonial politics and policies on the one hand and work on local colonial situations on the other. Until the 2000s, the French empire and the circuits of ideas, norms, products, and people that gave it a concrete existence were only rarely an object of research for French historians.

AN EMPIRE WITHOUT A CONSTITUTION

The most striking feature of the treatment of the colonies in France's constitutional history is the principle of "exception" (in French *spécialité coloniale*), according to which French colonies were governed not by general French laws but by "special" laws.[25] Thus the constitution introduced a major line of legal separation between the metropole and the colonies and a principle of fragmentation within the colonial world, since each territory was to be ruled by its own laws.

This trajectory started during the ancien régime. The colonies were considered to be a "special domain" governed and administered by the king without any of the rules limiting his power in the metropole.[26] This division between metropole and colonies persisted in the 1791 Constitution, which declared that the "French colonies and possessions in Asia, Africa, and America, although they form part of the French empire, are not comprised within the present Constitution" (Title VII, Article 8–the only occurrence of the word *empire* in a French constitutional document).[27] This text established the separation between France per se and its colonies, the status of which was left completely undefined—a constitutional terra uncognita. The decree of June 15, 1792, granted the National Assembly the power to pass laws specific to colonial territories. While the Constitution of 1793 mentioned neither "colonies" nor "empire," the Constitution of Year III (1795) reversed the direction and declared the colonies an "integral part of the Republic and . . . under the same constitutional law" (Article 6). This was an exceptional text in the sense that, unlike all other constitutional documents, it did not impose special laws on the colonies and did include them in the Republic. The article belongs to the section on the division of territory: it declares the colonies to be *départements*, assimilating them to the fundamental administrative units of French political geography and making them building blocks of the modern nation.[28]

The change between 1791 and 1795 should be understood in the light of important political and legal debates on the relationship between the metropolitan power and its overseas possessions, which started before the Revolution. The difficulties raised by geographical distance, especially in the domain of law, had been an important theme in the eighteenth century, from the writings of the creole member of the Royal Colonial Council, Emilien Petit, to those of Denis Diderot, in *L'Histoire des Deux Indes,* wondered, "At such great distance, what can be the efficacy of metropolitan laws on subjects and what can ensure the obedience of the subjects to these laws?"[29] Antimonarchic sentiment was associated with a position favoring a form of independence for the colonies within a federative structure. While this vision was taken quite seriously by members of the constituent assembly of 1791, by 1795 the political valence of independence had completely changed. In his report on the colonies, François-Antoine de Boissy d'Anglas proposed a vision of the relations between France and its colonies that would become commonplace in the nineteenth century, insisting on both the unequal capacity for self-government among different nations and the fundamental economic and strategic functions of the colonies. These two characteristics led him to push for a more powerful, more centralized colonial administration because "the further the government is from the people, the more powerful and firm it needs to be."[30] A crucial factor here is the radical transformation of the political landscape in the colonies, in the context of massive slave uprisings, the abolition of slavery in 1794, and the growing defiance of settlers toward the Revolution.

That this strict assimilationism was the result of an exceptional political context is confirmed by the reaffirmation of the legal exception in the Constitution of Year VIII (1799). Its Article 91 declared that the "legal status of the colonies (*régime des colonies*) is determined by special laws." Here *empire* and *départements* have disappeared and the older concept of colonies is revived, with the double implication of separation from the metropole and diversity of conditions.

All the constitutional texts of the nineteenth century repeated this "colonial exception." The continuity is all the more remarkable in that it applied to monarchic, imperial, and republican regimes. The affirmation that the colonies were "ruled by special laws and rules" (*lois et réglements particuliers*) in the constitutional charters of 1814 and 1830 would be repeated in all subsequent texts.

This inclusion/exclusion of the colonies from the constitutions led to contradictions that are perhaps most apparent in the 1848 Constitution—a text that might be the best illustration of the difficulty of the French elite to think "like an empire." Article 21 introduces the political representation of Algeria and the French colonies: from 1848 onward (with an interruption during the Second Empire) deputies from Guadeloupe, Martinique, Guiana, Réunion, Senegal, and India were called to participate in the production of French law. Yet, while Article 109 declared Algeria (conquered starting in 1830, officially annexed to France in 1834) and other colonies "French territories," it also specified that they were "ruled by specific laws until a special law applies the present constitution to them." With this step deferred, the short-lived Constitution never applied to the colonies—except for the article that allowed for their political representation.

The constitutional law of the Third Republic, a period associated with the apex of French modern imperialism, was, if possible, even more ambiguous. This very succinct document referred to the colonies only once to stipulate that the "departments of Algeria, [and] the four colonies of Martinique, Guadeloupe, Réunion and French India," would each elect a senator. In the absence of any mention of the legal nature of these territories, older texts, and most notably the Senatus-Consulte of 1854, were still applicable. Its Article 18 affirmed that "colonies, except for Martinique, Guadeloupe and Réunion, will be ruled by imperial decrees." Thus, during the entire Third Republic, a constitutional text from the regime of Napoleon III shaped the legal framework of the colonial possessions: it was literally an empire without a constitution.

Consequently, while the French parliament could legislate for colonial matters, its decisions were never automatically applicable to colonial territories. The parliament had to explicitly mention the colonial territories to which the law applied. In practice, the exception was the rule: during the Third Republic, the parliament only rarely mentioned the colonial extension of the laws it voted on, except for Algeria. In addition, the Senatus-Consulte of 1854 gave a prominent legislative role to the executive, since the president could rule colonial territories by "simple decrees." In reality during the Third Republic, an enormous body of colonial legislation, in all the territories, was the result of presidential decrees drafted by the Ministry of Colonies with the help of a body of experts nominated by the government and known as the High Colonial Council—comprised of law professors, colonial deputies, and members of the elite of the colonial administration. Colonial exception is thus characterized by the exclusion of colonial populations, including its elites, from decision making and by the overwhelming power of the executive branch at the expense of the legislative.

In a French political culture that was dominated, since the Revolution, by the "empire of law," the colonial exception was of paramount importance. Since law is first and foremost characterized by universality, "special laws" were a contradiction in terms: colonies were to be ruled by experts, not "rational laws." To the end, this constitutional organization entrenched a separation between the metropole, which was ruled through laws voted on democratically by the parliament, and colonies ruled by administrative fiat, or rather administrative fiats, since distinct bodies of expertise had been developed for different territories. This separation sheds some light on the history of the concept of "assimilation," often presented by actors at the time, and by historians afterward, as a distinctive trait of the French imperial project. Throughout most of the nineteenth century, "assimilation" meant the identity of the administrative apparatus and legislation between metropole and colonies: the process that would lead to this legal and administrative unification was the object of many debates, especially at the end of the century, which concentrated on the "ability" of natives to assimilate the cultural and political principles of French civilization.[31] These debates never mentioned the fact that French political culture and its constitutional tradition were also an important obstacle to this "rapprochement."

A Turn toward a Constitutional Empire

The 1946 Constitution represents an important rupture in this trajectory. By creating the French Union (Union française), which incorporated the metropole and overseas territories within the same constitutional framework, it became the first imperial constitution of France. At the same time, this Constitution of the Fourth Republic marked an apparent break with colonialism, as is suggested by the wording of the preamble. France is described as "forming with the peoples of overseas territories (*peuples d'outre-mer*) a Union based on equality of rights and duties, with no distinction of race or religion," with the intention of "eliminating any colonial system based on arbitrariness." One should resist the easy conclusion that in order to establish itself as imperial, France had to stop being colonial. As the rest of the preamble makes clear, there is a strong continuity between the colonial "humanism" of the interwar period, which promoted different but not divergent trajectories for France and its colonies, with the former serving as a guide for the latter, and the affirmation that "true to her traditional mission, France intends to lead toward freedom the people she has been in charge of, so that they can govern themselves and manage their own affairs democratically."[32] This sounds very much like Jules Ferry or, later, Albert Sarraut advocating the duty of the stronger to guide the weaker toward civilization.

The history of this period is well known. If World War II helped create an imperial consciousness, it also made it abundantly clear that the colonial republican order was in need of major reform. This observation and the international climate of the postwar period influenced the drafting of the 1946 Constitution, a two-step process. In the first version of the text, the articles defining the French Union were strongly influenced by a group of African representatives to the Constituent Assembly, led by Léopold Sedar Senghor. Thanks to their influence, the text envisaged a clear evolution toward self-government and democratization, with France and the other members participating in a federation of equals. The constitutional project—for reasons that have little to do with the provisions on the French Union—was rejected by referendum in May 1946. More conservative members of the colonial ministry were able to have their voices heard during the drafting of the second version of the document. This older generation was less prone to concessions and reforms.[33]

Many commentaries on the 1946 Constitution note that the attempt to find a compromise between these two positions led to a text that is, as far the French Union is concerned, both "ambiguous" and "misleading"—a text that was "dead from its inception" and made the decolonization process even more difficult.[34] But one could take a different view and insist on the "openness" of a text that was considered by both authors and critics as dynamic: it proclaimed equality without defining its terms and thus left space for political negotiation.

Thus, the 1946 Constitution could be described as the first imperial French charter in the sense that "the French Union française, like empires of the past, would be built out of different sorts of polities connected to an imperial center in different ways."[35] But the nature of the connection was highly ambiguous. While the preamble seemed to view it as a federative link in a community of equals, the articles in Title VIII showed continuity with the colonial tradition and introduced a strong distinction between the Republic on the one hand and its colonies on the other. Article 60 defines the French Union as composed of two ensembles: the "French Republic, comprising metropolitan France and overseas departments and territories"; and "associated territories and States." Once again, there was a reluctance to affirm the imperial nature of the Republic.

Conclusion

What were the consequences of this long-seated "denial" of empire on the process of decolonization in the French case? First, the lack of a unitary vision and the emphasis on bilateral relations between the metropolis and specific territories deeply shaped the different paths out of colonial domination. The French political elite did not see Algeria as a colony or a region of its empire but as an integral part of the French Republic: its coming to independence could not have the same meaning and consequences as that of the sub-Saharan colonies. In the 1950s and 1960s, decolonization was not regarded as a monolithic process of the demise of empire but rather as a series of accessions to sovereignty by territories that had different relationships with France. Second, the absence of a strong imperial political culture, and especially of an imperial constitutional tradition, left a lot of space for experimentation after World War II. From the debates on the French Union in 1946 to the creation of the French Community in 1958 (a looser and more egalitarian association between France and its "colonies"), many possibilities were explored. A noncolonial empire, in the sense of a less hierarchical federation characterized by equality within difference, was certainly one of them. But at the same time, older forms of repression were used in the violent crushing of anticolonial movements at Thiaroye (Senegal) in 1944, Sétif (Algeria) in 1945, Tonkin in 1946, and Madagascar in 1947. The path was everything but straightforward.

The "colonial exception" had also long-term consequences for the form of French postcolonial domination, especially in West Africa. The existence of a separate body of colonial legislation and policies led to the formation of an autonomous group of "colonial experts" in the metropole who advised the Ministry of Colonies; it also conferred great discretionary power on the highest local administrators, who behaved like proconsuls. These officials based their legitimacy on knowledge of local populations and participation in elite networks. Both were resources immediately available at the moment of independence. When French formal sovereignty ended, it was not difficult to mobilize these resources and reproduce the "special colonial domain" by setting up a "special office" for African affairs at the Elysée Palace, described by Robert Aldrich in this volume. In the end, the "colonial exception"—characterized by a constitutional division between France and its colonies, special colonial legislation devised by the executive, and the absence of a democratic process—facilitated the continuation of French domination, especially in West Africa, under a different name.

When Did Decolonization End?

France and the Ending of Empire

ROBERT ALDRICH

IN THE *LONGUE DURÉE* of imperial expansion and contraction, France experienced two periods of colonial downsizing, the first over the decades from the 1760s to 1815; the second, beginning in the 1940s, was largely complete by 1962. However, this eclipse of formal empire meant neither the end of France's international presence as a medium-range power nor its commercial, political, and cultural withdrawal from its former colonies. This essay argues that as the French refused to acquiesce to the new American empire in the ascendant after 1945, or to accept fully the end of their own empire by the early 1960s, their leaders devised ways to maintain powerful influence. This suggests that the boundaries between the colonial and postcolonial periods (and ideologies) are remarkably porous.

Constructing and Deconstructing Empires

France built the modern world's second-largest empire from the invasion of Algiers in 1830 through the acquisition of a League of Nations mandate over Syria and Lebanon after World War I. By the interwar years it had amassed domains of eleven million square kilometers encompassing one hundred million citizens and subjects: *la plus grande France*. At a grand *exposition coloniale* in Paris in 1931, fairgoers marveled at replicas of Angkor Wat and the Djenné mosque from West Africa, enjoyed performances by Khmer dancers and saluted parades of *tirailleurs sénégalais*, shopped at make-believe North African souks, and congratulated their colonial cousins on the achievements of settlers in Algérie française. Empire did not evoke unanimous support, however, and communists and surrealists organized a counterexhibition to show off the darker side of colonialism: violence and land spoliation, political disenfranchisement and corruption. Meanwhile, anticolonial nationalism gathered force. At the time of the colonial jamboree, France had only recently suppressed the Druze Rebellion in Lebanon and fought rebels in the Rif War in Morocco, it was sending increasing numbers of Vietnamese agitators and mutineers to the Maison Centrale prison in Hanoi or to the penal island of Con Dao, and it looked with mounting suspicion on anticolonial and autonomist movements in North Africa.

Nevertheless, few of the colonialists predicted that little more than thirty years after the 1931 fair, the overseas empire, except for a few redoubts, would have disappeared. The mandated territories gained independence at the end of World War II, as did the three countries of Indochina after a war that dragged on from 1946 to 1954; the protectorates of Morocco and Tunisia regained sovereignty in 1956, and India annexed the French *comptoirs* (enclaves, or trading outposts) on the subcontinent. The African colonies broke away in 1960 as fast as ministers could fly around to preside over the lowering of the Tricolour, and after eight years of fratricidal warfare Algeria became independent in 1962. It was a relatively rapid and largely unforeseen end to empire.[1]

The path to imperial disengagement, in retrospect, may look straight and narrow, but such was not the case. Like other imperialist powers, France proved a reluctant decolonizer, perhaps even more so because the defeat of 1940 and the German occupation had rendered France supine. Although Charles de Gaulle joined the Allied powers, France did not enjoy the "special relationship" that existed between London and Washington. The French political elite did not wish to cede the imperial great power mantle to the United States, as the British agreed to do. Later years would show that the French would try not only to establish and maintain their primacy in Western Europe but also to assert their distance from the United States through an assertive global diplomacy—marked by military withdrawal from the North Atlantic Treaty Organization (NATO), early recognition of the People's Republic of China, development of an independent nuclear capability, and criticism of U.S. policy in Southeast Asia. Indeed, much of French foreign policy was seen, especially by American critics, as an attempt to challenge the emergent hegemony of the United States in the "free world."

Meanwhile, at least through the 1950s, without the empire France was, as one senator declared, just a parcel of European landscape, but with it, France was a world power: a vocation for *grandeur* that the French never abandoned. A defeated power such as Italy or Japan might not have any choice but to relinquish its empire, and the Dutch retreated, unwillingly, from the East Indies, content with a diminished role in world affairs. Britain, victorious in the war, with greater or lesser grace nonetheless quit India. France did not envisage a similar fate, and empire—at least in the 1940s and 1950s—served as guarantor of its global status.

In the decade or so after the war, France tried to remold the empire the better to preserve it. In the 1944 Brazzaville conference, colonial leaders (all European, none indigenous) ruled out the possibility of "self-government" for the colonies, using that term in English. In 1946, the *vieilles colonies* (old colonies)—Martinique, Guadeloupe, Guiana, Réunion—became overseas *départements* (states) of France, just as were the three *départements* of Algeria, in principle indefectibly tied to the Republic, as much a part of France as Provence or Paris. The Constitution of 1946 extended citizenship, though not equal voting rights, to the colonized and ended the hated *code de l'indigénat*.[2] It established a Commonwealth-style French Union (Union française) with provisions for "associated states" that applied, though briefly, to Vietnam, Cambodia, and Laos while French soldiers fought a losing war to keep Indochina French.[3] But finally ignominious defeat at Dien Bien Phu spelled the end of the empire in Southeast Asia.

Some recommended further imperial retreat; the journalist Raymond Cartier in 1956 called for France to withdraw from empire for economic and political reasons, focusing modernization efforts on the provinces rather than the colonies, though few officials subscribed to *Cartiérisme*. In its sub-Saharan territories, France indeed appeared to be digging in—Paris invested more funding in black Africa in the last ten years of colonial rule than the grand total of all earlier investments. When the Algerian insurrection broke out in 1954, politicians of the Left and Right adamantly promised to defeat the nationalists, and to use all means fair and foul to achieve that objective—from the sending in of hundreds of thousands of French troops to a new Constantine Plan for economic development, from torture to extract information from nationalists to prosecution of antiwar activists in France and North Africa. In 1956, the French devised a new structure (under the *loi Defferre*) for a modest devolution of administrative power and the extension of universal suffrage to the colonies, but the reforms proved short-lived, as the Algerian War soon brought down the Fourth Republic and brought the return of de Gaulle. In a trip to Africa in 1958, de Gaulle famously said that he had "understood" the demands of the *pieds-noirs* (French residents), which many took as a resolve to keep Algérie française, although de Gaulle might already have been considering other options. He also visited black Africa, where he was welcomed by some but, to his anger, also saw signs of anti-French sentiment and heard calls for independence.

Back in Paris, de Gaulle designed a new constitution for the Fifth Republic, which turned the French Union into a Community (*Communauté* minus the "French" adjective) and engaged in other maneuvers in a last-ditch effort to preserve a dying empire. However, he soon conceded to Algerians the right of self-determination, foreseeing that this would mean independence. In the meantime, he crafted plans for black Africa, with the hope that France's sub-Saharan colonies would stay in the Republic. A referendum offered each the possibility of remaining a French territory or going it alone as an independent state; only Guinea, under Sékou Touré, made the latter choice. Most African leaders were unwilling to give up the aid and other funding that de Gaulle said would no longer be available to independent states, and many also feared the deleterious effects of independence on domestic politics and their own power bases. Very quickly, however, France and Africa moved toward formal separation; in less than two years, eighteen colonies had gained independence. Two years after that momentous change, following lengthy negotiations and continuous fighting, the Évian Accords proclaimed a truce in Algeria; the Algerians then voted in favor of independence, to which the French acceded.

French decolonization was a messy affair (not unlike the process elsewhere), brought about by war, nationalist pressure, and a decision in Paris that holding out was impossible, though with the dream that, even for Algeria, France might keep close ties with its former colonies. World War II, with the defeat of France, encroaching Japanese hegemony, and ultimately the occupation of Indochina, had provided a larger window of opportunity for the struggle that led to independence for Vietnam, Cambodia, and Laos, and in Vietnam, France suffered defeat on the battlefield. As for Algeria, the French army always maintained (and apologists for Algérie française still do) that it was not a nationalist military victory that forced the French out; rather the war of attrition against the French, the loss of thirty thousand soldiers, and the virtual civil war tearing France apart at home made it impossible to cling to the outpost. De Gaulle declared that decolonization had become France's policy because it was in France's interest, an admission of the impossibility, without ever greater bloodshed, expense, and international opprobrium, of retaining Algeria, but also a policy statement that France's interest was best served by devising other strategies to maintain *grandeur*.

By 1962, France had thus seen the eclipse of empire.[4] Anticolonial nationalism (the loss of support from colonized elites), changing international circumstances (changing alliances and military losses), and pressure for decolonization (not least due to economic concerns) at home are generally identified as the three pivots of decolonization. Anticolonialist nationalism, in the French case, played a major part: the ideological and guerrilla warfare of the Viet Minh and Algeria's National Liberation Front (FLN), as well as less violent but determined pressure in Morocco, Tunisia, West Africa, Equatorial Africa, and Madagascar. As the international winds blew against colonialism, France tried to shield itself with constitutional changes, military force (as in the disastrous Suez invasion), and influence in forums such as the United Nations, but lack of international support for imperial rule helped undermine the foundations of the empire. The Bandung Conference of 1955, the independence of Ghana in 1957, and the pan-Arabism championed by General Gamal Abdel Nasser in Egypt all contributed to tearing down French rule in the remaining colonies.[5]

Domestically, colonialism increasingly lost support. Many in France were simply indifferent to empire (as they always had been). Few really regretted the loss of Indochina. Only thirty-five thousand French people had lived in

"Vive Massu." Supporters of French General Jacques Massu construct barricades during the Algerian War of Independence, January 1960. (Michel Marcheux)

Indochina on the eve of World War II, so reintegrating them into France did not pose a major problem, and, in any case, some remained in a South Vietnam that for two decades longer seemed hospitable to a Western presence. (However, the Americans gradually displaced the French in South Vietnam, while France remained persona non grata in Ho Chi Minh's North Vietnam.) No one in France, other than the odd colonial adventurer, was willing to take up arms for empire in the Levantine or North African protectorates or sub-Saharan Africa, and all hoped that an amicable separation would preserve French stakes in the successor states.

Algeria was different, home to a million *pieds-noirs*, proximate to the mainland, and proclaimed to be part of France itself. Yet the long and bloody war whittled away support, first from sympathizers with the Algerians, intellectuals who opposed conscription of soldiers, and Christian activists tormented by the violence, then in a wider public skeptical about the benefits of fighting to retain French control and less and less convinced about the moral rightness of the settlers. Most greeted the end of the war with relief, though bitterness festered among *rapatriés* (the repatriated) who lost land and livelihood in the "abandonment" (as they saw it) of their homeland, old soldiers who felt unthanked for wartime service and sacrifice, diehard colonialists, *harkis* unceremoniously parked in resettlement camps in France in order to avoid massacre in Algeria, and those nostalgic for an idealized promised land across the Mediterranean.[6]

GRANDEUR WITHOUT EMPIRE

Yet not all was lost with the end of empire. *Pieds-noirs* assimilated surprisingly easily to French society, and migrant workers arrived in increasingly larger numbers than under colonial rule from Africa and elsewhere to provide cheap labor for France. Economically, the empire had never been the primary focus of French commerce—only about 10 to 15 percent of French trade had been with the colonies just before World War I, and only about a third during the Depression, a time of necessary imperial preference. Now postwar reconstruction and development, the consumer revolution, and demand created by population growth and urbanism provided jobs, healthy returns from investments, and openings for entrepreneurial acumen, with the *trente glorieuses* (1946–1975) of growth uninterrupted by decolonization. Colonial companies frequently changed names but carried on business as usual, and ex-colonies continued to furnish raw materials and markets for manufactured goods, the state now largely freed of the expenses attached to administration, defense, and the *mission civilisatrice*: a clear indication of the economic taproots of decolonization. A phrase attributed to François Mitterrand, "Partir pour mieux rester"—leaving in order to stay on more easily—provided the motto for decolonization *à la française*. France now successfully found new ways to make up for the loss of formal empire.

Colonialists had always argued that the empire provided geostrategic bases around the world and a reserve army of soldiers. Indeed France mobilized half a million indigenous soldiers, and 150,000 overseas citizens, during World War I, with over 80,000 *morts pour la France* (military personnel killed in action); colonial troops had played a major role in French liberation at the end of World War II. However, during the years of decolonization, France found something to compensate for the military benefits of a lost empire: nuclear weaponry. When de Gaulle returned to power, he sped forward with development of a nuclear arsenal, with the first nuclear devices exploded in 1960 deep in the Algerian desert.

With Algerian independence glimmering on the horizon, de Gaulle announced to a startled delegation from Oceania that the testing site would be transferred to French Polynesia, telling islanders that in return for hosting the installation, a manna of investments and jobs would rain down. From the early 1960s until the late 1980s, and again briefly at the start of Jacques Chirac's presidency in 1995 and 1996, France carried out atmospheric, then underground tests at Mururoa Atoll. Neighboring countries in the South Pacific were enraged. Although the French adamantly denied that there were deleterious ecological or health effects, recent revelations have proved that diseases that affected soldiers and workers, and environmental degradation, were in fact connected to radiation.[7]

Nuclear weaponry formed one of the foundations of France's power after the setting of the imperial sun. In addition to developing this new arsenal, leaders directed the country's attention back to Europe. They spearheaded establishment of the European Economic Community with the Treaty of Rome in 1957, the creation of a Paris-Bonn axis cemented with the rapprochement with Germany undertaken by de Gaulle. Military strength, a leading role in Europe, France's wealth as the second-largest European economy, and its seat as a permanent member of the United Nations Security Council ensured continued international leverage. France was a power, though a medium-sized one rather than a super-power, with which others had to contend. De Gaulle skillfully, if infuriatingly for his country's allies, jockeyed for international position to supplement that power: vetoing British entry into the Common Market, withdrawing from the military command of NATO, and promoting France in the Cold War years as an intermediary between East and West. Posing as the great decolonizer, de Gaulle also positioned France as privileged interlocutor of the Arab world and defender of the third world.

France also found ways to preserve some other benefits that empire had been said to offer. The French Republic still includes a dozen overseas outposts, a "miniempire" to be sure, with the vestigial territories sometimes labeled the "con-fetti of empire" or the "Republic's dancing-girls" (as President Valéry Giscard d'Estaing memorably referred to them, alluding to both exoticism and cost). Yet the real or perceived advantages that they give France have not been negligible. The nuclear testing site in Polynesia has now closed, but France maintains military bases in other territories. New Caledonia (where France struggled actively to avoid decolonization in the 1980s) contains one of the world's largest deposits of nickel, a strategic mineral, and because of the scattered and insular nature of the overseas territories, France lays claim to one of the world's largest exclusive economic zones of maritime area. As late at the 1970s, a French prime minister pointed to New Caledonia as one of the few places where French nationals might migrate and live under the French flag. The European space station is located at Kourou in Guiana. Ministerial communiqués speak about the opportunities that the territories provide for the *rayonnement* ("diffusion" or, literally, "radiance") of French culture. Champions of the *outre-mer* in the 1980s and beyond trumpeted these overseas territories as the good fortune (*la chance*, in former prime minister Michel Debré's formulation) not only of France but of Europe. In some ways, these justifications for retention of control over territories that prove constant financial drains on France, and where autonomist and independence movements, as well as civil strife, have punctuated recent history, constitute only a posteriori rationales for outposts where the majority electorally affirm a desire to remain part of France. These remnants of the colonial age nevertheless constitute part of France's geostrategic global positioning.[8]

France designed another particular connection between the colonial and the postcolonial: *francophonie*. The French have proclaimed their culture as universalistic, and colonialists prided themselves on spreading their language and civilization, even if the colonial schooling system restricted enrollments to a small fraction of the colonized. In 1962, the year of the Algerian debacle, Léopold Sedar Senghor—poet, former French minister, and first president of Senegal—along with other French-speaking politicians from Africa, called for the founding of an international francophone movement, one with certain parallels to the British Commonwealth but a more culturally focused agenda. The project did not register unanimous support, as Algeria and communist Vietnam refused to join (although Vietnam later became a member), but an infrastructure gradually developed, and France plays the leading role in the Organisation Internationale de la Francophonie, which furthers cultural links between the metropole and its former colonies. France still invests heavily in cultural and educational activities with *lycées* (schools), the Alliance Française, cultural institutes, and film and literary festivals, and many of the brightest students go to France for tertiary education. Even in places where the use of French has declined almost to extinction, such as Vietnam and Vanuatu, France steadfastly promotes its culture. Such efforts bespeak a desire to combat *les Anglo-Saxons* and English, a variation of cultural rivalries inherited from the colonial age and pursuit of international cultural politics that is a legacy of the *mission civilisatrice*.[9]

Neocolonialism? Soft and Hard

Francophonie represents an example of "soft imperialism," or soft postimperialism. France also engages in a harder sort of postcolonial undertaking, what some term a neocolonial approach to its former colonies. The countries of French West Africa and French Equatorial Africa, along with Madagascar and Djibouti, have a long history of entanglement with French merchants, slave traders, planters, and bankers. From western Africa, France in colonial times and at present has imported coffee, cocoa, tropical fruits, hardwoods, base and precious minerals, oil and gas, and other commodities; sub-Saharan Africa also served as a market for French manufactured goods and a place for investment, and in some of the countries France enjoyed a virtual commercial monopoly. After decolonization, France maintained cordial relations with local leaders, even nationalists such as Senghor and Félix Houphoët-Boigny, first president of the Ivory Coast. In contrast to the divorce between France and Indochina and Algeria, and despite occasional violence, the separation produced by decolonization was relatively amicable.[10]

French officials determined that it should remain so, and many African leaders agreed. In the years immediately preceding decolonization, there was talk in France and Africa of Eurafrique, a bicontinental bloc that could form an international force vis-à-vis the United States and the communist world. De Gaulle considered remodeling the Communauté established in 1958 as the "Communauté franco-africaine." Others suggested multicountry African federations linked to France, and one leader in Gabon proposed an entirely different type of evolution by mooting that his country be made a French *département*.[11] None of these alternatives eventuated, and the metamorphosis of 1960 brought to life separate, fully independent nation-states. But when they gained independence, the former colonies signed public and secret treaties with France concerning their future relationships. Paris placed African affairs under a new Ministry of Cooperation, but de Gaulle also set up a special office at the Élysée Palace, under Jacques Foccart, to manage Franco-African affairs outside the usual diplomatic channels.

French politicians publicly affirmed their intention to safeguard African relations, de Gaulle's Prime Minister Debré talking of "building a commonwealth, a group of states, grouped around France, and where the authority of France will be manifested by the maintenance of its influence, by the maintenance of its [development] aid and by its special cooperation." Prime Minister (and later president) Georges Pompidou declared to the National Assembly in 1964, "The policy of cooperation is the sequel to the policy of European expansion in the nineteenth century, which was marked by the creation of vast colonial empires or by the presence and economic and political influence of Europe in these immense areas." Referring to the special relationship between France and its old colonies, Houphouët-Boigny coined the term *Françafrique*, a word to which he gave a positive spin.[12]

A word needs to be said here about Foccart, often perceived as the éminence grise behind French African policy. Born in metropolitan France in 1913, Foccart came from a family of plantation owners in Guadeloupe, and he was engaged in the import-export business in his early life. Although allegedly he was initially involved in collaboration with the Germans at the start of the Vichy regime, he switched his allegiances and became a Resistance hero. This action created an almost symbiotic relationship between Foccart and de Gaulle, whom he thereafter faithfully served. In the 1950s, Foccart organized a paramilitary force, the Service d'Action Civique, which provided protection to Gaullist candidates and interests and played a role in the general's return to power in 1958. Foccart then assumed the role of "Mr. Africa" in the Gaullist administration, which he would hold until 1969 and intermittently thereafter, occupying various positions, including secretary-general of the short-lived French Community set up under the Fifth Republic and presidential adviser with an office near de Gaulle at the Élysée Palace. Foccart indubitably possessed an enormous knowledge of Africa and also benefited from close friendships with many of the pro-French African leaders who emerged from the decolonization process. Foccart had other arrows in his quiver as well. He enjoyed links with French companies eager to exploit African resources, notably the petroleum giant Elf. He was also closely involved with the French spying agency (SDECE, Service de documentation extérieure et de contre-espionnage), which in the name of French security carried out many covert intelligence-gathering and other operations in Africa before and after decolonization. Such a toolbox, at least according to his detractors, allowed Foccart to engineer French African policy.[13]

French intervention in Africa is well documented. In 1960, for instance, France took part in quashing a rebelling in Cameroon, with the SDECE accused of poisoning its leader, Félix Moumié. France supported failed secessionist movements in Katanga (in the former Belgian Congo) and Biafra (in Nigeria) in an attempt to weaken rivals to the old French colonies. In 1964, Foccart and his associates arranged an intervention in oil-rich Gabon in support of a French leader threatened by a coup; France exercised such a strong role, via Foccart's machinations, that the country was derided as "Foccartland." Interventions followed elsewhere, often, it would appear, with Foccart's direct backing (which he occasionally denied), the use of violent tactics, and the employment of mercenaries. The most famous of those hired hands was Bob Denard, a soldier of fortune involved in the Congo, Benin, and especially the Comoros Islands, where he was responsible for several coups—even overthrowing a leader he had effectively placed in power earlier when he lost the support of the French state. Such interventions in the 1960s and 1970s provided proof of France's determination, even when displaying ostensible deference to both democracy and the leaders of independent African states, to maintain France's overweening position. Military operations paralleled fiscal policy, aid, trade, and crony camaraderie between authorities in Paris and the African capitals.

Such actions led the political commentator François-Xavier Verschave to appropriate Houphoët-Boigny's term *Françafrique* to refer, in a damning manner, to the parallel and secret universe of French activities in Africa, remote-controlled by Foccart and his successors. Verschave posited a corrupt conspiracy among African leaders, French officials, and the companies that profited from business opportunities.[14]

In return for aid, much of it siphoned off by African rulers and elites, the French obtained access to natural resources, diplomatic support at the United Nations and other forums, and military bases. The French, in short, continued to treat their former African colonies as their preserve. The French African franc (CFA), dating back to 1939, continued as the legal currency of most of the independent countries, pegged to the French franc (and now the Euro), and down to the 1990s substantially overvalued; CFA countries were obliged to deposit more than half of their reserves in the French treasury. As many as a quarter of a million French people lived in sub-Saharan Africa in the 1980s, far more than in the colonial period, most holding high-ranking technical or commercial positions or working as *coopérants*. Seconded French civil servants worked as presidential advisers and staffed the upper echelons of African administrations. France turned a blind eye, Verschave and others revealed, to profiteering, corruption, and human rights abuses. It gave virtually unquestioning support to such long-lived leaders as Houphoët-Boigny, president of his country from 1960 to 1993, and Omar Bongo, president of the mineral-endowed Gabon for no fewer than forty-two years. Some rulers who enjoyed French support proved particularly dubious characters, the most egregious Jean-Bedel Bokassa of the Central African Republic, who with delusions of grandeur crowned himself emperor. Bokassa was alleged to have given a generous stash of diamonds to President Giscard d'Estaing, and France's patience only ran out when Bokassa made friends with Libya's Colonel Muammar Gadhafi; France saw to his overthrow in 1979 (but then allowed him to live in France). This was only one of the coups in which France was implicated; French forces have carried out military actions on some twenty occasions since 1960.[15] France continues to station thousands of troops on African soil.[16]

Françafrique, a cornerstone of postcolonial policy, has nevertheless begun to come apart. Stephen Smith dates the beginning of the end to 1994, the year of the death of Houphouët-Boigny, the devaluation (by half) of the CFA, and the failure of France to deploy its troops in Rwanda to stop genocide.[17] Somewhat belatedly, France started to redirect its energies to other areas of the world where commercial advantages presented themselves, perhaps because Africa no longer seemed such a solid investment as the French imagined in the 1960s. Some of the old dictators of Africa lost the support (in Africa and France) on which they had counted. France nurtured and expanded commercial ties with countries outside the francophone orbit, notably Angola, which holds large reserves of petroleum and natural gas, while maintaining close connections with former colonies such as Niger, which has large stocks of uranium.

Complex ties have nevertheless remained between France and Africa, and old habits die hard. When Nicolas Sarkozy became president in 2007, he promised a new African policy; he nevertheless gave a speech in Dakar that many condemned as an apologia for colonialism. When Sarkozy's minister of cooperation and *francophonie*, Jean-Marie Bockel, proclaimed in early 2008, "I want to sign the death certificate of Françafrique," adding that France must no longer give in to the "caprices" of African presidents and send aid that did not serve development, so strong were protests from African leaders that Sarkozy replaced the minister. "We are not going to fall out with those who do us great service," a presidential adviser admitted.[18] One news website titled an article: "La Françafrique est morte, vive la Françafrique."[19]

More recent signals, however, suggest further changes in Françafrique and other spheres of neocolonial sway. France notably refused to give refuge to its former friend Zine el-Abidine Ben Ali when he fled Tunisia in the wake of massive protests in 2011. The revolutionary movements in North Africa and the Middle East risk confounding some of France's carefully nurtured relationships with now contested rulers in those regions. In sub-Saharan Africa, the rocketing involvement of China in business, its demographic presence, and its expanding political relations have severely reduced France's relative position.[20] China has also challenged the clout of France (and other Western countries) elsewhere in the world. Yet France's privileged links with many of its former colonies are unlikely to disappear quickly or entirely, and retaining them remains one of the linchpins of French international policy even in the "post-post-colonial" age.

A final case of the porous boundaries between the colonial and postcolonial must be briefly mentioned: migration to France from the former colonies, an issue to which this essay has already alluded. Thousands of colonial migrants—after all, they were French subjects (and sometimes citizens)—poured into France in the early twentieth century. Though viewed with suspicion, and frequently objects of police surveillance, discrimination, and violence, they provided useful, inexpensive labor for farms and factories or served in the armed forces; a minority were businesspeople, civil servants, or students who emerged as the new African intelligentsia. During the growth years after World War II, the arrival of *travilleurs immigrés* accelerated (partly because of recruitment), although, contrary to expectations, not all of these "guest workers" returned home. Many settled down, their second- or now third-generation children French citizens with a dual, and perhaps inevitably ambiguous, identity.

This is not the place to recapitulate the history of modern migration to France. Suffice it to say that migration has changed the demographic complexion of France, a country that has more Muslim residents than any other in Europe. Issues involving migrants have become more aggravated in recent years with debates about multiculturalism, including the *affaire du foulard* (the conflict concerning the wearing of the Muslim head covering) and the banning of the burka.

"Ethnic" groups have become better organized and militant in demanding redress for their grievances and, in a few cases, recognition and compensation for colonial exactions. Some politicians, including those who make opposition to migration their primary platform, have charged migrants with delinquency and taking jobs from "true" French men and women, fomenting violence in the *banlieues* surrounding Paris and other cities, and giving support to extremist Islamism. Others point out that migrants are often the victims of unemployment and crime and that only a small proportion of French Muslims regularly practice their religion, let alone lend support to radicals or fundamentalists.

Keeping the door open to migrants—indeed, opening it wider—after the imperial sun set maintained a conduit of migration dating back to colonial times. The presence of migrants from the former colonies "brings the empire back home," often in ways that have culturally enriched French society. Because of this demographic change, France is no longer the country idealized in a misty-eyed manner by those who associate it with images of yesteryear. France now faces the major question of how these populations and their cultures fit into the country, and how France should (or can) adapt its institutions and expectations accordingly. The rather sterile discussion initiated by Sarkozy on "national identity" forms part of a real issue of the contours of postcolonial France. Imperial retreat did not leave the empire outside the metropolitan Hexagon.[21] The flags may have come down once and for all, but decolonization should perhaps be seen as a continuing process. Somewhat ironically, indeed, both policy makers promoting the benefits of continued engagement between France and its former colonies and critics of the nature of those links have emphasized the enduring nexus of French connections with the colonial, then noncolonial world.

CONCLUSION: THE "RETURN OF THE COLONIAL"

Debates on issues facing present-day France may seem removed from the decolonization of 1945 to 1962, but they point to the *retour du colonial*, a rediscovery of the French empire and its legacy that has been a major theme in recent years. Decolonization did not solve the problems of the colonial world, it did not sever the ties that bound France to its former empire, and it did not put to rest the demons of the colonial experience. Colonialism now haunts France: the colonial record and its moral and social legacies; relations between France (and the European Union) and the South; the complex problem of "national identity"; and issues of migration and multiculturalism that, at least indirectly, connect with the legacy of colonialism.

Both those who championed the independence of the colonies and those who, however reluctantly, acceded to it hoped that the change of sovereignty would turn a new page in France's relations with much of the world. Policymakers dreamed that a new model of relationship would preserve influence, raw materials, labor, and a cultural presence in the old colonies and allow France to ward off being subsumed into the postwar American imperium. So it did, at least in some ways, but the heritage of those intertwined histories and the successes and, more glaringly, failures of postimperial French policy still loom in contemporary life, as both international and domestic reconfigurations demand a French adaptation to the end of the old postcolonial order set in place with decolonization.

Decolonizing France

L. S. Senghor's Redemptive Program
for African Socialism

GARY WILDER

HOW MIGHT POSTWAR DECOLONIZATION, including the transition from European territorial colonialism to U.S. market imperialism, illuminate our historical present? This important question about decolonization as a process of global restructuring motivates this volume. But because much of the historiography on decolonization is premised on an uncritical methodological nationalism, it is ill-equipped to address this kind of question.

Histories of decolonization often tell stories of dyadic encounters between imperial states and colonized peoples in which the former are figured as powerful nations that possess colonial territories and the latter as not yet independent nations ruled by foreign colonizers. This type of approach leads paradoxically to imperial histories in which empires are not treated as fundamental units of analysis. It naturalizes national states as the primary actors in the drama of decolonization rather than recognizing them as its principal products. Whether written from the perspective of rapacious colonizers or tenacious liberators, these stories of confrontations between national states losing overseas possessions and oppressed nations liberating themselves from foreign conquerors rarely treat decolonization as an epochal process of global restructuring that unfolds on a vast political terrain that includes numerous and diverse actors and entails multiple levels of causation.

An understanding of imperialism and decolonization in terms of epochal global history has largely been the domain of Marxist political economy and world-systems theory. Such work, however, tends to treat empires as vehicles or expressions of global capitalism, which is considered the real agent of history and proper object of study. Alternatively, British imperial histories have treated empires as units of analysis and often seek to link long-term economic developments, conjunctural geopolitical conditions, and short-term maneuvering. International and diplomatic historians have also begun to recognize the grand terrain and large diversity of actors involved in postwar decolonization. But while they are alert to macrohistorical shifts among successive empires as complex systems of transnational governance, imperial and international historians still tend to treat history as an affair of powerful states and instrumental statesmen. In these accounts, rational actors typically pursue transparent interests by inviting or imposing strategic agreements, alliances, and allegiances. Deep structural transformations, systemic logics, and mass social movements do not typically figure in such stories of world hegemonic succession.

International, imperial, and world-systems approaches to decolonization often do recognize the role of non-European actors in these complex processes. But they tend to focus on the ways that colonized agency attempts more or less successfully to influence the process of decolonization without raising fundamental questions about the meaning of decolonization itself. Peripheral agents may be credited with helping to determine the pace of national liberation, the choice of national leaders, the terms of national sovereignty, or the place of new nations in the new global political and economic order. Colonial agents are typically treated as radical or moderate nationalists seeking to secure the best possible terms of state sovereignty for their new nations. Their national and provincial orientation is assumed. They are seen as instrumental actors extracting concessions and promoting interests by manipulating the large imperial players.

But we know that many of these peripheral actors were canny readers of the historical conjuncture in relation to the macrohistorical trends of imperial history. They often responded to this world-historical transition with their own epochal projects and projections. During the postwar opening, the world-making ambition to reconceptualize and reorganize the global order was not the exclusive preserve of imperial policy makers, American strategists, international lawyers, cosmopolitan internationalists, or revolutionary socialists. We need to move beyond the assumption that during decolonization many in the West thought globally while colonized peoples thought nationally. This idea derives from equally spurious assumptions, namely, that colonial emancipation could only be expressed in a territorial national form, that self-determination required state sovereignty, and that this sovereignty had to be unitary. From this perspective, colonized actors who did not support national independence could only be imperial apologists opposed to decolonization.

Such assumptions have been especially limiting in considerations of Léopold Sedar Senghor, who after World War II formulated an epochal project for African decolonization that, he claimed, would help to redeem, by reconciling, humanity on a planetary scale. In this essay, I will focus on his peculiar formulation of African socialism in order to illuminate the epochal and world-making ambitions of colonial actors. In the postwar opening, Senghor regarded decolonization as an opportunity not just to secure territorial sovereignty and national independence but to remake the global order and thereby disrupt the long-term history of imperial succession that has attended liberal political modernity from the start. He was not simply an instrumental nationalist but a visionary strategist and utopian pragmatist whose public initiatives attended to planetary possibilities by seizing a world-historical opportunity to transform (by elevating) and elevate (by transforming) the world that empires had made.

SITUATING SENGHOR

Whether celebrated as an avatar of African liberation or excoriated as a francophile imperial collaborator, Senghor is rightly recognized by scholars as an important figure whose writings and public interventions between the 1930s and 1980s had a significant impact on late colonial and postcolonial politics and consciousness. Best known either as one of the founders of the Negritude movement in interwar Paris or as the first president of independent Senegal in 1960, Senghor belonged to that generation of educated and engaged colonial elites who had intimate knowledge of imperial institutions, moved regularly between metropole and colony, and played central roles in designing postcolonial national states. Scholars have written about all aspects of Senghor's public life following his provincial African and devout Catholic upbringing in Senegal (as a poet, cultural activist, scholar, political critic, French national legislator, African politician, and postcolonial president) at each of the key moments in his career (in the black student and colonial literary expatriate world of interwar Paris, in the French National Assembly, and in Senegal after the war and during his presidency between 1960 and 1980).

Whether positively or negatively, Senghor is remembered primarily as a theorist of African subjectivity and black particularity who was more interested in cultural dignity than political liberty, as a moderate political reformer who collaborated with French rulers in the postwar period before independence, and as a cautious, socially conservative, and sometimes authoritarian, if never dictatorial, president who maintained close relations with the West during the Cold War. He is often caricatured as a classically educated apostle of "Negro African" values with a lifelong love of French high culture and European learning.

These one-sided portrayals, which typically bracket the cosmopolitan, socialist, and epochal dimensions of Senghor's thinking, reflect the territorial nationalist assumptions of postcolonial critics more than they do the actual content of Senghor's work. An unexamined territorialism has often treated Senghor's writings primarily as attempts to express or explain African subjectivity. And methodological nationalism has reduced debates to whether Senghor either promoted African independence or supported the French state. The limitations of these reductive optics are especially evident in accounts of Senghor's postwar public interventions, between 1948 and 1958, when he was a legislator in the French Fourth Republic and leader of an independent African political party. In comparison to Senghor's life as a Negritude poet before 1945 and his tenure as Senegalese president after 1960, this period of exceptional political creativity and audacity in Senghor's career has not been attended to adequately by scholars.

Critics often interpret Senghor's postwar interventions anachronistically from the perspective of his postcolonial presidency. Senghor's "African socialism" is then regarded as superficial, cynical, or opportunistic—a suspect state ideology rather than a considered engagement with Marx's writings and socialist politics. An a priori belief that real decolonization is synonymous with national sovereignty has made it difficult for scholars to recognize the utopian and cosmopolitan dimensions of Senghor's postwar vision of African socialism as one component of a program for colonial emancipation that transcended national autarchy and unitary states. Senghor's political project under the Fourth Republic is thus often treated as compromising or obstructing the path to genuine postcolonial freedom. He is misunderstood as accepting an alternative to decolonization rather than recognized as promoting an alternative form of decolonization. Such misprision affirms the very territorial nationalist logic and autarchic politics that Senghor's vision of African socialism sought to overcome.

Marxism and African Socialism

In the decade following World War II, Senghor pursued self-determination without state sovereignty on two fronts. First, as a legislator in the French National Assembly he waged a constitutional struggle to transform France into a federal republic that would include former colonial territories as freely associated member states that enjoyed juridico-political autonomy and equality, as well as socioeconomic solidarity, with metropolitan France. Second, as a Senegalese politician engaged in frequent electoral battles, Senghor founded an independent political party through which to fashion an original African socialism (and consolidate a local power base).

On both fronts, he made a crucial distinction between "the right of independence," which would only institute a limited (formal) sovereignty, and the "right of self-determination," which, for him meant existential disalienation and substantive self-management. Criticizing "the virus of independence" in a 1957 article in *Le Monde*, he explained that "in the interdependent world of the twentieth century, autarchy, whether economic, cultural, or simply political, equals stagnation."[1] The following year, on the eve of the collapse of the Fourth Republic, Senghor intervened in a National Assembly debate about the Algerian war and the prospect of rewriting the French Constitution. He argued that metropolitan France should agree to compromise its own sovereignty by transforming the unitary state into a federal republic and should allow Algeria to become independent after which it could join France in a broader union of confederated states. He called on his metropolitan counterparts to follow the lead of African parties that had decided to "desacralize" and thereby "transcend" the "notion of independence."[2]

Ten years earlier, in September 1948, Senghor had resigned from what he had come to regard as a corrupt and hypocritical French Socialist Party, which he accused of subordinating African interests to vulgar party politics. Along with his associate Mamadou Dia, he created the Bloc Démocratique Sénégalais (BDS). His aim in leaving the old Socialist Party was not to abandon socialism but to pursue "the socialist ideal" more faithfully.[3] This new independent party demanded autonomy over local affairs in Senegal and hoped to create an integrated West African federation that would itself be integrated into a new French federal republic.[4]

The BDS promoted a reformist socialism, at once mutualist and statist, that aligned itself with rural cultivators.[5] Linking nonviolence to economic realism, it sought to eliminate the excessive profit margins of a regressive colonial capitalism rather than abolish the relations of capitalist production altogether. Senghor and Dia placed their hopes for peaceful socialist transformation and humane economic development on agricultural cooperatives, which would be the focus of technical training, political organizing, and consciousness raising.[6] To this end, Senghor, in the name of the BDS, pursued legislative reforms in French West Africa that would "make real the rights inscribed in the Constitution."[7] These included extending suffrage, passing a formal labor code, and advocating for greater municipal autonomy, more local assemblies, workers' accident compensation, and the reform of agricultural cooperatives and credit systems.[8]

At the same time, Senghor also began a process of theoretical reflection on socialism in Africa. Many of the positions he would develop in the coming years were already present in a 1948 essay, "Marxism and Humanism," in which he challenged attempts by leftist Catholics and orthodox Soviets to reduce Marxism to vulgar materialism, positivism, or atheism.[9] Focusing on Marx's dialectical method, which Senghor believed recognized the underlying relation between matter and spirit, and on Marx's ethical critique of alienation, Senghor argued that Marx developed a holistic vision of *personal* freedom whereby the full human capacity of all individuals would be realized by reconciling labor and capital, the human and natural worlds, and man with his most essential self. Senghor argued that for Marx, socialist revolution would not only end labor exploitation and class antagonism. More fundamentally, the shift from private to social appropriation would establish a "new order" that would ensure "the development of the [total] person's intellectual and spiritual life."[10]

Attempting to reconcile Marx's ethical humanism with Jacques Maritain's Christian personalism, Senghor distinguished between *individual* liberty (based on the right to private property) and *personal* liberty (as "the possibility of the development of individual faculties" through community in a social state).[11] For Senghor, Marx's expansive vision of personal freedom was inseparable from his dialectical philosophy. He writes: "Marx . . . proposes neither a doctrine nor a system, but . . . a method of action in the service of total man, which excludes all totalitarianism, all fixity because man always remains to be realized. Marxism is not a catechism . . . it implies a continual process of overcoming. . . . It is dialectical . . . there is no definitive state: everything is movement, struggle, change."[12] Senghor's Marx is above all a philosopher and moralist who developed a dialectical ethics of human emancipation as both transcendent and worldly, which is to say ever incomplete and open-ended.

"Marxism and Humanism" was guided implicitly by the question that Senghor would address directly in a series of "Reports on Method" prepared for the annual BDS party congresses, namely, why Marx's critique of capitalism was relevant to the task of understanding African alienation. Senghor emphasized that social stratification in Africa was less a function of class exploitation than colonial and racial subjugation. In this context, he argued, workers were actually elites and peasants the real proletariat.[13]

But Senghor contended that despite these differences Marx's critique of European capitalism related directly to African societies insofar as they remained subject to the parasitic commercial capitalism of the *pacte colonial*.[14] He also argued that because French imperialism had created indissoluble bonds between metropolitan and overseas peoples Africa was an integral part of the "Europe" that Marx analyzed.[15] And warning against autarchic solutions to what he regarded as the global problem of capitalist alienation, Senghor insisted that African socialism could only succeed in alliance with metropolitan working classes and European socialist parties.[16] On another level, he believed that Marx's dialectical method and ethical project could be detached from the case of Europe and applied to particular African societies, which might pursue distinct roads toward socialism. Citing Marx's 1881 exchange with Vera Zassoulitch on rural communes in Russia, Senghor insisted that as a communal agrarian society, Africa already possessed institutions that could serve as the basis for precisely the kind of social production and solidarity that Marx had envisioned.[17]

But in order to reclaim Marx for Africa, Senghor had to confront the question of religiosity, which he regarded as "the very sap of Negro-African civilization."[18] He insisted that Marx's supposed atheism was only a conditional rejection of actually existing Christianity, which had been instrumentally deformed by capitalism into an ideological rationalization for systemic social misery.[19] Senghor believed that Marx's transformative vision of emancipation of the total person was consistent with religion's most fundamental aims and values. He denounced "atheistic" socialist parties as "churches" guilty of quasi-religious dogmatism that contravened the original spirit of Marx's writings. Conversely, he maintained that African spiritualism directly embodied Marx's ethical "integral humanism."[20] To denounce religion from the standpoint of socialism, Senghor suggested, was to "slip from a practice to a doctrine, from a method of action to a metaphysics or even a philosophy of history."[21] African religion, he explained, promoted social-ist *methods* by combining will and act with vital energy and popular emotion. African Christianity and African Islam, he explained, also promoted revolution-ary socialist *aims* by challenging "all sorts of despotisms" in order to restore "human dignity."[22] Senghor thus instructed party members that "we can quite legitimately be socialists while remaining believers (*croyants*)."[23]

This faithful socialism, grounded in both Marxist ethics and African religi-osity, would require the BDS to pursue organizing, education, and propaganda targeting indigenous cooperatives and syndicates. Senghor declared that through such political work the party would "begin to model the socialist face of the *cité* of the future."[24] Senghor's religiously grounded African socialism would be a fundamentally political project. He explained to BDS party members in 1953:

> It is not a question of collapsing or confusing politics and religion, of assigning one to the role of the other. *Politics*, as you know, is not exactly a religion, not even a philosophy—nor either a science. It is an art, the art of administering *la Cité*. It does not aim to discover and give the absolute truth. It is the art of using a method which, by ceaselessly corrected approximations, allows the greatest number [of people] to lead a more complete and happy life because more consistent with the *human condition*. Politics is an active humanism . . . it must be integral to and found itself upon an ethics. And religion still remains the most solid foundation of ethics.[25]

In this schema, in order to be authentically socialist and authentically African, the BDS had to undertake a political project rooted in vernacular religious ethics.

FEDERALIST SOCIALISM, SOCIALIST FEDERALISM

But Senghor's socialism did not simply fetishize African alterity. The party, he announced, would "also return socialism to its first vocation . . . that of coexistence and interdependence."[26] Because original socialism had a "federalist tendency," Senghor explained, the aim was to create "a balance which is local autonomy within union."[27] Strategically, this meant that "syndicalism because socialist is anti-autarchic" and must, in the spirit of "Eurafrican cooperation," "federate itself" within an international organization.[28] This meant that while the BDS should focus on African specificity and build on African religiosity, it should simulta-neously pursue socialist internationalism through close alliances with other working classes. But Senghor here is also making a stronger claim. He believed that the "federalist tendency" inherent in socialism would mean that the BDS party's aims—of economic self-management and humane development of the total person in ways that respected African cultural specificity yet promoted global solidarity—could best be pursued within the framework of a postcolonial federation.[29] As in the Proudhonian tradition of mutualism, Senghor considered socialism and federalism to be two sides of the same coin.[30]

It is crucial to remember that precisely when Senghor was forging this program for African socialism, he was also waging a constitutional struggle in the French National Assembly to transform the imperial republic into a decentralized federal democracy. Former colonies would organize themselves into regional federations, which would become member states. Each would possess a local territorial assembly and an autonomous administration through which to manage its own affairs. It would also send representatives to a federal parliament. Metropolitan France, Senghor explained, would become "one state among others, no longer the federator, but the federated."[31] Overseas peoples would be self-governing and subject to their own civil law even as they also enjoyed full French citizenship, juridical equality within the federation, and socioeconomic solidarity with the rest of France.[32] "Economic relations between the metropole and the overseas territories," he explained in 1954, "would cease to be dictated unilaterally. We would no longer be satellites of the metropole, our economy would thus be complementary and not a supplement."[33] These freely associated states would also be charter members of the emergent European Economic Community. Senghor envisioned a reciprocal relationship between this postcolonial federation and an ongoing process of civilizational complementarity, interdependence, and mutual interpenetration. *Eurafrique* referred both to the federal political framework and the corresponding cultural formation that would be its product and its precondition.[34] Senghorian decolonization would be based on partnership, reciprocity, and *métissage* (cultural mixture).

Senghor thus hoped to exploit the world-historic opportunity, following the postwar liberation of France—in that political opening between the secession of Vietnam and the loss of Algeria—to end colonialism and remake the republic. He was not simply demanding that overseas peoples be fully integrated within the existing nation-state. He was proposing a type of integration that would reconstitute France itself by quietly exploding the existing unitary republic from within. Legal pluralism, disaggregated sovereignty, and territorial disjuncture would be constitutionally grounded. The presumptive unity of culture, nationality, and citizenship would be ruptured. As he put it, "[S]overeignty would be a function of the . . . state, not . . . of the *patrie*."[35] This untimely project to transform France immanently was at once gradualist and radical, instrumental and ethical, pragmatic and utopian.[36] Senghor instructed party organizers that federalism, socialism, and religion were "interdependent . . . acts of the trilogy [which] form a single drama, that of the *human condition*."[37] He explained, "[U]sing the method of socialism . . . we discovered federation as the only solution to our problem and *to that of France*."[38] In other words, socialism required federalism, and federalism would renew socialism. Together they would resolve Africa's local problems, its problems with France, and France's own problems.[39] In the Cold War era, Senghor maintained, France and Africa would each need socialism and federalism and each other.

Senghor's program was driven by the insight that true decolonization could not simply target the legal status of African colonies. It would have to recognize their entwined relationship with metropolitan France by transforming the entire empire, metropole included, into a democratic socialist federation. Senghor, in other words, called neither for France to decolonize Africa nor for Africa to liberate itself but for Africans to decolonize France. African socialism would play a vanguard role in a process whereby the imperial nation-state would be sublated, with the national republic elevated into a plural democracy. In turn, this unprecedented state form (within which multiple peoples, civilizations, and legal orders would coexist) could serve as the elemental unit for an alternative global order. Senghor wagered that this postnational socialist state would allow humanity to pursue the dreams of solidarity and reciprocity proclaimed by various currents of postwar internationalism. Senghorian decolonization would seek to inaugurate a new epoch of human history through a process of interdependent overcoming. Colonial capitalism would be superseded by cooperative socialism. Illiberal empires would become postnational federations. International conflict would be displaced by civilizational rapprochement. Cold War antagonism would be transcended. Marxism and spiritualism would be reunited, ethics and politics reintegrated, multiplicity and democracy reconciled. This was a redemptive vision of African-led decolonization as planetary salvation.

REDEMPTIVE DECOLONIZATION

Senghor's program for postcolonial redemption proceeded from the postulate that because "veritable alienation" was moral as well as economic, emancipation could not be restricted to material well-being.[40] African socialism would have "to return man to himself."[41] Senghor warned the BDS against "conflating means and ends"; its aim was not merely to raise Africans' "standard of living" but to restore to them their "reason to live."[42] European socialist parties, he explained, failed precisely insofar as they inverted means and ends—by focusing on material rather than moral improvement, on superficial rational rather than deeper spiritual dimensions of human being.[43]

But Senghor was less interested in rejecting socialism than in *realizing* it, by returning to its Marxian sources in order to overcome socialism's actually existing party forms. He reminded BDS cadres that "the failure of socialists is not a failure of socialism."[44] He thus directed them to "the works of Marx . . . not to recite them, like the Bible, or the Koran, like a *dogma*, but to recuperate from them their spirit, their living and vivifying substance." Marx, he explained, recognized that man's "generic activity consists in transforming [the world] in his image . . . so that this material world responds, beyond his animal needs, to his spiritual exigencies of liberty and artistic creation, to his human dignity. Because man, to be fully human, must escape his alienation by capital and be a *creator* of beauty."[45]

According to Senghor, the objective of culture is "above all to satisfy the spiritual exigencies of life in society" though art that leads "man to commune with men, [and] all men with all the forces of nature," making "him more free by allowing him to *realize* himself."[46] African art, culture, and religion, Senghor argues, express these very aims of Marxian socialism. "Negro-African" art, he wrote, "is about . . . leading the people to participate in the collective life of the *cité* . . . [it is] precisely not [meant] to satisfy animal needs, but these needs being satisfied, to give life (*faire vivre*). . . . It is about creating a communion of men . . . with the vital forces of other men, and through this, with the cosmic forces of the universe. . . . In short, it is a matter of transforming our spiritual life by integrating it within social life to make it more intense because more human."[47]

Senghor thus figured black art as a crucial medium of human, social, and cosmic reconciliation and transcendence through which Africans could revitalize Marxism and redeem socialism. In turn, an ethical and vitalist socialism rooted in African culture, aesthetics, and religiosity would save Europe itself, which had been alienated by an instrumental rationality that reduced the human person to material utility, confused standard of living with reason for living, and perversely inverted human means and ends.

Senghor suggested that European "discursive reason" was only "a method, an instrument" that provided "practical recipes for utilizing nature" to improve material existence. But, he argued, the *moral* transformation of "true life" also required the kind of "analogic reason" or "sympathetic intuition" that he believed subtended both Marx's actual writings and specifically African ways of being, knowing, and making.[48] This was not a nativist gesture meant to reify incommensurable differences between Europe and Africa but a reminder that the postcolonial prospects of each depended on the other.[49] Europe and Africa would help one another to develop in ways that would also facilitate worldwide human self-realization within what Senghor called the civilization of the universal.

Although this program was partly based on an immediate practical concern with how best to promote moral and material development in the given postwar world, it was also guided by a utopian commitment to act as if a seemingly impossible future was already at hand. Senghor believed that if colonial emancipation were to institute a new epoch of human solidarity, it could best do so by inventing a sociopolitical form that did not yet exist for a world that had not yet arrived.[50] He treated socialism as a pragmatic means to the transcendent ends of happiness and public good, not as a doctrinal or dogmatic end in itself.[51]

Senghor's African socialism posited a dialectic relation whereby politics reveals the truth about religion and religion the truth about politics. Each discloses the end toward which the other should strive. His vision implied that politics becomes more political when routed through religion and religion more religious when routed through politics. For Senghor, authentic politics, like religion, addresses itself to transcendent potentiality. And authentic religion, like politics, addresses itself to worldly possibility. He thus developed a critique of religious absolutism from the standpoint of Marxist dialectics and a critique of vulgar Marxism from the standpoint of religious ethics. He challenged fixity and foundationalism whether expressed in religious or political idioms. Senghor envisioned *religion without dogma* and *socialism without orthodoxy*. The ultimate aim was religious humanism and secular transcendence. And this revolutionary hope was tethered to a gradualist program of concrete acts (social reforms and constitutional adjustments).

Senghor's redemptive program contained numerous tensions: his federalist convictions about mutualism and self-management as the basis for socialism, on the one hand, and his statist commitment to planning and development on the other; his critique of instrumental reason versus his faith in scientific management; his celebration of Marx's dialectical method and his critique of alienation, which identify immanent contradictions leading to crises within capitalist societies, on the one hand, and his assertions about reciprocity, interdependence, and social solidarity *without* overcoming capitalist social relations on the other; his invocations of popular spirit, collective emotions, and revolutionary action, on the one hand, and his reformist faith in constitutionally driven societal transformation without a corresponding social movement on the other; his emphasis on cooperative syndicalism and democratic self-management, on the one hand, and his alliances with conservative ethnic, religious, and regional power brokers across rural Senegal on the other; his pragmatic belief in socialist federalism as the best solution at this moment to francophone Africa's attempt to create a framework for self-determination, on the one hand, and his tendency at times to imply that federalism is an intrinsic and self-evident good for colonized peoples; his recognition that Marx's dialectical analysis was relevant to African social realities insofar as they were shaped according to capitalist social relations, on the one hand, and his belief that Marxian dialectics as a method could be detached from European social realities and simply applied in what he sometimes suggested were noncapitalist African societies. Senghor's federalist vision of African socialism (and socialist vision of federal democracy) implicitly raised a whole set of thorny problems that he never addressed (concerning African natural resources, capitalist polarization, and structural economic dependence).

Senghor's program for African socialism also changed over time. From 1948 to 1958 he attempted to recuperate Marx's writings to challenge economic determinism and mechanical materialism, to produce an immanent critique of actually existing socialist parties, and to create an authentic African socialism. After that he began to use African socialism to criticize Marxism *as such*, which, in an about-face, he accused of economism, determinism, and atheism. This shift occurred as a territorial national form of decolonization for Senegal seemed inevitable and Senghor became more interested in the vitalist and futurist phenomenology of Pierre Teilhard de Chardin and Gaston Berger.[52] Senghor's commitment to federalism was rescaled to focus on creating multinational African states. And as the president of Senegal, Senghor also deployed African socialism instrumentally to authorize state planning, party rule, and national unity.

But such contradictions and limitations do not warrant our treating Senghor's socialist project for postnational decolonization as a charter for the very territorial nationalist logic that it forcefully challenged. Such an interpretation is only possible if one separates Senghor's socialism from his federalism, if one reduces his socialism to a realist state project and brackets its transcendent ambitions, or if we treat it as the political ideology of a national state rather than a utopian project born of sustained reflection on the prospects for nonnational self-determination under late imperial conditions.

Reconsidering Senghorian Decolonization

Scholars have yet to attend adequately to Senghor's insights that real decolonization must operate on an imperial scale by transforming overseas and metropolitan societies simultaneously and that socialism, federalism, and decolonization in Europe and Africa had to be integrated within a single transformative project whose aim was not only African liberation or European redemption but planetary reconciliation and human realization. Senghor's program for a socialist federation hoped to fashion a legal and political framework that would recognize the history of interdependence that bound metropolitan and overseas peoples to one another and would protect the latter's material and political claims on a metropolitan society and state that Africans had helped to create even as it also established conditions for substantive self-government.

According to our inherited political metrics, we are supposed to counterpose a gradualist like Senghor to the anticolonial revolutionaries who led the African independence movement. But we should recall that while territorial nationalists like Sékou Touré and Pan-Africanists like Kwame Nkrumah sought to improve Africa's position in the postwar interstate system, Senghor envisioned transforming that system itself through new forms that superseded state sovereignty. While they hoped to replace colonial capitalism with African socialism in new nations or regional associations, Senghor believed that a socialist decolonization that did not also seek to revolutionize *metropolitan* states (and social relations) could never succeed.

This antiautarchic and postnational orientation toward decolonization also distinguished Senghor from iconic figures associated with the Bandung project such as Sukarno, Jawaharlal Nehru, and Gamal Abdel Nasser. At their most radical, these anticolonial visionaries sought to overcome imperialism through national development, popular democracy, third world solidarity, ideological nonalignment, and a commitment to international peace. They were nationalist internationalists and internationalist nationalists whose anti-imperial politics were premised on a residue of autarky. They envisioned an independent third world composed of allied national states that could catch up to the West by delinking themselves from the larger global economy while pursuing state planning and development initiatives.

But whereas they sought to seize a place for themselves (whether as nation-states, panethnic or regional blocs, or "the" third world) within the existing geopolitical order, Senghor's aim was to transform and transcend that order altogether through his dream of a peaceful socialist-federalist revolution. If the Bandung project imagined liberation through separation, Senghor proposed a type of revolutionary integration. Each, in different ways, pursued a variant of internationalism grounded in novel forms of solidarity. Both sought to overcome the limitations of narrow territorial independence in the context of postwar capitalism and Cold War geopolitics. These were distinct solutions to the challenges, which each rightly recognized, of global economic polarization and neocolonialism.

We should not pretend that Senghor's aversion to violence or caution about sudden change was revolutionary. But we can appreciate the revolutionary implications of his redemptive vision. Just as Senghor identified immanent potentialities within the politically variegated and socioeconomically interdependent French Union, we can identify unrealized political potential within Senghor's redemptive vision of African socialism. Rather than dismiss Senghor as a failed revolutionary nationalist, perhaps we should revisit him as flawed postnational visionary. His attempt to end colonial imperialism *and* transcend territorial nationalism should be considered a moral and utopian project whose "ambition," in Mohandas Gandhi's legendary formulation, was "much higher than independence."[53]

Thinking with Senghor about African socialism—taking seriously his cosmopolitan ruminations about postnational democracy and his cosmological reflections on planetary reconciliation—allows us to conjure the history of a decolonization that might have been. The point is not that his program for African socialism would have redeemed humanity. But it is worth examining why Senghor claimed that it might. Engaging Senghor's redemptive vision on its own terms points to a more nuanced understanding of decolonization as a process and period of global restructuring rather than a dyadic story of national liberation or transfer of power. Senghor's unrealized "future past" may also illuminate our present predicament, which is defined partly by the collapse of the Bandung project, the resurgence of resource imperialism, the supposed inability to imagine emancipatory alternatives to a seemingly unsurpassable neoliberal capitalism, and the democracy deficit of our postnational constellation.[54] Senghor's prescient plea to end empire *and* desacralize national independence as the necessary form for democratic self-determination may be a fruitful starting point for political reflection in and on our imperial present.

PART 6

SUBORDINATE ELITES AND
IMPERIAL DECLINE IN SOUTHEAST ASIA

Just a day after the transfer of sovereignty from the Netherlands to the United States of Indonesia on December 28, 1949, President Sukarno addressed the people for the first time from his new headquarters, the Palace in Koningsplein, Jakarta, declaring that the nation will live at peace with the world. (United Nations)

Informal Empire

The Case of Siam and the Middle East

GREGORY A. BARTON

"THESE HALF-CIVILIZED GOVERNMENTS such as those in China, Portugal, Spanish America all require a dressing every eight or ten years to keep them in order," Lord Palmerston remarked in Parliament. The year was 1850, and these words marked the high noon of British power under the influence of Henry Temple Palmerston. First as foreign secretary (in and out of office) and then as prime minister, Lord Palmerston exerted a great deal of influence on the British approach to informal empire between 1830 and 1865.[1] He laid the foundations for the expansion of the formal and informal empire and reflected the prevailing idea in the mid-Victorian period that Britain stood "at the head of moral, social, and political civilization" with the task to "lead the way and direct the march of other nations." Few doubted in this period that Britain had the role of "world bettering," as he put it.

Under his leadership Latin America, Africa, the Far East, and the Middle East were scenes of mounting British influence. By 1880, Britain's informal empire included much of Latin America, the Ottoman Empire, Egypt, Persia, and China—as well as points in between—a vast swath of the globe larger, in population terms, than its formal empire. Although the precise mix varied, this informal influence was exercised through a combination of naval power, bond loans, local merchants, trade ties, and diplomacy. This informal empire in particular molded the direction of the modern world well into the twentieth century through a system of subordinate elites, and it lasted until the baton of power itself passed to a former possession that some scholars claim Britain once held as an informal empire as well—the United States.[2]

DEFINITION OF INFORMAL EMPIRE

Opening markets involved opening opportunities for trade, but it also involved changing the nature of elites. Europe globalized the world largely through the process of imperialism, formal and informal. The argument for using the term *informal empire* as a model for world history is strong: massive investment in a foreign economy; large numbers of settlers or guest workers that run major sections of an economy or produce critical amounts of labor; outside interventions, whether military, diplomatic, or economic; relations between elites that determine the economic, cultural, and political direction of a country; new identities among elite groups that link them to the imperial power. All these factors justify the term. But scholars have defined *informal empire* more in passing than by means of any direct treatment of the subject.

Informal empire means the substance of empire without the form of empire. *Informal empire* almost always refers to relations between nations, including trade, investment, immigration, government and private aid, and cultural exchanges— not always all of these, but almost always one or more. Within these parameters I suggest the following definition of *informal empire*.

> Informal empire is a relationship in which a national or regional imperial elite intentionally or unintentionally exercises a dominant influence over the elite formation, identity, and conditions of exchange of the subjected elite in another nation or region with none of the formal structures of empire.

This definition steers clear of setting the perimeters too wide. Neither trade alone, nor cultural exchange, nor immigration or other relations between a more powerful and weaker nation necessarily means informal empire, at least not in the sense that scholars use the term. Rich and poor, powerful and weak are polarities that can exist side by side without dominance by one partner. Yet the above definition is narrow enough to focus on the real issues that historians investigate within informal empire—a dominant influence that permanently alters the substantial characteristics of a subjected nation. It also addresses the need to discuss elites—usually the missing factor in our analysis of the formation of the modern world—and the role they played in the extension of power outside the structures of formal empire.

To understand the "eclipse of empires" much depends on the definition of *empire*, particularly *informal empire*. Power flows through many channels, and this includes development aid, trade, immigration, capital, and cultural influences such as mass media, as well as through formal structures of empire. The British experience preceded and set the pattern for informal empire in the last two centuries and accordingly has much to tell us about the informal empire held by the United States, and how power accumulates and recedes. For instance, while the British failed to establish an informal empire over most of the Middle East after World War II, they had marked success in the Gulf States and shared this power with the United States. In Siam the elites very deliberately worked to minimize the dominant influence of Britain while remaining dependent on British influence to stave off advances by the French. This is a common response by any secondary power that is incorporated into an informal empire, whether British or American. Examining the "end of empires" through the lens of elite formation and influence may help clarify to what extent—if at all—Britain, the United States, and other European powers have in fact abandoned—or not abandoned—the imperial role.

THE PALMERSTON PROJECT

In Palmerston's era, the Foreign Office used its considerable power to open markets. Britain relied on trade for its livelihood, and most of this commerce was conducted outside of continental Europe, where intervention sometimes seemed a necessary evil. On the continent, liberalism—though it had its adherents—had never been fully embraced by any government, and so Britain looked outward to the world. In 1860 Britain produced 25 percent of all world trade, and 60 percent of this trade came from outside Europe.

With the livelihood of its economy so dependent on international commerce, Britain pursued free trade and opened markets not just to itself but to all, calling it "fair trade," a veneer of justice that the British found irresistible. If British policy were chained to the "cash nexus," as Carlyle called it, this same nexus allowed Britain to pursue open markets draped with the virtue of humanitarian concern. When a country opened its markets to Britain, it opened them to the world. When Britain used its influence to open a country to free trade, it helped that country modernize, step into the future, and join a mature body of nations that sought mutual benefits. Force sometimes had to be used. Policing the world to ensure a global market may not have been, and often was not, altruistic, but the mid-Victorians made a strong case that such police activity benefited more than Britain alone.[3]

Palmerston's diplomacy during the Belgian affair (in which Belgium gained independence in 1830) laid down his three basic operating assumptions, which would appear again and again throughout the following decades. First, the British fleet was of incalculable value for diplomacy. After the Napoleonic Wars the British maintained a small army, but it had the largest navy in the world—larger than the next four naval powers combined. Even if all the naval powers of the world had opposed the British, the British could have cleared the seas of enemy ships at any time in the nineteenth century. This gave the British a powerful reach and the option to blockade, bombard from the sea, level coastal forts, and even topple opposition far inland by sailing up rivers and bays. Thus force guaranteed free trade. Second, British interest was allied to strong, independent, commercially healthy states under the sway of no superpower outside of Britain itself. In 1850 Britain maintained 28 percent of the world's economic output and

25 percent of the market share of all world trade, producing 60 percent of the world's supply of coal, 50 percent of the world supply of iron, and 70 percent of the world's supply of steel. Of its exports, 90 percent were manufactured goods.[4] Third, necessary wars were never avoided. British interventions in Latin America, the Middle East, the Far East, and Africa illustrate how Palmerston, and even his more peace loving successors, like William Gladstone and Lord Salisbury (Robert Gascoyne-Cecil), utilized these three principles, and interfered whenever necessary to open markets.[5]

Palmerston showed little hesitancy to interfere, and interfere in such a way that makes the term *informal empire* applicable. In defending interference, in this case in Portugal, Palmerston argued that "if by 'interference' is meant intermeddling, and intermeddling in every way, and to every extent, short of actual military force; then I must affirm, that there is nothing in such interference, which the law of nations may not in certain cases permit."[6] Whatever his view of the law of nations, Palmerston often promoted armed intervention to open markets and create new alliances.

Palmerston laid down a flexible doctrine that enabled Britain to support regimes friendly to British influence and to oppose others. In the turmoil on the continent over Italian independence, Palmerston in 1860 opposed the censures of the king of Sardinia and the annexations that laid the foundation for Italian unity put forth by other European powers. John Russell, the secretary of state under Palmerston, stated in a dispatch to the European powers that "when a people from good reasons take up arms against an oppressor, it is but an act of justice and generosity to assist brave men in the defence of their liberties. . . . Her Majesty's Government will turn their eyes . . . to the gratifying prospect of a people building up the edifice of their liberties, and consolidating the work of their independence."[7]

This proved a handy doctrine for it gave the British government leeway to support any movement of self-determination that was in its interest, while allowing Britain to withhold support from any government or movement that did not fit its interest. To aid or oppose revolution gave Britain one tool among many to shape the political landscape of the world outside of its own formal empire. Palmerston felt that "commerce is the best pioneer of civilization . . . [free trade joined] civilization with one hand and peace with the other," making men "happier, wiser, better." Most important, free trade challenged the traditional landowning elites of "backward nations" and allowed a new set of people to take over the reins of these societies. When the merchant class gained more money from trade, it took over the reins of government, slowly displacing the old landed elites. Trade meant change, civilization, and republican forms of government. As Canning remarked in 1824, supremely confident of the benefits of trade, "Spanish America is free and if we do not mismanage our affairs sadly, she is English."[8]

Moreover, Britain kept a policy of isolationism toward Europe precisely to avoid a costly war on the continent that would drain men away from productive economic work, force higher taxes, increase the power of continental-style bureaucrats, and transform Britain socially and politically into a mirror image of the continent. Isolationism kept Britain unentangled (except for very particular and temporary occasions) and allowed it to remain both liberal at home and international in scope. Under what conditions, then, did Britain go to war to secure markets? Britain went to war outside of Europe when a particular market in Africa, China, Latin America, or elsewhere was worth the expense. If interventions occurred in Europe, they took place, outside of the Crimean War, in weaker states like Spain, Greece, or Naples to push for constitutional rule. And while new markets were important, Britain intervened most often to maintain old markets. It was when Britain had an economic stake in a region such as China, and the rulers of that region either would not or could not maintain order or conditions of free trade, that Britain intervened.

In 1810, Britain signed a peace treaty with Brazil that gave preferential treatment to British interests. After this Britain intervened often in Latin America between the 1830s and 1860s to remove obstacles to trade, investment, and finance.[9] When the Spanish colonies rebelled against Spain, Britain was slow to recognize the new governments, but it eventually did recognize the independent republics by signing trade treaties with them. This amounted to holding out the carrot of recognition if the republics met Britain on the ground of open trade and thus opened their economies to British penetration. Britain also played an instrumental role in the creation of Uruguay as a buffer zone between Brazil and Argentina to guarantee open river systems for British trade in the region.[10] Other intrusions to keep trade open occurred frequently up the Río de la Plata, and as far as Mexico. In 1848–49, Britain threatened naval action off the coast of Brazil to stop the trade in slaves. It threatened Peru in 1857 to ensure its compliance for British bondholders, and then against Chile in 1863, among other actions.

In the Levant, the British signed a treaty with the modernizing Muhammad Ali (1805–48) in 1838. This treaty demolished Ali's state monopolies and in consequence forced the Egyptian government to take loans. With the treaty came the "capitulations," which included the right of foreigners to be exempt from Egyptian courts and to be tried by their own European peers. After this, foreigners flooded into Egypt to trade. In 1838, a free trade treaty with Turkey, the Convention of Balta Liman, gave control of customs and tariffs to European powers, eliminated state monopolies, and forced the Ottoman government also to take out foreign loans in order to survive. Foreign traders paid no internal customs duty. A year later Britain intervened to protect Turkey from Muhammad Ali, ruler of Egypt, and also annexed Aden. In 1850, Palmerston established a British version of Civis Romanus in the Don Pacifico affair, sending the navy to blockade the port of Athens in defense of the principle that British citizens anywhere in the world had the right to be tried only by the British. Palmerston also intervened to protect Turkey against Russia in 1853–56, fighting the Crimean War to keep the Ottoman Empire independent and open to British commerce. The British established the Ottoman Bank in London in 1856, and after 1863 renamed it the Imperial Ottoman Bank, which issued that empire's currency. When Benjamin Disraeli purchased the Egyptian Khedive's share in the Suez Canal in 1869, it effectively gave control of that strategic waterway to Britain. After Egypt went bankrupt in 1876 (a year after Ottoman government went bankrupt), Britain and other European powers took control of the finances of the Egyptian government to oversee the repayment of debts to bondholders. When this proved insufficient, Britain occupied Egypt militarily in 1882.

Between 1840 and 1860, the British campaigned against the slave trade in Africa. This in turn increased trade and missions, particularly in Niger, Dahomey, Abyssinia, and Zanzibar. Palmerston called the slave trade a "foul and detestable crime," thus conferring the mantle of absolute virtue on its opponents. Slave treaties, he said, "are indirectly treaties for the encouragement of commerce." Private expeditions were supported by the government into Niger in 1841 and 1857, Dahomey in 1850, and Lagos in 1851 (which the British annexed in 1861), in addition to numerous military interventions against the slave trade. All this did not mean that Britain wanted formal colonies in the region. Indeed, Palmerston turned down opportunities for the colonization of Abyssinia in the 1840s and the occupation of Egypt in 1859. Of Abyssinia, Palmerston said, "All we want is trade and land is not necessary for trade; we can carry on commerce very well on ground belonging to other people."[11] Only when other European powers, particularly Germany, threatened this commerce with formal annexations did Britain join a scramble for formal colonies in the sub-Sahara.[12]

Despite this busy schedule, the British also found time to intervene in the Far East. The Opium War of 1839–42 ended with the Treaty of Nanking, which gave Britain Hong Kong and opened five "treaty ports" with special trading concessions and extraterritoriality for foreigners. Along the China coast, the French and British intervened repeatedly in 1847, 1856, and 1860. In 1863, Robert Hart, an Englishman, governed the Chinese Imperial Maritime Customs and used its revenues to repay loans from Western banks. Soon afterward the British took over the local salt administration. Palmerston, as well as his immediate successors, played a key role in these global interventions. The question of informal empire hinges on such interventions, and the economic penetrations that occurred because of them.

Palmerston sought the prosperity of Britain through trade but also had far-reaching ambitions to change the nature of Britain's trading partners—in Lord Canning's famous phrase, to "make them English." Palmerston combined force, diplomacy, and trade to create a large informal empire of influence that paralleled and even surpassed the influence of Britain's growing formal empire. At his death in 1865, much of the modern world had been cast in the mold that Palmerston advocated—a world where constitutional government commanded the greatest respect, free trade defined the economic relationship between countries, and a new business and professional elite acted like a solvent against traditional culture-cum-economic life and helped usher in the globalized world that we understand today. He also launched Britain on a path that led to resentment from those so forced into a modern mold.

But as the Industrial Revolution continued to evolve in European countries, Britain saw its relative—if not absolute—economic power slipping. Palmerston observed, "The rivalship of European manufacturers is fast excluding our productions from the markets of Europe and we must unremittingly endeavor to find in other parts of the world new vents for the produce of our industry." Interestingly, he goes on to mention both the Middle East and the Far East as potential partners in commerce, areas where he had initiated many interventions.[13]

We see, in the Palmerston era at least, a desire of the elites of one nation, in this case Britain, to alter the conditions of exchange that foster elite formation in other countries. We see also—in fits, starts, and even reversals—a discernible intentionality of purpose. Although such intentionality does not prove that Britain succeeded in its purpose of constructing a durable informal empire in the nineteenth and twentieth centuries, it was a step in that direction.

In addition, comparisons between a mammoth Victorian British informal empire and an even larger twentieth-century American informal empire have topical urgency—especially when informal empire projects a form of enlightened globalism under the rubric of democratic and libertarian principles. What follows are two brief case studies in which British officials attempted to establish an informal empire based on the formation of Western-oriented elites. One led to success, the other to failure. Both are instructive of how the formation of subordinate elites provides the key to tracing the influence of power, and of informal empire in particular.

SIAM AND ELITES, 1888 TO 1932

In the late nineteenth century, Siam, a nominally independent kingdom, remained at the edge of the southeastern flank of the Indian empire and the western edge of French Indochina. In the 1880s and 1890s, British Foreign Office officials were trying to create a "buffer state" in Siam that would keep the French in Indochina from bordering directly on India.[14] The Foreign Office and India Office wanted to keep Siam nominally independent so that the British—who dominated Siam's finance, trade, and shipping—could maintain an informal empire without the burdens and costs of running Siam directly, or of waging war with France.[15]

Historians studying Britain's relationship with Siam have debated vigorously whether Siam was part of Britain's "informal empire."[16] Robinson and Gallagher first brought the term into wide use in their classic article "The Imperialism of Free Trade," published in the *Economic History Review* in 1953. Following their model, Anthony Webster, in *Gentlemen Capitalists: British Imperialism in Southeast Asia, 1770–1890,* argued that Britain maintained an informal empire in Southeast Asia through finance and trading companies. While other scholars, such as Ian Brown, disagree that this control constituted imperialism, Webster's work lays out a broad outline of influence in the formation of Siam's economy by British capital. Many other scholars, such as David Wyatt, Nicholas Tarling, and Michael Vickery, have traced the Siamese turn toward Britain as an attempt to resist French encroachment. All accounts agree that the Bangkok elites used Britain to develop a Western-style military, court system, and professional bureaucracy. Vickery in particular traces how the Bangkok monarchy utilized a British model of administration to replace local and regional elites with royal commissioners to modernize the state and bring in new revenue. Given the definition of *informal empire* discussed above, Siam provides a revealing example of British informal empire's alliances with subordinate elites that lasted from the late nineteenth century until World War II.[17]

Britain's informal empire in Siam is usually dated to King Mongkut's signing of the Bowring Treaty in 1855, which gave British subjects extraterritorial privileges in parts of the Kingdom of Siam. In his famous metaphor—"to swim upriver and make friends with the crocodile [the French] or to swim out to the sea and hang on to the whale [the British]"—King Mongkut illustrates how Siam's elites chose to swim with the whale for nearly a century after 1855, making the country, as Paul Ktratoska and Ben Batson concluded, "in some degree . . . a part of Britain's informal empire, in which British interests, particularly economic, predominated without the exercise of formal sovereignty."[18]

British consuls, merchants, and advisers took actions that allowed British firms to dominate the teak industry in northern Siam, created British consular courts, gave British officials representation on the international court in the northern city Chiangmai, and enabled the Foreign Office to influence Royal Forest Department policies and negotiations. Although the Bangkok monarchy and ministries had their own internal policies toward northern Siam, they consistently required British capital and power to achieve unification from the 1870s to the 1890s, the critical period when Chulalongkorn and his government integrated the diffuse vassalage surrounding the Kingdom of Siam into a centralized nation-state centered in Bangkok.

Informal empire functioned through networks of collaboration.[19] The Foreign Office used British timber merchants to help control a sensitive region bordering on British Burma and French Indochina. British timber merchants, notably the

Bombay Burmah Trading Corporation (BBTC), sought to protect profits by keeping out French and other foreign competitors. In turn, King Chulalongkorn and his coterie of ministers used British pressure in northern Siam to increase Bangkok's control over the region. Chulalongkorn used Western ideas of governance and economics to assert his own power while maintaining Siam's formal independence. Despite modernization, Chulalongkorn, his ministers, and the northern chiefs feared that Britain or France might annex northern Siam. This fear of annexation is one of the main reasons why Chulalongkorn initially allowed British trading firms to dominate teak leases in the 1890s and early 1900s. Britain's domination of these concessions in northern Siam also helped Bangkok gain more control over the north, a process akin to an internal colonization.[20] Economic factors, such as the large capital reserves held by the BBTC and the Borneo Company, help explain the dominance of British trading firms in Siam, but these economic factors must be viewed in light of the Foreign Office's purposeful strategic and political actions to install British businesses combined with Chulalongkorn's fear of annexation.[21]

The Kingdom of Siam remained as the last bastion of the laissez-faire ideal of forestry in the 1890s. Under the protective gaze of the Indian empire and the Foreign Office, British timber merchants rapidly moved into the Siamese timber market during the late 1880s and early 1890s. Northern Thai aristocrats controlled northern Siam and its vast teak forests. These local leaders paid vassalage and taxes to the monarchy in Bangkok. With no formal regulations for leasing in place, the aristocrats and foreign leaseholders of teak forests often feuded over the legality of teak claims in the region. Because of these fights the British Foreign Office created extraterritorial courts in northern Siam during the early 1880s to protect the rights of Burmese and Indian subjects who worked in the forests.[22] Powerful British timber corporations, which had little or no hand in the creation of consular courts in 1882–83, eventually sought to exploit these extraterritorial privileges. The first British company to take advantage of them and enter into the teak trade in Siam was the Borneo Company.

After scouting the northern forests in 1884, the BBTC followed in the wake of the Borneo Company and started purchasing teak in Siam beginning in the late 1880s.[23] The BBTC began buying teak from preexisting leaseholders and picked up leases as quickly as it could during the 1890s. Both the BBTC and the Borneo Company began lobbying the Foreign Office to protect their holdings because of their increasing interest in Siamese teak. They first lobbied for protection when France blockaded Bangkok over supposed grievances in eastern Siam during the French crisis of 1893. The Foreign Office assiduously replied to the letters of the BBTC and Borneo Company, guaranteeing the protection of British businesses.[24] It also promised that the Royal Navy would protect British businesses if problems arose.

British firms continued to dominate the teak trade after 1901. Moreover, British foresters W. F. L. Tottenham (1901–4) and W. F. Lloyd (1904–25) served as the chief conservators until the mid-1920s. During the first decade of the twentieth century, the Foreign Office reflected happily on the British monopoly over the teak trade. In 1905, Ralph Paget, who served as the Foreign Office chargé d'affaires in Siam, assured Lord Lansdowne, the foreign secretary, that Britain dominated the teak trade in Siam: "As it is scarcely worth while to take into consideration the small forests owned by the East Asiatic Company [out of Denmark], it may practically be said that the whole of the teak trade in north of Siam is now controlled by British Companies."[25] Accordingly, British firms signed new thirty-year leases on teak forests in 1909.[26] Until World War II and the rise of Thai nationalization in the late 1940s and 1950s, the only serious rival to the BBTC was the Borneo Company.[27] It was no accident that the BBTC and other British firms came to dominate the teak trade for much of the twentieth century; it was part of a conscious attempt by the Foreign Office to use British companies headed by well-known gentlemen capitalists to dominate the teak trade and keep France away from the borders of Burma and India.

The example of Siam shows that throughout the early part of the twentieth century, the British special relationship with Siam enabled Bangkok elites, particularly those surrounding the monarchy, to extend control over the vast territories of the north and transform a loose, traditional feudal relationship with local aristocrats and petty princes into a unified modern state. In effect, the British expanded and sustained the elites of Siam throughout this period. While forestry policy and the teak trade played a central part in the formation of elites in Siam, broader influences, not the subject of this essay, were at work as well.

THE MIDDLE EAST AND ELITES, 1946 TO 1960

After World War II, Britain attempted to create an informal empire in the Middle East and used the British Middle East Office to sponsor development work precisely to attain significant influence that would salvage a fair share of its previous imperial power.[28] It had a long history of intervention in the region, and the resentment against British power played a role in the failure to attract and retain subordinate elites in the Middle East during postwar decades.

The Convention of Balta Liman (1838) gave control of customs and tariffs to European powers, eliminated state monopolies, and forced the Ottoman government to take out foreign loans to survive. Britain went on to purchase the Egyptian Khedive's share in the Suez Canal in 1869 and then occupied Egypt militarily in 1882. Continuing this long history of dominion, Britain used a number of administrative instruments to govern the Middle East in the years surrounding World War II. The Anglo-Iraqi Treaty (1930) and Anglo-Egyptian Treaty (1936) gave the peoples of the Middle East "a modicum of independence."[29] But by war's end, Britain had brought much of the region under outright military occupation. Aden and Cyprus were Crown colonies. The British controlled the flow of oil from Iran through the Anglo-Iranian Oil Company. Somaliland, Qatar, and Kuwait were British protectorates, while Transjordan and Palestine were under a British mandate. The Anglo-Egyptian condominium over the Sudan, created in 1899, was still operative. The war, however, had drained substantial resources from the British economy, and public opinion, as well as the Treasury, increasingly balked at the idea of sacrificing domestic social programs to retain vast colonial possessions in the face of mounting nationalist resistance. But giving up control over this strategically important region did not prove easy.

World War II and the tide of rising nationalism changed the imperial picture forever. While Winston Churchill certainly accused the Labour Party of scuttling the British Empire after the war, Roger Louis points out that Labour attempted to build a replacement for the loss of India and other areas with an informal empire of influence in the Middle East and Africa. F. S. Northedge has described Foreign Office personnel as certain that Britain's old position in the Middle East would sooner or later be restored to its former role. Arabs, Iranians, and even Jews would get used to the idea that Britain, by reason of its long experience, was the natural agency to govern them, to define their various needs, including defense, and to guide them on their way to prosperity and security.[30]

While London sponsored the British Middle East Office (BMEO) to gain influence through development initiatives, it is also true that an informal empire did not ensue. The British attempted to use appointments of their personnel in important government and private positions as a "mechanism of control." Informal empire failed in the Middle East because "the right sort" of appointments did not occur, and thus the British failed to form and sustain a new elite in this region after World War II.

There were numerous reasons for this failure. The push for British personnel went against a natural local resistance to give up authority.[31] Collaborating elites in the region had their own agendas and often played the Soviet Union, United Kingdom, and United States against each other. The freshly decolonized countries in the region had no intention of being absorbed by any one of them, and national leaders used the competitive spirit of the Cold War to increase both economic and military support. Nationalism, surging through the territories held by the colonial powers, strongly affected the countries of the Middle East and posed severe challenges to the British and Americans (to say nothing of the French) in the region. Nationalism was a tide that could not be entirely stayed by reestablishing the shah of Iran after the reign of Prime Minister Mohammed Mosaddegh, nor by diplomatically isolating Gamal Abdel Nasser as a new Hitler. Nationalists expressed a certainty of British malfeasance that proved impossible to override with development aid alone. Mosaddegh's attitude toward the British was shared widely in the region when he said, "You do not know how crafty they are. You do not know how evil they are. You do not know how they sully everything they touch."[32]

Officials at the Foreign Office and BMEO attempted to set up broad-based programs in the Middle East to develop its economic resources, which in turn would add political stability to a region where the British wished to protect their prestige and influence. The interests of the Soviet Union in the Middle East and the critical supply of oil to Western Europe gave added urgency to these development plans. Caught between virulent nationalism and American anticolonialism, Britain had few possibilities for maintaining its own influence in the region. A development agenda seemed like an obvious choice. A succession of prime ministers—Clement Attlee, Ernest Bevin, and then Anthony Eden—saw every reason for British success in a region that lacked money and experts but held large reserves of oil and a strategic position in the world.[33]

The British did not succeed in establishing an informal empire in the region through development initiatives because they failed to recruit subordinate elites. They had based their hopes for influence on getting "the right sort" placed close to the centers of power. That meant British personnel running the Anglo-Persian Oil Company in Abadan, and it also meant placing administrators in key posts within government ministries.[34] The influence of the BMEO never rivaled that of the wartime occupation or approached the level of imperial power. In marked contrast to Washington, London simply did not answer expectations with ready loans and hefty direct aid. British influence in the region was reduced to a handful of experts resisting the receding tide of influence—in vain after the Suez Crisis in 1956.

The Suez Crisis marked the end of significant British influence in the region. Without Washington's backing, Britain, France, and Israel attempted to seize the Suez Canal back from Egypt on October 29, 1956, in response to President Nasser's wildly popular proclamation that Egypt intended to nationalize this strategic waterway, still owned by an Anglo-French corporation. The British had eighty thousand troops garrisoned at Suez, and military facilities around the region, particularly in Aden. In the first phase of a combined offensive by three hundred thousand allied forces, the Israeli army swept across nearby Sinai and halted just ten miles from the canal on November 2, destroying the Egyptian defenders. Just three days later, French and British airborne and amphibious forces, backed by overwhelming air support from an armada of six aircraft carriers, landed near Port Said and quickly occupied key choke points along the canal. As his army collapsed with some three thousand dead and over thirty thousand captured, Nasser responded to the bombing attacks by sinking forty ships under Egyptian control in the canal, effectively closing it to shipping.

Condemnation by the United States, and a draft resolution of the United Nations Security Council denouncing the invasion, soon turned military victory into diplomatic defeat, making occupation of the canal untenable. International diplomatic pressure, the threat of economic retaliation, and a crisis in foreign exchange reserves the week before the invasion led Harold Macmillan, the British chancellor of the exchequer, to inform Prime Minister Eden that the artificial exchange rate set for the pound sterling could not be held. Given American opposition to the Suez invasion, and in need of further cooperation with the United States as a key ally, the British called off the invasion, accepted a cease-fire in November, and withdrew all of their troops a month later.

The British suffered a massive loss of prestige in the area. The Suez Crisis did not strategically dissolve British power or economic clout. But the loss of prestige led to a hardening of the resolve of elites in the Middle East, indeed around the British Empire, to resist further British influence. This denouement demonstrates how relationships with subordinate elites provide the key to informal empire. When relationships between elites dissolve, so, too, does informal empire.

Egyptian President Gamal Abdel Nasser greets a cheering crowd in Cairo after announcing the nationalization of the Suez Canal, August 1956. (Central Intelligence Agency)

The British vastly overestimated the degree to which Middle Eastern governments would defer to their judgment and advice, even on seemingly neutral matters. In this tense atmosphere, Britain, the United States, the Soviet Union, and
Arab nationalists were jockeying for power, and the attempt to transplant an
ambitious development program directly from the imperial nursery was a surprising development. But while development reforms, advocated by London, were
a "mechanism of control" that did help Britain to influence events in the region,
they did not, as Roger Louis points out, achieve a dominant role: in the end, the
British lacked the money, and the Arabs (and Iranians) lacked the patience. Citizens of the region wanted to run their own affairs and assumed that the "right
sort" were born and bred in the Middle East.

In contrast to its generalized failure across the wider Middle East, Britain did
hang on successfully in the Persian Gulf, drawing on its long history of informal
empire over these small sheikhdoms to achieve the grand aims that failed elsewhere in the region. After decades of episodic naval operations along this "pirate
coast," the British had signed a General Treaty with local sheiks in 1820, seeking
security for the East India Company's shipping and an end to the slave trade.
Starting in the Palmerston era, the British consolidated their control over the
gulf, first under a Perpetual Treaty of Maritime Peace in 1853, enforced by the
Royal Navy's Gulf Squadron, and later under a protectorate agreement of 1892.
The long British presence suppressed piracy and maintained stability in an imperial backwater whose main export was, for several centuries, natural pearls.[35] After
the discovery of oil in Bahrain in 1931, two British firms, the Anglo-Persian Oil
Company and its affiliate, the Iraq Petroleum Company, dominated drilling in the
gulf, developing the rich oil and gas resources that eventually brought extraordinary wealth to this arid, impoverished coast.[36] In 1952, following a century of such
indirect rule, the British presided over confederation of the gulf's sheikhdoms
into the Trucial Council, the direct precursor of the United Arab Emirates (UAE).
Two years later, after Iran's Mosaddegh government nationalized Anglo-Persian
Oil and its massive Abadan refinery at the north end of the gulf, the company
reincorporated as British Petroleum (BP) and remained an active player among
the sheikhdoms along the gulf's oil-rich southern shores.[37]

In 1968, the British announced their withdrawal and three years later presided over independence for Bahrain, Qatar, and the seven sheikhdoms of the
Trucial Council, now called the United Arab Emirates. At independence in 1971,
the British turned over their colonial constabulary, the Trucial Oman Scouts,
which became the basis of the Union Defence Force (UAE), and gave up the
Royal Navy base at Bahrain, which was occupied by the U.S. Navy.[38] For the next
two decades, Britain trained many UAE officers at Sandhurst and remained a
major source of defense support until the 1991 Gulf War, which Washington
fought to secure another of these oil-rich sheikhdoms, Kuwait. That conflict

served as the final act in this long imperial transition, and thereafter the United States became the preeminent power in the gulf, establishing the Fifth Fleet there in 1995 as a naval patrol force with headquarters at Bahrain.[39]

Whether voluntarily or involuntarily, London was gradually forced to give way to Washington throughout the Middle East. The United States, in marked contrast to Britain, had ample resources with which to build alliances with emergent elites through economic and military aid. Despite this seeming rupture in informal empire, American policy after the Suez Crisis quickly took a form quite similar to the role once held by Britain. Across the Middle East, the United States cultivated Arab autocrats, whether monarchs or military, as reliable subordinate elites and built an effective mechanism of control that would persist for another half century.

Conclusion

Just as officials used a colonial environmental discourse in the nineteenth and early twentieth centuries to construct imperial power in Siam, so, too, we see in a largely postcolonial setting the use of both development aid and environmental initiatives to replace at least some of the influence lost after the collapse of formal empire. In the case of Siam, informal empire succeeded because the British played a dominant role in the formation of the Bangkok elite in a newly emerging, unified modern state. In the Middle East after World War II, the British—although they had played a large role in elite formation in this region in the past—no longer had the cooperation of elites and could not form or sustain new elites that had other alliances to consider with countries such as the United States, were inspired by a rising tide of nationalism, and were backed by newfound oil money. Informal empire failed in this second instance precisely because an imperial elite failed to play a formative role with elites in the Middle East, as it had, earlier in the century, in Siam.

The examples of Siam and the Middle East are two slivers of the "Palmerston project," the first successful, the second a failure. The two examples help illustrate the importance of defining *informal empire* as a relationship in which a national or regional imperial elite intentionally or unintentionally exercises a dominant influence over the elite formation, identity, and conditions of exchange of the subjected elite in another nation or region with none of the formal structures of empire. This definition provides a "mechanism of control" that cuts to the most important issues of power and influence. The mechanisms can vary, but one constant remains. Informal empire is about elites in an imperial power that substantially alter elite behavior in another setting. The British experience accordingly has much to tell us about informal empire with the United States, as well as about how imperial power is built and how it is lost in the eclipse of empires.

Scientific Patriotism

Medical Science and National Self-Fashioning
in Southeast Asia

WARWICK ANDERSON AND HANS POLS

PHYSICIANS AND SCIENTISTS DOMINATED the first generation of nationalists in at least three East Asian colonies in the late nineteenth and early twentieth centuries: the Philippines under the Spanish and U.S. regimes, the Dutch East Indies, and the Japanese territory of Taiwan. There is substantial evidence that in each place decolonization was practically and symbolically yoked to scientific progress. Members of the first generation to receive training in biological science and to become socialized as professionals used this education to imagine themselves as eminently modern, progressive, and cosmopolitan. Their training gave them special authority in deploying organic metaphors of society and state and made them deft in finding allegories of the human body and the body politic. These scientists and physicians saw themselves as representing universal laws, advancing natural knowledge, and engaging as equals with colleagues in Europe, Japan, and North America. Science gave them a new platform for communication. This essay examines how scientific training shaped anticolonialism and nationalism in the Philippines and the East Indies, concluding with a brief comparison of the situation in Taiwan.

The modern roots of anti-imperial nationalism are widely recognized. It seems national sensibility finds its earliest and most explicit expression in sectors of society that are meritocratic, qualification based, mobile, and atomized. Intellectuals and professionals trained in the manipulation of abstract, technical data and skilled in the development of wide-ranging networks often constitute the nationalist avant-garde.[1] Ironically, their Enlightenment or universal projects could assume romantic or contingent form. Thus, as Ernest Gellner observes, "[N]ationalism is a phenomenon of Gesellschaft using the idea of Gemeinschaft: a mobile, anonymous society simulating a closed community."[2] Benedict Anderson also recognizes the contributions of "emerging nationalist intelligentsias" in the imagining of these political formations. National awakening tends to occur in "the *first* generation in any significant numbers to have acquired a European education." These young men bonded through schooling and their enhanced access to contemporary models of the nation and went on to fill "subordinate echelons of the colony's bureaucracy and larger commercial enterprises."[3]

Gellner notes the shift in the late nineteenth century "from history to biology as the main mythopoetic science" of nationalism, thereby rendering the nation natural, making it into a sort of necessary organism.[4] Yet neither Gellner nor Anderson critically interrogate the *biological* character and scope of nationalism. They repeatedly emphasize the importance of education, bureaucratization, and communication in the humanistic imagining of the nation, but the specific role of science in these modern processes receives scant attention. Pheng Cheah provides further elaboration on the philosophical origins of the "organismic metaphors" and "political organicisms" undergirding national aspirations, but he, too, mines few medical or scientific sources. Using Indonesian and Kenyan literary texts as illustrations, Cheah argues that both nationalism and cosmopolitanism are based on "the same organismic ontology."[5] Not surprisingly, the texts he cites happen to be full of examples of how scientific training cultivates national sensibility and the ways in which medicine can diagnose and treat the colonial or protonational body politic.

Some historians of science, focusing on isolated case studies, do make claims for the scientific shaping of national consciousness. Most important, Gyan Prakash argues that "the emergence and existence of India is inseparable from the authority of science and its functioning as the name for freedom and enlightenment, power and progress." Prakash also identifies a Western-educated indigenous elite enchanted by science, even though few local nationalist leaders boasted scientific training: "They saw reason as a syntax for reform, a map for the rearrangement of culture, a vision for producing Indians as a people with scientific traditions of their own."[6] For nationalists and colonizers alike, science possessed cultural authority and progressive legitimacy. In the Indian setting Prakash gives especially close attention to those nationalists who tried to reinscribe Western science, to translate "tradition" into a distinctive Hindu modernity, refiguring it as indigenous science. Prakash therefore cautions that his story concerns India alone, yet his recognition of the significance of science seems pertinent to a more general line of inquiry.[7]

Our argument has an unavoidable tendency to conflate science and medicine. In general, medical training provided the first, sometimes only, exposure of the colonized elite to science. Of course, one can identify a few exceptions, but throughout late colonial Southeast Asia, advanced science education commonly meant training in medical science. Even if these scientifically minded physicians went on to study other biological and natural sciences, medicine was their first port of entry. Therefore, to extricate immersion in a world of scientific thought and practice from socialization into a modern profession when gauging relative contributions to the national awakening would be reductive and anachronistic. Additionally, we should make it clear that not all those who invoked science, even medicine, in the national struggle were physicians or medical students—but those who did so most rigorously and consistently generally were. Above all, physicians and medical students were the most successful popularizers of organic analogies and evolutionary models. Of course, not all physicians became ardent nationalists—yet the ranks of nationalists were disproportionately medical. Why should this be so?

In this essay we examine the entanglement of science (especially medical or biological science) and nationalist self-fashioning in the Philippines under the Spanish and U.S. regimes and in the Dutch East Indies.[8] Thus we take the two great colonial archipelagoes of Southeast Asia and assay the role of the scientific imaginary in making the nation visible. The Philippines endured hundreds of years of Spanish clerical colonialism before the United States intervened in 1898; though mostly Catholic, it remained Muslim in the southern islands. In the East Indies, the Dutch exerted less control until the late nineteenth century; focused on commerce, they did not try to convert the majority Muslim population. Early in the twentieth century, both colonies intensified the production of minerals and export commodities and developed state bureaucracies. The Americans in the Philippines attempted a progressive reform of the customs and habits of ordinary Filipinos. The local elite soon took up this "civilizing" project and came to dominate interventionist state bureaucracies. In the East Indies, the so-called Ethical Policy, introduced in 1901, required at least a show of concern for the exploited colonized. The Dutch claimed to promote economic development and health and welfare reform, although by the 1920s, increasingly rancorous relations with Indonesian intellectuals and politicians led to their abandonment. Despite their proximity, these colonial regimes therefore manifested different patterns of governance, education, and inclusiveness—and yet, as comparative study suggests, exposure to science seems in each place to have given form and force to nationalist movements.[9]

Building on Prakash's pioneering study of science as a sign of modernity in late colonial India, we argue more generally for a scientific dynamic in decolonization movements and imperial transitions, distinct from conventional literary and historicist concomitants. That is, we seek to recover through comparative inquiry an anticipatory nationalism derived from scientific enthusiasm and sensibility, a sense of invention and expectancy different from the more familiar nostalgic or atavistic visions of the new nation. At the same time, we hope to indicate here the multiply contingent and hybrid character of science, nationalism, and modernity—how they could be accomplished only locally and laboriously.

The Philippines: Spanish and American

Though recognized primarily as the writer of two brilliantly sardonic novels, José Rizal, the leading opponent of Spanish colonialism in the Philippines, learned science from the Jesuits at the Ateneo de Manila and trained in medicine locally with the Dominicans at the University of Santo Tomás, and then in Madrid, before specializing in ophthalmology in Paris and Heidelberg. In the 1880s, he observed that the "Jesuits, who are backward in Europe, viewed from here, represent Progress; the Philippines owe to them their nascent education, and to them the Natural Sciences, the soul of the nineteenth century."[10] But Santo Tomás—which had offered Filipinos medical training since 1872—disappointed him. According to Rizal, the friars would point to a forbidden cabinet that contained modern equipment and exonerate themselves by saying that it was really "on account of the apathy, laziness, limited capacity of the natives, or some other ethnological or supernatural cause [that] until now no Lavoisier, Secchi, nor Tyndall has appeared, even in miniature, in this Malay-Filipino race!!"[11] Rizal therefore left for Europe where he undertook studies of the new bacteriology, antiseptic surgery, and physical anthropology. In Berlin he met the liberal pathologist Rudolf Virchow, along with physical anthropologists such as Fedor Jagor and Ferdinand Blumentritt. Rizal was treated as an equal, a cosmopolitan intellectual.[12] Heeding Virchow's advice to think microscopically, Rizal took up the ophthalmoscope. It allowed intense scrutiny of human pathology, scaling up otherwise imperceptible defects.

"Politics is nothing else but medicine on a large scale," Virchow frequently asserted. "Medicine, as a social science, as the science of human beings, has the obligation to point out problems and to attempt their theoretical solution."[13] It was this doctrine of social medicine and Virchow's own politics that inspired Rizal's campaign against the diseased Spanish clerical-colonial state in the Philippines. Both medicos regarded their societies as sick organisms—implicitly ailing female bodies, according to Raquel Reyes—requiring treatment and recuperation.[14] As Rizal has Elías assert in his novel *Noli Me Tangere* (1887), "The treatment applied to the evils of the country is so destructive as to affect even a sound organism, whose vitality weakens and conditions it for evil. Would it not be more reasonable to strengthen the sick body and lessen somewhat the violence of the treatment?"[15]

While studying in Europe, Rizal wrote copiously on the infected, corrupt, and repressive character of Spanish colonialism in the Philippines, and he completed his coruscating novels *Noli Me Tangere* and *El Filibusterismo* (1891). After returning to Manila in 1892, he was implicated in an aborted rebellion and declared guilty of sedition. The "First Filipino"—eventually the national hero—was executed by firing squad on December 30, 1896. At the Anthropological Society in Berlin, Virchow delivered the eulogy, lamenting—perhaps too hastily—the loss of the "only man with sufficient knowledge and resolution to open a way for modern thought into that distant island world."[16]

Beyond Rizal, the Propaganda Movement, the group of striving young anti-clerical Filipinos agitating against Spanish control, was saturated with scientists, physicians, and pharmacists. Among these self-confident *ilustrados* (or "enlightened ones") was Graciano López Jaena, the founder of the newspaper *La Solidaridad* in Barcelona. Failing to gain admittance to the medical school at Santo Tomás, he had worked as an apprentice at San Juan de Dios Hospital in Manila and practiced informally in Iloilo before leaving for Spain. He enrolled in medicine at the University of Valencia but did not complete his studies and succumbed to tuberculosis in his late thirties. Another leading *propagandista*, Mariano Ponce, took his medical degree at Santo Tomás, moved to Spain, wrote incendiary articles for *La Solidaridad*, and eagerly tried to supply the Filipino revolutionary forces with weapons. In the early twentieth century, under the U.S. regime, Ponce joined the National Party and established another paper, *El Ideal*.[17] The chief of the revolutionary army, General Antonio Luna, studied chemistry at Santo Tomás and qualified in pharmacy in Spain. Before taking up arms against the colonizers, he wrote a treatise on malaria and investigated acclimatization in the tropics. His brother, José Luna, sometimes was called the "physician of the revolution."[18] And so the roll call continues . . .

We should consider whether engagement with science, training in medicine, and exposure to professional colleagues across the globe changed the way the colonized elites thought of themselves and the world. Their scientific accomplishments must have appeared striking in a colonial regime that discredited Filipino scientific and technological achievements, thus securing and legitimizing fixed colonial hierarchies.[19] The later American regime would be perhaps more deft, proclaiming its civilizing mission and mobilizing Filipinos on modern intellectual and cultural trajectories, though refusing to recognize them as professional equals and proper citizens.[20] Yet the *propagandistas* and their successors stood out as self-conscious and confident scientific figures, adroitly applying universal knowledge in a variety of settings, including Europe, and developing diverse ties and networks. They came to believe they could diagnose and treat social and political pathologies just as they restored frail human constitutions. Above all, they came to view themselves as modern and cosmopolitan intellectuals, not mere colonial subjects.

Among Rizal's mentors was Trinidad H. Pardo de Tavera, a physician and leading *ilustrado* who wrote essays on Philippine medicinal plants, as well as regularly issuing civic exhortations. During the Philippine-American War he launched the newspaper *La Democracia* and founded the Federal Party, advocating autonomy for the islands within the United States. In Manila, his teachings led the next generation of Filipino scientists and physicians down the path of liberal reform and assimilation. Pardo de Tavera and his followers sought to transform Filipinos into modern civic subjects suitable for the future nation.

"America came to the Philippines to aid them, to sustain them and to give them the principles of liberty and free government," Pardo de Tavera wrote in 1902.[21] Filipinos were yet to achieve the necessary "triumph over one's self"—instead they remained lamentably "infected with the leprosy of superstition (*contagiodos con la lepra de la superstición*)." Accordingly, attainment of true self-government required the formation of a "hygienic consciousness (*el sentimento de la higiene*)." Despite the Filipino clamor for more hygiene, the Spanish had failed to prepare them for corporeal and political independence. Now they could take advantage of America's "regime of liberty, industry, work, and rationality (*mentalidad lógica*)."[22] In 1921, addressing graduates of the University of the Philippines, Pardo de Tavera imagined his people eventually "capable of following the infinite, progressive, and ascendant road of civilization." Anticipating the future nation, he urged graduates to develop the qualities of "confidence in one's own self, of appreciation, respect and love for work, of hygiene and care of our body, of disregard for suffering." "Let us therefore lay aside sentimental patriotism," he declared, "and let us adopt scientific patriotism."[23]

In the early twentieth century scientists and physicians often adapted or deferred their nationalist ardor, seeking instead to extend some sort of modernity into the Philippine hinterland and prepare the people for eventual self-government. Through science education, public health, and social welfare—Pardo de Tavera's "scientific patriotism" and Michel Foucault's biopolitics—they would organize rural and insular societies for the future nation. By way of illustration, Fernando Calderón, a suave obstetrician and president of the revolutionary municipal junta in Ormoc, Leyte, during the Philippine-American War, went on to become the first Filipino director of the Philippine General Hospital and dean of the medical school of the University of the Philippines.[24] Although he was a target of American racial disparagement, Calderón shared his colleagues' modernizing ambitions. Like them, he regarded himself as a pragmatist. After the war he became devoted to hygiene and the improvement of the masses, declaring the "nerve of civilization in the present epoch" to be "public hygiene in the towns in general and the health of each citizen in particular."[25] With the support and protection of his close friend Manuel Quezon, the nationalist leader, Calderón dominated clinical medicine in Manila for more than twenty years.

By 1920 a Filipinized colonial public health bureaucracy had led to hygiene programs directed at developing the *masses*, unlike the racial policies of white health officers, allowing, in effect, the normalization of social medicine and welfare provision. Erstwhile nationalist physicians like Vicente de Jesús, the first Filipino director of health, concentrated on educating and mobilizing the poor, thereby reproducing hygienic social citizens.[26] They were administering state medicine in a late colonial government. The need for education and reform of the masses was a truism of progressive public health in the early twentieth century. Thus Agerico B. M. Sison, a leading physician and later dean of the medical school, urged the emergent Philippine state to teach proper care of the body and fastidious behavior in the public schools in order to "inculcate the principles of hygiene and sanitation in the more plastic minds of the schoolchildren."[27] Furthermore, Jacobo Fajardo, the director of health in 1931, instructed nursing graduates to become "exemplary as a good citizen, interested always in the best solution of public questions, social and health problems, and in everything that pertains to the community."[28] These physicians were not only imagining a national community: they were inventing one.

During the 1930s science was conventionally linked to nation building and governmentality, supplanting the redundant and insulting American emphasis on its role in a more general civilizing mission. In 1936 Camilo Osias, the president of the National University, observed that "under the new order, there is a special call to men and women of science. More men and women need to be yoked for science." He went on: "If we as a people are to surmount the difficulties ahead we must apply to our life the ways and methods of science. We need to follow the careful laboratory method of fact finding, the scientific way of conducting research and sifting the facts, and the relentless procedure of science without partisanship or prejudice."[29] Leopoldo B. Uichanco, from the University of the Philippines, welcomed "the greater extension of science-consciousness in Filipino life."[30] Angel S. Arguelles, the director of the Bureau of Science, declared that "a nation dedicated to science, that applies it in various complex national activities, can look forward with confidence to its future and is bound to survive through the vicissitudes of time." Applied science, he believed, "would evolve a virile and progressive nation."[31] Indeed, the constitution of the Philippine Commonwealth, written in 1934, provided that "the State shall promote scientific research and invention," an extraordinary national commitment to science, indicating also, perhaps, the depth of scientific commitment to the nation.[32]

FROM THE DUTCH EAST INDIES TO INDONESIA

As Minke, Pramoedya Ananta Toer's double of pioneering nationalist Tirto Adi Suryo, arrived in Tanjung Priok, the harbor of Batavia (Jakarta), in 1901 to attend the local medical school, he mused:

> Farewell to you, ship. Farewell to you, sea. Farewell to all that is past. And the dark times, neither are you exempt—farewell.
>
> Into the universe of Betawi [Batavia] I go—into the universe of the twentieth century. . . . People say only the modern man gets ahead in these times. In his hands

lies the fate of humankind. You reject modernity? You will be the plaything of all forces of the world operating outside and around you. I am a modern person. I have freed my body and my thoughts of all ornamentations.

And modernity brings the loneliness of orphaned humanity, cursed to free itself from unnecessary ties of custom, blood—even from the land, and if need be, from others of its kind.[33]

Minke boarded the tram to the center of Weltevreden, Batavia's new suburb in the hills, traveling first class—"white class"—aware that he was a "native who prefers European clothes, who carries on like a *sinyo* [Indo-European man]." For Minke, Batavia was the epitome of modernity—and his studies at the medical school would ensure that he became a participant in this modern world.

Already we know Minke believed that "the science and knowledge that I received from school and the truth of which I witnessed in life made my personality very different from that of my people in general." He was becoming a modern person, a citizen of the world. As a young medical student, Minke was especially impressed that both José Rizal and the Chinese nationalist Sun Yat-sen were doctors. Like them, he placed "greater trust in scientific knowledge, reason. At least with them there are certainties that one can hold onto."[34]

Pramoedya notes the pathos of Minke's travels to medical school and into modernity. Most students had come from afar, leaving their villages and extended families, loosening the hold of *adat* (customary law). Yet most students resisted nostalgia, attracted to the potential of modernity, which brought with it the promises of science and progress. Many of them hoped to advance their social position by receiving an education, enabling them to take their place in the new order—as well as to improve social conditions in the colony with the tools modernity pledged to them. It was this sense of promise and potential that guided them into nationalist activism.

Edification at the medical schools in the Indies decisively shaped the subjectivities and self-conceptions of Indonesian students, prompting the formation of new and hybrid identities. For some this created a sense of turmoil, even vertigo. One of the less sanguine students, writing in the almanac of the Nederlandsch-Indische Artsen School (NIAS, the Netherlands-Indies School for Physicians in Surabaya), described vividly the estrangement that exposure to science and modernity was inducing.

I am, with my Western knowledge, snatched from my Oriental environment! From primary school on I have become increasingly and systematically alienated from the warmth of my Indonesian culture, while the cold and sober Western civilization could never become completely my own. . . . I hang suspended between heaven and earth, rudderless and unable to keep my balance, back and forth I am swept by the fierce waves of seething sea of life! I have no advice to Western ideas, which I never fully understand. . . . I am not able to blow the warmth of life into the Western ideas that I have received. . . . At the same time, the warm Oriental civilization is cold . . . and dead to me.[35]

The sense of living uncomfortably between two worlds was conveyed also in Abdul Moeis's 1928 novel *Salah Asuhan* (Wrong Upbringing).[36] A medical school dropout and political radical, active in the Sarekat Islam (Islamic Union), Moeis crafted a story that illuminated the horizon of Western possibility in the Indies, while drawing attention to the conflicts between old customs and modern aspirations.[37] Few such reservations were expressed in the Philippines during this period.

The Batavia medical school grew out of a small course for vaccinators and native medical assistants, which began in 1851. After repeated reorganization, it was renamed the School ter Opleiding van Inlandsche Artsen (STOVIA, the School for the Education of Native Physicians) in 1903, boasting a medical course lasting six years.[38] In 1927, it was transformed into a proper medical college (Geneeskundige Hoogeschool) conferring degrees equivalent to those in the Netherlands. The Surabaya medical school NIAS opened in 1913.[39] Both STOVIA and, to a lesser extent, NIAS became hotbeds of Indonesian nationalism. For example, Tirto Adi Suryo—Pramoedya's model for Minke—dropped out of medical school and in 1909 became involved in the founding of the Sarekat Dagang Islam, an influential syncretic political movement.[40] In 1908, Sutomo, then a student, cofounded Budi Utomo (Glorious Endeavor), an organization dedicated to developing Javanese culture, commonly regarded as the original national movement. After becoming a dermatologist at NIAS, Sutomo founded the first Indonesian study club and headed the Partai Indonesia Raya (Parindra), which established educational bodies and even a bank providing small loans to farmers. Medical graduate R. M. Cipto Mangunkusumo also assisted in the founding of Budi Utomo and, in 1912 he founded the Indische Partij (Indies Party), together with Ernest F. E. Douwes Dekker—a relative of Multatuli—and Suwardi Suryaningrat, yet another nationalist who spent some time at STOVIA before turning to journalism, teaching, and popularizing the name "Indonesia." The Indische Partij was the first to advocate complete independence for the Indies, while presenting itself as fostering unity between Indo-Europeans and Indonesians. The colonial government disbanded it after a rather short period of activity and exiled its leaders to the Netherlands.

Medical politics and professional rivalries further radicalized many of these incipient nationalists. In 1912, the executive of the (European) Association of Physicians in the Dutch East Indies sharply criticized the proposal of the colonial government to open a medical school in Surabaya—later to be known as NIAS.

Dutch physicians felt that opening a second medical school in the Indies would only allow underqualified Indonesians, Indo-Europeans, and those of Chinese descent to become physicians, thus degrading both the profession and medical care.[41] The statement generated outrage in the indigenous press and embarrassment in the European press. It became a rallying cry in the propaganda of the Indische Partij. As a consequence, indigenous physicians redoubled their support for the nationalist cause.[42]

While in the Netherlands, Cipto and Sutomo joined a small, highly select, somewhat elite, and very bright group of cosmopolitan students. They established contact with a variety of politicians, especially those from the Labor Party and communist movement, and representatives of Marxist science. Several Indonesian students in the Netherlands became members of the Indische Vereeniging (Indies Association), where, in the 1920s, far-reaching ideas about nationalism and Indonesian independence were formulated. The participation of Suwardi Suryaningat, Douwes Dekker, Cipto, and later Sutomo further radicalized the organization. It changed its name to Indonesische Vereeniging in 1923 and Perhimpunan Indonesia [Indonesian Association] late in 1924 (the translation into the new national language is significant). One prominent member was the economics student Mohammad Hatta, later the nation's first vice president and foreign minister.[43] The ideas developed by these students—most of them with some medical training—would be exceptionally compelling in the nationalist movement in the Indies.

As in the Philippines, scientists and physicians in the East Indies eventually developed some accommodation with the late colonial state, choosing to educate and enlighten the masses, thus preparing them for citizenship in the coming nation. At the same time, nationalists debated whether modernization and independence would be reached faster through collaboration with the colonial government or active opposition to it.[44] In the 1920s, Sukarno and many followers embarked on a policy of noncooperation, refusing to participate in the activities of the Volksraad (parliament). Many of them were exiled (within Indonesia this time) or jailed. Indonesian physicians, on the other hand, increasingly concentrated on hygiene education and social medicine. Usually they worked for the colonial public health service or as medical officers on plantations. Though apparently careerist, most of these physicians sympathized with the nationalist movement and demonstrated strong convictions about the social role medicine could play in improving conditions among Indonesians.

According to Abdul Rasyid, a member of the Volksraad and president of the Vereeniging van Indonesische Geneeskundigen (VIG, the Association of Indonesian Physicians) beginning in the late 1930s, Indonesian physicians were the principal mediators between the cultures of East and West, a task that conferred on them unusual responsibility in the uplift of the Indonesian population. As he stated, "The vision can already be imagined that Indies physicians will have to be one of the levers for the development of the Indonesian population."[45] Rather than explicit political campaigning, the VIG published numerous articles in its journal, *Medisch Tribune*, arguing for public health programs and hygiene education. Rasyid and his cohort of physicians were committed to improving and mobilizing Indonesian society through scientific initiatives—just as an earlier generation had used science to refashion themselves—even if that meant serving, or at least functioning within, a political system they were seeking to abolish.

Professional organization and even nomenclature are inextricable from rising nationalism in the early twentieth century. The VIG began in 1910 as the Vereeniging van Inlandsche Geneeskundigen (Association of Native Physicians) and changed its name to Vereeniging van Indische Geneeskundigen (Association of Indies Physicians) in 1926. At this time, a proposal from Indonesian physicians studying in the Netherlands to call the association "Indonesian" was

The director the Philippine nationalist newspaper *La Independencia*, General Juan Luna (*middle row, far left*), and his editor Dr. Mariano del Rosario (*back row, far left*), both qualified pharmacists, with their staff of writers and historians—including Fernando Ma. Guerrero (*front row, left*), Clemente José Zulueta (*back row, second from left*), and Epifanio de los Santos (back row, second from right), Manila, 1898. (Library of Congress Prints and Photographs Division)

rejected because the word had distinct nationalist implications. The students in the Netherlands could not comprehend this response, since to them it was self-evident that the association was already politically involved. If the name "Indonesian" were rejected, they would prefer the designation "native" rather than "Indies," because at least it correctly indicated the membership of the association, which ought to promote the interests of indigenous physicians. For radical students in the Netherlands—who had just engaged in an extensive debate about the reactionary views of two Dutch psychiatrists on the nature of the native mind—the association should be a vehicle for the advancement of *Indonesians*, not merely medicine in the Indies.[46]

When the name of the association was finally changed in 1938 to Vereeniging van Indonesische Geneeskundigen, few objected. At the first congress, it was resolved to send a friendly letter to the Association of European Physicians, expressing the hope that both associations would collaborate in the future—or even that the European colonial vestige might be incorporated in the national body.[47] A motion adopted at the same meeting opposed "the existing dualism in the medical corps."[48] Through its many activities in improving the working conditions of Indonesian physicians and protesting against discriminatory colonial practices, the VIG would attempt to realize the ideals of social medicine for the entire Indonesian population. Of necessity, it had to stay within the boundaries of what was legally allowed in the Indies at the time. Many members of the VIG remained employed as physicians during the Japanese occupation.[49] A few became actively involved in the armed struggle against the Dutch in 1946 after the outbreak of the Indonesian revolution. The *asrama* (dormitory) of the medical students at Prapatan 10 became one of the three centers of armed revolt in Jakarta.[50] After national independence in 1949, Indonesian physicians followed varied career paths. Some built a system of medical education to train physicians for the newly independent nation and developed health policy in the Ministry of Health. A smaller number became leading businessmen and generals. All of them were involved in nation building—albeit through different channels.

CONCLUSION

In her study of the relations of the Taiwanese medical profession and the Japanese colonial state, Ming-Cheng M. Lo describes a shift from resistance to assimilation and quiescence. During the 1920s, the first generation of Taiwanese doctors "channeled their resources and power into anti-colonial struggles, positioning themselves as major movement leaders in the nascent Taiwanese civil society," but in the *kominka* (assimilationist) period of imperial expansion (1937–1945), medicos became the "professionals who carried forth Japanese colonial modernity." She argues that for the earlier "national physicians" ethnic ties influenced their professional identities, while the more accommodating "medical modernists" managed to displace ethnic allegiance in favor of professional identity.[51] The pattern is similar to those we discerned in the Philippines and East Indies, although we find the later cohort advancing national goals through mass mobilization, rather than withdrawing completely from the struggle. However, we can confirm Lo's observation that indigenous physicians under the late colonial state tended to embrace "modernity's promise of progress. . . . The modern, for them, stood for an ideal situation in which human lives could be continually improved by rational thinking and action"—by science, in effect.[52]

Like Prakash and Lo, we believe it is time for historians of imperial transitions and national emergence to take more seriously contemporary scientific vision and medical training. From the late nineteenth century on—and maybe earlier—science and medicine offered new ways of seeing humans, their societies, and their place in nature. Evolutionary biology proved an inexhaustible source of organic metaphor and model, a guide for intellectuals chafing against fixed social hierarchies and ossified colonial structures. As we have seen, social medicine and bacteriology could also shape political perceptions and suggest radical solutions to social problems and mass organization. They might alter views of agency, control, and scale. They implied a diagnostic relation to the state and prescribed new strategies for intervention. For the first generation of "native" physicians, the first cohort exposed to science, their training gave them an entry point into what felt like the laboratory of modernity. Science not only changed their view of the world; it refashioned their sense of themselves, sometimes with painful and distressing consequences. They became scientists and physicians rather than mere colonized subjects, transformed into mobile cosmopolitan agents, modern intellectuals, and nationalists. Science could give them a sense of anticipation, of limitless potential, of national futures. Yet historians until recently have focused mostly on history, law, and other, more retrospective and nostalgic narratives of national emergence.

From our vantage point, science made available within the colonial sphere a mode of modern self-consciousness and offered the anticolonial intelligentsia a means of social reproduction, a professional identity and agenda. Importantly, this emergent professionalism did not lead to a withdrawal from politics, as Weber would have predicted. Rather, it organized and consolidated a means of constituting other national subjects—it operationalized the biopolitical project of developing the population into hygienic citizens, of disciplining the emergent nation-state. These professionals could mobilize the masses for the nation.[53]

We do not mean to suggest that science alone explains everything or that poetry is impotent. In the Philippines, a vigorous anticlerical reaction, masculine *amor propio*, and enthusiasm for freemasonry also contributed to the assertiveness of the intellectual elite's positivism and liberalism. In the East Indies, nationalism was more syncretic, a tense and unstable combination of Islam, ethnic filiation, and science, an amalgam that transformed its constituents in unpredictable ways. The patterns were different again in Taiwan, as Lo demonstrates, and in India, where Prakash argues that science exerted its pull a little later and was more thoroughly indigenized. Our goal here is simply to show the scientific dimensions and scope of nationalism in the early twentieth century, not to imply a single cause for national awakening or a uniform configuration.

Additionally, we wanted to trace, lightly and perhaps too enigmatically, a genealogy for the "globalization" of Western science and medicine, connecting their spread with colonial structures and national aspirations. One might argue that this was not a story about nationalism and independence but rather an account of neocolonialism and dependence.[54] In a sense, we have described the shift from formal political and economic imperialism to the neocolonial intellectual hegemony of science and technical reason. For most recent analysts of the globalization of science, the phenomenon excites a feeling of euphoria and perception of novelty—whereas we offer here an anhedonic and critical reading of this and other neocolonial developments.[55] Ostensibly we were writing about nationalism and the end of empire, but of course we were also charting another imperial transition, albeit an exceptionally complex and ambiguous one.

Decolonization and the
Roots of Democracy

REMCO RABEN

THE INSTITUTION OF DEMOCRACY was a crucial ingredient of the transition of the colonized world toward independence. The democratic turn many countries took—often characterized as the "second wave" of democratization—was instigated by the Western powers, which looked for a legitimate successor regime and a stable political system.[1] Democracies were established with an urgency that had been inconceivable during the heyday of colonial rule. Although decolonization and democracy are closely connected, and at the time both were championed by international forums such as the United Nations, they have rarely been investigated in conjunction. All too often, the discussion of democracy outside the West has been dominated by its failure and demise; this stimulated the study of authoritarian tendencies rather than democratic forces. It seems relevant to revisit the stirrings of and experiments with democracy in the decolonizing world, as it can shed light on several fundamental claims on the origins of democracy in the non-Western world, on decolonization, and on the nature of postcolonial society.

The widely accepted view on the history of modern democracy is that it originated in the West and from there spread over the rest of the world. But is the narrative of a sudden Western-driven democratization telling the entire story? Was democracy a parting gift from the Western powers, irrespective of whether or not it fitted local wishes and political traditions—which would explain the failure of most democratic regimes within a generation of independence? Or was democratic rule in keeping with certain established or emerging political practices and principles in the colony? The issue urges us to investigate the genealogies of democracy in the non-Western world, in particular its meaning and practices in the era of decolonization. We cannot explain the crystallization of democracy by looking at just this moment of changing regimes. Decolonization is not only the process of political deal making around the imperial retreat and national independence. To understand the deeper dynamics of decolonization, a longer time frame is called for.[2]

The example of Indonesia urges us to look beyond the seemingly clear characterizations of a West-driven modernization and awkward indigenous adoption. It will demonstrate the quintessentially heterogeneous genealogy of democracy. Moreover, it will demonstrate that the process of democratization on the doorstep of independence was wrought with contradictions. Authoritarian colonial traditions, transitional and emergency politics, and sometimes warfare and internal power struggles worked against the development of fully democratic structures. On the other hand the claim of self-determination and the advent of international discourses on democracy provided strong motivations for establishing forms of representative politics. Maybe most important, impending decolonization made the issue of legitimation by the people acute.

The development of democracy will be analyzed from several angles: the formal democratic structures that were established under colonial rule and at independence, the influences of local practices of participatory politics, and the political conceptualizations by political leaders. Above all, Sukarno became, as the leader of anticolonial nationalism in the 1920s and early 1930s, and later as Indonesia's first president, a pivotal figure in the development and ultimate breakdown of democratic tendencies. Not only was Sukarno a leader of undeniable charm and charisma, but he was, like his contemporaries Jawaharlal Nehru and Léopold S. Senghor, a political visionary who maneuvered across the local, national, and international in a bold bid to change all three. At home, these efforts meant advancing, then curtailing, the country's democracy; abroad, first seeking the support of Western powers in 1945, then spurning them to fight neocolonialism at the 1955 Asia-Africa Conference; and, internationally, first joining the UN to win independence and then resigning in 1965 to form the Beijing-Jakarta axis.

COLONIAL DEMOCRACY

By the 1940s and 1950s, colonial powers pushed democratization as part of their exit strategies; before that, they had not been very fervent and principled democratizers. Still, beginning in the late nineteenth century authorities in several European colonies took the initiative to institute representative assemblies. Most notoriously this happened in British India, where the Indian Council Act of 1861 provided for provincial legislative councils of appointed representatives, without much power to initiate or amend laws and decrees of the viceroy. In the early twentieth century, the councils evolved into an India-wide Legislative Council, in which British and Indian representatives were chosen by a limited but growing electorate. The Philippines, in the hands of the United States since 1898, received its Assembly in 1907, which tellingly was inaugurated in the Manila Grand Opera. In the Netherlands Indies, a People's Council (Volksraad) was established in 1917. Other colonies did not have any kind of formal representation, or they were introduced only after World War II. This happened in the British colonies in Africa, where colonial officials looked for new forms of political legitimation and new political roles for the indigenous elites. Ahead of all other colonies was the Gold Coast, where the first universal elections on the African continent were held in 1951.

Before World War II, colonial electoral constituencies were extremely limited. Among colonial democracies, the Philippine franchise was the most extensive. Just prior to the war, about 14 percent of the population had voting rights. In the Netherlands Indies, the members of the Volksraad were chosen by a small electorate: just 2,228 members of municipal and regional councils, who themselves were only partly elected by a minimal franchise and partly appointed by the government. Moreover, its competence remained very limited; the council had the right of amendment and initiative, but in case of nonagreement between council and government the Dutch Crown was authorized to proclaim the decree.[3]

In most places, the colonial assemblies had been preceded by municipal councils. At the same time that the Dutch colonial government started expanding and formulating its policies in ethical terms of development, the first municipal councils were established. In the Netherlands Indies, this happened from 1905 onward, based on the 1903 Decentralization Law. Their institution was not the result of a democratic movement but of the tendency to modernize government and intervene more actively in local society. These local councils were dominated by Dutchmen and had very restricted means and powers. Generally only a few Indonesians (and Chinese) could become members of these councils, and most of them came from the aristocratic class of officials. Plans to increase the number of Indonesians on the councils met with fierce resistance from local Dutch administrators in 1930, many of whom thought that indigenous Indonesians were not capable of acting as worthy members of city councils.[4]

Despite the severe limitations, the early experiences with these semidemocratic institutions and procedures were the testing ground of later democratic practices. Although many nationalists refused to cooperate with the Dutch (the so-called non-co), others continued to serve in municipal and regional councils and the Volksraad, where, in many ways, they learned the trade of party politics and parliamentary debate. Quite a few became members of Indonesia's parliament after independence. Moreover, the existence of these representative councils influenced the expectations of the people, not only by means of what these councils did but also by default. This trend was demonstrated most clearly in the emergence, in 1939, of Gaboengan Politik Indonesia (the Indonesian Political Federation or GAPI), the joint factions of "cooperating nationalists" in the Volksraad, which on the brink of World War II called for a full democracy—a demand that was high-handedly declined by the Dutch Indies' government.[5]

New Civic Traditions

According to modern definitions and standards of democracy, these early democratic institutions were very shallow beginnings—although we should be aware that even in the West universal suffrage was very rare in the 1910s. Trying to gauge the genealogies of democracy at empire's end, we should also look beyond the formal institutions of representation. Strong tendencies of popular participation developed outside the formal democratic agencies, which presumably also helped to spread the idea of popular representation.

One of the new phenomena of the late nineteenth and early twentieth centuries was the emergence of new civic traditions of organization and collective action. These were crucial in the development of political awareness among the people. With the expansion of the colonial state and its increasing intervention in the daily lives of its subjects, people's distrust, but also their expectations of the state, grew. The people responded to the insecurities of urbanization and heightened mobility by instituting mutual aid societies.[6] Besides, Indonesians increasingly learned to voice their claims and wishes on the streets. Even if political and civil rights were denied to the great majority of Indonesians, cultures of participation did develop, in the form of membership of parties, social organizations, and labor unions or more informally through demonstrations and petitions.

An interesting example comes from the large harbor city Surabaya in eastern Java. In the first half of 1928, inhabitants of Surabaya assembled in large numbers at meetings of the Comité Perasaan Pendoedoek Soerabaja—the Committee for the Sentiments of the Inhabitants of Surabaya.[7] The catalyst for the meeting was the government's intention to take over the administration of autonomous *desa* (villages or wards) lying within the municipal boundaries. The committee was able to mobilize a crowd of several thousand people. Their message was that the *desa* people did not appreciate the intervention of the state and they opposed the annexation and *kampung* (city wards) improvement schemes, especially as long as the number of Indonesian representatives in the municipal council was not brought up to a level at which the people would feel themselves to be properly represented. Similar organizations sprang up in other cities.[8]

The Indonesians did not feel that their interests were sufficiently represented by the municipal councils, and quite understandably so. Only a tiny minority of Indonesians had the right to vote, and everywhere Indonesian council members remained a small minority. As such the protests were a clear sign of the expectations of representational government, but also of disenchantment with the *workings* of the colonial state. There seems to have been a fairly general belief that a real, modern state would make use of representational politics. On the other hand, a tradition was established in which collective action became part and parcel of the political process. This was a lesson learned during the colonial period and not forgotten after independence.

NATIONALISTS AND DEMOCRACY

On a broader geographic and more ideological level, emerging conceptions of nationhood placed the notion of the people's will at the center of politics. Not only did anticolonial nationalism rely on its power to mobilize large numbers of inhabitants for its cause, but the claims nationalist leaders made for autonomy or independence were made in the name of the collectivity of the nation. The intellectual explorations and imaginings of the 1920s and 1930s had diverse inspirations, but they generally gravitated toward popular representation and civic rights.

Although ideas of people's sovereignty were strong, the precise form it should take was less clear. Experiences with colonial forms of representative politics were disappointing, as they were ineffective and more exclusionary than democratic. But they did not inhibit the aspirations for fuller democracy, and often even stimulated them. Nevertheless, some leaders and ideologues had serious misgivings about Western-style democracy. There was a widespread belief that Indonesian society was much more collectivist than European societies. The early nationalist and leader of the independent school movement, Soewardi Soerjaningrat (Ki Hadjar Dewantara), wrote in 1931 that "democracy must not be allowed to violate overall interests." He made a distinction between Western democracy, with its emphasis on individuality, and Eastern democracy, which "attaches greatest importance to establishing a unity."[9]

Sukarno, who since the mid-1920s had emerged as the most powerful and vocal leader of the nationalist movement, also had his reservations about the Western democratic model; in his eyes it had failed to protect the poorer classes from the onslaught of capitalism.[10] On the other hand, he was too much aware of the importance of popular legitimation of power to discard democracy altogether. After a strong infatuation with Marxist ideology during adolescence, he had by the late 1910s turned to Sun Yat-sen's *san min chui*, the trinity of nationalism, socialism, and democracy.[11] For Sukarno this amalgam seemed to offer a much more viable perspective than socialist internationalism, which had attracted him in his adolescent days. To this he added some indigenous elements based on conceptions of "Indonesian" culture and the centrality of Islam. For the time being, at least until the outbreak of World War II, he concentrated much more on the coordination of nationalist activities and on the mobilization of the people than on political theory.

Even early in his career as a political activist, Sukarno was convinced that Western-style politics was based on individualism, which, he felt, did not suit the Indonesian character. Influenced by conceptions of Indonesian collectivism, an awareness that the people needed strong guidance on their path to independence and nationhood, and a distrust of Western democracies as instruments of capitalist cliques, Sukarno was swayed toward corporatist solutions.[12] These corporatist ideas seem to have reached their temporary apex in the hectic days of mid-1945, when Sukarno and other nationalist leaders were ordered by the Japanese authorities to formulate a political structure for an independent Indonesia.

On June 1, 1945, Sukarno delivered his famous Pancasila speech before the Investigating Committee for the Preparation of Independence, which was instituted by the Japanese occupation authorities. In this speech, Sukarno presented the five principles on which he wanted to build the Indonesian state, which became known as the Pancasila (Five Pillars). The third principle concerned the centrality of *permusjawaratan-perwakilan* (deliberation among representatives). He saw Western democracy as a very limited form of representational politics, as it offered political democracy but allowed people to be dominated by capitalists. He therefore added notions of economic democracy and social justice.[13] But at that moment he was unclear about how he envisioned the Indonesian political structure.

One day earlier, Supomo, the most important Indonesian law expert of his time and member of the committee, had been more specific. Supomo, who was to hastily draft the first, temporary constitution of the Indonesian Republic of August 18, 1945, was convinced that a consultative assembly should be part of the state structure and would function as a sounding board and mouthpiece through which to convey the wishes of the people to the head of state. Another prominent nationalist, Mohammad Hatta, was an advocate for ministerial accountability. Sukarno asserted that the head of state embodied the sovereignty of the people, not the assembly.[14] These notions were supported by Supomo and reflected his and Sukarno's ideas of an integralist state. Those ideas were rooted in Javanese conceptions of authority but were enhanced by the urgencies of the revolutionary times, which called for strong leadership, and plans for the Indonesian state had at this stage still to be in concordance with Japanese wishes and political principles. As a consequence, the 1945 Constitution bore traces of Japanese politics, with its emphasis on strong executive leadership. New were Sukarno's ideas of a one-party system. He was convinced that party politics would fragment the precious solidarity of the Indonesians, and he hoped to guarantee their unanimity in the anticolonial struggle.

COLONIALISM'S DEMOCRATIC TURN

It would seem, then, that the prospects for democracy were bleak at war's end. In the minds of the draftees of the constitution-to-be, Western-style democracy was not the most prominent option, colonized peoples had little experience with free democratic politics, and the Western powers demonstrated a much stronger commitment to safeguarding their interests or recovering their rule than to promoting participatory politics. However, World War II had also created an international environment that strongly favored democratization. The war against the Axis powers was increasingly proclaimed as a war against antidemocratic forces. This attitude, although it became severely compromised in the colonial crises after the war's end, had many repercussions on European attitudes in molding the new politics in their overseas possessions.

In the case of the Netherlands Indies, the Dutch government had shown an increasing willingness to provide for the political participation of Indonesians. Dutch Queen Wilhelmina, in exile and dependent on her allies for the reconquest of her country, spoke on August 6, 1942, before the U.S. Congress. On that occasion she explained, of course very conscious about the place and the audience for her speech, that the Netherlands would organize a conference with the colonies, but "in concordance with sound democratic principles no final decision would be made without cooperation of all after liberation." Suddenly in Dutch discourse new terms such as *democracy* were linked to the older colonial tenets of popular well-being and popular development.

The idea that democracy had to be developed in the Netherlands Indies achieved some urgency after the Japanese capitulation. The colonial rulers had to look for new bases of legitimation among both the Indonesian elites and the people. Confronted with the proclamation of an Indonesian Republic, the issue of national self-determination became acute. Moreover, the Dutch were aware that the international community, in particular the United States and Great Britain, would expect the Dutch to introduce "massive suffrage" and a parliamentary system.[15] In the Indies, too, voices were raised in favor of democratic reform. In October 1945, several Dutch social democrats in Java petitioned to the minister of economic affairs in The Hague to guarantee democratic institutions for an independent Indonesia in the near future.[16] But how and how fast the Netherlands Indies should democratize was subject to debate—and in the increasingly violent situation of late 1945 it was not the most urgent issue. In government circles, the idea dominated that forms would have to be found "to guarantee democratic values by accommodating to the particular social structure of the Netherlands Indies."[17]

Interestingly, despite the reservations, democratic principles became a yardstick for a successful future for postwar Indonesia. In this vein, Dutch Chief Civil Affairs Officer C. O. van der Plas communicated to the supreme Allied commander in Southeast Asia, General Louis Mountbatten, that his policy of nonintervention in Indonesian affairs would cause Indonesians, who were still under the influence of the Japanese, to turn away from "Western democracies."[18] And Minister of Overseas Territories J. H. A. Logemann wrote to Governor-General A. W. L. Tjarda van Starkenborch Stachouwer in October 1945 that "nationalist, democratic and communist tendencies had become global forces" that could not be denied.[19] Tjarda's successor, H. J. van Mook, argued that the central government of Indonesia would have to be structured on democratic principles of popular representation with an Indonesian majority—an enormous step given the abortive claims for greater representative powers for Indonesians before the war.[20] Minister Logemann confirmed the principle but emphasized that "in fact only that small elite thinks in the same manner as we do, [and] is capable and willing to co-operate in shaping a society in which the values of our democracy really count."[21] The democratic turn colonialism had taken was exemplified by one Catholic member of the Netherlands Senate, who argued that the Dutch should not deal with quasi democrats such as Sukarno and Prime Minister Sutan Sjahrir but should instead work toward revitalizing "the democratic institutions as known from old. . . . We should be able to say: *we* are the real democrats—which is true; the others are fascists who are under Japanese influence—which is also true."[22]

Not everybody was convinced about the worth of democratization. A member of the Dutch Raad van State, J. W. Meijer Ranneft, thought that a democratic system, forced on the Netherlands Indies by Britain and the United States for internal political reasons, would not work well.[23] Apparently he abhorred the possibility of having to work with the revolutionaries, whom he saw as puppets of Japan, and he therefore supported a continuation of the prewar authoritarian model. But voices like Meijer Ranneft's would become marginalized in the acute bid for new legitimacies. The first Dutch plans for a future Indonesia, dating from late 1945, concerned a commonwealth, based on democratic principles and giving "special guarantees" for religious freedom, minority rights, and protection of persons and possessions.[24]

From 1946 onward, the Dutch started to work toward a federal Indonesia consisting of several states—and, indeed, by the time of the transfer of sovereignty there would be sixteen of them. Only a few developed a good working administrative system, most prominently the Negara Indonesia Timur (NIT) or State of East Indonesia. Apart from the occasional—indirect—elections for *negara* (federal state) parliaments, elections were also held for municipal councils. Thus on August 9, 1946, the people of Makassar chose their municipal council.[25] The limits of democratization became clear in areas where Republican candidates threatened to get the upper hand. One such instance was in Madoera, where the evolution of the Negara Madoera was stalled when pro-Republican politicians threatened to win the majority vote.[26]

It would be easy to characterize the Dutch policies of and arguments for democratization as opportunistic or hypocritical. The Dutch had to be democratic to remain true to their own heightened democratic awareness and to counter Republican claims that they were acting according to the people's will. They feared that Republican politicians would get the upper hand and thwart the construction of the federation. A second concern was the protection of the interests of minority groups, such as Chinese and Europeans (including Eurasians). The result was a cautious development of representative institutions, with the central

negara councils elected by indirect vote, and with ethnically separated constituencies—a remnant of the ethnic segregation of the prewar period.

REPUBLICAN DEMOCRACY

How did democracy fare on the other side of the colonial conflict? Sukarno's
one-party structure only lasted for two months after the proclamation of Indonesia's independence. Whatever the second thoughts several national leaders had
about "Western" democratic models, the necessity of people's representation was
generally acknowledged, for the simple reason that a revolutionary government
fighting for the self-determination of the people and in the name of a nation had
to create forms of representation. Despite Sukarno's reservations about the suit-
ability of multiparty democracy, he seemed to put them aside to appease several
other powerful nationalist leaders and to appeal to the victorious Allied powers
and thus win their support for Indonesia's independence.

In late August 1945, Sukarno instituted the Komite Nasional Indonesia Pusat
(KNIP, the Central Indonesian National Committee), a presidential advisory
council with no legislative powers of its own. A majority of its 137 members, in
its initial composition, were supportive of the Republic. Islamic forces and more
radical youth members were relatively poorly represented.[27] In the deliberations
preceding the proclamation of independence, Sukarno had advocated a government system with corporatist features and a strong presidency. However, he also
was aware of the international discourse of democracy, and he did not hesitate to
capitalize on that issue. In October 1945, he wrote to the British commander of
the Allied forces in Indonesia, Philip Christison, inserting the word *democracy* or
its synonyms into almost every sentence.

> In the name of the Indonesian people I call on the British Government to clarify its
> position regarding the Indonesian struggle for self-determination. My people have
> unquestioned faith in the declared war aims of the Allies, especially in the promise
> to afford all peoples the right to form a government of their own choosing.... If the
> British want to see the spread of real democracy, Indonesia is ideal ground. The
> structure of Indonesian society, from the little villages up, is essentially democratic.
> We now hold power in our hands and we want to see the whole of Indonesia
> democratised.... The opportunity is now ours and we want to demonstrate to the
> world that we are able and willing to make democracy a living and vital force in
> Indonesia.[28]

The Indonesian leaders were well aware of the international atmosphere. This
became obvious in their political manifesto, published on November 1, 1945,
which explicitly referred to the principles of the San Francisco Charter (the foundational treaty of the United Nations), which did not mention democracy but

did stress the axiom of the self-determination of people. The Indonesian manifesto testified to the shift to parliamentary democracy that had taken place in
October.[29]

Among nationalist leaders, adherence to democratic values was uneven.
Sukarno himself had instituted a presidential system in which KNIP had advisory powers only—a model based on his experiences under the Japanese. Many
members preferred a much stronger role for KNIP and pushed for reform. Their
petition of October 7 was accepted by Sukarno, who gave KNIP legislative powers. These were primarily to be performed by a working committee—the Badan
Pekerdja (BP-KNIP)—which would be responsible to the plenary KNIP. The
number of members was expanded to 188. When President Sukarno made Sutan
Sjahrir first minister in November 1945, the latter pushed through the principle that he and his cabinet were responsible to KNIP (or rather its Working
Committee) only, and not to the president.[30] Indeed, Sjahrir was among the
most principled advocates of parliamentary democracy; just a few weeks before
his appointment as prime minister he had published a pamphlet in which he
pointed to the dangers of nationalism as the main platform for politics, as it
would inevitably lead to fascism.[31]

The first weeks of the new government brought many changes: the Working
Committee regulated the setup of national committees in the regions and cities,
replaced Sukarno's one-party system by a multiparty one, and pushed for a
speedy general election for a Council of People's Representatives (scheduled for
January 1946).[32] November and December saw the birth of most political parties
that would dominate Indonesian politics in the next parliamentary period. In late
December the government still held out the prospect of elections for the People's
Representative Council, but due to the military pressures from the Dutch, the
internal struggles in the Republic, and the frequent succession of cabinets, elections were postponed and did not materialize until September 1955.[33]

Was the institution of KNIP a halfhearted strategy to show democratic intentions to the world and the Indonesian people? Or was it meant to be a real first
step toward a fully developed parliamentary system? There is no doubt that
the proponents of reform in October 1945—most prominently Vice-President
Mohammad Hatta and Sutan Sjahrir—wished to establish a parliamentary democracy, and most political parties that came into being after November 1945 championed the swift institution of democratic procedures. Among them was of course
Sjahrir's Socialist Party but also the major Islamic party, Masjumi. A meeting of
Masjumi at Magelang on February 20, 1946, resulted in a plea for representative
government and direct elections for a parliament.[34]

But a true parliamentary democracy would not be accomplished as long as
the revolution lasted. After negotiations with the Dutch failed in 1947 and their
military pressure mounted, Republican leaders were reluctant to democratize

institutions at the central level. Given the emergency situation and the constant threat of annihilation by Dutch forces, the Republican government was little interested in establishing full democracy. Moreover, a paramount parliament would always carry the risk of opposing groups taking power.

Local Democracies

The state of democracy cannot be gauged solely from the events at the center. Democracy was not only a venture of state making and national programming. Far removed from the motivations and intentions of the national leaders, democratic notions appeared to be very much alive in many places, as was demonstrated in local initiatives and the response to instructions from the Republican headquarters. In the colonial past, it was customary in Java that the holders of village lands elected the village head (lurah). The regional colonial officer then formally appointed the official. The practice of electing village administrators was taken up during the revolution and extended to village councils, an institution that had not existed before the revolution. In many places local committees were spontaneously formed, often on the basis of local elections.[35] In particular, during the early months of the revolution, many of these local committees and administrators would operate in a fairly autonomous manner.

In some places, local nationalists formed committees very quickly after the news of independence became known. This happened in Surabaya as early as August 23, 1945, and the committee pledged loyalty to the new Republic on September 3.[36] In several other places, the entire population assembled to create a Komite Nasional—the local version of the KNIP—and elect its members.[37] In other places, too, local people elected their administrators.[38] The procedure deviated greatly from the practice under Japanese rule and should be seen as a serious attempt to establish new forms of legitimacy for local administration.[39] It was not a mere return to old practices: in colonial times village heads often came from one family, and there were relatively few changes. In the early revolution, large numbers of villages saw changes in their leadership, often caused by pressure from the inhabitants.[40] It seems that village head elections were democratized: choices were real, and many candidates came from new families. The Republican government tried to bring some order to the situation and appoint chairmen to the local committees, in order to institute a regular administration.

Municipal and regency councils, which had existed in the major cities since the late colonial period, had continued to operate during the Japanese occupation, though without elections. After August 1945, new councils were formed. Elections were held in Republican areas for all government levels. In Palembang successful elections were held for the residential council in December 1946 (chosen by representatives from various groups and classes) and for the municipal council in mid-August 1946.[41] In Yogyakarta, local democracy was greatly expanded under the guidance of the sultan; People's Representative Councils were formed in each *kelurahan* (village cluster or urban quarter), the members of which were elected by all inhabitants, men and women, eighteen years and older.[42]

Apparently, the notion of popular participation was widespread. It drew its inspiration from older Javanese customs of electing or acclaiming local village functionaries and from the Republican slogan of "people's sovereignty" (*kedaulatan rakyat*), which was one of Sukarno's Five Pillars of the Indonesian state (Pancasila) formulated in early June 1945. This slogan struck a chord in the minds of many citizens and, like its brother "social justice" (*keadilan sosial*), would continue to echo in the media and social organizations throughout the 1940s and 1950s.

ACCOMPLISHING DEMOCRACY

There was not a single version or vision of democracy on the threshold of independence. Several models circulated, and none was fully crystallized, not on the Republican side, nor in one of the other polities that sprang up under Dutch control. In the Indonesian Republic the KNIP performed a predominantly advisory role, but it did provide a site for debate and consensus making. Truly democratic it was not; it operated without elections, and due to the war it could not meet for long periods. In the meantime, local participatory politics continued to exist in various forms. On the Dutch side of the archipelago several states were building a parliamentary structure and instituting elections for local officials, on the level of both the *negara* (states) and the cities and residencies. The most accomplished of them was the NIT. Even there, no general elections were held; only at municipal levels were councils elected by ballot.

The political landscape was therefore extremely varied. Not only did several systems of government exist side by side, but the situation also varied within the Republican and Dutch territories. To complicate matters further, in areas that were reconquered by the Dutch during their second attack in December 1948, mixed forms of government were introduced. These different forms had to be brought into line when the United States of Indonesia was formed in the final negotiations with the Netherlands in late 1949. The federal constitution lasted only eight months, until August 1950, when the federal state was dissolved and a unitary Indonesian state was formed. The federal constitution provided for a bicameral system, not unlike the Dutch one, but with special arrangements for the representation of the sixteen states and a few minorities. The 1950 unitary constitution was an amended form of the federal one.

Postcolonial democracy was fairly well developed in theory and institutionally, and elections were usually successful where and when they were held. By and large, democratic institutions and practices were strengthened and expanded. In municipalities, Dewan Perwakilan Rakyat Daerah (Regional People's Representative

Councils) were installed, as successors of the provisional councils from the days of the revolution. At several moments in the 1950s, local elections were held.[43] Local political life was thriving, as political parties and elections were considered effective means through which to pursue one's goals and stake out a position for oneself or a community.[44]

However, soon after the general elections of 1955, which in fact were a resounding success for parliamentary democracy, President Sukarno would discard the system, most famously in his "Let us bury the parties" speeches of October 1956.[45] At that moment, Sukarno once again balanced domestic changes with international circumstances and reasserted his grip on both Indonesian domestic politics and world affairs, detaching Indonesia from the Western international system at the famed Bandung Conference of African and Asian leaders in 1955, in a bid to shape a global order of newly independent states, creating thereby the nonaligned movement as a middle path amid the bipolar divisions of the Cold War. Just as neocolonialism was condemned at Bandung, so Sukarno blamed democracy for the chaos in Indonesian society, and Western politics of parliamentary contestation were to be discarded as unfit for Indonesian society.

As the fifteenth session the UN General Assembly opens, leaders of the nonaligned bloc meet, including President Kwame Nkrumah of Ghana (*left*), Prime Minister Jawaharlal Nehru of India (*center*), and President Sukarno of Indonesia (*right*), New York, October 4, 1960. (United Nations)

Sukarno's political notions were notoriously inarticulate, but despite his strong prodemocratic signals to the international powers in the early days of the revolution, he was fairly consistent in his conviction that Indonesia would be better off without party democracy. Under the pressure of serious regional uprisings in Sulawesi and Sumatra, both armed by Washington in retaliation for Jakarta's move toward international neutralism, the president proclaimed martial law in March 1957. In the next two years he would dismantle the parliamentary system and institute Guided Democracy, which bore a strong resemblance to Sukarno's corporatist ideas about the politics of deliberation and avoidance of contention.

Decolonization and Democracy

The history of participatory politics in Indonesia points to a far more hybrid genealogy than a Western or Dutch legacy or an internationally propagated ideology that materialized at independence. During colonial times, Indonesia had developed several forms of participatory or representational politics. Although formal procedures were inconsistent and had not been fully crystallized, perceptions of political participation seem to have been widespread. "Democratic" reflexes occurred at many levels. Although in many ways local leaders and elites took the initiative, there are also many examples of democratic tendencies "from below." Just as many young men were eager to take up arms against the Dutch (and others), large numbers of Indonesians, too, were taken in by ideas of participation and the promise of people's sovereignty—even if the precise form they would take could not have been very clear to most.

From the official angle, popular participation in politics was an important tenet on both Dutch and Indonesian sides during decolonization, and it became a central instrument of legitimation. In both areas, the protoparliaments were necessary places for debate and consensus seeking in a politically insecure environment. Despite the antagonism between the departing colonial power and nationalist leaders, they seemed to be in agreement on the main principles of government, and political alternatives (such as an Islamist or communist state) were shunned by both.

We can only conclude that notions of democracy, participatory politics, and people's sovereignty were strong at empire's end. In many places in Java, sincere interest in electing officials, participating in political decision making, and representative government was visible. Of course, this is only part of the story. Attitudes toward democracy were ambiguous on both sides of the colonial divide, and policies of democratization were often halfhearted and distrustful. Under the circumstances of national struggle against the imperial power and the necessity to formulate national identities and a shared purpose, the idea of political opposition was not welcomed, and the departing colonial power showed its true face by postponing real elections until after its departure.

Indonesia's example makes clear how various traditions and contingencies influence initiatives toward participatory politics and the establishment of democratic institutions. It urges us to question several accepted ideas. First is the assumption that colonial rule primarily left a legacy of authoritarianism. A close look at Indonesia during the long period of decolonization offers a different picture and points to other traditions too. Colonial experiments with representative bodies at the local and colonial levels, as well as the exclusion of the majority from these institutions, incited political awareness among Indonesians. Colonial governance had created expectations among at least part of the urban population. Even if citizenship was withheld from them, colonial rule had created a political public that developed and fostered ideals of participation.

A second view holds that the Japanese period dealt a severe blow to whatever democratic forces existed in Indonesia.[46] In actual fact, although the Republican leadership was, especially during the first weeks and months after the proclamation, reluctant to organize political fragmentation through democratic institutions, the drive for participatory politics at the local level was intense.

Third, the idea is often voiced that decolonization was the decisive influence in building democratic institutions in Indonesia. Independence was unimaginable without popular representation, although its form and status were debated. But it can be argued that forms of democratization would have taken place even without the acute impulse of a national uprising. Returning to the point made in the beginning, the turn to democracy that is visible at all levels in Indonesian society during the revolution can best be seen as one link in a much longer development of state expansion, which had stimulated collective action and expectations of participatory politics, above all in Java.

Finally, it is said that democracy should be considered primarily as a Western form forced on Indonesian society. It was certainly not just a Western medium forced on the Indonesian state. Nor was it, as Dutch Lieutenant Governor-General H. J. van Mook later suggested, the case that "modern, representative democracy was often grafted on the ancient, communal democracy of the village meeting."[47] It took its dynamics from a quickly changing society, where communications were revolutionized, horizons widened dramatically within one or two generations, and public life became increasingly organized, not necessarily in a nationalist movement or political party but also in one of the innumerable professional or cultural associations. These were parapolitical organizations that prepared the way for fuller democracy.

Both on the side of the governments and on that of the governed, wishes for political participation were a logical step in the crystallization of a "big" interventionist state. In other words, it was not primarily the result of European-driven modernization but of the widening scope and ambitions of the state. Not coincidentally, this trend had immediate effects on politics at the local level, where people could draw on other traditions of political participation. At the national level, on the other hand, attitudes tended to be much more ambiguous. For both the colonial state and its successor, representation offered opportunities for legitimation, but it also presented a threat to colonial or national unity and claims to power, and, after independence, to the interests of the new rulers. This ambiguity was one of the causes for the postcolonial crises of democracy. Significantly, the failures in the system were blamed on the heterogeneity of parliamentary democracy, in effect ignoring the local fundamentals of democracy. In this sense, democracy more often than not had to take the blame when the performance of the state failed.

Sukarno's dilemmas were those of most of the world, but his visions were bold and original. His search for a political format that would fit the cultural specificities of Indonesia and the political needs of the immediate postcolonial situation parallels that of Senghor. Like him, Sukarno looked for alternatives to a world that followed Western dictates and models. They dared look beyond the simple dichotomies of great power politics and tried to stimulate solidarities beyond national boundaries. In so doing, they offered the world a cosmopolitan vision of solidarity and justice that had a lasting influence on global politics. At home, they both envisioned a form of democracy in line with the assumed cultural models available—Sukarno's *musyawarah* was not far removed from Senghor's "feeling of the nation." However, in practical politics they failed to develop viable alternative forms of democracy. They both experimented with multiparty systems but soon resorted to muted forms in the face of internal opposition.

PART 7

IMPERIAL DECLINE AND NATIONAL IDENTITIES

Declaration of independence and folding of the Portuguese flag in Mozambique, June 1975. (Alfredo Cunha)

Natives Who Were "Citizens" and Natives Who Were *Indígenas* in the Portuguese Empire, 1900–1926

CRISTINA NOGUEIRA DA SILVA

THE NATURE OF NATIVE political participation within the colonies is a central issue relevant to imperial eclipse and transition. It is often assumed that elites suddenly deprived of acquired historic rights and privileges will automatically question the legitimacy of the metropole. It is also sometimes assumed that metropolitan republicanism leads inexorably to claims for colonial independence. In the case of the Portuguese empire, a key period for examining both issues was the First Republic, which began in 1910 and lasted until the beginning of the military dictatorship in 1926. This chapter will examine twentieth-century legal doctrines concerning citizenship and political participation and discuss the limits of republican culture. Even though many elites harshly criticized the inequities of the republican system, this did not lead to the birth of independence movements like those that emerged in the Spanish and Portuguese empires a century earlier. Nor did it lead to discussions of "national self-determination," which came into vogue following World War I and the Versailles Peace Conference of 1919. Like its French counterpart, Portuguese republicanism proved highly prejudicial to native colonial elites but did not give rise to political or doctrinal attitudes furthering the eclipse of Portuguese empire.

In order to understand the colonial policies of the First Republic, it is best to start with the simple but important premise that the political culture of early-twentieth-century Portuguese republicanism was a rather familiar creature in line with European norms.[1] From its modern conception, republicanism defined political participation as its central value; republican society essentially consisted of citizens participating in government and being subject to laws they had been involved in drafting.[2] A secondary component entailed a society of individuals exercising civil rights. What complicated matters was that the Portuguese Republic was a colonial regime. Who, then, among the native populations within the empire, would or would not exercise the rights of citizenship?

Portugal was not the first republic forced to confront this question. In many respects, the Portuguese solution, the *indigenato* system, resembled that which existed in the French colonies in the last quarter of the nineteenth century.[3] This system was based on a legal division of the native population into civilized and uncivilized individuals. The "uncivilized" were, by definition, those who could not be included in the "ordered space" of civil society and hence were denied key political and judicial rights. The "already civilized," in contrast, were accepted as citizens; in theory, they served as living proof that Portugal took its civilizing mission seriously.[4] Some Portuguese politicians contended that the goal of the republican system was to enlarge the number of individuals in this latter group. The system, however, did not meet such goals. The *indigenato* included mechanisms that were supposed, in theory, to enable individuals to achieve access to full citizenship, yet in practice such mechanisms often undermined the ability of individuals to acquire such citizenship. These mechanisms also threatened the forms of social and political "identification" of some native groups that comprised the colonial elites in Portuguese Africa, thereby provoking conflicts and fierce debates with metropolitan authorities.[5]

SUBJECTION, AUTONOMY, OR ASSIMILATION?

In the early twentieth century, international law—in addition to mainstream European colonial doctrines—rejected the notion that economic exploitation and political coercion were legitimate exercises of imperial power. As was the case in other countries, the consensus in Portugal was that government should be morally guided by the "science of colonial administration," which provided a range of models for tutelage and governance adapted to diverse colonial scenarios. One such model was the "subjection" regime, characterized by "unity in authority, concentration of all colonial business in a single ministry and extensive powers granted to the colonial governors."[6] Under this system, the metropole imposed all legislation, from the top down, without previously consulting colonists or defining a "civilizing purpose." By the early twentieth century, European and Portuguese literature had discarded the validity of this type of regime, given that modern colonial rule needed to include a tutelage obligation toward native populations.

Instead of *subjugation*, Portuguese colonial literature recognized the viability of two other systems, known respectively as *autonomy* and *assimilation*. The former was based on the policies of the British government in the so-called settlement colonies, where local representative bodies held ample legislative powers and metropolitan governors possessed oversight and emergency authority but intervened minimally in direct government. As these colonies had no parliamentary representation in the metropole, colonial representatives produced the lion's share of local legislation. To be sure, considerable autonomy could cause significant problems for the metropole, especially when colonial parliaments threatened its economic and geopolitical interests. Another frequent problem was that colonists often ran roughshod over native concerns and even undertook, or turned a blind eye toward, extermination campaigns. The disregard, not to mention the murder, of natives clashed with international norms obligating colonizers to guarantee the "preservation of native tribes and to work towards the continued improvement of the conditions of their moral and material well-being."[7]

The second alternative to *subjugation* was known as *assimilation*. Under this regime, colonists elected deputies who were given a seat in a metropolitan parliament, which drafted domestic and colonial legislation. Accordingly, metropolitan laws and institutions, unless specified otherwise, were applicable to the colonies. All inhabitants, including colonial natives, would enjoy equal rights and duties. While the purpose of *autonomy* was to create a separate society in the colonies, the purpose of *assimilation* was to gradually merge the colonies into the "motherland."

These three systems were, of course, ideal types rather than inflexible formulas. Portuguese republican politicians and academics tinkered with various combinations and modifications. *Subjection*, in its purest form, was deemed to be unsuitable. It was not only incompatible with the international obligation to improve native societies but it was also perceived to run contrary to Portuguese "colonial traditions." All the same, neither *autonomy* nor *assimilation* was thought to be workable. With respect to the former, demographic reasons weighed heavily. While the British colonies were populated with significant numbers of men and women of European origin, Portugal's "plantation" colonies were comprised chiefly of natives. José Ferreira Marnoco e Sousa, the first professor of colonial administration in the Law Faculty at the venerable University of Coimbra, believed that such a system would cause serious conflict, arguing that "without the moderating power of the metropole, European and the indigenous elements within our colonies would wage war until one or the other was eliminated, exterminated or forced into full submission."[8] Consequently, he expressed the widespread belief that the majority of the colonial population had not yet reached the stage in which they could exercise political rights, an opinion that echoed the teachings of John Stuart Mill. What is more, he opined that autonomous colonial government would surely lead to "racial conflict."[9] As such, he argued against granting political rights to natives and allowing colonists direct political participation. Such logic was also applied to white colonists who clamored for increased rights. It was argued that this would inevitably lead to extending such rights to natives, causing upheaval and racial conflict. On the basis of this belief, some early-twentieth-century authors even advocated abolishing the election of representatives of the overseas territories to the Portuguese parliament, which had taken place since the establishment of the country's liberal regime in 1822. This elimination would avoid the inevitable "electoral preponderance of native peoples," to borrow the words of Lopo Vaz de Sampayo e Mello, a professor at the Colonial School, founded in 1906.[10]

Marnoco e Sousa was one of the few who defended an *assimilation* regime. Most who dissertated on such issues came out strongly against this solution. Few such individuals espoused such radical opinions as Sampayo e Mello. Nevertheless, they argued that the assimilationist policies adopted by the constitutional monarchy (1820–1910) were the root cause of the troubled state of the colonial administration, and hence needed to be remedied. They espoused the nearly unanimous belief that the great weakness of an *assimilation* regime was that it granted citizenship to native populations. Even the proassimilationist Marnoco e Sousa shared this view. For him, *assimilation* did not have to include equal rights for European and native populations. The essence of *assimilation*, he argued, was that colonies send deputies to a metropolitan parliament. In this way, neither the colonial populations (as in the case of a *subjection* regime) nor those of the metropole (as in the case of an *autonomous* regime) saw their rights or interests sacrificed. To him, the ultimate goal of *assimilation* was to end the distinction between the metropole and the colonies so that both would form a single nation in the future with a "parliament composed of men speaking the same language, despite their different origins, coming from all over the world . . . to discuss the general interests of a shared motherland."[11]

Another advantage of the *assimilation* regime, Marnoco e Sousa reasoned, was that the "moderating power of the metropole" protected native populations from the predatory actions of the colonists. All the same, he stressed that such protection did not mean more political rights would be granted to native populations. On the contrary, he agreed that the possibility of the overseas deputies being elected by "men of color, and by the native people" would result in "a situation where a white minority would be oppressed by a majority of uneducated, coarse men."[12] In this respect, he was a man of his time. Like most academics, politicians, and colonial administrators, he believed it was urgent to put an end to the outdated monarchical "traditions" of granting Portuguese citizenship to native people in the colonies.

To be clear, this assertion—that the monarchy had systematically granted Portuguese citizenship to native colonists—was not accurate. What was true was that some native elites in Portuguese Africa, particularly in key coastal areas, possessed significant local power and autonomy. All the same, it must be underscored that neither the various constitutions of the constitutional monarchy nor any of the accompanying legislation provided for an explicit and unconditional extension of citizenship. What is more, the widespread powers granted to such elites originated from the time when Portugal's presence in Africa had been constructed on the base of an understanding with local powers.[13] In a few such coastal areas, native individuals together with a few *reinóis* (those coming from Portugal) did occupy various intermediate and lower positions within the colonial administration. Native elites in Portuguese Africa had significant municipal powers and even possessed some capacity to influence the election of parliamentary deputies.[14] Such elites took part in colonial trade as intermediaries between colonial and African societies. Many of the richer families, by means of their involvement in plantation agriculture, had participated in the slave trade, a thriving business for many centuries. Such elites were generally Christian converts, although many metropolitan figures were skeptical about their capacity to become "genuine" Catholics.[15] They spoke Portuguese but often communicated among themselves in the local African languages. They were, in short, the legacy of a long process of cultural and biological miscegenation.[16]

In the late nineteenth century, the ordinarily peaceful coexistence between these elites and the Portuguese began to change. The understandings, or implicit pacts, inherited from the old colonial regime could not withstand the pressures of the industrial era. Rising competition among European nations for African territories led the Portuguese to dedicate serious resources to developing a more effective and profitable way to exploit their territories. Though not always successful, their efforts did transform colonial rule. Portuguese reforms were threefold. First, the Portuguese sought to extend direct governance over a much larger sector of the native population. Not everyone was in agreement, as many administrators were hesitant to take on such a daunting task. However, politicians felt that such measures were necessary to prove to other countries that Portugal was capable of being a proper and hence virile "colonial nation." Second, a growing plantation economy demanded the building of infrastructure and the provisioning of a labor force. To this end, the Portuguese sought to submit native populations to a special (forced) labor regime, a policy revealing of the economic interests behind the *indigenato* system.[17] Third, the number of white settlers was growing, albeit slowly. As such, native colonial elites were forced to compete on increasingly unfavorable terms with new arrivals from Europe, causing a decline in their influence and status.[18] All this suggests that these elites were one of the groups targeted by the "*antiassimilation*" discourse described above. They were also one of the groups negatively affected by the *indigenato* system. All the same, the legal categories within the system gave such elites the formal possibility to become "citizens of the Republic." It is to this system that we shall now turn.

REFORM OF COLONIAL ADMINISTRATION (1910–1926)

After rejecting *assimilation* and admitting the impossibility of "true autonomy," republican politicians reached an agreement by fixing on and implementing a hybrid solution. The Organic Law of Overseas Civil Administration (1914) created "government councils," intended to represent the "vital forces" in each colony, granting them "wide autonomy." In reality, however, such councils were consultative bodies, since the core legislative power resided with the metropolitan government and the parliament. Politicians also reinforced the supremacy of the colonial governor by ensuring that such bodies had minimal ability to limit his actions. Local and municipal institutions would operate with some degree of representation, but their basic theoretical purpose was to educate people in "municipal life" rather than acting as an instrument of empowerment. As liberal institutions required educated citizens, it was deemed necessary to educate first with the goal to provide for more advanced forms of association in the future.

The Organic Law also established the *indigenato* system, which in turn was based on principles that colonial administrators had already identified as the rules of a good "indigenous policy." Accordingly, legislators deemed that native peoples, due to their "civilizational condition," could not be allowed to exercise political rights within European institutions; rather, they should be subject to special legislation. Liberal principles of governance—such as the separation of powers—were unsuitable, given that natives did not understand the difference between justice and administration. The Organic Law further stipulated that the private lives of natives, now called *indígenas*, were to be regulated by customary laws, provided these did not clash with "basic rights of life and human liberty."[19] The role of colonial authorities was to codify these laws, intervening in a paternalistic way by modifying custom in consonance with liberal principles.[20] Another immediate goal was to draft special versions of criminal law, land law, and labor law for *indígenas*.

One of the central purposes of the *indigenato* system was to subject most natives to an exceptional regime of civil, criminal, and political law that served the ideological and economic aims of colonization. However, this system also had a less explicit, though by no means subsidiary, aim. This was to limit the possibility of political participation of native peoples, especially those who were considered "civilized" or what was called "assimilated" in official jargon.

Classifying populations was the fulcrum of an "indigenous policy," which theoretically aimed to improve the material and spiritual welfare of the people. For this end, it was necessary to delineate who, among the natives, was incapable of exercising political rights (and hence was to be subject to special laws) and who could be considered for citizenship. The draft version of the Organic Law of 1914 defined an *indígena* as an individual "of color" who failed to meet a series of criteria. According to provision 15, only those *indígenas* who met all such requirements would be considered "assimilated" and hence deemed citizens of the Republic. To comply, a person needed to speak Portuguese, one of its dialects, or another educated language; to practice European law rather than native "customary law"; and to be either engaged in an occupation, trade, or industry or in possession of enough property to support himself. In concrete terms, the classification of subjects and citizens divided natives into two groups: those who were subordinated to special rules but were unable to participate in formulating them and those subject to the rules of the Republic and able to vote for parliamentary representatives who formulated them. With time, legislation, as well as administrative parlance, came to refer to these rights-deprived subjects as *indígenas*. Citizens, in turn, were known as "assimilated" (*assimilados*) or sometimes "nonindigenous" individuals.

In 1917, the Portuguese colonies of Angola, Mozambique, and Guinea passed laws enshrining the *indígena* system and hence depriving the great majority of natives of civil and political rights. This legislation did not represent a major change since the monarchy had employed a property-based electoral system and had also used similar criteria with respect to literacy and education. However, these laws and regulations also introduced a number of new filters for natives who wished to exercise political rights, such as voting or standing for political office. It was stipulated that government councils should include public servants in addition to representatives of the local population, elected by restricted suffrage. The reason for this provision was that there were few citizens among "the mass of a backward population."[21] In order for a municipal institution to be recognized by the Portuguese, it was not mandatory for it to contain a minimum number of Europeans. Under the monarchy, the overseas minister, Aires de Ornelas, had promulgated such a decree for Mozambique in May 1907.[22] Nevertheless, a similar situation later re-emerged under the Republic. Voters had to be resident individuals who could read and write in any language; were engaged in an occupation, trade, or industry; and possessed sufficient property to support themselves. Candidates had to possess academic qualifications to be decided by each colony. This latter criterion was critical, as it gave rise to legislative and administrative acts requiring qualifications that could only be obtained at educational institutions located in the metropole.[23]

The "civilizational criteria" was the name given to another filter used to separate those who could exercise political rights from those who remained under a tutelary regime. In 1917, the colony of Mozambique published a provincial ordinance regulating what soon was to be called the "assimilation process." Accordingly, a person of the "black race" seeking citizenship had to produce documents issued by municipal or local authorities that proved he had abandoned the "habits and customs characteristic of their race." Such persons were also obliged to declare that they practiced monogamy. Moreover, it was preferable that such declarations were accompanied by birth, baptism, or marriage certificates, if they had them. After the publication of this ordinance, all those wishing to obtain an *alvará de assimilado* (assimilation certificate) had to attach, in addition to the certificates already mentioned, a letter written by the applicant attesting to monogamy and a certificate from the district administrator stating that the applicant had abandoned indigenous "habits and customs," could speak and write Portuguese, and had sufficient means to support himself.[24] It must be stressed that an implicit condition for obtaining rights was that local administrators were willing (or even available) to issue these documents.[25] Another implied condition was that applicants had to have a certain degree of proximity to, or familiarity with, the colonial administration. These conditions were not, of course, made explicit. However, in practice it was almost as difficult to gain necessary access to administrative officials as it was to meet the formal criteria of the law.

Angola and Guinea followed Mozambique, issuing similar regulations which remained in effect until 1961.[26] It has yet to be determined how many individuals underwent and succeeded in becoming assimilated, although experts agree that the number was proportionally quite low.[27] Contemporary research has focused on the socioeconomic origins of those who took advantage of the procedure, the reasons behind the low numbers, the ambiguous legal meaning of being classified as an *assimilado*, and the effects of such regulations on those who did not qualify for citizenship. With respect to origins, recent research covering the republican period suggests that most such people came from the middle strata of the culturally "assimilated" population (cobblers, low-level public officials, artisans, teachers, mission school students, etc.).[28]

The reasons for the low numbers are also well known. As was the case in the French colonies, where similar mechanisms for access to citizenship were in place, many encountered insurmountable hurdles in producing the necessary documentation.[29] Furthermore, some persons who could have qualified were not interested in obtaining the *alvará*. All in all, the Mozambican ordinance from 1917 turned the *assimilados* into a tiny minority and ensured that natives wishing to be "equated to Europeans" would remain a miniscule proportion of the population. Because of the documentary requirements, the administration essentially controlled the numerical growth of *assimilados*, ensuring that the number would not rise above desired levels.[30] Unsurprisingly, even these individuals had trouble translating acquired rights into opportunities. Such "citizens" were increasingly subject to various—and usually far from subtle—forms of discrimination that reduced their chances of entering the administration or investing in business ventures.[31] Finally, with respect to the great mass of the population, the law had a great effect. Native *indígenas* were left bereft of persons who could represent their interests. Since few persons could fulfil the requirements for full political participation, this reduced the number of persons who could even nominally be considered natives in colonial institutions.

In the immediate aftermath of the approval of the Organic Law and its ordinances, critics tended to focus on its immediate effects rather than the long-term consequences. Before the Organic Law, colonial elites of native origin had considered themselves Portuguese citizens, in spite of the ambiguities that had always surrounded this form of identification. After the law, however, they were instantly converted into subjects (*indígenas*) until they put together the requisite paperwork to obtain the *alvará de assimilado*. This change meant that, in order to be Portuguese citizens, most of these individuals were now obliged to undergo a process similar to a naturalization process applied to foreigners. These elites therefore suffered what they felt was a process of double declassification. In the first place, until they applied for citizenship, they were considered *indígenas*, or subjects, a term loaded with negative political and "civilizational" connotations. Given that they were temporarily grouped together with the "native masses," they were, at least in theory, subject to labor and criminal regulations that were specifically designed for persons who could not understand modern laws. Second, until they applied for citizenship, they were left in legal limbo. It was not clear whether they were "Portuguese" or not, although it was clear that they could not be considered foreigners.

To protest this situation, some members of the higher strata of native Mozambican elites engaged in a risky method of resistance by refusing to undergo the formal assimilation process in 1917. They formed associations, aired their grievances in the press, tried to elect representatives to local political bodies, and exerted pressure on metropolitan politicians. At one point, they even threatened to bring their grievances directly to the U.S. president, Woodrow Wilson.[32] As a general rule, their attempts to change the law and its procedures failed in the long-term. What is worth emphasizing, however, is that, regardless of their success or failure, such elites, especially in Mozambique, never questioned the sovereignty of Portugal. In Angola, some elites were more radical. Yet, all in all, most accepted the colonial situation that had led to their subalternization, believing that they would ultimately benefit from the system once they could work out the problems. Mozambican journalists and intellectuals made endless references to Portuguese constitutional texts, both monarchist and republican, which they interpreted as having offered citizenship to all those born in Portugal "and its dominions," including native peoples. For such persons, citizenship provisions—such as Article 7 of the 1826 Constitutional Charter—represented the beneficent traditions of Portuguese colonial administration that the *indigenato* system threatened to destroy. Interestingly, the defenders of the *indigenato* system also relied on this constitutional tradition, which was supported by an extensive body of interpretation from jurists and politicians developed throughout the nineteenth century. However, these defenders of the *indigenato* system interpreted this tradition negatively, arguing that it was absurd "that natives born in colonial territory have the same rights as Portuguese citizens."[33] What is worth highlighting, though, is that both sides argued from and recognized the legitimacy of the same constitutional texts consecrating colonial rule.

This debate, therefore, concerned the nature rather than the legitimacy of the empire. It serves to reinforce the maxim, articulated by Fred Cooper and Anne

Laura Stoler, that "visions of Empire were created and clarified out of metropolitan discourses as well as by those fashioned in the colonies themselves."[34] What is more, the press campaigns of native elites not only invoked the good monarchical traditions of the empire, but they also invoked republican values, which they argued clashed with the *indigenato* system. Much like metropolitan academics and politicians, they never pushed beyond this narrow legal debate to question the compatibility of republican culture with colonialism. Mozambican elites did not seek to put an end to the Portuguese presence but to restore what they perceived to be an inclusive colonial tradition. As happened in other parts of the Portuguese empire, their identity remained linked to a distant center, a faraway metropole on the Iberian Peninsula, a *mentalité* that prevented this generation from acting against the imperial political order.

CONCLUSION

To conclude, it is also worth noting that the Wilsonian doctrine of national "self-determination," stemming from the Versailles Peace Conference of 1919, did not have an impact on or even serve to discredit such imperialist-constitutionalist debates taking place in Portuguese Africa. Practically all the leading figures from the peace conference, including President Wilson himself, believed that "Africa would need outside control"—a principle that led to a series of colonial mandates, which were practically indistinguishable from direct annexations.[35] Portugal was, of course, not alone. The French, British, and Americans also believed that the doctrine only applied to "civilized nations" capable of governing themselves in the near future and not to those territories under imperial tutelage regimes, which were not yet deemed mature enough for self governance. National self-determination did have some effect on the "informal" structure of British and French rule in the Middle East, but these areas were viewed differently, since they were inherited from the Ottoman Empire. In an age when anthropological ideas concerning racial superiority and inferiority were at their height, sub-Saharan Africa was a different matter.

The opinions of the Africans themselves were, of course, more complex. In February 1919, the First Pan-African Congress convened for three days in Paris at a hotel on the Boulevard de Capucins. Led by Blaise Diagne, an African French deputy from Senegal, and the African American civil rights activist W. E. B. Du Bois, the congress counted sixteen delegates from the United States and twelve more from nine African territories. With Diagne serving as president and Du Bois as secretary, the congress adopted resolutions requesting gradual self-government for Africans, safeguards for their land, and education for all. Its proceedings attracted press coverage on both sides of the Atlantic and led to a succession of conferences that inspired a later generation of African nationalists. The immediate impact of the congress, though, was minimal. None of the Versailles Peace

Conference delegates attended, and no one thought to bring up these resolutions at the Paris Peace Conference itself.[36]

Moreover, it must be stressed that African opinion did not rally behind Wilson's call for self-determination either. At the conference, most native elites within European empires, such as Blaise Diagne and native Mozambicans, were more interested in the extension of metropolitan citizenship rights to Africans than in breaking up colonial empires. In sum, republican culture in Portugal and all of Europe—unlike that of the previous century—did not lead to imperial collapse but instead to the birth of citizenship debates within the empire itself.

From Subjecthood to Citizenship in South Asia

Migration, Nationality, and the
Post-imperial Global Order

JOYA CHATTERJI

THE FALL OF GREAT EMPIRES has often prompted migration. But by all accounts, in the past these were relatively small flows, made up chiefly of soldiers, skilled artisans, and comprador elites who had failed to forge fresh strategic alliances with new rulers at home, and who migrated abroad in search of political patrons.[1] The fall of the great European empires, in contrast, and the rise of nation-states in the twentieth century were accompanied by mass migrations on a wholly unprecedented scale.

Why was this the case, and what have been the implications of these massive flows for the new global order? This essay will follow Aristide Zolberg in arguing that nation formation is a "refugee-generating process."[2] It will also explore the global consequences of the mass migrations that complicated Britain's retreat from its erstwhile imperial possessions. India's independence and partition in 1947, the independence of Ceylon and Burma in 1948, the wave of nation formation in anglophone Africa in the 1950s and 1960s, and the breakaway of Bangladesh from Pakistan in 1971 all provoked both vast migrations and drives by states to fortify their frontiers. The new nation-states of the later twentieth century—not least those of the Indian subcontinent—were more concerned than their imperial predecessor had been with controlling flows across borders. They also had far more pressing reasons to define who was, and who was not, a citizen.

This essay will highlight the central role that India and Pakistan, and their South Asian neighbors, played in this process. In their drive to manage and control mass migration, the new states of South Asia developed concepts of citizenship that rolled back the hitherto dominant idea of British imperial subjecthood. In its stead they erected an ethnically defined model of nationality founded on the right to enter, the right to remain, and the right to return. In due course, this model spread throughout the erstwhile British empire, eventually being adopted in 1971 by the former metropole itself.

First, however, a few words are in order about "British subjecthood" and what it had come to mean by the mid–twentieth century. As Caitlin Anderson has argued, British subjecthood was founded on the doctrine of allegiance, a complicated and "quasi-mythical" idea whose antecedents date back to the medieval period. According to that doctrine, subjecthood derived from an individual's loyalty to the Crown, and because that relationship was founded in natural law ("written with the finger of God in the heart of man"), it was indelible and unalterable by either sovereign or subject.[3] Since 1608, when Sir Edward Coke, in *Calvin's Case*, insisted that all the king's subjects were equal, subjecthood had also implied the equal legal status of all those born within the king's dominions.[4] This was the celebrated principle of jus soli, or subjecthood by virtue of birth in the realm.[5]

By the end of the nineteenth century, this principle of legal equality had been eroded in practice, and "natural born" Britons had come to enjoy greater rights and protections than those born in the empire.[6] All British subjects did not enjoy equal and unfettered rights to move wherever they wanted within an empire on which the sun never set. Some Indian migrants enjoyed greater freedom of mobility than others. The "passenger" classes, who paid their own fares and were, in the main, traders, were, in theory at least, free to travel when they pleased. Indentured "coolies" were legally obliged to serve out their contracts abroad, and "assisted" migrants recruited by agents known as *kanganis* were shackled even more firmly by the bonds of debt.[7] By the late nineteenth century, over a million Indians working on labor-hungry tropical plantations all over the empire found themselves tied down in a variety of ways.[8] During World War I, moreover, passports were introduced in India, and thereafter all private travelers leaving India by sea had to carry this document. By this time, several British dominions had devised racially inflected stratagems for barring unwanted persons from South Asia: notably Australia's Immigration Restriction Act of 1901, which used a dictation test to exclude the unwanted; Canada's exclusionary head tax aimed at nonwhites; and South Africa's Immigrants Regulation Act of 1913, which prohibited persons whose "standards and habits of life" rendered them "unsuited to the requirements of the Union."[9] By the 1930s, even the imperial territories of the Indian Ocean rim had begun to restrict the immigration of Indians: Malaya and the Straits Settlements now imposed controls. After its separation from India in 1937, Burma, too, began negotiations for a treaty to limit Indian immigration, and in 1939 Ceylon banned it altogether.[10]

Nor was entry into India itself unregulated. Wars in the twentieth century generated a regime of controls designed to keep out of India persons seen as a threat to imperial security. With the Great War, even "troublemakers" of Indian origin were denied ingress into India, and the Passport Act of 1920 made travel documents compulsory for all persons wishing to travel there.[11] In 1939, "the needs of the war emergency" justified the enactment of a Foreigners Ordinance and an Enemy Foreigners Order, giving the imperial state powers to detain and expel foreigners.[12]

The British imperial past was thus not some halcyon age of unrestricted mobility for all His Majesty's subjects; nor was that subjecthood equal in practice. Yet there is no doubt that British decolonization and the emergence of new nations ushered in a new migration regime whose interlocking and overlapping laws, policies, and practices are a crucial dimension of the new global order.

PARTITION AND INDEPENDENCE IN INDIA AND PAKISTAN

The most dramatic and far-reaching changes were first witnessed in India and Pakistan. In 1947, the complex high politics of decolonization culminated in a decision to divide Britain's Indian empire between two independent successor states, India and Pakistan. The contentious boundary between them was drawn on the basis of religion: contiguous Muslim-majority districts in the northwest and east were carved out to produce the new state of Pakistan. In the negotiations for the transfer of power, Britain was able to persuade India and Pakistan to stay within the Commonwealth. The architects of the partition agreements assumed that citizens of India and Pakistan would remain British subjects, and as such continue to have "free" access to the other dominions and all parts of the empire.[13] Astonishing as it may seem in retrospect, in August 1947 the leaders of India and Pakistan still believed that, partition notwithstanding, the peoples of the subcontinent would stay where they were. The consensus was that open borders between the two states would facilitate the orderly transfer of power to two separate dominions, with little or no social and economic disruption.

This proved to be a vain hope. The fires of civil violence that broke out on August 15, 1947, spread rapidly across the western plains of the subcontinent. Massive migrations began: millions of ordinary Hindus, Sikhs, and Muslims stranded on the wrong side of the border began to flee their homes in terror. As a humanitarian catastrophe of unprecedented proportions unfolded, India and Pakistan acted in concert to set up a Military Evacuation Organisation (MEO) to protect "stranded refugees" and escort them across the new border. By the end of 1947, it had evacuated five million refugees across the borders between India and Pakistan.[14] By 1951, some twenty million refugees had crossed the borders in both directions.

The MEO was a response to an emergency that neither state was equipped to handle on its own, but it proved to be the first step down a slippery slope, toward a new policy with far-reaching ramifications. If partition's refugees in their millions were to be allowed to move across borders between India and Pakistan (and

Lord Louis Mountbatten, the British viceroy of India, handing over power to Quaid-i-Azam Mohammad Ali Jinnah, the first governor-general of Pakistan, August 14, 1947. (Library of Congress Prints and Photographs Division)

indeed to be assisted by the MEO in so doing), this raised the question of what was to happen to the property they left behind. Who was to protect it and by what means? Both India and Pakistan started out with the firm intention of protecting the property of the emigrants (or "evacuees," as they were labeled), guaranteeing their continued rights of ownership. Both governments appointed Custodians of Evacuee Property "to take possession of the property and effects of evacuees and to take such measures as he considers necessary or expedient for preserving such property or effects."[15]

But problems soon arose about how to deal with incoming refugees who had occupied property abandoned by evacuees during the riots. Everywhere incoming refugees had begun to break into and squat in any vacant property they could find, resolutely (and often violently) resisting efforts to oust them. Local policemen proved reluctant to take action to evict refugees of their own faith. Increasingly, the Indian government began to draw a distinction between refugees and "ordinary looters," acknowledging the special claims of refugees.[16] However, this in its turn raised another conundrum. What would happen if Muslim evacuees came back home to India once order was restored (and many were known to want to return)?[17] Where would they go if their houses had been taken over by refugees? And what would happen to Hindu and Sikh refugees who wanted to return to homes in Pakistan?

In early 1948, Nehru's government came to the momentous conclusion that the only way forward was to prevent evacuees from returning to reclaim their homes. The Influx from Pakistan (Control) Ordinance held that "no person shall enter India from any place in Pakistan, whether directly or indirectly unless . . . he is in possession of a permit."[18] One year later, when it had become plain that the permit system was impossible to enforce in a society where few people had any identity documents, the Evacuee Property Ordinance came onto the statute book. This draconian ordinance empowered provincial governments in every part of India (except the eastern states of West Bengal, Assam, and Tripura) to acquire evacuee property "as it may need for a public purpose which may include the rehabilitation of refugees . . . or payment of fair compensation [to them]."[19] At a stroke, the ordinance effectively nationalized *all* evacuee Muslim property, adding it to the pool of resources out of which India hoped to rehouse and rehabilitate incoming Hindu and Sikh refugees. Pakistan's officials protested vociferously, and with justification, that these measures effectively "disinherited" India's Muslim displacees. But very soon Pakistan followed with its own identical legislative and executive measures.[20] Faced with a situation in which India had slammed the door shut on Muslim refugees and made it impossible to recover their properties, Pakistan could see that it had little option but to appropriate all abandoned evacuee Hindu and Sikh property in its turn.

These measures repudiated the fundamental doctrines of British subjecthood, namely, that it was forged by birth within the realm and was an indelible and unalterable bond. The "permit system" stripped partition's refugees of the right to return to the land of their birth.[21] The Evacuee Property Ordinances made their flight an irrevocable step. Once the very act of leaving one's home rendered it liable to seizure, people were forced to stay where they were. And for those who had already left, there was no alternative but to remain where they now found themselves, or to seek some new destination outside South Asia where they could settle. Migration was endowed with a new finality and novel political resonances. Muslim migrants to Pakistan were deemed by India to have chosen citizenship in Pakistan *by the very act of* moving there and to have renounced forever their right to Indian citizenship. Hindus and Sikh refugees born in Pakistan, likewise, were banned from returning to their homes there. The imperatives of responding to mass migrations that neither had desired or anticipated pushed both nations toward redefining nationality in ethno-religious terms.

These regulatory regimes had a profound impact on South Asia. They effectively sealed the western borders between India and Pakistan. The eastern borders between them, too, were gradually closed. After 1952, passports and visas were required for travel between India and East Pakistan. The Enemy Property Acts of 1967, promulgated by both countries, applied to *all* their territories, bringing East Pakistan, West Bengal, Assam, and Tripura (hitherto excluded from the purview of the evacuee property regime) firmly within its remit. These acts not only made it more difficult than ever to cross the borders; it also made it hazardous for people even to maintain contact with relatives on the other side, since fraternizing with "the enemy" across the border rendered property liable to seizure.[22] In 1972, after its secession from Pakistan in a war that produced ten million refugees, Bangladesh, too, enacted its own Vested Property Ordinance. This mirrored the provisions of the evacuee property acts of its neighbors, with calamitous implications for its large Hindu populations, and also for its Urdu-speaking Muslim minorities.[23] Today South Asia's borders are among the most violently policed frontiers in the world.[24]

The impact of these upheavals was not restricted to the subcontinent. They had a ripple effect that soon touched South Asians in the diaspora. By 1947, there were three million people of South Asian origin scattered over fifty-eight countries of the world. Perhaps one in three of these "overseas Indians" was a Muslim.[25] Many of these Muslims came from parts of the subcontinent that after partition went to India, not Pakistan, and they had relatives and properties there. Questions were now raised about their "nationality." The External Affairs Ministry was much exercised, for instance, by the case of one Mr Gardee, a Muslim of Indian origin and a longtime resident of Johannesburg. Mr Gardee, reputedly one of South Africa's richest men, came from Bombay, where he had substantial properties. Indian officials believed (with no definite evidence to support their belief) that he had "pro-Pak leanings" and had traveled to Pakistan to buy property there. This led to a move to enlarge the scope of the Evacuee Property Act to apply to Indian Muslims overseas of "doubtful loyalty."[26] Gardee's properties in Bombay were seized by the Custodian of Evacuee Property, as were the properties of many other Indian Muslims living abroad.[27]

Not surprisingly, finding themselves in a position similar to that of Mr Gardee, many overseas Indians rushed to register themselves as Indian citizens. The position of those whose homes were in the erstwhile Princely States was further complicated by the passage of British Nationality Act of 1948 (of which more later), which extended British nationality to all former British Indian subjects. Since technically inhabitants of the Princely States had never been British Indian subjects—owing allegiance first and foremost to their own rulers rather than the king emperor—they now found themselves at risk of being rendered stateless by the new legislation.[28] This prompted a flood of applications for Indian citizenship, to which many were technically entitled under the Indian Constitution of 1950.

However, this rush among diasporic South Asians for Indian citizenship did not play well in their host countries. Ethno-nationalists in East and South Africa now seized on the phenomenon as proof that Indian migrants had no loyalty to their countries of adoption.[29] In South Africa, where the Afrikaner National Party had long been pressing for the repatriation of "Asiatics," the question had more delicate ramifications. If South Africa's "Asiatics" *were* Indian nationals, the party claimed, it was well within South Africa's rights to ask them to leave. If, on the other hand, they were South African citizens by virtue of birth and domicile, then India had no business interfering in South Africa's internal affairs and proselytizing in the United Nations on their behalf.[30]

For its part, the Indian government began now to see compelling reasons why its diasporic peoples should be encouraged to take on the citizenship of their host countries. This would allow India to sidestep the sticky question of who, among these three-million-odd people abroad, was entitled to Indian citizenship, who among them was a "closet" Pakistani, and who it was safe to allow back home. It would—or so the officials in New Delhi's South Block hoped—give these people a more secure claim to political rights in their host nations than if they were deemed to be migrants.[31] It would also prevent a flood of returning migrants seeking shelter back in India at a time when the government was stretched to the limit by the challenge of rehabilitating millions of partition refugees. But, as subsequent events would show, this policy was no guarantee that the "host" countries would accept Indian migrants as their own people.

NATIONALITY IN THE NEIGHBORHOOD AND WIDER EMPIRE

In 1948, Burma and Ceylon gained independence and stood forth as new nations. Both countries set immediately to drafting new citizenship laws that distinguished between "ethnic" citizens and immigrants. In August 1949, Ceylon enacted an Indian and Pakistani Residents (Citizenship) Act, which allowed persons of Indian and Pakistani origin to register, within two years of the passage of the act, for citizenship in Ceylon. But it distinguished between citizens "by descent" and citizens by registration, who were not entitled—as defined by various new development initiatives—to the "goods" of development.[32] According to the Indian Mission in Colombo, Ceylonese officials had no intention of making registration easy for Indian migrants, and were "deliberately dragging their feet in registration of Indians as citizens."[33] Already in 1939, any further migration of Tamil plantation workers to Ceylon had been banned. But among the seven or eight hundred thousand Tamils who had migrated to Ceylon before this date, many had left their wives and children behind in South India. This population, for the most part unlettered and unorganized (few independent unions were allowed to operate on the plantations), had now to negotiate the complex business of acquiring Ceylonese citizenship for themselves and their families.[34] The Indian Mission in Colombo concluded that "the best thing would be for all Indians who were qualified to be Ceylonese citizens to apply for citizenship without hesitation."[35]

For its part, in 1948 Burma defined its own nationality law on frankly ethnic grounds, giving citizenship only to persons deemed to belong to an "indigenous race" or having one grandparent from an "indigenous race." Indians who had lived in British Burma since before 1942 could register as citizens, but they were soon to be victims of government drives forcibly to acquire their land without fair compensation.[36] This generated a new wave of migration (or rather repatriation) as Indians from Burma began to trickle back into India as refugees and, in the case of Arakanese Muslims, into East Pakistan. Neither India nor Pakistan— both still struggling to rehabilitate millions of partition refugees—was able to do much to do much to help them beyond allowing them (with greater or lesser degrees of reluctance) the right to enter and remain in their countries of origin. In the case of "Anglo-Indian" residents of Burma, even granting this limited concession was rather more than the Indian government was prepared to do: the Indian Mission in Burma was advised only to issue these hapless relics of the Raj temporary papers rather than register them as full-fledged Indian citizens. Because of their doubtful claims to ethnic Indian antecedents, their loyalty to India was deemed suspect.[37] The rising tides of ethnically defined nationalisms throughout the Indian Ocean region meant that the Anglo-Indians, too, would now have to seek new destinations in other parts of the world where their British subjecthood still allowed them entry, in yet another new stream of migration in the South Asian diaspora.

The Decline, Revival, and Fall of "British Subjecthood"

By 1948, Canada and Australia had adopted their own citizenship laws. Even as they paid lip service to the idea of a shared British subjecthood in the empire and Commonwealth, they reaffirmed their commitment to keeping nonwhite migrants—whether from the Commonwealth or elsewhere—out of their territories. Australia and Canada stuck obstinately to this position, invoking their sovereign right to determine who could, and could not, enter their territories, and they held fast, until the mid-1960s, to an immigration policy in which color and race were the determinants. "British imperial subjecthood" was beginning to look like a tattered inheritance, its contradictions exposed to the world.

These were the circumstances under which London brought the British Nationality Act onto the statute book in 1948. The act introduced the new legal statuses of "citizens of the United Kingdom and Commonwealth" (CUKC) and "citizens of independent Commonwealth countries" (CICC).[38] It allowed both categories free entry into the United Kingdom, with the right to take employment, while citizens of the old (white) dominions were given the right to register as British citizens after a year's residence.[39] It therefore extended, on paper at least, free access to the United Kingdom to all citizens of both the "old" and "new" Commonwealth, and hence to Indians, Pakistanis, and Ceylonese.

Enacted at a time of cross-party consensus about the importance of defending the traditional ideal of British subjecthood and the necessity of maintaining close relations with the Commonwealth, the act was passed before immigration from the "new" Commonwealth had become a concern in Britain. But the context changed almost immediately with the arrival on British shores of 492 Jamaicans onboard the *Empire Windrush* in June 1948. After this "incursion" (as Clement Attlee famously described it), every U.K. government would face demands that Britain's doors be closed to "colored immigrants."[40]

Between 1948 and 1962, Whitehall admittedly resisted pressures to introduce controls that were openly discriminatory and hung on to what remained of the common subjecthood in the empire and Commonwealth. But is it not the case, as is often claimed, that Britain in this period remained open to all comers. Interestingly, Britain now used its good offices with governments in the "source" countries to encourage them to introduce their own controls to prevent unregulated emigration from their shores. In the mid-1950s, when South Asian migrants replaced those from the Caribbean as the prime focus of official concern, Britain asked India and Pakistan not to issue their citizens passports for travel to the United Kingdom. They agreed to deny passports to their own people if they lacked adequate resources and could not prove sufficient literacy and knowledge of English. Both countries instituted police checks into the character and antecedents of would-be migrants. For its part, by means of unpublicized arrangements with the U.K. Home Office, India began to weed out applications for passports from "low-class citizens," checking their claims that they had secured work and accommodation in Britain.[41] It was only in 1960, when India's Supreme Court declared it to be discriminatory, that this strange practice—of "outsourcing" U.K. migration controls against Indians to India—came to an end. In 1961, Pakistan, too, lifted its restrictions on emigration to the United Kingdom.[42]

Finally, after a decade of mounting domestic pressure for restrictions, the Commonwealth Immigrants Act went onto the statute book in 1962.[43] Although it did not openly discriminate on the grounds of race, it was specifically designed to restrict the admission of "colored immigrants"; and this was the outcome in practice. Prospective migrants from South Asia now had to obtain employment vouchers from the Ministry of Labour before being allowed into Britain. These were given mainly to people who had specific jobs to go to in Britain, or to those who had particular skills and qualifications that Britain wanted. Only the wives and children of migrants already in Britain still had an absolute right to entry into the United Kingdom.

Since 1962, the immigration laws of Britain have become ever more complex and restrictive, even, for a brief and inglorious episode in the 1980s, subjecting migrant brides from South Asia to virginity tests. Space does not permit a detailed discussion of these laws, but two points need to be noted. In 1963, Kenya gained independence, and four years later, in 1967, it passed an Immigration Act that obliged all those without Kenyan citizenship to acquire work permits. It also introduced laws that deliberately targeted South Asians in business and trade. This followed a drive to "Africanize" the newly independent national government and economy of Kenya. Uganda followed suit, setting up a committee to African-ize commerce and industry in 1968 and introducing discriminatory systems of trade licenses and work permits in 1969. Many of the South Asians who left East Africa at this time were British citizens, having opted to retain their CUKC status in 1963. In 1968, Britain passed a new Commonwealth Immigration Act, which restricted the number of Asian families from East Africa permitted to enter the United Kingdom to fifteen hundred. This broke an explicit pledge, given in 1963 to East African Asians who retained their CUKC status, that they would have unrestricted rights of entry into the United Kingdom. It also meant that Britain now had denied the right of return to a specific class of its own citizens.

In 1971, a Conservative government passed an Immigration Act that intro-duced "patriality" as a condition for the right of abode in the United Kingdom. This was a thinly disguised form of ethnic qualification—"patriality" being "in-digenous" antecedents by another name. Commonwealth citizens were now deemed to have the same status as "aliens" in Britain. After a quarter of a century of prevarication, with this step Britain repudiated its own historic conception of subjecthood. Faced with the triple challenge of economic and geopolitical decline and potentially huge postcolonial immigration, as Christian Joppke has suggested, Britain refashioned itself from a "civic" to an "ethnic" nation in which member-ship is defined by the tests of birth and ancestry.[44] Finally, as the last vestiges of its empire faded away, Britain joined the new world of ethnic nation-states as a full-fledged member, abandoning its legacy as architect of a liberal and (in this matter) universalist empire and turning in on itself to keep outsiders at bay.

THE WORLD OF THE "GREEN CARD HOLDER," "GULF" SUBORDINATION, AND HUMAN TRAFFICKING

Since the mid-1960s, the international migration regime (as it affects South Asians) has been dominated by two main trends. The first is the move—heralded by passage of the Hart-Celler Act by the United States in 1965—explicitly to em-brace a hierarchy of preferences for certain *types* of migrants within a system of controls that caps overall numbers but does not bar certain peoples or races. In the United States, preference has been given to two groups.[45] The first, based on the notion of "family reunion," are the children and dependents of migrants who are already legal permanent residents. The second are for highly accom-plished migrants whose skills match the needs of the domestic economy. By and large, with local and temporal variations, these preferences have also guided the immigration policies of the other developed countries of the English-speaking West since the 1970s. Australia, Canada, and Britain have all adopted this model. The common perception is that Britain "closed" its doors to South Asians at the same time as the rest of the world began to open them.[46] But the facts point to a different conclusion: widely different regimes have converged since the 1960s and 1970s on a broadly common ground.

The second trend has been the reemergence—side by side with a rapidly growing global labor market—of familiar forms of subordination among poor and unskilled migrants. These migrants are predominantly young and able-bodied men, although increasingly they have been joined by large numbers of single women working as cooks, maids, child minders, or sex workers. The oil-rich Persian Gulf emirates are merely the most visible parts of a labor market segmented by race and hierarchy, in which a few highly skilled and well-paid elite migrants enjoy freedoms and mobility, while poorer South Asian workers are employed on astonishingly illiberal terms.[47] These new helots enjoy few, if any, rights.[48] The noxious practice of employers confiscating the passports of "labor-class" employees has become commonplace. Gang masters lure poor migrants to destinations all the way from Malaysia or Dubai to Britain with great expectations of pay and good working conditions, only to confiscate their (often forged) papers on arrival, withhold pay, and in effect incarcerate them until they have worked enough notionally to pay off the inflated costs of their passage. The brutalities of human trafficking in the twenty-first century are reminiscent of many of the horrors of indenture and *kangani* in the 1900s.

On the face of it, then, the migration regimes of the twenty-first century bear an uncanny resemblance to those of the old imperial world. Just as the old order was stratified by class and status, with a clear legal distinction between the self-funded free "passenger class" and "assisted" unfree "coolie class," the new order is characterized by a chasm that separates the legal status of increasingly hyper-mobile "green card holders" (and their ilk) and trafficked or otherwise "assisted" migrants drawn from larger poor communities, who are "stuck."[49]

But there are important distinctions, and this essay concludes by pointing to them. In the nineteenth century, it was well understood that free and assisted migrants alike would usually leave families behind, remitting monies home and returning periodically to see them. Now the tendency for Western governments is to promote "family reunion." It would be churlish to deny that this bias owes something to genuine humane concerns in receiving states. But it would be naive to believe that when Western governments endorse family reunion they are not also concerned to ensure that those few migrants whom they have been forced to accept as permanent inhabitants have all their eggs in one national basket, and that it is the basket the host controls. These states are anxious to ensure that migrants deposit all their emotional ties and loyalties safely within the borders of the nation-state in which they now live.

The final distinction between the old and the new is the preference today for "permanent settlement" by those chosen few deemed eligible for entry and who have "earned" their right to stay in Western industrialized nation-states. To get a green card in the United States, the applicant has to demonstrate *continuous unbroken residence* and legal employment. In Britain, those with "leave to remain" have not only to demonstrate an unbroken stretch of domicile before they are granted that leave, but they also cannot leave the United Kingdom for any length of time *without losing that entitlement.* The paradox for today's "green card migrants" is that they can only regain their freedom to come and go by taking the ultimate step of applying for the citizenship of their host country and renouncing affiliation with their homeland. Only by professing loyalty to the adopted nation through ever more elaborate rituals of citizenship can today's migrant regain the right freely to leave it. And yet, ironically, the technologies of today also enable that person ever more easily to resort to the many forms of subversion of the nation-state that are collectively understood as "transnationalism."

CONCLUSION

The imperatives behind the passage of the Hart-Celler Act have been debated; some argue persuasively that it had much to do with the civil rights movement in the United States.[50] But few would deny that it was as much a response to the new international context of decolonization and the Cold War, as well as to America's assumption of leadership of the "free world." America's imperial role required that it, like every successful empire before it, had to elaborate a universalist and inclusive discourse. Restrictive U.S. policies in the pre–World War II era—with their emphasis on national quotas that favored "assimilable" Western Europeans, their espousal of "Asiatic Barred Zones," and measures to prevent Chinese and Japanese immigration—were at odds with America's image as the beacon of liberty and had to be abandoned.[51] Older liberal republican traditions of civic citizenship, which promised that anyone could become an American if he or she embraced its love of liberty, were instead revived and reworked as the ideological underpinnings of the free world.

One question that the decline of Britain's imperium poses for the future of America is this: will America, like Britain before it, retreat from its confident universalism? Just as Britain retreated from a universalist liberal notion of subjecthood to a narrow, increasingly ethnically understood conception of national citizenship, might America's view of itself (however rose tinted) as a multicultural nation of migrants be undermined by the realities of its economic decline? Faced by the challenges of globalization, the exodus of capital, and the multiplicity of allegiances of migrants in a global labor market, will America be pushed, as Britain had been, into embracing a revived nativism? Can America respond to the challenge of refashioning its citizenship in ways that do not alienate or exclude sections of its postimperial plural society?

PART 8

U.S. GLOBAL HEGEMONY

U.S. Marines take down the flag and transfer control of the Subic Bay naval base to the Republic of Philippines, 1992. (U.S. Department of Defense)

The "Three R's" and the Making of a New World Order

Reparation, Reconstruction, Relief, and U.S. Policy, 1945–1952

GREG BANKOFF

THE POST–WORLD WAR II TRANSITION from a European imperial order to an American world system was not so much a military affair as a financial project. The Truman administration had to rely more on economic than military power to achieve its foreign policy objectives as Congress initiated a precipitous dismantling of the postwar U.S. military machine.[1] The trade and monetary agreements reached at Bretton Woods in July 1944 represented an attempt to build a new American world order founded on commerce rather than coercion. The United States set about transforming a regional, informal empire of islands, itself the product of a successful earlier war, the Spanish-American (1898), into something much more enduring—a global empire of financial and market mechanisms. If *colonial* is the appropriate adjective to describe the former, then *developmental* best expresses the new policy agendas that inform the latter. Overseas development assistance (ODA) had its origins in postwar aid premised on the three "R's" of reparation, reconstruction, and relief. By going back to the basics of development and tracing its manifestations in three discrete geopolitical arenas—Greece, the Philippines, and Japan in the formative years between 1945 and 1952—the dynamics of what began as a practical program for postwar recovery and reconstruction are revealed as a new tool of imperial ambition.

THE THREE "R's"

Postwar recovery, at least for the victors, has historically been premised on reparations imposed on the vanquished: peace treaties are as much about compensation for damages as they are about the cessation of hostilities. Since the nineteenth century, the vanquished have paid a heavy price for defeat that was calibrated in monetary terms. The destruction wrought upon life and property by mechanized warfare and large-scale aerial bombardment both heightened the moral claim to compensation for those affected and made the demands of war indemnities more difficult for the defeated nation to sustain.[2] At the conclusion of World War I, the victorious Allies imposed on Germany the requirement to compensate those who had suffered losses through its "aggressions" and established an inter-Allied Reparations Commission to mediate such claims according to the defeated state's ability to pay. Initial Allied pronouncements during World War II were of a similar ilk, with the Yalta declaration of February 1945 obliging Germany to make reparations in kind of U.S.$22 billion. A similar policy was imposed on Japan under the terms of surrender on September 2, 1945.[3]

While matters of retribution were never far from popular consciousness, as early as December 1941 American officials in the State and Treasury Departments were plotting an alternative course.[4] Mindful that the peace terms of 1919 had contributed to the major depression, mass unemployment, and social evils of the interwar years, they set about establishing conditions that would give rise to economic recovery and stressed reconstruction more than retribution. Reparations, consequently, would be tempered by the need to rebuild a devastated Europe and revive world trade. Anglo-American negotiators were able to reach a remarkable degree of consensus over what this postwar blueprint should entail: a relatively open world economy but with international supervision of national monetary and trade policies, and a high degree of toleration of state intervention to promote national concerns.[5]

An example of this shift from retribution toward reconstruction is provided by the Treaty of Peace with Italy signed on February 10, 1947. The United States sought to ensure that the terms imposed were not so onerous as to retard Italy's reestablishment of "sound economic conditions" and "healthy relations with other members of the family of nations." In the words of Walter Surrey, deputy U.S. negotiator of the subsequent economic agreement with Italy, it was widely recognized that "chaos, hunger and desperation, while a barren soil for the birth of a democratic system of government, were admirably suited for the quick growth of a dictatorship, including a communist dictatorship."[6] Accordingly, reparations were only provided to Yugoslavia, Greece, the Soviet Union, Ethiopia, and Albania. The U.S. government waived its own claims and confined its demands to a modest U.S.$5 million to satisfy those of American nationals. A similar policy was followed with respect to claims against the minor Axis powers Bulgaria, Hungary, and Romania. No reparations at all were exacted from Austria as it was deemed not to have been an independent state during the war.[7]

The causes of this remarkable shift in U.S. attitudes were varied and overlapping. Foremost among them was a simple matter of political necessity. One of the least remembered consequences of the war in Europe is the thoroughgoing destruction of property rights caused by Nazi occupation policies and forced or voluntary population movements at the war's end. Most European states faced the immense task of having to disentangle property rights, undo forced transfers of property, and reestablish some semblance of property relationships that was more consistent with the political viewpoint of the liberated governments. Matters were complicated by the fact that many property titles could not be restored as their owners were either dead or missing and their heirs could not be traced. There was also the emotive question of the large landholdings and industrial concerns acquired by people who had collaborated with German authorities and, for moral and political reasons, could not be allowed to retain ownership of them. Individual Nazis and occupation government instrumentalities had also acquired a vast amount of property and loot, which also required divesture and redistribution. Added to the effects of the occupation were the forced evacuations of Sudeten Germans from Czechoslovakia, the Germanic inhabitants in areas of East Germany granted to Poland, and those from the new territorial acquisitions awarded to Yugoslavia.[8] While the situation in Western Europe was not of the same magnitude as it was in the East, the property of collaborating manufacturers or resource owners in France and of war-related industries and utilities in Italy confronted these states with similar problems.[9]

This drastic modification to prewar property titles and rights "unparalleled" in history left postwar states with little alternative but to assume immediate control over such holdings. Nor at the outset were these decisions controversial since they were recognized even by private enterprise as an economic necessity.[10] Concern was not over nationalization per se but to what purposes it served. If such measures were taken according to the accepted dictates of international law that nationalization was accompanied by prompt, adequate, and effective compensation, then it was within the rights of sovereign states to take such steps. The U.S. position was more extreme and posited that a state's right to expropriate private property was actually "conditional" on its ability to make such payments in freely convertible currency.[11] Between 1945 and 1947, it became apparent that Eastern European governments, under pressure from the Soviet Union, were using the cloak of postwar economic necessity to carry out programs of political restructuring, making nationalization not a measure to restore democracy but to facilitate the eventual establishment of communist states. To this end, compensation paid in long-term state securities held in inconvertible currencies ushered in state ownership of the means of production.[12] Even more alarming, the large, influential communist parties in France and Italy were pressing their governments for an extension of public ownership.[13] As European states (including the British government) resorted to nationalization to deal with their economic plights, the question of reparations became less a matter of compensation and more one of reconstruction to contain the spread of communism.

Reconstruction, however, not only saved democracy from another authoritarian tyranny, but it was also good for business. In fact, the shift in American

thinking was already taking place prior to 1945. Many in U.S. government circles were convinced that the imposition of reparations after World War I had
caused the subsequent conflict. Moreover, the liberal establishment was alarmed
at the prospect of a massive postwar depression in the United States unless the
world's markets were thrown open to American goods. Already in 1942, the State
Department had established an Office of Foreign Relief and Rehabilitation that
was later subsumed into the United Nations Relief and Rehabilitation Administration (UNRRA) headed by Herbert Lehman and reporting directly to the secretary of state, Cordell Hull. Lehman was charged with coordinating all federal
agencies dealing with rehabilitation and the Allies. Officials at UNRRA followed
in the wake of Allied armies dispensing goods and supplies, wherever possible of
U.S. provenance, in both Europe and China before handing over its operations
to the United Nations in 1947.[14]

However, it was the threat of economic collapse in Europe in the winter of
1946–47 that persuaded President Harry Truman and his cabinet of the need for
a comprehensive program of economic aid. By the end of 1946, European postwar recovery began to stall as a direct result of drastic shortages of key commodities such as coal and food exacerbated by some of the severest weather in
a century. Moreover, there was also evidence by the beginning of 1947 that the
United States was headed for recession, a downturn in domestic demand that
might be cushioned by exports to Europe. The problem was that Europe no longer
had the dollar reserves to pay for these goods; there was now a worldwide dollar shortage that threatened international trade. Providing foreign aid, however, would assure the world of a ready supply of dollars with which to purchase
American goods and maintain high levels of industrial production.[15] It was in
America's self-interest to offer economic assistance to the distressed peoples of
Europe and the world, and if that aid also limited the appeal of communist parties, so much the better. As Colonel William Eddy, a senior State Department
official, made clear to the Committee on the Extension of U.S. Aid to Foreign
Governments in March 1947, "In determining the basis for granting assistance
it will be necessary to ask whether the stabilization and strengthening of the
country in question will rebound as a material benefit to the position of the
United States."[16]

These considerations of political motivation and economic self-interest in
Europe lay at the core of the principal foreign aid program of the period, the Marshall Plan (1948–51), although Asia was also a major theater of action. Named
after the then secretary of state, George Marshall, the plan was an ambitious
four-year program meant to inject U.S.$12.5 billion into the economies of West-
ern Europe. Officially called the European Recovery Program (ERP), it allocated
grants and loans according to each country's dollar balance of payments deficit,
with Britain and France together receiving 43 percent of the total amount. About

one-third of all imports were agricultural with grains sourced from surplus American production. This assistance encompassed much more than simple aid in kind: American contractors refurbished the Corinth Canal and modernized mines in Turkey, American technicians installed U.S. equipment in the oil refinery at Trieste, and European businessmen were sent to the United States to study production techniques.[17] American officials attempted to shape European monetary and fiscal policy, conducted economic surveys of Europe's infrastructure, and aspired toward initiating European integration with their designs to pool and coordinate inland transport systems and to establish a regional coal commission.[18] The same federal agency that managed the ERP, the Economic Cooperation Administration, however, was also responsible for managing export controls to Eastern Europe and the Soviet Union with the aim of limiting the flow of strategic materials to the communist bloc.

As a wartime ally, the Soviet Union was invited to take part in discussions, but any steps toward European integration were viewed by Moscow as threats to its security. The Soviet press denounced Marshall's June 1947 address at Harvard University outlining the aid to Europe, calling it "a plan for political pressure with dollars" and a means of "interference in the internal affairs of other countries." A Tass news broadcast on June 29 accused the United States of "making use of its credit possibilities for expanding its external markets."[19] In fact, according to Adolf Berle, a member of President Franklin Roosevelt's "Brain Trust," the Soviet fear of losing influence over Eastern Europe unintentionally made the plan the *causa belli* of the Cold War. "The historical fact is that the Soviet Union opened her general European offensive as a direct answer to the Marshall Plan," he wrote in 1948, "and has elected to make the United States its chief target."[20] His views were shared by others.[21] Over a few years, a combination of political necessity and economic self-interest transformed a policy of extracting reparations from defeated enemies into a program of national reconstruction, supplying billions of dollars to build stable democracies in Europe and Asia. In the process, it may also have started the Cold War.

A GLOBAL ARENA

The Marshall Plan was not so much a product of the Cold War as an integral part of a concerted U.S. program to effect postwar recovery in Europe, with bilateral counterparts in Asia. The Philippine War Damage Commission (1947–51) and the nature of the U.S. Occupation regime in Japan achieved much the same outcomes as the Marshall Plan did in European countries like Greece. An examination of developments in these three countries highlights the similarities in approach and outcome of what had become U.S. government policy to use the supply of aid in the guise of postwar reconstruction as a means of furthering its own political and economic interests.

Greek Civil War

In many respects, the Marshall Plan in Europe started with the bilateral grants of aid made to Greece and Turkey in 1947. In particular, the Greek Civil War (1946–49) served as a "test tube" for the world of American resolve to halt both economic collapse and communist aggression. The Greek Communist Party and its military wing, the Democratic Army of Greece (DSE) were seen as serious obstacles to American goals in that country. The ERP imposed "semicolonial rules" in an attempt to refashion Greek society, interfering in the internal affairs of state agencies and threatening to withhold funds if its advice was ignored. Economic reconstruction emphasized basic infrastructure development such as roads, mines, and electricity supplies, as well as improvements to agriculture. State institutions were overhauled under American tutelage, strengthening their ability to intervene directly to limit black market practices, control inflation, police tax evasion, and address low productivity. At the same time, U.S. officials made it clear to labor unions that continuing assistance depended on increasing productivity and maintaining industrial peace.

All these measures were basic ERP policies implemented in one form or another across Western Europe, although they were applied rather more forcefully in Greece than elsewhere. A significant dimension of the Marshall Plan in Greece was its political agenda linking assistance to democratization, blocking all attempts to negotiate with the communists, sponsoring the temporary resettlement of over seven hundred thousand people from areas in northern Greece to deprive the DSE of supplies and recruits, and engineering the merger of centrist political parties.[22] Reconstruction in postwar Greece became a matter of nation building along lines acceptable to Washington. Moreover, the United States' continued patronage of the Greek armed forces inadvertently paved the way for the military dictatorship of 1967–74.

Philippine War Damage Commission

Outside of Europe and away from the historical limelight cast by the Marshall Plan, the same processes were at work under different guises. Much of Asia had also been devastated during the war, not least the Philippines, an erstwhile American colony till 1946. Invaded and fought over twice, its cities, industries, and farms lay in ruins. Manila, the archipelago's capital, was described by General Dwight D. Eisenhower as the "worst damaged city in the world with the possible exception of Warsaw."[23] Much of the destruction had been perpetrated by American armed forces during the liberation battles of 1944 and 1945. At the war's height, President Roosevelt had promised Filipinos that they would be paid for everything they lost right down to "the last nipa hut and last carabao."[24]

To honor such pledges, Congress passed the Philippine Rehabilitation Act (PRA) in 1946, which allocated U.S.$602 million and established a Philippine

War Damage Commission (PWDC) to administer the program over a four-year period. Funds were viewed as both providing appropriate compensation to Filipinos for their property losses during the war and acting as a "rehabilitation stimulus" to the soon to be independent nation. Put somewhat more graphically in the PWDC's final report, "[F]reedom without financial aid would have been comparable to putting a friend to sea in an unprovisioned open boat."[25]

The United States' motives behind funding the PWDC are in many ways more complex than those behind the Marshall Plan in Europe. Certainly gratitude was an important factor, expressing a deep appreciation for the loyalty Filipinos had shown during the war. A memorandum submitted by PWDC commissioner Frank Waring to a House of Representatives committee hearing in 1950 spoke of the United States taking "this unprecedented step as a token of appreciation for

Senator Millard Tydings, Secretary of the Interior James A. Krug, and Resident Commissioner Carlos P. Romulo of the Philippines stand behind President Harry Truman at the signing of the Philippine Rehabilitation Act, April 30, 1946, authorizing U.S. payment for private and public war damage in the Philippines. (Library of Congress Prints and Photographs Division)

the valiant aid given to American Armed Forces throughout the last war." The very next sentence further qualified this action, adding that "the establishment and maintenance of a strong democracy in the Philippines is the desire of our own country."[26]

In addition to the genuine feelings of indebtedness, the economic and political self-interest of the United States was also a significant driver. The provisions for delivering aid through the PRA of April 30, 1946, were made dependent on the Filipino authorities' acceptance of a trade agreement that heavily favored the United States. The Philippine Trade Act placed restrictions on the duty levied on U.S. imports, fixed quotas on primary exports to the United States, set the exchange rate between the two currencies, subjected any change to an American veto, and even granted U.S. citizens unilateral parity with Filipinos in the ownership and exploitation of their country's natural resources, a right whose implementation required amending the new Philippine Constitution.[27] Even Assistant Secretary of State William Clayton denounced the act, telling the Senate Finance Committee that these provisions deprived the Philippine government of "a sovereign prerogative."[28]

Although the threat of communism is never mentioned in the published PWDC material, it is there as an underlying theme in the subsequent House of Representatives hearings. As the Huk Rebellion raged throughout Central Luzon between 1946 and 1954, the Philippines was cast as "a beacon" whose "struggling young democracy" had been imperiled by the infiltration of twenty-five thousand Red Chinese.[29]

Occupation of Japan

Americans had an even freer hand in Japan than in Western Europe or the Philippines. The initial intention of U.S. policy toward Japan was not noticeably conciliatory and anticipated the country undergoing a period of "stern discipline as the inevitable retribution for military aggression." The planned reparations were to strip Japan of all war-related industries, demilitarize the country, and provide compensation to neighboring states. With respect to the latter, a provision ensured that recipients were not made "unduly dependent on the Japanese economy" or would "contribute to the Japanese war potential."[30] A special reparations committee began its work in Tokyo in November 1945. The mission's head, Edwin Pauley, wrote that while Japan might again play a major part in the Asian economy, it was no longer to be "a place of leadership and control."[31]

While avoiding a policy of collective punishment, General Douglas MacArthur, in his role as supreme commander of the Allied powers, carried out a sweeping restructuring of Japanese society. The much vaunted postwar Constitution of 1946, for example, a remarkable document that ensured a wide array of political, social, and economic liberties, was actually drafted by a secret committee of twenty-four American military officers and then delivered to the Japanese Diet to present as its own authorship.[32]

Yet here, too, the matter of reparations was soon overtaken by more pressing questions about the reconstruction of Japan. If Pauley's report in December 1945 suggested using reparations to correct a history of physical and economic abuse inflicted on the rest of Asia, General Frank McCoy spoke a very different language just four years later.[33] The considered view of the U.S. government in May 1949 was no longer to limit Japanese production but rather to revive these industries. Such a change in attitude amounted to rescinding the entire reparations program.[34] Under the Treaty of Peace signed with Japan on September 8, 1951, the country was to be turned into a workshop utilizing its trained manpower and obsolete industrial capacity to process its neighbors' raw materials. Though unfavorable when compared with the terms offered other belligerent nations, the 1951 treaty was described by one of its architects, John Foster Dulles, as one of "reconciliation, eliminating from it all trace of hatred and vengeance." Certainly Robert Menzies, the Australian prime minister, considered it so, calling it "soft."[35]

The reason behind this reversal of policy was the worsening security situation in East Asia: the declaration of the People's Republic of China in 1949 and the outbreak of the Korean War in 1950. If the first purpose of the treaty had been to break the vicious cycle of war, victory, peace, and war, the second aim was a no less important task, "to translate Japan from a defeated enemy into a positive contributor to collective security in the Pacific."[36] A security treaty was signed that granted the United States the right to freely distribute its armed forces throughout Japan and to suppress internal disturbances if called on. Nor should the economics of the relationship with Japan be completely overlooked. As in the case of the Marshall Plan and the Philippine War Damage Commission, the United States supplied over U.S.$2 billion in direct assistance during its Occupation of Japan.[37] Substantial additional sums were also channeled indirectly through U.S. armed services procurement spending (exempt from the "Buy America" Act and invisible to a hostile public opinion), which intentionally awarded contracts to supply naval and air force bases on Okinawa and to support military operations farther afield in Asia to Japanese companies. Even U.S. military aid to Southeast Asia was tied to the purchase of manufactured goods from Japan.[38] Working in tandem with the objectives of successive U.S. administrations, Japanese governments throughout the 1950s were able to settle reparation claims with regional governments by making their own payments in the form of services and capital goods and so further expand their heavy and chemical industries.[39]

Reconstruction and the Cold War

In all three cases, reconstruction increasingly became a matter of Cold War politics in the decades that followed 1945. A "bold new program" of technical assistance, the so-called Point Four, was proclaimed by President Truman in his inaugural address of January 1949 and formally constituted the following year with the establishment of the Technical Cooperation Administration (TCA). In 1951, the TCA and the Economic Cooperation Administration, which was responsible for administering the Marshall Plan in Europe, merged to form a single agency, the Mutual Security Administration. Distribution of aid, however, remained largely piecemeal in nature, self-serving and without any discernible pattern beyond U.S foreign policy interests, and heavily skewed in favor of military assistance. Fully 76 percent of all expenditures (in 1958) were in the United States.[40] Finally, the Foreign Assistance Act of 1961 created the U.S. Agency for International Development (USAID), the organization still in control of global development assistance. Over the next forty years (1962–2003), USAID dispensed a total of U.S.$273 billion on promoting health, education, transportation, and agricultural and economic development in 160 nations. It proved an indispensable weapon in successfully prosecuting the Cold War and presently constitutes an important element in the postinvasion reconstruction policies pursued in Iraq and Afghanistan.[41]

RELIEF AND THE DEVELOPMENTAL PARADIGM

So far this discussion has dealt mainly with the first two of the three "R's," reparation and reconstruction. Relief or aid was a central feature of U.S. policy across the globe as it sought to shape a world that simultaneously reflected its own values and served its economic and political ends. In examining American programs in Greece, the Philippines, and Japan, the terms *semicolony, former colony*, and *temporary colony* can be used to describe the relationship between the United States and the country in question. The aid supplied in those years was characterized as colonial because it reflected the prior history of relief as it had developed in the previous century. Overseas development assistance during the ensuing decades of the Cold War remained similar in nature because it served much the same ends of maintaining Western and now American hegemony.

Relief as an organized program of coordinated international assistance was first recognized in the second half of the nineteenth century. Given the imperial ethos and political composition of the times, aid was mainly framed in terms of colonial discourses. What this meant in practice is exemplified in the Indian Famine Codes of 1880, the first detailed articulation of what relief should constitute in the modern era. These codes had their foundations in the European philosophies of the day regarding both the role of the state and the proper market treatment of the poor, albeit transferred to a colonial setting. This meant blaming the poor for their poverty and holding the land and its people responsible for other hazards. The state's role in relief was to be minimal, based more on expediency than any other factor. The state only accepted any responsibility for relief as a matter of "good governance" based on past experiences such as the Irish Potato Famine of 1845–48 and the Indian Mutiny of 1857.[42] Of course, the United States of America was not a colonial power until the end of the nineteenth century, but it did have an internal frontier in its West. Policies in relation to Native American peoples were similar in kind to those described for British India.[43]

These colonial origins served as the precedent for development aid in the modern era, instilling a preoccupation with averting dependency through over-generous assistance, a heavy reliance on free market solutions, and, above all, the retention of external management and control of relief programs. The result was relief campaigns that often better served the interests of the "relievers" rather than the "relieved."[44] This link between colonial relief campaigns and modern aid programs is rarely made. Instead, development aid is mainly seen as the child of the Cold War, more specifically a product of U.S. foreign policy to halt the spread of communism in the third world. To Wolfgang Sachs and other post-developmental theorists, development was actually "invented" after World War II as a novel form of domination over peoples and states trying to free themselves from the yoke of colonialism.[45] The offer of aid promised elites an attractive alternative to the massive economic dislocation and social upheaval suggested by the Soviet model.

These more self-interested motives increasingly came to the fore during the Cold War. On the one hand, the rationale behind ODA was to contain the spread of communism. On the other hand, it was meant to facilitate American capital's penetration of newly emerging markets, build up the administrative capacity of the state, and provide the infrastructure for both public and private enterprise.[46] Development was a continuation of a discourse already started under colonialism and refined in the debates over postwar compensation. As the anticommunist agenda receded in the 1980s and 1990s, foreign direct investment and private capital flows began to replace ODA as the favored development paradigm. The focus, however, remained much as it had been in the nineteenth century in terms of its heavy reliance on free market mechanisms and the conditionality of funding dependent on the privatization of public services and infrastructure. The result-ant privatization programs and sell-off of state assets have commonly taken place in the absence of proper regulatory safeguards, placing many services beyond the reach of the poor, leaving others at the mercy of substantial rises in utility charges, and rendering all more vulnerable.[47]

Too much global public awareness that aid maintains forms of dependency reminiscent of the colonial era and that development primarily serves the agendas of the "developers" more than it does those to be "developed" is bad for democracy—even if it is good for business. The whole rationale of international aid giving is undermined and even the efficacy of welfare at home is called into question. Such home truths have proven embarrassing to the United States and other Western governments for which the last fifty years of development aid has only seen the gap between rich and poor widen. There is also an increasing number of countries, the so-called excluded states or nonintegrating gap, that remain outside the orbit of global capitalism and resist the penetration of external economic forces and the restructuring of international institutions.[48] For these states, very much in the forefront of U.S. foreign policy since 9/11, "other solutions" have had to be found that are more reminiscent of the "reconstruction" programs of the immediate post–World War II period.

CONCLUSION

Much has been written and rewritten about the Cold War and the role of the Marshall Plan. There have been at least three waves of revisionism: the initial inversion of Soviet aggression, which blamed the United States for its pursuit of open-door liberal multilateralism; the postrevisionism that replaced polemic with solid research (sometimes described more like "orthodoxy plus archives"); and the "new" history based on documentary evidence from behind the former iron curtain.[49]

Rather than regarding post–World War II recovery solely as a prelude to the Cold War, there is another narrative, one that views the matter of reparation and reconstruction as an episode in a much longer history about the nature of international relief and what is now called ODA. This is a story primarily about unequal relationships of power in the form of donor and recipient where the giving is not without self-interest and the receiving involves a loss of autonomy. This relationship had its genesis in nineteenth-century colonialism, which has clouded the subsequent history of aid. As the United States has been by far the largest donor in total dollar terms (though one of the least generous in percentage of gross national income), it is able to exert considerable influence on recipient countries both through bilateral assistance and through its sway over multilateral institutions such as the World Bank and associated agencies.

As this essay has shown, the period of post–World War II reconstruction was pivotal in transforming the United States from a regional colonial power into an international superpower able to exert its authority not only through its daunting military prowess but also through its ability to provide ODA to a relief-starved world. Moreover, this aid was not confined to simply Europe and the Marshall Plan but was truly global in scale, although here, as in the cases of the Philippines and Japan, the arrangements had more of a bilateral nature. State and Treasury officials were aware of the national advantages that might accrue through exercising this form of influence, but how far they systematically set out to use relief to further the United States' own economic and political ambitions is less certain. Perhaps it was more a policy that evolved with time and circumstance. As Robert Kramer claimed in 1951, "The immediate objective may be relief to the destitute, and the ultimate goal may be economic and social rehabilitation of an entire country, with the emphasis not on restoration of pre-war conditions but on long range economic and social development."[50] What else was that "long-range development" to be unless it was modeled on American values and served U.S. interests?

Entangled Empires

The United States and European Imperial Formations in the Mid-Twentieth Century

JULIAN GO

THERE IS A COMMON TALE about the rise of the United States after World War II premised on the assumption of American exceptionalism. Presumably, the United States emerged from the war as a benevolent, anti-imperial hegemon. Working from its own deep anti-imperial and democratic values, it pushed the European empires to dismantle and valiantly inaugurated a new global order of open trade, national sovereignty, and freedom. Matching its high morals to its new economic and industrial power, the United States became a new "anti-imperial" liberal empire, marking an imperial transition from the decaying old world of repression to the bright new world of liberty and freedom. This exceptionalism narrative is deep. It is entailed in popular and scholarly discourse alike. It is found, for instance, in George W. Bush's assertion that "America has never been an empire. We may be the only great power in history that had the chance, and refused." It is found, too, in the historian Jeremi Suri's claim that the United States has been an "anti-empire" guided by "American claims to freedom and opposition to empire."[1]

This essay reconsiders the narrative of transition that the story of American exceptionalism implies. First, it is not the case that American global power after World War II was anti-imperial. In fact, the United States itself was an empire, just a different type than traditional territorial empires. In this new "American way of empire," as Thomas Bender has called it, indirect rule and influence replaced colonialism and military bases, client states, and financial aid replaced pith helmets, jodhpurs, and rajas.[2] Harry Magdoff initially called this "imperialism without colonies."[3] More recently, others have relabeled it "empire by remote control" or "nonterritorial imperialism."[4] As the essay by Gregory Barton in this volume suggests, another term that might be used for this is *informal imperialism*.

Second, the transition from the European empires of the early twentieth century to the new American empire was not a tidy affair. As Alfred McCoy suggests in the introduction to this volume, scholars should keep in mind that imperial transitions are often marked by continuity as well as change. In this spirit, the present essay shows that the rise of the new U.S. empire was at first dependent on the European empires it presumably opposed. Rather than a simple transition from dying European empires to a new American empire, there was a tangled web of interimperial relations, forces, and networks between them.[5] And when this network of empires began to break down, the transition to America's informal empire did not occur by means of the valiant agency of the United States alone. It was rather effected by the agency of the very peripheral peoples that the empires, both old and new, sought to subdue. When the United States did take an anti-imperial stance, it was not because of its anticolonial liberal values but because the new global climate and American pragmatism demanded it to be so.

THE AGE OF IMPERIALISM HAS ENDED?

It is unsurprising that World War II has been taken as a monumental turning point away from Europe as the center of global power based on colonial empires and toward the new American informal empire. World War II weakened the old order. It devastated Europe's economies, unsettled colonial institutions, and thus contributed to the decolonization of long-standing colonies such as India and Indonesia. Still, the colonial empires did not just disappear. As late as 1951, the colonies and trusteeships of the five major European powers—Belgium, France, the Netherlands, Portugal, and the United Kingdom—numbered eighty-five separate territorial units. Those units covered 8.9 million square miles and held more than 170 million people.[6] How and why?

The traditional narrative of American exceptionalism implies that the United States—supposedly anti-imperial in character, given its exceptional history of anticolonial revolution and democratic development—pushed European powers to decolonize their empires. After all, Sumner Welles had declared that "the age of imperialism had ended" in 1942. In January of 1941, President Franklin D. Roosevelt articulated lofty anticolonial principles in his "Four Freedoms" speech, speaking of a new world order portending the United Nations.[7] Yet part of the reason why the colonial empires were still alive and well in 1951 was because of U.S. support rather than in spite of it. Washington supported the European empires because they provided economic benefits. As the business sector and policy makers repeatedly stressed, the best way for the United States to get new markets and materials was not by dismantling the existing imperial systems but by sustaining and tapping them. In the eyes of policy makers and business elites, the colonial world was critical for supplying the ever-increasing demand for various raw materials.[8] Analysts noted in the 1940s that the United States had been "the greatest ultimate consumer of colonial products."[9] Later strategists in Washington repeatedly insisted that Africa and other colonized regions of the world were vital for maintaining America's supply of minerals, metals, oil, and other raw materials.[10] The conclusion was that, to keep the supply incoming and in hopes of finding markets for American products, the United States should support European colonial structures. European rule, stressed a State Department report in 1950, offered "political and economic stability." As long as U.S. capital was afforded "equal treatment," America's "economic goals . . . should be achieved through coordination and cooperation with the colonial powers."[11] In 1953, Undersecretary of State Henry Byroade added that supporting Europe's empires would also serve to maintain Europe's economy (and so ultimately America's economy too). Therefore, "the granting of complete freedom to those who were not yet ready for it would serve the best interests neither of the U.S. nor the free world as a whole."[12]

By the time Byroade had made his point in 1953, the American state had already put its strategy of supporting the European empires into action. Decidedly retreating from Welles's and Roosevelt's anti-imperial rhetoric, the U.S. state pushed the European empires to open their doors to North American interests and in exchange offered to help keep those empires intact by providing financial aid. Such aid was sorely needed due to the devastation of the war. Without funds, Europe's empires would collapse. And the American state decided to provide them.[13] The Marshall Plan was aimed at helping Europe recover from the devastation of the war. But parts of that plan, carried out by the Economic Cooperation Administration (ECA), were also aimed at helping the European empires reassert themselves. In the 1950s, the ECA sent approximately 7.5 billion dollars to European empires, with the French and British colonial empires receiving approximately 6.5 billion and the Portuguese, Belgian, and Netherlands empires receiving the rest.[14]

In this way, Europe's postwar economies could be restored through continued colonialism. John Orchard, chairman of the ECA Advisory Committee on Underdeveloped Areas, explained that the program would help to reduce the "dollar gap" while also providing Europe with "increased supplies of essential commodities" and "wider markets for European factories."[15] In other words, the program would help restore the imperial economic relations between Europe and its colonies that had been disrupted by the war. At the same time, America would benefit. The United States would gain access to the colonies, which would "supply additional raw materials for our factories and foodstuffs to supplement our agricultural production" and provide markets in the colonial world. It would further increase Europe's own purchasing power, enabling an economic recovery that would be open to new products from across the Atlantic.[16] For these reasons and others, the State Department conceded in 1950, "[T]he colonial relationship [between Europe and its dependencies] . . . is still in many places useful and necessary."[17]

Postwar economics was only one string entangling the United States and the European empires together in mutual support. The other was security and defense, which became increasingly critical after 1947 when the Cold War intensified. One goal here was funding Europe's empires so that they could be used as defensive bulwarks against rival powers. As a State Department memo in 1952 explained, the United States must "rely upon the colonial powers of Western Europe to make an addition to American strength sufficient to deter and to hold in check the tremendous military power of the Soviet armies."[18]

The United States therefore supported and gave aid to the French military in Indochina and the Dutch in Indonesia. And America's support of the French military effort in Indochina in the late 1940s, which was covering 80 percent of French military costs by the early 1950s, was not only aimed at stopping Vietnamese communists from taking over the country but also at strengthening Britain's position in Malaysia against the spread of communism.[19] Likewise, in the mid-1950s, the United States relied on the long-established British presence in key areas like the Middle East as a bulwark against Soviet expansion, not least against expansion over the region's vital oil.[20] To stop dominoes from falling, the American state simply propped up the European empires against them. George Kennan of the State Department's Policy-Planning staff later declared, "The dissolution of the [British] empire was not in our interest as there were many things the Commonwealth could do which we could not do and which we wished them to continue doing."[21] Senator Henry Cabot Lodge Jr. told the Senate at its hearings on the North Atlantic Treaty, "[W]e need . . . these countries to be strong, and they cannot be strong without their colonies."[22]

Supporting Europe's empires was also important for America's own military base system. Prior to World War II, the United States had only a small network of military installations, with overseas bases only in its own colonies (e.g., the Philippines, Hawaii, and Puerto Rico).[23] By the end of war, however, military strategists planned for an extensive worldwide network of security. The war had already brought American forces to the far ends of the earth. But how to keep them there? Military advisers and policy planners in the executive branch landed on an easy answer: use the territorial domains already established by European colonialism.

The strategy had already begun in 1941 when the United States lent England war supplies in exchange for ninety-nine-year leases establishing military bases in the Britain's Caribbean colonies. After the war, the process continued: the United States gave loans so that Britain could reestablish its overseas empire after the war; in exchange the United States was granted the use of any and all of Britain's overseas colonies for military bases or transport nodes.[24] The United

States made similar arrangements with the French, especially in their northern African colonies. Rather than attempting to undo French colonial control, it became U.S. policy to support it financially because, as the Bureau of Near Eastern, South Asian, and African Affairs determined, French control provided "stability, even though such stability is obtained largely through repression."[25]

This stability would be important for halting future Soviet aggression and also for allowing the United States to maintain its own military presence in the region. An agreement with France in 1950, for instance, enabled Washington to construct five new air bases in Morocco for the Strategic Air Command while letting France maintain its own flag.[26] Even though "imperialism of the old school is practiced" in North Africa, concluded the State Department, "there is one favorable factor, that of U.S. strategic interests, since we are in a position to use this area in time of war."[27] Similarly, the United States was allowed by Portugal to set up an air base in the Azores but only if Washington supported Portugal's bid to reassert itself over East Timor. (That air base, at Lajes, would later stand as the vital ground for U.S. airlift missions to Israel during the Yom Kippur War of 1973.)

In the end, the United States was able to create its vast network of global military power by relying on rather than dismantling European colonialism. Out of the thirty-nine territories in Central America, the Caribbean, Africa, Asia, and the Pacific wherein the United States maintained the most troops from 1950 to 1960, eight were U.S. colonies (excluding Japan, which Washington ruled temporarily after World War II) and twenty more were colonies or protectorates of European countries.[28] A secret memo circulated in the State Department in 1950 stated that "the security interests of the U.S. at the present time will best be served by a policy of support for the Western Colonial Powers."[29]

REPUTATION AND EMPIRE

For at least a decade and a half after World War II, the American state did not rise like a phoenix from the flames of the European empires; it rather rode wing to wing with them in mutual support and interaction. But did not the United States *eventually* take an anticolonial stand and drop its support of the European empires? And did not the United States eventually construct its own imperial network of power, which took over where Europe's empires left off? The answer to both question is yes. But the reality of why and how these processes unfolded betrays any tale of valiant American anticolonialism and benevolent American agency.

To begin we must recognize the profound shift in the global political climate in the mid–twentieth century. That shift has to do the proliferation of anticolonial nationalism, and its associated principles of self-determination, around the globe. The earliest stirrings of anticolonial nationalism in the nonwhite world were already seen in the Indian National Congress (1885), the Islamic revival movements in the Middle East (beginning in the late nineteenth century), the Philippine Revolution against Spain (1896), and the Pan-African Congress (1900). The Japanese victory over Russia (1905) and the Xinhai Revolution in China (1911) added fuel to that fire, signifying to the colonial world that nonwhite peoples could determine their own destinies.[30] Seizing on this global development, V. I. Lenin joined the chorus, articulating anti-imperial rhetoric and calling for self-determination of all peoples.[31] It was in fact Lenin's discourse that compelled U.S. President Woodrow Wilson to add pronouncements on self-determination to his Fourteen Points. Rather than the originator of anticolonial nationalism, Wilson was just trying to keep up.[32]

The period between the world wars was a critical turning point. Wilson had received requests for aid from anticolonial nationalists around the world, but as he did nothing to help, disappointment if not ire resulted.[33] And imperial boundaries existing before World War I were reinscribed rather than dismantled in the postwar negotiations, much to the further disappointment of anticolonial nationalists. In India, Ghandian populism rose during the 1920s and, given a new global press and literate colonized elites, Ghandi's anticolonial stance received widespread attention in the colonial world. At the Fifth Pan-American Conference at Santiago Chile in 1923, Latin Americans joined the chorus, in this case charging the United States with imperialism for intervening in the Dominican Republic and Haiti.[34] The 1930s Depression then laid the socioeconomic conditions for protests across Asia, Africa, and the Caribbean. World War II helped hasten the trend. It weakened colonial structures, armed colonized peoples, and raised questions about the strength of European empires and their future viability.[35] After the war, anticolonial nationalism continued to spread. In 1951, the General Assembly of the United Nations offered a palpable marker for the end of the imperial age. It voted for a review of the UN system of territorial administration of mandates and for a statement to be inserted into covenants that "all peoples shall have the right of self-determination." The U.S. delegate voted against this measure.[36]

The emergence and proliferation of anticolonialism significantly altered the global landscape. Foremost, it became a powerful mobilizing device, making possible new coalitions and political formations. As a symbol, anticolonial nationalism and its principle of universal self-determination mobilized disparate groups within and across imperial space. Tribes or religious sectarians could unite on national grounds whereas they might not have before. And colonized peoples from different countries could find common cause. Italy's attempt to recolonize Ethiopia in 1935, for instance, was met with protests around the world—from Harlem to British Guiana—prompting one scholar to call it the "first of instance of a Third World-wide reaction to an instance of Western intervention."[37]

The spread of anticolonial nationalism is critical for our story. To be sure, it did not go unnoticed by the imperial powers. In 1952, the British Foreign Office prepared a memorandum on "The Problem of Nationalism" that circulated in Winston Churchill's cabinet. The memo warned of the "dangers inherent in the present upsurge of nationalism" around the world and in Britain's colonies and was especially concerned about the "intersections" of "Asian nationalism" and nationalism in "the Near East and Africa."[38] Such nationalism thus became a potent tool with which to accrue political support, and it thereby shifted the cultural terrain of geopolitical competition. The Soviet Union, for instance, tried to use it as symbolic capital. This effort had begun during World War I with Lenin's anti-imperial rhetoric, prompting Wilson, as mentioned earlier, to declare his support for self-determination. But as anticolonialists mobilized further during and after World War II, and as the Cold War heightened between 1947 and 1951, officials in Washington became increasingly worried that the Soviet Union would penetrate anticolonial nationalist movements and use this new powerful discourse for its own ends. A 1950 policy paper from the Bureau of Near Eastern, South Asian, and African Affairs assessed the situation in Africa.

> While Communism has made very little headway in most of Africa, European nations and the United States have become alert to the danger of militant Communism penetrating the area. The USSR has sought within the United Nations and outside to play the role of the champion of the colonial peoples of the world. While the greater portion of the areas of Africa have as yet no firm nationalist aspirations, there are certain areas such as French North Africa and British West Africa where the spirit of nationalism is increasing. The USSR has sought to gain the sympathy of nationalist elements.[39]

Due to the proliferation and dominance of anticolonial nationalism, the American state reconsidered its initial strategy of imperial outsourcing. When and where nationalism was perceived as relatively well developed, the United States came to dissuade the continuance of European colonialism. This approach was most clearly articulated in a series of policy papers in the State Department that reconsidered policy toward dependent areas of the world. The conclusion was that continued support of European powers would be fruitless, for strong anticolonial nationalist movements would effectively overthrow them and create instability and disorder.[40] More worrisome, it would damage America's "reputation" and push nationalist forces toward the Soviet Union. Of particular concern was Soviet "propaganda" in the colonial world that played on anticolonial sentiment: this would portray the United States as an imperialist and win over nationalists to the Soviets. Strategists in Washington therefore insisted that the United States would have to disavow its alliance with the European empires.[41]

This strategy was clearly stated in a famous 1952 State Department paper identifying the "General Objectives of U.S. Policy Toward Colonial Areas." It stated that America's main objective was to "favor the progressive development of all dependent peoples toward the goal of self-government."[42] The reason was that

> substantial advocates toward self-government have been made in a number of territories and more than 500 million people have achieved independence. Nationalist movements are gaining strength in non-self-governing territories throughout the world. United States policy must be based on the general assumption that nationalism in colonial areas is a force which cannot be stopped but may, with wisdom, be guided. . . . It is clearly in the interest of the United States to give appropriate encouragement to those movements which are non-communist and democratic in character. [This would] contribute toward the building of colonial areas into bulwarks against the spread of communism. The very fact of a demonstrated United States interest in democratic nationalist movements will strengthen the hand of these groups against their communist counterparts.[43]

American policy, therefore, should "seek the alignment with the democratic world of dependent peoples and those achieving self-government or independence; in particular to maintain and strengthen their friendship and respect for the United States. The importance of this objective is clear in view of the Soviet Union's obvious bid for the sympathies of colonial peoples."[44]

The fear that nationalism might lead to communism was clear in President Dwight D. Eisenhower's response to the Suez Crisis in 1956. The decision by Egyptian President Gamal Abdel Nasser to nationalize the Suez Canal threatened British and French interests, thereby summoning an Anglo-French invasion of Egypt (with Israel mounting a separate assault). The United States had strategic stakes in the Canal, too, but the Eisenhower administration condemned the invasion rather than supporting it exactly because it feared that the incursion would result in a nationalist and communist blowback throughout the region and across the colonial world.[45]

We see this same concern throughout the period after World War II, first in areas where nationalism developed earliest and was the most potent. In those areas, including India and Malaysia, the United States encouraged European powers to take concrete and well-publicized steps toward self-government. Similarly, the administration of President John F. Kennedy later pressured Portugal to decolonize its African colonies in the hopes that this would take some of the fire away from the communist movement (even though this would reverse the U.S. position as the importance of the American base in the Azores had made itself more clear in the wake of the Berlin crisis).[46] The United States also stopped supporting French suppression of colonial nationalists in Vietnam and Dutch rule in Indonesia, though only when anticolonial forces had proven far too resistant to repression or when anticolonial nationalists waved anti-Soviet banners.[47] One State Department official summarized the strategy for Vietnam simply enough. Suggesting that the United States end its support of French rule given the outpouring of anticolonial sentiment, he asked rhetorically, "Whether the French like it or not, independence is coming to Indochina. Why, therefore, do we tie ourselves to the tail of their battered kite?"[48]

CONCLUSION

In the end, not only did anticolonial nationalism's power compel the American state to reconsider imperial outsourcing. It likewise compelled Washington to shift its imperial tactics toward informal modes of influence. A famous National Security Council report stated it boldly. Noting the staggering development of nationalist consciousness in Southeast Asia, the council concluded simply that "nineteenth century imperialism is no longer a practicable system in SEA [Southeast Asia]."[49] In other words, to replace colonialism in an age of anticolonial urgency and competing Soviet bids for sympathy, the most the American state could do was turn to hidden tactics of informal empire for now nominally independent nations—propping up subordinate elites (aka clients) or covertly manipulating outcomes.

A memo by the U.S. consul general at Leopoldville, Congo, in 1957 is suggestive. First, he wrote that the United States should stop supporting European colonialism lest Africans turn to the Soviets: "Now that the issue of 'colonialism' is being moved front and center by the Soviets the essential thing it seems to me *is that we free ourselves from the vice.* . . . The U.S. should stand for freedom from all forms of oppression, for self-government, and for independence based upon self-determination." Second, he suggested that the United States should maintain influence in the region not through the colonial powers but through financial aid. In other words, rather than arouse the indignation of anticolonial nationalists, the United States should "maneuver . . . by abolishing the vestiges of the 'older' imperialism" and replacing them with new forms of influence such as direct economic support.[50] Only a few years later such a "maneuver" was indeed made in the Congo, but it did not involve economic support, nor was it a peaceful process. It involved the CIA, bribery, and a coup. In effect, Washington stopped supporting the Belgians only to replace them with a man named Joseph Mobutu who would then become a classic U.S. subordinate elite, for decades presiding over a brutal authoritarian regime in the Congo while doing America's bidding.

This pattern would be repeated throughout the disintegrating colonial world: the United States turned away from the colonial empires only to deploy in their place new mechanisms of power. Since European colonial rule was no longer tenable, and since a new round of colonization by Washington would face the ire of nationalists, the United States was constrained to outsource imperial functions locally. It thereby created a vast new imperial network based on clients, bribes, and bases rather than colonies. This was indeed an imperial transition. It was a succession from colonialism to informal rule, and from European metropoles to Washington, D.C. But this was not always if ever an easy process brought about by valiant U.S. agency. Nor was it a reflection of America's ostensibly democratic national character. It was an often violent process that was unleashed as a pragmatic American state sought to contain and channel the power of anticolonial nationalism around the world.

Cold War Transition

Europe's Decolonization and Eisenhower's
System of Subordinate Elites

BRETT REILLY

AT THE AMERICAN BAR ASSOCIATION's diamond jubilee in August 1953, Secretary of State John Foster Dulles delivered the keynote address juxtaposing 1872, the year of the association's founding, with 1953. "Because we are a principal source of free-world strength," he explained, "we face the intense hostility of the Soviet-dominated world." We would not, Dulles continued, "want to have to depend on our own unaided strength," so winning allies and finding means "to bind them to us and us to them in dependable ways is . . . an essential aspect of United States foreign policy."[1]

Within these sparse comments, Dulles indicated a major feature of U.S. strategy during the Cold War—an effort to create and control a global nexus of voluntary allies and subordinate elites within its "Free World" sphere. This policy emerged from practice and exigency as much as it did from design, developing slowly from 1953 to 1961 until it became a self-conscious strategy for the exercise of global power. From the vantage point of hindsight, we can see, within the Eisenhower administration's dealings with developing nations, tactics of local control similar to those that European colonial empires had employed for over a century.

During President Dwight D. Eisenhower's eight years in office, Europe's rapid decolonization and the Cold War's deepening tensions converged, compelling Washington to develop a new strategy for global control. While Harry S. Truman's presidency had faced similar problems, these pressures converged on a global scale only after 1953, when Europe's slow imperial retreat coincided with a spreading Cold War conflict. Amid the bipolar division between communist and capitalist blocs, the end of colonial rule unleashed new nations, leaders, and problems that represented serious threats to international stability. Illustrating these changing global conditions, the number of member nations in the United Nations increased from 60 in 1952 to 122 in 1966—a doubling of the world's sovereign states in just fourteen years.[2] These are not mere numbers, but rather indices of a fundamental reordering of geopolitics that required a radical adjustment by the major powers. Reflecting this change, in his first three years in office Dulles visited thirty-two heads of state, becoming the first U.S. secretary of state to travel to the Middle East, South Asia, Southeast Asia, and East Asia.[3]

To meet the challenge of this fast-changing world, the Eisenhower administration adopted a global policy of U.S. power projection through overseas military bases, formal military alliances, forceful diplomacy, covert operations, and foreign aid. The "leasehold empire" of military bases doubled in size in less than two decades, from 582 to 1,014 installations, offering security, monetary assistance, and protection to recipient countries, all while expanding the ambit of Washington's global reach.[4] Washington also sent military advisors abroad, training three hundred thousand foreign soldiers between 1946 and 1970.[5] Through strategic use of U.S. foreign aid, the monetary assistance of the International Monetary Fund, and the World Bank's development loans, American leaders held ample economic means for global control.

Institutionally, the president and his secretary of state sought to develop a comprehensive global strategy by revamping the U.S. National Security Council (NSC) and its Planning Board to develop broad recommendations that were translated into specific actions by the Operations Coordinating Board. Meeting an unprecedented 366 times in eight years, Eisenhower's NSC operated, according to one scholarly analysis, as "a rigorously analytical national security team."[6] Such an assessment of Dulles and Eisenhower's decision making must be tempered by an awareness that their analytical framework, while rigorous in a sense, also divided the leaders and countries of decolonizing Asia and Africa into a simple binary, free world versus communist.

National Leaders as Subordinate Elites

From 1952 to 1960, the NSC and State Department surveyed the global landscape, moving from country to country, continent to continent, identifying threats to American power and frequently prescribing the manipulation of national leaders, the so-called subordinate elites, as the solution to these problems. Indeed, the U.S. diplomatic documents of this period are peppered with the names of national leaders who seem to be the focus of American attention. In Asia, Secretary Dulles sought to make Philippine president Ramon Magsaysay a "dynamic symbol [of the] free world cause in Southeast Asia," capable of unifying that region's decolonizing nations under a pro-Western banner.[7] In Europe, the council awarded economic and military aid to "Tito's Yugoslavia," thereby building a bilateral relationship that was of "vital importance" in damaging the Soviet Union's hold on other bloc states.[8] Surveying Africa and the Middle East, Washington concluded by 1956 that Egyptian president Gamal Abdel Nasser was "not a leader with whom it will be possible to enter into friendly arrangements" and that the United States "should lose no time in implementing policies designed to reduce . . . Nasser as a force" in the region.[9] Closer to home, in Latin America the administration agreed that "the Castro regime is a threat to our security interests and the achievement of our objectives in Latin America . . . [so] consequently we seek a change in Cuba."[10] In general the NSC was concerned that many countries remained weakly committed or uncommitted to the United States, notably in former colonial areas where "the general unreliability of the governments of these states" had "complicate[d] the task of building firm ties with them." Improving this situation would require, as the NSC noted, working with local leaders to create "strong, independent, and self supporting groupings of nations, friendly to the United States" in Asia and the Middle East.[11]

When the Eisenhower administration wielded its diplomacy and military power, it defaulted to methods similar to British imperial policies of formal and informal control.[12] In their influential 1953 essay, historians Ronald Robinson and John Gallagher argued that the informal empire of the Victorian age existed insofar as "economic dependence and mutual good-feeling" could keep the local governments "bound to Britain while still using them as agents for further British expansion." Whenever "there was fear of a foreign challenge to British supremacy . . . imperial authorities intervened directly to secure their interests."[13] Washington followed a similar path, dispensing economic and military assistance to advance its strategic interests. But when these methods failed, the Eisenhower administration intervened directly, notably with the Central Intelligence Agency (CIA) in Iran in 1954 and the U.S. Marines in Lebanon in 1958. Invoking this parallel, historian Wm. Roger Louis has argued that British empire builders of Victoria's era "would have recognized the methods of post World War II Americans."[14] Within this British system, as Robinson noted in a later essay, subordinate elites served as the critical means for the exercise of informal influence. European imperialists could only operate in foreign lands if they could use their wealth, prestige, and military power to effect "mutual interest and interdependence" between themselves and "collaborating elites," which were usually a faction of indigenous leadership capable of translating foreign power into local political leverage. Hence, Robinson posited, "[I]mperialism was as much a function of its victims' collaboration or non-collaboration . . . as it was of European expansion."[15]

Just as cultivation and control of local allies proved vital to European imperialism in the nineteenth century, so they would prove key adjuncts of U.S. global power in the "American Century." The British Empire did not operate primarily by means of its military power, which was limited, but through local conduits that made "collaboration, rather than marginalization . . . the prevailing mode of management."[16] Thus, the British allied themselves with the sultans of Malaya, the French with the Vietnamese Nguyen emperors, and the Dutch with local aristocrats in the East Indies. Gregory Barton's essay in this volume explains how Britain's ability to cultivate subordinate elites provided "the key to informal empire" in Siam and beyond. Conversely, following World War II, when Britain failed "to build alliances with emergent elites through economic and military aid" in the Middle East, the region passed into Washington's orbit after American officials successfully "cultivated Arab autocrats, whether monarchs or military, as reliable subordinate elites." Thus, beginning with Eisenhower, the U.S. cultivation of national leaders as its subordinate elites "built an effective mechanism of control that would persist for another half-century."[17]

Eisenhower and Dulles were not scholars of dying empires but strategists seeking a policy to lead them through this tempestuous confluence of decolonization and Cold War conflict. Through close collaboration with their imperial allies, their own deductions, and their immersion in a succession of crises from Indochina to Suez, they developed new networks of subordinate elites to exercise leadership over a vast global bloc they termed the Free World. Unlike the centralized Soviet Comintern, the Eisenhower administration's mechanism of control was a diffuse array of national, bilateral, and multilateral agencies. By 1957, this system was so fully developed that the administration could reject an elaborate proposal from the Pentagon chief, Admiral Arthur W. Radford, "to create echelons of indigenous leadership" through an "indigenous training program" that would identify potential leaders worldwide—in Southeast Asia, South America, Africa, and the Middle East—for indoctrination into "Militant Liberty." In a terse rebuff, the NSC replied that "*existing* mechanisms are perfectly competent" to achieve this goal.[18]

Indeed, the mechanisms that allowed the exercise of American global power from Latin America to Asia were marked by five defining facets: selection, contingency, maintenance, change, and catastrophe. First, American envoys engaged, sometimes in conjunction with European empires, in the active selection of promising leaders for newly emerging nations. The Eisenhower administration approached this task with a decidedly militarized focus, increasing the number of officers trained from strategically significant countries. This shift was reflected in the U.S. Command and General Staff College's admissions of foreign military leaders, which rose sharply from just 38 graduates from twenty-four countries in 1951 to 170 graduates representing forty-five nations in 1959. In countries likely to experience military coups, Washington would develop "systemic, continuing relationships" with key officers and, as Eisenhower believed, thereby gain a unique ability to "orient the potential leaders in a pro-Western" direction.[19]

Second, beyond the sword, American policy makers recognized education as a potent source of political influence, attempting to use training of civil as well as military officials to cultivate leaders in areas where U.S. influence was weak.

To gain leverage over Southeast Asia's new nations, in 1955 the NSC's Operations Coordinating Board (OCB) argued for an expansion of education programs in the Philippines, which would serve as "an important means of assuring that the Filipinos in the future will hold ideas and objectives compatible with those which we hold." In the board's analysis, Manila's universities could operate as a regional education center, which would "extend Philippine influence" and, given the historically close relationship, "theoretically American influence" as well.[20]

Third, complementing their initial selection of local leaders, U.S. planners cultivated contingency elites—opposition figures, rising politicians, and military officers—they could employ to counterbalance or replace an undesirable leader. In support of this strategy, Washington attempted to dispense its economic,

The U.S. perspective on its subordinate elites, showing U.S. president Lyndon Johnson (*far right*) towering above his loyal Asian allies (*left to right*) Australian prime minister Harold Holt, South Korean president Park Chung Hee, Philippine president Ferdinand Marcos, New Zealand prime minister Keith Holyoake, South Vietnamese president Nguyen Van Thieu, and Thai Prime Minister Thanom Kittikachorn at the Manila Conference of the Southeast Asia Treaty Organization (SEATO) on the Vietnam War, October 24, 1966. (LBJ Library, photo by Frank Wolfe)

political, and military aid to develop or enhance a local ally's political influence. By 1958, the NSC's members determined that military aid was "the most readily available means and, in a pragmatic sense, the best means" to assure U.S. interests in foreign countries.[21] For this mechanism to remain responsive to changing political conditions, U.S. aid had to be appropriated without irrevocably identifying Washington with a particular leader, thus preserving, as the OCB concluded, "the possibility of under-cutting former free world leaders if they are not amenable to American suggested reforms."[22] Moreover, maintenance of an ally's power also came through economic aid or political influence that could build local support. Hence, a year before the 1957 Philippines general election, the Eisenhower administration instructed its Manila embassy that "care should be taken" in concluding political agreements "to avoid giving the impression the action was 'obtained' by any individual Filipino unless U.S. objectives would be furthered directly by giving such credit."[23] But allies, as we will see, often proved to be more adept at extracting greater autonomy or concessions than U.S. policy makers envisioned.

Fourth, this system showed a willingness to use means fair and foul to change subordinate elites—whether through diplomatic influence or CIA covert operations—if they proved too intractable or lost their credibility as a viable anticommunist ally. During Eisenhower's eight years in office, the CIA promoted coups and covert operations to alter the balance of local power in Central America (Guatemala), the Middle East (Iran, Iraq, Lebanon, Syria), and Asia (Korea, the Philippines, Vietnam, Tibet, Indonesia). In total, the Eisenhower administration initiated 170 major CIA operations, a number only surpassed by his successor, John F. Kennedy, who "launched 163 major covert operations" in less than three years.[24]

Finally, U.S. policy makers, recognizing the importance of local assets, developed management systems to retain global influence in the event of a Soviet invasion or hostile regime change in a strategic country. Most prominently, the NSC created the Inter-Agency Evacuation Committee to compile lists of "public or political leaders of established stature or promising potential who would be especially useful to the U.S. in the establishment of governments." If communists invaded or subverted any of the thirty-eight countries listed in the committee's plans for 1958, the U.S. military and CIA would evacuate, abduct, or somehow "deny" these "key indigenous persons" to the Soviet bloc. Further, the United States worked within the North Atlantic Treaty Organization (NATO) to expand Operation Gladio, a network of clandestine stay-behind armies and leaders designed to foment an insurgency in the event that Western Europe fell under communist rule.[25]

However, this American system of influence had inherent limits. Through alliances founded ultimately on the promise of democracy and development, U.S.

policymakers had devised a system of control that ceded, through disbursement of foreign aid and military assistance, the means for its allies to achieve greater autonomy. During the last half of the twentieth century, formerly subordinate allies across the globe would gain new capacities and build the internal stability that American strategists had originally hoped for, but, in the process, become less dependent upon access to U.S. aid or markets, allowing national leaders in Asia, Europe, and Latin America the independence to implement policies that often contravened Washington's priorities. As the South Korean case shows with striking clarity, this American system of global control would thus prove, like the British before it, "a self-liquidating concern."

To explore the character of this American system of subordinate elites in its most dominant form, two case studies, South Korea and South Vietnam, reveal the broad outlines of this evolving system of global management. As Cold War tensions increased, the western edge of the Pacific Rim became a hotly contested arena. The victory of the People's Republic of China, the division of the Korean Peninsula, and the escalation of France's colonial war in Indochina transformed Asia into a flashpoint of global conflict, placing, as the OCB observed in 1954, "a premium on nationalist leaders" in Vietnam.[26] Accordingly, South Korea and South Vietnam became not only major Cold War battlegrounds, but critical proving grounds for Washington's strategy of global control via subordinate elites.

South Korea

The Republic of Korea (ROK), also known as South Korea, provides an exemplary case for full-spectrum application of U.S. global power and the place of subordinate elites within this system. After the Korean War armistice in 1953, the Eisenhower administration maintained the U.S. position on the peninsula by providing Syngman Rhee's regime with 2.6 billion dollars in economic assistance and 1.8 billion in military aid.[27] Moreover, Washington stationed two U.S. Army divisions at the thirty-eighth parallel, supported by over two dozen military installations, and trained over seven thousand South Korean officers at military schools in the United States from 1950 to 1957.[28]

At the close of World War II, Syngman Rhee's reputation as a Korean patriot and staunch anticommunist had helped him win Washington's backing, particularly among more aggressive American officials. During nearly four decades spent living in the United States, Rhee had cultivated valuable relationships with U.S. officials and established himself as an attractive ally who, as the Office of Strategic Services (OSS) believed, harbored "more of the American point of view than other Korean leaders."[29] Indeed, Rhee frequently proclaimed that he ascribed to "Jeffersonian democratic" values.[30] At the outset of the postwar U.S. occupation of Korea, two of the most influential American officials in East Asia, Douglas McArthur and John R. Hodge, saw an advantage in working through a man like

Rhee and, over the State Department's objections, collaborated with the OSS to expedite his return to Korea before other prominent exiles.

Although Rhee soon established himself through force of personality and his own connections as the central figure in the early ROK, he remained highly dependent on U.S. support until the Korean War changed the dynamics of power. When Rhee attempted to postpone the 1950 spring elections, Secretary of State Dean Acheson threatened to withdraw American aid if there were any delay. Rhee quickly reversed course and went ahead with the elections. But when Rhee engaged in blatant intimidation during the 1953 presidential campaign, Washington found that, with vast resources committed to the Korean War, its influence was severely circumscribed. Rhee arrested opponents, telling the U.S. embassy to "keep out of this . . . it was not its business."[31]

Eisenhower and Dulles's determination to end the Korean War brought both concessions to the ROK government and contingency plans to remove Rhee if he attempted to disrupt the armistice. In the summer of 1953, the Korean president displayed his volatility, releasing twenty-five thousand North Korean prisoners of war, an act that threatened to end the peace negotiations. Incensed, Eisenhower spoke of withdrawing from Korea, but Dulles's opinion held sway. The NSC agreed that "we must take the strongest possible line with Rhee so that he will not imagine that he can actually run the show."[32] To ensure that Rhee could be controlled, Eisenhower signed a Mutual Defense Treaty with South Korea, which Rhee had in fact demanded, that gave the United States operational control of the ROK army. Moreover, the administration developed a contingency plan for toppling the Korean government. In the event that Rhee attempted to resume hostilities with North Korea, the U.S. Eighth Army's commander would initiate Operation Ever Ready with provisions to "secure custody of dissident military and civilian leaders . . . withdraw recognition of the Rhee government . . . initiate an anti-Rhee publicity campaign . . . [and] proclaim martial law."[33]

Despite these difficulties, American officials recognized that as long as they maintained a qualified control over the Korean president, he would be a useful ally. Certainly, U.S. officials knew there were far worse alternatives. When the NSC considered France's needs in Vietnam, one of the meeting's principals opined, "I hate to admit this because he's a real S.O.B., but what they need there is a Rhee."[34] As the Cold War came to Asia, such allies were increasingly advantageous, offering strong but conditional support for U.S. policies. When Britain refused to endorse a militant anticommunist position on Indochina in 1954, Dulles excoriated Britain's foreign secretary, Anthony Eden, telling him that the United States was thinking about "going it alone . . . [and] this would probably mean increasing the close relations with Syngman Rhee and Chiang Kai-shek, who, whatever their defects, were at least willing to stand strong against the Communists."[35]

While Operation Ever Ready provided the means to control Korea in the event of an emergency, Washington needed more immediate instruments to influence Seoul's government. Unwilling to force Rhee from the presidency, the U.S. embassy cultivated strategic allies within the Korean bureaucracy. By the late 1950s, according to a former American diplomat, the embassy had, in effect, installed "control knobs at almost all important points of Korean polity" and "devised many techniques for quietly influencing legislators and ROKG[overn-ment] executive branch." Furthermore, the 1953 Mutual Defense Treaty gave the United States the power of approval over all major South Korean military appointments, assuring that any significant command in the ROK army was staffed by a Korean officer whom the U.S. military had deemed acceptable.[36] Before mass demonstrations forced Rhee from office in 1960, these relationships and over 4.3 billion dollars in U.S. aid kept his regime within the bounds that Washington deemed acceptable.

Consequently, the sudden, unplanned regime change presented a major chal-lenge to U.S. foreign policy. After Rhee's ouster in 1960, the democratically elected Chang Myon government came to power, which was both pro-American and quite weak. When the Korean military launched a coup in 1961, General Carter Magruder, commander of U.S. and UN forces in Korea, quickly agreed to give General Park Chung Hee, the coup group's "strongman," an assurance that he would not interfere.[37] The main hurdle to U.S. support was cleared after the CIA reviewed its records and "consulted with one of its best sources" to confirm that Park was not a communist. From the summer of 1960 on, the U.S. embassy would, Washington instructed, "work with Pa[r]k, manifesting our support for him as basis to influence his courses of action along lines acceptable to us."[38] Accordingly, just months after overthrowing a democratically elected govern-ment, General Park was honored with an official state visit to Washington.

Even after endorsing Park's rule, the State Department still tried to check his authority, revealing the importance Washington placed on ensuring the compli-ance of local allies and the cultivation of alternatives. As Park was planning a shift to civilian rule in July 1963, U.S. ambassador Samuel Berger began "to work more closely with opposition elements, especially those which we believe are best suited to our purpose and *most responsive to our guidance* . . . to try to help create opposition to which we can turn as an alternative to junta in any situation that may develop. An opposition is needed . . . [and] our influence should be brought to bear as appropriate in order to help in its *formation* and *survival*." Upset by Park's dictatorial style and intransigence in the face of U.S. suggestions, Berger recommended encouraging American journalists to publish articles crit-ical of the ROK leadership.[39]

From 1953 to 1963, American policy makers thus sought, with varying degrees of success, to keep an anticommunist South Korea within Washington's global orbit and to shape the Republic's policies through the manipulation of its leaders. Yet only a year and a half after Berger called for measures to undermine him, President Park received a red-carpet welcome at the White House. By 1966, when the Korean government committed fifty thousand soldiers—under President Lyndon Johnson's "More Flags" program—to the U.S.-led counterinsurgency in South Vietnam, Park became Washington's most valuable ally in the war effort and, therefore, an indispensable foreign policy asset. Since Korea was "by ordinary standards in no position to play an important international role or to give economic or military assistance," American policy makers increased their foreign aid and enhanced the international prestige of South Korea's president—an effort marked by Park's two visits to Washington, visits by President Johnson and Vice President Hubert Humphrey to Seoul, and Park's attendance at the 1966 Manila Conference.[40]

Just a week after the Manila photo showing U.S. dominion over its subordinate elites (page 348), the South Korean perspective on the alliance was reflected in this poster at Seoul International Airport with a strong, forthright President Park Chung Hee, head noticeably higher than President Lyndon B. Johnson, whose downward glance seems weak and indecisive, October 31, 1966. (LBJ Library, photo by Frank Wolfe)

Behind the façade of this anticommunist alliance, Park extracted $4.6 billion in concessions tied to Vietnam that he used to finance Korea's rapid industrialization. While Park may have appeared the pawn in 1966, he was more the knight by 1968 when President Johnson visited Seoul. Beset by domestic political difficulties and economic problems from his mismanagement of the war economy, Johnson asked his once seemingly sycophantic ally to purchase $100 million in U.S. bonds. Noting that his own government's total budget was less than $1 billion, Park may well have surprised the American president by rejecting the proposal out of hand. In another exercise of this growing autonomy, Park proved aggressive about preserving his access in Washington when Johnson decided not to run for reelection. Preferring to deal with Hubert Humphrey, who had supported Seoul's second Vietnam troop deployment in 1966, Park donated "several hundred thousand dollars" to Humphrey's presidential campaign and, as discussed below, launched a parallel effort to buy the support of influential U.S. legislators.[41]

In another manifestation of the shift in this bilateral power balance, the Johnson and Nixon administrations, mindful of the Korean troops in Vietnam, acquiesced as Park tightened his authoritarian grip, culminating in the promulgation of the 1972 Yusin Constitution. Until the end of the Vietnam War, moreover, Washington concealed evidence of a scandal later known as "Koreagate." Beginning in 1968, Park initiated a program to ensure South Korea's interests in Washington by bribing dozens of U.S. congressmen, notably Richard T. Hanna, with cash payments up to $200,000. After Nixon announced the withdrawal of more U.S. troops from Korea in 1970, Park increased the scope of the bribery to ensure his continued influence beyond the end of the Vietnam War.[42] Though the United States played a central role in Park's emergence as South Korea's strongman—sanctioning his coup, legitimating his government, and providing his regime with an infusion of capital sufficient to spark the country's economic miracle—the relationship remained contingent. By the 1970s, as Nixon coordinated with China, Park moved to assert his autonomy, bribing congressmen, attempting to develop nuclear weapons, and continuing the state-led industrialization of the Korean economy. The economic concessions and political sacrifices of the Vietnam War effectively reduced American influence in Seoul and emboldened its regime to operate more assertively.

SOUTH VIETNAM

As the Korean War stalemated and France was forced to withdraw from Indochina, the Eisenhower administration inserted itself into the Vietnamese situation, sending 1.6 billion dollars in economic aid and another 650 million in military assistance during its eight-year term.[43] More directly, the Pentagon trained thousands of Vietnamese soldiers between 1954 and 1960, eventually sending 1,375 South Vietnamese officers annually to military schools in the United States.[44]

Diplomatically, Washington constructed the Southeast Asia Treaty Organization (SEATO) to offer its Saigon ally protection as a charter state to the treaty, thus counterbalancing the 1954 Geneva Accords' provision for the unification of North and South Vietnam. In this unilateral divided-nation strategy, the Eisenhower administration's success hinged on its chosen surrogate, Ngo Dinh Diem. During the transition from French to U.S. protection for South Vietnam, Diem soon consolidated his power, ruled as an autocrat for eight years, and then suffered a sudden downfall when he became insubordinate—a process that illustrates the importance of contingency elites in Washington's strategy.

When the United States began supplanting the French in Vietnam during the spring of 1954, Diem was still one contender among many for the country's leadership. His advantage was a reputation for patriotism and anticommunism, as well as contacts with notable U.S. leaders such as Cardinal Francis Spellman and Senator John F. Kennedy. By June 1954, Emperor Bao Dai had recognized that the French tide was receding and the American rising, and consequently he asked Diem to assume the premiership of Vietnam. As the emperor recalled in his memoirs, he chose Diem because he was "well-known to the Americans. . . . In their eyes, he was the man best suited for the job, and Washington would not be sparing in its support of him."[45]

Indeed, the transition from French to U.S. influence came soon after Diem arrived in Saigon. American authorities, notably CIA operative Edward Lansdale, began working with the new premier, courting support for him in both Saigon and Washington. By the fall, President Eisenhower had made plain his desire to supplant the French with a letter to Diem that established the U.S.–South Vietnam relationship. In recognizing Diem as "Chief of Government" and offering economic and military assistance contingent on "undertaking needed reforms" and the creation of a "viable state," Eisenhower's well-publicized letter served as notice of the selection of an ally.[46] Almost from the start, however, this alliance brought a long series of conflicts over exactly which "needed reforms" American officials could persuade Diem to adopt.

With U.S. advisers soon dissatisfied over Diem's unresponsiveness to guidance and the French increasingly upset over Diem's anticolonial attitude, Dulles agreed to consider removing the premier in late 1954 if the French could produce a suitable successor. After several months Washington demurred, concluding that France's candidates were too soft on communism and personally flawed.[47] But by the spring of 1955 U.S. advisers had grown increasingly frustrated when they found their "ability to influence Diem . . . limited," and the Eisenhower administration authorized the French to remove him. However, Lansdale, now a close confidant, warned Diem of the directive, prompting him to launch an attack on the rival political and military power center in Saigon, the Binh Xuyen police and paramilitary apparatus. The tactic succeeded. In a cable to Saigon dated April 27,

just hours after Diem launched his offensive, Secretary of State Dulles immediately canceled the orders, viewing the battle for Saigon as a turning point and
Diem "emerging [as] a hero" who had eliminated disruptive factions and consolidated his power.[48]

The 1955 battle for Saigon also consolidated support for Diem in Washington
that continued into the Kennedy administration. Diem's perceived importance
was so great in 1961 that Vice President Johnson proclaimed Diem "the Winston
Churchill of Southeast Asia." In pushing for closer relations, Johnson argued,
"Shit, man, he's the only boy we got out there."[49] But Diem's increasing authoritarianism and persecution of non-Catholics reversed the tide of opinion during
the Kennedy administration. By spring of 1963, the abuse of protesting Bud-
dhists, tumultuous riots, and self-immolation of bonzes combined with the corruption and callousness of Diem's inner circle to sap the regime's international
credibility. "No news picture in history," Kennedy said of the bonze Thich Quang
Duc's self-immolation, "has generated so much emotion around the world as
that one."[50] The Kennedy administration hardened its attitude quickly, sending
Henry Cabot Lodge to assume control of the embassy and, hopefully, to reel Diem
back in. Within weeks, however, Lodge's pessimistic dispatches and President
Kennedy's critical disposition set the course to replace this now insubordinate ally.

The forthcoming coup would employ contingency elites who were likewise
dissatisfied with the Diem regime. Roger Hilsman, assistant secretary of state for
Far Eastern affairs, responded to Ambassador Lodge's pessimistic August 1963
report with instructions of his own, approved by President Kennedy and Secretary of State Dean Rusk, directing the ambassador to identify "key military leaders" unhappy with Diem and inform them of Washington's concerns over the
current regime. Additionally, the cable tasked Lodge with examining "all possible
alternative leadership and mak[ing] detailed plans as to how we might bring
about Diem's replacement if this should become necessary."[51] For the next several months American support for regime change grew while Lodge managed the
interplay of actors, personally approving the meetings between the embassy's
military contact, army commander General Tran Van Don, and CIA operative
Lucien Conein. As the CIA's man in Saigon, Conein was an invaluable link to
the coup plotting among Army of the Republic of Vietnam (ARVN) generals,
employing his eighteen-year relationship with General Don to keep the embassy
apprised of plans being made by the group's leader, General Duong Van Minh.
If the general needed assistance, the embassy authorized Conein to deliver cash,
part of the Kennedy administration's "inducements (financial, political, or otherwise) to opportunists or recalcitrants" who would oppose Diem at the time of his
overthrow.[52]

While the Vietnamese generals planned, the administration in Washington
and its ambassador in Saigon worked to find a middle ground between control

of the incoming junta and plausible deniability. In assessing questions about "cutout and control" of the coup, National Security Advisor McGeorge Bundy cabled Lodge in late October to inform him that the White House could not direct the group and the "burden of proof" rested on the Vietnamese generals to develop a plan that would topple Diem quickly. If their plan met this burden, said Bundy, Washington would instruct Lodge to allow the coup; if their plans appeared unlikely to succeed, Lodge would discourage the coup; and if the generals went forward without Lodge's consent, the embassy would warn Diem of the impending attack and help defend him. Bundy reminded the ambassador that the hands-off management of this process was a perilous balancing act, since "a miscalculation could result in jeopardizing U.S. position in Southeast Asia."[53] When the coup came on November 1, 1963, such balance was lost as Ambassador Lodge rebuffed Diem's appeal for help and CIA operative Conein collaborated closely with the plotters.[54]

After deposing Diem and his brothers, the generals took control of the government, accomplishing the coup's short-term goals. As promised, Washington quickly extended recognition to the new regime and resumed the full array of U.S. aid programs. A hindsight judgment about the coup's advisability, or a "triumph forsaken," is irrelevant here.[55] Rather, we can see with surprising clarity a system of global-cum-local control that effected the removal of Diem through ties between U.S. officials and contingency elites inside the South Vietnamese military. Following the coup, the Kennedy White House could tell Congress— with a certain degree of truth—that the coup was a "Vietnamese affair."[56] Indeed, Washington's demand for plausible deniability had necessitated Diem's removal through independent Vietnamese action. Dissatisfied generals, cultivated partially through personal relationships, worked within, not at the behest of the American system of subordinate elites.

Returning to Robinson's argument about the indigenous foundations of European colonialism, we can see some parallels. Both Park's decision to deploy troops in Vietnam and Diem's defiance of Washington's advice in 1963 were instances of both "collaboration" and "noncollaboration" by subordinate elites within an expanding American imperium. Moreover, as Robinson argues for the British Empire, when economic and military assistance failed to maintain a reliable subordinate elite and threats to U.S. strategic interests loomed—as in Guatemala in 1954, Iran in 1954, and Lebanon in 1958—Washington often intervened directly.

Conclusion

Beginning in the early 1950s, volatile forces of decolonization and Cold War competition created a formidable challenge for American policy makers. Global power, once dispersed among a half dozen imperial powers, was now concentrated in just two competing blocs centered in Washington and Moscow. Moreover, dozens of new states were appearing on continents once controlled by a few European empires, necessitating a new strategy for global control that relied, in the main, on informal means. Employing mechanisms from foreign aid to covert operations, Eisenhower's system proved remarkably enduring through times of calm and crisis, building a free world bloc across Asia and Latin America that became the foundation for an "American Century."

Although military aid, military training, overseas bases, foreign aid, diplomatic alliances, and economic ties were interwoven to form the fabric of Washington's control, one element above all, subordinate elites, was critical for this entire apparatus. Even before taking office, General Eisenhower recognized that the dynamics of U.S. global power rested on allies when he stated, "We cannot be a modern Rome, guarding the far frontiers with our legions if for no other reason than because these are *not*, politically, *our frontiers*."[57] Thus, when relations foundered at moments of crisis or disagreement and U.S. policy makers deemed leaders insubordinate, as in Korea and Vietnam, Washington took measures to undermine, circumscribe, or eliminate the influence of those elites, who, as Dulles said, tried to "actually run the show."

By the end of Eisenhower's tenure, these factors were ingrained in Washington's statecraft in strategic areas of the third world, a change illustrated by the State Department's 1962 policy guidelines for Saudi Arabia. To support this key oil-producing ally, diplomats were instructed to "maintain friendly contact with all factions of the Royal Family." More specifically, the U.S. Embassy in Riyadh would respond favorably to the royal family's requests for loans and military training and would also encourage American investment in the country. U.S. policy makers also recommended "psychological" programs "stressing personal contact" with the full spectrum of Saudi elites, as well as developing American educational and cultural programs. To expand their network of possible allies and cultivate an alternative elite, the State Department planned to "enhance the influence of the U.S. on the Saudi military" and "discreetly cultivate the present and potential opposition . . . whose dissatisfaction with the present regime is evident," since "national leadership may some day emerge" from these factions.[58] These measures succeeded in cultivating a close U.S.-Saudi alliance, cemented in 1974 when Washington replaced Britain as trainers of the Saudi Arabian National Guard—part of the broader transition from British to American influence in the Middle East. Although the primary reason for involvement in Saudi Arabia— unlike Vietnam and Korea—was economic, U.S. policy makers still orchestrated the management of subordinate elites to ensure Washington's interests in the Kingdom and the neighboring sheikhdoms along the Persian Gulf.

When the Cold War ended forty years after Eisenhower forged this system of global control, Washington's interactions with subordinate elites remained the foundation for its exercise of world power. Indeed, several recent incidents reveal this system as still at work in America's relations with major allies in Europe and the Middle East. For example, when the United States went to war with Iraq in 1991, its allies paid 90 percent of that war's sixty-one-billion-dollar cost.[59]

A decade later, when President George W. Bush sought to attack Iraq without the United Nations' support, he assembled the "Coalition of the Willing," which included compliant allies from Italy to El Salvador—a latter-day reincarnation of President Johnson's "More Flags" program. Documents released by WikiLeaks reveal continuities between Washington's dealings with President Park in 1965 and those with Italian prime minister Silvio Berlusconi in 2002. Five months before the coalition invaded Iraq in March 2003, the U.S. Italian embassy relied on Berlusconi to build support in Italy and the European Union for Operation Iraqi Freedom. To raise his stature and build stronger ties, the White House granted him a private meeting with President Bush and high-level intelligence briefings. After building Berlusconi up as a counterweight to opposition from French president Jacques Chirac and German chancellor Gerhard Schröder, the State Department reasoned, "[O]ur ace is that Berlusconi understands—and should appreciate after his meetings in the United States—the strategic importance of defanging Baghdad. Moreover, Berlusconi has demonstrated a capacity for leading public opinion on foreign policy issues he knows are make or break for us."[60] Italy's support for Bush's foreign policy—as well as the thirty-two hundred Italian soldiers sent to Iraq—confirms the effectiveness of Washington's management of this subordinate ally. In the aftermath of the Iraq War, as Washington faces new challenges in an increasingly multipolar world, an important index of its future power will be the survival and strength of this system of subordinate elites.

Imperial Illusions

Information Infrastructure and the
Future of U.S. Global Power

AFTER A DECADE OF FIGHTING several, simultaneous wars on terror, contradictory signs of slippage began to appear in Washington's global dominion. By 2011, it appeared that U.S. military power, unchallenged for decades, was slowly being eroded by the country's fiscal crisis and waning economic influence.

Prominent among those who have predicted this decline, historian Eric Hobsbawm has long argued that America's attempt to achieve "global supremacy" would "almost certainly fail." For Hobsbawm, "empires were mainly built, like the British Empire, by aggression and war," and it was usually winning or losing big wars "that did them in." As a "middleweight country" Britain, he observed, "knew that it did not and could not rule the world," saving London from "the megalomania that is the occupational disease of would-be world conquerors." As U.S. economic power declines, Washington, he warned, might be "tempted to maintain an eroding global position by relying on political-military force."[1]

Though some trends seem to corroborate this gloomy prediction, Hobsbawm's focus on the old imperial verities of military, economy, and territory may well overlook less visible technological elements in a changing global architecture. Just as he grew up a British subject in a world shaped by war and empire, so I was raised, a generation later, the son of an American electronics engineer who told me childhood stories of continental radar shields and telecommunications satellites.[2] Beyond the spectacle of war, we are witnessing, from my generational perspective, a new global hegemony founded not on sea power or even air power but in aerospace and cyberspace.

From this technological viewpoint, the most significant feature of Washington's ascent to world power in the century past was not its victory or defeat in particular wars but the relentless rise of a powerful U.S. information infrastructure. If Britannia once ruled the waves and, lest we forget, the telegraph cables beneath, then America now reigns over sky, space, and cyberspace. Whatever the fate of

U.S. global power might be, Washington's mastery over these strategic domains is emerging as key to its plans for future global dominion.

INFORMATION AND U.S. GLOBAL POWER

My emphasis on information's role in Washington's global power admittedly departs from the conventional emphasis on military might, economic weight, or cultural influence. In its 2008 futurology exercise, the U.S. National Intelligence Council cited "the transfer of *global wealth and economic power* now under way—roughly from West to East— . . . without precedent in modern history" as the primary factor in predicting that by 2025 the "United States' relative strength—even in the military realm—will decline."[3] The council conceded that its analysis may have downplayed "the role of technology in bringing about radical change." But it still insisted that "over the past century, geopolitical rivalries . . . have been more significant causes of the multiple wars, collapse of empires, and rise of new powers than technology alone."[4]

Similarly, historian Paul Kennedy awarded technology a secondary status in the fate of world empires. The two tests that "challenge the *longevity* of every major power," he writes, are whether it can balance "the nation's perceived defense requirements and the means it possesses," that is, whether "it can preserve the technological and economic bases of its power" amid global economic change.[5] Even in this formulation, technology is subordinate to the determinative dyad of military power and economic means.

To focus on information is not to deny the undeniable import of economic or military factors but to argue that an evolving information infrastructure was nonetheless critical in America's past ascent to world power and may prove key in its future global leadership. Since the late nineteenth century, U.S. data management advanced largely from the stimulus of domestic demand. But at three points during the past century these technologies were plunged into crucibles of counterinsurgency in Asia and thereby transformed into innovative military information regimes. In the Philippines, Vietnam, and Afghanistan/Iraq, a mix of guerrilla resistance, protracted conflict, and unfamiliar Asian cultural terrain forced the U.S. military beyond conventional tactics into the unfamiliar domain of unconventional warfare. During each of these protracted conflicts, the U.S. military was pushed to the breaking point and responded by drawing together contemporary information technologies, fusing them into an infrastructure of unprecedented power, and forging an advanced array for data management. Over the span of a century, the U.S. military's information infrastructure thus advanced through three technological regimes—manual (Philippine-American War), computerized (Vietnam War), and robotic (Afghanistan and Iraq).

By applying America's first information revolution of the 1870s to the pacification of the Philippines after 1898, the U.S. Army developed sophisticated systems for collecting, codifying, and operationalizing voluminous amounts of data about whole societies. Despite an enormous expansion into a global system during World War II, Washington's data management remained, until the 1950s, largely *manual* with typewritten files, numeric codification, and limited mechanical assistance for transmission and tabulation. From the 1960s onward, however, a *computerized* information infrastructure emerged during the Vietnam War with automated data processing and electronic communications. After a decade of combat in Iraq and Afghanistan, the Pentagon was, by 2010, at the edge of a *robotic* information regime that will fuse aerospace, cyberwarfare, and biometrics into a worldwide surveillance and strike network of unprecedented power. Throughout these changes, the U.S. information infrastructure has developed in two defining directions: an incessant acceleration in the volume and velocity of data processing; and, in recent years, a gradual levitation of its global force projection into an ether of sky, space, and cyberspace.

Despite major changes in technology, a distinctive epistemology has remained central to America's exercise of world power—both its capacity for global dominion and its inclination to imperial disaster. Unlike major European powers, the U.S. imperial state has eschewed deep cultural knowledge of foreign societies and instead favored superficial yet serviceable data. By eschewing the cultural frame typical of other empires, the U.S. information paradigm can quickly reduce complex social formations to data, amass vast quantities of information, and deploy this analysis for lethal action. Even when defeated, this system seems to transform military reversal into technological advance, almost as if it contains an embedded engineering for ever-increasing efficiency.

Yet the system's strength is also its weakness. Although the U.S. information infrastructure is unequaled in its power to collect and collate data, its human operators often struggle to identify appropriate paradigms for accurate analysis, producing a succession of so-called intelligence failures—Pearl Harbor, the Cuban missile crisis, the Tet Offensive, 9/11, and, above all, Iraq's weapons of mass destruction.[6] By generally excluding cultural factors, this infrastructure's linear logic struggles to understand complex social formations, thus inclining it to a regular recurrence of such disasters. Though expertise about foreign cultures in the European manner might serve as something of a corrective, it is no panacea that can prevent the imperial hubris that seems to blind all great powers—whether Britain at Delhi in 1857 and Suez in 1956, or France at Dien Bien Phu in 1954. Ultimately, Washington's awesome mass of information can foster a self-referential illusion of omniscience or even omnipotence, creating the potential for miscalculation that can spiral downward from defeat into debacle.

AMERICA'S FIRST INFORMATION REVOLUTION

This distinctive imperial epistemology has its origins in "America's first information revolution" of the 1870s to 1880s, which created a capacity for surveillance of the many rather than the few—a defining attribute, in my view, of the modern state. During this dynamic decade, the sum of Thomas A. Edison's quadruplex telegraph (1874), Philo Remington's commercial typewriter (1874), and Alexander Graham Bell's telephone (1876) allowed the transmission of textual data with unprecedented speed and accuracy.[7] After engineer Herman Hollerith patented the punch card in 1889, the U.S. Census Bureau adopted this system in 1890 to quickly enumerate sixty-two million Americans—a success that later led Hollerith to become one of the founders of International Business Machines, better known as IBM.[8]

Parallel innovations in data storage allowed reliable encoding and rapid retrieval from this tide of information. In the mid-1870s, Melvil Dewey created an alphanumeric code to catalog the Amherst College Library, and Charles A. Cutter developed a similar method in Boston that later became the basis for the Library of Congress system.[9] Using a variation of these smart numbers for cataloguing and retrieval, the Office of Naval Intelligence created a card method for recording intelligence (1882), and the U.S. Army's Military Information Division expanded its intelligence cards from just four thousand in 1892 to over three hundred thousand a decade later.[10]

Since America's city police forces circa 1900 were cesspits of corruption, this information revolution came to crime detection from a mix of foreign and domestic sources. At Paris police headquarters in 1882, Alphonse Bertillon created modern criminal identification with a system of corporeal measurements and facial photographs that was soon adopted as the American standard. During the 1890s, the chief of India's colonial police, Sir Edward R. Henry, codified the modern system of fingerprint classification, which was introduced to America in 1904, superseding Bertillon's biometrics.[11]

While it was an imitator in criminal identification, America was an innovator in police and fire communications, with the Gamewell Corporation adapting telegraphy and telephony to create centralized alarm systems.[12] By 1900, America's cities were wired with a total of 764 municipal fire-alarm systems and 148 police-patrol networks handling 41 million messages annually.[13] But on the eve of empire in 1898, the United States was still a "patchwork" state with a weak central government. Congress, courts, and civil society barred application of these innovations to federal law enforcement, denying Washington any investigative capacity beyond the Customs barrier.[14]

AN EXCEPTIONAL EMPIRE

By its victory in the Spanish-American War of 1898, Washington suddenly acquired a string of island colonies stretching halfway around the globe from Puerto Rico to the Philippines, joining the ranks of imperial powers. This sudden conquest created an immediate need for an imperial epistemology to govern this far-flung insular empire. Were the early American empire builders in Cuba, Puerto Rico, and the Philippines "orientalists" who used deep cultural knowledge for colonial rule, or was there another intellectual architecture that informed Washington's overseas occupations? Indeed, today at the peak of U.S. global power, we might at long last ask what kind of empire is this American imperium—that is, how does it manage its administration, its pacification, and, most important, its information?[15]

The historical record provides little evidence for an American orientalism. At base, there was a striking contrast between European and American educational standards for colonial service circa 1900. Over 90 percent of the 362 British officials selected for the Sudan Political Service from 1899 to 1952 were graduates of universities such as Oxford and Cambridge. By contrast, among the 509 schoolteachers who landed at Manila in 1901, arguably the most carefully vetted of American colonial officials, 31 had high school diplomas, 121 normal school training, and the rest "some college."[16] In 1919, French trainees for the Moroccan native affairs directorate took 140 hours of Arabic and studied ethnography, while comparable American recruits for the Philippines Constabulary were military school cadets with little training beyond drill and discipline.[17]

Emerging from Oxford and Cambridge, English imperialists headed east of Suez to learn languages and probe subject societies for a timeless cultural essence that would unlock the "native mind."[18] With their vocational training, American colonials headed west across the Pacific for superficial surveys of the Philippine present through census, mapping, and taxonomy. Few Americans bothered to learn Filipino languages; but thousands taught Filipinos to read English. Instead of career colonials, American overseas rule relied on a transitory A-to-Z army of consultants in fields ranging from agronomy to zoology.[19]

The utilitarian nature of U.S. imperial knowledge emerges by comparing the leading journals for colonial scholarship from British Malaya, French Indochina, and the Philippine Islands.[20] Tabulating topics for all 604 articles published in three official journals from 1906 to 1916 indicates that Americans focused on the natural sciences, with 57 percent of the essays based on primary research; the French work was diametrically skewed toward classical orientalist studies (art, archaeology, history, philology); and the British were in between with a mix of applied and classical research. (See table on the next page.)

While European imperialists thus emphasized deep cultural knowledge for the manipulation of subject societies from within, American colonials amassed contemporary data for control from without. Instead of archaeology or philology, Americans favored pragmatic research on crops, forests, technology, and geography. If the prime aim of the modern state is, as James C. Scott argues, to establish metrics for rendering "a social hieroglyph into a legible and administratively more convenient format," then U.S. imperial epistemology was unrivaled

Topics of Articles in Learned Colonial Journals, Southeast Asia, 1906–1916

	Art	Ethnography	Miscellaneous		History	Folklore	Literature	Natural Science	Social Science	Total Applied[a]	Total Cultural
			Culture								
United States	—	22	—		2	—	1	317	4	321	25
Britain	—	19	4		21	26	21	60	13	73	91
France	28	21	1		20	2	24	—	2	2	96

SOURCES: *Philippine Journal of Science*, vols. 1–10; *Journal of the Straits Branch of the Royal Asiatic Society*, vols. 45–77; *Bulletin de l'École Française d'Extrême-Orient*, vols. 6–9, 11–13, 16–18.

[a] *Applied* means natural or social science articles with pragmatic implications for colonial administration.

in its ability to read alien terrains through such surface reconnaissance.[21] European scholars of empire such as Niall Fergusson who fault the contemporary American aversion to foreign languages and cultural knowledge fail to grasp the guiding genius of a U.S. imperial style grounded in short-term service and serviceable information.[22]

PHILIPPINE PACIFICATION

The U.S. pacification of the Philippines from 1898 to 1913 represents the first sustained application of America's information systems to surveillance of an entire society, producing important innovations in the technology of social control. From the moment it landed at Manila in August 1898, the U.S. Army faced a fifteen-year insurgency that strained its coercive capacities to the limit. To contain this ferment, the U.S. regime elaborated its information technologies into colonial controls through a three-tiered security apparatus—the U.S. Army's Division of Military Information, the Manila Police, and the Philippines Constabulary.

As it struggled to uproot guerrillas, the U.S. Army discovered the imperative of accurate information and formed the first field intelligence unit in its hundred-year history. In December 1900, the Philippine command instructed Captain John Taylor to establish the Division of Military Information (DMI) with the mission of "fixing the identity" of the enemy. Without any established doctrine for tactical intelligence, the new unit defaulted to library methods by cataloging the mass of two hundred thousand captured documents, from which Captain Taylor later selected fifteen hundred for his five-volume study, *The Philippine Insurrection against the United States.* Blind to the cultural wellsprings of Filipino nationalism, however, Taylor portrayed the revolution's leaders as primitives driven by "race hatred and envy and blood lust" to establish a "Malay despotism."[23] Indicative of a recurring problem within the U.S. information system, the lack of an appropriate paradigm neutralized this prodigious data gathering.

Taylor's successor in command, Captain Ralph Van Deman, who was later known as the "father of U.S. military intelligence," soon developed innovative doctrines for categorizing and operationalizing this encyclopedic information on the Filipino resistance.[24] In March 1901, the DMI launched a "confidential" project to compile information cards for every influential Filipino with details of physical appearance, finances, property, loyalties, and kinship. While Van Deman developed new methods for amassing and disseminating vast amounts of information, his analysis also suffered the pitfalls of data without paradigm, often seeing a serious threat when, in fact, there was none.[25]

During its pacification of Manila (1898–1901), the U.S. Army also created a metropolitan police force that applied data management to domestic counterintelligence. After colonial rule began in 1901, Manila's civilian police added a centralized phone network, Gamewell police-fire alarms, electrical street lighting,

Bertillon's photo identification, and fingerprinting. Within just twenty years, Manila's police files would amass photographic file cards on two hundred thousand residents, equivalent to 70 percent of the city's total population.[26] Moreover, in July 1901, the first U.S. civil governor, William Howard Taft, established the Philippines Constabulary as a mobile force of five thousand men to control the countryside and contain anticolonial subversives.[27] Through this application of data management to systematic surveillance, U.S. colonial officials pacified Asia's first national revolution, turning armed resistance into political collaboration. Through its emerging information infrastructure, Washington had developed the coercive power to control whole societies.

The OSS in World War II

The global intelligence demands of World War II strained the U.S. information infrastructure and brought this manual regime to the breaking point. By establishing the Office of Strategic Services (OSS) as its first global espionage agency in 1941, Washington created a potent mechanism for both covert operations and intelligence gathering. Among the new agency's nine branches, Research and Analysis (R&A) was distinctive for its application of academic methods to advance beyond the "haphazard and indiscriminate" foreign data then held by federal agencies. With a staff of 1,950 academics, R&A quickly amassed 50,000 books, 300,000 photographs, 350,000 foreign serials, a million maps, and 3 million file cards—sources for over 3,000 wartime staff studies.[28] Through the work of these scholar-sleuths, the OSS's Central Information Division created a system with "indexing, cross-indexing, and counter-indexing" of those 3 million file cards for quick data retrieval and cross-referencing.[29]

In the postwar period, this combination of omnivorous data gathering and agile array was evident in institutions inspired by the OSS. Following a design developed during the war by the Library of Congress, the Carnegie Foundation, and the OSS, some fifty-four major university libraries agreed to divide the globe and, by 1961, were collecting materials from 145 nations. Similarly, the OSS influenced postwar creation of the Human Relations Area Files (HRAF) at Yale University, which compressed all extant ethnographic data into a single, capacious file, with a copy deposited at Central Intelligence Agency (CIA) headquarters in Virginia.[30] Building on this wartime experience, the CIA's Foreign Broadcast Information Service (FBIS) monitored radio and television broadcasts worldwide throughout the Cold War.[31]

In a sense, the OSS represents the apotheosis of voracious data gathering by America's first information regime. During this wartime mobilization of information, Washington recruited a legion of educated scholars and dedicated clerks who worked tirelessly to operationalize America's first international data set. Yet this same system required, from its origins in 1901 through its apogee in 1945, that these masses of information be processed manually—laboriously typed, coded, filed, and retrieved. By early 1944, the OSS found itself "drowning under the flow of information," with rising masses of data stockpiled, uncodified, and unread.[32] In its global reach, this manual information regime, absent techno- logical change, might eventually have imposed some restraint on U.S. imperial epistemology.

SECOND INFORMATION REVOLUTION IN INDOCHINA

Under the pressures of protracted war in Indochina from 1964 to 1974, the U.S. information infrastructure made rapid strides in computerized data manage- ment whose sum was America's second information revolution. While the CIA and military applied automated data processing to pacify the country's villages, the U.S. Air Force (USAF) developed an electronic battlefield in southern Laos and deployed the first surveillance drones over North Vietnam. In this second symbiosis of industrial capacity and military innovation, such automation mir- rored America's emergence as the world's first "technetronic" society shaped by what Zbigniew Brzezinski called "the impact of technology and electronics."[33]

From the outset, counterguerrilla strategy in Vietnam reflected the Kennedy administration's new doctrine of "special warfare."[34] According to Dr. Adam Schesch, from 1961 to 1975 the Pentagon's Advanced Research Projects Agency (ARPA) contracted nearly five thousand studies of insurgency and counterin- surgency. By weighing dozens of "measurable and mechanical" variables, these studies reduced "research findings to the narrowest explanations" in an ambitious effort "to construct the equivalent of a chemical Table of the Elements for . . . 'unconventional warfare.'"[35] Once again, U.S. imperial epistemology reduced com- plex social problems to measurable units and performance metrics.

For nearly fifteen years, the CIA and U.S. military applied advanced informa- tion technology to eradicate the Communists' shadow government in South Vietnam, the so-called Viet Cong Infrastructure (VCI).[36] In May 1967, President Lyndon Johnson appointed CIA official Robert W. Komer as his "pacification czar" and sent him to Saigon as head of Civil Operations and Rural Development Support (CORDS). But this tough CIA official soon learned that "no effective attack has yet been devised for . . . degradation of VC [Viet Cong] infrastructure."[37] One agency analyst recommended borrowing an automated "reporting and infor- mation system" from the Ford Motor Company that allowed "a greatly expanded capacity for storing, manipulating and reproducing information."[38] With this technology, Komer launched the Infrastructure Intelligence Coordination and Exploitation (ICEX) program for "the identification and destruction of the [Viet Cong] infrastructure."[39] Within a year, the CIA's Phoenix Program was using computers to centralize all data on the Communist underground, identifying key cadres for interrogation or elimination by the agency's counterguerrilla teams.[40]

In theory, centralized data dissemination would catalyze arrests and generate more names for the computers, sweeping the Viet Cong from the villages. Instead, this circular flow of data within the Phoenix Program's cycle of intelligence and operations created a hermetic information architecture without any external check against false identification of Viet Cong suspects.[41]

By 1972, after five years of "intensive effort at computer mechanization," Phoenix claimed 81,740 Viet Cong somehow eliminated and 26,369 prisoners killed.[42] However, the program's founder, Komer, later described it as "a small, poorly managed, and largely ineffective effort." Indeed, one Pentagon study found that in 1970–71 only 3 percent of the suspects "killed, captured, or rallied were full or probationary Party members above the district level," and over half the supposed Viet Cong captured or killed "were not even Party members."[43] One veteran of the CIA, Ralph McGehee, was even blunter, stating, "The truth is that never in the history of our work in Vietnam did we get one clear-cut, high-ranking Viet Cong agent."[44]

In a parallel effort, CORDS conducted the computerized Hamlet Evaluation Survey (HES), which contributed to these data-driven illusions of progress. "Since subjective judgments had already proven so far off base," CORDS chief

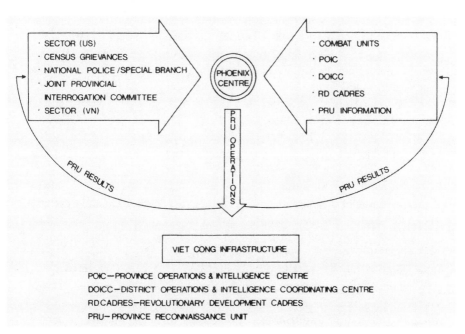

POIC—PROVINCE OPERATIONS & INTELLIGENCE CENTRE
DOICC—DISTRICT OPERATIONS & INTELLIGENCE COORDINATING CENTRE
RD CADRES—REVOLUTIONARY DEVELOPMENT CADRES
PRU—PROVINCE RECONNAISSANCE UNIT

Self-referential information loop within the Cycle of Intelligence and Operations, Phoenix Program, South Vietnam, 1968–69, indicating the lack of any external check on misidentification of civilians as Communist cadres.

Komer recalled, "the pressure was for solid, quantifiable data." Indeed, he added, "the whole question of how to . . . measure what was actually going was one of the trickiest and most painful in this highly atypical war." In late 1966, Defense Secretary McNamara ordered the CIA to "design me something that will tell us the status of control in the countryside." Consequently, agency and military intelligence specialists identified eighteen variables for an assessment model that balanced development and security. Using a five-point scale from A (secure) to E (contested), 220 U.S. military advisers submitted monthly security ratings for all of South Vietnam's 12,600 hamlets, which were then processed for display on a consolidated IBM dot-matrix map. Beneath the high-tech patina, an essentially subjective assessment pronounced 75 percent of South Vietnam's population pacified by late 1967—just before the disastrous Tet Offensive shattered such illusions of progress. To correct such bias, in late 1968 CORDS contracted with Control Data Corporation to develop an automated survey as "a highly integrated *man-machine* interface."[45]

Komer insisted he had "few illusions as to how well we divined the undivinable," and called the HES "a crude measurement of several physically measureable . . . factors," which was "full of weaknesses." Nonetheless, he "personally used the HES figures extensively" and considered this data "our best reporting from the field on a systematic basis." Unable to measure the critical variable of "popular commitment, because we couldn't," the HES faced an impossible dilemma. "We were trying desperately to find countrywide indicators," said Komer, "and naturally the only indicators we could use were those that were statistically comparable and measureable." Though these measures were "very gross and oversimplified," they were, he said, "much better than the previous subjective evaluations or impressionistic reporting."[46]

If we are to believe Komer, U.S. officials, needing data on the critical but unquantifiable issue of popular loyalties, measured a few unrelated variables that happened to be quantifiable and then based their policies on the resulting statistics—even though fully aware of the imperfect, incomplete, illusory nature of those same numbers. Consequently, the share of the South Vietnamese population rated "secure" climbed relentlessly to 84 percent, even as the Saigon regime lost popular support and plunged toward defeat. In the end, automated indices led South Vietnam's government, said CIA director William Colby, "to delude itself about its standing with its own people."[47]

The final element in this automated pacification was the Combined Documents Exploitation Center (CDEC), which started in October 1966 as a computerized effort by army intelligence to classify the three million pages of enemy documents captured annually. At CDEC's Saigon warehouse, clerks copied documents on reels of cinema film stock with bar-code identification encrypted inside the sound track, allowing automated retrieval with the "state-of-the-art"

FILE/SEARCH computer system. But the system proved "cumbersome," and analysts "took to wandering into the warehouse to grope for what they needed." Through the combined failure of these multiple metrics, as a recent study reported, the U.S. command "increasingly lost the ability to draw accurate conclusions from the massive amount of data it was collecting," with the result that "insufficient analysis often led to faulty evaluations . . . in large part because MACV had created no verification procedures or feedback mechanisms for its metrics system."[48]

The U.S. experiment with electronic bombing of the Ho Chi Minh Trail proved equally illusory. As Hanoi's manpower and matériel flowed down the trail through southern Laos in 1966, Washington realized that victory in Vietnam required cutting this vital infiltration route. Instead of creating a physical barrier with an estimated 140,000 troops and ten million land mines, Secretary of Defense Robert McNamara mobilized the military's most advanced technology to build a billion-dollar "electronic barrier" anchored by an "air-supported anti-infiltration subsystem" astride the trail in nearby Laos.[49]

Within the 6.7 million tons of bombs the U.S. dropped on the whole of Indochina during the Vietnam War (1965 to 1973), the air force concentrated a full 25 percent, or 1.7 million tons, on southern Laos. Under an advanced program dubbed Operation Igloo White, the U.S. combined sensors, computers, and fighter-bombers for an electronic bombing campaign against North Vietnam's truck convoys. To detect these enemy trucks, the air force laced this forested mountain corridor through southern Laos with twenty thousand acoustic, seismic, thermal, and ammonia-sensitive sensors. The "Acoubuoy" was parachuted into trees to listen, while "Spikebuoy" was dropped into soil with antennae camouflaged like local weeds, and both sent signals to EC-121 communications aircraft circling overhead.[50]

At the nearby U.S. base in Nakhorn Phanom, Thailand, the massive Infiltration Surveillance Center employed four hundred airmen and two powerful IBM 360/65 mainframe computers equipped with the first visual display monitors to translate all those sensor signals into "an illuminated line of light" called a worm, which "moved down the map at a rate equal to the computed target speed." After confirming coordinates, the center launched F-4 Phantom jets over Laos where Loran radio signals guided them to the target and the IBM computers discharged laser-guided bombs automatically.[51] Concerned about losing the lumbering EC-121s to antiaircraft fire, the air force experimented unsuccessfully with unmanned aircraft, retrofitting several Beechcraft Debonairs as "radio controlled drones" and testing Nite Gazelle helicopters "as hovering killer drones" to destroy trucks.[52]

In its internal assessments of this electronic barrier, the air force was surprisingly sanguine. A 1970 evaluation found that "the Igloo White system was both effective and accurate," hitting 40 percent of enemy targets.[53] A year later, the program reportedly destroyed an incredible twenty-five thousand North Vietnamese trucks. The digital worm crawling across Igloo White computer screens identified a truck's coordinates, aircraft bombed that location, and the worm, after a twenty-minute lag, disappeared—data sufficient to convince the air force that the trucks were destroyed. Within the project's sealed information loop (shown below) there was no external check on such inflated estimates of success.[54]

Even when the war was raging, such optimism attracted sharp criticism. Skeptical CIA analysts reduced air force damage claims by 75 percent.[55] While the air force raised its estimates to 80 percent of enemy trucks destroyed in southern Laos, Hanoi reported only 15 percent lost.[56] After tanks, trucks, and over one hundred thousand North Vietnamese troops poured down the Ho Chi Minh Trail undetected for a massive attack in 1972, one analyst for the Pacific air force advised his commander, "Due to the duration, intensity, and geographical extent of the current NVN [North Vietnamese] offensive . . . everyone now recognizes that our estimates were in error." An official air force history later concluded that Igloo White's sophisticated sensors had been defeated by the "thousands of North Vietnamese soldiers and local laborers [who] kept the Ho Chi Minh Trail open by constructing, camouflaging, and repairing . . . the roads."[57]

In retrospect, Igloo White was but one example of the way that these massive air operations over Indochina encouraged innovation. Throughout the war, the air force accelerated the development of unmanned aircraft by adapting the Ryan

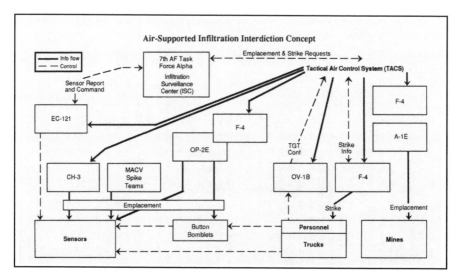

Self-contained data loop, Air-Supported Infiltration Interdiction, U.S. Air Force, for bombing the Ho Chi Minh Trail in southern Laos, 1968–73. (U.S. Air Force)

Model 147 "Firebee" target drone for surveillance over China, North Vietnam, and Laos. Indicative of the rapid progress, the "Lightning Bug" series achieved a 2,400-mile range and flew 3,500 sorties in the Vietnam theater equipped with ever more sophisticated electronics. In 1965, a Lightning Bug intercepted the electronic signal from an enemy surface-to-air missile (SAM), allowing later U.S. fighters to carry missile jammers, a success the Pentagon called "the most significant contribution to electronic reconnaissance in the last 20 years." By 1972, the air force developed the "SC/TV" model drone with a camera in the nose so the "airborne remote control officer . . . could now navigate using a low-resolution television image." Though slowed for twenty years after Vietnam, air force experiments with unmanned aircraft were revived in the 1990s to build the "Predator" combat drone.[58] Through the pressure of history's largest air war over Indochina, drones were thus transformed from dumb training targets to agile surveillance aircraft and launched on a technological trajectory toward full weaponization that would be realized in the next major conflict, Afghanistan.

At great cost, the Vietnam War thus marked a watershed for Washington's global information architecture. Within the long arc of technological progress, Igloo White proved transformative, integrating electronic sensors in lieu of human intelligence and computerized targeting in lieu of visual contact, moving warfare, over the longer term, toward a future electronic battlefield. In the short term, of course, automated bombing in Laos created the illusion that North Vietnam's supply effort had been thwarted, while computerized data collection in South Vietnam also fostered the delusion that pacification was defeating the Viet Cong guerrillas—both harbingers of future information failures. Moreover, the Vietnam debacle, at the cost of fifty-eight thousand dead and a hundred billion dollars in wasted capital, was a sharp blow to U.S. power, sparking deep domestic divisions for a generation and weakening Washington's global military posture for over a decade.[59] At a deeper level, however, these information failures proved self-correcting, transforming even these defeats into experiments leading to the development of electronic technologies that would prove effective thirty years later in Afghanistan.

GLOBAL WAR ON TERROR

Building on advances during the Vietnam conflict, Washington fought the Global War on Terror after 2001 through an expanded information infrastructure with electronic surveillance, biometric identification, and aerial force projection. Just as Vietnam accelerated the military's computerized data processing, so the Global War on Terror has served as a de facto laboratory for the integration of space, cyberspace, and robotics into a third information regime. This war's voracious appetite for information produced, after 2001, a veritable "fourth branch" of federal government with 854,000 vetted security officials, 263 security organizations, over 3,000 private and public intelligence agencies, and 33 new security complexes. All of these agencies were, by 2010, pumping out a total of 50,000 intelligence reports annually, many redundant, many unread.[60] "The complexity of this system defies description," said Lieutenant General John R. Vines, who reviewed this information infrastructure for the Pentagon, adding, "Because it lacks a synchronizing process, it inevitably results in message dissonance, reduced effectiveness and waste. We consequently can't effectively assess whether it is making us more safe."[61]

From Bush to Obama, there has been an underlying continuity in the development of a cyberwarfare capability at home and abroad. Starting in 2002, President George W. Bush gave the National Security Agency (NSA) secret orders to monitor domestic communications, and the agency later launched its top-secret "Pinwale" database to scan countless millions of electronic messages.[62] Similarly, the Federal Bureau of Investigation (FBI) opened its Investigative Data Warehouse in 2004 as a "centralized repository for . . . counterterrorism"; and by 2009 it held a billion individual records.[63]

In 2009, digital surveillance grew into "cyberwarfare" after the formation of the U.S. Cyber Command (CYBERCOM), with headquarters at Fort Meade and a cyberwarfare center at Lackland Air Base staffed by seven thousand air force employees.[64] Two years later the Pentagon declared cyberspace an "operational domain"—like air, land, or sea—and moved beyond defense of the military's seven million computers to train its cyberwarriors for offense.[65] While developing a formidable cyberwarfare capacity, Washington has been cautious in its deployment to avoid creating precedents for attacks from Russia (which crippled Estonia's computers in 2007 and Georgia's in 2008) or China (which repeatedly hacked Pentagon servers since 1999). Thus, the U.S. used computer viruses with devastating effect against Iran's nuclear facilities from 2006 to 2010 but opted for conventional strikes against Libya's air defenses in 2011.[66]

Overseas, the pressure of pacifying foreign societies has again produced innovation in the U.S. information infrastructure. The occupation of Iraq from 2003 to 2011 served as a crucible of counterinsurgency, creating a new fusion of biometric surveillance and digital warfare. Advanced biometrics first appeared in 2004 during the aftermath of the bitter battle for Falluja when Marines stopped the 250,000 returning residents at desert checkpoints for fingerprinting and iris scans.[67] By mid-2008, the U.S. Army was checking the identities of Baghdad's population via satellite link to a biometric database in West Virginia with a million Iraqi fingerprints and retinal scans on file.[68] Starting in 2010, the Pentagon deployed an upgraded identification system in Afghanistan, allowing U.S. patrols to scan Afghani eyes into the Biometric Automated Toolset (BAT)—a laptop computer equipped with "separate plug-in units that record mug shots, fingerprints and retinal characteristics" for instantaneous satellite transmission.[69]

In Afghanistan, the unmanned aerial vehicle became a potent weapon in Washington's aerospace arsenal, accelerating drone development slowed since the Vietnam War. Launched as an experimental craft in 1994, the Predator drone was first deployed in 2000 for surveillance under the CIA's Operation Afghan Eyes.[70] In July 2008, the air force developed the larger MQ-9 "Reaper" drone with "persistent hunter killer" capabilities—sixteen hours flying time, sensors for "real time data," and fourteen air-ground missiles.[71] Indicating the torrid pace of drone development, between 2004 and 2010 total flying time for all unmanned vehicles rose from just 71 hours to 250,000.[72] Launched in 1994 without weapons or even GPS (Global Positioning System), these drones were eventually equipped, circa 2011, with sensors so sensitive they could read disturbed dirt at five thousand feet and backtrack footprints to an enemy bunker.[73] By 2009, the number of air force drones deployed over Afghanistan and Iraq had increased to 28 Reapers and 195 Predators collecting 16,000 hours of video daily while firing hundreds of Hellfire missiles that killed over 1,900 insurgents inside Pakistan's tribal areas from 2006 to 2011.[74] Moreover, by then there were seven thousand drones in the U.S. armada of unmanned aircraft operated largely by the army, air force, and CIA.[75] Although the second-generation Reaper drones seemed stunningly sophisticated, one defense analyst called them "very much Model T Fords."[76]

The media has generally focused on these airborne assassinations, but the drone's real significance lies in its future role as the lowest tier in an emerging global network of sky/space surveillance. By late 2008, night flights over Afghanistan were using sensors to give American ground forces real-time images of Taliban targets as small as a few warm bodies.[77] All such information from the air force's "$5 billion global surveillance network" was fed into a secret warehouse at Langley Air Base in Virginia where "cubicle warriors" conducted a daily review of "1,000 hours of video, 1,000 high-altitude spy photos, and hundreds of hours of 'signals intelligence," phoning actionable data directly to dozens of field commanders in Afghanistan.[78]

By 2011, the air force was planning to quadruple its drone fleet to 536 unmanned aircraft and was training 350 drone pilots, more than the number of all bomber and fighter pilots combined, for an armada ranging from the hulking Global Hawk, with a 116-foot wingspan, to the agile Shadow, with an 11-foot span.[79] The sophistication of this technology was exposed in December 2011 when an RQ-170 Sentinel drone came down in Iran revealing a dart-shaped, 65-foot wingspan for flight at altitudes of fifty thousand feet—equipped with radar-evading stealth capacity, active electronically scanned array (AESA) radar, and advanced optics "that allows operators to positively identify terror suspects from tens of thousands of feet in the air."[80]

Despite all this technological wizardry, Washington's war effort in Afghanistan may yet founder on another dense social formation akin to Vietnam, with

data divorced from local realities. In January 2009, the Pentagon released its periodic report *Progress toward Security and Stability in Afghanistan*—a document
whose masses of information quantified indices of purported allied progress and
ignored unquantifiable factors such as culture and ideology.[81] Despite ten years
of pacification, the surge in U.S. ground forces to one hundred thousand, and
intensified drone strikes, the Taliban, according to a 2010 Pentagon report, had
continued to spread throughout the Afghan countryside.[82]

In late 2009 as President Barack Obama was announcing the surge in troops
for Afghanistan, an NBC News correspondent in Kabul uncovered a PowerPoint
slide prepared by the Joint Chiefs of Staff emblematic of the underlying weakness in America's imperial epistemology. Titled "Afghan Stability/COIN [Coun-
terinsurgency] Dynamics," the graphic purported to reduce every element in this
complex war to a single chart with thirteen major variables ("Popular Support")
and a dozen subfactors ("Perception of Coalition Intent"). "For some military
commanders," NBC reported, "the slide is genius, an attempt to show how all
things in war—from media bias to ethnic/tribal rivalries are interconnected."
Other military officers saw it as "an assault on logic."[83] One general who had
banned PowerPoint when he commanded U.S. forces in northern Iraq commented, "It's dangerous because it can create the illusion of understanding and
the illusion of control." Similar PowerPoint presentations had been used by General Tommy Franks in launching the 2003 Iraq invasion while ignoring variables
that soon erupted into lethal insurgency, and by President Obama in planning
his Afghan surge in 2009.[84] As in Vietnam, the "illusion of control" derived from
hermetic information loops has encouraged ten years of incessant escalation in
Afghanistan without success or sustainable progress.

Yet even as this critique circulated, Pentagon strategists were already addressing the epistemological flaw in their warfare planning. In 2008, the army's Training and Doctrine Command (TRADOC) released a new cognitive model for
planning solutions to "ill-structured or wicked problems" called the Commander's Appreciation and Campaign Design (CACD). Instead of "engineering" fixed
responses to complex situations *ab initio*, this doctrine instructed field commanders to "design" steps forward though an ongoing "discourse" with the evolving
situation.[85]

In the future, however, even this supple decision-making process might be
superseded by automation from the Information Processing Techniques Office
(IPTO), a branch of the Pentagon's Defense Advanced Research Projects Agency
(DARPA). With the motto "Information lifts the fog of war," IPTO was building, as of 2010, new "communication systems [that] continuously generate . . .
information at rates beyond which humans can assimilate" through "machine
intelligence techniques that can identify patterns . . . and adapt to changing circumstances."[86] By confronting its disastrous planning for Iraq, the army was

Afghanistan Stability / COIN Dynamics

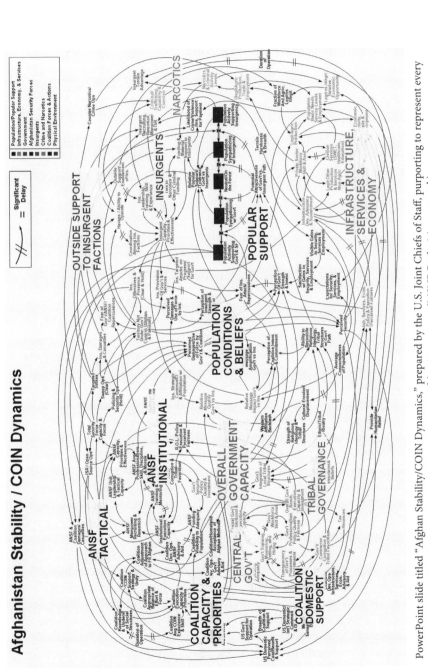

PowerPoint slide titled "Afghan Stability/COIN Dynamics," prepared by the U.S. Joint Chiefs of Staff, purporting to represent every element of the coalition's counterinsurgency campaign in Afghanistan, 2009. (MSNBC television network)

inserting apertures, human and computerized, into the self-referential information loops that had proven so problematic in past cognitive schema—another
instance of the self-correcting engineering embedded within the U.S. information infrastructure.

THIRD INFORMATION REVOLUTION

Even as the army was correcting a conceptual flaw within its second information
regime, this infrastructure was being superseded by a third information revolution taking shape inside DARPA and the air force. Through prototype testing
and war-gaming, the Pentagon was developing a triple-canopy aerospace apparatus for global force projection that would, within a decade, be integrated into a
multi-domain information system with robotic controls.

After a decade of ground warfare in Afghanistan and Iraq, the Obama administration announced, in early 2012, a leaner defense strategy with a 14 percent cut in infantry, a marked shift from the Middle East to check "the growth of
China's military power," and an increased emphasis on space and cyberspace.
Although this new strategy would maintain the capability to counter a major
aggressor in "a combined arms campaign across all domains—land, air, maritime, space, and cyberspace," the growing threat of asymmetric attacks, by both
state and non-state actors, now placed a premium on investments in "critical
space-based capabilities."[87] By 2020, this new defense architecture will integrate
space, cyberspace, and terrestrial combat through robotics for seamless information and action.

In its plans for the future, the air force has defined the full weaponization of
space as central to the next generation of warfare. In 2004, a strategic study defined
space assets as "critical to achieving information superiority," which is imperative for "gaining supremacy in all environments."[88] Two years later, experience
in Afghanistan convinced the air force to develop a strategy for "Battlespace
Awareness (space and terrestrial) . . . and prompt global strike . . . capabilities."
Consequently, the Pentagon established the Joint Functional Component Command for Space to manage military operations in what was fast becoming the
ultimate strategic high ground.[89]

To prepare for these challenges, the air force has held periodic combat simu-
lations, such as the 2009 Future Capabilities Game, to gain "a better understanding of how air, space and cyberspace overlap in warfare."[90] Although the results
remain classified, we can infer, from the specifications for its components, that
by 2020 the Pentagon will deploy a three-tiered space shield to envelope the earth
from stratosphere to exosphere.

The age of space warfare dawned in April 2010 when the Defense Department
quietly launched the X-37B Orbital Test Vehicle, an unmanned space shuttle just
twenty-nine feet long, into orbit 250 miles above the earth for a seven-month

The first X-37B Orbital Test Vehicle waits for launch in the encapsulation cell of the Evolved Expendable Launch vehicle at Titusville, Florida, April 5, 2010. (U.S. Air Force)

mission. By removing pilots and their costly life-support systems, the air force created a miniaturized, militarized spacecraft with multiple advantages—thrusters for in-orbit maneuvers to elude missile attacks, solar batteries for an extended flight, and a capacious cargo bay for signals-intercept sensors, satellite deployment, and possible air-to-air missiles.[91] By the time the second X-37B prototype landed at Vandenberg Air Force Base in June 2012 after a fifteen-month flight, this classified mission represented a successful test of "robotically controlled reusable spacecraft" and established the viability of unmanned space drones in the exosphere, the outermost level of the Pentagon's emerging three-tiered space/sky canopy.[92]

At the next tier closer to earth in the upper stratosphere, DARPA and the air force are collaborating in the development of the Falcon Hypersonic Cruise Vehicle, which, flying thirteen thousand miles per hour at twenty miles altitude, "could deliver 12,000 pounds of payload at a distance of 9,000 nautical miles from the continental United States" within an hour, destroying any target "anywhere in

Artist's conception, circa 2008, of the U.S. Falcon Hypersonic Cruise Vehicle, an unmanned aircraft that will fly at an altitude of twenty miles and destroy targets anywhere in the world within an hour. (Defense Advanced Research Projects Administration)

the world on 30 minutes notice, with no need for a nearby airbase." Although the first test launches in April 2010 and August 2011 crashed midflight, they achieved twenty-two times the speed of sound and sent back "unique data" to resolve remaining aerodynamic problems.[93]

In the lower stratosphere, within striking distance of the earth, the Defense Department is working with aerospace contractors in developing high-flying drones to supersede manned aircraft within the closest tier of this triple-canopy array. To replace the piloted U-2 surveillance aircraft by 2015, the Pentagon has, since 2006, procured an armada of ninety-nine Global Hawk drones for the air force and navy at a cost of $218 million each. Flying at sixty thousand feet elevation with an extended wingspan, the Global Hawk is equipped with high-resolution cameras to photograph individual soldiers within a hundred-mile radius, electronic sensors to intercept radio and telephone communications, and efficient engines for a continuous twenty-four-hour flight, allowing close surveillance of forty thousand square miles daily.[94]

By late 2011, the air force and CIA had ringed the entire Eurasian land mass with a network of sixty bases for Reaper and Predator drones—in Sicily, the

The Global Hawk, an unmanned aerial vehicle capable of surveillance flights for twenty-four hours at sixty thousand feet, is one of a hundred that will be operational by 2015, shown here on a test flight from Tinker Air Force Base, Oklahoma, in 2011. (U.S. Air Force)

Middle East (Iraq, Oman, Qatar), Central Asia (Afghanistan, Uzbekistan), the Indian Ocean (Djibouti, Somalia, Seychelles, Diego Garcia), and Guam. With a flying range of 1,150 miles when armed with its full payload of Hellfire missiles and GBU-30 bombs, U.S. Reaper drones could strike targets anywhere in Europe, Africa, and Asia.[95]

Moreover, by 2014 the "Vulture," a solar-powered, unmanned aircraft with a massive four-hundred-foot wingspan, will patrol the globe ceaselessly at twelve miles altitude with sensors capable of "unblinking" surveillance. To establish the viability of this new technology, NASA's "Pathfinder" reached 71,500 feet with a solar-powered, 100-foot wingspan in 1997, and its fourth-generation successor, the "Helios," flew at 97,000 feet with a 247-foot wingspan in 2001, two miles higher than any previous aircraft.[96] More experimentally, the Pentagon has explored the possibility of unmanned fighters, notably the MQ-X jet equipped with versatile missiles and wide-area cameras.[97]

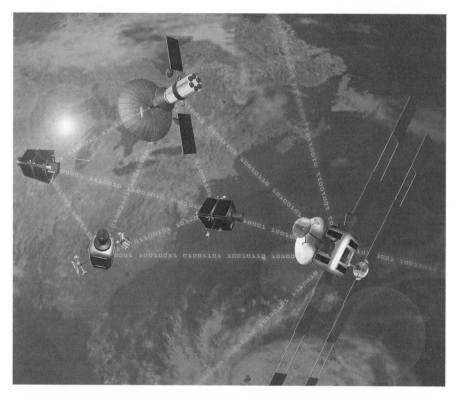

System F6, a cluster of wirelessly interconnected modules that will form an orbital U.S. satellite, shown in this artist's representation over North America, circa 2009. (Defense Advanced Research Projects Administration)

To arm all tiers of this triple-canopy array, DARPA has tested a multitask missile, the Triple Target Terminator (T3), which can "engage air, cruise missile, and air defense targets [from] fighters, bombers and UAVs [unmanned aerial vehicles]," allowing any aircraft to switch "rapidly between air-to-air and air-to-surface." Hypothetically, the Vulture, Falcon, or Predator could fire this missile to strike a terrestrial target, while the X-37B or similar space drones could use it to deflect an attack or destroy an enemy satellite.[98]

At the apex of this triple canopy, orbital satellites are the prime targets, a vulnerability that became painfully obvious in 2007 when China used a ground-to-air missile to shoot down one of its own satellites.[99] To counter this threat, in May 2011 the U.S. Air Force launched the GEO-1 satellite, at a cost of $1.2 billion, into a high, geostatial orbit where it was designed to serve as a component in the Space-Based Infra-Red System (SBIRS) with rapid-response sensors to detect missile launches anywhere in the world.[100] Simultaneously, DARPA was developing the F-6 modular satellite system, scheduled for "an on-orbit demonstration in 2015," which will "decompose a large monolithic spacecraft into a group of wirelessly linked elements, or nodes [, that] executes a specific spacecraft function," increasing its "resistance to . . . a bad part breaking or an adversary attacking."[101] Ultimately, this entire three-tier system will be self-maintaining through "robotic manipulator technologies" such as the Front-End Robotic Enabling Near-Term Demonstration (FREND), which can automatically deliver fuel, provide repairs, or reposition satellites.[102]

Operation of this complex worldwide apparatus will require, as one DARPA official explained in 2007, "an integrated collection of space surveillance systems—an architecture—that is leak-proof." For this new global optic, DARPA is building the wide-angle Space Surveillance Telescope (SST) for a quantum leap in "space surveillance."[103] Future space warriors seated at a single console will track every object in earth's orbit continuously through a global network of SSTs based at Maui, Diego Garcia, and other stations worldwide. Since 2004, the Defense Department has expanded the National Geospatial-Intelligence Agency into a supersecret bureau. In 2010, it had sixteen thousand employees, a five-billion-dollar budget, and a two-billion-dollar headquarters at Fort Belvoir, the fourth-largest federal building in Washington, housing 8,500 staffers wrapped in electronic security—all aimed at coordinating the flood of surveillance data pouring in from SSTs, Predators, Reapers, Vultures, U-2 spy planes, Global Hawks, X-37B space drones, Google Earth, and orbiting satellites.[104]

Ultimately, the impact of this third technological regime will be shaped by the integration of this aerospace array into a robotic command apparatus that will coordinate operations across all combat domains—space, cyberspace, sky, sea, and earth. To defend against asymmetric terror strikes, moreover, civil defense and cyberwarfare will incorporate biometric identification and electronic surveillance across the electromagnetic spectrum. To control this complexly integrated system, cybernetics and robotics will necessarily play a significant role in both vigilance and actual combat.

Looking forward into the future, the core of this new technology will be operational within a decade to create the infrastructure for this third U.S. information regime by 2020, about the same time that China will be ready to contest American dominion over space and cyberspace, thereby creating new frontiers for interstate conflict. After human space flight in 2003, a spacewalk in 2008, and module docking in 2011, China was on track to launch its own space station by 2020, just about the time the U.S.-led International Space Station will be retired without replacement, making Beijing the sole power with a manned presence in space.[105] In the years following 2020, both powers will have the capability for space warfare, creating the potential for armed conflict over control of the ultimate strategic high ground.

CONCLUSION

In contrast to Britain's dominion over land and sea, America's global reach seems bent on a century-long trajectory beyond sovereign territory toward control over interstitial domains—space, cyberspace, sky, and the electromagnetic spectrum. Over the past half century, the U.S. information infrastructure has grown into an apparatus of unimaginable power and precision, moving far beyond the conceptual framework of the second, computerized information regime whose flaws were so painfully evident in Indochina. Yet even these advances are but intimations of a third U.S. information revolution brewing within the Pentagon, which seeks to build a network of aerospace robotics, advanced cyberwarfare, and pervasive biometrics to envelop the earth in an electronic grid—allowing elimination of entire enemy battlefield formations through "networkcentric warfare" or incineration of a single insurgent with a drone-fired missile.

At the risk of joining that long line of historians who have proven so inept at prediction, there seems, simply put, to be at least two interpretations of America's Vietnam past and its global future. After a century's growth through manual and automated technological regimes, the United States seemed, circa 2012, at the cusp of creating a uniquely potent third information revolution to exercise global dominion in excess of its economic strength. Looking forward, the question remains whether this U.S. military technology can somehow break the historic binary between financial means and military power. Just as an edge in maritime technology allowed Portugal, Holland, and Britain to build overseas empires that dwarfed their small, poorly endowed homelands, so the United States might gain a similar advantage in space and cyberspace. With an agile force directed via a robotic information infrastructure, the United States could, in principle, parlay its military power into a second American century. If this interpretation is correct, then continuing technological advances could possibly exempt Washington from past patterns of imperial decline, creating something akin to an endless American empire.

Alternatively, if military technology is, in fact, Washington's best chance to extend its global dominion, then recent history is not all that reassuring. As the tide turned against the Third Reich in 1944, German technology produced wonder weapons, rockets and jets that threatened to dominate the skies over Europe. Indeed, in January 1945, just three months before the war's end, Britain's Air Ministry warned gravely that if Berlin were not defeated by July "she will have dominance in the air over Germany and above the armies." In the end, however, the waves of Allied aircraft, tanks, and troops—marshaled by superior U.S. economic strength—simply overwhelmed Hitler's "secret weapons."[106]

Moreover, in a globalizing age of rapid information transfer, any technological edge will likely prove ephemeral as rivals quickly gain access to advances through espionage, cyberpenetration, or open-source science. Instead of securing a strategic edge for a decade or two with a new weapons system, the maintenance of dominance in space and cyberspace will require constant renewal through relentless scientific innovation. With America's education system in decline, its science and technology will, as discussed in this volume's introduction, lose its competitive edge within a generation, eventually equalizing the competition for control over space and cyberspace.

In its overwhelming wealth of data, this evolving U.S. robotic information regime can also foster, like its predecessors, an imperial hubris, an illusion of omniscience and omnipotence that can lead to some latter-day Vietnam debacle. In Indochina data divorced from cultural context created an "illusion of control" and an elusive quest for victory, transforming a limited intervention into a micro-military disaster. Regardless of particular structures, international information management is an enterprise generally bedeviled, often fatally, by imperial illusions. Despite academic rigor and linguistic sophistication, British intelligence grounded in deep cultural knowledge was stunned by the Indian Mutiny of 1857. Similarly, the U.S. computerized pacification in Vietnam, designed to penetrate even the smallest hamlet, somehow missed the mobilization of the enemy's entire army for offensives in 1968 and 1972. Just as sophisticated U.S. counterinsurgency foundered amidst social complexities in Vietnam and Afghanistan, so any future exercise of global control via robotic drones might prove politically counterproductive—a possibility given weight by polling in twenty-one nations such as Brazil, Japan, Turkey, and Russia that found, in mid-2012, strong, often overwhelming disapproval of U.S. drone attacks on extremists in the Middle East.[107] If this interpretation obtains, then Washington's reliance on technological solutions might someday incline it toward a devastating defeat, a succession of reverses, or a slow erosion of power through future military misadventures.

There is an obvious ambiguity to this predicted outcome. Only the future can tell whether Washington's bid to extend its global dominion through techno-logical innovation will fare any better than the Third Reich's defense of its con-tinental empire with wonder weapons. Whether we are witnessing the triumph of the machine or the collapse of the system, this U.S. information infrastructure, now reaching rapidly into space and cyberspace, will remain a key factor in Washington's future as a global power.

NOTES

McCoy / Fatal Florescence

This essay benefited from thoughtful readings by my coeditors Stephen Jacobson and Josep Maria Fradera, research by Wisconsin students Samuel Finesurrey and Brett Reilly, and a critical reading by my old friend Peter Kinder.

1. At its completion in 1841, the Washington statue's classical allusions aroused mixed reactions, both complementary and critical. An editorial in a Washington, D.C., newspaper described it approvingly as a "domestic Jupiter," while a letter writer to a New York paper criticized the sculptor Horace Greenough for "distrusting alike the American character and the American taste" and rendering "the father of our country, like some Roman despot," calling ancient Rome the "most arrogant, presumptuous, and miserable empire of barbarians that ever existed." *Daily National Intelligencer*, October 20, 1841; *New York Herald*, December 6, 1841. For other sources on this statue see, Oliver Larkin, "The Great Stone Paradox," *American Quarterly* 1, no. 3 (1949): 221–24; Nathalia Wright, *Horatio Greenough: The First American Sculptor* (Philadelphia: University of Pennsylvania Press, 1963), 117–59; "George Washington sculpture by Horatio Greenough, 1840," *Legacies*, Smithsonian Institution Press, http://www.smithsonianlegacies.si.edu/objectdescription.cfm?ID=66; "Landmark Object: George Washington Statue, 1841," National Museum of American History, http://americanhistory.si.edu/news/factsheet.cfm?key=30&newskey=779. Virgil, *The Aeneid*, translated by Robert Fitzgerald (New York: Vintage, 1990), 13 (1:371–75).

2. Alan P. Wallach, "Cole, Byron, and the Course of Empire," *The Art Bulletin* 50, no. 4 (1968): 375–79.

3. The White House, Office of the Press Secretary, "Remarks by the President in the State of the Union Address," January 27, 2010, http://www.whitehouse.gov/the-press-office/remarks-president-state-union-address.

4. E. J. Dionne Jr., "Off-Message Biden Recasts the Obama Agenda," *Washington Post*, February 4, 2010.

5. Cullen Murphy, *Are We Rome? The Fall of an Empire and the Fate of America* (Boston: Houghton Mifflin, 2007), 1–6; Vaclav Smil, *Why America Is Not a New Rome* (Cambridge: MIT Press, 2010), ix–xii.

6. Anne-Marie Slaughter, "Preface," in Mr. Y, *A National Strategic Narrative* (Washington, D.C.: Woodrow Wilson Center, 2011), 2, http://www.wilsoncenter.org/sites/default/files/A%20National%20Strategic%20Narrative.pdf; Robert Kagan, "Not Fade Away: The Myth of

American Decline," *The New Republic*, February 2, 2012, http://www.tnr.com/article/poli
tics/magazine/99521/america-world-power-declinism; Schuyler Null, "New Security Narrative: The National Conversation Series Launches at the Wilson Center," *New Security Beat*,
Woodrow Wilson International Center for Scholars, April 13, 2011, http://www.new
securitybeat.org/2011/04/in-search-of-new-security-narrative.html.

7. John Darwin, *After Tamerlane: The Rise and Fall of Global Empires, 1400–2000* (New
York: Bloomsbury, 2008), 16–17.

8. Piers Brendon, *The Decline and Fall of the British Empire* (New York: Vintage Books,
2010), 605.

9. Charles Maier, "The End of Empire and the Transformations of the International System," in Sarvepalli Gopal and Sergei L. Tikhvinsky, eds., *History of Humanity: Scientific and
Cultural Development*, vol. 7, *The Twentieth Century* (London: Routledge, 2008), 54.

10. Alfred W. McCoy, Francisco A. Scarano, and Courtney Johnson, "On the Tropic of
Cancer: Transitions and Transformations in the U.S. Imperial State," in Alfred W. McCoy
and Francisco A. Scarano, eds., *Colonial Crucible: Empire in the Making of a Modern American State* (Madison: University of Wisconsin Press, 2009), 4–7.

11. Fred T. Jane, *Jane's Fighting Ships: All the World's Fighting Ships* (London: William
Clowes and Sons, 1900), 68–70; Clark G. Reynolds, *Navies in History* (Annapolis: Naval
Institute Press, 1998), 104–20.

12. Niall Ferguson, *Empire: The Rise and Demise of the British World Order and the Lessons
for Global Power* (New York: Basic Books, 2002), 201–4; Brendon, *The Decline and Fall of the
British Empire*, 98–99. The figure of 99,000 soldiers includes only those units serving in the regular British Army that were funded by Great Britain's defense budget. The British Empire had
other forces, imperial and British, paid for by local colonial governments. In 1898, the total
regular force of the British Army was 211,000. But, as of 1903, 100,436 of these British troops
were serving in the Indian Army, which also had 175,000 Indian troops—and both of these
colonial contingents were sustained by Indian taxes. In sum, the British Empire had a standing
army of some 386,000 men, but Britain paid for less than third of its total cost. T. A. Heath-
cote, "The Army of British India," in David Chandler, ed., *The Oxford History of the British
Army* (Oxford: Oxford University Press, 1994), 379; *The World Almanac and Encyclopedia,
1899* (New York: Press Publishing, 1899), 342; e-mail from John Darwin, August 10, 2011.

13. Edward Gibbon, *The Decline and Fall of the Roman Empire* (New York: Everyman
Library, 1994), 4:117–27.

14. Harold James, *The Roman Predicament: How the Rules of International Order Create
the Politics of Empire* (Princeton: Princeton University Press, 2006), 21–23.

15. Paul Kennedy, *The Rise and Fall of the Great Powers* (New York: Random House,
1987), xv–xxv, 447, 528–40.

16. Eric Hobsbawm, *On Empire, War, and Global Supremacy* (New York: New Press,
2008), 62, 69–71, 87–91.

17. D. A. Low, *Eclipse of Empire* (Cambridge: Cambridge University Press, 1991), xii–xiii;
D. K. Fieldhouse, *The Colonial Empires: A Comparative Survey from the Eighteenth Century*
(New York: Macmillan, 1982), 395–97.

18. Brendon, *The Decline and Fall of the British Empire*, xviii–xx, 660–62.

19. Ronald Robinson, "Non-European Foundations of European Imperialism: Sketch for
a Theory of Collaboration," in Roger Owen and Bob Sutcliffe, eds., *Studies in the Theory of
Imperialism* (London: Longman, 1972), 138–39.

20. Darwin, *After Tamerlane*, 22–23, 493–94.

21. William Roger Louis, *Ends of British Imperialism: The Scramble for Empire, Suez, and
Decolonization* (London: I. B. Tauris, 2006), 455.

22. William Roger Louis and Ronald Robinson, "The Imperialism of Decolonization,"
Journal of Imperial and Commonwealth History 22, no. 3 (1994): 465.

23. Brendon, *The Decline and Fall of the British Empire*, 100.

24. John Gallagher and Ronald Robinson, "The Imperialism of Free Trade," *Economic History Review* 6, no. 1 (1953): 1–15.

25. Darwin, *After Tamerlane*, 492–93.

26. David Cannadine, *Ornamentalism: How the British Saw Their Empire* (New York: Oxford, 2001), 58–64.

27. Darwin, *After Tamerlane*, 14–15.

28. Robinson, "Non-European Foundations of European Imperialism," 139.

29. Brendon, *The Decline and Fall of the British Empire*, 61.

30. Alan Knight, "Britain and Latin America," in *The Oxford History of the British Empire*, vol. 3, *The Nineteenth Century* (Oxford: Oxford University Press, 1999), 135–36.

31. Kaye Whiteman, "The Man Who Ran Françafrique," *The National Interest* 49 (Fall 1997): 92–99.

32. Edward Heath, "Realism in British Foreign Policy," *Foreign Affairs* 48, no. 1 (October 1969): 39.

33. Prosser Gifford and William Roger Louis, *The Transfer of Power in Africa: Decolonization, 1940–1960* (New Haven: Yale University Press, 1982); William Roger Louis, *The British Empire in the Middle East, 1945–1951: Arab Nationalism, the United States, and Postwar Imperialism* (Oxford: Oxford University Press, 1984).

34. Arend Lijphart, *The Trauma of Decolonization: The Dutch and West New Guinea* (New Haven: Yale University Press, 1966), 192–249.

35. Richard Norton Taylor, "Not So Secret: Deal at the Heart of UK-US Intelligence," *The Guardian*, June 24, 2010, http://www.guardian.co.uk/world/2010/jun/25/intelligence-deal-uk-us-released; "Minutes of the Inauguration Meeting British Signal Intelligence Conference, 11–27 March 1946," National Security Agency, "UKUSA Agreement Release 1940–1956," http://www.nsa.gov/public_info/declass/ukusa.shtml.

36. Nick Cullather, *Secret History: The CIA's Classified Account of Its Operations in Guatemala, 1952–1954* (Stanford: Stanford University Press, 2006), 111; Stephen Dorril, *MI6: Fifty Years of Special Operations* (London: Fourth Estate, 2000), 586–96, 718, 721; Richard Aldrich, *The Hidden Hand: Britain, America, and Cold War Secret Intelligence* (London: John Murray, 2001), 467–76, 612.

37. William Roger Louis, "American Anti-colonialism and the Dissolution of the British Empire," *International Affairs* 61, no. 3 (1985): 395–420.

38. Wm. Roger Louis, *Imperialism at Bay: The United States and the Decolonization of the British Empire* (Oxford: Oxford University Press, 1977), 566.

39. Miles Kahler, *Decolonization in Britain and France: The Domestic Consequences of International Relations* (Princeton: Princeton University Press, 1984), 330–33, 348–53.

40. Brendon, *The Decline and Fall of the British Empire*, 487–506; J. G. Darwin, "The Fear of Falling: British Politics and Imperial Decline since 1900," *Transactions of the Royal Historical Society*, 5th ser., 36 (1986): 27–43.

41. Lijphart, *The Trauma of Decolonization*, 285–91.

42. Frederick Winterbotham, *The Ultra Secret* (London: Weidenfeld and Nicolson, 1974).

43. David M. Kennedy, "The Origins and Uses of American Hyperpower," in Andrew J. Bacevich, ed., *The Short American Century: A Postmortem* (Cambridge: Harvard University Press, 2012), 16, 28–29, 32; Christopher Chase-Dunn, Andrew K. Jorgenson, Thomas Reifer, and Shoon Lio, "The Trajectory of the United States in the World-System: A Quantitative Reflection," *Sociological Perspectives* 48, no. 2 (2005): 233–54; William H. Branson, Herbert Giersch, and Peter G. Peterson, "Trends in United States International Trade and Investment since World War II," in Martin Feldstein, ed., *The American Economy in Transition* (Chicago, University of Chicago Press, 1980), 191; Walter LaFeber, "Illusions of an American Century," in Bacevich, *The Short American Century*, 163.

44. Darwin, *After Tamerlane*, 470–71.

45. Kennedy, "The Origins and Uses of American Hyperpower," 33.

46. G. John Ikenberry, "The Future of the Liberal World Order: Internationalism After America," *Foreign Affairs* 90, no. 3 (May/June 2011): 61.

47. Ibid., 57–59.

48. Arnold J. Toynbee, *America and the World Revolutions* (New York: Oxford University Press, 1962), 105–13; *Chicago Daily Tribune*, September 11, 1954, February 14, 1955; James R. Blaker, *United States Overseas Basing: An Anatomy of the Dilemma* (New York: Praeger, 1990), table 2.

49. Francis Fukuyama, "The End of History?" *The National Interest* 16 (Summer 1989), 3–18.

50. Julian Go, *Patterns of Empire: The British and American Empires, 1688 to Present* (Cambridge: Cambridge University Press, 2011), 170.

51. The World Bank, World Development Indicators, Current GPD (US$), 1987–1991, http://data.worldbank.org/indicator/NY.GDP.MKTP.CD?page=5; Chase-Dunn et al., "The Trajectory of the United States in the World-System."

52. For figures on overseas bases, see Report of the Defense Secretary's Commission, *Base Realignments and Closures* (Washington, D.C.: Department of Defense, 1988), 15; for fighters and missiles, U.S. Department of the Air Force, *United States Air Force Statistical Digest, FY 1998* (Washington, D.C.: Government Printing Office, 1999), 92; for naval strength, U.S. General Accounting Office, *Navy Aircraft Carriers: Cost-Effectiveness of Conventionally and Nuclear-Powered Carriers* (Washington: U.S. General Accounting Office, 1998), 4.

53. "Table 3.1: Outlays by Superfunction and Function: 1940–2009," in Office of Management and Budget, *Historical Tables, Budget of the United States Government, Fiscal Year 2005 (2004)*, Washington, 50, http://www.whitehouse.gov/sites/default/files/omb/budget/fy 2005/pdf/hist.pdf.

54. C. Fred Bergsten, *The United States and the World Economy: Foreign Economic Policy for the Next Decade* (Washington, D.C.: Institute for International Economics, 2005), 20; Go, *Patterns of Empire*, 170.

55. World Trade Organization, 2009 Press Releases, PRESS/554, March 23, 2009, "World Trade 2008, Prospects for 2009," http://www.wto.org/english/news_e/pres09_e/pr554_e.htm; United Nations, Statistics Division, Commodity Trade Statistics Database, "UN comtrade," http://comtrade.un.org.

56. *New York Times*, July 22, August 16, 2010; Associated Press, "China Passes U.S. in Energy Use," *Wisconsin State Journal* (Madison), July 21, 2010.

57. Michael T. Klare, "Twenty-first Century Energy Superpower: China, Energy, and Global Power," *TomDispatch*, September 19, 2010, http://www.tomdispatch.com/post/175 297/tomgram%3A_michael_klare%2C_china_shakes_the_world.

58. Dominic Wilson and Roopa Purushothaman, *Global Economics Paper No. 99: Dreaming with BRICs: The Path to 2050* (New York: Goldman Sachs, October 1, 2003), 9–10, 21; Dominic Wilson and Anna Stupnytska, *Global Economics Paper No. 153: The N-11: More Than an Acronym* (New York: Goldman Sachs, March 28, 2007), 8, http://www.chicago booth.edu/alumni/clubs/pakistan/docs/next11dream-march%20'07-goldmansachs.pdf.

59. *New York Times*, August 16, 2010.

60. *New York Times*, September 11, 2011.

61. International Monetary Fund, "World Economic Outlook Database," April 2011 edition, http://www.imf.org/external/pubs/ft/weo/2011/01/weodata/index.aspx; Mark Weisbrot, "2016 When China Overtakes the US," *The Guardian*, April 27, 2011, http://www .guardian.co.uk/commentisfree/cifamerica/2011/apr/27/china-imf-economy-2016.

62. World Bank Group, "World Development Indicators: Patent Applications, Residents," http://data.worldbank.org/indicator/IP.PAT.RESD.

63. Robert D. Atkinson and Scott Andes, *The Atlantic Century: Benchmarking EU and U.S. Innovation and Competitiveness* (Information Technology and Innovation Foundation, February 2009), 2–4, http://www.itif.org/files/2009-atlantic-century.pdf.

64. *New York Times*, October 28, 2010. Two years later, the U.S. regained the number one slot with the Sequoia supercomputer designed by IBM for the National Nuclear Security Administration. See, Deborah Netburn, "U.S. Wins: Fastest Supercomputer in World Is Right Here," *Los Angeles Times*, June 18, 2012, http://www.latimes.com/business/technol ogy/la-fi-tn-fastest-super-computer-20120618,0,4055242.story.

65. Claudia Goldin and Lawrence F. Katz, *The Race between Education and Technology* (Cambridge: Harvard University Press, 2008), 324–30.

66. *New York Times*, December 7, 2010.

67. *New York Times*, July 23, 2010; World Economic Forum, *The Global Competitiveness Report, 2010–2011* (Geneva: World Economic Forum, 2010), 421, http://www3.weforum .org/docs/WEF_GlobalCompetitivenessReport_2010-11.pdf.

68. James Clay Moltz, "Russia and China: Strategic Choices in Space," in Damon Coletta and Frances T. Pilch, eds., *Space and Defense Policy* (London and New York: Routledge, 2009), 277, 281.

69. *New York Times*, October 27, 2010; Members of the 2005 "Rising above the Gather-ing Storm" Committee, *Rising above the Gathering Storm Revisited: Rapidly Approaching Category 5* (Washington, D.C.: National Academies Press, 2010), 5, http://www.cra.org/gov affairs/blog/wp-content/uploads/2010/09/RAGS-Revisited.pdf.

70. United Nations Development Program, "Human Development Index 2007 and Its Components," in *UN Development Report, 2009*, http://hdrstats.undp.org/en/indicators/91 .html; NationMaster.com, Economy Statistics>GINI index (most recent) by country, http:// www.nationmaster.com/graph/eco_gin_ind-economy-gini-index.

71. Rohini Hensman and Marinella Correggia, "US Dollar Hegemony: The Soft Under-belly of Empire," *Economic and Political Weekly* 40, no. 12 (March 19, 2005): 1093–95.

72. Michael Hudson, "Washington Can't Call the Shots Anymore," *Financial Times*, June 15, 2009.

73. Peter S. Green, "Volcker Says Dollar's Role in Danger as U.S. Influence Declines Globally," *Bloomberg*, December 1, 2010, http://www.bloomberg.com/news/2010-12-01/vol cker-says-dollar-s-global-role-is-in-danger-as-u-s-influence-declines.html.

74. *New York Times*, August 7, 2011.

75. U.S. National Intelligence Council, *Global Trends, 2025: A Transformed World* (Wash-ington, D.C.: Government Printing Office, 2008), vi, 97, 42.

76. For Portugal and U.S. natural gas, see *New York Times*, August 9, 2010, June 10, 2012. For Germany, see *New York Times*, December 26, 2008. For China, see *New York Times*, December 14, 2010, September 2, 2011; and Michael Richardson, "China's Green Ambition, US Sees Red," *Yale Global*, January 5, 2011, http://yaleglobal.yale.edu/content/chinas-green-ambition-us-sees-red. For France, see World Nuclear Association, "Nuclear Power in France," http://www.world-nuclear.org/info/inf40.html. For Denmark, see Bryan Walsh, "Denmark's Wind of Change," *Time*, February 25, 2009. For the Netherlands, see *New York Times*, August 29, 2008, August 10, 2010, and December 15, 2010.

77. U.S. Energy Information Administration, "Annual Energy Outlook 2010 with Pro-jections to 2035," May 11, 2010, http://www.eia.doe.gov/oiaf/aeo/execsummary.html.

78. *New York Times*, November 5, 2011.

79. Amy Belasco, *The Cost of Iraq, Afghanistan, and Other Global War on Terror Opera-tions since 9/11* (Washington, D.C.: Congressional Research Service, September 2, 2010), 1–3, http://www.fas.org/sgp/crs/natsec/RL33110.pdf.

80. *New York Times*, November 6, 2010.

81. Michael Mandelbaum, *The Frugal Superpower: America's Global Leadership in a Cash-Strapped Era* (Philadelphia: Perseus, 2010), 20, 46–52, 185.

82. Tim Weiner, *Legacy of Ashes: The History of the CIA* (New York: Random House, 2008), 29–30, 39–40, 44–54, 61–70, 84–87, 92–105, 133–40, 142, 187–89, 321–22; William

Rosenau, *U.S. Internal Security Assistance to South Vietnam: Insurgency, Subversion and Public Order* (New York: Routledge, 2005), 18–26.

83. LaFeber, "Illusions of an American Century," 169–70.

84. U.S. Department of State, *Foreign Relations Series of the United States, 1952–1954*, vol. 2, *National Security Affairs*, part 2 (Washington, D.C.: Government Printing Office, 1984), 838.

85. Memorandum, William H. Godel (Deputy Director, Office of Special Operations, DOD) to William J. Donovan (former Ambassador to Thailand), July 26, 1955, Box 9, William J. Donovan Papers, U.S. Army Heritage and Education Center, Carlisle Barracks, Pennsylvania.

86. Weiner, *Legacy of Ashes*, 157, 322–23, 717; Samuel P. Huntington, *The Third Wave: Democratization in the Late Twentieth Century* (Norman: University of Oklahoma Press, 1991), 16–21; Robert Kagan, *The World America Made* (New York: Knopf, 2012), 23–24; John Charmley, *Churchill's Grand Alliance: The Anglo-American Special Relationship, 1940–1957* (New York: Harcourt Brace, 1995), 97.

87. *New York Times*, February 12, February 20, 2011.

88. Embtel 496, Embassy Manama to Embassy Baghdad, July 25, 2008, Wikileaks Cablegate Archive, Reference ID: 08MANAMA496, http://wikileaks.org/cable/2008/07/08MANAMA496.html.

89. Frank Baldwin, "America's Rented Troops: South Koreans in Vietnam," *Bulletin of Concerned Asian Scholars* 7, no. 4 (1975): 33–40.

90. Tony Blair, *A Journey: My Political Life* (New York: Knopf, 2010), 407.

91. *New York Times*, February 8, 2012.

92. *Washington Post*, December 13, 2010.

93. *New York Times*, August 30, September 1, 2011; Aluf Benn, "WikiLeaks Cables Tell the Story of an Empire in Decline," *Haaretz*, December 12, 2010, http://www.haaretz.com/print-edition/opinion/wikileaks-cables-tell-the-story-of-an-empire-in-decline-1.328145.

94. Deptel 37561, State to Embassy Bujumbura, April 16, 2009, Wikileaks Cablegate Archive, Reference ID: 09STATE37561, http://wikileaks.org/cable/2009/04/09STATE37561.html.

95. Deptel 105048, State to Embassy Manama, October 8, 2009, Wikileaks Cablegate Archive, Reference ID: 09STATE105048, http://wikileaks.org/cable/2009/10/09STATE105048.html.

96. "U.S. Embassy Cables: Bomb al-Qaida Where You Want, Yemen Tells US, but Don't Blame Us if They Strike Again," *The Guardian*, December 3, 2010, http://www.guardian.co.uk/world/us-embassy-cables-documents/225085; "U.S. Embassy Cables: Profile of 'Intellectually Curious' but 'Notoriously Mercurial' Gaddafi," *The Guardian*, December 7, 2010, http://www.guardian.co.uk/world/us-embassy-cables-documents/167961; "U.S. Embassy Cables: King Hamad and Bahrain's Relationship with the US," *The Guardian*, February 15, 2011, http://www.guardian.co.uk/world/us-embassy-cables-documents/237626.

97. *New York Times*, February 20, 2011.

98. "U.S. Embassy Cables: Tunisia—a U.S. Foreign Policy Conundrum," *The Guardian*, December 7, 2010, http://www.guardian.co.uk/world/us-embassy-cables-documents/217138.

99. Embtel 2543, Embassy Cairo to State, December 13, 2008, Wikileaks Cablegate Archive, Reference ID: 08CAIRO2543, http://wikileaks.org/cable/2008/12/08CAIRO2543.html.

100. Embtel 874, Embassy Cairo to State, May 19, 2009, Wikileaks Cablegate Archive, Reference ID: 08CAIRO783, http://wikileaks.org/cable/2008/04/08CAIRO783.html.

101. "Obama Interview: The Transcript," *BBC News World Service*, June 2, 2009, http://www.bbc.co.uk/worldservice/news/2009/06/090602_obama_transcript.shtml.

102. Lisa Hajjar, "Suleiman: The CIA's Man in Cairo," *Al Jazeera*, February 7, 2011, http://english.aljazeera.net/indepth/opinion/2011/02/201127114827382865.html.

103. Geoffrey Wheatcroft, "America's Unraveling Power," *New York Times*, February 10, 2011; *New York Times*, July 10, 2012

104. *New York Times*, February 8, 2011.

105. Ikenberry, "The Future of the Liberal World Order," 66.

106. Kagan, *The World America Made*, 58.

107. Zbigniew Brzezinski, *Strategic Vision: America and the Crisis of Global Power* (New York: Basic Books, 2012), 44–45.

108. *New York Times*, November 12, 2010.

109. *New York Times*, November 4, 2011.

110. *TR Defence*, November 7, 2010, http://www.trdefence.com/?p=1768; *Atlantic Council*, October 6, 2010, http://www.acus.org/natosource/new-questions-about-turkeys-secret-military-exercise-china.

111. VOANews.com, September 25, 2010, http://www.voanews.com/english/news/Australia-China-Conduct-Live-Fire-Naval-Exercise-in-Yellow-Sea-103780194.html.

112. Andrew F. Krepinevich, *Why AirSea Battle?* (Washington, D.C.: Center for Strategic and Budgetary Assessments, 2010), 2–11, http://www.csbaonline.org/wp-content/uploads/2010/02/2010.02.19-Why-AirSea-Battle.pdf.

113. David Vine, *Island of Shame: The Secret History of the U.S. Military Base on Diego Garcia* (Princeton: Princeton University Press, 2009), 10; Richard G. Burgess, "Guam's Return to Prominence," January 25, 2007, Military.com, http://www.military.com/forums/0,15240,123418,00.html.

114. *New York Times*, September 12, 2010; Peter Ford, "China and the U.S. Battle to Assert Presence in South China Sea," *Christian Science Monitor*, August 17, 2010, http://www.csmonitor.com/World/Asia-Pacific/2010/0817/China-and-the-US-battle-to-assert-presence-in-South-China-Sea.

115. Office of the Secretary of Defense, *Military and Security Developments Involving the People's Republic of China, 2010* (Washington, D.C.: Department of Defense, August 2010), i, 1–3, 7, 25–26, 30, 34–37; *New York Times*, August 17, 2010; "China Launches New Global Positioning Satellite," *Reuters*, July 31, 2010, http://www.reuters.com/article/idUSTRE67005R20100801.

116. Brzezinski, *Strategic Vision*, 122.

117. *New York Times*, May 4, 2011.

118. Edward Helmore, "US Air Force Prepares Drones to End Era of Fighter Pilots," *The Guardian*, August 22, 2009, http://www.guardian.co.uk/world/2009/aug/22/us-air-force-drones-pilots-afghanistan.

119. David Ignatius, "Transforming U.S. Military Might into 21st-Century Weapons," *Washington Post*, January 2, 2011.

120. U.S. National Intelligence Council, *The 2020 Global Landscape* (Washington, D.C.: U.S. National Intelligence Council, 2005), Executive Summary, http://www.dni.gov/nic/NIC_globaltrend2020_es.html.

121. Tom Bower, *The Paperclip Conspiracy: The Hunt for Nazi Scientists* (Boston: Little Brown, 1987), 35–37, 40–45, 49–51, 53–59, 64–66, 73–78, 87.

122. Jim O'Neil, *The Growth Map: Economic Opportunity in the BRICs and Beyond* (New York: Penguin, 2011), introduction; *New York Times*, January 23, 2012; Wilson and Stupnytska, *Global Economics Paper No. 153: The N-11*, 9, 15.

123. *New York Times*, December 3, December 24, 2011.

124. Kagan, *The World America Made*, 92–93. See the essay by Courtney Johnson in this volume exploring the major changes in Anglo-American and Pan-American amity that accompanied the U.S. emergence as a major power circa 1900.

125. Akira Iriye, "Toward Transnationalism," in Bacevich, *The Short American Century*, 141; Brzezinski, *Strategic Vision*, 115–19.

126. Ikenberry, "The Future of the Liberal World Order," 57–58, 61–68.

127. Michael Hardt and Antonio Negri, *Empire* (Cambridge: Harvard University Press, 2000), xi–xvii, 179–90, 214–18, 325–48, 393–403; Michael Hardt and Antonio Negri, *Multitude: War and Democracy in the Age of Empire* (New York: Penguin, 2005), xii–xiii, 30–32, 59–61, 129–38, 163–76; Brzezinski, *Strategic Vision*, 115–16; Mike Davis, *Planet of Slums* (London: Verso, 2007), 151, 199, 205–6.

128. U.S. National Intelligence Council, *The 2020 Global Landscape*, Executive Summary.

129. Jeffrey A. Frieden, "From the American Century to Globalization," in Bacevich, *The Short American Century*, 156.

130. Brzezinski, *Strategic Vision*, 76–77.

131. Mark Twain, "Passage from 'Outlines of History' (suppressed.) Date 9th Century," in Jim Zwick, ed., *Mark Twain's Weapons of Satire: Anti-imperialist Writings on the Philippine-American War* (Syracuse: Syracuse University Press, 1992), 78–79.

Delgado Ribas / Eclipse and Collapse of the Spanish Empire

1. Niall Ferguson, "Complexity and Collapse. Empires on the Edge of Chaos," *Foreign Affairs* 26 (March–April 2010): 18–32; Carl Boggs, *Imperial Delusions: American Militarism and Endless War* (Lanham: Rowman and Littlefield, 2005), 192–212. For an ultraconservative perspective, see Gene W. Heck, *The Eclipse of the American Century: An Agenda for Renewal* (Lanham: Rowman and Littlefield, 2008).

2. Herbert B. Gray and Samuel Turner, *Eclipse of Empire?* (London: Nisbet, 1916); Richard Jebb, *The Empire in Eclipse* (London: Chapman and Hall, 1926).

3. For a full historiographic review of end-of-empire perspectives, see John Darwin, "Decolonization and the End of Empire," in Robin W. Winks, ed., *The Oxford History of the British Empire*, vol. 5, *Historiography* (Oxford: Oxford University Press, 201), 541–57. For an analysis of the strategies—ranging from indirect rule to a "special relationship" with the United States—that Great Britain pursued between 1918 and the 1960s to counteract its loss of influence in the world, see Ronald Hyam, *Britain's Declining Empire. The Road to Decolonisation* (Cambridge: Cambridge University Press, 2006), 12–29.

4. This is, though, beginning to change. See, J. H. Elliot, "The Eclipse of Empire in British and Spanish America," in *Spain, Europe, and the Wider World, 1500–1800* (New Haven: Yale University Press, 2009), 211–30.

5. *Calcutta Review* 106, no. 2 (1898): 70. For the text of the speech, see *Times of London*, May 5, 1898, 18; or *New York Times*, May 18, 1898, 5–6.

6. See, for example, "Spain Ready to Collapse," *Omaha Sunday Bee*, November 27, 1898.

7. For an overview of these, see Gabriel Paquette, "The Dissolution of the Spanish Atlantic Monarchy," *Historical Journal* 52, no. 1 (2009): 175–212.

8. David Ringrose, *Spain, Europe, and the "Spanish Miracle," 1700–1900* (Cambridge: Cambridge University Press, 1996), 83.

9. On industry and trade, see Leandro Prados de la Escosura, *De imperio a nación: Crecimiento y atraso económico en España (1780–1930)* (Madrid: Alianza Editorial, 1988). On Spain's fiscal difficulties, see Josep Fontana, *La quiebra de la monarquía absoluta, 1814–1820: La crisis del Antiguo Régimen en España* (Barcelona: Crítica, 2002), 31–36.

10. Melchor Fernández Almagro, *La emancipación de América y su reflejo en la conciencia española* (Madrid: Hispánica, 1944), 11.

11. Emiliano Fernández de Pinedo, "La recuperación del comercio español con América a mediados del siglo XIX," in A-Miguel Bernal, *Antiguo Régimen y liberalismo: Homenaje a Miguel Artola*, vol. 1, *Visiones generales* (Madrid: Alianza Editorial, 1994), 51–66.

12. Angel Bahamonde and José Cayuela, *Hacer las Américas: Las élites coloniales españolas en el siglo XIX* (Madrid: Alianza Editorial, 1992). Martin Rodrigo y Alharilla, *Los*

marqueses de Comillas, 1817–1925: Antonio y Claudio López (Madrid: LID Editorial, 2000); *Indians a Catalunya: Capitals cubans en l'economia catalana* (Barcelona: Fundació Noguera, 2007); and "Empresarios en la distancia: Con el negocio en Cuba y la vivienda en Cataluña," *Illes i Imperis* 10–11 (2008): 153–66.

　13. This argument is forcefully made in Enric Ucelay-Da Cal, *El imperialismo catalán: Prat de la Riba, Cambó, D'Ors y la conquista moral de España* (Barcelona: Edhasa, 2003), 64–76. See also José Álvarez Junco, "La nación en duda," in Juan Pan-Montojo, ed., *Más se perdió en Cuba: España, 1898, y la crisis de fin de siglo* (Madrid: Alianza Editorial, 1998), 405–75.

　14. Gonzalo de Reparaz, "Lo que fue y *lo que resta*," *Blanco y Negro*, August 13, 1898, 9–10 (my italics).

　15. Alejandro R. Díez Torre, "África y el africanismo del iberista Gonzalo de Reparaz," in Alejandro R. Díez Torre, ed., *Ciencia y memoria de África: Actas de las III Jornadas sobre expediciones científicas y africanismo español, 1898–1998* (Madrid: Universidad de Alcalá de Henares, 2002), 243–76; José A. Rocamora, "Un nacionalismo fracasado: El iberismo," *Espacio, Tiempo y Forma*, ser. 5, *Historia Contemporánea* 2 (1989): 29–56.

　16. Reparaz, "Lo que fue y *lo que resta*," 10.

　17. Matthew Restall, "The Decline and Fall of the Spanish Empire," *William and Mary Quarterly* 64, no. 1 (2007): 1–8. The first to point in this direction was John Elliott in "The Decline of Spain," *Past and Present* 20 (1961): 52–75.

　18. Henry Kamen describes this discourse as a "myth." However, I would argue that the frequency of such discourse means that the sensation of decline has to be regarded as a reality. See Henry Kamen, *Empire: How Spain Became a World Power, 1492–1763* (New York: Harper Collins, 2003), 489.

　19. I have dealt with this issue in greater depth in Josep M. Delgado Ribas, *Dinámicas imperiales (1650–1796): España, América y Europa en el cambio institucional del sistema colonial español* (Barcelona: Bellaterra, 2007), 45–71.

　20. John Leddy Phelan, "Authority and Flexibility in the Spanish Imperial Bureaucracy," *Administrative Science Quarterly* 5, no. 1 (June 1960): 47–65.

　21. Stanley Stein and Barbara Stein, *Silver, Trade, and War: Spain and America in the Making of Early Modern Europe* (Baltimore: Johns Hopkins University Press, 2000), 57–105.

　22. Reparaz, "Lo que fue y *lo que resta*," 9.

　23. Joaquim Albareda, *La Guerra de Sucesión de España (1700–1714)* (Barcelona: Crítica, 2010), 131–33.

　24. A copy can be found in the Spanish Archivo Histórico Nacional: Estado, leg. 2927.

　25. Allan J. Kuethe, "Las milicias disciplinadas de América," in J. Marchena and A. J. Kuethe, eds., *Soldados del Rey: El ejército borbónico en América colonial en vísperas de la Independencia* (Castellón: Universitat Jaume I, 2005), 151–59; Juan Marchena, *Oficiales y soldados en el ejército de América* (Seville: Escuela de Estudios Hispano-Americanos—Consejo Superior de Investigaciones Científicas, 1983), 79–80.

　26. Allan J. Kuethe, *Cuba, 1753–1815: Crown, Military, and Society* (Knoxville: University of Tennessee Press, 1986).

　27. From 1760 to 1766 the monarchy's annual military spending fell by 55 percent as a result of the savings that Esquilache made in the army and navy; see Delgado Ribas, *Dinámicas imperiales*, 367.

　28. Carlos Corona Baratech, "Las Milicias Provinciales en España durante el siglo XVIII como ejército peninsular de reserva," in *Congreso Internacional de Historia Militar: Temas de Historia Militar*, vol. 1 (Zaragoza: Consejo Superior de Investigaciones Científicas, 1982).

　29. Viceroy of New Spain Bucareli to Secretary of State Grimaldi, Mexico, April 26, 1772, Archivo General de las Indias, Serie: Indiferente General, leg. 1630.

30. Josep M. Torras Ribé, *Los mecanismos del poder: Los ayuntamientos catalanes durante el siglo XVIII* (Barcelona: Crítica, 2003), 35–54.

31. For a theoretical cost-benefit analysis of secession processes, see Viva Ona Bartkus, *The Dynamic of Secession* (Cambridge: Cambridge University Press, 1999), 8–30.

FRADERA / EMPIRES IN RETREAT

1. For an exhaustive description of the Portuguese imperial crisis, see Valentim Alexandre, *Os sentidos do Império: Questão Nacional e Questão Colonial na Crise do Antigo Regime Português* (Lisbon: Edições Afrontamento, 1993), 595–97.

2. Essential reading is C. A. Bayly, *The Birth of the Modern World, 1780–1914* (Oxford: Blackwell, 2004), 86–120.

3. Kirsten Schulz, *Tropical Versailles: Empire, Monarchy, and the Portuguese Royal Court in Rio de Janeiro, 1808–1821* (New York: Routledge, 2001); José Luis Cardoso, "The Transfer to the Court to Brazil, 200 Years Afterwards," *Journal of Portuguese History* 7, no. 1 (2007): 1–10.

4. Carlos Antolín Cano, "Una contienda diplomática durante el reinado de Carlos IV: Las relaciones hispano-portuguesas en el periodo revolucionario, 1780–1802," *Hispania* 153 (1983): 65–87.

5. João Paulo Garrido Pimenta, *Estado e Nação no fim dos impérios ibéricos no Prata (1808–1828)* (São Paulo: Hucitec, 2006); Maximiliano M. Menz, *Entre Impérios: Formação do Rio Grande na Crise do Sistema Colonial Português (1777–1822)* (São Paulo: Alameda, 2009).

6. This document is reproduced in José Luis Cardoso, *A economia política e os dilemas do império luso-brasileiro (1790–1822)* (Lisbon: Comissão para as Commemoraçoes dos Descobrimentos Portugueses, 2001), 202.

7. This argument is convincingly and explicitly made in Luiz Felipe de Alencastro, *O Trato dos Viventes: Formação do Brasil no Atlântico Sul* (São Paulo: Companhia das Letras, 2000).

8. See J. M. Delgado Ribas, *Dinámicas imperiales: España, América y Europa en el cambio institucional del sistema colonial español* (Barcelona: Ediciones Bellaterra, 2007).

9. Kenneth Maxwell, *Conflicts and Conspiracies in Brazil and Portugal, 1750–1808* (London: Routledge, 2004); Itsván Jancsó, *Na Bahia, Contra o Império: História do Ensaio de Sediçao de 1798* (São Paulo: Editora Hucitec, 2000).

10. For an overall view, see Tulio Halperín Donghi, *Reforma y disolución de los imperios ibéricos, 1750–1850* (Madrid: Alianza, 1985).

11. Roberto Breña, *El primer liberalismo español y los procesos de emancipación de América, 1808–1824: Una revisión historiográfica del primer liberalismo hispánico* (Mexico City: El Colegio de México, 2006).

12. A. M. Hespanha, *As Vesperas do Leviathan: Instituçoes e Poder Político em Portugal, Sec. XVII* (Coimbra: Almadina, 1994).

13. Márcia Regina Berbel, "A constitução espanhola no mundo luso-americano (1820–1823)," *Revista de Indias* 68, no. 242 (2008): 225–54.

14. J. M. Fradera. "Raza y ciudadanía: El factor racial en la definición de los derechos de los americanos," in *Gobernar colonias* (Barcelona: Ediciones Península, 1999), 51–70.

15. For a further development of these questions in the Portuguese world, see Cristina Nogueira da Silva, *Constitucionalismo e Império: A Cidadania no Ultramar Portugués* (Coimbra: Almedina, 2009).

16. Márcia Berbel, Rafael Marquese, and Tâmis Parron, *Escravidão e política: Brasil e Cuba, 1790–1850* (São Paulo: Hucitec, 2010).

17. This issue is discussed in José María Portillo Valdés, *Revolución de Nación: Orígenes de la cultura constitucional en España* (Madrid: Instituto de Estudios Políticos, 1991).

18. For the Portuguese case, see Valentim Alexandre, *A Questão Colonial no Parlamento*. vol. 1, *1821–1910* (Lisbon: Publicaçoes Dom Quixote, 2008).

19. Márcia Regina Berbel, *A Nação como Artefato: Deputados do Brasil nas Cortes Portuguesas (1821–1822)* (São Paulo: Hucitec, 1999).

20. For an excellent collective work on the formation of monarchic Brazil, see Keila Grinberg and Ricardo Salles, eds., *O Brasil imperial*, vol. 1, *1808–1831* (Rio de Janeiro: Civilisação Brasileira, 2009).

21. Regarding the Spanish enclaves, see Manuel Moreno Fraginals, *El ingenio: Complejo económico social cubano del azúcar*, 3 vols. (Havana: Editorial de Ciencias Sociales, 1978); and Francisco A. Scarano, *Sugar and Slavery in Puerto Rico: The Plantation Economy of Ponce, 1800–1850* (Madison: University of Wisconsin Press, 1984).

22. Stuart B. Schwartz, *Sugar Plantations in the Formation of Brazilian Society: Bahia, 1550–1835* (Cambridge: Cambridge University Press, 1985); A. J. R. Russell-Wood, *The Black Man in Slavery and Freedom in Colonial Brazil* (London: Macmillan, 1982).

23. For a detailed description, see J. M. Fradera, *Colonias para después de un imperio* (Barcelona: Ediciones Bellaterra, 2005).

24. Franklin W. Knight, *Slave Society in Cuba during the Nineteenth Century* (Madison: University of Wisconsin Press, 1970); Rebecca J. Scott, *Slave Emancipation in Cuba: The Transition to Free Labor, 1860–1899* (Princeton: Princeton University Press, 1985). The *chinos de Manila* were mainland Chinese indentured servants sent to Cuba and Puerto Rico via Manila.

25. Ed. de Jesus, *The Tobacco Monopoly in the Philippines: Bureaucratic Enterprise and Social Change, 1766–1880* (Quezon City: Ateneo de Manila Press, 1980).

26. Arthur F. Corwin, *Spain and the Abolition of Slavery in Cuba, 1817–1886* (Austin: University of Texas Press, 1967); David Murray, *Odious Commerce: Britain, Spain, and the Abolition of the Cuban Slave Trade* (Cambridge: Cambridge University Press, 1980).

27. Fradera, *Colonias para después de un imperio*, 327–438.

28. For a general description of the new empire, see Francisco Bethencourt and Kirti Chaudhury, eds., *Nova Historia da Expansão Portuguesa*, vol. 4, *Do Brasil para África (1808–1930)* (Lisbon: Editorial Estampa, 1998); and Gervase Clarence-Smith, *The Third Portuguese Empire, 1825–1975: A Study in Economic Imperialism* (Manchester: Manchester University Press, 1985).

29. José C. Curto, *Enslaving Spirits: The Portuguese Brazilian Alcohol Trade at Luanda and Its Hinterland* (Leiden: Brill, 2004).

30. Jeremy Adelman, *Sovereignty and Revolution in the Iberian Atlantic* (Princeton: Princeton University Press, 2007), 230–241.

31. Leslie Bethell, "Britain, Portugal, and the Suppression of the Brazilian Slave Trade: The Origins of Lord Palmerston's Act of 1839," *English Historical Review* 80, no. 317 (1965): 761–84.

32. Leslie Bethell, *The Abolition of the Brazilian Slave Trade: Britain, Brazil, and the Slave Trade Question, 1807–1868* (Cambridge: Cambridge University Press: 1970).

33. João Estevão, "Cabo Verde," in *O Imperio Africano, 1825–1890*, vol. 10 of *Nova História da Expansão Portuguesa* (Lisbon: Editorial Estampa, 1996), 169–210.

34. M. A. Klein, "The Impact of the Atlantic Slave Trade on the Societies of Western Sudan," in Joseph E. Inokori and Stanley Engerman, eds., *The Atlantic Slave Trade: Effects on Economies, Societies, and Peoples in Africa, the Americas, and Europe* (Durham: Duke University Press, 1992), 25–48; M. A. Klein, "The Slave Trade and Decentralized Societies," *Journal of African History* 42 (2001): 49–65.

35. Giuseppe Papagno, *Colonialismo e Feudalismo: A questão dos Prazos da Coroa em Moçambique nos finais do século XIX* (Lisbon: A Regra do Jogo, 1980).

36. J. M. Fradera, *Filipinas, la colonia más peculiar: La hacienda pública en la definición de la política colonial, 1762–1868* (Madrid: Consejo Superior de Investigaciones Científicas, 1999).

37. Benito J. Legarda Jr., *After the Galleons: Foreign Trade, Economic Change, and Entre-preneurship in the Nineteenth-Century Philippines* (Quezon City: Ateneo de Manila University Press, 1999).

38. J. Darwin, *After Tamerlane. The Rise and Fall of Global Empires, 1400–2000* (London, Penguin Books, 2007).

39. Christopher Schmidt-Nowara, *Empire and Antislavery: Spain, Cuba, and Puerto Rico, 1833–1874* (Pittsburgh: University of Pittsburgh Press, 1999).

JACOBSON / IMPERIAL AMBITIONS IN AN ERA OF DECLINE

1. See, for example, John Darwin, *The Rise and Fall of Global Empires, 1400–2000* (London: Bloomsbury, 2008); and Ian Morris, *Why the West Rules—For Now* (New York: Farrar, Straus and Giroux, 2010).

2. For an evaluation and critique of this argument, see Felipe Fernández-Armesto, "The Improbable Empire," in Raymond Carr, ed., *Spain: A History* (Oxford: Oxford University Press, 2000), 116–51. For the latest word, see Henry Kamen, *Empire: How Spain Became a World Power, 1492–1763* (London: Penguin, 2002); and, of course, the essays in this volume.

3. Emmanuel Todd, *After the Empire: The Breakdown of the American Order* (New York: Columbia University Press, 2003), 134.

4. I borrow this term from John Darwin, *The Empire Project: The Rise and Fall of the British World System, 1830–1970* (Cambridge: Cambridge University Press, 2009). He, in turn, derived the expression from Adam Smith.

5. For the Spanish-American War and the insightful comparison with Russia, see John Tone, *War and Genocide in Cuba, 1895–98* (Chapel Hill: University of North Carolina Press, 2006), 8–9. For the Ten Years' War, see César R. Yáñez Gallardo, "La última invasión armada: Los contigentes militares españoles en las guerras de Cuba, siglo XIX," *Revista de Indias* 52, no. 194 (1992): 107–27, esp. 113.

6. Manuel Moreno Fraginals, *El ingenio complejo económico social cubano de azúcar* (Barcelona: Crítica, 2001), 536; Ada Ferrer, *Insurgent Cuba: Race, Nation, and Revolution, 1868–1898* (Chapel Hill: University of North Carolina Press, 1999), 2.

7. For the reform and peculiarities of the Spanish empire in the nineteenth century, see Josep M. Fradera, *Colonias para después de un imperio* (Barcelona: Edicions Bellaterra, 2005).

8. As demonstrated by Seymour Drescher, slavery was economically viable and profitable despite the advent of abolition. Seymour Drescher, *From Slavery to Abolition: Comparative Studies in the Rise and Fall of Atlantic Slavery* (New York: New York University Press, 1999).

9. This is explained in detail in Josep M. Fradera, *Indústria i mercat: Les bases comercials de la indústria catalana moderna (1814–1845)* (Barcelona: Crítica, 1989), 236–41.

10. This was obviously in violation of treaties signed with Britain in 1817 and 1835. From 1819 to 1861, Britain brought 244 slave ships, 182 of which carried the Spanish flag, to trial in the Court of Sierra Leone. See Arturo Arnalte, "El Tribunal Mixto Anglo-Español en Sierra Leona, 1819–1865," *Cuadernos de Historia Moderna y Contemporánea* 6 (1985): 197–215.

11. For these routes, see Pere Pascual, *Agricultura i industrialització a la Catalunya del segle XIX* (Barcelona: Crítica, 1990), 196–97; and César Yáñez, "El perfil ultramarí de l'economia catalana," in Josep M. Fradera, César Yañez, Albert Garcia Balañà, Doria González, Miguel Ángel Puig-Samper, Luis Ángel Sánchez, Martín Rodrigo Juan José Lahuerta, *Catalunya i ultramar: Poder i negoci a les colònies espanyoles (1750–1914)* (Barcelona: Museu Marítim Drassanes de Barcelona, 54–76, esp. 61–62.

12. Albert Garcia Balañà notes that as of December 31, 1858, Spain had purchased some 4,046 shares. This number was considerably below those of France (207,111) and the Ottoman Empire (96,517). However, it was higher than those of Holland, Belgium, and Prussia.

British and Austrian shares had yet to be announced. See Albert Garcia Balañà, "'El comercio español en África' en la Barcelona de 1858: Entre el Caribe y el Mar de China, entre Londres y París," *Illes i Imperis* 10–11 (1998): 167–86. esp. 186.

13. For a biography of this interesting person, see Martín Rodrigo y Alharilla, *Los Marqueses de Comillas, 1817–1925* (Madrid: LID Editorial, 2000).

14. For the latest word on the Liberal Union, see Francesc A. Martínez Gallego, *Conservar progresando: La Unión Liberal (1856–1868)* (Valencia: Historia Social Biblioteca, 2001), 11–116;. For O'Donnell's Cuban circles, see José G. Cayeula Fernández, "Estrategias político militares y sistema defensivo de la isla de Cuba (1854–1859)," *Estudios históricos: Homenaje a los profesores José María Jover y Vicente Palacio Atard* (Madrid: Universidad Complutense, 1990), 553–77.

15. For a good summary of these actions, see Nelson Durán, *La Unión Liberal y la modernización de la España isabelina: Una convivencia frustrada, 1854–1868* (Madrid: Akal, 1979), 225–76. For a recent analysis incorporating the latest bibliography, see Juan Antonio Inarejos Muñoz, *Intervenciones coloniales y nacionalismo español: La política exterior de la Unión Liberal y sus vínculos con la Francia de Napoleón III (1856–1868)* (Madrid: Sílex, 2010).

16. J. Mañé y Flaquer, "Las grandes potencias," *Diario de Barcelona*, August 19, 1860, 7707–8.

17. For the annexation of the Dominican Republic, see Eduardo González Calleja and Antonio Fontecha Pedraza, *Una cuestión de honor: La polémica sobre la anexión de Santo Domingo vista desde España (1861–65)* (Santo Domingo: Fundación García Arévalo, 2005); and Cristóbal Robles, *Paz en Santo Domingo (1854–65): El fracaso de la anexión a España* (Madrid: Consejo Superior de Investigaciones Científicas, 1987).

18. J. Molá y Martínez "El abandono de Santo Domingo," *Diario de Barcelona*, April 5, 1865, 3492–94.

19. For the War of the Pacific, see William Columbus Davis, *The Last Conquistadores: The Spanish Intervention in Peru and Chile, 1863–1866* (Athens: University of Georgia Press, 1950). Despite the presence of various assumption that reek of the "Black Legend," this dated study is an informed analysis based on Spanish, Peruvian, Chilean, and British press accounts.

20. For a discussion of the number of deaths, see Joan Serrallonga Urquidi, "La Guerra de África (1859–60): Una revisión," *Ayer* 29 (1998): 139–59, esp. 157. Martínez Gallego lists sixteen thousand dead, nine thousand from disease; however, he does not reveal his source (*Conservar progresando*, 131).

21. Simón Segura, "La desamortización de 1855," *Economía Financiera Española* 19–20 (1967): 95–104.

22. José Doménech y Coll, "Presupuesto de obligaciones generales del Estado," *Diario de Barcelona* 6 (August 1860): 7375.

23. Manuel García Arévalo, "Presentación," in Eduardo González Calleja and Antonio Fontecha Pedraza, *Una cuestión de honor*, xviii; Fradera, *Colonias para después de un imperio*, 658.

24. Davis, *The Last Conquistadores*, 242.

25. For the colonial dimensions of Prim's biography, see Josep M. Fradera, "Juan Prim y Prats (1814–1870): Prim conspirador o la pedogía del sable," in *Liberales, agitadores y conspiradores*, ed. Isabel Burdiel and Manuel Pérez Ledesma (Madrid: Espasa, 2000), 239–66; and Albert Garcia Balañà, "Patria, plebe, y política en la España isabelina: La guerra de África en Cataluña (1859–1860)," in *Marruecos y el colonialismo español (1859–1912): De la guerra de África a la "penetración pacífica,"* ed. Eloy Martín Corrales (Barcelona: Edicions Bellaterra, 2002).

26. For the "Second Empire" argument, see Durán, *La Unión Liberal y la modernización de la España isabelina*, 228. For nationalism, see José Álvarez Junco, *Mater Dolorosa: La idea*

de España en el siglo XIX (Madrid: Taurus, 2001), 509–31; and Muñoz, *Intervenciones colo-niales y nacionalismo español*. Economic motives are emphasized in Martínez Gallego, *Conservar progresando*, 117–64.

27. Garcia Balañà, "El comercio español en África en la Barcelona de 1858." For figures concerning African slaves, he relies on Laird W. Bergad, Fe Iglesias García, and María del Carmen Barcia, *The Cuban Slave Market, 1790–1880* (Cambridge: Cambridge University Press, 1995), 26–31. For Chinese coolies, he cites Lisa Yun and Ricardo René Laremont, "Chinese Coolies and African Slaves in Cuba, 1847–74," *Journal of Asian American Studies* 4, no. 2 (June 2001): 99–122, esp. 111, table 5.

28. Fradera, *Colonias para después de un imperio*, 568.

29. The "ideological justification" for the invasion of Vietnam came from a Philippine missionary, who relied heavily on the information received from Macao. Manuel de Rivas, *Idea de Imperio de Annam o de los Reinos Unidos de Tunquin y Cochinchina* (Manila: Amigos del País, 1858). This is explained in Sara Rodicio García, "Una encrucijada en la historia de España: Contribución hispánica a la expedición de Cochinchina" (PhD thesis, Universidad Complutense de Madrid, 1987), 1:605.

30. Antonia Pi-Suñer, *El general Prim y la cuestión de México* (Mexico City: Universidad Nacional Autónoma de México, 1996), 31–59.

31. Ángel Bas, "La crisis algodonera," *Diario de Barcelona*, September 16, 1863, 8404–5.

32. Davis, *The Last Conquistadores*, 53.

33. "Cortes, Senado, Estracto de la sesion celebrada el dia 21 de Junio," *Diario de Barcelona*, June 21, 1864, 6137–40.

34. John Gallagher and Ronald Robinson, "The Imperialism of Free Trade," *Economic History Review* 6, no. 1 (August 1953): 1–15.

35. For Latin America, see H. S. Ferns, "Britain's Informal Empire in Argentina, 1806–1914," *Past and Present* 4, no. 1 (November 1953): 60–75; Peter Winn, "British Informal Empire in Uruguay in the Nineteenth Century," *Past and Present* 73, no. 1 (November 1976): 100–126; Andrew Thompson, "Informal Empire? An Exploration in the History of Anglo-Argentine Relations, 1810–1914," *Journal of Latin American Studies* 24, no. 2 (May 1992): 419–36; Alan Knight, "Britain and Latin America," in Andrew Porter, ed., *Oxford History of the British Empire: The Nineteenth Century* (Oxford: Oxford University Press, 1999), 122–45; and Mathew Brown, ed., *Informal Empire in Latin America: Culture, Commerce, and Capital* (Oxford: Blackwell, 2008). For the French version, see David Todd, "A French Imperial Meridian, 1814–1817," *Past and Present* 210, no. 1 (February 2011): 155–86.

36. Omar Rodríguez Esteller, "La intervención española en las aduanas marroquíes (1862–1885)," in *Marruecos y el colonialismo español (1859–1912)*, 79–131, esp. 80–81.

37. The Spaniards believed that the British were surreptitiously aiding the Chileans. Estanislao Reynals y Rabassa, "Las amistades inglesas," *Diario de Barcelona*, February 1, 1866, 996–98.

38. Luis Ortega Martínez, *Chile en ruta al capitalismo: Cambio, euforia, y depresión, 1850–1880* (Santiago: LOM Ediciones, 2005).

39. For a similar point, see Fradera, *Colonias para después de un imperio*, 675.

40. For example, in 1856, Spain had only had 578 kilometers of rail, fewer than those of one of its colonies, Cuba, which had 741. Compare this to the United States (20,552 kilometers), Britain (14,017), France (6,211), or Prussia (2,911). Due to the railway boom, by 1863 Spain had 3,569 kilometers of rail. For the 1856 figures, see "Estado de los Ferro-Carriles del Mundo de 1856," *Diario de Barcelona*, May 19, 1857, 4041–42. For the 1863 figures, see Durán, *La Unión Liberal y la modernización de la España isabelina*, 170. In 1864, Spain had a population of 16 million people, had an agricultural sector valued at 7 billion reales (U.S.$273 million) per year, and registered a total of 3.29 billion reales (U.S.$128.3 million) in exports and imports. The corresponding numbers for France, were 37.4 million people, 24

billion reales (U.S.$936 million) in agriculture, and 21.8 billion reales (U.S.$850.2 million) in imports and exports. For these figures, see Ángel Bas, "Presupuestos," *Diario de Barcelona*, May 19, 1864, 4812–15. In 1861, Spanish customs collected approximately 247 million reales (U.S.$9.6 million) in duties per annum, while England collected 2.3 billion reales (U.S.$89.7 million) and France 666 million reales (U.S.$26 million). For these figures, see Durán, *La Unión Liberal y la modernización de la España isabelina*, 195. The Spanish fleet grew from 31 vessels with 172 canons in 1856 to 83 vessels and 712 canons in 1862. This was still a far cry from the size of the British and French navies. For these figures, see Martínez Gallego, *Conservar progresando*, 130–31.

41. For troop numbers and other above-mentioned figures, see Sebastian Balfour, *Deadly Embrace: Morocco and the Road to the Spanish Civil War* (Oxford: Oxford University Press, 2002), 26, 89, 98, 102, 109, 113, 147. As Balfour notes, the mustard gas estimate by a German officer does not include the gas produced after the third quarter of 1925.

42. For the importance of Morocco to the rise of Primo de Rivera, see Carolyn Boyd, *Praetorian Politics in Liberal Spain* (Chapel Hill: University of North Carolina Press, 1979), 160–235. For the relationship between Morocco and the Spanish Civil War, see Balfour, *Deadly Embrace*.

43. For economic interests, see Víctor Morales Lezcano, "Las minas del Rif y el capital financiero Peninsular, 1900–1930," *Moneda y Crédito* 135 (1975): 61–77; and Martín Rodrigo, "Una avanzadilla española en África: El grupo empresarial Comillas," in *Marruecos y el colonialismo español (1859–1912)*, 133–65.

44. For this, see Boyd, *Praetorian Politics in Liberal Spain*, 183–235.

45. For the "world role" debates in Britain, see Darwin, *The Empire Project*, 642–45.

46. Paul Preston, "Mussolini's Spanish Adventure: From Limited Risk to War," in Paul Preston and Anne L. Mackenzie, eds., *The Republic Besieged: Civil War in Spain, 1936–39* (Edinburgh: Edinburgh University Press, 1996), 21–52.

47. Enrique Moradiellos, *Francisco Franco.: Crónica de un caudillo casi olvidado* (Madrid: Biblioteca Nueva, 2002), 105–8.

GARCIA BALAÑÀ / "THE EMPIRE IS NO LONGER A SOCIAL UNIT"

This essay has greatly benefited from generous comments on an initial and quite different version from participants at the Eclipse of Empires conference (Barcelona, June 2010). The final editorial format has also been enhanced by observations from editors Alfred W. McCoy, Josep M. Fradera, and Stephen Jacobson. The text is part of the Project Ref. HAR2009-14099-C02-01 funded by the Spanish Ministry of Science and Innovation (MICINN).

1. See Albert Garcia Balañà, "Patria, plebe y política en la España isabelina: La Guerra de África en Cataluña (1859–1860)," in Eloy Martín Corrales, ed., *Marruecos y el colonialismo español (1859–1912)* (Barcelona: Edicions Bellaterra, 2002), 13–77, 40, esp. 71–72.

2. Joan Connelly Ullman, *The Tragic Week: A Study of Anticlericalism in Spain, 1875–1912* (Cambridge: Harvard University Press, 1968); Sebastian Balfour, *The End of the Spanish Empire, 1898–1923* (Oxford: Clarendon Press, 1997), 123–31; Sebastian Balfour, *Abrazo mortal: De la guerra colonial a la Guerra Civil en España y Marruecos (1909–1936)* (Barcelona: Península, 2002), 23–70.

3. U.S. National Archives and Records Administration, Despatches from U.S. Consuls in Barcelona, Spain (1797–1906), T 121: letter from the Consul, Perkins, to Fish, the Secretary of State (Barcelona, December 10, 1869). Albert Garcia Balañà, "Tradició liberal i política colonial a Catalunya: Mig segle de temptatives i limitacions (1822–1872)," in Josep M. Fradera and César Yáñez, eds., *Catalunya i Ultramar: Poder i negoci a les colònies espanyoles (1750–1914)* (Barcelona: Museu Marítim, 1995), 77–106, esp. 94–102.

4. José Martí, "La Solución," in *La Cuestión Cubana* (Seville), April 26, 1873.

5. Garcia Balañà, "Tradició liberal i política colonial a Catalunya," 95, 105.

6. José Joaquín Moreno Masó, *La petjada dels catalans a Cuba* (Barcelona: Comissió Amèrica i Catalunya, 1993), 53–78, 69.

7. César Yáñez, *Saltar con red: La temprana emigración catalana a América (1830–1870)* (Madrid: Alianza Editorial, 1996), 52–54, 83–90.

8. Ibid., 56–70, 169–209; Josep M. Fradera, *Indústria i mercat: Les bases comercials de la industrialització catalana moderna (1814–1845)* (Barcelona: Crítica, 1987).

9. Martín Rodrigo y Alharilla, *Indians a Catalunya: Capitals cubans en l'economia catalana* (Barcelona: Fundació Noguera, 2007), 21–23.

10. César Yáñez, "Saltar con red: La emigración catalana a América, 1830–1930" (PhD thesis, Universitat Autònoma de Barcelona, 1994), 264–66.

11. Ibid., 257–58, 275–80.

12. César Yáñez, *La emigración española a América (Siglos XIX y XX)* (Colombres: Archivo de Indianos, 1994), 241–50.

13. Ibid., 114–15, esp. 24–26; Blanca Sánchez Alonso, *Las causas de la emigración española, 1880–1930* (Madrid: Alianza Editorial, 1995), 281–84.

14. These numbers do not include the numerous of migrants who returned home nor the considerable number of those who arrived on military expeditions. Yáñez, *La emigración española a América*, 42, 48–51.

15. Ibid., 48–49.

16. Imilcy Balboa Navarro, *Los brazos necesarios: Inmigración, colonización y trabajo libre en Cuba, 1878–1898* (Valencia: Biblioteca Historia Social, 2000), 227–29.

17. Jose C. Moya, *Cousins and Strangers: Spanish Immigrants in Buenos Aires, 1850–1930* (Berkeley: University of California Press, 1998), 13–14, 60–68, 228–32, 259–67.

18. Cited in Ibid., 66.

19. Stephen Constantine, "Migrants and Settlers," in Judith M. Brown and William Roger Louis, eds., *Oxford History of the British Empire*, vol. 4, *The Twentieth Century* (Oxford: Oxford University Press, 1999), 163–87, 165–67.

20. María Dolores García Cantús, "Fernando Poo: Una aventura colonial española en el África occidental, 1778–1900" (PhD thesis, Universitat de València, 2003), 343–564.

21. Fernando Poo Census (1901), cited in ibid., 564–66. Fernando Poo is now Bioko Island in Equatorial Guinea.

22. Sánchez Alonso, *Las causas de la emigración española*, 286–87.

23. C. R. Yáñez, "La última invasión armada: Los contingentes militares españoles a las guerras de Cuba, Siglo XIX," *Revista de Indias* 194 (1992): 107–27, esp. 110, 114.

24. Balfour, *Abrazo mortal*, 60–63.

25. Garcia Balañà, "Patria, plebe y política en la España isabelina," 27–50.

26. Albert Garcia Balañà, "Significados de República: Insurrecciones federales, redes milicianas y conflictos laborales en la Cataluña de 1869," *Ayer* 71, no. 3 (2008): 213–43.

27. *Lo Somatent: Periódich Polítich Liberal*, April 17, 1869, 2–3.

28. Evaristo Ventosa (pseudonym of Fernando Garrido), *La regeneración de España* (Barcelona: Salvador Manero, 1860), 129–30.

29. Garcia Balañà, "Patria, plebe y política en la España isabelina," 48–50.

30. "Isla de Cuba," *La Federación*, 157 (August 18, 1872), 4; Joan Casanovas, *Bread, or Bullets! Urban Labor and Spanish Colonialism in Cuba, 1850–98* (Pittsburgh: University of Pittsburgh Press, 1998), 109–11, 114–19.

31. Albert Garcia Balañà, "'Ya no existe Partido Progresista en Barcelona': Experiencia social y protesta obrera en la insurrección republicana de 1869," *Hispania* 230 (2008): 735–60.

32. Rafael Núñez Florencio, *Militarismo y antimilitarismo en España (1888–1906)* (Madrid: Consejo Superior de Investigaciones Científicas, 1990), 225.

33. Juan Pan-Montojo, "El atraso económico y la regeneración," in Juan Pan-Montojo, ed., *Más se perdió en Cuba: España, 1898, y el crisis fin de siglo* (Madrid: Alianza, 1998), 267–340, esp. 292–94.

34. Joan Casanovas, *¡O pan, o plomo! Los trabajadores urbanos y el colonialismo español en Cuba, 1850–1898* (Madrid: Siglo XXI, 2000), 55.

35. Manuel Pérez Ledesma, "La sociedad española, la guerra y la derrota," in Juan Pan-Montojo, ed., *Más se perdió en Cuba: España, 1898, y el crisis fin de siglo* (Madrid: Alianza, 1998), 97–155, esp. 101.

36. Carlos Serrano, *Final del Imperio: España, 1895–1898* (Madrid: Siglo XXI, 1984), 99–112; Pérez Ledesma, "La sociedad española, la guerra y la derrota," 114–16, 123.

37. Benedict Anderson, *Under Three Flags: Anarchism and the Anti-colonial Imagination* (London: Verso, 2005), 169–95.

38. Carlos Serrano, "Prófugos y desertores en la Guerra de Cuba," *Estudios de Historia Social* 22–23 (1982): 253–78.

39. C. A. Bayly, *The Birth of the Modern World, 1780–1914* (Oxford: Blackwell, 2004), 228–33.

40. Catherine Hall and Sonya O. Rose, eds., *At Home with the Empire: Metropolitan Culture and the Imperial World* (Cambridge: Cambridge University Press, 2006).

41. Garcia Balañà, "Patria, plebe y política en la España isabelina," 58–63.

42. Garcia Balañà, "Tradició liberal i política colonial a Catalunya," 93, 94–102.

43. Catherine Hall, *Civilising Subjects: Metropole and Colony in the English Imagination, 1830–1867* (Cambridge: Polity Press, 2002), 380–433.

44. Cited in Xavier Garcia Olivé, "'Moros de dos menas': Republicanismes barcelonins i la 'Guerra de Margallo' (1893)" (MA thesis, Universitat Pompeu Fabra, 2008), 26–32, 35.

GRANDIN / FACING SOUTH

1. Review of D. Gregorio Funes, *Ensayo de la historía civil del Paraguay: Buenos-Ayres, y Tucuman, North American Review* 12 (1821): 435.

2. Louis Hartz, "American Historiography and Comparative Analysis: Further Reflections," *Comparative Studies in Society and History* 5, no. 4 (July 1963): 365–77.

3. Michael Rogin, *Fathers and Children: Andrew Jackson and the Subjugation of the American Indian* (New Brunswick: Transaction Publishers, 2009 [1975]), 7; Uday Mehta, "Liberal Strategies of Exclusion," *Politics and Society* 18, no. 4 (1990): 427–541; Robert A. Williams, *The American Indian in Western Legal Thought: The Discourses of Conquest* (New York: Oxford University Press, 1992), 246–48.

4. Rogin, *Fathers and Children*, xxvii.

5. James Madison, *Letters and Other Writings of James Madison*, vol. 3, *1816–1828* (New York: R. Worthington, 1884), 516. See also United States Congress, *Abridgment of the Debates of Congress, from 1789 to 1856*, vol. 9, *March 13, 1826–Feb. 6, 1828* (New York: D. Appleton, 1858); and Jeffrey Malanson, "The Congressional Debate over U.S. Participation in the Congress of Panama, 1825–1826: Washington's Farewell Address, Monroe's Doctrine, and the Fundamental Principles of U.S. Foreign Policy," *Diplomatic History* 30, no. 5 (2006): 813–38.

6. Review of D. Gregorio Funes, *Ensayo de la historía civil del Paraguay*, 438.

7. Brian Loveman, *No Higher Law: American Foreign Policy and the Western Hemisphere since 1776* (Chapel Hill: University of North Carolina Press, 2010).

8. Michael Paul Rogin, *Subversive Genealogy: The Politics and Art of Herman Melville* (Berkeley: University of California Press, 1985), 20.

9. Merle Curti, "Young America," *American Historical Review* 32, no. 1 (October 1926): 34–55.

10. Calvin Colton, ed., *The Works of Henry Clay* (New York: Barnes & Burr, 1863), 5:485.

11. John Mason Hart, *Empire and Revolution: The Americans in Mexico since the Civil War* (Berkeley: University of California Press, 2002).

12. See Mary A. Renda, *Taking Haiti: Military Occupation and the Culture of U.S. Imperialism, 1915–1940* (Chapel Hill: University of North Carolina Press, 2001), 89–130, 333, and Mark T. Gilderhus, *Pan American Visions: Woodrow Wilson in the Western Hemisphere, 1913–1921* (Tucson: University of Arizona Press, 1986), 134–35.

13. Henry Stephens Randall, *The Life of Thomas Jefferson* (Philadelphia: J. B. Lippincott, 1871), 3:181.

14. Arthur P. Whitaker, *The Western Hemisphere Idea: Its Rise and Decline* (Ithaca: Cornell University Press, 1954).

15. Bernard Mayo, *Jefferson Himself: The Personal Narrative of a Many-Sided American* (Charlottesville: University of Virginia Press, 1998), 302.

16. Anthony Pagden, "The Savage Critic: Some European Images of the Primitive," *Yearbook of English Studies* 13 (1983): 32–45; Anthony Pagden, *European Encounters with the New World: From Renaissance to Romanticism* (New Haven: Yale University Press, 1994).

17. Anthony Pagden, *Spanish Imperialism and the Political Imagination: Studies in European and Spanish-American Social and Political Theory, 1513–1830* (New Haven: Yale University Press, 1998), 133–53; 146 for the quotes.

18. Ibid., 142–44, 151–53.

19. Francisco de Miranda, *The New Democracy in America: Travels of Francisco de Miranda in the United States, 1783–84*, translated by Judson P. Wood, edited by John S. Ezell (Norman: University of Oklahoma Press, 1963), 163.

20. Review of D. Gregorio Funes, *Ensayo de la historía civil del Paraguay*, 438.

21. Glen Dealy, "Prolegomena on the Spanish American Political Tradition," *Hispanic American Historical Review* 48, no. 1 (February 1968): 37–58.

22. Robert Williams, *The American Indian in Western Legal Thought: The Discourses of Conquest* (New York: Oxford University Press, 1992).

23. Ada Ferrer, *Insurgent Cuba: Race, Nation, and Revolution, 1868–1898* (Chapel Hill: University of North Carolina Press, 1999).

24. Compare Steve Stern's *Peru's Indian Peoples and the Challenge of Spanish Conquest: Huamanga to 1640* (Madison: University of Wisconsin Press, 1993) to Richard White's *The Middle Ground: Indians, Empires, and Republics in the Great Lakes Region, 1650–1815* (Cambridge: Cambridge University Press, 1991).

25. Williams, *The American Indian in Western Legal Thought*; Jill Lepore, *The Name of War: King Philip's War and the Origins of American Identity* (New York: Knopf, 1998), 158–67; Peter Silver, *Our Savage Neighbors: How Indian War Transformed Early America* (New York: Norton, 2007).

26. Howard Berman, "The Concept of Aboriginal Rights in the Early History of the United States," *Buffalo Law Review* 27 (Fall 1978): 637–67, 643–44 for quote. See also Stuart Banner, *How the Indians Lost their Land: Law and Power on the Frontier* (Harvard: Harvard University Press, 2005), 152; Tim Alan Garrison, *The Legal Ideology of Removal: The Southern Judiciary and the Sovereignty of Native American Nations* (Athens: University of Georgia Press, 2009), 94.

27. Quoted in Helmut de Terra, "Alexander von Humboldt's Correspondence with Jefferson, Madison, and Gallatin," *Proceedings of the American Philosophical Society* 103, no. 6 (1959): 783–806.

28. Paolo G. Carozza, "From Conquest to Constitutions: Retrieving a Latin American Tradition of the Idea of Human Rights, *Human Rights Quarterly* 25, no. 2 (May 2003): 281–313.

29. Cass Sunstein, "The Enlarged Republic—Then and Now," *New York Review of Books*, March 26, 2009.

30. U.S. Department of State, *Papers Relating to the Foreign Relations of the United States* (Washington, D.C.: Government Printing Office, 1896), 558.

31. Greg Grandin, "The Liberal Traditions in the Americas: Rights, Sovereignty, and the Origins of Liberal Multilateralism," *American Historical Review* 117, no. 1 (February 2012): 68–91, 71.

32. Alejandro Alvarez, *The Monroe Doctrine: Its Importance in the International Life of the States of the New World* (New York: Oxford University Press, 1924), 13. See also Walter LaFeber, *The New Empire: An Interpretation of American Expansion, 1860–1898* (Ithaca: Cornell University Press, 1998 [1963]), 242–83, for the importance of the Venezuela-British boundary dispute to international norms.

33. *Reports of Committees and Discussions Thereon: Patents and Trade-Marks; Extradition of Criminals; International American Monetary Union; International American Bank; International Law; Arbitration; Miscellaneous Business of the Conference* (Washington, D.C.: Government Printing Office, 1890), 2:1079.

34. LaFeber, *The New Empire*, 249, 261 for quotations.

35. Whitaker, *The Western Hemisphere Idea*, 86–107.

36. Alejandro Alvarez, "Latin America and International Law," *American Journal of International Law* 3, no. 2 (April 1909): 269–353.

37. Mark T. Gilderhus, *Pan American Visions: Woodrow Wilson in the Western Hemisphere, 1913–1921* (Tucson: University of Arizona Press, 1986), 136.

38. Ira Jewell Williams, "Confiscation of Private Property of Foreigners under Color of a Changed Constitution," *Law Notes*, March 1919, 231.

39. Raoul E. Desvernine, *Claims against Mexico: A Brief Study of the International Law Applicable to Claims of Citizens of the United States and Other Countries for Losses Sustained in Mexico during the Revolution of the Last Decade* (New York: n.p., 1921), 51–53.

40. See "To Oppose Alien Rights in Mexico," *New York Times*, January 23, 1919, for the quotations. See also Merrill Rippy, *Oil and the Mexican Revolution* (Leiden: Brill, 1972), 157–58.

41. Lloyd Gardner, *Economic Aspects of New Deal Diplomacy* (Madison: University of Wisconsin Press, 1964); Thomas Ferguson, "Industrial Conflict and the Coming of the New Deal: The Triumph of Multinational Liberalism in America," in Steve Fraser and Gary Gerstle, eds., *The Rise and Fall of the New Deal Order, 1930–1980* (Princeton: Princeton University Press, 1989).

42. "New League of Americas Is Proposed," *Christian Science Monitor*, April 13, 1936.

43. Luigi Einaudi, "Remarks to Organization of American States" (December 22, 1989), U.S. Department of State Current Policy Document, no. 1240, reprinted in *Panama: A Just Cause* (Washington, D.C.: US Department of State, 1989), 3.

44. Richard Allen, "For the Record," *Washington Post*, June 4, 1981.

45. House of Representatives, *Review of the 37th Session and Upcoming 38th Session of the U.N. Commission on Human Rights: Hearing Before the Subcommittee on Human Rights and International Organizations of the Committee on Foreign Affairs*, 97th Cong., 1st sess., November 16, 1981, vols. 88–981 (Washington, D.C.: Government Printing Office, 1982), 12–14. For Abrams's authorship, see Aryeh Neier, *Taking Liberties: Four Decades in the Struggle for Human Rights* (New York: Public Affairs, 2003), 185–86.

46. Louis Hartz, *The Liberal Tradition* (New York: Harcourt, Brace and World, 1955), 14.

JOHNSON / "ALLIANCE IMPERIALISM" AND ANGLO-AMERICAN POWER AFTER 1898

1. Bradford Perkins, *The Great Rapprochement: England and the United States, 1895–1914* (New York: Atheneum, 1968).

2. Quoted in W. T. Stead, *The Last Will and Testament of Cecil John Rhodes* (London: Review of Reviews Office, 1902), 73–74.

3. See Michael L. Gerlach, *Alliance Capitalism: the Social Organization of Japanese Business* (Berkeley: University of California Press, 1997); and especially John H. Dunning, *Alliance Capitalism and Global Business* (London: Routledge, 1997).

4. Paul Kennedy, *The Rise and Fall of the Great Powers* (New York: Random House, 1987), 251.

5. H. J. Mackinder, "The Geographical Pivot of History," *Geographical Journal* 23 (1904): 421–37.

6. Halford J. Mckinder, *Democratic Ideals and Reality: A Study in the Politics of Reconstruction* (New York, Henry Holt, 1919), 75–76.

7. Ibid., 216.

8. Quoted in W. T. Stead, *The Americanization of the World or The Trend of the Twentieth Century* (London: *Review of Reviews* Office, 1902), 435.

9. Ibid., 162.

10. W. T. Stead, "W. T. Stead's Statement," *New York Times*, April 5, 1902.

11. Stead, *The Last Will and Testament of Cecil John Rhodes*, 82.

12. Thomas J. McCormick, *China Market: America's Quest for Informal Empire, 1893–1901* (Chicago: Elephant Paperbacks, 1990).

13. See W.T. Stead, "The Anglo-American Association," *Review of Reviews* 18 (1898), 77; and *An American Response to Expressions of English Sympathy* (New York: Anglo-American Committee, 1899), http://www.archive.org/stream/expressionsengoonewyrich/expression sengoonewyrich_djvu.txt.

14. John Hay to Henry D. White, September 24, 1899, quoted in William Roscoe Thayer, *The Life and Letters of John Hay, Volume 2* (Boston and New York: Houghton Mifflin, 1915), 221.

15. Dana Munro, *Intervention and Dollar Diplomacy in the Caribbean, 1900–1921* (Westport: Greenwood Press, 1980).

16. Elihu Root, "The Real Monroe Doctrine," *Proceedings of the American Society of International Law at Its Eighth Annual Meeting Held at Washington D.C.* (Washington D.C., 1914), 6–21.

17. Quoted in Robert Bacon and James Brown Scott, eds., *Latin America and the United States: Addresses by Elihu Root* (Cambridge: Harvard University Press, 1917), xv.

18. Cited by Federico de Onís in Beatrice Gilman Proske, ed., *Archer Milton Huntington* (New York: Hispanic Society of America, 1963).

SCARANO / PRO-IMPERIALIST NATIONALISTS AT THE END OF SPAIN'S CARIBBEAN EMPIRE

1. Here, "nationalism" is the desire for substantial disentanglement from existing economic, social, and political arrangements of subordination to another, often colonial, power; see Josep M. Fradera, "Reading Imperial Transitions: Spanish Contraction, British Expansion, and American Irruption," in Alfred W. McCoy and Francisco A. Scarano, eds., *Colonial Crucible: Empire in the Making of the Modern American State* (Madison: University of Wisconsin Press, 2009), 34–62. Thus, nationalism need not be only an ideology of separate nation-statehood, although it is a predominant form. After 1800, most nationalisms articulated their goals in terms of making new states coterminous with recognizable ethnic groups.

2. Lillian Guerra, *The Myth of José Martí: Conflicting Nationalisms in Early Twentieth-Century Cuba* (Chapel Hill: University of North Carolina Press, 2005), 15–18.

3. Manuel Moreno Fraginals, "Plantaciones en el Caribe: El caso Cuba-Puerto Rico-Santo Domingo (1860–1940)," in *La historia como arma y otros estudios sobre esclavos, ingenios y plantaciones* (Barcelona: Crítica, 1983), 56–117; César J. Ayala, *American Sugar Kingdom: The Plantation Economy of the Spanish Caribbean, 1898–1934* (Chapel Hill: University of North Carolina Press, 1999).

4. For an analysis of subtle accommodations of subaltern groups with imperial designs, see Eileen Findlay, *Imposing Decency: The Politics of Sexuality and Race in Puerto Rico*

(Durham: Duke University Press, 1999); and Julian Go, "The Provinciality of American Empire: 'Liberal Exceptionalism' and U.S. Colonial Rule, 1898–1912," *Comparative Studies in Society and History* 49, no. 1 (2007): 74–108.

5. Mariano Negrón Portillo, "Puerto Rico ante la invasión norteamericana de 1898," *La Toga* 10, no. 2 (1978): 18–21; Laura Náter Vázquez, "El 98 en la historiografía puertorriqueña: Del político entusiasta al héroe popular," *Boletín del Centro de Investigaciones Históricas* 4 (1988–89): 101–22; Consuelo Naranjo Orovio, Miguel Angel Puig-Samper, and Luis Miguel García Mora, eds., *La nación soñada: Cuba, Puerto Rico y Filipinas ante el 98* (Madrid: Ediciones Doce Calles, 1996).

6. Gervasio L. García, "I Am the Other: Puerto Rico in the Eyes of North Americans, 1898," *Journal of American History* 87, no. 1 (June 2000): 39–64.

7. Walter LaFeber, *The New Empire: An Interpretation of American Expansion, 1860–1898* (Ithaca: Cornell University Press, 1963).

8. See, for example, Ada Ferrer, "Cuba, 1898: Rethinking Race, Nation, and Empire," *Radical History Review*, no. 73 (Winter 1999): 22–46; and Stuart B. Schwartz, "The Hurricane of San Ciriaco: Disaster, Politics, and Society in Puerto Rico, 1899–1901," *Hispanic American Historical Review* 72, no. 3 (August 1992): 303–34.

9. For example, see Consuelo Naranjo Orovio, Miguel Angel Puig-Samper, and Luis Miguel García Mora, *La nación soñada*; Antonio Santamaría García and Consuelo Naranjo Orovio, "El 98 en América: Últimos resultados y tendencias recientes de la investigación," *Nuevo Mundo Mundos Nuevos*, no. 2 (2002), http://nuevomundo.revues.org/document590 .html; and Juan Pan-Montojo, coord., *Más se perdió en Cuba: España, 1898 y la crisis de fin de siglo* (Madrid: Alianza Editorial, 1998).

10. Ada Ferrer, *Insurgent Cuba: Race, Nation, and Revolution, 1868–1898* (Chapel Hill: University of North Carolina Press, 1999). See also her "Cuba, 1898."

11. This is Carmelo Rosario Natal's contention in *Puerto Rico y la crisis de la Guerra Hispanoamericana, 1895–1898* (Hato Rey: Ramallo Brothers, 1975).

12. Juan Manuel Carrión, "The Making of Puerto Rican National Identities under U.S. Colonialism," in Juan Manuel Carrión, ed., *Ethnicity, Race, and Nationality in the Caribbean* (Río Piedras: Institute of Caribbean Studies, University of Puerto Rico, 1997), 159–91. Astrid Cubano Iguina details the shifting political scene in *El hilo en el laberinto: Claves de la lucha política en Puerto Rico (siglo XIX)* (Río Piedras: Ediciones Huracán, 1990).

13. Cubano Iguina, "Political Culture and Male Mass-Party Formation in Late Nineteenth-Century Puerto Rico," *Hispanic American Historical Review* 78, no. 4 (November 1998): 631–62.

14. Francisco A. Scarano, "The Jíbaro Masquerade and the Subaltern Politics of Creole Identity Formation in Puerto Rico, 1745–1823," *American Historical Review* 101, no. 5 (December 1996): 1398–1431.

15. See especially Isabel Gutiérrez del Arroyo, *El reformismo ilustrado en Puerto Rico* (Mexico City: Asomante and El Colegio de México, 1953). My conception of the Liberal Pact owes much to her work. See my "Liberal Pacts and Hierarchies of Rule: Approaching the Imperial Transition in Cuba and Puerto Rico," *Hispanic American Historical Review* 78, no. 4 (November 1998): 583–601. See also Josep M. Fradera, "De la periferia al centro (Cuba, Puerto Rico y Filipinas en la crisis del Imperio español)," *Anuario de Estudios Americanos* 61, no. 1 (2004): 161–99; and his *Gobernar colonias* (Barcelona: Ediciones Península, 1999).

16. José A. Piqueras, "La siempre fiel isla de Cuba, o la lealtad interesada," *Historia Mexicana* 58, no. 1 (September 2008): 478.

17. Manuel Tuñón de Lara, *Estudios sobre el siglo XIX español* (Madrid: Siglo XXI de España, 1972).

18. David R. Murray, "Statistics of the Slave Trade to Cuba, 1790–1867," *Journal of Latin American Studies* 3, no. 2 (November 1971): 136.

19. This is a point made by Franklin W. Knight, *Slave Society in Cuba during the Nineteenth Century* (Madison: University of Wisconsin Press, 1969). Note that Knight contrasts Cuba's "slave society" with Puerto Rico's "society with slaves."

20. Robert L. Paquette, *Sugar Is Made with Blood: The Conspiracy of 'La Escalera' and the Conflict between Empires over Slavery in Cuba* (Middletown: Wesleyan University Press, 1988).

21. Luis Martínez-Fernández, *Torn Between Empires: Economy, Society, and Patterns of Political Thought in the Hispanic Caribbean* (Athens: University of Georgia Press, 1994).

22. Oscar Loyola Vega, "El anexionismo en el primer año de la Guerra Grande," *Santiago* 35 (1979): 157–206.

23. In arguing that for Cubans the term *raza de color* was, as in the United States, a catchall category of racist exclusion, Aline Helg notes that Cuba's racialist discourse often did not use a skin-tone gradient to make exclusionary classifications. See her *Our Rightful Share: The Afro-Cuban Struggle for Equality, 1886–1912* (Chapel Hill: University of North Carolina Press, 1995).

24. For the various strands of nationalism present in the rebel camp, see Guerra, *The Myth of José Martí*. For the rightward trend within the rebel camp, see Ferrer, *Insurgent Cuba*; and her "Rustic Men, Civilized Nation: Race, Culture, and Contention on the Eve of Cuban Independence," *Hispanic American Historical Review* 78, no. 4 (November 1998): 663–86.

25. See Laird W. Bergad, "Towards Puerto Rico's Grito de Lares: Coffee, Social Stratification, and Class Conflicts," *Hispanic American Historical Review* 60, no. 4 (November 1980): 617–42; and Olga Jiménez de Wagenheim, *El Grito de Lares: Sus causas y sus hombres* (Río Piedras: Ediciones Huracán, 1984).

26. On Betances's life and revolutionary passion, see especially Félix Ojeda Reyes, *El desterrado de París: Biografía del doctor Ramón Emeterio Betances, 1827–1898* (San Juan: Ediciones Puerto, 2001).

27. The short-lived First Spanish Republic of 1873–74 entertained the idea of granting the overseas colonies a status of autonomy similar to that bestowed on Canada five years earlier. Like the Republic itself, the project did not outlive a conservative backlash. See Agustín Sánchez Andrés, "La alternativa federal a la crisis colonial: Las colonias en los proyectos de organización federal del estado (1872–73)," *Revista Complutense de Historia de América* 23 (1997): 193–208.

28. Jorge I. Domínguez, "Responses to Occupations by the United States: Caliban's Dilemma," *Pacific Historical Review* 48, no. 4 (November 1979): 591–605.

29. Ada Ferrer forcefully raised this point in "Cuba, 1898" and "Rustic Men, Civilized Nation."

30. Angel G. Quintero Rivera, *Patricios y plebeyos: Burgueses, hacendados, artesanos y obreros—las relaciones de clase en el Puerto Rico de cambio de siglo* (Río Piedras: Ediciones Huracán, 1988).

31. Ileana Rodríguez-Silva has documented the silencing of race in Puerto Rico during this period in "A Conspiracy of Silence: Blackness, Class, and Nation in Post-emancipation Puerto Rico, 1850–1920" (PhD diss., University of Wisconsin–Madison, 2004).

32. Stuart Hall, "Race, Articulation, and Societies Structured in Dominance," in *Sociological Theories: Race and Colonialism* (Paris: United Nations Educational, Scientific, and Cultural Organization, 1980), 305–45.

33. Scarano, "Liberal Pacts and Hierarchies of Rule," 591–92.

ELIZALDE / IMPERIAL TRANSITION IN THE PHILIPPINES

1. William Schurtz, *The Manila Galleon* (New York: Dutton, 1939).

2. Josep M. Fradera, *Colonias para después de un Imperio* (Barcelona: Editions Bellaterra, 2005); Edilberto de Jesús, *The Tobacco Monopoly in the Philippines: Bureaucratic Enterprise and Social Change, 1766–1880* (Quezon City: Ateneo de Manila University Press, 1980).

3. Ronald Robinson, "Non-European Foundations of European Imperialism: Sketch for a Theory of Collaboration," in Roger Owen and Bob Sutcliffe, eds., *Studies in the Theory of Imperialism* (London: Longman, 1972); D. A. Lowe, *Eclipse of Empire* (Cambridge: Cambridge University Press, 1991).

4. That was the verdict of all the analysts whose opinions were canvassed, from Francisco Leandro de Viana to Sinibaldo de Mas, Segismundo Moret, Manuel Becerra, Antonio Maura, and Víctor Balaguer.

5. John Bowring, *A Visit to the Philippine Islands* (London: Smith, Elder, 1859), 94–95.

6. Jean Baptiste Mallat, *Les Philippines: Histoire, geographie, moeurs, agriculture, industrie et commerce des colognes espagnoles dans l'Oceanie, 1846* (Manila, National Historical Institute, 1983), 507–8.

7. Bowring, *A Visit to the Philippine Islands*, 99–100.

8. Fedor Jagor, *Travels in the Philippines, 1874* (Manila: Filipiana Book Guild, 1965), 112.

9. The Spanish basically occupied the island of Luzon and the most important townships, the river valleys, and the most strategic ports in the main islands. However, Spain exercised little control over the territory and its inhabitants in the mountains, the denser forests, many parts of the Visayas, and much of Mindanao.

10. John Foreman, *The Philippine Islands, 1890, 1899, and 1906* (New York: Charles Scribner's Sons, 1899), 217–18; Bowring, *A Visit to the Philippine Islands*, 117–18; Mallat, *Les Philippines*, 241–47.

11. Bowring, *A Visit to the Philippine Islands*, 212.

12. Ibid., 95.

13. Edward Said, *Orientalism* (New York: Pantheon Books, 1987); *Culture and Imperialism* (New York: Vintage Books, 1993).

14. Foreman, *Philippine Islands*, 237.

15. Ibid., 241.

16. Ibid., 643.

17. See, for example, Henry C. Lodge, ed., *Selections from the Correspondence of Theodore Roosevelt and Henry Cabot Lodge, 1884–1918* (New York: Charles Scribner's Sons, 1925); Alfred T. Mahan, *The Influence of Sea Power upon History* (Boston: Little, Brown, 1890); and Brook Adams, "The Spanish War and the Equilibrium of the World," *Forum* 25 (1898): 641–51. I have dealt with this subject in depth in María Dolores Elizalde, "De Nación a Imperio: La expansión de los Estados Unidos por el Pacífico durante la guerra hispano-norteamericana," *Hispania* 196 (1997): 551–88; and "1898: El fin de la relación entre España y Filipinas," in María Dolores Elizalde, ed., *Las relaciones entre España y Filipinas, siglos XVI–XX* (Madrid: Consejo Superior de Investigaciones Científicas—Casa Asia, 2003), 273–301.

18. John Barret, "The Cuba of the Far East," *North American Review* 164 (1897): 173–80.

19. Richard Kagan, "Prescott's Paradigm: American Historical Scholarship and the Decline of Spain," *American Historical Review* 101, no. 2 (1996): 423–46; Gerald F. Linderman, *The Mirror of War: American Society and the Spanish American War* (Ann Arbor: University of Michigan Press, 1974).

20. William McKinley, 55th Cong., 3d sess., House of Representatives, Instructions to the Peace Commissioners, Washington, 16 September 1898, in *Papers Relating to the Foreign Relations of the United States*, 1898 (Washington, D.C.: Government Printing Office, 1901), 906–8.

21. Recent studies have shown that Spain's situation was not as exceptional as historians have traditionally depicted it. In 1875 Spain commenced a process of modernization and progress, which brought it close to the European standards of the time. However, elements

of weakness and instability still persisted, and Spain was not counted among the elite of the most powerful nations.

22. Alfred W. McCoy, "Fatal Florescence: Europe's Decolonization and America's Decline," in this volume.

Schmidt-Nowara / The Broken Image

Support for research and writing came from grant number HAR2009-07103 from Spain's Ministry of Science and Innovation.

1. Richard Kagan, ed., *Spain in America: The Origins of Hispanism in the United States* (Urbana: University of Illinois Press, 2002); Iván Jaksić, *The Hispanic World and American Intellectual Life, 1820–1880* (New York: Palgrave Macmillan, 2007).

2. On Rome and Britain, see Dane Kennedy, "On the American Empire from a British Imperial Perspective," *International History Review* 29 (March 2007): 83–108.

3. Mike Wallace, "Nueva York, the Back Story: New York City and the Spanish-Speaking World from Dutch Days to the Second World War," in Edward J. Sullivan, ed., *Nueva York, 1613–1945* (New York: New York Historical Society, 2010), 19.

4. Richard Kagan, "Prescott's Paradigm: American Historical Scholarship and the Decline of Spain," *American Historical Review* 101 (April 1996): 423–46.

5. Jaksić, *The Hispanic World and American Intellectual Life*, 185.

6. Ibid., 154.

7. Ibid., 119; Christopher Schmidt-Nowara, "Centers and Peripheries of U.S. Hispanism," *A Contracorriente* 6 (Spring 2009): 321–26.

8. Herbert Eugene Bolton, *The Spanish Borderlands: A Chronicle of Old Florida and the Southwest* (New Haven: Yale University Press, 1921). For an example of Hispanism in the American metropolis, New York, see the study of the vogue for Spanish art by Edward J. Sullivan, "Art Worlds of Nueva York," in Sullivan, *Nueva York, 1613–1945*, 172–215.

9. "Da cuenta del incidente suscitado por la insolación que recibió de la Ciudad de Chicago," letter to the Ministro de Estado, dated Washington, 20 de Abril de 1900, Archivo del Ministerio de Asuntos Exteriores, Correspondencia, Embajadas y Legaciones (AMAE/CEL) EE Unidos, 1892–1903, leg. H1481, no. 63. The note scribbled across the copy sent to Madrid reads "Aprobar su conducta en términos laudatorios."

10. "Da cuenta de su viaje a Chicago," letter to the Ministro de Estado dated Washington, 4 de Septiembre de 1900, AMAE/CEL, EE Unidos, 1892–1903, leg. H1481, no. 132.

11. "Da cuenta de su viaje a San Francisco en cumplimiento de la Real Orden No 84, de 20 de Julio último," dated Washington, 3 de Noviembre de 1909, AMAE/CEL, EE Unidos, leg. H1482, no. 149. He also noted his warm welcome by a local Clavé chorus, important associations among working class Spaniards.

12. "Thousands Attend Ceremony at Memorial Church Site," *Palm Beach Daily News*, March 16, 1925.

13. "San Agustín Ciudad por Don Pedro Menédez Avilés. La Florida," 1924–1926, Palacio Real, Reinados, Alfonso XIII, 12.427/24; "Conmemoración del 20 Centenario de la Fundación de San Antonio de Tejas (EEUU)," 1930, Palacio Real, Reinados, Alfonso XIII, 16.230/29; "Semi-Centenario que la Universidad de Southern California, ha de celebrar durante los días 4, 5, 6 y 7 del próximo mes de Junio en Los Angeles, California," 1930, Palacio Real, Reinados, Alfonso XIII, 8.899/27.

14. On history and commemoration in Southern California during this period, see Kevin Starr, *Americans and the California Dream, 1850–1915* (New York: Oxford University Press, 1973); William Deverell, *Whitewashed Adobe: The Rise of Los Angeles and the Remaking of Its Mexican Past* (Berkeley: University of California Press, 2004); Matthew F. Bokovoy, *The San Diego World's Fairs and Southwestern Memory, 1880–1940* (Albuquerque: University of New Mexico Press, 2005); Phoebe Kropp, *California Vieja: Culture and Memory in a*

Modern American Place (Berkeley: University of California Press, 2006); Stephen Aron, "Missions, Myth, and Memory in the Making of Modern Southern California," *Reviews in American History* 35 (March 2007): 83–88; and Christopher Schmidt-Nowara, "Spanish Origins of American Empire: Hispanism, History, and Commemoration, 1898–1915," *International History Review* 30 (March 2008): 32–51. Much of this work draws its inspiration from Carey McWilliams, *North from Mexico: The Spanish-Speaking People of the United States* (Philadelphia: J. B. Lippincott, 1949).

15. "El Cónsul de España da cuenta de la Exposición Panamá-California de San Diego (California)," letter dated San Francisco, 11 de Enero de 1915, AMAE/Política/Política Exterior/Exposiciónes y Concursos, leg. H 3222 (Sa-San) Expediente "Exposición en San Diego de Agricultura, Pesqueria, Mineria, Colonias, Bosques, Transportación, Colonización, Aviación, Arte que se ha de celebrar en 1915" (313), no. 2.

16. Charles Fletcher Lummis, *The Spanish Pioneers* (Chicago: McClurg, 1893).

17. Bolton, *The Spanish Borderlands*, vii.

18. See Mark Thompson, *American Character: The Curious Life of Charles Fletcher Lummis and the Rediscovery of the Southwest* (New York: Arcade Publishing, 2001); and John Nieto-Phillips, *The Language of Blood: The Making of Spanish-American Identity in New Mexico, 1880s–1930s* (Albuquerque: University of New Mexico Press, 2004).

19. Rafael Altamira, "A manera de prólogo," in Charles F. Lummis, *Los exploradores españoles del siglo XVI: Vindicación de la acción colonizadora española en América*, trans. Arturo Cuyás (Barcelona: Araluce, 1916), 17–18. This edition was subsidized by J. C. Cebrián, who also supported the revised edition of Julián Juderías's *La leyenda negra* (Barcelona: Araluce, 1917). At the same time, Cebrián was providing the financial backing for the *Hispanic American Historical Review*, founded after the Panama-Pacific Exposition. On Cebrián, Lummis, and the reception of Lummis's work in Spain, see Ana Varela-Lago, "Conquerors, Immigrants, Exiles: The Spanish Diaspora in the United States, 1848–1948" (PhD diss., University of California, San Diego, 2008).

20. "City of East San Diego, California Office of the Mayor," letter from Harvey M. Holleman, on letterhead, dated 22 March 1913, Papers of Charles Fletcher Lummis (PCFL), Box 13, File 1, Special Collections Library, University of Arizona.

21. "To the Honorable the Supreme Body of the Order of Panama," dated 12 June 1913, PCFL, Box 13, File 1.

22. "Lummis Knighted by Alfonso XIII," *New York Times*, August 3, 1915.

23. Mike Davis, Kelly Mayhew, and Jim Miller, *Under the Perfect Sun: The San Diego Tourists Never See* (New York: New Press, 2003); Bokovoy, *The San Diego World's Fairs and Southwestern Memory*.

BALLANTYNE / INFORMATION AND INTELLIGENCE IN THE
MID-NINETEENTH-CENTURY CRISIS IN THE BRITISH EMPIRE

1. Tony Ballantyne, "Colonial Knowledge," in Sarah Stockwell, ed., *British Empire: Themes and Perspectives* (Oxford: Blackwell, 2008), 177–98.

2. C. A. Bayly, *Empire and information: Intelligence Gathering and Social Communication in India, 1780–1870* (Cambridge: Cambridge University Press, 1996).

3. Partha Chatterjee, *The Nation and Its Fragments: Colonial and Postcolonial Histories* (Princeton: Princeton University Press, 1993).

4. James Belich, *The New Zealand Wars and the Victorian Interpretation of Racial Conflict* (Auckland: Auckland University Press, 1986); T. R. Metcalf, *Ideologies of the Raj* (Cambridge: Cambridge University Press, 1996); Catherine Hall, *Civilising Subjects: Colony and Metropole in the English Imagination, 1830–1867* (Chicago: University of Chicago Press, 2002), esp. 378–79.

5. Christine Bolt, *Victorian Attitudes to Race* (London: Routledge and Kegan Paul, 1971); George Stocking, *Victorian Anthropology* (New York: Macmillan, 1987); Douglas

Lorimer, *Colour, Class, and the Victorians: English Attitudes to the Negro in the Mid-Nineteenth Century* (Leicester: Leicester University Press, 1978).

6. Robert Young, *Colonial Desire: Hybridity in Theory, Culture, and Race* (London: Routledge, 1995), 109, 119–20.

7. This entailed responsibility for revenue collection and the administration of the law.

8. Michael Fisher, "The Office of Akhbar Nawis: The Transition from Mughal to British Forms," *Modern Asian Studies* 27, no. 1 (February 1993): 45–82.

9. Durba Ghosh, *Sex and the Family in Colonial India: The Making of Empire* (Cambridge: Cambridge University Press, 2006).

10. David Ludden, "Orientalist Empiricism," in Carol A. Breckenridge and Peter van der Veer, eds., *Orientalism and the Postcolonial Predicament: Perspectives on South Asia* (Philadelphia: University of Pennsylvania Press, 1993); Marika Vicziany, "Imperialism, Botany, and Statistics in Early Nineteenth Century India. The Surveys of Francis Buchanan (1762–1829)," *Modern Asian Studies* 20, no. 4 (1986): 625–61.

11. See, e.g., G. J. Christian, *Report on the Census of the North-West Provinces of the Bengal Presidency Taken on the 1st of June 1853* (Calcutta: J. Thomas, 1854); Bayly, *Empire and Information*, 316.

12. C. A. Bayly, "Knowing the Country: Empire and Information in India," *Modern Asian Studies* 27, no. 1 (1993): 30–31.

13. William Dalrymple, in *The Last Mughal: The Fall of a Dynasty—Delhi, 1857* (London: Bloomsbury, 2006), 24, suggests that up to one-third of the forces assembled at Delhi were made up of "jihadis."

14. Marina Carter and Crispin Bates, "Empire and Locality: A Global Dimension to the 1857 Indian Uprising," *Journal of Global History* 5, no. 1 (2010): 51–73.

15. John William Kaye, *A History of the Sepoy War in India, 1857–1858*, 7th ed. (London: W.H. Allen & Co., 1875), 491.

16. Tony Ballantyne, "The Changing Shape of the Modern British Empire and Its Historiography," *Historical Journal* 53, no. 2 (2010): 429–52.

17. See e.g., *Daily Southern Cross*, June 5, 1857, 3.

18. Browne to Newcastle, April 27 and November 1, 1860, *Great Britain Parliamentary Papers*, 1861 (2798) XLI, 33 and 160.

19. Browne to Newcastle, March 22, 1860, *Great Britain Parliamentary Papers*, 1861 (2798) XLI, 17.

20. *Daily Southern Cross*, June 5, 1857, 3.

21. John Stenhouse, "Church and State in New Zealand, 1835–70: Religion, Politics, and Race," in Hilary Carey and John Gascoigne, eds., *Church and State from Old to New Worlds* (Leiden: Brill, 2010).

22. David McCan, *Whatiwhatihoe: The Waikato Raupatu Claim* (Wellington: Huia, 2001), 51, 67–68;

23. See, e.g., *Daily Southern Cross*, June 5, 1857, 3; James Cowan, *The New Zealand Wars: A History of the Maori Campaigns and the Pioneering Period*, 2 vols. (Wellington: W.A.G. Skinner, 1922), 1:446; and Tony Ballantyne, *Orientalism and Race: Aryanism in the British Empire* (Basingstoke: Palgrave, 2002), 161–69.

24. Quoted in the *Wanganui Herald*, March 1, 1883, 2.

25. C. A. Bayly. *Indian Society and the Making of the British Empire* (Cambridge: Cambridge University Press, 1987), 180.

26. See F. W. Buckler, "The Political Theory of the Indian Mutiny," *Transactions of the Royal Historical Society*, ser. 4, 5 (1932): 71–100. In this view, it was actually the British who were rebels.

27. Bayly, *Indian Society and the Making of the British Empire*, 184; Jill Bender, "Sir George Grey and the 1857 Indian Rebellion: The Unmaking and Making of an Imperial

Career," in Crispin Bates and Marina Carter, eds., *Mutiny at the Margins: Global Perspectives on 1857* (Delhi: Sage, 2010).

28. Clare Anderson, *The Indian Uprising of 1857-8: Prisons, Prisoners, and Rebellion* (London: Anthem, 2007), 134.

29. Ibid., chap. 5, esp. 129; Satadru Sen, *Disciplining Punishment: Colonialism and Convict Society in the Andaman Islands* (Oxford: Oxford University Press, 2000).

30. Belich, *The New Zealand Wars and the Victorian Interpretation of Racial Conflict*; James Belich, *I Shall Not Die: Titokowaru's War, New Zealand, 1868-9* (Wellington: Allen & Unwin, 1989).

31. Belich, *The New Zealand Wars and the Victorian Interpretation of Racial Conflict*, 138.

32. Cowan, *The New Zealand Wars*, 1:351; Belich, *The New Zealand Wars and the Victorian Interpretation of Racial Conflict*, 162.

33. Monty Soutar, "Kupapa; A Shift in Meaning," *He Pukenga Korero* 6, no. 1 (2001): 35–39.

34. See, e.g., Cowan, *The New Zealand Wars*, 1:455.

35. Judith Binney, *Redemption Songs: A Life of Te Kooti Arikirangi Te Turuki* (Wellington: Bridget Williams, 2005), 84.

36. See, e.g., *Wellington Independent*, August 20, 1863, 3.

37. In fact there were only a total of eighty-three executions in New Zealand between 1842 and 1957. There was certainly an increase during the 1860s. The year 1866 alone saw ten executions, while there were twenty-one in the decade as a whole (at least ten of which were Maori). http://www.nzhistory.net.nz/culture/the-death-penalty/notable-executions.

38. Sir John Lawrence reflected, "I am lost in astonishment that any of us are alive. But for the mercy of God we must have been ruined. Had the Sikhs joined against us, nothing, humanly speaking could have saved us." *Lahore Chronicle*, November 17. 1858. For "points of recognition," see Tony Ballantyne, *Between Colonialism and Diaspora: Sikh Cultural Formations in an Imperial World* (Durham: Duke University Press, 2006), 26–28, 33–35.

39. Ballantyne, *Between Colonialism and Diaspora*, 63–66, 71–74; Thomas R. Metcalf, *Imperial Connections: India in the Indian Ocean Arena, 1860-1920* (Berkeley: University of California Press, 2007), 102–35.

40. Bayly, *Indian Society and the Making of the British Empire*, 194–97.

41. Section 6 of Maori Representation Act, 1867, *New Zealand Statutes*, 1867.

42. James Belich, *Making Peoples: A History of the New Zealanders from Polynesian Settlement to the End of the Nineteenth Century* (Auckland: Penguin, 1996), 244, 265.

43. Tony Ballantyne, "State, Power, and Politics," in Giselle Byrnes, ed., *New Oxford History of New Zealand* (Melbourne: Oxford University Press, 2009), 117.

44. Lawrence Stone, ed., *An Imperial State at War: Britain from 1689 to 1815* (London: Routledge, 1994).

45. James Belich, *Making Peoples*, 249–56.

46. Ian J. Kerr, *Engines of Change: The Railroads That Made India* (Westport: Praeger, 2007) 12, 23, 87, 89.

SANTIAGO-VALLES / THE FIN DE SIÈCLES OF GREAT BRITAIN AND THE UNITED STATES

1. Oliver C. Cox, *Capitalism as a System* (New York: Monthly Review Press, 1964), x, xi–xii, xiii, 3–16, 136–38, 141; Samir Amin, *Empire of Chaos* (New York: Monthly Review Press, 1992), 28–55; Giovanni Arrighi, *The Long Twentieth Century* (London: Verso, 1994), 27–84; István Mézáros, *Socialism or Barbarism* (New York: Monthly Review Press, 2001), 23–50; Atilio Borón, *Empire and Imperialism* (London: Zed Books, 2005), 111–16.

2. Giovanni Arrighi and Beverly Silver, "Introduction," in Giovanni Arrighi and Beverly Silver, eds., *Chaos and Governance in the Modern World System* (Minneapolis: University of Minnesota Press, 1999), 30, 31, 33.

3. Michel Foucault, *Discipline and Punish* (New York: Pantheon Books, 1977), 195–217; Martha Kaplan, "Panopticon in Poona: An Essay on Foucault and Colonialism," *Cultural Anthropology* 10, no. 1 (1995): 88–91; Gyan Prakash, *Another Reason* (Princeton: Princeton University Press, 1997), 123–300; Michael J. Shapiro, *Violent Cartographies* (Minneapolis: University of Minnesota Press, 1997).

4. Michel Foucault, *The History of Sexuality* (New York: Vintage Books, 1990), 1:139 (original emphasis); Michel Foucault, *Society Must Be Defended* (New York: Picador, 2003), 60.

5. Foucault, *Society Must Be Defended*, 254; Fernand Braudel, "History and the Social Sciences," in Peter Burke, ed., *Economy and Society in Early-Modern Europe* (New York: Harper and Row, 1972), 16–18. Braudel's essay was originally published in 1958.

6. On fifty-year cycles, see Fernand Braudel, *Civilization and Capitalism, 15th-18th Century*, vol. 3, *The Perspective of the World* (Berkeley: University of California Press, 1992), 72, 80–83, 246, 604; and Arrighi, *The Long Twentieth Century*, 13–16, 74–84, 235–38, 330–31.

7. Pasquale Pasquino, "Criminology: The Birth of a Special Savoir," *Ideology and Consciousness* 7 (Autumn, 1980): 20; Stephen Jay Gould, *The Mismeasure of Man* (New York: W. W. Norton, 1981), 73–233; Nancy Leys Stepan, *"The Hour of Eugenics"* (Ithaca: Cornell University Press, 1991), 96–97; Pedro Trinidad Fernández, *La defensa de la sociedad: Cárcel y delincuencia en España (siglos XVIII–XX)* (Madrid: Alianza Editorial, 1991), 248–82; Gail Bederman, *Manliness and Civilization* (Chicago: University of Chicago Press, 1996); Lee D. Baker, *From Savage to Negro* (Berkeley: University of California Press, 1998), 26–98.

8. Richard Drinnon, *Facing West* (New York: New American Library, 1980), 232–332; Edwin Bliss, *Turkey and the Armenian Atrocities* (Fresno: Meshag Publishers 1982 [1896]), 476–81; Adrian Graves, "Colonialism and Indentured Labour Migration in the Western Pacific, 1840-1915," in P. C. Emmer, ed., *Colonialism and Migration* (Dordrecht: Martinus Nijhoff Publishers, 1986), 237–59; Michael Taussig, "Culture of Terror—Spaces of Death: Roger Casement's Putumayo Report and the Explanation of Torture," in Nicholas B. Dirks, ed., *Colonialism and Culture* (Ann Arbor: University of Michigan Press, 1992), 135–73; Gunther Peck, "Reinventing Free Labor: Immigrant Padrones and Contract Laborers in North America, 1885-1925," *Journal of American History* 83 (December 1996): 848–71; V. G. Kiernan, *Colonial Empires and Armies, 1815-1960* (Montreal: McGill-Queen's University Press, Sutton Publishing Ltd., 1998), 160–66; Mike Davis, *Late Victorian Holocausts* (London: Verso, 2001).

9. Michel Aglietta, *A Theory of Capitalist Regulation* (London: New Left Books 1979), 79–85, 111–19; Peter Duus, *The Abacus and the Sword: The Japanese Penetration of Korea, 1895-1910* (Berkeley: University of California Press, 1995); Laura Tabili, *"We Ask for British Justice": Workers and Racial Difference in Late Imperial Britain* (Ithaca: Cornell University Press, 1994); David. B. Abernathy, *Global Dominance* (New Haven: Yale University Press, 2000), 92–103, 278–99; Bruce Nelson, *Divided We Stand* (Princeton: Princeton University Press, 2001), 8–45; Howard Winant, *The World Is a Ghetto* (New York: Basic Books, 2001), 83–129.

10. W. E. B. DuBois, "The Negro Problems," in David Levering Lewis, ed., *W. E. B. DuBois: A Reader* (New York: Henry Holt, 1995), 49 (originally published in 1915).

11. Foucault, *Discipline and Punish*, 219; Kelvin Santiago-Valles, "American Penal Forms and Colonial-Spanish Custodial-Regulatory Practices in Fin-de-Siècle Puerto Rico," in Alfred W. McCoy and Francisco A. Scarano, eds., *Colonial Crucible: Empire in the Making of the Modern American State* (Madison: University of Wisconsin Press, 2009), 87–94.

12. Pasquino, "Criminology"; Martha Knissey-Huggins, *From Slavery to Vagrancy in Brazil* (New Brunswick: Rutgers University Press, 1985); Alex Lichtenstein, *Twice the Work of Free Labor: The Political Economy of Convict Labor in the New South* (New York: Verso, 1996); Satadru Sen, *Disciplining Punishment: Colonialism and Convict Society in the Andaman Islands* (Oxford: Oxford University Press, 2000), 166–261; Peter Zinoman, *The Colonial Bastille: A History of Imprisonment in Vietnam, 1862-1940* (Berkeley: University of California

Press, 2001), 28–97; Frank Dikötter, *Crime, Punishment, and the Prison in Modern China* (New York: Columbia University Press, 2002), 27–58; Stephen Pierce, "Punishment and the Political Body: Flogging and Colonialism in Northern Nigeria," in Stephen Pierce and Anupama Rao, eds., *Discipline and the Other Body* (Durham: Duke University Press, 2006), 186–214.

13. Jean Chesneaux, *Peasant Revolts in China, 1840–1949* (W. W. Norton, 1973), 50–55; Miguel Martínez Cuadrado, *La burguesía conservadora (1874–1931)* (Madrid: Alianza Universidad, 1976), 82–85, 135, 138–44; Manuel Tuñón de Lara, *La España del siglo XIX* (Barcelona: Editorial Laia, 1977), 55–83; Stuart Creighton Miller, *"Benevolent Assimilation": The American Conquest of the Philippines, 1899–1903* (New Haven: Yale University Press, 1982); Kiernan, *Colonial Empires and Armies*, 78–82, 86–90, 98–99, 109–110; Jeremy Black, *War and the World* (New Haven: Yale University Press 1998), 181–88; Sen, *Disciplining Punishment*, 42–49; Nigel Bolland, *The Politics of Labour in the British Caribbean* (Kingston, Jamaica: Ian Randle, 2001), 174; Robert Utley and Wilcomb Washburn, *Indian Wars* (New York: Mariner Books, 2002), 220–85.

14. E. J. Hobsbawm, *The Age of Empire, 1876–1914* (New York: Vintage Books, 1989), 37; Beverly Silver and Giovanni Arrighi, "Polanyi's 'Double Movement': The *Belle Époques* of British and U.S. Hegemony Compared," *Politics and Society* 31, no. 2 (June 2003): 327–29, 332–34.

15. For the burden on laborers, see Hobsbawm, *The Age of Empire*, 123–24; Beverly Silver and Eric Slater, "The Social Origins of World Hegemonies," in Giovanni Arrighi and Beverly Silver, eds., *Chaos and Governance in the Modern World System*, 186, 191–92; and Silver and Arrighi, "Polanyi's 'Double Movement,'" 336. For the peasant wars, see Chesneaux, *Peasant Revolts in China*, 56–77; Alison des Forges, "'The drum is greater than the shout': The 1912 rebellion in northern Rwanda," in Donald Crummey, ed., *Banditry, Rebellion, and Social Protest in Africa* (London: James Currey, 1986), 311–332; Paul Vanderwood, *Disorder and Progress: Bandits, Police, and Mexican Development* (Wilmington: Scholarly Resources, 1992), 139–178.

16. Henry K. Carroll, *Report on the Island of Porto Rico: Population, Civil Government, Commerce, Industries, Productions, Roads, Tariffs, and Currency with Recommendations by Henry K. Carroll* (Washington, D.C.: Government Printing Office, 1899), 602–3; George M. Davis, *Report of Brigadier General George M. Davis, U.S.V., on Civil Affairs of Porto Rico* (Washington, D.C.: Government Printing Office, 1900), 19; George M. Davis, *Annual Reports of the War Department for the Fiscal Year Ended June 30, 1900*, part 13, *Report of the Military Governor of Porto Rico on Civil Affairs* (Washington, D.C.: Government Printing Office, 1902), 97, 102; Blanca Silvestrini, *Violencia y criminalidad en Puerto Rico, 1898–1973* (Río Piedras: Editorial de la Universidad de Puerto Rico, 1980), 25; Fernando Picó, *1898: La guerra después de la guerra* (Río Piedras: Ediciones Huracán, 1987); Mariano Negrón Portillo, *Cuadrillas anexionistas y revueltas campesinas en Puerto Rico, 1898–1899* (Río Piedras: Centro de Investigaciones Sociales, Universidad de Puerto Rico, 1987), 32, 40–42.

17. Silver and Slater, "The Social Origins of World Hegemonies," 185–190.

18. Winston Churchill, *The Second World War*, vol. 1, *The Gathering Storm* (New York: Houghton Mifflin, 1948), xiii. See also Siegmund Neumann, *The Future in Perspective* (New York: G. P. Putnam's Sons, 1946); Silvio Pons and Andrea Romano, eds., *Russia in the Age of Wars, 1914–1945* (Milan: Fondazione Giangiacomo Feltrinelli, 2000), xii; and Immanuel Wallerstein, "The Global Picture, 1945–90," in Terence K. Hopkins and Immanuel Wallerstein, eds., *The Age of Transition* (London: Zed Books, 1998), 215.

19. Giorgio Agamben, *Means without End* (Minneapolis: University of Minnesota Press, 2000), 22, 23; Gargi Bhattacharyya, John Gabriel, and Stephen Small, *Race and Power* (New York: Routledge, 2002), 73–87, 123–26; Paul Farmer, *Pathologies of Power* (Berkeley: University of California Press, 2003).

20. For example, see R. Travis Osborne, ed., *Human Variation* (New York: Academic Press, 1978); and Richard Herrnstein and Charles Murray, *The Bell Curve* (New York: Free Press, 1994).

21. For example, see Samuel Huntington, *The Clash of Civilizations and the Remaking of World Order* (New York: Simon and Schuster, 1996); and Bernard Lewis, *What Went Wrong?* (Oxford: Oxford University Press, 2001).

22. Fred Halliday, *The Making of the Second Cold War* (London: Verso, 1983); Larry Everest, *Oil, Power, and Empire* (Monroe: Common Courage Press, 2004).

23. Immanuel Wallerstein, "The Global Possibilities, 1990–2025," in Terence K. Hopkins and Immanuel Wallerstein, eds., *The Age of Transition* (London: Zed Books, 1998), 229–42; David Held, Anthony McGrew, David Goldblatt, and Jonathan Perraton, *Global Transformations* (Stanford: Stanford University Press, 1999), 97–109; Stephen Lendman, "Resource Wars: Can We Survive Them?" *Global Research*, June 6, 2007, http://www.globalresearch.ca/index.php?context=viewArticle&code=LEN20070606&articleId=5892, viewed August 2, 2007.

24. Michael K. Tabb, *The Amoral Elephant* (New York: Monthly Review Press, 2001), 51–78, 161–79; Bhattacharyya, Gabriel, and Small, *Race and Power*, 28–59, 92–116; Ronaldo Munck, *Globalisation and Labour* (London: Zed Books, 2002); Anna Marie Smith, *New Right Discourse on Race and Sexuality* (Cambridge: Cambridge University Press, 2004); Philip McMichael, *Development and Social Change* (Thousand Oaks: Pine Forge Press, 2008), 128–227.

25. Midnight Notes Collective, eds., *The New Enclosures*, Midnight Notes, no. 10, 1990, http://www.midnightnotes.org/newenclos.html, viewed March 5, 2001; Saskia Sassen, *Globalization and Its Discontents* (New York: New Press, 1998); David Kyle and Rey Koslowski, eds., *Global Human Smuggling* (Baltimore: Johns Hopkins University Press, 2001); Ellen Rosen, *Making Sweatshops* (Berkeley: University of California Press, 2002); International Labour Conference, *A Global Alliance against Forced Labour* (Geneva: International Labour Office, 2005), http://www.ilo.org/dyn/declaris/DECLARATIONWEB.DOWNLOAD_BLOB ?Var_DocumentID=5059, viewed March 10, 2005; Silvia Federici, "Precarious Labor: A Feminist Viewpoint," *Upping the Anti*, June 7, 2008, http://auto_sol.tao.ca/node/3074, viewed December 2, 2008; George Caffentzis, "The End of Work or the Renaissance of Slavery? A Critique of Rifkin and Negri," *Common Sense: Journal of the Edinburgh Conference of Socialist Economists*, no. 24 (December, 1999): 20–38.

26. Neil Smith, *The New Urban Frontier* (London: Routledge, 1996); Teresa Caldeira, *City of Walls* (Berkeley: University of California Press, 2000); Saskia Sassen, *The Global City* (Princeton: Princeton University Press, 2001), 305–23, 329–44; Bhattacharyya, Gabriel, and Small, *Race and Power*, 124–34; Chris Webster, George Glasze, and Klaus Frantz, "The Global Spread of Gated Communities," *Environment and Planning B: Planning and Design* 29, no. 3 (2002): 315–20; Mike Davis, *Planet of Slums* (New York: Verso, 2007).

27. Melissa Spatz, "A 'Lesser' Crime: A Comparative Study of Legal Defenses for Men Who Kill Their Wives," *Columbia Journal of Law and Social Problems* 24, no. 4 (Fall 1991): 597–638; Kathryn Olmsted, *Challenging the Secret Government* (Berkeley: University of California Press, 1996); Ruth Gilmore, "Globalization and U.S. Prison Growth: From Military Keynesianism to Post-Keynesian Militarism," *Race and Class* 40, nos. 2–3 (1998): 171–88; Loïc Wacquant, "'Suitable Enemies': Foreigners and Immigrants in the Prisons of Europe," *Punishment and Society* 1, no. 2 (October 1999): 215–23; Jonathan Simon, "'Entitlement to Cruelty': The End of Welfare and the Punitive Mentality in the United States," in Kevin Stenson and Robert Sullivan, eds., *Crime, Risk, and Justice* (London: Willan Publishing, 2000), 125–43; Martha K. Huggins, "Urban Violence and Police Privatization in Brazil: Blended Invisibility," *Social Justice* 27, no. 2 (Summer 2000): 113–34; Peter Singer, *Corporate Warriors* (Ithaca: Cornell University Press, 2003); David Lyon, "Globalizing Surveillance,"

International Sociology 19, no. 2 (2004): 135–49; Fox Butterfield, "Trouble in Private U.S. Jails Preceded Job Fixing Iraq's," *New York Times*, June 6, 2004, http://www.common dreams.org/headlines04/0606-02.htm, viewed October 5, 2004; Liz Fekete, *The Deportation Machine* (London: Institute of Race Relations, 2005); Lynn Welchman and Sara Hossain, *"Honor": Crimes, Paradigms, and Violence against Women* (London: Zed Books, 2005); Alfred W. McCoy, *A Question of Torture* (New York: Metropolitan Books, 2006), 108–90; Jasmin Hristov, *Blood and Capital: The Paramilitarization of Colombia* (Athens: Ohio University Press, 2009).

28. Clarence Lusane, *Pipe Dream Blues* (Boston: South End Press, 1991); Held et al., *Global Transformations*, 97–104, 113–15, 123; Bhattacharyya, Gabriel, and Small, *Race and Power*, 51–57; Greg Campbell, *Blood Diamonds* (Boulder: Westview Press, 2002); Michael C. Ruppert, *Crossing the Rubicon* (Gabriola Island, British Colombia: New Society Publishers, 2004), 22–150, 527–69; Naomi Klein, "The Rise of Disaster Capitalism," *Nation*, May 2, 2005, http://www.thenation.com/docprint.mhtml?i=20050502&s=klein, viewed May 10, 2005; David Phinney, "A U.S. Fortress Rises in Baghdad: Asian Workers Trafficked to Build World's Largest Embassy," *CorpWatch*, October 17, 2006, http://www.corpwatch.org/arti cle.php?id=14173&printsafe=1, viewed October 24, 2006; Eric Mann, *Katrina's Legacy* (Los Angeles: Frontline Press, 2006); Ellen Brown, "Libya: All about Oil, or All about Banking?," *Global Research*, April 14, 2011, http://www.globalresearch.ca/PrintArticle.php?articleId=24306, viewed April 15, 2011.

29. John Walton and David Seddon, *Free Markets and Food Riots* (Oxford: Basil Blackwell, 1994); Eric Holt-Gimenez and Raj Patel, eds., *Food Rebellions* (Oakland: Food First Books, 2009); David DeGraw, "Global Insurrection against Neo-liberal Economic Domination," *Global Research*. February 23, 2011, http://www.globalresearch.ca/PrintArticle.php?articleId=23350, viewed February 24, 2011; Vicente Navarro, "Crisis and Class Struggle in the Eurozone: The Cases of Spain Greece, Ireland, and Portugal," *CounterPunch*, August 19–21, 2011, http://www.counterpunch.org/navarro08192011.html, viewed August 21, 2011.

30. Siriporn Skrobanek, Nataya Boonpakdee, and Chutima Jantateero, *The Traffic in Women* (London: Zed Books, 1997), 80–91; José Bové, "A Farmers' International?," *New Left Review*, new ser., no. 12 (November–December 2001), http://newleftreview.org/A2358, viewed September 12, 2003; Munck, *Globalisation and Labour*, 154–94; Notes from Nowhere, *We Are Everywhere* (London: Verso, 2003), 22, 34–38, 80–88, 102–5, 140–49, 184–95, 204–10, 286–89, 328–70, 418–27, 464–71; Coalition of Immokalee Workers (CIW), "CIW Anti-slavery Campaign," 2004, Coalition of Immokalee Workers Online Headquarters, http://www.ciw -online.org/slavery.html, viewed January 2, 2005; Rajeev Patel and Philip McMichael, "Third Worldism and the Lineages of Global Fascism: The Regrouping of the Global South in the Neoliberal Era," *Third World Quarterly* 25, no. 1 (2004): 247–51; Laith Al-Saud, "The Resistance in Context: An Anatomy of the Resistance to the American Occupation of Iraq," *CounterPunch*, May 21–22, 2005, http://www.counterpunch.org/laith05212005.html, viewed June 1, 2005; Alain Gresh, "After Hizbullah and Hamas: Middle East—What Will Emerge from the Ruins?" *Le Monde Diplomatique*, August 2006, http://mondediplo.com/2006/08/02leb anon, viewed September 2, 2006; Michael Watts, "Oil Inferno: Crisis in Nigeria," *Counter-Punch*, January 2, 2007, http://www.counterpunch.org/watts01022007.html, viewed January 20, 2007; "Leading Indicators of Revolt in the Middle East and North Africa: Corruption, Unemployment, and Percentage of Household Money Spent on Food," *Washington's Blog*, February 20, 2011, http://georgewashington2.blogspot.com/2011/02/numbers-behind-middle-eastern-and-north.html, viewed February 21, 2011.

31. October 22 Coalition, "Mission Statement of the National Day of Protest to Stop Police Brutality, Repression, and the Criminalization of a Generation," 1996, October 22 Coalition, http://october22.org/, viewed March 10, 2003; "Prison Riot in Mexico City," *New York Times*, September 17, 1998, http://query.nytimes.com/gst/fullpage.html?res=9802E3D

61E31F934A2575ACA96E958260, viewed April 4, 2003; Sara Callaway and Benoit Martin, "The *Sans Papiers* Defend Their Autonomy with New Protests and Occupations," *Archives de la liste "zpajol,"* June 1998, http://www.bok.net/pajol/sanspap/blackwomen/blackwomen 2.en.html, viewed March 12, 2007; Notes from Nowhere, *We Are Everywhere*, 38–45, 326–27; Staughton Lynd, *Lucasville* (Philadelphia: Temple University Press, 2004); "28 Killed in Philippines Prison Uprising," *USA Today*, March 15, 2005, http://www.usatoday .com/news/world/2005-03-15-philippines-prison-uprising_x.htm, viewed May 8, 2005; Fatima Khafagy, "Honor Killing in Egypt," UN Division for the Advancement of Women, Expert Group Meeting, Vienna, May 17–20, 2005, http://www.un.org/womenwatch/daw/egm /vaw-gp-2005/docs/experts/khafagy.honorcrimes.pdf, viewed February 10, 2007; Martha Alicia Duque, "Indígenas señalan nuevos caminos de resistencia en Colombia," *Le Monde Diplomatique*, Colombian edition, April 2005, http://www.eldiplo.info/mostrar_articulo.php ?id=66&numero=33, viewed May 17, 2005; International Women's Health Coalition, "Justice, Community, and Spirituality: A Conversation with Nigerian Activist Ngozi Iwere," 2006, International Women's Health Coalition, http://www.iwhc.org/programs/africa/nige ria/iwereinterview.cfm, viewed March 10, 2007; Rashid Khalidi, *The Iron Cage* (Boston: Beacon Press, 2007), 140–200; Kevin R. Johnson and Bill Ong Hing, "The Immigration Rights Marches of 2006 and the Prospects for a New Civil Rights Movement," *Harvard Civil Rights-Civil Liberties Law Review* 42 (2007): 99–138.

32. Bruce Porter and Marvin Dunn, *The Miami Riot of 1980* (Lexington: D. C. Heath, 1984); Anders Corr, *No Trespassing* (Boston: South End Press, 1999), 97–184; Notes from Nowhere, *We Are Everywhere*, 196–201, 264–77; Chittaroopa Palit, "Monsoon Risings: Mega-dam Resistance in the Narmada Valley," *New Left Review*, new ser., no. 21 (May–June 2003), http://newleftreview.org/?page=article&view=2450, viewed October 5, 2003; Perry Keisha-Khan, "The Roots of Black Resistance: Race, Gender, and the Struggle for Urban Rights in Salvador, Bahia, Brazil," *Social Identities* 10, no. 6 (2004): 811–31; Everest, *Oil, Power, and Empire*, 286, 296, 298; Dominique Vidal, "The Fight against Urban Apartheid." *Le Monde Diplomatique*, December 2005, http://mondediplo.com/2005/12/03apartheid, viewed January 5, 2006; Mann, *Katrina's Legacy*; Nir Hasson, "Thousands of Protesters Rally against Jewish Presence in East Jerusalem," *Ha'aretz*, March 6, 2010, http://www.haaretz .com/news/thousands-of-protesters-rally-against-jewish-presence-in-east-jerusalem- 1.264238, viewed March 20, 2010; Joseph Harker, "For Black Britons, This Is Not the 80s Revisited: It's Worse," *The Guardian*, August 11, 2011, http://www.guardian.co.uk/comment isfree/2011/aug/11/black-britons-80s-mps-media, viewed August 12, 2011. See also note 31.

33. Immanuel Wallerstein, *The End of the World as We Know It* (Minneapolis: University of Minnesota Press, 1999), 46–48.

34. Silver and Slater, "The Social Origins of World Hegemonies," 213.

35. Wallerstein, "The Global Possibilities, 1990–2025," 229–32, 241, 243.

Darwin / The Geopolitics of Decolonization

1. The classic account is J. Gallagher and R. Robinson, "The Imperialism of Free Trade," *Economic History Review*, new ser., 6. no. 1 (1953): 1–15. For the Chinese case, see J. Osterhammel, "Britain and China, 1842–1914," in Andrew N. Porter, ed., *Oxford History of the British Empire*, vol. 3, *The Nineteenth Century* (Oxford: Oxford University Press, 1999), 146–69.

2. See Gerrit W. Gong, *The "Standard of Civilisation" in International Society* (Oxford: Oxford University Press, 1984).

3. Benjamin Kidd, *Social Evolution* (London: Macmillan, 1894).

4. Paul W. Schroeder, *The Transformation of European Politics, 1763–1848* (Oxford: Oxford University Press, 1994), esp. 575–82.

5. Hew Strachan, *The First World War*, vol. 1, *To Arms* (Oxford: Oxford University Press, 2001), chaps. 6, 7.

6. See Lord Lugard, *The Dual Mandate in Tropical Africa* (Edinburgh: William Blackwood, 1922).

7. Akira Iriye, *After Imperialism: The Search for a New Order in the Far East, 1921–1931* (New York: Oxford University Press, 1965), is the classic account.

8. See Edmund S. K. Fung, *The Diplomacy of Imperial Retreat: Britain's South China Policy, 1924–1931* (Hong Kong: Oxford University Press, 1991).

9. See Greg Kennedy, *Anglo-American Strategic Relations in the Far East, 1933–1939* (London: Frank Cass, 2002); Joseph A. Maiolo, *The Royal Navy and Nazi Germany, 1933–39: A Study in Appeasement and the Origins of the Second World War* (Basingstoke: Macmillan, 1998); and Lawrence R. Pratt, *East of Malta, West of Suez: Britain's Mediterranean Crisis, 1936–1939* (Cambridge: Cambridge University Press, 1975).

10. See Harold James, *The End of Globalization: Lessons from the Great Depression* (Cambridge: Harvard University Press, 2001).

11. John Darwin, *The Empire Project: The Rise and Fall of the British World System, 1830–1970* (Cambridge: Cambridge University Press, 2009), chap. 11.

12. Robert Skidelsky, *John Maynard Keynes: Fighting for Britain, 1937–1946* (London: Macmillan, 2000).

13. See Michael Roberts and A. E. G. Trollip, *The South African Opposition, 1939–1945: An Essay in Contemporary History* (London: Longmans, Green, 1947), chap. 6.

14. For the Dutch case, see H. W. van den Doel, *Het Rijk van Insulinde* (Amsterdam: Prometheus, 1996), 284, 286.

15. See Darwin, *The Empire Project*, 533–36, 555–56.

16. William Roger Louis, *Imperialism at Bay: The United States and the Decolonization of the British Empire, 1941–1945* (Oxford: Oxford University Press, 1977).

17. William Roger Louis, *The British Empire in the Middle East, 1945–1951: Arab Nationalism, the United States, and Postwar Imperialism* (Oxford: Oxford University Press, 1984), part 5.

18. Darwin, *The Empire Project*, chap. 13.

19. W. R. Louis and R. Robinson, "The Imperialism of Decolonization," *Journal of Imperial and Commonwealth History* 22, no. 3 (1994): 462–511.

20. LM 089, Roll 37, Caffery (Cairo) to State Department, May 23, 1950, State Department Central Files (Egypt), U.S. National Archives and Records Administration.

21. John Darwin, "The Central African Emergency, 1959," *Journal of Imperial and Commonwealth History* 21, no. 1 (1993): 217–34. For Kenya, see David Anderson, *Histories of the Hanged: The Dirty War in Kenya and the End of Empire* (London: Weidenfeld and Nicolson, 2005).

22. Nigel John Ashton, "Harold Macmillan and the 'Golden Days' of Anglo-American Relations Revisited, 1957–63," *Diplomatic History* 29, no. 4 (2005): 700–702.

23. See Stephen Kotkin, *Armageddon Averted: the Soviet Collapse, 1970–2000* (Oxford: Oxford University Press, 2008).

Saada / The Absent Empire

1. Gary Wilder, *The French Imperial Nation-State: Negritude and Colonial Humanism between the Two World Wars* (Chicago: University of Chicago Press, 2005). The imperial nature of France is also partly the object of the recent massive comparative project by Jane Burbank and Frederick Cooper, *Empires in World History: Power and the Politics of Difference* (Princeton: Princeton University Press, 2010).

2. Examples include Laurent Dubois, *Soccer Empire: The World Cup and the Future of France* (Durham: Duke University Press, 2010); George R. Trumbull IV, *An Empire of Facts: Colonial Power, Cultural Knowledge, and Islam in Algeria, 1870–1914* (New York: Cambridge University Press, 2009); and Benjamin Claude Brower, *A Desert Named Peace: The*

Violence of France's Empire in the Algerian Sahara (New York: Columbia University Press, 2009).

3. As a rapid comparative search between the Amazon.fr and the Amazon.us websites would suggest, this association is still far more frequent in English than in French. If there has been a "turn" in recent French historiography, it has been more "colonial" than "imperial."

4. Lauren Benton, "Constitutions and Empires," *Law and Social Inquiry* 31, no. 1 (2006): 177–98.

5. While he does not use the phrase "noncolonial empire," Frederick Cooper has suggested in his analysis of the constitutional debates of 1946 that the French government tried to make its empire "less colonial." See Frederick Cooper, "From Imperial Inclusion to Republican Exclusion? France's Ambiguous Postwar Trajectory," in Charles Tshimanga, Didier Gondola, and Peter J. Bloom, eds., *Frenchness and the African Diaspora: Identity and Uprising in Contemporary France* (Bloomington: Indiana University Press, 2009), 91–119, esp. 104.

6. Bernard Porter, *The Absent-Minded Imperialists: What the British Really Thought about Empire* (Oxford: Oxford University Press, 2005).

7. Jacques Marseille, *Empire colonial et capitalisme français: Histoire d'un divorce* (Paris: Albin Michel, 1984); Raoul Girardet, *L'Idée coloniale en France de 1871 à 1962* (Paris: La Table Ronde, 1972); Charles-Robert Ageron, *France coloniale ou parti colonial?* (Paris: Presses Universitaires de France, 1978).

8. See, among other works, Martin Evans, "Culture and Empire, 1830–1962: An Overview," in *Empire and Culture: The French Experience, 1830–1940* (New York: Palgrave, 2004), 1–23; Pascal Blanchard and Sandrine Lemaire, eds., *Culture coloniale: La France conquise par son empire (1871–1931)*, "Mémoires," no. 86 (Paris: Éditions Autrement, 2003); and Pascal Blanchard and Sandrine Lemaire, eds., *Culture impériale, 1931–1961: Les colonies au cœur de la République*, "Mémoires," no. 102 (Paris: Éditions Autrement, 2004).

9. Reine-Claude Grondin, *L'Empire en province: Culture et expérience coloniales en Limousin (1830–1939)* (Toulouse: Presses Universitaires du Mirail, 2010).

10. Burbank and Cooper, *Empires in World History*, 8. They continue, "The concept of empire presumes that different peoples within the polity will be governed differently."

11. Laurent Dubois, *A Colony of Citizens: Revolution and Slave Emancipation in the French Caribbean, 1787–1804* (Chapel Hill: University of North Carolina Press, 2004); Fanny Colonna, *Instituteurs algériens, 1883–1939* (Paris: Presses de la Fondation nationale des sciences politiques, 1975); Frederick Cooper, "Labor, Politics, and the End of Empire in French Africa," in *Colonialism in Question: Theory, Knowledge, History* (Berkeley: University of California Press, 2005), 204–30.

12. The term *second French colonial empire* was canonized by French historiography as a shorthand way to describe the mostly African, Asian, and Pacific empire of the twentieth century.

13. Jennifer Pitts, *A Turn to Empire: the Rise of Imperial Liberalism in Britain and France* (Princeton: Princeton University Press, 2005).

14. The association with these emperors has recently been noted by David Todd in "A French Imperial Meridian, 1814–1870," *Past and Present* 210 (February 2011); 155–86, esp. 158.

15. Raymond Carré de Malberg, "La condition juridique de l'Alsace-Lorraine dans l'Empire allemand," *Revue de Droit public* 1 (January–March 1914): 5–47.

16. Raymond Carré de Malberg, *Contribution à la théorie générale de l'État, spécialement d'après les données fournies par le droit constitutionnel français* (Paris: Sirey, 1920–22).

17. William B. Cohen, *Rulers of Empire: The French Colonial Service in Africa* (Stanford: Hoover Institution Press, 1971), 39.

18. Cooper and Burbank, *Empires in World History*, 8.

19. Quoted in Charles-Robert Ageron, "L'Exposition coloniale," in Pierre Nora, ed., *Les Lieux de mémoire*, vol. 1, *La République* (Paris: Gallimard, 1984), 584.

20. Gaston Pelletier and Louis Roubaud, *Empire ou Colonies?* (Paris: Plon, 1936), 231.

21. Quoted in Ageron, *France coloniale ou parti colonial?* 260–61.

22. Ibid.

23. René Maunier, *L'Empire français: Propos et projets* (Paris: Librarie du Recueil Sirey, 1943).

24. Wilder, *The French Imperial Nation State*; Olivier Le Cour Grandmaison, *La République impériale: Politique et racisme d'État* (Paris: Fayard, 2009).

25. To my knowledge, the only recent historical analysis of this important phenomenon is to be found in the work of Josep M. Fradera, especially "L'esclavage et la logique constitutionnelle des empires," *Annales, Histoire, Sciences Sociales*, 3 (May–June 2008): 533–60.

26. See Pierre Dareste, *Traité de droit colonial*, 2 vols. (Cannes: Imprimerie Robaudy, 1931), 1:227.

27. Here I mean *empire* as a way to describe the ensemble made up of the metropole and its colonies. Of course *empire* was used in the Senatus-Consulte of Year XII (1804) and in the 1852 Constitution to refer to Napoleonic regimes. The constitution project undertaken by Marshall Pétain, which was never promulgated, is an exception to this trajectory in that it devotes its last section to the definition of the empire as "the overseas territories over which the French state [*l'Etat français*, i.e., the Vichy regime] exercises its sovereignty." Nonetheless, it repeated that the empire was ruled by "particular legislations."

28. Marie-Vic Ozouf-Marigier, *La formation des départements: La représentation du territoire français à la fin du 18e siècle* (Paris: Éditions de L'École des hautes études en sciences sociales, 1989).

29. Emilien Petit, *Droit Public ou Gouvernement des colonies françaises d'après les lois faites pour ces pays* (Paris: Librairie Paul Geuthner, 1911 [1771]); Abbé de Raynal, *Histoire philosophique et politique des établissements et du commerce des Européens dans les deux Indes*, 5 vols. (Paris: Bibliothèque des Introuvables, 2006). The passage by Denis Diderot is quoted in Yves Benot, *La Révolution française et les colonies, 1789–1794* (Paris: la Découverte, 2004), 189.

30. On Boissy d'Anglas's report, see Jouda Guteta, "Le refus d'application de la constitution de l'an III à Saint-Domingue (1795–1797)," in Florence Gauthier, ed., *Périssent les colonies plutôt qu'un principe! Contributions à l'histoire de l'abolition de l'esclavage, 1789–1804* (Paris: Société des Etudes Robespierristes, 2002), 81–90.

31. Martin Deming Lewis, "One Hundred Million Frenchmen: The 'Assimilation' Theory in French Colonial Policy," *Comparative Studies in Society and History* 4, no. 2 (January 1962): 129–53.

32. The preamble states, "La France forme avec les peuples d'outre-mer une Union fondée sur l'égalité des droits et des devoirs, sans distinction de race ni de religion. L'Union française est composée de nations et de peuples qui mettent en commun ou coordonnent leurs ressources et leurs efforts pour développer leurs civilisations respectives, accroître leur bien-être et assurer leur sécurité. Fidèle à sa mission traditionnelle, la France entend conduire les peuples dont elle a pris la charge à la liberté de s'administrer eux-mêmes et de gérer démocratiquement leurs propres affaires; écartant tout système de colonisation fondé sur l'arbitraire, elle garantit à tous l'égal accès aux fonctions publiques et l'exercice individuel ou collectif des droits et libertés proclamés ou confirmés ci-dessus."

33. James I. Lewis, "The French Colonial Service and the Issues of Reform, 1944–1948," *Contemporary European History* 4, no. 2 (1995): 153–88.

34. Alain Fenet, "Les dispositions du préambule de 1946 relatives aux peuples d' Outre-mer," in CURAPP [Centre universitaire de recherches administratives et politiques de

Picardie], *Le Préambule de la Constitution de 1946* (Paris: Presses Universitaires de France, 1996), 147–55.

35. Burbank and Cooper, *Empires in World History*, 421.

ALDRICH / WHEN DID DECOLONIZATION END?

1. Martin Thomas, Bob Moore, and L. J. Butler, *Crises of Empire: Decolonization and Europe's Imperial States, 1918–1975* (London: Hodder, 2008); Martin Shipway, *Decolonization and Its Impact: A Comparative Approach to the End of the Colonial Empires* (Oxford: Wiley-Blackwell, 2008). See also Tony Chafer, *The End of Empire in French West Africa: France's Successful Decolonization?* (Oxford: Berg, 2002); Todd Shepard, *The Invention of Decolonization: The Algerian War and the Remaking of France* (Ithaca: Cornell University Press, 2006); and Mark Atwood Lawrence and Fredrik Logevall, eds., *The First Vietnam War: Colonial Conflict and Cold War Crisis* (Cambridge: Harvard University Press, 2006). The most recent French overview is Bernard Droz, *Histoire de la décolonisation au XXe siècle* (Paris: Seuil, 2009).

2. The *code de l'indigénat* made it possible in certain colonies for administrators to impose penalties and sentences, including corporal punishment, on "natives" without judicial procedure, trial, or conviction.

3. The French ruthlessly, and successfully, repressed an insurrection in Madagascar in 1947.

4. Three other outposts subsequently gained independence: the Comoros Islands (minus Mayotte, which remains attached to France) in 1974–75, Djibouti in 1977, and the Anglo-French condominium of the New Hebrides (Vanuatu) in 1980.

5. Martin Thomas, *The French North African Crisis: Colonial Breakdown and Anglo-French Relations* (London: Palgrave Macmillan, 2000); Irwin M. Wall, *France, the United States, and the Algeria War* (Berkeley: University of California Press, 2001).

6. *Harkis*, the Muslim "auxiliaries" who fought in the French armies, were considered by Algerian nationalists to be traitors. Around ninety thousand *harkis* and their families sought refuge in France in 1962.

7. Robert Aldrich, *France and the South Pacific since 1940* (London: Macmillan, 1993); Nathalie Mrgudovic, *La France dans le Pacifique Sud: Les enjeux de la puissance* (Paris: L'Harmattan, 2008); Sarah Mohamed-Gaillard, *L'Archipel de la puissance? La Politique de la France dans le Pacifique Sud de 1946 à 1998* (Brussels: Peter Lang, 2010).

8. See Robert Aldrich and John Connell, *France's Overseas Frontier: Départements et Territoires d'Outre-Mer* (Cambridge: Cambridge University Press, 1992); Suzanne Dracius, Jean-François Samlong and Gérard Théobald, *La Crise de l'outre-mer français* (Paris: L'Harmattan, 2009).

9. Yvette Rocheron and Christopher Rolfe, eds., *Shifting the Frontiers of France and Francophonie* (Oxford: Peter Lang, 2004); D. E. Ager, *"Francophonie" in the 1990s: Problems and Opportunities* (Clevedon: Multilingual Matters, 1996).

10. Trade and investment ties with Algeria nevertheless remained strong and have increased in recent years with economic liberalization in Algeria and with French interest in the country's supplies of natural gas. With Vietnam's policy of *doi moi*, or reform, France has also reengaged with that former colony.

11. Such a suggestion was not necessarily as odd as it now seems. France made the *vieilles* colonies into *départements d'outre-mer* in 1946 (and the island of Mayotte in the Indian Ocean became a *département* in 2011).

12. Debré and Pompidou are quoted in Pierre Kipré, "De la Françafrique à l'afro-pessimisme," *L'Histoire*, no. 350 (February 2010): 61.

13. On France's "Mr. Africa," see Pierre Péan, *L'Homme de l'ombre* (Paris: Fayard, 1990). Kaye Whiteman ("The Man Who Ran Françafrique," *The National Interest* 49 [Fall 1997]:

92–99) gives a good, critical overview of his activities. *Les Cahiers du Centre de recherches historiques*, no. 30 (2002, http://ccrh.revues.org/612, accessed February 19, 2012), has a useful set of articles on "Foccart—Entre France et Afrique," including, Jean-François Médard, "'La politique est au bout du réseau': Questions sur la méthode Foccart," and Jean-Pierre Dozon, "L'état français contemporain et son double, l'état franco-africain." These last two articles analyze links among Foccart, the SDECE, Elf, French investment agencies, government ministries in Paris, and African leaders. Douglas Porch, *The French Secret Service* (New York: Farrar, Straus and Giroux, 1995), provides a reliable history of French intelligence gathering and covert operations.

14. See François-Xavier Verschave, *La Françafrique: Le plus long scandale de la République* (Paris: Stock, 1994), and his many other works.

15. Gordon Cumming and Rachael Langford, eds., "France and Africa in the Global Era," special issue, *Modern and Contemporary France* 13, no. 1 (February 2005); Bruno Charbonneau, "Dreams of Empire: France, Europe, and the New Interventionism in Africa," *Modern and Contemporary France* 16, no. 3 (August 2008): 279–96.

16. France maintains bases in Djibouti, Senegal, and Gabon. "France hasn't fully abandoned its traditional bilateral structure," and it " has yet to officially revise or renegotiate the secret and public defense treaties signed with a select number of African countries," according to Washington's Council on Foreign Relations, http://www.cfr.org/publication/12578/, accessed April 6, 2010.

17. Stephen W. Smith, "Nodding and Winking," *London Review of Books*, February 11, 2010, 10–12. Also see his *Voyage en postcolonie: le nouveau monde franco-africain* (Paris: Grasset, 2010).

18. Christophe Boisbouvier, "50 Years Later, Françafrique Is Alive and Well," *RFI English*, February 16, 2010, http://www.english.rfi.fr/africa,/20100216-50-years-later-francafrique-alive-and-well, accessed April 7, 2010.

19. La Françafrique est morte, vive la Françafrique," *Africa Confidential* 49, no. 7 (March 28, 2008), http://www.africa-confidential.com/article-preview/id/2519/No-Title, accessed April 7, 2010.

20. See Deborah Brautigan, *The Dragon's Gift: The Real Story of China in Africa* (New York: Oxford University Press, 2010); and Serge Michel and Michel Beuret, *China Safari: On the Trail of China's Expansion in Africa* (New York: Nation Books, 2009).

21. Alec G. Hargreaves, *Multi-ethnic France: Immigration, Politics, Culture, and Society* (London: Routledge, 2007).

Wilder / Decolonizing France

1. L. S. Senghor, "La décolonisation, condition de la communauté Franco-Africaine," *Le Monde*, September 4, 1957, reprinted in L. S. Senghor, *Liberté*, vol. 2, *Nation et voie africaine du socialisme* (Paris: Editions de Seuil, 1971) (hereafter *Liberté* 2), 216–19.

2. Assemblée nationale, May 13, 1958, reprinted as "Indépendance nominale et confederation," in *Liberté*, 2:221.

3. L. S. Senghor, Lettre à Guy Mollet, Sécrétaire Général du Parti Socialiste, Dakar, le 27 septembre 1948, reprinted as "Vers un socialisme africain," in *Liberté*, 2:45–50.

4. Ruth Schachter Morgenthau, *Political Parties in French Speaking West Africa* (Oxford: Clarendon Press, 1964), 145–53.

5. "Rapport sur la méthode, VIe congrès du B.D.S. 21 avril 1954," reprinted as "La conscience: Vertu majeure du socialisme," in *Liberté* 2:125.

6. Ibid., 136–40.

7. Ibid., 125.

8. Ibid., 126.

9. L. S. Senghor, "Marxisme et humanisme," *La Revue socialiste* 19 (March 1948): 201–16, reprinted in Senghor, *Liberté* 2:29–44.

10. L. S. Senghor, "Rapport sur la méthode du Parti, IIe Congrès du B.D.S., 22–24 avril 1950," reprinted as "Le népotisme contre la révolution sociale," in *Liberté* 2:67–68.

11. Senghor, "Marxisme et humanisme."

12. Ibid., 44.

13. L. S. Senghor, "Rapport sur la méthode au 1er congrès du B.D.S., 15, 16, 17 avril 1949 à Thies," reprinted as "Naissance du Bloc Démocratique Sénégalais," in *Liberté* 2:57.

14. Ibid., 56.

15. Senghor, "Marxisme et humanisme"; Senghor, "La conscience," 135.

16. Senghor, "La conscience," 137–38.

17. Senghor, "Marxisme et humanisme, 35.

18. Senghor, "Rapport sur la méthode, Ve congrès du Bloc démocratique sénégalais, juillet 1953" reprinted as "Socialisme, fédération, religion," in *Liberté* 2, 106.

19. Senghor, "Marxisme et humanisme," 33; Senghor, "Naissance du Bloc Démocratique Sénégalais," 57–58, Senghor, "Socialisme, fédération, religion," 101.

20. Senghor, "Le népotisme contre la révolution sociale," 72.

21. Senghor, "Socialisme, fédération, religion," 106–7.

22. Senghor, "Le népotisme contre la révolution sociale," 72.

23. Senghor, "Socialisme, fédération, religion," 107.

24. Senghor, "Le népotisme contre la révolution sociale," 68–70.

25. Senghor, "Socialisme, fédération, religion," 108.

26. Senghor, "La conscience," 141.

27. Ibid., 141, 137.

28. Ibid., 137–38.

29. Ibid., 140.

30. Pierre-Joseph Proudhon, *Du principe fédératif et de la nécessité de reconstituer le parti de la revolution* (Paris: E. Dentu, 1863).

31. L. S. Senghor, "Union française et fédéralisme," *Université des Annales*, November 21, 1956, reprinted in *Liberté* 2:205.

32. See L. S. Senghor, "L'avenir de la France dans l'Outre-Mer," *Politique étrangère* 19, no. 4 (1954); L. S. Senghor, "Pour une solution fédéraliste," in "Où va l'Union française," special issue, *La Nef*, June 1955, reprinted in *Liberté* 2:161–63; and Senghor, "Union française et fédéralisme."

33. Senghor, "La conscience," 140.

34. See Gary Wilder, "*Eurafrique* as the Future Past of Black France: Sarkozy's Temporal Confusion and Senghor's Postwar Vision," in Trica Danielle Keaton, T. Denean Sharpley-Whiting, and Tyler Stovall, eds., *France Noire—Black France* (Durham: Duke University Press, 2012); and Jonathan K. Gosnell, "France, Empire, Europe: Out of Africa?," *Comparative Studies of South Asia, Africa, and the Middle East* 26, no. 2 (2006): 203–12.

35. Senghor, "Pour une solution fédéraliste," 167.

36. This part of my argument parallels and complements Frederick Cooper's essays, "Provincializing France," in Ann Laura Stoler, Carole McGranahan, and Peter Purdue, eds., *Imperial Formations* (Santa Fe: School for Advanced Research Press, 2007); and "Alternatives to Empire: France and Africa after World War II," in Douglas Howland and Luise White, eds., *The State of Sovereignty: Territories, Laws, Populations* (Bloomington: Indiana University Press, 2009).

37. Senghor, "Socialisme, fédération, religion," 109.

38. Ibid., 106 (my emphasis).

39. Ibid.

40. Senghor, "La conscience," 141.

41. Ibid., 135.

42. Ibid., 141.

43. Senghor, "Socialisme, fédération, religion," 107.

44. Senghor, "La conscience," 136.

45. Senghor, "Rapport sur la méthode, VIIIe congrès du Bloc démocratique sénégalais, mai 1956" reprinted as "Socialisme et culture," in *Liberté* 2, 184.

46. Ibid., 185.

47. Ibid., 190–91.

48. L. S. Senghor, "L'Afrique et l'europe: Deux mondes complémentaires," *Marchés coloniaux*, May 14, 1955, reprinted in *Liberté* 2:154.

49. Ibid., 155.

50. See Gary Wilder, "Untimely Vision: Aimé Césaire, Decolonization, Utopia," *Public Culture* 21, no. 1 (Winter 2009): 101–40.

51. Here I am using *pragmatic* to refer to the antifoundational and experimental approach to truth and politics that refuses a priori certainties about the best means to desirable ends.

52. On Senghor's philosophical vitalism, see Jacques Louis Hymans, *Léopold Sédar Senghor: An Intellectual Biography* (Edinburgh: Edinburgh University Press, 1971); Souleymane Bashir Diagne, "Senghor et Bergson," paper presented at conference on Canonical Works and Continuing Innovation in African Arts and Humanities, CODESRIA, Accra Ghana, September 17–19, 2003; Diagne, "On Prospective: Development and a Political Culture of Time," *Africa Development* 29, no. 1 (2004): 55–69; Diagne, "Bergson in the Colonies: Intuition and Duration in the Thought of Senghor and Iqbal," *Qui Parle* 16, no. 1 (Summer 2007); Wilder, *The French Imperial Nation-State.*

53. Rudrangshu Mukherjee, ed., *The Penguin Gandhi Reader* (New York: Penguin Books, 1993), 74.

54. Rienhart Kosellek, *Futures Past: On the Semantics of Historical Time* (New York: Columbia University Press, 2004).

Barton / Informal Empire

I owe a great debt to Alfred W. McCoy who, as coeditor of this volume, persistently engaged and improved this essay.

1. He served as foreign secretary in 1830–34, 1835–41, and 1846–51, and then as prime minister in 1855–58 and 1859–65.

2. Lord Palmerston, quoted in W. Baring Pemberton, *Lord Palmerston* (London: Batchworth Press, 1954), 141; George Canning, quoted in Martin Lynn, "Policy, Trade, and Informal Empire," *Oxford History of the British Empire*, vol. 3, *Nineteenth Century* (Oxford: Oxford University Press, 1999), 102; See also the *Commons' Committee Report* of 1837; "Report from the Select Committee on Aborigines (British Settlements)," *Parliamentary Papers* (1837) (425), VII, 76. Anthony Hopkins has recently made the claim that Britain possessed the southern portion of the United States as an informal empire before the Civil War. See his keynote address, "The United States, 1783–1861: Britain's Honorary Dominion?," British Scholar Annual Conference, Austin, Texas, April 1, 2011.

3. William Woodruff, *Impact of Western Man: A Study of Europe's Role in the World Economy, 1750–1960* (London: Macmillan, 1966), 313.

4. T. W. Heyck, *The Peoples of the British Isles* (Chicago: Lyceum, 2002), 297–98.

5. Phillip S. Bagwell and G. E. Mingay, *Britain and America: A Study of Economic Change, 1850–1939* (London: Routledge, 1987), 93–95.

6. Quoted in Pemberton, *Lord Palmerston*, 34.

7. Quoted in Pemberton, *Lord Palmerston*, 283.

8. Augustus Granville Stapleton, *George Canning and His Times* (London: John W. Parker and Son, 1859), 407–11.

9. Rory Miller, *Britain and Lain America in the Nineteenth and Twentieth Centuries* (London: Longman, 1993), 67, 243–44.

10. Peter Winn, "British Informal Empire in Uruguay in the Nineteenth Century," *Past and Present* 73, no. 1 (1976): 100–126.

11. Minute by Palmerston, 30 Aug. 1847, on Plowden to Foreign Office [hereafter FO], 28 Aug. 1847, FO 1/4.

12. Lord Palmerston, 10 Aug. 1842, *Parliamentary Debates* (Commons), Col. 1251–52.

13. Palmerston to Auckland, 22 Jan. 1841, Broadlands Papers, quoted in Martin Lynn, "Policy, Trade, and Informal Empire," in *Oxford History of the British Empire: Nineteenth Century*, vol. 3 (Oxford: Oxford University Press, 1999), 106. See also Alan Knight, "Britain and Latin America," *Oxford History of the British Empire: Nineteenth Century*, vol. 3(Oxford: Oxford University Press, 1999), 122–45.

14. The classic history of foreign policy during this period is C. Jesharaun, *The Contest for Siam, 1889–1902: A Study in Diplomatic Rivalry* (Kuala Lumpur: University of Malaya Press, 1977).

15. Anthony Webster, *Gentlemen Capitalists: British Imperialism in Southeast Asia, 1770–1890* (London: Tauris, 1998), 155–62, 229–45.

16. For an overview of the theory of informal empire, see John Gallagher and Ronald Robinson, "The Imperialism of Free Trade," *Economic History Review* 6, no. 1 (1953): 1–15; and William Roger Louis, ed., *Imperialism: The Robinson and Gallagher Controversy* (New York: New Viewpoints, 1976). Key works on Siam include Richard S. Horowitz, "International Law and State Transformation in China, Siam, and the Ottoman Empire during the Nineteenth Century," *Journal of World History* 15, no. 4 (2004): 445–86; Ian Brown, "British Financial Advisers in Siam in the Reign of King Chulalongkorn," *Modern Asian Studies* 12, no. 2 (1978): 193–215; D. R. Sardesai, *British Trade and Expansion in Southeast Asia* (New Delhi: Allied, 1977); Chayan Rajchagool, *The Rise and Fall of the Thai Absolute Monarchy* (Bangkok: White Lotus, 1994); and Anthony Webster, *Gentleman Capitalists: British Imperialism in Southeast Asia, 1770–1890* (London: Tauris, 1998).

17. One of the richest areas of inquiry into Thai history has been the examination of how the Kingdom of Siam warded off British and French imperialism by modernizing and centralizing its state in the late nineteenth century. Of special interest are books such as David K. Wyatt, *The Politics of Reform in Thailand: Education in the Reign of King Chulalongkorn* (New Haven: Yale University Press, 1969); Tej Bunnag, *Provincial Administration of Siam, 1892–1915* (Kuala Lumpur: Oxford University Press, 1977); Tej Bunnag, *The Ministry of Interior under Prince Ranajubhab* (Kuala Lumpur: Oxford University Press, 1977); Ian Brown, *The Elite and the Economy in Siam* (Singapore: Oxford University Press, 1989); Thongchai Winichakul, *Siam Mapped: A History of the Geo-body of a Nation* (Honolulu: University of Hawaii Press, 1994); Akiko Iijima, "The 'International Court' System in the Colonial History of Siam," *Taiwan Journal of Southeast Asian Studies* 5, no. 1 (2008): 3–64. A seminal article on regional elites and the modernizing reforms between 1893 and 1915 is Michael Vickery, "Thai Regional Elites and the Reforms of King Chulalongkorn," *Journal of Asian Studies* 29, no. 4 (August 1970): 863–81. In particular see his discussion of the British colonial administration model on page 875.

18. Paul Kratoska and Ben Batson, "Ethnic Nationalism," in Nicholas Tarling, ed., *The Cambridge History of Southeast Asia*, vol. 2, *The Nineteenth and Twentieth Centuries* (Cambridge: Cambridge University Press, 1993), 292.

19. For a theoretical sketch of collaboration, see Ronald Robinson, "Non-European Foundations of European Imperialism: Sketch for a Theory of Collaboration," in R. Owen and B. Sutcliffe, eds., *Studies in the Theory of Imperialism* (London: Longman, 1972), 117–42; reprinted in Louis, *The Robinson and Gallagher Controversy*, 128–51.

20. This is the argument of Iijima, "The 'International Court' System in the Colonial History of Siam" 3–64.

21. Brown, *The Elite and the Economy in Siam*, 118–19.

22. For the discussions leading to the creation of the treaty that created the extraterritorial courts, see "Chiengmai Treaty, 1882–1883," FO 69/95, National Archives Kew. There is no discussion of British overseas corporations.

23. Nigel Brailey, "The Scramble for Concessions in 1880s Siam," *Modern Asian Studies* 33, no. 3 (1999): 516.

24. See especially the printed correspondence between the Foreign Office and both companies in *Correspondence Respecting the Affairs of Siam* (London: Printed for Her Majesty's Stationary Office by Harrison and Sons, 1894).

25. National Archives (PRO), "Mr. Paget to Marquis of Lansdowne," March 11, 1905, FO 422/59.

26. Malcolm Falkus, "Early British Business in Thailand," in R. P. T. Davenport Hines and Geoffrey Jones, eds., *British Businesses in Asia since 1860* (Cambridge: Cambridge University Press, 1889), 144–45.

27. For discussions relating to the end of Britain's dominance in Thailand's teak industry, see National Archives (PRO), FO 371/101185 and FO 371/106912.

28. Roger Louis, *Ends of British Imperialism: The Scramble for Empire, Suez, and Decolonization* (London: Tauris, 2007); Paul Kingston, *Britain and the Politics of Modernization in the Middle East, 1945–1958* (Cambridge: Cambridge University Press, 1996); Wesley K. Wark, "Development Diplomacy: Sir John Troutbeck and the British Middle East Office, 1947–50," in John Zarnetica, ed., *British Officials and British Foreign Policy, 1945–50* (Leicester: Leicester University Press, 1990).

29. Salisbury used the phrase "A modicum of independence" to describe the essential control of a region with a facade of self-governance. See Lady Gwendolen Cecil, *Life of Robert Marquis of Salisbury*, vol. 2, *1868–1880* (London: Hodder and Stoughton, 1921), 239. Sir John Shuckburgh used a similar phrase when immediately after World War I he described the protectorates of the Middle East as an unnecessary "pantomime." See Peter Sluglett, *Britain in Iraq, 1914–1932* (London: Ithaca Press, 1976), 31.

30. F. S. Northedge, "Britain and the Middle East," in Ritchie Ovendale, ed., *The Foreign Policy of the British Labour Governments, 1945–51* (Leicester: Leicester University Press, 1984), 11.

31. For example, Ibrahim Kaibni, director of the Jerusalem Office of the Transjordan, resisted the appointment of an agricultural assistant "if he had to relinquish some of his authority." J. C. Eyre, to Sir John S. Bennett, April 2, 1954, National Archives (PRO) FO 371/1052/14.

32. Quoted in Louis, *Ends of British Imperialism*, 733. For a discussion of nationalism and British policy, see Elie Kedourie, "Pan Arabism and British Policy," in *The Chatham House Version and Other Middle Eastern Studies* (Waltham: Brandeis University Press, 1970), 213–35. Albert Hourani provides a good analysis of nationalism in this period in his *History of the Arab Peoples* (Cambridge: Cambridge University Press, 1991). See also Rashid Khalidi, "Arab Nationalism: Historical Problems in the Literature," *American Historical Review* 96, no. 5 (1991): 1363–73.

33. Eden read a number of forestry reports by Mooney. See Herbert F. Mooney, "Some Notes on Forestry in Jordan," June 30, 1954, BMEO, confidential memo no. 27 12943/1/2, from BMEO/Political Division to Anthony Eden, foreign secretary.

34. Louis, *Ends of Imperialism*, 754.

35. James Onley, *The Arabian Frontier of the British Raj: Merchants, Rulers, and the British in the Nineteenth-Century Gulf* (Oxford: Oxford University Press. 2007), vii, 2–5, 104–33, 153–54.

36. James Bamberg, *The History of the British Petroleum Company*, Vol. 2, *The Anglo-Iranian Years, 1928–1954* (Cambridge: Cambridge University Press, 1994), 142–73; "Historical Overview," for R. N. Schofield and P. L. Toye, eds., *Oil Concessions in Five Arab States,*

1911–1953: Kuwait, Bahrain, Qatar, Trucial States, and Oman (Cambridge: Cambridge University Press, 1989), http://www.archiveeditions.co.uk/titledetails.asp?tid=71, accessed September 28, 2011.

37. Stephen Dorril, *MI6: Inside the Covert World of Her Majesty's Secret Intelligence Service* (London: Free Press, 2000), 595–96.

38. This agrees with James Onley's assertion that strategy, not economics, compelled Britain into diplomatic relations with the Persian Gulf sheikhdoms up to 1971. See James Onley, *The Arabian Frontier of the British Raj*, 35; and Michael A. Palmer, *Guardians of the Gulf: A History of America's Expanding Role in the Persian Gulf, 1883–1992* (New York: Simon and Shuster, 1999), chap. 4, 5.

39. Marc J. O'Reilly, *Unexceptional: America's Empire in the Persian Gulf, 1941–2007* (New York: Lexington Books, 2008), 180.

ANDERSON AND POLS / SCIENTIFIC PATRIOTISM

This essay benefited from comments and criticisms from Prasenjit Duara, Carol Hau, Alfred W. McCoy, Vicente Rafael, and Glenda Sluga. Unless otherwise stated, Warwick Anderson is responsible for translations from Spanish and Hans Pols for translations from Dutch. A longer version of this essay appeared under the same title in *Comparative Studies in Society and History* 54, no. 1 (2012): 93–113.

1. Edward A. Shils, "The Intellectual in the Political Development of New States," *World Politics* 12 (1960): 329–68; Harry J. Benda, "Non-Western Intelligentsias as Political Elites," in J. H. Kautsky, ed., *Political Change in Under-developed Countries: Nationalism and Communism* (New York: Wiley, 1963), 235–52; J. D. Legge, *Intellectuals and Nationalism in Indonesia: A Study of the Following Recruited by Sutan Sjahrir in Occupied Jakarta* (Jakarta: Equinox Publishing, 2010 [1988]).

2. Ernest Gellner, *Nationalism* (London: Phoenix, 1998), 74.

3. Benedict Anderson, *Imagined Communities: Reflections on the Origins and Spread of Nationalism*, rev. ed. (London: Verso, 1991), 118, 119 (original emphasis), 126. See also Benedict Anderson, *Under Three Flags: Anarchism and the Anti-colonial Imagination* (London: Verso, 2005).

4. Gellner, *Nationalism*, 74.

5. Pheng Cheah, *Spectral Nationality: Passages of Freedom from Kant to Postcolonial Literatures of Liberation* (New York: Columbia University Press, 2003), 6, 2.

6. Gyan Prakash, *Another Reason: Science and the Imagination of Modern India* (Princeton: Princeton University Press, 1999), 3, 6.

7. Anderson explains how science in the Philippines also "functioned as both index and generator of civic responsibility." Warwick Anderson, "Science in the Philippines," *Philippine Studies* 55 (2007): 309.

8. This challenges sociological claims that professions withdraw from the public sphere. Max Weber, *Economy and Society: An Outline of Interpretive Sociology*, ed. Guenther Roth and Claus Wittich, trans. Ephraim Fischoff et al. (New York: Bedminster Press, 1968).

9. For a justification of sociological comparison, see Warwick Anderson, "Racial Hygiene and the Making of Citizens in the Philippines and Australia," in Ann Laura Stoler, ed., *Haunted by Empire: Geographies of Intimacy in North American History* (Durham: Duke University Press, 2006), 94–115.

10. José Rizal, *Noli Me Tangere*, trans. Jovita Ventura Cruz (1886; repr., Manila: Nalandangan, 1990), 318.

11. Ibid.

12. John N. Schumacher, "Rizal and Blumentritt," *Philippine Studies* 2 (1954): 85–101.

13. Rudolf Virchow, quoted in Henry E. Sigerist, *Medicine and Human Welfare* (New Haven: Yale University Press, 1941), 93.

14. On Rizal's "pathological vision," see Raquel A. G. Reyes, *Love, Passion, and Patriotism: Sexuality and the Philippine Propaganda Movement, 1882–1892* (Seattle: University of Washington Press, 2008), chap. 5.

15. José Rizal, *Noli Me Tangere*, trans. Ma. Soledad Lacsin-Locsin (Honolulu: University of Hawaii Press, 1997), 325.

16. Rudolf Virchow, "Don José Rizal," *Verhandlungen der Berliner Gesellschaft für Anthropologie, Ethnologie und Urgeschichte* (1897).

17. Ponce figures in Anderson, *Under Three Flags*.

18. John N. Schumacher, *The Propaganda Movement, 1880–1895* (Manila: Solidaridad, 1973); "Philippine Higher Education and the Origins of Nationalism," *Philippine Studies* 23 (1975): 53–65; *The Making of a Nation: Essays on Nineteenth Century Filipino Nationalism* (Manila: Ateneo de Manila University Press, 1991).

19. Michael Adas, *Machines as the Measure of Men: Science, Technology, and Ideologies of Western Dominance* (Ithaca: Cornell University Press, 1989); "Contested Hegemony: The Great War and the Afro-Asian Assault on the Civilizing Mission Ideology," in Prasenjit Duara, ed., *Decolonization: Perspectives from Now and Then* (London: Routledge, 2004), 78–100.

20. Warwick Anderson, *Colonial Pathologies: American Tropical Medicine, Race, and Hygiene in the Philippines* (Durham: Duke University Press, 2006).

21. T. H. Pardo de Tavera, "Filipino Views of American Rule," *North American Review* 174 (January 1902): 74.

22. T. H. Pardo de Tavera, *El Legado del ignorantismo* (Manila: Bureau of Printing, 1921), 33, 36, 4, 41.

23. T. H. Pardo de Tavera, "The Conservation of the National Type," 11th Annual Commencement Address, University of the Philippines, April 4, 1921, 19–20, 13, 21, Pardo de Tavera Collection, B2 E16, Rizal Library, Ateneo de Manila University.

24. Juan Fuentes, "The First Filipino PGH Director," in Enrique T. Ona, ed., *The Hospital: The First 75 Years of the University of the Philippines–Philippine General Hospital Medical Center (1910–1985)* (Manila, 1986), xxiv–xxvi; Warwick Anderson, "Modern Sentinel and Colonial Microcosm: Science, Discipline, and Distress at the Philippine General Hospital," *Philippine Studies* 57 (2009): 3–48.

25. Fernando Calderón, 1908, quoted in John E. Snodgrass, *Source History and Description of the Philippine General Hospital (1900–1911)* (Manila: Bureau of Printing, 1912), 25.

26. Anderson, *Colonial Pathologies*, chap. 7.

27. Agerico B. M. Sison, "Educating Our Educators," *Bulletin of the San Juan de Dios Hospital* 1 (1927): 123, 124.

28. Jacobo Fajardo, "Commencement Address," *Bulletin of the San Juan de Dios Hospital* 5 (1931): 174, 175.

29. Camilo Osias, "Utilizing Science for Human Needs," in Zoilo M. Galang, ed., *Encyclopedia of the Philippines: The Library of Philippine Literature, Art, and Science* (Manila: P. Vera and Sons, 1936), 7:624–25, 625–26.

30. Leopoldo B. Uichanco, "The Philippines in the World of Science," in Galang, *Encyclopedia of the Philippines*, 7:190.

31. Angel S. Arguelles, "Progress of Research in the Philippines," in Galang, *Encyclopedia of the Philippines*, 7:29, 28.

32. Article XIII, section 4.

33. Pramoedya Ananta Toer, *Footsteps*, trans. Max Lane (New York: Penguin, 1990), 15–16.

34. Pramoedya Ananta Toer, *This Earth of Mankind*, trans. Max Lane (New York: Penguin, 1996), 16, 16, 19.

35. Sizaru Veralina, "Mijn Nood" [My distress], in Dj. Siregar, Soeharso, and C. Schreuder, eds., *NIAS Almanak: Lustrumnummer 1933–1934* (Surabaya: Nederlandsch-Indische Artsen School, 1934), 208.

36. Abdoel Moeis, *Never the Twain*, Modern Library of Indonesia (Jakarta: Lontar, 2010). The translator opted for the title *Never the Twain* because it would resonate with English readers. The literal translation of the original title is "Wrong Upbringing."

37. Keith Foulcher called Moeis a Minke-like character in "Biography, History, and the Indonesian Novel: Reading *Salah Asuhan*," *Bijdragen tot de Taal-, Land- en Volkenkunde* 161, nos. 2–3 (2005): 247–68.

38. A. de Waart, ed., *Ontwikkeling van het Geneeskundig Onderwijs te Weltevreden, 1851–1926 (Uitgave ter Herdenking van het 75-Jarig Bestaan van de School tot Opleiding van Indische Artsen [STOVIA])* [The development of medical education in Weltevreden] (Weltevreden: Kolff, 1926); M. A. Hanafia SM, Bahder Djohan, and Surono, *125 Tahun Pendidikan Dokter di Indonesia, 1851–1976* [125 years of medical education in Indonesia] (Jakarta: Fakultas Kedokteran Universitas Indonesia, 1976); Ahmad Sujudi, H. Ali Sulaiman, and H. Sofyan Ismael, eds., *150 Tahun Pendidikan Dokter di Indonesia: Menuju Persaingan Global* [150 years of medical education in Indonesia: Towards global competition] (Jakarta: Ikatan Alumni Universitas Indonesia—Fakultas Kedokteran Universitas Indonesia, 2002).

39. Widohariadi and Bambang Permono, *Peringatan 70 Tahun Pendidikan Dokter di Surabaya, 15 Sept. 1983* [Commemorating 70 years of medical education in Surabaya] (Surabaya: Gideon, 1983); Widohariadi and Bambang Permono, *Peringatan 90 Tahun Pendidikan Dokter di Surabaya* [Commemorating 90 years of medical education in Surabaya] (Surabaya: Fakultas Kedoktoran Universitas Airlingga, 2003).

40. Pramoedya Ananta Toer, *De Pionier: Biografie van Tirto Adhisoerjo* [The pioneer: Biography of Tirto Adhisoerjo] (Amsterdam: Manus Amici–Novib, 1988).

41. [O. Deggeler and J. J. van Lonkhuyzen], "Het Indisch Ontwerp, 1913" [The Indies proposal, 1913], *Bond van Geneesheeren in N.-I.*, nos. 52–53 (1912): 25–29.

42. E. F. E. Douwes Dekker, "De Indische Partij: Rapport der Propaganda-Deputatie" [The Indies Party: Report by the propaganda delegation], *Het Tijdschrift* 2, no. 4 (1912): 97–146, esp. 100, 114–21, 133–36.

43. Harry A. Poeze, *In het Land van de Overheerser*, Vol. 1: *Indonesiërs in Nederland, 1600–1950* [In the land of the ruler, vol. 1: Indonesians in the Netherlands, 1600–1950] (Dordrecht: Foris, 1986).

44. Susan Abeyasekere, *One Hand Clapping: Indonesian Nationalists and the Dutch, 1939–1942* (Melbourne: Centre of Southeast Asian Studies, Monash University, 1976).

45. Abdul Rasyid, "Beschouwingen over de Positie van den Ind.-Arts" [Reflections on the position of the Indonesian physician], in *Het Eerste Congres van de Vereeniging van Indonesische Geneeskundigen Gehouden op 24, 25, en 26 December 1938 te Semarang* [First congress of the Association of Indonesian Physicians, Semarang] (Batavia: Kenanga, 1938); Abdul Rasjid, quoted in *Medisch Tribune* 27 (March 1939): 10.

46. Hans Pols, "The Nature of the Native Mind: Contested Views of Dutch Colonial Psychiatrists in the Former Dutch East Indies," in Sloan Mahone and Megan Vaughan, eds., *Psychiatry and Empire* (London: Palgrave Macmillan, 2007), 172–96.

47. "De Bond van Geneesheeren in Ned. Ind." [The association of physicians in the Dutch Indies] *Medisch Tribune* 27 (March 1939): 4.

48. "Verslag over het 1e Congres van de Vereeniging van Indonesische Geneeskundigen, 1938" [Report on the first congress of the Association of Indonesian Physicians], *Medisch Tribune* 27(March 1939): 16.

49. Gunseikanbu, *Orang Yang Terkemuka Di Jawa* [Leading men on Java] (1944; repr. Yogyakarta: Gadjah Mada University Press, 1986).

50. Benedict Anderson, *Java in a Time of Revolution: Occupation and Resistance, 1944–1946* (Ithaca: Cornell University Press, 1972); O. E. Engelen, Aboe Bakar Loebis, Abdullah Ciptoprawiro, Soejono Joedodibroto, Oetarjo, and Idris Siregar, *Lahirnya Satu Bangsa dan Negara* [The birth of a nation and a state] (Jakarta: Penerbit Universitas Indonesia, 1997).

51. Ming-Cheng M. Lo, *Doctors within Borders: Profession, Ethnicity, and Modernity in Colonial Taiwan* (Berkeley: University of California Press, 2002), 5, 6, 7.

52. Ming-Cheng M. Lo, "Between Ethnicity and Modernity: Taiwanese Medical Students and Doctors under Japan's Kominka Campaign, 1937–1945," *positions: east asia cultures critique* 10, no. 2 (2002): 299.

53. Prasenjit Duara, *Sovereignty and Authenticity: Manchukuo and the East Asian Modern* (Oxford: Rowman and Littlefield, 2003), 19.

54. Vincanne Adams discusses "science fetishism" in *Doctors for Democracy: Health Professionals in the Nepal Revolution* (Cambridge: Cambridge University Press, 1998).

55. Warwick Anderson and Vincanne Adams, "Pramoedya's Chickens: Postcolonial Studies of Technoscience," in Edward J. Hackett, Olga Amsterdamska, Michael Lynch, and Judy Wajcman, eds., *The Handbook of Science and Technology Studies*, 3rd ed. (Cambridge: MIT Press, 2007), 181–204; Warwick Anderson, "From Subjugated Knowledge to Conjugated Subjects: Science and Globalisation or Postcolonial Studies of Science?," *Postcolonial Studies* 12 (2009): 389–400.

RABEN / DECOLONIZATION AND THE ROOTS OF DEMOCRACY

1. The most famous analysis is of course Samuel P. Huntington, *The Third Wave: Democratization in the Late Twentieth Century* (Norman: University of Oklahoma Press, 1991), 18–19. For a criticism, see Renske Doorenspleet, "Reassessing the Three Waves of Democratization," *World Politics* 52, no. 3 (2000): 384–406.

2. See Els Bogaerts and Remco Raben, eds., *Beyond Empire and Nation: The Decolonization of African and Asian Societies, 1930s–1960s* (Leiden: KITLV Press, 2012).

3. *Verslag van de commissie tot bestudeering van staatsrechtelijke hervormingen* (Batavia: Landsdrukkerij, 1941), 1:95–98.

4. Arsip Nasional Republik Indonesia, Jakarta (hereafter ANRI), Arsip Binnenlands Bestuur, inv.nr. 1653, Concept-afdelingsverslag commissie van rapporteurs van de Volksraad, zittingsjaar 1930–1931, Wijziging samenstelling van enige stadsgemeenteraden.

5. Susan Abeyasekere, *One Hand Clapping: Indonesian Nationalists and the Dutch, 1939–1942* (Clayton: Centre of Southeast Asian Studies, Monash University, 1976).

6. John Ingleson, "Worker Consciousness and Labour Unions in Colonial Java," *Pacific Affairs* 54, no. 3 (Autumn 1981): 485–501, esp. 493.

7. ANRI, Arsip Binnenlands Bestuur, inv.nr. 1687, Opheffing desa autonomie binnen gemeente Soerabaya, 1928.

8. They could be found in Yogyakarta, Palembang, and elsewhere. See Harry A. Poeze, ed., *Politiek-politioneele overzichten van Nederlandsch-Indië*, vol. 1, *1927–1928* (The Hague: Martinus Nijhoff, 1982), 225, 279, 306.

9. Kenji Tsuchiya, *Democracy and Leadership: The Rise of the Taman Siswa Movement in Indonesia* (Honolulu: University of Hawaii Press, 1987), 140–41.

10. R. E. Elson, *The Idea of Indonesia: A History* (Cambridge: Cambridge University Press, 2008), 51.

11. Very little attention has been given to Sun's influence on Sukarno's thinking. See Bernhard Dahm, *Sukarno and the Struggle for Indonesian Independence* (Ithaca: Cornell University Press, 1969), 34.

12. Chusnul Mar'iyah, "Soekarno dan demokrasi," in Nazaruddin Sjamsuddin, ed., *Soekarno; Pemikiran politik dan kenyataan praktek* (Jakarta: Rajawali Pers, 1988), 173–208, esp. 177; Dahm, *Sukarno and the Struggle for Indonesian Independence*, 200–203.

432   Notes to pages 281–286

13. Soekarno, *Lahirnja Pantja Sila*, in Herbert Feith and Lance Castles, eds., *Indonesian Political Thinking, 1945–1965* (Ithaca: Cornell University Press, 1970), 40–49, esp. 44–47.

14. Adnan Butung Nasution, *The Aspiration for Constitutional Government in Indonesia: A Socio-legal Study of the Indonesian Konstituante 1956–1959* (Jakarta: Pustaka Sinar Harapan, 1992), 96.

15. Minister of Overseas Territories Logemann to members of the Council of Ministers, October 11, 1945, in S. L. van der Wal, P. J. Drooglever and M. J. B. Schouten, eds., *Officiële bescheiden betreffende de Nederlands-Indonesische betrekkingen, 1945–1950*, 20 vols. (The Hague: Martinus Nijhoff and Instituut voor Nederlandse Geschiedenis, 1971–96) (hereafter *NIB*), 1:324.

16. S. I. van Creveld a.o. in Bandung to W. Drees, October 2, 1945, in *NIB*, 1:226.

17. Minister J. H. A. Logemann to members of the Council of Ministers, October 11, 1945, in *NIB*, 1:324.

18. Report by the the representative at the Allied Supreme Command in South-East Asia, C. O. van der Plas about his conversations with Mountbatten, no date, in *NIB*, 1:229–30.

19. Minister Logemann to Gov. Gen. A. W. L. Tjarda van Starkenborgh Stachouwer, October 9, 1945, in *NIB*, 1:282–83.

20. Lt. Gov. Gen. H. J. van Mook to Logemann, October 29, 1945, in *NIB*, 1:473–74.

21. Memorandum of Minister Logemann, December 16, 1945, in *NIB*, 2:367.

22. Ch. Welter (member of the Upper Chamber of parliament) to Minister Logemann, December 24, 1945, in *NIB*, 2:438–39.

23. J. W. Meijer Ranneft to Prime Minister W. Schermerhorn, December 22, 1945, in *NIB*, 2:416.

24. Memorandum of Minister Logemann to the Council Of Ministers, December 24, 1945, in *NIB*, 2:423.

25. Survey of Borneo and East-Indonesia (with exception of Bali and Lombok), September 10, 1947, in *NIB*, 11:73.

26. C. O. van der Plas (Commissioner Eastern Java) to Lt. Gov. Gen. van Mook, April 22, 1948, in *NIB*, 13:503–8.

27. Benedict R. O'G. Anderson, *Java in a Time of Revolution; Occupation and Resistance, 1944–1946* (Ithaca: Cornell University Press, 1972), 91.

28. President Sukarno to Philip Christison, October 9, 1945, in *NIB*, 1:289.

29. Feith and Castles, *Indonesian Political Thinking*, 53, 55.

30. George McTurnan Kahin, *Nationalism and Revolution in Indonesia*, 2nd ed. (Ithaca: Cornell University Press, 1970), 168; see also *NIB*, 2:113.

31. Sutan Sjahrir, *Perdjoeangan kita* (Djakarta: Pertj. Repoeblik Indonesia 1945). See also Kahin, *Nationalism and Revolution in Indonesia*, 165.

32. *Warta Indonesia*, October 8, 1945; *Berita Repoeblik Indonesia*, November 17, 1945.

33. *Berita Repoeblik Indonesia*, January 1, 1946.

34. National Archives, The Hague, Archive NEFIS/CMI, inv.nr. 3123, Resolution meeting Masjoemi, February 20, 1946.

35. Kahin, *Nationalism and Revolution in Indonesia*, 140; Deliar Noer and Akbarsyah, *KNIP: Komite Nasional Indonesia Pusat. Parlemen Indonesia, 1945–1950* (Jakarta: Yayasan Risalah, 2005).

36. H. W. Dick, *Surabaya, City of Work* (Athens: Ohio University Press, 2002), 79.

37. *Tjahaja*, September 4, 1945; *Toedjoean-rakjat*, October 26, 1945.

38. *Soeloeh merdeka*, December 11, 1945.

39. For changes in village administration under Japanese rule, see Aiko Kurasawa, "Japanese Occupation and Leadership Changes," in J. van Goor, ed., *The Indonesian Revolution*. Utrechtse historische cahiers 7, nos. 2–3 (Utrecht: Rijksuniversiteit Utrecht, 1986), 57–78.

40. Kurasawa, "Japanese Occupation and Leadership Changes in Javanese Villages," 65.

41. *Soeloeh merdeka*, December 24, 1945; Political Report on Sumatra, August–September 1946, in *NIB*, 5:468.

42. *Berita Repoeblik Indonesia*, December 15, 1945. See also Suhartono, *Parlemen desa: Dinamika DPR Kalurahan dan DPRK-Gotong Royong* (Yogyakarta: Laperan Pustaka Utama, 2000), 60–61.

43. See Dick, *Surabaya*, 99–100.

44. Clifford Geertz, *The Social History of an Indonesian Town* (Cambridge: MIT Press, 1965). See also Remco Raben a.o., "Nation, Region, and the Ambiguities of Modernity in the 1950s," in Henk Schulte Nordholt and Ireen Hoogenboom, eds., *Indonesian Transitions* (Yogyakarta: Pustaka Pelajar, 2006), 115–62.

45. Feith and Castles, *Indonesian Political Thinking*, 81–83.

46. This is also suggested for other areas in Southeast Asia. See Jose Veloso Abueva, "Filipino Democracy and the American Legacy," *Annals of the American Academy of Political and Social Science* 428 (November 1976): 114–33, esp. 114.

47. H. J. van Mook, *The Stakes of Democracy in South-East Asia* (London: George Allen and Unwin, 1950), 113.

DA SILVA / NATIVES WHO WERE "CITIZENS" AND NATIVES WHO WERE *INDÍGENAS* IN THE PORTUGUESE EMPIRE

1. Fernando Catroga, "In the Name of the Nation," in Fernando Catroga and Pedro Tavares de Almeida, eds., *Res Publica: Citizenship and Political Representation in Portugal, 1820–1926* (Lisbon: Biblioteca Nacional de Portugal, Assembleia da República, 2011).

2. On the subject, see Quentin Skinner's classic work *Liberty before Liberalism* (Cambridge: Cambridge University Press, 1998).

3. On the *indigenato* system, see Jane Burbank and Frederick Cooper, "Empire, droits et citoyenneté, de 212 à 1946," *Annales Histoire, Sciences Sociales* 63, no. 3 (May–June 2008): 514–56; and Josep M. Fradera, "Esclavage et la logique constitutionnelle des empires," *Annales Histoire, Sciences Sociales* 63, no. 3 (May–June 2008): 536, 559–60. On this system in the French empire, see Emmanuelle Saada, *Les enfants de la colonie: Les métis de l'Empire français entre sujétion et citoyenneté* (Paris: La Découverte, 2007), 109–35.

4. On the idea of gradual extension of the "rule of law" as a means of concealing the repressive aspect of the *indigenato* system, see Gregory Mann, "What Was the 'Indigénat'? The 'Empire of Law' in French West Africa," *Journal of African History* 50, no. 3 (2009): 331–53, esp. 336.

5. I use the term *identification* (or *self-understanding*) in the sense used in Rogers Brubaker and Frederick Cooper, "Beyond 'Identity,'" *Theory and Society* 29 (2000): 1–47, and Frederick Cooper, *Colonialism in Question: Theory, Knowledge, History* (Berkeley: University of California Press, 2005), 71–77.

6. Ruy Ulrich, *Política colonial: Lições feitas ao Curso do 4o ano jurídico no anno de 1908–1909* (Coimbra: Imprensa da Universidade, 1909), 60.

7. Article 6 of the General Act of the Conference of Berlin, http://africanhistory.about.com/od/eracolonialism/l/bl-BerlinAct1885.htm.

8. José Ferreira Marnoco e Sousa, *Administração Colonial, Prelecções feitas ao curso do 4o ano jurídico* (Coimbra: França Amado, 1906), 115.

9. On John Stuart Mill and colonialism, see Uday Singh Metha, *Liberalism and Empire: A Study in Nineteenth-Century British Liberal Thought* (Chicago: University of Chicago Press, 1999); and Jennifer Pitts, *A Turn to Empire: The Rise of Imperial Liberalism in Britain and France* (Princeton: Princeton University Press, 2005).

10. Lopo Vaz de Sampayo e Mello, *Política indígena* (Porto: Magalhães e Moniz Editores, 1910), 205–6.

11. Marnoco e Sousa, *Administração colonial*, 116–17.

12. José Ferreira Marnoco e Sousa, *Direito Político, Poderes do Estado, sua organização segundo a ciência política e o direito constitucional português* (Coimbra: França Amado, 1910), 52–53.

13. Valentim Alexandre, "Administração colonial," in António Barreto and Maria Filomena Mónica, eds., *Dicionário de História de Portugal*, (Lisbon: Figueirinhas, 1999), 7:45–46.

14. Jill Dias, "A Sociedade colonial de Angola e o liberalismo português," in Miriam Halpern Pereira, ed., *O Liberalismo na Península Ibérica na primeira metade o século XIX*, vol. 2 (Lisbon: 1981); "Angola," in Joel Serrão and A-H. de Oliveira Marques, eds., *Nova História da Expansão Portuguesa* (Lisbon: Estampa, 1998), 10:508–42.

15. Cristina Nogueira da Silva, "Liberdade e tolerância religiosa: 'Portugueses não católicos' no Ultramar do século XIX," in *Historia Constitucional, Revista Electrónica de Historia Constitucional* (E-journal of Constitutional History), no. 8 (2007), http://hc.rediris.es/08/articulos/pdf/04.pdf. See also Cristina Nogueira da Silva, "Political Representation and Citizenship under the Empire," in Fernando Catroga and Pedro Tavares de Almeida, eds., *Res Publica: Citizenship and Political Representation in Portugal, 1820–1926* (Lisbon: Biblioteca Nacional de Portugal, Assembleia Da Republica, 2011), 90–111.

16. On the situation of these elites in the various Portuguese colonies in Africa, see Gervase Clarence-Smith, *O terceiro Império Português (1825–1975)* (Lisbon: Teorema, 1985), 30–56, originally published as *The Third Portuguese Empire* (Manchester: Manchester University Press, 1985). For Mozambique, see Jeanne Penvenne, *Trabalhadores de Lourenço Marques (1870–1974)* (Maputo: Arquivo Histórico de Moçambique, 1993); and Jeanne Penvenne, "A History of African Labor in Lourenço Marques, Mozambique, 1877 to 1950" (PhD diss., Boston University, 1982). For Angola, besides the works by the British-born historian Jill Dias, see Douglas Wheeler and René Pélissier, *História de Angola* (Lisbon: Tinta-da-China, 2009), esp. 147–224; Jacopo Corrado, "The Rise of a New Consciousness: Early Euro-African Voices of Dissent in Colonial Angola," *E-Journal of Portuguese History* 2 (2007), http://www.scielo.oces.mctes.pt/pdf/ejph/v5n2/v5n2a03.pdf; and Jacopo Corrado, *The Creole Elite and the Rise of Angolan Protonationalism, 1870–1920* (Amherst: Cambria Press, 2008).

17. On the various types of these special forms of labor in Mozambique, see Jeanne Marie Penvenne, *African Workers and Colonial Racism: Mozambican Strategies and Struggles in Lourenço Marques, 1877–1962* (Portsmouth: Heinemann, Social History of Africa Series, 1995).

18. Clarence-Smith, *O Terceiro Império Portugués*, 112–13, 141. On the growing conflicts and their expression in the press and native associations, see Malyn Newitt, *A History of Mozambique* (Bloomington: Indiana University Press, 1995), 443–44; and Wheeler and Pélissier, *História de Angola*, 152–92. See also the texts by Augusto Nascimento (for São Tomé e Príncipe), Aida Faria Freudenthal (for Angola), and Olga Neves (for Mozambique) in A. H. de Oliveira Marques and Joel Serrão, eds., *Nova História da Expansão Portuguesa*, vol. 10 (Lisbon: Estampa, 2001).

19. Base 18 of the Organic Law ratified what had been decided in the 1900 Congrès de Sociologie Coloniale. See *Curso de Administração colonial segundo as prelecções do Dr. Rocha Saraiva ao curso jurídico de 1913–1914* (Coimbra: Livraria Neves Editora, 1914), 244–45.

20. Cristina Nogueira da Silva, "'Missão civilizacional' e codificação de 'usos e costumes' na doutrina colonial portuguesa (séculos XIX–XX)," *Quaderni Fiorentini per la Storia del Pensiero Giuridico Moderno* 33–34 (2004–5): 899–919.

21. *Diário da Câmara dos Deputados*, February 13, 1914, 9, http://debates.parlamento.pt/page.aspx?cid=r1.cd.

22. This decree had limited the granting of municipal rights to villages with over two thousand European inhabitants. See *Colecção Geral da Legislação Portuguesa, 1907* (Lisbon: Imprensa Nacional, 1908), 342.

23. Examples of this can be found in Wheeler and Pélissier, *História de Angola*, 152.

24. Arquivo Histórico de Moçambique, *Direcção dos Serviços dos Negócios Indígenas*, section M (1902–1967), case file 108.

25. Newitt, A History of Mozambique, 443.

26. After the fall of the First Republic, the indigenato system was confirmed by the dictatorship of the Estado Novo in the Estatuto Político, Civil e Criminal dos Indígenas de Angola e Moçambique (1926) and in the Estatuto Político, Civil e Criminal dos Indígenas (1929).

27. Although it corresponds to a later period, see the data collected in the 1950 census by Douglas L. Wheeler and René Pélissier. According to these authors, among the 4 million Africans who then lived in Angola, only 30,089 had achieved the status of *assimilados*. Wheeler and Pélissier, *História de Angola*, 200.

28. This information was collected within the context of the research project entitled "The Government of Difference: Political Imagination in the Portuguese Empire (1496–1961)," funded by the Portuguese Foundation for Science and Technology.

29. On similar processes in French Empire, see Gary Wilder, "Practicing Citizenship in Imperial Paris," in John Comaroff and Jean Comaroff, eds., *Civil Society and Political Imagination in Africa: Critical Perspectives* (Chicago: University of Chicago Press, 1999).

30. "Map on the Acquisition of Citizenship (1954–1960)," in Arquivo Histórico de Moçambique, *Direcção dos Serviços dos Negócios de Indígenas*, secção M, tribunais indígenas, Cx. 1628, Mç. 3 (1961). Note that this was drafted during a time when political reforms, aimed at increasing levels of citizenship within the African empire, were being enacted. We can count 1,356 cases of successful "assimilation" during this period.

31. Newitt, *A History of Mozambique*, 443–44; Penvenne, *African Workers and Colonial Racism*, 65–116; Wheeler and Pélissier, *História de Angola*, 152–92.

32. José Moreira, *Os assimilados: João Albasini e as eleições, 1900–1922* (Maputo: Arquivo Histórico de Moçambique, n.d.), 134. See also Jeanne Marie Penvenne, "João dos Santos Albasini, 1876–1922: The Contradiction of Politics and Identity in Colonial Mozambique," *Journal of African History* 37, no. 3 (1996): 419–64.

33. Ulrich, Política Colonial, 103.

34. Frederick Cooper and Ann Laura Stoler, *Tensions of Empire: Colonial Cultures in a Bourgeois World* (Berkeley: University of California Press, 1997), 12.

35. Margaret MacMillan, *Paris, 1919: Six Months That Changed the World* (New York: Random House, 2001), 98, 104.

36. Clarence G. Contee, "Du Bois, the NAACP, and the Pan-African Congress of 1919," *Journal of Negro History* 57, no. 1 (January 1972): 13–28.

CHATTERJI / FROM SUBJECTHOOD TO CITIZENSHIP IN SOUTH ASIA

Claire Davies lent invaluable help with research on the evolution of British and American migration controls after World War II.

1. For related accounts of migration, see Tirthankar Roy and Douglas Haynes, "Conceiving Mobility: Weavers' Migrations in Pre-colonial and Colonial India,'" *Indian Economic and Social History Review* 36, no. 1 (1999): 35–67; and Robert Nichols, *A History of Pashtun Migration, 1775–2006* (New York: Oxford University Press, 2008).

2. Aristide R. Zolberg, "The Formation of New States as a Refugee-Generating Process," *Annals of the American Academy of Political and Social Science*, no. 467 (May 1983): 24–38.

3. Caitlin Anderson, "Aliens at Home, Subjects Abroad: British Nationality Law and Policy, 1815–1870" (PhD thesis, University of Cambridge, 2008).

4. Clive Parry, *British Nationality, Including Citizenship of the United Kingdom and Colonies and the Status of Aliens* (London: Steven and Sons, 1951); Keechang Kim, *Aliens in Medieval Law: The Origins of Modern Citizenship* (Cambridge: Cambridge University Press, 2004).

5. Parry, *British Nationality*.

6. Anderson, "Aliens at Home, Subjects Abroad."

7. On *kanganis*, see Hugh Tinker, *A New System of Slavery: The Export of Indian Labour Overseas, 1830–1920* (London: Hansib, 1974).

8. Ibid., 61–115.

9. Radhika Mongia, "Race, Nationality, Mobility: A History of the Passport," *Public Culture* 11, no. 3 (Fall 1999): 527–57; Ministry of External Affairs, India, *Question of Treatment of Indians in the Union of South Africa before the United Nations: Documents and Proceedings* (Simla: Government of India Press, 1947) (henceforth MEAI), F. 3-1/OSI-1948.

10. Sunil Amrith, "Indians Overseas? Governing Tamil Migration to Malaya, 1870–1941," *Past and Present* 208 (August 2010): 231–61.

11. Radhika Singha, "A 'Proper Passport' for the Colony: Border Crossing in British India, 1882–1920," unpublished manuscript.

12. "Statement of Objectives and Reasons," *The Foreigners Act, 1946 (Act No. 31 of 1946) [India]: An Act to confer upon the Central Government certain powers in respect of foreigners.*

13. Statement on Partition by the Deputy Prime Minister in the Constituent Assembly, December 12, 1947, in MEAI/ F. 9-2/48-Pak I.

14. M. S. Randhawa, *Out of the Ashes; An Account of the Rehabilitation of Refugees from West Pakistan in Rural Areas of East Punjab* (Chandigarh: Public Relations Department, Punjab, 1954).

15. See the introduction to the Government of East Punjab's law titled the *East Punjab Evacuees' (Administration of Property) Act, 1947 (E.P. Act XIV of 1947)*.

16. Jawaharlal Nehru to Sardar Vallabhbhai Patel, October 6, 1947, in Durga Das, ed., *Sardar Patel's Correspondence, 1945–50* (Ahmedabad: Navajivan, 1972), 4:400.

17. Ibid.

18. Ordinance XXXIV of 1948, NAI/MEACR/ F.26–189/48-Pak I (Secret).

19. The reasons for the exclusion of West Bengal, Assam, and Tripura from the emerging evacuee property regime is a complex subject in itself that cannot, for reasons of space, be discussed here.

20. Pakistan promulgated a central Evacuee Property Ordinance in October 1949. "The Problem of Evacuee Property and Efforts Made to Solve It," enclosure in Memo from the Indian Ministry of External Affairs to India's Permanent Representative at the UN, December 31, 1949, MEAI/11(21)/49-Pak III (Secret).

21. Vazira F. Zamindar, *The Long Partition and the Making of Modern South Asia: Refugees, Boundaries, Histories* (New York: Columbia University Press, 2007).

22. Joya Chatterji, *The Disinherited: Migrants, Minorities, and Citizenship in South Asia* (Cambridge: Cambridge University Press, forthcoming).

23. Abul Barkat et al., *Political Economy of the Vested Property Act in Rural Bangladesh* (Dhaka: Association for Land Reform and Development, 1997); M. I. Farooqui, *Law of Abandoned Property* (Dhaka: Khaja Art Press, 2000); Papiya Ghosh, *Partition and the South Asian Diaspora: Extending the Subcontinent* (London: Routledge, 2007).

24. Willem van Schendel, "The Wagah Syndrome: Territorial Roots of Contemporary Violence in South Asia," in Amrita Basu and Srirupa Roy, eds., *Violence and Democracy in India* (Calcutta: Seagull Books, 2007).

25. Memo by B.F.H.B. Tyabji dated August 23, 1952, MEA (AFR II Branch)/AII/53/ 6491,31 (Secret).

26. MEA/AII/ 52/6423/31 (1952, Secret).

27. File note dated April 20, 1950, MEA/17–39/49-AFRI (Secret).

28. Technically, they were "British protected persons." After the Nationality Act of 1948, they could become citizens of the United Kingdom and its colonies by means of naturalization,

but they did not receive this citizenship automatically, as did other British Indian subjects. See Parry, *British Nationality*, 95.

29. MEA/17–39/49-AFRI (Secret); MEA/AII/ 52/6423/31 (1952, Secret).

30. India had been campaigning against the Asiatic Land Tenure Act since its promulgation in 1946 and took the matter to the United Nations.

31. Note by M. L. Mehta dated April 5, 1950, GOI/ MEAI/7/49/BCI (C) (Secret).

32. No Indian (or Pakistani) registered under the act would have rights under the Land Development Ordinance, the Fisheries Ordinance, and the Omnibus Licensing Ordinances, which were designed to promote the welfare of Ceylonese citizens. Ibid.

33. Ministry of External Affairs (CAP Branch) file note dated ?/5/1951, MEAI/7/49-BCI (C).

34. Patrick Peebles, *The Plantation Tamils of Ceylon* (London: Leicester University Press, 2001).

35. Note by M. L Mehta dated April 5, 1950, GOI/ MEAI/7/49/BCI (C) (Secret).

36. "Note on Land Nationalisation in Burma," GOI/ MEAI/F. 9-8/48-o.s.II/1948.

37. Indian Ministry of Home Affairs (MHAI)/33/32/49-FII (1949).

38. The act created five different categories of citizens. In addition to CUKC and CICC, these included "Irish British subjects," "British subjects without citizenship," and "British protected persons." The latter category included former subjects of the Indian Princely States.

39. Randall Hansen, *Citizenship and Immigration in Postwar Britain: The Institutional Origins of a Multicultural Nation* (Oxford: Oxford University Press, 1999), 46–47.

40. Ibid., 57.

41. Pakistan agreed, in addition, to give publicity to the difficulties encountered by Pakistanis in finding work in Britain. Cabinet Memorandum, Commonwealth Immigrants, memorandum by the Lord President of the Council, June, 20, 1958, PRO/CAB/129/93.

42. Judith Brown, *Global South Asians: Introducing the Modern Diaspora* (Cambridge: Cambridge University Press, 2004), 42.

43. Roger Kershaw and Mark Pearsall, *Immigrants and Aliens: A Guide to Sources on UK Immigration and Citizenship* (Kew: Public Record Office, 2004).

44. Christian Joppke, "Multiculturalism and Immigration: A Comparison of the United States, Germany, and Great Britain," in David Jacobson, ed., *The Immigration Reader: America in Multidisciplinary Perspective* (Oxford: Blackwell, 1998).

45. Refugees and asylum seekers are the third category of migrants who still have access under these systems, but for reasons of space, they cannot be discussed here.

46. See, e.g., Sandhya Shukla, *India Abroad* (Princeton: Princeton University Press, 2003), 49.

47. Roger Ballard, "The Political Economy of Migration: Pakistan, Britain, and the Middle East," in Jeremy Eades, ed., *Migrants, Workers, and the Social Order* (London: Tavistock, 1987).

48. Nicholls, *Pashtun Migration*.

49. Robert Gooding-Williams, "On Being Stuck," in Robert Gooding-Williams, ed., *Reading Rodney King, Reading Urban Uprising* (New York: Routledge, 1993).

50. Joppke, "Multiculturalism and Immigration," 292–99.

51. William Bernard, "Immigration: History of U.S. Policy," in David Jacobson, ed., *The Immigration Reader: America in Multidisciplinary Perspective* (Oxford: Blackwell, 1998).

BANKOFF / THE "THREE R's" AND THE MAKING OF A NEW WORLD ORDER

1. Robert Pollard, *Economic Security and the Origins of the Cold War, 1945–1950* (New York: Columbia University Press, 1985), 20–23.

2. Quincy Wright, "War Claims: What of the Future?" *Law and Contemporary Problems* 16, no. 3 (1951): 543–45.

3. Joseph Stetler, "To What Extent Should Congress Appropriate to Distribute the Burden of War Loss, Given the Insufficiency of War Reparation," *Law and Contemporary Problems* 16, no. 3 (1951): 476–77.

4. Staving Desk, Jan T. Gross, and Tony Judd, eds. *The Politics of Retribution in Europe: World War II and Its Aftermath* (Princeton: Princeton University Press, 2000).

5. John Isenberg, "A World Economy Restored: Expert Consensus and the Anglo-American Postwar Settlement," *International Organization* 46, no. 1 (1992): 289–321.

6. Walter Sterling Surrey, "Problems of the Italian Peace Treaty: Analysis of Claims Provisions and Description of Enforcement, "*Law and Contemporary Problems* 16, no. 3 (1951): 436–38.

7. Stetler, "To What Extent Should Congress Appropriate to Distribute the Burden of War Loss," 480–81.

8. Samuel Herman, "War Damage and Nationalization in Eastern Europe," *Law and Contemporary Problems* 16, no. 3 (1951): 499.

9. Mario Einaudi, "Nationalization in France and Italy," *Social Research* 15, nos. 1–4 (1948): 22–43.

10. Herman, "War Damage and Nationalization in Eastern Europe," 501.

11. Seymour Rubin, "Nationalization and Compensation: A Comparative Approach," *University of Chicago Law Review* 17, no. 3 (1950): 460–61.

12. Nicholas Doman, "Compensation for Nationalised Property in Post-war Europe," *International Law Quarterly* 3, no. 3 (1950): 332–41.

13. Einaudi, "Nationalization in France and Italy," 25–27.

14. Andrew Williams, "'Reconstruction' before the Marshall Plan," *Review of International Studies* 31, no. 3 (2005): 548–51.

15. Scott Jackson, "Prologue to the Marshall Plan: The Origins of the American Commitment for a European Recovery Program," *Journal of American History* 65, no. 4 (1979): 1046–54.

16. National Archives, Minutes of the Committee on the Extension of U.S. Aid to Foreign Governments, M-1, March 18, 1947, Box 17, Department of State, Lot 122, quoted in Jackson, "Prologue to the Marshall Plan," 1052.

17. Diane Kunz, "The Marshall Plan Reconsidered: A Complex of Motives," *Foreign Affairs* 76, no. 3 (1997): 167–69.

18. Adolf Berle, "The Marshall Plan in the European Struggle," *Social Research* 15, nos. 1–4 (1948): 6.

19. Sidney Fay, "The Marshall Plan," *Current History* 88, no. 534 (1989): 30–31, 51 (originally published in 1947).

20. Berle, The Marshall Plan in the European Struggle, 1.

21. Fay, "The Marshall Plan."

22. Konstantina Botsiou, "New Policies, Old Politics: American Concepts of Reform in Marshall Plan Greece," *Journal of Modern Greek Studies* 27, no. 2 (2009), 209–40.

23. *Final Report on Public Property Rehabilitation in the Philippines Pursuant to the Philippine Rehabilitation Act of 1946* (Manila: Philippine War Damage Commission, 1950), 2.

24. Ernest Schein, "War Damage Compensation through Rehabilitation: The Philippine War Damage Commission," *Law and Contemporary Problems* 16, no. 3 (1951): 523.

25. *Final Report on Public Property Rehabilitation in the Philippines*, 5.

26. U.S. House of Representatives, 81st Congress, 1st and 2d Sessions, *Hearings before the Committee on Foreign Affairs, S.1033 and H.R.7600 Bills to Further Amend the Philippine Rehabilitation Act of 1946* (Washington, D.C.: Government Printing Office, 1950), 68.

27. Mamerto Ventura, *United States–Philippine Cooperation and Cross-Purposes: Philippine Post-war Recovery and Reform* (Quezon City: Filipiniana Publications, 1974), 92–99.

28. Bernard Seeman and Laurence Salisbury, *Cross-Currents in the Philippines* (New York: American Council Institute of Pacific Relations, 1946), 58.

29. *Hearings before the Committee on Foreign Affairs*, 107, 123, 129, 139.

30. National Diet Library, Japan, Summary of United States Initial Post-defeat Policy relating to Japan (Informal and without Commitment by the Department of State), April 12, 1945, Records of State-War-Navy Coordinating Committee, Records of the Subcommittee for the Far East, 384.1 Surrender Term, Japan 1945.4.18–1945.8.30, SFE-1 Roll No. 2, http://www.ndl.go.jp/constitution/e/shiryo/01/007/007_001r.html.

31. Michael Schaller, *The American Occupation of Japan: The Origins of the Cold War in Asia* (New York: Oxford University Press, 1985), 35.

32. Ray Jennings Ray, *The Road Ahead: Lessons in Nation Building from Japan, Germany, and Afghanistan for Postwar Iraq* (Washington, D.C.: United States Institute for Peace, 2003), 18.

33. Schaller, *The American Occupation of Japan*, 37–38.

34. Stetler, "To What Extent Should Congress Appropriate to Distribute the Burden of War Loss," 477–78.

35. John Foster Dulles, "Security in the Pacific," *Foreign Affairs* 30, no. 2 (1952): 175; Stanley Metzger, "The Liberal Japanese Peace Treaty," *Cornell Law Quarterly* 37 (1952): 383.

36. Dulles, "Security in the Pacific," 175.

37. Ibid., 184.

38. Peter Leitner, "Japan's Post-war Economic Success: Deming, Quality, and Contextual Realities," *Journal of Management History* 5, no. 8 (1999): 493; Suehiro Akira, "The Road to Economic Re-entry: Japan's Policy towards Southeast Asian Development in the 1950s and 1960s," *Social Science Japan Journal* 2, no. 1 (1999): 90.

39. Akira, "The Road to Economic Re-Entry," 88.

40. Louis Picard and Terry Buss, *A Fragile Balance: Re-examining the History of Foreign Aid, Security, and Diplomacy* (Sterling: Kumarian Press, 2009), 88, 94.

41. General Accounting Office, *Foreign Assistance: USAID's Operating Expense Account Does Not Fully Reflect the Cost of Delivering Foreign Assistance*, September 30, 2003, GAO-03-1152R USAID Operating Expenses, http://www.gao.gov/products/GAO-03-1152R.

42. David Hall-Matthews, "Historical Roots of Famine Relief Paradigms: Ideas on Dependency and Free Trade in India in the 1870s," *Disasters* 20, no. 3 (1996): 216–30.

43. William Beinart and Peter Coates, *Environment and History: The Taming of Nature in the USA and South Africa* (London: Routledge, 1995).

44. Hall-Matthews, "Historical Roots of Famine Relief Paradigms," 228–29.

45. Wolfgang Sachs, *The Development Dictionary: A Guide to Knowledge and Power* (London: Zed Books, 1992).

46. Henry Veltmeyer, "Development and Globalization as Imperialism,"" *Canadian Journal of Development Studies* 26, no. 1 (2005): 89–106.

47. John Hilary, *Profiting from Poverty: Privatisation Consultants, DFID, and the Public Services* (London: War on Want, 2004).

48. Susanne Soederberg, "American Empire and 'Excluded States': The Millennium Challenge Account and the Shift to Pre-emptive Development," *Third World Quarterly* 25, no. 2 (2004): 280.

49. Michael Cox and Caroline Kennedy-Pipe, "The Tragedy of American Diplomacy? Rethinking the Marshall Plan," *Journal of Cold War Studies* 7, no. 1 (2005): 97–100.

50. Robert Kramer, "Foreword," *Law and Contemporary Problems* 16, no. 3 (1951): 346.

Go / Entangled Empires

I would like to thank Alfred W. McCoy and anonymous readers for University of Wisconsin Press for their comments on this essay.

1. Jeremi Suri, "The Limits of American Empire," in Alfred W. McCoy and Francisco A. Scarano, eds., *Colonial Crucible: Empire in the Making of the Modern American State* (Madison: University of Wisconsin Press, 2009), 524. See also Charles S. Maier, *Among Empires: American Ascendancy and Its Empires* (Cambridge: Harvard University Press, 2006); Anthony Pagden, "Imperialism, Liberalism, and the Quest for Perpetual Peace," *Daedalus* 134, no. 2 (2005); Arthur Schlesinger Jr., "The American Empire? Not So Fast," *World Policy Journal* 22, no. 1 (2005); and Tony Smith, *America's Mission: The United States and the Worldwide Struggle for Democracy in the Twentieth Century* (Princeton: Princeton University Press, 1994). For more critical discussions of exceptionalism and the U.S. empire, see Julian Go, *Patterns of Empire: the British and American Empires Compared, 1688–Present* (Cambridge: Cambridge University Press, 2011).

2. Thomas Bender, "The American Way of Empire," *World Policy Journal* 22, no. 1 (2006).

3. Harry Magdoff, "Imperialism without Colonies," in Roger Owen and Bob Sutcliffe, eds., *Studies in the Theory of Imperialism* (London: Longman, 1972).

4. Engseng Ho, "Empire through Diasporic Eyes: A View from the Other Boat," *Comparative Studies in Society and History* 46, no. 2 (2004).

5. Louis and Robinson have intimated some of these relations, but the relations were probably more extensive than even they uncovered. See William Roger Louis and Ronald Robinson, "The Imperialism of Decolonization," *Journal of Imperial and Commonwealth History* 22, no. 3 (1994).

6. John E. Orchard, "ECA and the Dependent Territories," *Geographical Review* 41, no. 1 (1951).

7. John J. Sebrega, "The Anticolonial Policies of Franklin D. Roosevelt: A Reappraisal," *Political Science Quarterly* 101, no. 1 (1986).

8. Gabriel Kolko, *Confronting the Third World: United States Foreign Policy, 1945–1980* (New York: Pantheon Books, 1988).

9. Arthur N. Holcombe, *Dependent Areas in the Post-war World* (Boston: World Peace Foundation, 1941).

10. Phillip Darby, *Three Faces of Imperialism: British and American Approaches to Asia and Africa, 1870–1970* (New Haven: Yale University Press, 1987), 205; Philip W. Bell, "Colonialism as a Problem in American Foreign Policy," *World Politics* 5, no. 1 (1952), 97.

11. U.S. Department of State, *Foreign Relations of the United States 1950, The Near East, South Asia, and Africa*, vol. 5 (Washington, D.C.: Government Printing Office, 1950), 1527 (hereafter FRUS 1950, vol. 5).

12. *Times* (London), November 2, 1953, 6.

13. FRUS 1950, vol. 5:1527, 1535; Louis and Robinson, "The Imperialism of Decolonization."

14. Orchard, "ECA and the Dependent Territories," 67–72.

15. Ibid., 67.

16. Ibid.

17. FRUS 1950, vol. 5:1527.

18. U.S. Department of State, *Foreign Relations of the United States 1952–54, United Nations Affairs*, vol. 3 (Washington, D.C.: Government Printing Office, 1979), 1104–5 (hereafter FRUS 1952–54, vol. 3).

19. Andrew J. Rotter, "The Triangular Route to Vietnam: The United States, Great Britain, and Southeast Asia, 1945–1950," *International History Review* 6, no. 3 (August 1984).

20. U.S. Department of State, *Foreign Relations of the United States 1947, The Near East and Africa*, vol. 5 (Washington, D.C.: Government Printing Office, 1971), 575–623; FRUS 1950, vol. 5:491–99, 521–26; Kolko, *Confronting the Third World*, 20.

21. Louis and Robinson, "The Imperialism of Decolonization," 499, n. 42.

22. Quoted in ibid., 468.

23. Robert E. Harkavy, *Great Power Competition for Overseas Bases: The Geopolitics of Access Diplomacy* (New York: Pergamon Press, 1982), 66–67, 100.

24. Louis and Robinson, "The Imperialism of Decolonization"; Harkavy, *Great Power Competition for Overseas Bases*, 127–53; C. T. Sandars, *America's Overseas Garrisons: The Leasehold Empire* (Oxford: Oxford University Press, 2000), 42–61.

25. FRUS 1950, vol. 5:1528.

26. Harkavy, *Great Power Competition for Overseas Bases*.

27. FRUS 1950, vol. 5:1573.

28. Figures were calculated from U.S. Department of Defense, Statistical Information Analysis Division, "Military Personnel Historical Reports," http://www.dior.whs.mil/mmid/military/history/309hist.htm, accessed January 2006. This counts countries that later received independence but were colonies when the United States first established troop bases in them.

29. U.S. Department of State, *Foreign Relations of the United States, 1950 Western Europe*, vol. 3 (Washington, D.C.: Government Printing Office, 1977), 1078–79; see also FRUS 1952–4, vol. 3:1081.

30. Frank Furedi, *Colonial Wars and the Politics of Third World Nationalism* (London: I. B. Tauris, 1994), 27–28.

31. Richard Koebner and Helmut Dan Schmidt. *Imperialism: The Story and Significance of a Political Word, 1840–1960* (Cambridge: Cambridge University Press, 1964), 282–84.

32. Erez Manela, *The Wilsonian Moment: Self-Determination and the International Origins of Anticolonial Nationalism* (Oxford: Oxford University Press, 2006).

33. Ibid.

34. Koebner and Schmidt, *Imperialism*, 299.

35. On the development of anticolonial nationalism in the early twentieth century through World War II, see R. F. Holland, *European Decolonization, 1918–1981* (New York: St. Martin's Press, 1985). Also see Furedi, *Colonial Wars and the Politics of Third World Nationalism*.

36. Julius William Pratt, "Anticolonialism in United States Policy," in Robert Strauz-Hupé and Harry W. Hazard, eds., *The Idea of Colonialism* (New York: Frederick A. Praeger, 1958).

37. Furedi, *Colonial Wars and the Politics of Third World Nationalism*, 23.

38. "The Problem of Nationalism," with covering letter by Sir William Strang (Permanent Secretary at the Foreign Office), June 21, 1952, Foreign Office 936–217, Public Records Office (Kew, U.K.).

39. FRUS 1950, vol. 5:1525.

40. On the reconsideration of policy, see John Kent, "The United States and the Decolonization of Black Africa, 1945–63," in David Ryan and Victor Pungong, eds., *The United States and Decolonization* (New York: St. Martin's Press, 2000).

41. Darby, *Three Faces of Imperialism*, 175.

42. FRUS 1952–54, vol. 3:1082.

43. Ibid., 1083–85.

44. Ibid., 1087.

45. See especially Scott Lucas, "The Limits of Ideology: U.S. Foreign Policy and Arab Nationalism in the Early Cold War," in David Ryan and Victor Pungong, eds., *The United States and Decolonization* (New York: St. Martin's Press, 2000). See also William Roger Louis, "American Anti-colonialism and the Dissolution of the British Empire," *International Affairs* 61, no. 3 (1985).

46. Cary Fraser, "Understanding American Policy Towards the Decolonization of European Empires, 1945–64," *Diplomacy and Statecraft* 3, no. 1 (1992).

47. Robert J. McMahon, "Toward a Post-colonial Order: Truman Administration Policies toward South and Southeast Asia," in Michael J. Lacey, ed., *The Truman Presidency* (Cambridge: Cambridge University Press, 1989).

48. Quoted in Lloyd C. Gardner, "How We 'Lost' Vietnam, 1940–1954," in David Ryan and Victor Pungong, eds., *The United States and Decolonization* (New York: St. Martin's Press, 2000).

49. Quoted in Odd Arne Westad, *The Global Cold War: Third World Interventions and the Making of Our Times* (Cambridge: Cambridge University Press, 2005), 113.

50. U.S. Department of State, *Foreign Relations of the United States 1955–57, Africa*, vol. 18 (Washington, D.C.: Government Printing Office, 1989), 27.

REILLY / COLD WAR TRANSITION

1. "Text of Mr. Dulles's Address before American Bar Association," *New York Times*, August 27, 1953.

2. "Member States," United Nations, http://www.un.org/en/members/growth.shtml# text, accessed April 4, 2011.

3. "How Dulles Averted War," *Life*, January 16, 1956.

4. C. T. Sandars, *America's Overseas Garrisons* (Oxford: Oxford University Press, 2000), 15; James R. Blaker, *United States Overseas Basing* (New York: Praeger, 1990), 33.

5. John Charmley, *Churchill's Grand Alliance* (New York: Harcourt Brace, 1995), 97.

6. Carnes Lord, *The Presidency and the Management of National Security* (New York: Free Press, 1988), 70; Fred Greenstein and Richard Immerman, "Effective National Security Advising: Recovering the Eisenhower Legacy," *Political Science Quarterly* 115, no. 3 (2000): 343.

7. Dulles to Embassy Manila, November 27, 1953, in *Foreign Relations of the United States, 1952–1954* (hereafter FRUS), 13:883.

8. Planning Board Report to NSC, December 11, 1953, FRUS 1952–54, 8:121.

9. State Paper, August 4, 1956, FRUS 1955–57, 16:141–42.

10. Dulles to Manila, November 27, 1953, FRUS 1952–54, 13:883.

11. "Report to the National Security Council by the Executive Secretary," October 30, 1953, FRUS 1952–54, 2:587; Memo, President for National Security Affairs to NSC, July 31, 1953, FRUS 1952–54, 2:440.

12. For a justification of the use of the "imperial" as an analytical tool for understanding U.S. global history, see Paul Kramer's recent essay, in which he argues, "While debates have generally centered on questions of semantics—what the imperial 'is'—we should instead emphasize what it does, what kinds of analyses it enables and forecloses. Specifically, the imperial facilitates the pursuit of very specific historiographic ends essential, in this case, to the placement of the United States in the world." See, "Power and Connection: Imperial Histories of the United States in the World," *American Historical Review* 116, no. 5 (December 2011): 1349.

13. John Gallagher and Ronald Robinson, "The Imperialism of Free Trade," *Economic History Review* 6, no. 1 (1953): 7, 4.

14. Wm. Roger Louis, "American Anti-Colonialism," in Wm. Roger Louis and Hedley Bull, eds., *The Special Relationship* (Oxford: Oxford University Press, 1986), 262.

15. Ronald Robinson, "Non-European Foundations of European Imperialism," in Roger Owen and Bob Sutcliffe, eds., *Studies in the Theory of Imperialism* (London: Longman, 1972), 129, 132, 142.

16. David Cannadine, *Ornamentalism* (Oxford: Oxford University Press, 2001), 58–59.

17. Gregory A. Barton, "Informal Empire: The Case of Siam and the Middle East," in this volume.

18. Memo, "Problems of Cold War Planning," S. Everett Gleason (Dep. Exec. Secretary, NSC) to James S. Lay (Exec. Secretary, NSC), and attachment "Militant Liberty," August 26,

1957, DDEL, WHO [White House Office], OSANA [Office of the Special Assistant for National Security Affairs], "Militant Liberty" (emphasis mine).

19. Miles Wolpin, *Military Aid and Counterrevolution in the Third World* (Lexington: Lexington Books, 1972), 84; "410th Meeting of the National Security Council," June 18, 1959, Dwight D. Eisenhower Library, Papers as President, 1953–61, NSC Series, "410th Meeting of NSC" (hereafter DDEL); Minutes of OCB Meeting," October 22, 1958, DDEL, WHO, NSC, OCB [Operations Coordinating Board] Secretariat Series, "Southeast Asia (NSC 6012) (5)."

20. OCB to Philippine Working Group, August 17, 1955, DDEL, WHO, NSC, OCB, "OCB 091, Philippine Islands (File #2) (3) [June 1955–September 1956]"; Lilly to MacDonald, May 6, 1955, OCB, WHO, NSC, "OCB 091, Philippine Islands (File #1) (10) [November 1953–June 1955].

21. Harr to Draper, January 21, 1959, DDEL, WHO, OSANA, OCB Series, Subject Subseries, "Military Assistance Program."

22. "Planning Board Discussion of Southeast Asia Revisions," PB [Planning Board], July 11, 1960, DDEL, WHO, NSC, OCB Secretariat Series, "Southeast Asia (NSC 6012) (3)."

23. "Outline Plan of Operations with Respect to the Philippines," OCB, December 27, 1956, DDEL, WHO, NSC, OCB, "OCB 091, Philippines Islands (File #3) (2) [October 1956–June 1957]."

24. Tim Weiner, *Legacy of Ashes: The History of the CIA* (New York: Random House, 2008), 321.

25. "Progress Report on NSC 123," October 8, 1957, DDEL, WHO, NSC, OCB Secretariat Series, "Evacuation of Key Indigenous Persons [NSC 123]"; Daniele Ganser, *NATO's Secret Armies* (New York: Frank Cass, 2005).

26. "Political Conditions in Vietnam," Senior Representative in Indochina, August 25, 1954, DDEL, WHO, NSC, OCB Central File Series, "OCB 091, Indo-China (File #2) (2) [August–December 1954]."

27. U.S. Agency for International Development [USAID], *U.S. Overseas Loans and Grants* (Washington, D.C.: USAID, 2009), 127.

28. James R. Blaker, *United States Overseas Basing* (New York: Praeger, 1990), 42; Gregg Brazinsky, *Nation Building in South Korea* (Chapel Hill: University of North Carolina Press, 2007), 90.

29. Bruce Cumings, *The Origins of the Korean War: Liberation and the Emergence of Separate Regimes, 1945–1947* (Princeton: Princeton University Press, 1981), 189.

30. "Korea: The Walnut," *Time*, March 9, 1953.

31. William Stueck, *Rethinking the Korean War* (Princeton: Princeton University Press, 2002), 199.

32. 150th Meeting of the NSC, June 19, 1953, FRUS 1952–54, 15:1202.

33. Director of the Executive Secretariat to State, October 28, 1953, FRUS 1952–54, 15:1570–71.

34. 177th Meeting of the NSC, December 23, 1953, FRUS 1952–54, 13:930.

35. Memcon, Dulles and Eden, April 30, 1954, FRUS, Microfiche Supplement, Document 440.

36. Quee-Yong Kim, *The Fall of Syngman Rhee* (Berkeley: Institute of East Asian Studies, 1983), 141–42.

37. Oral History [original version], General Carter B. Magruder, 1972, Magruder Papers, U.S. Army Military History Institute, Carlisle Barracks, PA.

38. Rusk to Seoul, August 5, 1961, John F. Kennedy Library, NSF [National Security File], Korea, "Korea Cables, 7/21/62–8/3/62."

39. Tae Yang Kwak, "The Anvil of War" (PhD diss., Harvard University, 2006), 79 (emphasis mine).

40. Embtel 12908, Seoul to State, April 16, 1965, Lyndon B. Johnson Library, NSF, Vietnam, "Vol. 2 (A), NODIS-LOR 3/65–9/65 [2 of 2]."

41. For total ROK earnings see Kwak, "The Anvil of War," 152; Summary of discussion between Johnson and Park, April 17, 1968, Lyndon B. Johnson Library, NSF, CF, Korea, "Memos and Cables [2 of 2] Vol. VI 4/68-12/68"; U.S. House of Representatives, 95th Congress, 2d Session, Subcommittee on International Organizations, *Investigation of Korean-American Relations, Report* (Washington, DC: Government Printing Office, October 31, 1978), 132–34.

42. Kwak, "The Anvil of War," 2–3, 222; Chae-jin Lee, *A Troubled Peace: U.S. Policy and the Two Koreas* (Baltimore: Johns Hopkins University Press, 2006), 95–102.

43. U.S. Overseas Loans and Grants, 139.

44. James Lawton Collins, *The Development and Training of the South Vietnamese Army, 1950–1972* (Washington, D.C.: Department of the Army, 1975), 15.

45. Bao Dai, quoted in Edward Miller, "Vision, Power, and Agency," *Journal of Southeast Asian Studies* 35, no. 3 (2004): 455; Seth Jacobs, *America's Miracle Man in Vietnam* (Durham: Duke University Press, 2004), 1–25.

46. *Department of State Bulletin,* November 15, 1954, 735–36.

47. "Draft, First Progress Report on NSC 5429/5," OCB, January 19, 1955, DDEL, WHO, NSC, OCB Central File Series, "OCB 091, Indo-China (File #3) (2) [January–March 1955]."

48. Telegram, State to Embassy Saigon, April 27, 1955, FRUS 1955–1957, 1:301 n. 1.

49. Quoted in David Halberstam, *The Best and the Brightest* (New York: Random House, 1972), 135.

50. Seth Jacobs, *Cold War Mandarin* (Lanham: Rowman and Littlefield, 2006), 148.

51. Ibid., 145.

52. *The Pentagon Papers,* Senator Gravel ed. (Boston: Beacon Press, 1971), 2:782; Department of State, "Check-List of Possible U.S. actions in Case of Coup," October 25, 1963, http://www.gwu.edu/~nsarchiv/NSAEBB/NSAEBB101/vn17.pdf, accessed April 25, 2011.

53. The Pentagon Papers, 782–83.

54. Stanley Karnow, *Vietnam: A History* (New York: Penguin Books, 1983), 297–311.

55. Mark Moyar, *Triumph Forsaken: The Vietnam War, 1954–1965* (New York: Cambridge University Press, 2006), 285–287.

56. "Congress Briefed on Saigon Rising," *New York Times,* November 2, 1963.

57. Quoted in Charmley, *Churchill's Grand Alliance,* 207.

58. "Guidelines of United States Policy Toward Saudi Arabia," February 26, 1962, National Archives and Records Administration, College Park, MD, Record Group 59, Office of Arabian Peninsular Affairs, Records Relating to the Persian Gulf and Arabian Peninsular, 1952–1975, "Saudi Arabia 1962."

59. Harry G. Summers, *Persian Gulf War Almanac* (New York: Facts on File, 1995), 99; U.S. Department of Defense, *Conduct of the Persian Gulf War* (Washington, D.C.: Government Printing Office, 1992), 633–38, appendix P, http://www.ndu.edu/library/epubs/cpgw .pdf, accessed April 25, 2011.

60. Embtel 4484, Embassy Rome to State Department, September 13, 2002, Wikileaks Cablegate Archive, Reference ID:02ROME4484, http://wikileaks.org/cable/2002/09/02ROME 4484.html, accessed September 20, 2011.

McCoy / Imperial Illusions

This essay benefited from close readings by my colleagues John W. Hall and Brett Reilly.

1. Eric Hobsbawm, *On Empire, War, and Global Supremacy* (New York: New Press, 2008), 62, 69–71, 87–91; Eric Hobsbawm, *The Age of Empire, 1875–1914* (New York: Pantheon, 1987), 1–3.

2. My father was Alfred M. McCoy Jr., the systems engineering director for the world's first system of global telecommunications satellites, which was developed during the 1960s

by Aerospace Corporation under a contract with the U.S. Air Force. After the successful launch of test satellites in 1967, the system, known as the Initial Defense Communication Satellite Program, was fully operational within a year, managing heavy communications traffic between South Vietnam and Washington, D.C. See Donald H. Martin, "A History of U.S. Military Satellite Communication Systems," *Crosslink* [El Segundo: Aerospace Corporation] 3, no. 1 (Winter 2001/2002), http://www.aero.org/publications/crosslink/winter2002/01 .html.

3. National Intelligence Council, *Global Trends, 2025: A Transformed World* (Washington, D.C.: Government Printing Office, November 2008), vi, 97, http://www.dni.gov/nic/ PDF_2025/2025_Global_Trends_Final_Report.pdf.

4. Ibid., 3–5.

5. Paul Kennedy, *The Rise and Fall of the Great Powers* (New York: Random House, 1987), 514–15.

6. See Roberta Wohlstetter, *Pearl Harbor: Warning and Decision* (Stanford: Stanford University Press, 1962); Don Oberdorfer, *Tet! The Turning Point in the Vietnam War* (Baltimore: Johns Hopkins University Press, 2001); *The 9/11 Commission Report: Final Report of the National Commission on Terrorist Attacks on the United States* (Washington, D.C.: Government Printing Office, 2004).

7. G. Tilghman Richards, *The History and Development of Typewriters* (London: Her Majesty's Stationery Office, 1964), 23–25; Lewis Coe, *The Telegraph: A History of Morse's Invention and Its Predecessors in the United States* (Jefferson: McFarland, 1993), 89.

8. F. H. Wines, "The Census of 1900," *National Geographic*, January 1900, 34–36; Friedrich W. Kistermann, "Hollerith Punched Card System Development (1905–1913)," *IEEE Annals of the History of Computing* 27, no. 1 (2005): 56–66; Emerson W. Pugh, *Building IBM: Shaping an Industry and Its Technology* (Cambridge: MIT Press, 1995), 1–36.

9. Wayne A. Wiegand, *Irrepressible Reformer: A Biography of Melvil Dewey* (Chicago: American Library Association, 1996), 14–24; Leo E. LaMontagne, *American Library Classification with Special Reference to the Library of Congress* (Hamden: Shoe String Press, 1961), 52–60, 63–99, 179–233.

10. Elizabeth Bethel, "The Military Information Division: Origin of the Intelligence Division," *Military Affairs* 11, no. 1 (Spring 1947): 17–24.

11. Henry T. F. Rhodes, *Alphonse Bertillon: Father of Scientific Detection* (London: Harrap, 1956), 71–109; E. R. Henry, *Classification and Uses of Fingerprints* (London: G. Routledge and Sons, 1900), 61.

12. Gamewell Fire Alarm Telegraph Co., *Emergency Signaling* (New York: Gamewell Fire Alarm Telegraph Co., 1916), chap. 8.

13. U.S. Bureau of the Census, *Abstract of the Twelfth Census of the United States, 1900* (Washington, D.C.: Government Printing Office, 1904), 421–22.

14. Stephen Skowronek, *Building a New American State: The Expansion of National Administrative Capacities, 1877–1920* (Cambridge: Cambridge University Press, 1982), 8–18, 39–46.

15. Reynaldo C. Ileto, *Knowing America's Colony: A Hundred Years from the Philippine War* (Honolulu: Center for Philippine Studies, University of Hawaii, 1999), 19–40, 41, 56.

16. J. A. Mangan, *The Games Ethic and Imperialism: Aspects of the Diffusion of an Ideal* (New York: Viking, 1986), 79, 86–90; Glenn Anthony May, *Social Engineering in the Philippines: The Aims, Execution, and Impact of American Colonial Policy* (Westport: Greenwood Press, 1980), 85.

17. Martin Thomas, *Empires of Intelligence: Security Services and Colonial Disorder after 1914* (Berkeley: University of California Press, 2008), 62–64; letter from W. C. Rivers to Harry H. Bandholtz, November 15, 1907, Reel 2, Harry H. Bandholtz Papers, Michigan Historical Collections, Ann Arbor.

18. Mangan, *The Games Ethic and Imperialism*, 71–100, 130–31; J. A. Mangan, *Athleticism in the Victorian and Edwardian Public School: The Emergence and Consolidation of an Educational Ideology* (Cambridge: Cambridge University Press, 1981), 122–40; Bernard S. Cohn, *Colonialism and Its Forms of Knowledge* (Princeton: Princeton University Press, 1996), 4–5.

19. Alfred W. McCoy, Francisco A. Scarano, and Courtney Johnson, "On the Tropic of Cancer: Transitions and Transformations in the U.S. Imperial State," in Alfred W. McCoy and Francisco A. Scarano, eds., *Colonial Crucible: Empire in the Making of the Modern American State* (Madison: University of Wisconsin Press, 2009), 24–26.

20. "L'École Française d'Extrême-Orient," *Pacific Affairs* 25, no. 3 (September 1952): 292–96; Tiew Wai Sin, "History of *Journal of the Malaysian Branch of the Royal Asiatic Society* (JMBRAS), 1878–1997: An Overview," *Malaysian Journal of Library and Information Science* 3, no. 1 (July 1998): 43–60; Lewis E. Gleeck Jr., *American Institutions in the Philippines, 1898–1941* (Manila: Historical Conservation Society, 1976), 150–54.

21. James C. Scott, *Seeing Like a State: How Certain Schemes to Improve the Human Condition Have Failed* (New Haven: Yale University Press, 1998), 2–3, 65–71.

22. Niall Ferguson, *Colossus: The Price of America's Empire* (New York: Penguin, 2004), 205–11.

23. John R. M. Taylor, *The Philippine Insurrection against the United States*, 5 vols. (Pasay City: Eugenio Lopez Foundation, 1971), 1:1–3, 62, 67–69, 101.

24. Alfred W. McCoy, *Policing America's Empire: The United States, the Philippines, and the Rise of the Surveillance State* (Madison: University of Wisconsin Press, 2009), 77–80.

25. Ibid., 77–81.

26. Ibid., 28–29, 70–74.

27. Heath Twitchell Jr., *Allen: The Biography of an Army Officer, 1859–1930* (New Brunswick: Rutgers University Press, 1974), 4–6, 19, 24, 26, 36–59, 65–67, 75–84, 86, 290.

28. Robin W. Winks, *Cloak and Gown, 1939–1961: Scholars in the Secret War* (New York: William Morrow, 1987), 60, 74–75, 104, 111, 113–14.

29. Ibid., 87–88, 99–101, 110.

30. Ibid., 108–9, 44–47.

31. Joseph E. Roop, *Foreign Broadcast Information Service: History*, part 1, *1941–1947*, Central Intelligence Agency, https://www.cia.gov/library/center-for-the-study-of-intelligence/csi-publications/books-and-monographs/foreign-broadcast-information-service/index.html.

32. Winks, *Cloak and Gown*, 104–5.

33. Zbigniew Brzezinski, *Between Two Ages: America's Role in the Technetronic Era* (New York: Viking Press, 1970), 10.

34. Michael McClintock, *Instruments of Statecraft: U.S. Guerrilla Warfare, Counterinsurgency, and Counter Terrorism, 1940–1990* (New York: Pantheon Books, 1992), 161–88.

35. Adam Bertram Schesch, "Popular Mobilization during Revolutionary and Resistance Wars: Vietnam, China, Yugoslavia, Ireland, and Algeria" (PhD diss., University of Wisconsin–Madison, 1994), v, x–xiii, 22–29; Dr. Adam B. Schesch, personal communication, Madison, Wisconsin, May 28, 2010.

36. Victor Marchetti and John D. Marks, *The CIA and the Cult of Intelligence* (New York: Alfred A. Knopf, 1974), 245–46.

37. Douglas Valentine, *The Phoenix Program* (New York: William Morrow, 1990), 130–33; Nelson H. Brickham, Memorandum For: Ambassador R. W. Komer, Subject: Personal Observations, May 26, 1967, http://www.thememoryhole.org/phoenix/.

38. Brickham, Memorandum For: Ambassador R. W. Komer, Subject: Personal Observations, May 26, 1967.

39. ICEX Briefing, n.d., http://www.thememoryhole.org/phoenix/icex_briefing.pdf; Valentine, *The Phoenix Program*, 133–34; L. Wade Lathram, MACCORDS, Memorandum For:

Ambassador R. W. Komer, Subject: Action Program for Attack on VC Infrastructure, 1967–1968, July 27, 1967, http://www.thememoryhole.org/phoenix/action_program.pdf.

40. Ian McNeill, *The Team: Australian Army Advisers in Vietnam, 1962–1972* (Saint Lucia: University of Queensland Press, 1984), 385–411; Central Intelligence Agency, Internal Security in South Vietnam—Phoenix, December 12, 1970, http://www.thememoryhole.org/phoenix/internal-security.pdf\.

41. McNeill, *The Team*, 397.

42. Valentine, *The Phoenix Program*, 253–56, 276–79; Central Intelligence Agency, Internal Security in South Vietnam—Phoenix, December 12, 1970; Dale Andradé, "Pacification," in Stanley Kutler, ed., *Encyclopedia of the Vietnam War* (New York: Charles Scribner's Sons, 1996), 423; Dale Andradé and James H. Willbanks, "CORDS/Phoenix: Counterinsurgency Lessons from Vietnam for the Future," *Military Review* (March–April 2006): 20.

43. Andrew F. Krepinevich Jr., *The Army and Vietnam* (Baltimore: Johns Hopkins University Press, 1986), 228–29.

44. Ralph W. McGehee, *Deadly Deceits: My 25 Years in the CIA* (New York: Sheridan Square Publications, 1983), 156.

45. James William Gibson, *Perfect War: The War We Couldn't Lose and How We Did* (New York: Random House, 1986), 305–15; Robert Lester, *A Guide to the Microfilm Edition of the Records of the Military Assistance Command Vietnam*, part 3, *Progress Reports on Pacification in South Vietnam, 1965–1973* (Bethesda: University Publications of America, 1990), 2–5; R. W. Komer, *Organization and Management of the "New Model" Pacification Program—1966–1969* (Santa Monica: Rand Corporation, May 7, 1970), 198–99.

46. Komer, *Organization and Management of the "New Model" Pacification Program—1966*, 198–204, 207–8, 243.

47. Richard A. Hunt, *Pacification: The American Struggle for Vietnam Hearts and Minds* (Boulder: Westview Press, 1990), 185–86, 194–95, 197–99, 260–61; Lester, *A Guide to the Microfilm Edition*, 2.

48. William Turley, "Captured Vietnamese Documents, (CDEC Microfilm Collection), University of Massachusetts, Boston," *CORMOSEA Bulletin* 17, no. 1 (June 1988): 21–30; James J. Wirz, *The Tet Offensive: Intelligence Failure in War* (Ithaca: Cornell University Press, 1991), 93–94. On-line posts by Christopher Jenner, "Subject: FW: Combined Document Exploitation Center and Combined Military Interrogation Center," October 31, 2005; and Dan Duffy, "Subject: Re: Captured Documents from the Vietnam War," October 30, 2005, Vietnam Studies Group, "Captured Documents from the Vietnam War," http://www.lib.washington.edu/SouthEastAsia/vsg/guides/cdec.html. Gregory A. Daddis, *No Sure Victory: Measuring U.S. Army Effectiveness and Progress in the Vietnam War* (New York: Oxford University Press, 2011), 223, 227.

49. Jacob Van Staaveren, *Interdiction in Southern Laos, 1960–1968* (Washington, D.C.: Center for Air Force History, 1993), 255–69; HQ PACAF, Directorate Tactical Evaluation, Project Contemporary Historical Examination of Current Operation (hereafter CHECO), "Igloo White July 1968–December 1969 (U)," January 10, 1970, 1–5.

50. U.S. Congress, *Congressional Record—Senate: May 14, 1975* (Washington, DC: Government Printing Office, 1975), 14265–66; Raphael Littauer and Norman Uphoff, eds., *The Air War in Indochina* (Boston: Beacon Press, 1972), 9–11, 168, 281; Gibson, *Perfect War*, 396–97; John T. Correll, "Igloo White," *airforce-magazine.com*, November 2004, http://www.airforce-magazine.com/MagazineArchive/Pages/2004/November%202004/1104igloo.aspx; CHECO, "Igloo White July 1968–December 1969 (U)," 21–28.

51. Gibson, *Perfect War*, 397; Staaveren, *Interdiction in Southern Laos*, 271–72; Correll, "Igloo White"; Littauer and Uphoff, *The Air War in Indochina*, 154; CHECO, "Igloo White July 1968–December 1969 (U)," 17–19; Bernard C. Nalty, *The War against Trucks* (Washington, D.C.: Air Force Museums and History Program, 2005), 103.

52. CHECO, "Igloo White July 1968–December 1969 (U)," 30–31; Nalty, *The War against Trucks*, 41, 85–88, 126–27, 217; Thomas P. Ehrhard, "Unmanned Aerial Vehicles in the United States Armed Services: A Comparative Study of Weapon System Innovation" (PhD diss., John Hopkins University, 2000), 162n.

53. CHECO, "Igloo White July 1968–December 1969 (U)," 20, 35.

54. Gibson, *Perfect War*, 398–99; Staaveren, *Interdiction in Southern Laos*, 278.

55. Correll, "Igloo White."

56. Military History Institute of Vietnam, *Victory in Vietnam*, trans. Merle Pribbenow (Lawrence: University of Kansas Press, 2002), 320; Correll, "Igloo White."

57. Nalty, *The War against Trucks*, 294, 301–2.

58. Ehrhard, "Unmanned Aerial Vehicles in the United States Armed Services," 413, 417–18; Greg Goebel, "The Lightning Bug Reconnaissance Drones," http://www.vector site.net/twuav_04.html#m3; U.S. Air Force, *The U.S. Air Force Remotely Piloted Aircraft and Unmanned Aerial Vehicle Strategic Vision* (2005), 1–2, http://www.af.mil/shared/media/doc ument/AFD-060322-009.pdf.

59. Stephen Daggett, *Costs of Major U.S. Wars: CRS Report for Congress* (Washington, D.C.: Congressional Research Service, July 24, 2008), 2, http://www.fas.org/sgp/crs/nat-sec/RS22926.pdf.

60. Dana Priest and William M. Arkin,"Top Secret America," *Washington Post*, July 18, July 19, July 20, July 21, 2010.

61. Priest and Arkin, "Top Secret America," *Washington Post*, July 19, 2010.

62. *New York Times*, December 16, 2005, June 16, 2009.

63. Robert S. Mueller III, "Testimony United States Senate Committee on the Judiciary: FBI Oversight," May 2, 2006, http://fas.org/irp/congress/2006_hr/050206mueller.html; *Washington Post*, August 30, 2006; Kurt Opsahl, "EFF Issues Report on FBI Investigative Data Warehouse," Electronic Frontier Foundation, April 28, 2009, http://www.eff.org/deeplinks /2009/04/eff-issues-report-fb.

64. *New York Times*, June 12, 2009.

65. David Alexander, "Pentagon to Treat Cyberspace as 'Operational Domain,'" *Reuters*, July 14, 2011, http://www.reuters.com/article/2011/07/14/us-usa-defense-cybersecurity-idUSTRE76D5FA20110714.

66. *New York Times*, August 12, 2008, October 18, 2011, June 1, 2012; Ian Traynor, "Russia Accused of Unleashing Cyberwar to Disable Estonia," *The Guardian*, May 16, 2007, http://www.guardian.co.uk/world/2007/may/17/topstories3.russia; Joel Brenner, *America the Vulnerable: Inside the New Threat Matrix of Digital Espionage, Crime, and Warfare* (New York: Penguin Press, 2011), introduction; Lolita C. Baldior, "Pentagon Takes Aim at China Cyber Threat," *Associated Press*, August 19, 2010, http://www.guardian.co.uk/world/feedar ticle/9227669; Lolita C. Baldior, "U.S., China to Cooperate More on Cyber Threat," *Associated Press*, May 7, 2012, http://www.salon.com/2012/05/07/us_china_to_cooperate_more_on_cyber_threat/.

67. *Washington Post*, April 19, 2005.

68. *Washington Post*, December 1, 2007; Robert Parry, "Mobile Labs to Target Iraqis for Death," consortiumnews.com, December 13, 2007, http://www.consortiumnews.com/Print/2007/121307.html.

69. Richard Tompkins, "Biometrics Play Important Role in Afghanistan," *Human Events*, February 23, 2010, http://www.humanevents.com/article.php?id=35735; *New York Times*, April 21, 2010.

70. *The 9/11 Commission Report*, 189–90, 210–14.

71. "Air Force Report," *Air Force News*, October 27, 2008, http://www.youtube.com/watch?v=ureJE68i5q4&feature=related.

72. Nick Turse, "The Drone Surge: Today, Tomorrow, and 2047," *TomDispatch*, January 24, 2010, http://www.tomdispatch.com/archive/175195/nick_turse_the_forty_year_drone _war.

73. Peter W. Singer, "Do Drones Undermine Democracy?" *New York Times*, January 22, 2012.

74. Jane Mayer, "The Predator War," *New Yorker*, October 26, 2009; *New York Times*, April 15, 2009, December 17, 2010, June 20, 2011; Edward Helmore, "US Air Force Prepares Drones to End Era of Fighter Pilots," *The Guardian*, August 22, 2009, http://www.guardian .co.uk/world/2009/aug/22/us-air-force-drones-pilots-afghanistan.

75. Singer, "Do Drones Undermine Democracy?"

76. *New York Times*, March 16, 2009.

77. *New York Times*, February 23, 2009.

78. *New York Times*, January 17, 2011.

79. *New York Times*, June 20, 2011.

80. Kimberly Dozier, "Iran Puts U.S. Drone on Television," Associated Press, *Wisconsin State Journal*, December 9, 2011; David Fulghum and Bill Sweetman, "U.S. Air Force Reveals Operational Stealth UAV," *Aviation Week*, December 4, 2009, http://www.aviationweek .com/aw/; Northrop Grumman, Electronic Systems, "AESA Radar: Revolutionary Capabilities for Multiple Missions," http://www.es.northropgrumman.com/solutions/aesaradar/assets /review_aesa.pdf.

81. U.S. Department of Defense, *Report on Progress toward Security and Stability in Afghanistan* (Washington, D.C.: Department of Defense, January 2009), 17, 19, 28, 32, 36–39, 42, 48, 67.

82. *New York Times*, November 23, 2010.

83. Richard Engel, "So What Is the Actual Surge Strategy?" *NBC News World Blog*, December 2, 2009, http://worldblog.msnbc.msn.com/archive/2009/12/02/2140281.aspx.

84. *New York Times*, April 27, 2010.

85. T. C. Greenwood and T. X. Hammes, "War Planning for Wicked Problems," *Armed Forces Journal*, December 2009, http://www.afji.com/2009/12/4252237/; U.S. Army Training and Doctrine Command, *The U.S. Army Commander's Appreciation and Campaign Design (CACD)*, Pamphlet no. 525-5-500, version 1.0 (Fort Monroe: TRADOC, January 28, 2008), 12–15.

86. "IPTO Mission," "Understand," and "Deep Green," Information Processing Techniques Office (IPTO), Defense Advanced Research Projects Agency (DARPA), http:// www.darpa.mil/ipto/.

87. Julian E. Barnes and Nathan Hodge, "Military Faces Historic Shift," *Wall Street Journal*, January 6, 2012; U.S. Department of Defense, *Sustaining U.S. Global Leadership: Priorities for 21st Century Defense* (Washington, D.C.: U.S. Department of Defense, January 2012), 2–5, http://www.defense.gov/news/Defense_Strategic_Guidance.pdf.

88. HQ, USAF/XPXC, Future Concepts and Transformation Division, *The U.S. Air Force Transformation Flight Plan, 2004* (Washington, D.C., 2004), 48, 53, http://www.af.mil/shared /media/document/AFD-060328-005.pdf.

89. Air Force Space Command, *Strategic Master Plan, FY06 and Beyond* (Washington, D.C., 2006), 8, 11, 36, http://ddaybarcelona.com/DOCUMENTS/masterplan.pdf; United States Strategic Command, "Joint Functional Component Command for Space," http:// www.stratcom.mil/factsheets/USSTRATCOM_Space_Control_and_Space_Surveillance/.

90. HQ, USAF/XPXC, *The U.S. Air Force Transformation Flight Plan, 2004*, 27. See also Air University Public Affairs, "Air Force Wargaming Institute Hosts CSAF Wargame," October 30, 2009, http://www.aetc.af.mil/news/story.asp?id=123175083.

91. *New York Times*, May 23, 2010; Brian Weeden, "X-37B Orbital Test Vehicle Fact Sheet," www.SecureWorldFoundation.org; U.S. Air Force, "X-37 Orbital Test Vehicle," posted May 21, 2010, http://www.af.mil/information/factsheets/factsheet.asp?fsID=16639.

92. Paul Rincon, "X-37B US Military Spaceplane Returns to Earth," *BBC News*, December 3, 2010, http://www.bbc.co.uk/news/science-environment-11911335; Alicia Chang, "Unmanned Air Force Space Plane Lands in Calif.," *Associated Press*, June 16, 2012, http://www.washingtontimes.com/news/2012/jun/16/unmanned-air-force-space-plane-lands-calif/.

93. Defense Advanced Research Projects Agency, "Falcon Technology Demonstration Program HTV-3X Blackswift Test Bed," October 2008, http://www.darpa.mil/Docs/Falcon-Blackswift%20FS%20Octo8.pdf. See also P. W. Singer, *Wired for War: The Robotics Revolution and Conflict in the 21st Century* (New York: Penguin Press, 2009), 121; and *New York Times*, August 12, 2011.

94. *New York Times*, August 3, 2011.

95. Nick Turse, "America's Secret Empire of Drone Bases: Its Full Extent revealed for the First Time," *TomDispatch*, October 16, 2011, http://www.tomdispatch.com/blog/175454/tomgram%3A_nick_turse%2C_mapping_america%27s_shadowy_drone_wars; Nick Turse, "The Crash and Burn Future of Robot Warfare," *TomDispatch*, January 15, 2012, http://www.tomdispatch.com/archive/175489/.

96. Noah Schachtman, "DARPA Vision: 'Unblinking' Spy Drones, Veggie-Powered Killer Bots," *Danger Room*, August 8, 2007, http://www.wired.com/dangerroom/2007/08/the-pentagons-f/; Defense Advanced Research Projects Agency, Tactical Technology Office, "Vulture," http://www.darpa.mil/Our_Work/TTO/Programs/Vulture/Vulture.aspx; "Dr. Paul MacCready Biography," August 29, 2007, AeroVironment, Inc., http://www.avinc.com/careers/benefits/nextPage.

97. Helmore, "US Air Force Prepares Drones to End Era of Fighter Pilots," *The Guardian*, August 22, 2009; Amber Corrin, "Future UAVs Must Multitask, Air Force Says," *Defense-Systems*, April 29, 2010, http://www.defensesystems.com/Articles/2010/04/29/Unmanned-aerial-vehicle-versatility.aspx.

98. Defense Advanced Research Projects Agency, Tactical Technology Office, "Triple Target Terminator (T3)," http://www.darpa.mil/Our_Work/TTO/Programs/T3/Triple_Target_Terminator.aspx.

99. *Washington Post*, January 19, 2007.

100. Mark Brown, "Missiles, You've Been Warned," *Wired*, May 9, 2011, http://www.wired.com/dangerroom/2011/05/missiles-youve-been-warned-new-sats-have-their-orbiting-eye-on-you/.

101. Speech by Dr. Owen Brown, Program Manager, Virtual Space Office, DARPA's 25th Systems and Technology Symposium, Anaheim, California, August 8, 2007, http://archive.darpa.mil/DARPATech2007/proceedings/dt07-vso-brown-access.pdf; Defense Advanced Research Projects Agency, Tactical Technology Office, "System F6," http://www.darpa.mil/Our_Work/TTO/Programs/System_F6.aspx.

102. Defense Advanced Research Projects Agency, Tactical Technology Office, "Front-End Robotic Enabling Near-Term Demonstration (FREND)," http://www.darpa.mil/tto/programs/frend/index.html; Frank J. Cepollina and Jill McGuire, "Viewpoint: Building a National Capability for On-Orbit Servicing," *ASK: Academy Sharing Knowledge* 34 (Spring 2009), http://askmagazine.nasa.gov/issues/34/34i_national_capability_on_orbit_servicing.html.

103. Speech by Dr. Owen Brown, August 8, 2007; Defense Advanced Research Projects Agency, Tactical Technology Office, "Space Surveillance Telescope (SST)," http://www.darpa.mil/tto/programs/sst/index.html.

104. Greg Easterbrook, "Undisciplined Spending in the Name of Defense," *Reuters*, January 20, 2011, http://blogs.reuters.com/gregg-easterbrook/2011/01/20/undisciplined-spending-in-the-name-of-defense/; National Geospatial-Intelligence Agency, *Geospatial Intelligence Standards: Enabling a Common Vision* (Washington, D.C.: National Geospatial-Intelligence Agency, November 2006), http://www.fas.org/irp/agency/nga/standards.pdf;

National Geospatial-Intelligence Agency, *National System for Geospatial Intelligence (NSG), Statement of Strategic Intent* (Washington, D.C.: National Geospatial-Intelligence Agency, March 2007), https://www1.nga.mil/About/Documents/nsg_strategic_intent.pdf; Dana Priest and William M. Arkin, "Top Secret America," *Washington Post*, December 20, 2010, http://projects.washingtonpost.com/top-secret-america/articles/a-hidden-world-growing-beyond-control/4/.

105. *New York Times*, November 4, 2011.

106. Tom Bower, *The Paperclip Conspiracy: The Hunt for Nazi Scientists* (Boston: Little Brown, 1987), 32–37, 40–45, 49–51, 53–59, 64–66, 73–78, 87.

107. Kimberly Dozier et al., "A Question of Secrecy vs. Safety," Associated Press, *Wisconsin State Journal*, June 17, 2012; Pew Global Attitudes Project, Pew Research Center, "Drone Strikes Widely Opposed," June 12, 2012, http://www.pewglobal.org/2012/06/13/global-opinion-of-obama-slips-international-policies-faulted/.

CONTRIBUTORS

ROBERT ALDRICH is professor of European history at the University of Sydney, author of *Vestiges of the Colonial Empire in France: Monuments, Museums, and Colonial Memories* (2005), which was published in an expanded and updated French edition as *Les Traces coloniales dans le paysage français* (2011), and editor of *The Age of Empires* (2007).

WARWICK ANDERSON is an ARC Laureate Fellow and Professor in the Department of History and Centre for Values, Ethics, and the Law in Medicine at the University of Sydney. He is author of *Colonial Pathologies: American Tropical Medicine, Race, and Hygiene in the Philippines* (2006).

TONY BALLANTYNE is professor of history at the University of Otago and author of *Between Colonialism and Diaspora: Sikh Cultural Formations in an Imperial World* (2006).

GREG BANKOFF is professor of modern history at the University of Hull and author of *Flammable Cities: Urban Fire and the Making of the Modern World* (with Uwe Luebken and Jordan Sand, 2012), *A History of Natural Resources in Asia: The Wealth of Nature* (with Peter Boomgaard, 2007), and *Breeds of Empire: The "Invention" of the Horse in Maritime Southeast Asia and Southern Africa, 1500–1950* (with Sandra Swart, 2007).

GREGORY A. BARTON is research fellow in the Research School of Social Sciences at the Australian National University and author of *Lord Palmerston and the Empire of Trade* (with Peter Sterns, 2009). He is editor-in-chief of the journal *Britain and the World* (Edinburgh University Press) and the book series Britain and the World (Palgrave Macmillan).

JOYA CHATTERJI is reader in modern South Asian history at the
University of Cambridge, fellow of Trinity College, and author of
Bengal Divided: Hindu Communalism and Partition (2002) and
The Spoils of Partition (2007).

JOHN DARWIN teaches imperial and global history at Oxford University
where he is a fellow of Nuffield College. His recent publications include
After Tamerlane: The Rise and Fall of Global Empires, 1400–2000 (2008),
which won the Wolfson Prize in History, and *The Empire Project:
The Rise and Fall of the British World System, 1830–1970* (2009),
which won the Trevor Reese Prize.

CRISTINA NOGUEIRA DA SILVA is professor of the history of law at
the Universidade Nova de Lisboa and author of *Constitucionalismo e Império:
A cidadania no Ultramar português* (2009).

JOSEP M. DELGADO RIBAS is professor of history at the Universitat
Pompeu Fabra (Barcelona) and author of *Dinámicas imperiales (1650–1796):
España, América y Europa en el cambio institucional del sistema
colonial español* (2007).

MARÍA DOLORES ELIZALDE is scientific researcher at the Consejo
Superior de Investigaciones Científicas (Spain) and editor of *Las relaciones
entre España y Filipinas* (2003), *Repensar Filipinas: Política, Identidad,
Religión* (2009), and *Filipinas, un país entre dos imperios* (2011).

JOSEP M. FRADERA is professor of history at the Universitat Pompeu
Fabra (Barcelona) and author of *Gobernar colonias* (1999) and *Colonias
para después de un imperio* (2009).

ALBERT GARCIA BALAÑÀ is associate professor of modern and
contemporary history at Universitat Pompeu Fabra (Barcelona) and
author of *La fabricació de la fàbrica: Treball i política a la Catalunya
cotonera (1784–1874)* (2004).

JULIAN GO is associate professor of sociology at Boston University
and author of *Patterns of Empire: The British and American Empires,
1688–Present* (2011).

GREG GRANDIN is professor of history at New York University and a
member of the American Academy of Arts and Sciences. He is author of
Fordlandia (2009), a finalist for the Pulitzer Prize, the National Book Award,
and the National Book Critics Circle Award.

STEPHEN JACOBSON is associate professor of history at the Universitat Pompeu Fabra (Barcelona) and author of *Catalonia's Advocates: Lawyers, Society, and Politics in Barcelona, 1759–1900* (2009).

COURTNEY JOHNSON is research fellow at the Consejo Superior de Investigaciones Científicas (Spain) and author of *Imperial Vernacular: The Paradox of Hispanism in the Age of Empire* (forthcoming).

ALFRED W. McCOY is the J. R. W. Smail Professor of History at the University of Wisconsin–Madison. His recent publications include *Policing America's Empire: The United States, the Philippines, and the Rise of the Surveillance State* (2009), which won the George Kahin Prize, and *Torture and Impunity: The U.S. Doctrine of Coercive Interrogation* (2012).

HANS POLS is associate professor of history and philosophy of science at the University of Sydney and studies the history of medicine in the Dutch East Indies.

REMCO RABEN teaches Asian and colonial history at Utrecht University, the Netherlands, and is author of *Being "Dutch" in the Indies: A History of Creolisation and Empire, 1500–1920* (with Ulbe Bosma, 2008) and *Representing the Japanese Occupation of Indonesia: Personal Testimonies and Public Images in Indonesia, Japan, and the Netherlands* (2000).

BRETT REILLY is a doctoral student at the University of Wisconsin–Madison specializing in the study of Vietnam and U.S. diplomatic history in Asia.

EMMANUELLE SAADA is associate professor of French and history at Columbia University and author of *Empire's Children: Race, Filiation and Citizenship in the French Colonies* (2012).

KELVIN SANTIAGO-VALLES is associate professor of sociology at Binghamton University–State University of New York and author of *"Subject People" and Colonial Discourses: Economic Transformation and Social Disorder in Puerto Rico, 1898–1947* (1994).

FRANCISCO A. SCARANO is professor of history at the University of Wisconsin–Madison and editor, with Stephan Palmié, of *The Caribbean: A History of the Region and Its Peoples* (2011).

CHRISTOPHER SCHMIDT-NOWARA is Prince of Asturias Chair in Spanish Culture and Civilization at Tufts University and author of *Slavery, Freedom, and Abolition in Latin America and the Atlantic World* (2011).

GARY WILDER is associate professor in the anthropology PhD program and Director of the Mellon Committee on Globalization and Social Change at the Graduate Center, City University of New York. He is the author of *The French Imperial Nation-State: Negritude and Colonial Humanism between the Two World Wars* (2005).

INDEX